D0536795

BASIC RETAILING

THE IRWIN SERIES IN MARKETING

Consulting Editor
Gilbert A. Churchill, Jr.
University of Wisconsin, Madison

BASIC RETAILING

Irving Burstiner
Bernard M. Baruch College
City University of New York

1986
IRWIN
Homewood, Illinois   60430

Cover Photos: Eric Oxendorf
Front Cover Insert Photo: Courtesy of Milwaukee County Historical Society

© RICHARD D. IRWIN, INC., 1986

All rights reserved. No part of this publication may be
reproduced, stored in a retrieval system, or transmitted,
in any form or by any means, electronic, mechanical,
photocopying, recording, or otherwise, without the prior
written permission of the publisher.

ISBN 0-256-02842-7
Library of Congress Catalog Card No. 85–81543
Printed in the United States of America
1 2 3 4 5 6 7 8 9 0 K 3 2 1 0 9 8 7 6

**With love and deep appreciation to Razel,
my wife and helpful partner**

PREFACE

Basic Retailing is the end product of nearly five years of effort and dedication by a career retailer-turned-college professor. Its content reflects a well-integrated blend of over three decades of hands-on experience and the conceptual and disciplined perspective of scholarly research.

Since entering the academic world in 1971, I have taught retailing, marketing, and management to thousands of college students and to industry groups. I have also written several books in these fields for the general public. Throughout my academic career, my objectives in teaching and in writing have remained constant: to kindle excitement about the dynamic, exciting nature of retailing in our economy. Realism, relevance, clarity, and comprehension have been primary concerns, as well as promoting a genuine respect and appreciation for retailing as a career. I kept those same goals before me while writing this book. My aim was to make the world of contemporary retailing come alive in a highly readable and attractive textbook.

Basic Retailing has been designed for the introductory retailing course at both two-year and four-year colleges. The writing is conversational; the vocabulary is basic and easy to understand. The reading level is consistent with that of the first-semester college student. Readers without prior exposure to finance, marketing, or general business coursework will have little difficulty following the material.

How *Basic Retailing* Differs from Other Textbooks While the text has been amply documented with many references, there is less emphasis on theory and more on retailing applications than in many competitive works.

Basic Retailing covers all topics traditionally taught in the introductory course and more. It shies away from an unjust dependence on large-scale retailing and accords independent retailing its full and proper status. Throughout the book, many different types of both merchandise and service retailers are described.

There is an expanded, two-chapter treatment of human resources management, in contrast to the single chapter commonly found in other textbooks. Four chapters focus on the vital area of retail promotion. Contrary to most elementary retailing texts, *Basic Retailing* devotes an entire chapter to retail display and another to personal selling. Store services are the central theme of still another chapter.

The Book   *Basic Retailing* contains 22 chapters and is organized into seven parts.

Part 1 lays the foundation for student understanding and appreciation of modern retailing. Chapter 1 introduces the reader to retailing's role in our marketing system, traces its evolution since colonial times, and identifies various types of retail enterprises. Chapter 2 begins with a thorough discussion of small-scale, independent retailing. It then discusses the topics of service, nonstore, and international retailing. In Chapter 3, the socioeconomic and technological environments within which retail companies must work are examined. Also discussed are such topics as the firm's social responsibility and ethical considerations. Chapter 4 provides useful, up-to-date information about several retail types including, among others, department stores, chains, off-price retailers, and franchises. Opportunity analysis, positioning, planning and forecasting, and retail research are all addressed in Chapter 5. Chapter 6 concludes Part 1 with a detailed overview of the financial end of the retail business. Balance sheet and operating statement terms are clearly defined. Applications of ratio analysis are demonstrated, and such important areas as expense management, insurance, and store security are covered in some detail.

Part 2 centers on the consumer, the focal point of all retailing activity. Chapter 7 explores the psychology of the consuming public. After depicting consumers as both information processors and problem solvers, it delves into such aspects of the human personality as motivation, perception, learning, the self-concept, and attitudes. Chapter 8 examines the effects on shopping behavior of culture, subcultures, reference groups, and one's stage in the family life cycle. It also presents the major techniques that firms use to segment consumer markets.

Part 3 provides specifics about the location and design of retail facilities. After identifying the different types of retail shopping areas, Chapter 9 underscores the significance of the trading area concept. It also demonstrates how retailers find and evaluate locations, and offers information relating to store occupancy. Chapter 10 concentrates on the retail facility itself, giving details of store construction, lighting, decor, layout patterns, space allocation, and fixturization.

Part 4 deals with the human resources area in retailing. Chapter 11 addresses the subjects of organization, staffing, employee compensation, training, performance evaluation, and other aspects of human resources administration. The management and supervision of employees is the main thrust of Chapter 12. Also dealt with are such topics as managerial leadership, communication, motivation, and productivity.

Part 5 relates to the merchandise and services component of the retailing mix. Chapter 13 initiates the discussion of merchandise planning and control. Approaches to product classification are discussed, along with implications for retail buyers of the product life cycle concept. Also reviewed are procedures for ordering staple items and the merchandising of fashion goods. Chapter 14 introduces more advanced concepts of merchandise management: inventory planning, stock turnover, merchandise budgeting, the retail method of inventory valuation, and FIFO/LIFO. Pricing is the central theme of Chapter 15. The student is introduced to the price-setting approaches, pricing policies, and promotional pricing techniques used by retail firms. Markups of different types are defined and their use illustrated in detail. The chapter also presents concise and lucid treatments of markdowns and discounts. Devoted to retail buying, Chapter 16 describes the buying process and furnishes details about sources of both information and merchandise. Resident buying offices, vendor relations, and the handling of incoming goods are other topics treated here. In Chapter 17, the student comes to appreciate the significant role of services in the retailing sector. An introduction to the management of customer credit completes the chapter.

Part 6 presents a comprehensive overview of retail promotion. Chapter 18 identifies the components of the promotion mix, stresses the importance of store image, and describes sales promotion techniques. Public relations and publicity are also discussed. Chapter 19 deals with retail advertising. It covers a wide range of topics—from truth-in-advertising and cooperative advertising to budgeting methods, the media, and advertising agencies. It also reviews methods retailers use to evaluate their advertising.

Chapter 20 targets the impact of retail display. It presents the basic principles of design, popular display patterns, and aesthetic color schemes for both window and interior displays. Chapter 21 stresses the value of personal selling in store retailing. After identifying and comparing different types of selling jobs, the text delineates the steps in the retail selling process. Also addressed is the problem of improving sales effectiveness.

In **Part 7,** a single, forward-looking chapter brings the text to its logical conclusion. Following a short epilogue, Chapter 22 provides a prologue to the 21st century. Expected changes in population demographics, technology, and the sociological environment give rise to speculation about the next 20 years or so. Specific predictions of value to retail management are also made.

Pedagogical Aids   The material in each chapter is supported by the following learning aids:

1. Chapter Outline
2. Study Objectives
3. Chapter Summary
4. List of Key Terms (terms also appear in text in bold type)
5. Review Questions
6. Discussion Questions
7. Notes

In addition, the book contains:

Case Studies that involve many different types of retailers.
A useful, end-of-text *Glossary of Key Terms* with clear and concise definitions.
"Retailing As a Career"—an informative Appendix that encourages students to begin thinking about their careers, shows them how to prepare a resume, and gives worthwhile hints about employment interviews. It also includes a listing of the names, addresses, and telephone numbers of over 100 retail companies.
Author Index.
Subject Index.

Finally, well over 100 photographs lend interest and timeliness to the text. Figures, charts, tables, and an occasional cartoon underscore important concepts.

The Instructor's Manual   There are four parts to the Manual:

1. *Chapter Aids*—This section contains the following helpful material for each of the 22 chapters: chapter outline, study objectives, key terms (and their definitions), answers to end-of-chapter review questions, comments on the discussion questions, list of selected readings, and both true-false and multiple-choice questions.
2. *Case Notes*—Thorough discussions of all cases in order of their appearance in the textbook.
3. *Test Bank*—Two midterms and two final examinations, along with their answer keys.
4. *Overhead Transparency Masters*—Useful and well-designed transparency masters of charts, figures, tables, and other text material.

ACKNOWLEDGMENTS

Before concluding this Preface, I would like to express my gratitude to my wonderful wife, Razel, for the consistent encouragement and support she has given me all throughout the preparation of the manuscript. I also wish to thank Jeffrey Daniels and Clare Recht, my two able, former graduate assistants, for their help with this project. A special note of appreciation goes to my friend and aide, Dr. Sherif El-Aasi.

This book could not have appeared in print without the help and know-how of the professionals at Richard D. Irwin. I owe a great deal to those professors who critically reviewed the manuscript as it was being developed. My thanks are owed to Gilbert A. Churchill, Jr., Donald C. Slichter Professor in Business Research, University of Wisconsin–Madison, for his insightful comments and encouragement throughout the entire writing process; and to Ben C. Butcher, California State University–Long Beach; Loretta Franklin Kilgore, Spokane Community College; and Edward W. Wheatley, East Carolina University–Greenville. Their helpful suggestions and comments have been greatly appreciated.

Irving Burstiner

CONTENTS

PART 2

THE CUSTOMERS

Some Basic Definitions. The Consumer: Information Processor, Problem-Solver: *Consumer Decision Making.* Motivation and Human Behavior: *What Motives Are Like. Consumer Motivation. Shopping Orientations.* The Basic Human Needs: *Physiological Needs. Safety Needs. Love and Belongingness Needs. Esteem Needs. Self-Actualization Needs. Closing Comments.* Perception. Learning: *Theories of Learning.* The Self-Concept. Attitudes: *Attitudes and Consumption Behavior.* Personality. The Adoption of New Ideas: *The Diffusion of Innovations: A Macro Perspective. The Micro View: The Consumer's Adoption Process.*

Cultural Influences on Buyer Behavior: *Some Basic American Values. Social Class. Warner's Social Class Structure.* Subcultures in America: *The Black Subculture. The Spanish Subculture. Subcultures Based on Age. The Senior Citizen Subculture.* Reference Groups: *The Family.* The Family Life Cycle: *An Alternate Profile.* Market Segmentation: Selecting Consumer Targets: *Segmenting Markets. Outshoppers.*

CASES FOR PART 2 238

PART 3

THE RETAIL FACILITY

Retail Shopping Areas: *In-city Retail Shopping Sections. Shopping Centers.* Evaluating Trading Areas: *Extent of the Trading Area.*

Gravitational Models in Trading Area Estimation. Nongravitational Approaches. Finding and Evaluating New Locations: *Growth Areas for Retailers. Information Sources for Location Analysis. Factors to Consider when Evaluating Locations. Factors to Check in the Larger Community. The Store's Neighborhood and the Site Itself. Location Research.* Store Occupancy: *Building a Store. Buying a Store. Renting a Store.*

Store Construction: *The Store as a Machine.* The Store Exterior: *Signing. Display Windows. Store Entrances. Awnings.* Interior Design and Decor: *Atmospherics. Interior Walls. Flooring. Ceilings. Lighting.* Store Layout Patterns: *The Grid(iron) Layout. Freeform Layout. Combinations.* Allocating Space for Greater Productivity: *Concern over Productivity. Approaches to Selling-Space Allocation.* Fixtures and Equipment: *Fixtures. Equipment.*

PART 4

THE RETAIL EMPLOYEE

Human Resources: An Introduction: *Retail Stores Are Powered by People. Employees Are Critical to Store Success. Personnel Administration in Transition.* Organizing the Retail Company: *Organization. Basic Principles of Management. Departmentizing. Small Store Organization. Large Store Organization.* Staffing the Retail Enterprise: *Personnel Sources. Aids in Selection.* Compensation: Paying Retail Employees: *Characteristics of a Sound Pay Plan. Setting up a Pay Plan. Types of Pay Plans. Supplemental Benefits.* Training and Development: *Why Retailers Train Employees. Designing Training Programs. Training Methods. Management Development.* Evaluating Employee Performance: *Rating Forms in Employee Evaluation.*

Managerial Leadership: *The Basic Managerial Functions.* Communication in Management: *Types of Communications. Problems in Communicating.* Leadership Basics: *Styles of Leadership. Leader Decision Making.* Motivating Employees and Improving Productivity: *Organizational Morale. Training Supervisory Personnel.* Motivation Theory: A Brief Review: *The Human Relations Era. Newer Insights.*

PART 5

MERCHANDISE AND STORE SERVICES

Some Basic Inventory Decisions: *Merchandise Concerns of Retailers. Merchandise Classifications.* Two Planning and Control Aids: *Gross Margin Return on Investment. ABC Analysis.* Analyzing Shoppers' Needs: *Internal Sources of Information. External Sources of Information.* Classifying Products: *Industrial Goods. Consumer Goods.* The Product Life Cycle: *Product Introduction Stage. Growth Stage. Maturity Stage. Decline Stage. Length of the PLC.* Ordering Staple Merchandise: *The Basic Stock Plan.* Merchandising Fashion Goods: *Model Stock. Fashion Merchandise.*

Inventory Planning and Control: *Unit Control. Dollar Control.* Stock Turnover: *The Basic Stockturn Formula. Stockturn at Retail. Calculating Stockturn for the Entire Store. Calculating Stockturn at Cost: An Illustration. Turnover Expressed in Merchandise Units.* Merchandise Budgeting: *Forecasting Sales. Translating Sales Objectives into Monthly Projections. Planning the Merchandise Inventory. Compensating for Inventory Reductions. Projected Purchases. Calculating the Open-to-Buy.* Retail Method of Inventory Valuation: *Nature of the Retail Method.* Inventory Methods: *Physical Inventory. Perpetual Inventory. Observation. The Tickler Method.* FIFO and LIFO.

The Meaning of Price: *Factors that Influence Pricing Decisions. The Price-Quality Relationship.* Setting Prices: *Manufacturers' Objectives in Pricing. Retailers' Objectives in Pricing. Pricing Approaches.* Pricing Policies: *Variable or Fixed Pricing. Price Lining. Psychological Pricing. Unit Pricing.* Promotional Pricing Methods: *Leader Pricing.*

Loss Leader Pricing. Bait Pricing. Comparative Pricing. Trade-Ins.
Markups: *Individual Markups. Markup Percentages. Working
with Both Percentages and Dollars-and-Cents Figures. Average Markup.
Cumulative Markup. Initial Markup. Maintained Markup. Maintained
Markup and Gross Margin.* Markdowns: *Reasons for Taking
Markdowns. Calculating Markdown Percentages. Other Considerations.*
Understanding Discounts: *Trade Discounts. Cash Discounts. Quantity
Discounts. Seasonal Discounts. Special-Purpose Discounts.
Allowances.* Legal Considerations: *Resale Price Maintenance.
Pertinent Federal Legislation.*

Company Size and the Buying Function. The Retail Buyer. The Buying
Process: *Other Buying Approaches.* Information Sources: *Internal
Sources. External Sources.* Sources of Merchandise: *Manufacturers.
Wholesalers. Limited-Service Wholesalers. Other Types of Wholesaling
Establishments. Agents and Brokers.* Resident Buying Offices: *Types of
Buying Offices. Independent Buying Offices.* Dealing with Vendors:
Channel Conflict. Buyer-Supplier Relations. Rating Suppliers. Handling
Incoming Merchandise: *Receiving Merchandise. Marking.*

Services in the Retail Sector: *Service Retailers. Services Offered by
Merchandise Retailers.* Customer Satisfaction. Frequently Offered
Services: *Some Popular Services.* Managing Customer Credit: *Why Credit
Is Offered. How Retail Credit Is Handled. Credit Plans for Shoppers.
Outside Credit Card Plans. Billing the Charge Customer. Collecting
Past-due Accounts.*

PART 6

PROMOTION IN RETAILING

Promotion in Action: *Significance of Retail Promotion. Objectives of
Promotion.* Developing the Store Image. Sales Promotion: *Need for a*

Year-Round Program. Techniques of Sales Promotion: *Advertising Specialties. Audiovisual Methods. Catalogs. Consumer Information and Instruction. Contests and Games. Coupons. Demonstrations. Exhibits and Shows. Premiums and Giveaways. Push Money and Other Incentives. Rain Checks. Sampling. Special Promotional Events. Tie-in Promotions. Trading Stamps. Trade-in Promotions.* Public Relations: *Defining Public Relations. Publicity.*

BASIC RETAILING

Chicago Historical Society

MODERN
RETAILING

RETAILING: ESSENCE AND EVOLUTION

Your Study Objectives

After you have studied this chapter, you will understand:

1. What retailing is and its role and significance in our marketing system.
2. Some of the principal developments in the evolution of American retailing.
3. Major types and classifications of retail enterprises.

The retailing sector is bustling, colorful, vibrant, and stimulating. No other arena of marketing activity carries more excitement or sense of immediacy. None is as close, as familiar, or more often participated in by the American consumer. Through numerous outlets, we are continually exposed to and tempted by goods and services in almost unlimited variety.

The first two chapters of this book take you on an introductory tour of this dynamic field. In Chapter 1, you will learn about the place of retailing in our marketing system and its contributions to our economy. We trace the evolution of modern American retailing from early colonial times to the present. You will learn how to identify and classify various retail enterprises: general merchandise and specialty retailers, leased departments, wholesaler-sponsored voluntary chains and other vertical marketing systems, food retailers, and so on. Chapter 2 continues your introduction with a detailed presentation of the small independent retailer. Other topics presented include large-scale, service, nonstore, and international retailing.

Retailing's Role in the Marketing System

Retailers sell merchandise and/or services to consumers to satisfy their personal and household needs. Retailing activity differs from industrial selling, which involves marketing goods and/or services to industry, commerce, government, nonprofit, and other types of organizations *for their own use* in conducting their affairs. It is distinct from manufacturing, where the major emphasis lies in making or producing goods. Typically, manufacturers sell their products through distributors—individuals and firms engaged in the so-called distributive trades, wholesaling and retailing. Wholesalers purchase goods from manufacturers in large quantities and resell them in smaller amounts to business and other organizations. Among them are retail companies. Products and services consumed by the organizations themselves are called *industrial goods.* Those that are resold by retailers to the consuming public are known as *consumer goods.*

The retailing process involves a number of specific functions or areas of activity. Among these are:

buying merchandise for resale to consumers
selling and other forms of promotion
storing, or warehousing, merchandise
transporting merchandise
taking business risks
financing operations
obtaining information for management decisions
providing information to consumers

The Many Faces of Retailing

Retailing takes place in many diverse settings. The few entries listed below contribute, at best, only an introductory exposure to the different types of retail environments:

shoppers swarming through the entrances of a department store at opening time in response to a heavily publicized pre-holiday promotion

an Avon representative displaying samples of cosmetics to a housewife

the bleep of the register as a checkout clerk draws a box of Kellogg's Rice Krispies across the window of a laser scanner

the owner of a Trans Am filling the tank with unleaded gasoline

young adults standing in line to purchase tickets for a concert

at a Burger King, a salesclerk collecting from a customer for a hamburger, order of fries, and a Pepsi

a youngster on a bicycle tossing the morning newspaper at the door of a suburban home

in a furniture warehouse, a homeowner signing an installment agreement for the purchase of a bedroom suite

a young adult selecting a pair of eyeglass frames at an optician's

at a neighborhood savings bank, a consumer putting away $2,000 in an individual retirement account

a family on vacation checking in at a Holiday Inn

a customer purchasing two quarts of milk and a loaf of bread at a convenience store just before midnight

an insurance agent stressing the need for a term life policy to a married couple with two young children

at a Waldenbooks branch, a shopper browsing through the books in the history section

a saleswoman at a chic boutique complimenting a customer on her choice of blouse

a mail-order advertisement in *House Beautiful* for monogrammed belts

outside a 15-story office building at noon, a street vendor hawking umbrellas in the rain

motorists stopping at a roadside stand to buy melons

a TV commercial offering a new country music album

Yes, retailing is carried on in stores; in homes and offices; at roadside stands and on city streets; via TV, radio, newspapers, magazines, and other media; in banks, hotels, and restaurants; and a hundred other types of locations. **Retailing** is a form of distribution. It involves selling goods and/or services to final consumers to fulfill their needs and wants. The term also embraces all those activities that must take place in order for the retailer to sell those goods and/or services. Each retail transaction involves an exchange between consumer and retailer. The consumer exchanges money for an article of merchandise or a service offered by the retailer.

Windward Mall, Kaneohe (Oahu) Hawaii: Retailing takes place in many and diverse settings.

Courtesy Winmar Company, Inc., Seattle, WA

Economic Aspects   Figure 1.1 indicates biennial sales for all of retailing, in current dollars, for selected years from 1967. Sales since 1981 have exceeded $1 trillion annually. From another perspective, some $5,018 were spent in 1982 for every man, woman, and child in the United States. This can be seen in Figure 1.2 (solid line). More than two thirds of all retail sales dollars were spent on nondurable goods—the thousands of products

---

Figure 1.1   Total retail sales in current dollars, selected years ($ billions)

1967	$293
1970	$368.4
1975	$588.1
1978	$807.4
1981	$1,047.6

Source: U.S. Department of Commerce, Bureau of the Census, *Statistical Abstract of the United States 1984–1985*, 105th ed. (Washington, D.C.: U.S. Government Printing Office, 1984), p. 799.

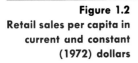

Figure 1.2
Retail sales per capita in current and constant (1972) dollars

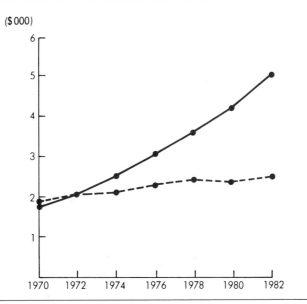

Source: U.S. Department of Commerce, Bureau of the Census, *Statistical Abstract of the United States, 1984–1985*, 105th ed. (Washington, D.C.: U.S. Government Printing Office, 1984), p. 782.

and services that are quickly consumed. Foods and many household items are examples. (Durables, nondurables, and other classifications of goods are discussed in more detail in Chapter 13.)

When per capita sales are expressed in constant 1972 dollars, rather than current dollars, retailing's growth curve over the years appears rather flat. See the dotted line in Figure 1.2. A major contributing factor is graduated price increases due to the effects of inflation.

A labor-intensive industry, retailing is among the country's largest employers. Over 13 million people are engaged in some kind of retailing activity. There are approximately 1.6 million retail establishments. Of these, 300,000 or so are chain stores. Thus, the independent retailer is more characteristic of this segment of the economy than are the chains. We can, however, expect the number of independents to decline over time, as established chains continue to expand and new ones are formed. Additional causes of this decline include the growth of the franchising method of distribution, acquisitions and mergers, and other changes in the retail sector. Independents may be unable to compete in price with the larger companies.[1] Chain store operations already account for nearly half of all retail sales.

Other Aspects Aside from its evident impact on the health of our economy, we ought to recognize retailing's ongoing contribution to our culture. Retailers may be viewed as "change agents, gatekeepers, opinion leaders, and innovators in the process of diffusion of popular culture."[2] Through stores across the nation as well as through house-to-house selling and other nonstore methods, we are continually exposed to a wealth of products and services. We partake of many, and often. They help us to eat, sleep, work, play, travel, rest, and generally participate in society.

A major characteristic of the retailing industry in general is that it is continually evolving. In recent decades, we have witnessed a number of significant changes and trends.[3] Among them are:

the appearance of the boutique
the spread of nonstore retailing
the expansion of mass merchandising companies
the growth of vertical marketing systems[4]
chains of specialty shops being launched by department stores and
   other general merchandise retailers[5]
an increasingly competitive retailing environment
growing consumer interest in at-home shopping
lifestyle marketing
a new professionalism in management ranks and more attention to
   the firm's return on investment
increasing stress on productivity

The Wheel of Retailing

Originated by Harvard Professor Malcolm P. McNair in the late 1950s, the **Wheel of Retailing** theory describes the behavior of new types of retail institutions that have entered our economy over the decades. It holds that an innovative retailer initially tries to gain a foothold in the highly competitive marketplace by launching a different kind of low margin–low cost operation. An excellent illustration is the discount house, which appeared shortly after the end of World War II. At the outset, the new company's overhead expenses and the retail prices of the merchandise it sells are kept low. Service offerings are limited, and the enterprise is managed on a below-average gross margin percentage.[6] If the new operation proves successful, competitors are bound to spring up. Each attempts to outperform the originator by accenting distinguishing strategies. To counter the competition, the innovative retailer widens the assortment of goods, invests more heavily in fixtures and store decor, spends more on advertising, and so on. Thus, it finds its operating costs rising steadily. As it continues to grow, the firm hires additional personnel, including supervisors and other managers. As its gross margin percentage of sales slips, the company will need to raise its retail prices. Eventually, consumers come to perceive little difference between the new institution and the retailers it originally competed against. Room is thus made once again for a low-status operation to appear on the scene. A new cycle then begins.

The theory applies to a number of retail types besides the discount house: the supermarket, furniture warehouse, off-price store, and box store (a small, low-priced, limited-line food store) are some examples. There are obvious exceptions, however. Among them are convenience food stores, automatic vending machines, and department store branches. The value of the Wheel of Retailing concept lies more in understanding some of the evolutionary aspects of American retailing than in anything else.

It has been claimed that the wheel may be slowing down, largely because of the use of modern marketing in the retailing sector.[7] Such factors as the increasing sophistication of advertising, the growth of shopping centers, and the rise of "conglomerchants" have created a more stable retail environment. A **conglomerchant** is a retail conglomerate—a large organization that owns a variety of retail businesses. In effect, it is "a multiline merchandising empire under central ownership, usually combining several styles of retailing with behind-the-scenes integration of some distribution and management functions."[8] Among the more notable examples are companies like the Minneapolis-based Dayton-Hudson Corporation, the Melville Corporation (offices in Harrison, New York), and U.S. Shoe, headquartered in Cincinnati.[9] The conglomerchant may own a number of chain store organizations, each tailored to a specific market position.[10]

Whether or not the Wheel of Retailing does slow down, it remains to be seen if the concept will apply to the developing fields of telecommunications and teleshopping. What institutional changes these new areas will bring about are still a subject for conjecture.[11]

Retailing in America: A Capsulized Evolution

In the next page or two, we briefly trace the development of the retailing industry in the United States. We hope this condensed presentation will give you a rudimentary understanding of some complexities of modern retailing.

From the Beginning to the 19th Century

In colonial times, *trading posts* served as America's first retail outlets. At these small frontier outposts, settlers and trappers bartered flax, corn, other farm products, furs, and skins for whiskey, gunpowder, and goods brought over from Europe. *Peddlers* were the next merchants to appear on the scene. Forerunners of today's direct, or door-to-door, retailers, these were enterprising people who sold their wares from one settlement or village to the next. Traveling at first on foot, then on horseback, and eventually by wagon, these peddlers carried pots and pans, knives, notions, and household goods. Because currency and coins were scarce, they would often exchange their merchandise for food and clothing produced by the villagers, rather than for money. They came to be known as Yankee peddlers because of their popularity in New England.

The settlements grew into villages and towns. A third retailing institution emerged to answer the needs of an expanding population. This was the **general store,** a small outlet that stocked a number of different basic lines of goods. In addition to groceries and household items, these stores offered farm equipment and supplies, animal feed, tools and hardware, clothing, and even some medicines. By the end of the 18th century, general stores were prevalent in the nation's more populous areas. Modern general stores can still be seen here and there in the more rural sections of the country.

The 19th Century Westward expansion, the growth of the railroads, and the appearance of our first manufacturing plants all contributed to the development of another innovative retail type. Though popular, general stores were ill-equipped to handle the vast output of the new factories. The new **single-line store** specialized in one type of merchandise, such as dry goods, men's clothing, hardware, or drugs. These retailers were the precursors of today's single- and limited-line specialty stores, discussed later in this chapter.

Shortly after the end of the Civil War, a few merchants established the first American *department stores.* Patterned after a successful European concept, these large retailers evolved from dry goods stores or other single-line outlets. Over the following two or three decades, *mail-order houses* like Montgomery Ward and Sears, Roebuck started up operations. They began distributing catalogs and filling orders by mail. The new method of distribution offered consumers a startling innovation, the ultimate in convenience. Public acceptance was immediate. Mail-order growth accelerated even more with the institution of parcel post service by the federal government just before the outbreak of World War I.

The 20th Century By the early 1900s, food, variety, and other *chain store organizations* were already well established. Actually, the first unit of what would become a major chain decades later had been conceived back in 1859— a small specialty tea shop in New York City. Eventually, this modest store grew into the Great Atlantic & Pacific Tea Company. Chain organizations continued to expand, demonstrating even more rapid growth during the 1920s.

James Cash Penney made his philosophy clear when he opened his first Golden Rule store in Wyoming in 1902. The successful business incorporated as the J. C. Penney Company in 1913.

James Cash Penney
1875–1971

"No man can be himself alone; he is the sum of all the influences of all his associations. I am not inclined to think of the Penney Company as a creation of mine. It is bigger than anything one individual could ever create or be. It is the finest example I know of cooperative effort; people sharing in what they helped to create have made it what it is. Whatever I had to do with its beginning, by injecting a few cardinal ideas into the selling of merchandise, has come back to me a hundred-fold in the confidence—and I think I may say, humbly, the love—of my associates. All along the way they have strengthened me with their esteem; the desire to be worthy of them has made me a better man."

James Cash Penney

Courtesy J. C. Penney Company, Inc.

Early Kroger stores and a modern Kroger supermarket.

Photos courtesy Kroger Co., Cincinnati, OH

The collapse of the stock market and the rigors of the Great Depression spawned a new retailing institution: the *supermarket*. Consumers responded favorably to its strong appeals: prices substantially lower than those found at the neighborhood grocery, self-selection and self-service, and an atmosphere very much in keeping with the difficult times people were then experiencing. These low-overhead, low-profit enterprises were housed in premises that were poorly illuminated and sparsely furnished. Goods were displayed on the floor in opened cartons. Over the next 15 years, another low-price, low-overhead retail type began to spring up: the *discount house.* By the end of World War II, a number of discounters had launched large, starkly outfitted stores, mostly in secondary locations. They offered famous brands of radios, TVs, and other appliances, cameras and photographic equipment, and other articles at reduced prices. Their marketing strategy was to undersell department stores and other traditional retailers of similar merchandise. A few were membership operations; they closed their doors to the general public, admitting only card holders.

During the 1950s and 1960s, the continuing flight of in-city residents to suburbs all across the nation lent impetus to the construction of *planned shopping centers.* Within a few years, centers of all kinds, sizes, and shapes began to dot the countryside as more and more retailers followed their clienteles into suburbia. Interest in the *franchise system of distribution* grew in the 1960s, and the numbers of franchised outlets and franchisors proliferated during the 1970s. Newer types of retailers continued to grow in popularity, among them the furniture warehouse, catalog showroom, and combination store. Some of today's types are described in the next section. Others, because of their significance to the economy, are treated in greater detail in Chapter 4.

Beverly Center, a regional retail development in Los Angeles, California. Shopping centers evolved as consumers began to relocate to the suburbs.

Courtesy The Taubman Company, Inc., Troy, MI/Richard Gordon photo

Types and Classifications of Retail Enterprises Today

It would be difficult to embrace the enormous range and variety of today's retail types in a single chapter. Any number of approaches might be followed in attempting to portray the complexities of the industry. An obvious starting point would be to divide retailers into store or nonstore types. Examples of nonstore retailers include mail-order and door-to-door selling operations. We might also classify companies as either merchandise or service retailers. Still another approach would be to categorize existing ownership arrangements: those maintained contractually (like franchises) and those that are not. This would lead us to consider categories such as independent retailers, chain organizations, franchises, wholesaler-sponsored voluntary chains, consumer cooperatives, military commissaries and post exchanges, and so on. Moreover, it would be of value to treat the complex food retailing industry separately. Aside from restaurants of all kinds (sit-down, fast-food, carry-out), there are groceries, meat markets, fruit-and-vegetable stands, bakeries, and other traditional types. We also buy food at convenience stores, delicatessens, supermarkets, combination stores, superstores, box stores, warehouse outlets, food cooperatives, and the like.

Perhaps the most reasonable avenue would be to classify today's retail firms by the kinds of goods they carry. Under this scheme, most operations may be categorized as general merchandise, single-line, limited-line, or specialty retailers. Figure 1.3 presents an overview of total sales produced during 1983 by selected merchandise types.

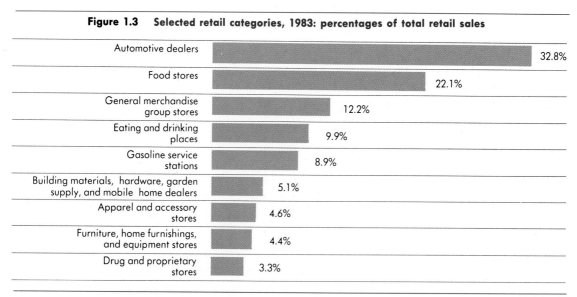

Figure 1.3   Selected retail categories, 1983: percentages of total retail sales

Automotive dealers	32.8%
Food stores	22.1%
General merchandise group stores	12.2%
Eating and drinking places	9.9%
Gasoline service stations	8.9%
Building materials, hardware, garden supply, and mobile home dealers	5.1%
Apparel and accessory stores	4.6%
Furniture, home furnishings, and equipment stores	4.4%
Drug and proprietary stores	3.3%

Source: U.S. Department of Commerce, Bureau of the Census, *Statistical Abstract of the United States, 1984–1985,* 105th ed. (Washington, D.C.: U.S. Government Printing Office, 1984), p. 782.

Table 1.1 **Selected store types,** **1982**		

Type of Retail Store	Number of Establishments with Payrolls, 1982 (000)	Total Sales ($ billions)
Auto and home supply stores	40.0	$ 20.4
Building materials, supply stores	33.9	34.7
Department stores	10.0	107.1
Drinking places (alcoholic beverages)	61.2	8.6
Drug and proprietary stores	48.6	35.8
Eating places	257.6	92.2
Family clothing stores	17.9	13.5
Florists	20.9	3.1
Furniture stores	29.6	17.2
Gasoline service stations	116.2	94.8
Gift, novelty, and souvenir stores	22.3	2.2
Grocery stores	128.1	225.7
Hardware stores	19.6	8.4
Jewelry stores	22.2	8.3
Liquor stores	34.1	17.1
Men's and boys' clothing and furnishings stores	17.4	7.7
Motor vehicle dealers	25.6	152.0
Radio, TV, and music stores	28.6	7.7
Shoestores	36.0	11.3
Sporting goods stores and bicycle shops	20.1	7.5
Variety stores	10.8	7.9
Women's clothing, specialty stores and furriers	51.0	22.2

Source: U.S. Department of Commerce, Bureau of the Census, *Statistical Abstract of the United States, 1984–85,* 105th ed. (Washington, D.C.: U.S. Government Printing Office, 1984), p. 786.

You will note that automotive dealers and food stores alone accounted for over half of the nearly $1.2 billion in retail sales that year.

Table 1.1 contains sales and other information for 1982 for selected types of stores.

General Merchandise Retailers

Because they offer a number of different product lines, department stores, variety stores, and discount houses are frequently referred to as **general merchandise retailers.** Present-day department stores are large departmentized facilities that enjoy annual sales in the millions of dollars. They offer a number of merchandise lines, among them family apparel, furniture, appliances, linens, cosmetics, and others. Dayton-Hudson, Macy's, Dillard's, Foley's, and Bullock's are some examples. The modern discount stores have evolved since their beginnings in the 1940s. Many have expanded their assortments to include family apparel, housewares, linens and dry goods, stationery, and other lines. New discounters have also entered the field. Today, these retail companies may be better described as mass merchandisers, rather than discounters. Among the more popular names today are Zayre, K mart, and Wal-Mart.

Department stores and discount houses are treated in more depth in Chapter 4—along with chain store organizations, supermarkets, and franchises.

Variety stores typically offer as many as 18 or 20 different lines: household items, dry goods, some apparel, kitchen utensils, stationery, notions, candy, and so on. Goods are displayed prominently and sold through self-selection and self-service.

A more recent low-price retail type, the **catalog showroom** has demonstrated an even faster rate of growth than the discount store. Operating with low overhead, this aggressive retailer sells name-brand goods at prices substantially below those at other stores. Usually offered are high-markup goods such as cameras, small appliances, jewelry, and the like. The full-color catalogs are printed with product descriptions, code numbers, and both regular and discount selling prices. When shoppers come to the showroom, they consult the catalogs at desks and write up order blanks. Next, they bring the completed forms to a sales counter where a clerk fills the order from inventory held in the back room. The customers pay for their merchandise and take it with them. Showroom patrons tend to be price and brand conscious.[12]

The catalog showroom concept has spawned another interesting retail type. A store in Richmond, Virginia, combines mail-order shopping with electronic retailing. It is the outcome of a merger between two companies: Catalogia, of Tuxedo Park, New York, and World Catalog Centers.[13] Shoppers screen catalogs for specific articles using a computer terminal. The firm receives a fee on every order, an amount that varies with ticket size and sales volume. Plans are to open hundreds of such units over the next few years, most of them as franchises.

Single-line and Limited-line Specialty Retailers

A clear line cannot easily be drawn between single-line and limited-line stores, since both types basically specialize in a single merchandise line. Thus, both are often referred to as *specialty retailers*. Among the better-known specialty chains are Radio Shack, Toys "R" Us, Lerner's, Levitz, and Thom McAn. (See the section on chain store operations in Chapter 4.) The major point of distinction between the two appears to be the width and depth of the assortment carried. **Single-line retailers** offer a broad selection in one category. They also usually stock additional merchandise to round out their offerings. **Lim-**

Specialty retailers include franchise merchandise outlets and consumer service businesses.

Courtesy Wild Tops Franchising, Inc., Ashland, MA

Courtesy Cutco Industries, Inc., Jericho, NY

ited-line retailers typically have smaller stores and carry a reduced number of offerings in one line. There are specialty bookstores, for instance, that offer only Catholic or Protestant works or books written in Spanish, Greek, or some other language. There are book dealers who specialize in only the arts or the physical sciences. Single-line and limited-line outlets are found in most merchandise lines: jewelry, hardware, flowers and plants, shoes, liquor, linens, and sporting goods are a few common examples. Beauty salons, travel agencies, opticians, hand laundries, upholsterers, automotive repairs, theaters, and many other service operations are also regarded as specialty retailers.

Miscellaneous Retail Types

Although many other types of retail operations exist, we will mention only a few. **Boutiques** are small specialty shops that feature a narrow range of exclusive, fashionable merchandise in an attractive atmosphere. They are often found in jewelry, women's apparel, bathroom accessories, gourmet foods, and a number of other lines. Many department stores have adapted the boutique approach as a welcome relief from the monotony of conventional departmental layouts. In effect, they set up mini-stores, stocked with related merchandise and built around individual lifestyle themes to pique shopper interest. **Leased departments** are sections of discount houses, department stores, and other large outlets that are rented to and managed by outside individuals or firms. Retail management often tries to incorporate new merchandise lines or new services at reduced risk. They rent the necessary space, utilities, and support services (such as store credit) to operators who have the know-how and skills to run that type of business successfully. Rent paid to the store by the operator is usually a percentage of the department's sales. Many service operations in larger stores are leased departments: coffee or snack shop, optical department, travel agency, beauty parlor, dental clinic, and the like. Among the kinds of goods often sold in this manner are men's clothing, shoes, and children's apparel. **Furniture warehouses** are large promotional mass-merchandising operations that combine warehouse facilities with an extensive showroom operation. The typical outlet is a maze of room settings and open areas stocked with armchairs and recliners, living-room suites, dining-room furniture, and the like. The premises are huge, frequently occupying many times the area of the average furniture store. In the warehouse section, couches, tables, and other furniture are stored on racks, stacked up to 40 feet or more by forklifts. Levitz and other furniture warehouse retailers offer national-brand goods at reduced prices.

Vertical Marketing Systems (VMSs)

Retailers obtain most of their merchandise from wholesalers for resale to consumers. The wholesaling intermediaries procure their goods from manufacturers. Normally, then, two or more independent companies operate collectively, forming a network, or *marketing channel*. It is through this channel that manufactured items flow from producers to consumers, who buy them at retail stores. Not all channel arrangements involve independent members working together, however. There

Franchise companies like Swiss Colony Stores, Inc., are a form of vertical marketing system.

Courtesy Swiss Colony Stores, Inc., Monroe, WI

are manufacturers, for example, who prefer to maintain complete control over the distribution of their products. They may integrate forward by setting up their own warehouses and stores, thus establishing a private *vertical marketing system (VMS)*. With a VMS, the company can administer the pricing approaches they desire, maintain quality control, gainfully assign specialized personnel, benefit by tried-and-proven internal systems, controls, and accounting procedures, and retain all profits. Sherwin-Williams (paints), Kodak (film), and Hart, Shaffner, & Marx (clothing) are among the many producers who operate their own retail outlets.

Contractual approaches to channel management and control are also very much in evidence. Franchising, discussed in more depth in Chapter 4, is a case in point. Names like McDonald's, Holiday Inn, Howard Johnson's, Kentucky Fried Chicken, Bonanza, Baskin-Robbins, Pizza Hut, and Dunkin' Donuts attest to the popularity of this form of VMS. Also worthy of mention are two other kinds of contractual systems: the **wholesaler-sponsored voluntary chain** and the **retailer cooperative**. As the name indicates, the first channel arrangement is launched by a strong wholesaling company in search of wider distribution and more product-market control. The distributor urges independent retail firms in its field to become members, offering them such advantages as lower wholesale prices (feasible because of the greater buying power it can command), assistance in inventory control and bookkeeping procedures, promotional aid, and the like. These chains are commonly found in hardware, drugs, and some other retail lines.

Retailer cooperatives are associations, or federations, of independent retailers who have joined in order to enjoy the benefits of acting in concert. In effect, they integrate backwards by setting up their own wholesaling operation. They buy merchandise in larger quantities at lower prices. They establish a common warehouse, share advertising expenses, and may even issue their own private-label products. Retailer cooperatives operate in the groceries, hardware, automotive supplies, and other merchandise lines.

Food Retailers: Selected Types   As mentioned earlier, groceries and other food products are distributed through a variety of store types. These retailers range from small convenience-food units to giant superstores. Several types are identified and briefly discusssed in the next section.

Convenience Stores Occasionally referred to as "bantam stores," the **convenience store** is a mini-grocery with a strong convenience appeal for the local community. It carries a limited assortment of groceries and impulse goods, usually stocking only the more popular brands. Customer convenience stems from its neighborhood location and its extended store hours. Many of these small stores are open around the clock. Largest of all convenience chains are the 7-Eleven units, franchised by the Dallas-based Southland Corporation. Other well-known chains include the Circle K, Little General, and UtoteM stores.[14]

During the 1970s, Texaco and other oil companies began converting their gasoline service stations into convenience outlets. Early in 1984, Mobil Oil (owner of Montgomery Ward), followed suit. The company announced plans to convert its "full-service stations into self-service gas islands in combination with convenience stores." Mobil, supplier to some 12,000 stations, refers to these new outlets as snack shops.[15]

Supermarkets By the early 1970s, nearly four out of every five dollars in grocery sales nationally were being recorded at supermarket outlets.[16] Unlike their Depression-years counterparts, today's **supermarkets** are large, high-volume stores with wide aisles, ample illumination, and attractive decor. In addition to groceries, fruits and vegetables, dairy products, meats, and other edibles, they stock a wide variety of household necessities, health and beauty aids, and other nonfood lines. Among the more popular chains in the field are Kroger, Safeway, Winn-Dixie, and A&P. (More details about this important retail institution appear in Chapter 4.)

Box and Combination Stores Intense competition, high overhead costs, and low gross margins on grocery items have traditionally held down supermarket profits. When profits are expressed as a percentage of sales, supermarkets have historically shown a narrow range of below 1 percent to perhaps 3 percent. Some operators have tried to slash overhead by opening smaller outlets called **box stores.** These are low-price, self-service food stores that carry a much narrower assortment than the supermarket. They also do not offer perishable merchandise or extra services. Some require shoppers to bring their own paper bags. The PLUS stores and A&P's LoLo units are examples. Following an opposite strategy, other managements acquire larger premises to combine drugs and pharmaceuticals, or general merchandise, and a supermarket. Generally double or triple the size of a conventional supermarket, these **combination stores** run from 30,000 to 50,000 square feet and even more.

Superstores and Hypermarkets Even larger than the combination store, the **superstore** is a truly modern mass merchandiser. Not only does it encompass a large and complete supermarket and prescription pharmacy, but it also stocks many other merchandise lines: housewares, garden supplies, personal care items, appliances, wines, apparel, bakery products, and so on. Snack shops and other service operations are also often present. Many Kroger and Pathmark stores fall into this category. Finally, much bigger than the superstore and at the opposite end of the size spectrum from the small convenience store lies the giant European **hypermarket.** This is a huge, general merchandise outlet that combines the equivalent of a large discount house—and a sizable supermarket and drugstore—under a single roof.[17] Furniture, large household appliances, and automotive repairs are also offered. To handle the high volume of sales requires as many as 40 or more checkout stations. The first hypermarket, opened by Carrefour, appeared in a Parisian suburb in the early 1960s. By 1973, there were more than 250 such outlets in France.[18] Despite two or three attempts at launching a similar store in the United States (such as those by Fed-mart), this innovative retail institution has yet to succeed here.

Other Food Retailers Before leaving food marketing, we should mention two other types of retail outlets: the **consumer cooperative** and the **military commissary.** Most consumer cooperatives are food stores, although there are some nonfood operations. These stores are established by consumers who are anxious to save on their food budgets. Members usually pay regular market prices for their purchases, but because they own shares in the enterprise, they receive dividends. In effect, then, the returned monies reduce their food costs. Cooperatives in the United States have never enjoyed the popularity that they have in France, England, and other countries.[19]

The federal government operates military retail stores such as army post exchanges, navy stores, and commissaries—large grocery outlets for service personnel. Prices at these commissaries are generally below those of regular consumer supermarkets. Indeed, sales levels in these outlets have been found to be directly influenced by the physical attractiveness of the store, the relative pricing advantage, and the present service level.[20]

Summary   The retailing sector is a busy and vital link in our distribution system. Retailers buy goods from manufacturers and wholesalers and resell them to consumers to satisfy their needs and wants. Buying, selling, storing, transportation, and risk-taking are among the major functions performed by retail enterprises.

Total sales of the approximately 1.6 million retail establishments in operation now exceed $1 trillion annually. More than 13 million people work in the industry.

Our earliest retail institution was the trading post. This was followed by the Yankee peddler, general store, and single-line store. Department stores and mail-order houses first appeared after the end of the Civil War. The first two decades of the 20th century saw the rapid proliferation of chain stores. Supermarkets became popular during the Depression years. Planned shopping centers began to take hold during the 1950s, and their construction accelerated in the 1960s and 1970s. We also witnessed a tremendous expansion in franchising, a method of distribution that had been around since the turn of the century.

Most of today's retail enterprises can be classified as general merchandise, single-line, limited-line, or specialty retailers. Department stores, discount houses, variety stores, and other general merchandise retailers offer shoppers a number of different product lines. Single-line stores offer a broad selection of goods in one merchandise line. The smaller limited-line stores carry fewer offerings in one line.

Among other retail categories of interest are boutiques, leased departments, furniture warehouses, franchises and other vertical marketing systems such as the wholesaler-sponsored voluntary chain and the retailer cooperative.

A number of store types are engaged in food marketing. Among them are convenience stores, supermarkets, box stores, combination stores, superstores, consumer cooperatives, and commissaries.

Key Terms

retailing	furniture warehouses
Wheel of Retailing	wholesaler-sponsored voluntary chain
conglomerchant	retailer cooperative
general store	convenience store
single-line store	supermarket
general merchandise retailer	box stores
variety store	combination stores
catalog showroom	superstore
single-line retailer	hypermarket
limited-line retailer	consumer cooperative
boutiques	military commissary
leased departments	

Review Questions

1. Offer a brief definition of retailing and explain how it differs from manufacturing or wholesaling.

2. Name and describe at least five major functions that are performed in the retailing process.

3. List a minimum of six significant developments or trends witnessed in the retailing sector in recent years.

4. Cite two factors that have contributed to the belief by some authorities that the Wheel of Retailing may be slowing down.

5. Arrange the following innovations in their order of evolution:

   a. Supermarkets.   d. Chain store organizations.
   b. Discount houses.   e. Mail order houses.
   c. Department stores.   f. Planned shopping centers.

6. Cite three approaches for classifying today's retail enterprises. other than by merchandise categories.

7. Clearly distinguish between general merchandisers and single-line retailers.

8. Describe the major characteristics of each of the following retail types:

   a. Boutique.   d. Convenience store.
   b. Leased department.   e. Superstore.
   c. Furniture warehouse.   f. Commissary.

9. What are vertical marketing systems?

10. What benefits might an independent retailer gain by joining a wholesaler-sponsored voluntary chain?

Discussion Questions

1. In your opinion, what is meant by the trend toward professionalism among retail managers?

2. Within little more than a decade, the total volume of retail sales nearly tripled over that recorded for 1970. Yet when sales per capita are expressed in constant (1972) dollars, the growth curve appears rather weak. Speculate about some reasons why this may be so.

3. In your own words, explain the Wheel of Retailing hypothesis. Suggest three newer types of retailers to which the theory does not seem to apply.

4. Briefly trace the evolution of retailing in America from early colonial days to the end of the 19th century.

Notes

[1]John F. Cady, "Structural Trends in Retailing: The Decline of Small Business?" *Journal of Contemporary Business* 5 (Spring 1976), pp. 67–96.

[2]Elizabeth C. Hirschman and Ronald W. Stampfl, "Roles of Retailing in the Diffusion of Popular Culture: Microperspectives," *Journal of Retailing* 56 (Spring 1980), p. 36.

[3]For example, see: William R. Davidson, "Changes in Distributive Institutions," *Journal of Marketing* 34 (January 1970), pp. 7–10; William R. Davidson and Alice L. Rodgers, "Changes and Challenges in Retailing," *Business Horizons* 24 (January–February 1981), pp. 82–87.

[4]These are explained later in the chapter.

[5]David P. Schulz, "Expansion," *Stores* 65 (August 1983), p. 30.

[6]Stanley C. Hollander, "The Wheel of Retailing," *Journal of Marketing* 24 (July 1960), pp. 37–42.

[7]Dillard B. Tinsely, John R. Brooks, Jr., and Michael d'Amico, "Will the Wheel of Retailing Stop Turning?" *Akron Business and Economic Review* 9 (Summer 1978), pp. 26–29.

[8]Rollie Tillman, "The Rise of the Conglomerchant," *Harvard Business Review* 49 (November–December 1971), p. 45.

[9]See Chapter 4 for more information about these companies.

[10]Tinsely et al., "Will the Wheel Stop?" p. 29.

[11]Malcolm P. McNair and Eleanor G. May, "The Next Revolution of the Retailing Wheel," *Harvard Business Review* 56 (September–October 1978), pp. 81–91.

[12]Pradeep K. Korgaonkar, "Shopping Orientations of Catalog Showroom Patrons," *Journal of Retailing* 57 (Spring 1981), pp. 78–90; Pradeep K. Korgaonkar, "Consumer Preferences for Catalog Showrooms and Discount Stores: The Moderating Role of Product Risk," *Journal of Retailing* 58 (Fall 1982), pp. 76–87.

[13]"Catalogia Weds Old and New," *Chain Store Age, General Merchandise Edition* 60 (February 1984), pp. 34*ff.*

[14]"Convenience Stores: A $7.4 Billion Mushroom," *Business Week* (21 March 1977), p. 61.

[15]Carol E. Curtis, "Mobil Wants to Be Your Milkman," *Forbes* (13 February 1984), pp. 44–45.

[16]Walter J. Salmon, Robert D. Buzzell, and Stanton G. Cort, "Today the Shopping Center, Tomorrow the Superstore," *Harvard Business Review* 52 (January–February 1974), p. 89.

[17]Eric Langeard and Robert A. Peterson, "Diffusion of Large-scale Food Retailing in France: *Supermarché et Hypermarché,*" *Journal of Retailing* 51 (Fall 1975), pp. 43–63*ff.*

[18]Ibid., p. 58.

[19]For an introduction to this comparatively small area, see: Ronald C. Curhan and Edward G. Wertheim, "Consumer Food Buying Cooperatives Revisited: A Comparison from 1971 to 1974," *Journal of Retailing* 51 (Winter 1975–76), pp. 22–32*ff;* Robert Sommer, William E. Hohn, and Jason Tyburczy, "Motivation of Food Cooperative Members: Reply to Curhan and Wertheim," *Journal of Retailing* 57 (Winter 1981), pp. 114–16; Robert Sommer et al., "Customer Characteristics and Attitudes at Participatory and Supermarket Cooperatives," *Journal of Consumer Affairs* 17 (Summer 1983), pp. 134–49; Elizabeth A. Schifert and Robert D. Boynton, "A Comparative Performance Analysis of New Wave Food Cooperatives and Private Food Stores," *Journal of Consumer Affairs* 17 (Winter 1983), pp. 336–53.

[20]Richard C. Morey, "Measuring the Impact of Service Level on Retail Sales," *Journal of Retailing* 56 (Summer 1980), p. 90.

CHAPTER 2

Courtesy Hilton Hotels Corporation, Beverly Hills, CA

RETAILING TODAY

Your Study Objectives

After you have studied this chapter, you will understand:

1. The role of the independent retailer.
2. What services are and the growing importance of service retailing.
3. The three major categories of nonstore retailers.
4. The overseas expansion of American retailers and foreign interests in domestic retailing.

The Small Independent Retailer

Independent retailers represent the foundation and the bulwark of the retailing industry. Nearly 8 out of every 10 retailers own and operate only one store. Despite the small size of their operations, these business owners collectively account for over one half of the $1 trillion-plus in retail sales each year. Today's giant department store and chain store organizations were the small independent retailers of yesteryear. Hundreds of thousands of new retail enterprises are launched annually. Unfortunately, a similar number also close down.

Among the more common types of independent retail establishments are restaurants, bars, groceries, gasoline service stations, car dealerships, furniture and home furnishings outlets, and women's apparel and specialty shops. Many consumer services are also popular. These include, for example: banking services, automotive repairs, beauty salons and barber shops, dry cleaning and laundry services, motels and hotels, dental and medical services, colleges and universities, and other types. Much less popular are bookstores, variety stores, household appliance stores, toy and hobby shops, and retail bakeries. Fewer than 20,000 of each of these types are to be found across the country.

New kinds of retail businesses continue to appear. Among the more notable types seen in recent years are soup-and-salad restaurants, frozen yogurt shops, cookie stores, plant shops, VCR rental services, computer stores, and computer repair shops.

Owning Your Own Business

At some time in our lives, many of us daydream about self-employment as an alternative way to earn a living. Many actively explore its possibilities. In recent years, more and more people seem to be taking the plunge; the number of new business starts grows from one year to the next. For decades, business writers have pegged the formation of new ventures at around 350,000 to 400,000 a year. The actual figure, however, may be much higher—perhaps as high as 2 million or more.[1] According to one report, the total number of new enterprises of all types launched in 1983 was close to 581,000.[2]

Why Go into Business? People launch businesses of their own for any number of reasons. Some simply seek independence. They are willing to undertake all challenges and responsibilities, prefer making their own decisions, and do not like taking orders from others. Other people look forward to the opportunity of accumulating wealth, believing that they could never hope to become rich by working for someone else. Still others enter retailing because they enjoy interacting with shoppers, or they like the idea that sales dollars are taken in every day, or they are knowledgeable about and adept at buying the kinds of merchandise they plan to offer.

Dissatisfaction with a job is often a precipitating factor in the decision to seek self-employment.[3] We also see thousands of people switch-

Independent retail businesses like this successful sandwich shop are the foundation and the bulwark of the retailing industry. Today's giant retailers were the small independents of yesteryear.

Eleanore Snow

ing careers in their late 30s and 40s. Many of these individuals start their own businesses. More mid-career changes can be expected in the years ahead because of the changing composition of the population. Among the contributing factors are an increasing life expectancy, a rising median age, and growing numbers of women who seek employment.[4] Many of these new business owners will be former company executives, civil service employees, and women who have worked in many different fields.[5]

Drawbacks to Self-Employment There are disadvantages attached to starting an enterprise. For one thing, business owners must bear considerable responsibility. They cannot pass the buck to others. Entrepreneurs may have to perform tasks they do not like, put in long hours, and take work home with them after closing up. They need to learn how to cope with change, unexpected events, disappointments, and setbacks. Often, during the first months of operation, they are unable to take any income out of the business. Other typical limitations of the small-scale retail firm include initial undercapitalization, inability to secure merchandise at favorable prices, inability to afford specialized personnel, lack of managerial know-how, and a modest promotion budget.

Laypeople and business writers alike have often speculated about the personal characteristics required to succeed in your own business. Research has suggested that more successful entrepreneurs are flexible, willing to take risks, tolerant of frustration, creative, and persistent.[6]

Other traits that have been linked to entrepreneurial success are the need for achievement, a high level of motivation, self-discipline, and self-confidence.[7]

New Business Failures in Retailing

Retailing is easy to enter, but it also reflects a high mortality rate. A substantial percentage of new businesses fail in their first few years. The Dun & Bradstreet Corporation issues an annual *Business Failure Record*. In this publication, recent failures in different types of businesses are analyzed. As you can see in Figure 2.1, the major underlying causes of failures among retail companies in 1981 were incompetence, unbalanced experience, lack of experience in the line, and lack of managerial experience.

The odds of failure are linked, in part, to the specific type of retailing entered. Shown in Table 2.1 are the failure rates for various retail lines the same year. Topping the list were infants' and children's clothing stores. Among the types reflecting lower failure rates were drugstores; groceries, meat, and produce stores; and women's accessories shops. It should be understood, however, that actual business failures represent only a small percentage of the enterprises that are discontinued each year. The majority of these do not go into bankruptcy.

Figure 2.1
Underlying causes of 6,882 retail failures

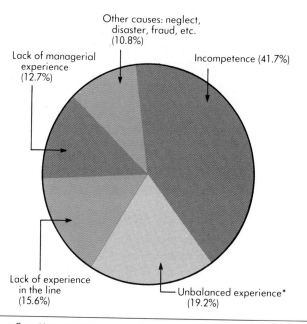

Other causes: neglect, disaster, fraud, etc. (10.8%)

Incompetence (41.7%)

Lack of managerial experience (12.7%)

Lack of experience in the line (15.6%)

Unbalanced experience* (19.2%)

* Owner(s) or corporation officers not well rounded in sales, finance, purchasing, and production.
Source: Economic Analysis Department, *The 1981 Dun & Bradstreet Business Failure Record* (New York: The Dun & Bradstreet Corporation, 1983), p. 12. Used with permission.

Table 2.1 **Retail lines ranked by** **failure rates**	

Lines of Business	Failure Rate per 10,000 Operating Concerns
Infants' and children's wear	114
Furniture and furnishings	84
Dry goods and general merchandise	78
Sporting goods	78
Lumber and building materials	64
Women's ready-to-wear	61
Menswear	57
Appliances, radio and TV	56
Cameras and photographic supplies	46
Auto parts and accessories	46
Shoes	42
Books and stationery	40
Bakeries	39
Eating and drinking places	37
Hardware	37
Automobiles	34
Gifts	33
Toys and hobby crafts	26
Jewelry	24
Women's accessories	23
Groceries, meats and produce	21
Drugs	20
Department stores	16

Source: Economic Analysis Department, *The 1981 Dun & Bradstreet Business Failure Record* (New York: The Dun & Bradstreet Corporation, 1983), p. 6. Used with permission.

One research study tracked thousands of new enterprises in the state of Illinois over a five-year period. Its findings contradicted the popular belief that 85 to 90 percent of all new businesses fail in the first few years of operation. About one third of these retailers were still open after more than five years.[8] Among the more successful were hardware and drugstores, car dealers, and retailers of farm equipment. Restaurants, groceries, and gasoline service stations reflected the poorest survival rate. It appeared that the larger the size, the higher the rate of survival.

Problems of Small Independents Generally, small businesses of all kinds encounter difficulties in such areas as advertising and promotion, accounting records, inventory control, inadequate sales, and cash flow.[9] Among independent retailers in small towns, marketing may be the most troublesome area, and advertising the most common marketing problem.[10] Small-town merchants also have problems with accounting and finance. Among the operating difficulties reported by small retailers in one major metropolitan area were shoplifting, getting and keeping competent employees, and maintaining proper inventory levels.[11]

Large-scale Retailing

Small independent operations constitute by far the bulk of American retailers. At the other end of the spectrum are the larger firms, which, while far fewer in number than the independents, have a powerful impact on our economy. The size of their holdings is indeed difficult to imagine. Many count their assets in the billions of dollars.

Table 2.2 presents 1983 sales results for the top 20 retailing companies. As you can see, revenues for the first five listed totaled more than $100 billion. To give you some idea of their size and scope,

Table 2.2
Top 20 retailers in 1983

Rank	Name of Company (Home Offices)	Sales ($ billions)	Number of Employees
1	Sears, Roebuck (Chicago, Ill)	$35.9	450,000
2	K mart (Troy, Mich.)	18.6	250,000
3	Safeway Stores (Oakland, Calif.)	18.6	162,100
4	Kroger (Cincinnati, Ohio)	15.2	162,000
5	J. C. Penney (New York, N.Y.)	12.1	175,000
6	Southland (Dallas, Tex.)	8.8	60,800
7	Federated Department Stores (Cincinnati, Ohio)	8.7	123,700
8	Lucky Stores (Dublin, Calif.)	8.4	65,000
9	American Stores (Salt Lake City, Utah)	8.0	60,000
10	Household International (Prospect Heights, Ill.)	7.9	77,000
11	Winn-Dixie Stores (Jacksonville, Fla.)	7.0	66,500
12	Dayton-Hudson (Minneapolis, Minn.)	7.0	100,000
13	Montgomery Ward (Chicago, Ill.)	6.0	78,500
14	Jewel Companies (Chicago, Ill.)	5.7	36,600

Table 2.2
(concluded)

Rank	Name of Company (Home Offices)	Sales ($ billions)	Number of Employees
15	BATUS (Louisville, Ky.)	5.5	64,000
16	F. W. Woolworth (New York, N.Y.)	5.5	114,600
17	Wal-Mart Stores (Bentonville, Ark.)	4.7	62,000
18	Great Atlantic & Pacific Tea (Montvale, N.J.)	4.6	40,000
19	Albertson's (Boise, Idaho)	4.3	34,000
20	May Department Stores (St. Louis, Mo.)	4.2	70,200

Source: Fortune, "The 50 Largest Retail Companies," June 11, 1984 issue, "© 1984 Time Inc. All rights reserved."

these same five firms controlled assets amounting to more than $69 billion. They also employed nearly 1.2 million people.[12]

Because of their significance in retailing, further discussion of some large-scale retailers will be found in Chapter 4. That chapter elaborates on some notable types: their characteristics, advantages and disadvantages, operating methods, and so on. It focuses on department stores, chain organizations, supermarkets, discount stores and other mass merchandisers, and retail franchising systems.

Service Retailing

Services now account for well over 15 percent of our national income. This percentage is higher than that derived from both of the distributive trades (retailing and wholesaling). As indicated in Table 2.3, income from our service industries grew from $44.7 billion in 1960 to some $426.6 billion by 1983. This represents more than a ninefold increase in only 23 years. By way of contrast, national income from the retail trades in 1983 totaled $209.7 billion, while another $152.4 billion were produced through wholesaling activity.[13] In the years ahead, we can look forward to the service sector accounting for even higher proportions of our national income. Topping the list of services in 1983 were medical and other health services, for a total yield of nearly $145 billion.

Over 20 million people work in the service sector. This is a larger number than all who earn their livelihoods in retailing and wholesaling combined.

Table 2.3
National income from
service indiustries*

Industry	Income ($ billions)			
	1960	**1970**	**1980**	**1983**
Amusement and recreational services	$ 1.7	$ 3.2	$ 9.0	$ 11.9
Auto repair, services, and garages	1.7	3.7	11.2	13.7
Educational services	2.2	7.0	15.4	19.8
Hotels and other lodging places	2.0	4.5	13.8	17.4
Legal services	2.7	6.7	21.3	32.5
Medical and other health services	10.7	29.4	99.6	144.9
Membership organizations†	4.5	10.0	24.9	31.4
Motion pictures	0.9	1.7	3.8	5.2
Miscellaneous business services	5.4	15.0	53.0	77.9
Miscellaneous professional services	3.4	8.8	31.0	40.4
Miscellaneous repair services	1.1	2.2	6.8	7.5
Personal services	4.6	7.6	13.3	16.4
Private household services	3.8	4.5	6.6	7.8
All services	44.7	104.1	310.0	426.6

* Refers to national income without capital consumption data. Data for 1960 exclude Alaska and Hawaii.
† Includes social services.

Source: U.S. Department of Commerce, Bureau of the Census, *Statistical Abstract of the United States, 1984–85,* 105th ed. (Washington, D.C.: U.S. Government Printing Office, 1984), p. 780.

What Services Are   **Services** are difficult to define. We can, however, agree on a basic distinction between services and products. Products are tangible objects that are made, manufactured, fabricated, or produced. The Committee on Definitions of the American Marketing Association describes services as "activities, benefits, or satisfactions which are offered for sale or are provided in connection with the sale of goods."[14]

Many factors have contributed to the strong growth of the service sector. An obvious one is the steadily increasing number of wives who work, bringing second incomes into their households. Thus, more disposable funds are available for discretionary spending: on luxury products and services, leisure-time activities, travel, and the like. Another significant factor is the rapid rise in household formations, most notably the surprising surge in the nonfamily type.[15] As a direct consequence, demand for home buying and rental services has been growing. More and more, consumers want to rent rather than purchase expensive goods outright: cars, sports equipment, videocassette recorders, TVs, and so on. The selling prices of such articles have gone up considerably, fueled by escalating costs of labor and materials. Similarly, the costs of medical care, hospitalization, and other health-related services have skyrocketed since the 1970s.

The Hilton Hawaiian Village. Retail service businesses like this flourish when consumer disposable income becomes available for luxury products and services, leisure activities, and travel.

Courtesy Hilton Hotels Corporation, Beverly Hills, CA

Distinguishing Features of Service Offerings Three characteristics distinguish services from product offerings: intangibility, inseparability, and perishability.[16]

Intangibility As we have already noted, products are concrete objects, things that can be seen and touched. Services, on the other hand, are intangible. We buy admission tickets to a theater, see the show, are (we hope) entertained, and leave the theater with little more than a satisfied feeling and a pleasant memory. If we take a taxi home, we pay the driver for the transportation provided, but take only ourselves home. This quality of **intangibility**—something that cannot be touched or felt—makes it difficult for consumers to shop around for a particular service. Merchandise selection decisions are more easily made. We are able to choose the goods we buy from among several brands. We base our selections on our personal evaluations of such criteria as size, color, style, materials, and other product characteristics. The service retailer must furnish far more information to enable shoppers to make buying decisions than does the merchandise retailer.

Inseparability Another attribute of most services is **inseparability.** Because labor is a crucial component, we cannot separate the service from the person who performs it or from the employees we must speak with. How can we sever the ties between the services we seek and the beautician or barber; dentist, physician, or ophthalmologist; teacher at a school of music or a dance conservatory; plumber who

Some service retailers cater to the consumer's need for recreation.

Courtesy Putt-Putt Golf Courses of America, Inc. "Putt-Putt Golf Course" and "Putt-Putt Golf & Games" are U.S. Registered Trademarks, © 1984. All rights reserved.

replaces a leaky faucet; mechanic who repairs a carburetor; or airline pilot and crew that take us to our destination?

Perishability Many services reflect a third characteristic, that of **perishability.** Their shelf life is short. Unlike tangible goods, they cannot be warehoused or stored. The car that is not rented for even one day by a car rental agency represents a loss of income to the firm. If not used on the specified date, tickets for seats at a concert or on an airplane are worthless.

In general, these three characteristics have worked against the successful marketing of services. Being intangible and perishable, service offerings cannot be kept for long. Nor can retailers produce them at one location and transport them to sell at another. Consequently, many services are sold through multiple retail outlets combining promotion and production activities.[17] Consumers seem to prefer service operations that are close to their homes. The quality of inseparability also tends to localize service marketing by limiting the number of alternatives from which the consumer can choose.[18] The outputs of those who perform services can differ greatly since the production of services resists standardization. The manufacturer of goods can employ quality control methods to ensure standardization. The producer of a service cannot, without a great deal of difficulty. Indeed, "with services, contact personnel are the service."[19]

Figure 2.2 Examples of service businesses	**Industrial Services**	**Consumer Service Retailers**
	Accounting	Amusement parks
	Advertising	Car repairs
	Architectural	Beauty parlors
	Consulting	Car washes
	Insurance	Dry cleaners
	Legal	Garages
	Machinery repair	Hospitals
	Maintenance	Hotels
	Plant security	Insurance agencies
	Public relations	Movie theaters
	Research	Private schools
	Transportation	Securities dealers

Service retailers can move further toward mass marketing by routinizing operations and systems and through mechanization. We have already seen evidence of progress in the spread of automatic teller machines, automatic car washes, coin-operated machines at toll bridges, group insurance plans, and prepackaged vacation tours.[20]

Retail Services   Services may be categorized according to their ultimate users. **Industrial services** are those destined for consumption by business and other organizations that need them to conduct their operations. **Consumer services** exist to satisfy the needs and wants of consumers. Examples of both categories are shown in Figure 2.2.

For traditional goods retailers, many services hold enormous potential. Most retail services can be divided into two major classifications: (1) those that accompany the merchandise—like the installation of carpeting or draperies and (2) services that are sold independently of store merchandise. The greatest opportunities lie in the second area.[21] Services in this category include dental, financial, and legal services.

As early as 1977, dental clinics were operating at some Sears stores. We now find such clinics at units of People's Drug, Montgomery Ward, Alexander's, Times Square Stores, and other chains. Like Dentalworks and Dentcare Systems, many are franchised outlets. Dental clinics are expanding even more rapidly into shopping malls across the country, along with optical, podiatry, and other services.[22] Financial services are in an even more enviable position today. By the early 1980s, for example, five of J. C. Penney's California stores were offering money market and checking accounts, loans, second mortgages, and other services through an arrangement with a California-based bank.

Financial centers offer a broad range of consumer services in selected Sears stores.

Courtesy Sears, Roebuck & Co., Chicago

In 1983, J. C. Penney signed an agreement to acquire its own banking facility—the First National Bank of Harrington, in Delaware.[23]

Nonstore Retailing

Not all retailing requires the use of store premises. Consumer goods and services are distributed by nonstore methods as well. In fact, the sales of **nonstore retailing** have been expanding at a more accelerated pace than that of total retail sales.[24] The major categories in this classification are: (1) direct selling companies, (2) vending machine operators, and (3) mail-order houses. There are, of course, other types: flea marketers, food wagon vendors, scissors grinders, ice cream vendors, street vendors, and so on.[25]

Direct Selling Companies

Of all nonstore approaches, **direct selling** is the most costly and at the same time the most personalized. Firms and individuals engaged in direct retailing work with their customers one to one without the benefit of a store environment. As in Table 2.4, some 8,000 companies with payrolls were in operation in 1982. Sales for the category totaled nearly $4 billion.

Basically, most direct selling activities fall into two categories: canvassing and party-plan selling. **Canvassing** is door-to-door selling. Salespeople cover a neighborhood or community by knocking on doors.

Table 2.4 Nonstore retailers, 1977 and 1982						
Type of Operation	Number of Companies (000)		Total Sales ($ billions)		Five-Year Growth Percentage	
	1977	1982	1977	1982	Number of Companies	Sales
Direct selling*	8.4	8.0	$2.9	$ 3.9	−4.8%	+34.4%
Mail-order houses	6.7	7.4	7.4	10.9	+10.4	+47.3
Vending machine operators	5.7	5.4	3.7	4.6	−5.3	+24.3

* Companies with payrolls.

Source: Bureau of the Census, U.S. Department of Commerce, *Statistical Abstract of the United States: 1984–85*, 105th ed. (Washington, D.C.: U.S. Government Printing Office, 1984), p. 786.

They introduce themselves and try to gain admittance so they can make their presentations. The public's attitude toward them is, unfortunately, not at all favorable. Nowadays, most consumers are afraid to open their doors to strangers.[26] Many resent unexpected visits that interrupt their daily routines. Still others are suspicious of canvassers. They feel that these salespeople often try "to trick or influence people into buying what they do not need."[27]

In **party-plan selling,** a salesperson interests a homeowner or apartment dweller in hosting a gathering of neighbors and friends. Usually the host is rewarded with one or two token gifts. Merchandise is shown at the gathering, and orders are taken from the guests. Office parties are also popular today because so many women work.

Direct marketing companies distribute many kinds of products. Some of the better-known names in the field and the merchandise lines they are noted for are:

Amway	cleaning supplies
Avon	cosmetics and jewelry
Fuller Brush	personal and home care articles
Mary Kay	cosmetics
Sara Coventry	jewelry
Shaklee	vitamins
Stanley	housewares and cleaning products
Tupperware	plastic household items
Wear-ever Aluminum	pots and utensils
World Book	encyclopedias

Vending Machine Operators

A wide variety of merchandise is sold by means of automatic equipment. Typically, the equipment is placed in busy locations. **Vending**

From *The Wall Street Journal*, with permission of Cartoon Features Syndicate.

machine operators rent space for their coin-actuated machines in office buildings, places of entertainment, large stores, subway and train stations, airports, and the like. They fill and service the machines regularly. Among the many kinds of products sold in this manner are soft drinks and other beverages, sandwiches, snack foods, candy, cigarettes, toiletries and personal items, music, flight insurance, and computer games. As Table 2.4 indicates, the sales of these nonstore retailers reached $4.6 billion in 1982.

Mail-Order Retailing

Table 2.4 also shows some 7,400 mail-order houses in operation that same year. These companies accounted for nearly $11 billion in sales, up 47.3 percent over 1977 sales. The figure is, however, severely misleading. Not taken into account are the thousands of other retail organizations that are not mail-order houses yet transact a great deal of business by mail. The field has burgeoned so in the past several decades that practitioners now prefer the label direct marketing to mail-order retailing. According to one report, by 1984, direct marketing accounted for about 14 percent of all retail transactions.[28] Back in 1977, the Small Business Administration advised that consumers were buying more than $1 billion worth of products and services by mail every week.[29] A rapidly growing method of distribution, mail-order selling

Mail-order retailers depend on the mail and on United Parcel Service to deliver merchandise orders to their customers.

Gary Csuk

is discussed in more depth in Chapter 19. Mail-order houses offer shopping convenience and assure customer satisfaction (in the form of a money-back guarantee). Some, like Spiegel, sell general merchandise. Others, such as L.L. Bean and Herrschner's, retail specialty goods. Still others offer novelty items; Sunset House is an example. Mail-order firms distribute catalogs and mailing pieces to consumers. Shoppers place orders by mail; the merchandise is generally forwarded to them through the mails or by the United Parcel Service (UPS). The companies develop and maintain mailing lists of both buyers and prospective customers. They may also advertise in the print and broadcast media. Typically, shoppers respond to offers made on TV or in radio commercials by calling a toll-free number.

Organizations of all types and sizes engage in direct marketing these days. Gulf, Shell, and other oil companies and bank card systems such as MasterCard and VISA regularly circulate special offers to vast numbers of cardholders. Encyclopedia firms, producers of records and tapes, book publishers, and jewelry manufacturers are among the many direct marketers that advertise frequently over TV and radio. Department stores, specialty chains, and other retailers who maintain charge account lists use mailings to produce additional revenues and expand their trading areas. At Sears, Roebuck branches and at other stores, shoppers can peruse catalogs and place orders for merchandise at special desks. Thousands of catalog stores have appeared around the country in areas where demographics would make a regular outlet unprofitable.

The computer revolution has accelerated direct marketing activity. Although telecommunication retailing is still a fledgling industry, its popular acceptance may grow until it imperils traditional retail stores—especially the small independents.[30] Of course, consumer resistance, costs, and other barriers to the growth of interactive cable TV systems still exist.[31]

The mail-order field holds fascinating promise for thousands of people. Most view it as a way of starting up in business with only a modest investment. Many subscribe to the widespread notion that "Just about anything that can be sold at all can be sold by mail: products, services, even knowledge."[32] Owners of established businesses are often eager to explore this method for additional sales volume. Segmentation approaches aimed at specific markets have produced notable success stories. To cite just a few in insurance alone, there is Colonial Penn for the over-50 market, Gerber Life for families with young children, and Academy Life for veterans of our armed forces.[33]

International Retailing

Although quite modest in scope when compared to established international trade, the overseas expansion of American retailers has been growing slowly but steadily. When conducting business in other lands, these firms confront many problems. Among them are cultural differences, the preferences and dislikes of foreign consumers (as distinct from Americans), fluctuations in the rate of exchange between our currency and those of other nations, ethical differences, and the like. There is also the need to compete with the established department stores, chains, and independent retailers in the host country. Rarely do other governments have "well articulated, coherent policies toward the retail trades" and those policies in effect "are usually fragmentary, unconnected, and even inconsistent."[34]

American firms seeking outlets abroad mostly rely on franchising, joint venture, and direct investment strategies. In a franchising arrangement, the domestic retailer licenses a foreign investor to operate a business under the format of the domestic company. The **joint venture** involves a domestic firm entering into partnership with a foreign company to establish facilities overseas. **Direct investment** is the costliest approach of the three. Yet it can provide the American retailer with the greatest degree of control over the foreign marketing operation. The domestic firm infuses both capital and management know-how into the construction and operation of the overseas facility.

American Retailers Abroad

By the early 1970s, a number of U.S. franchising organizations had already established units in foreign lands. Among their ranks were

In 1984, Toys "R" Us announced plans to expand into the Middle East, Canada, Great Britain, and Singapore.

Eleanore Snow

such fast-food restaurants as McDonald's and Burger King and lodging chains like Howard Johnson and Holiday Inn. At the outset, these franchisors encountered a variety of difficulties, not the least of which were legal and governmental restraints.[35] By 1974, Tandy Corporation (parent of the Radio Shack outlets and other chain operations) had more than 100 stores abroad. Some were as far away as Australia. Plans were made for launching additional stores in Europe.[36] By the late 1970s, the Pittsburgh-based Athlete's Foot chain had facilities in Japan, England, and other countries—and contemplated opening outlets in South Africa, France, and Australia as well.[37]

Not all American retailers operating overseas are franchisors. There are general merchandise stores like J. C. Penney and Sears, Roebuck; supermarket chains such as Safeway; and direct selling organizations, including Avon and Tupperware. In 1982, the F. W. Woolworth Company tried to sell a 51 percent interest in its 24 profitable units in Mexico. Mexican law prohibits expansion by firms that are not majority owned by a native company.[38] In 1983, K mart established a subsidiary, K mart Trading Services, Inc., to provide management services for export and imports, barter and counter trade, and retail marketing of consumer goods. By that time, K mart already had offices in Japan, West Germany, and several other countries.[39] In 1984, Toys "R" Us announced plans for expansion into the Middle East, Canada, Great Britain, and Singapore, through both joint ventures and wholly owned subsidiaries.[40]

In 1982, BATUS, the American arm of London's BAT Industries, purchased the Marshall Field department store chain.

Eleanore Snow

Foreign Interests in Domestic Retailing

Foreign corporations have also been investing in American retailing. As one writer pointed out in 1980: "Over 10% of the U.S. grocery business is now owned by Europeans, including two of the top ten supermarket chains, A&P and Grand Union."[41] A German conglomerate owns A&P; Loblaw's and National Tea are owned by a Canadian company. We can expect even more involvement in U.S. retailing in the future by Oriental and Middle Eastern companies as well as European firms. Again, these will be through joint ventures as well as direct investment.[42]

Already well established in South Florida by the late 1970s, Shoppers Drug Mart (Canada's largest drugstore chain) announced plans to open some 200 stores across the country during the 1980s.[43] BATUS, of Louisville, Kentucky, is the American arm of London's BAT Industries. BATUS owns both Saks Fifth Avenue and Gimbel's. In 1982, the company purchased the Marshall Field department stores and a chain of furniture outlets for $310 million.[44]

Summary   Most retail firms in the United States are small one-store operations. These independent retailers account for more than one half of total retail sales. Every year, hundreds of thousands of new businesses are established, while nearly equal numbers close down. People start their own businesses for a variety of reasons: to be independent, a chance to become rich, dissatisfaction with a job, and so on. Most likely, such personal traits as flexibility, need for achievement, self-motivation, and self-discipline are needed to be successful in retailing.

Many new enterprises shut down in their first few years of operation. Incompetence and lack of experience are two of the more significant causes. Small-scale retailers typically have problems in both the marketing and accounting areas.

Services are a strong and fast-growing part of the economy. More than 20 million are employed in the service sector. The intangibility, inseparability, and perishability of services make it difficult to mass market them. Consumer services are of two types: those offered with goods and those sold independently. For traditional goods retailers, the second area holds great potential. Examples of such services include, among others, financial, health-related, and legal services.

Goods and services are also sold by nonstore methods. Three major types of nonstore retailers are the direct selling company, vending machine operator, and mail-order retailer.

American retailers have been expanding overseas through franchising, joint venture, and direct investment strategies. Hotels, restaurants, and specialty chains are among the more popular franchises abroad. General merchandise chains, supermarkets, direct selling organizations, and variety store chains are also represented overseas. Some foreign companies have a stake in American retailing in domestic supermarkets, department stores, and other types.

Key Terms

services	direct selling
intangibility	canvassing
inseparability	party-plan selling
perishability	vending machine operators
industrial services	joint venture
consumer services	direct investment
nonstore retailing	

Review Questions

1. List five reasons why some people go into their own business.
2. What are some of the disadvantages of self-employment?
3. Specify four underlying causes of retail failures.
4. Name 6 of the leading 20 retail organizations in 1983.
5. Differentiate between products and services.

6. *Intangibility* and *inseparability* are characteristic of most services. Explain the meaning of each of the terms.

7. Contrast industrial and consumer services. Furnish six examples of each type.

8. Identify three major categories of nonstore retailers and briefly describe each one.

9. Distinguish between door-to-door canvassing and party-plan selling.

10. Name five well-known direct marketing companies and specify the type(s) of merchandise each one offers.

Discussion Questions

1. Prepare a list of five personal characteristics you believe are essential for success in independent retailing. Give your reasons why each of these is necessary.

2. In one study of new retail enterprises, restaurants and groceries were among the store types with poor survival rates. Speculate about why this may be so.

3. Many consumer magazines carry mail-order advertising. Some examples are: *House Beautiful, Family Circle, American Legion Magazine, Good Housekeeping, Redbook, Field & Stream, Elks Magazine, Popular Mechanics,* and *Car and Driver.* At your local library, review two or three issues of any one of these publications. Make a list of the kinds of merchandise offers that appear to be popular.

4. Mass marketing has remained an elusive goal for service retailers. What recommendations can you make for the following types of retailers to move further along the road to mass marketing their services?
   a. A national motel chain.
   b. A local chain of beauty parlors.
   c. An independent dance studio.

Notes

[1]Alvin D. Star and Chem L. Narayana, "Do We Really Know the Number of Small Business Starts?" *Journal of Small Business Management* 21 (October 1983), pp. 44–48.

[2]*U.S. News & World Report* (2 April 1984), p. 18.

[3]Robert H. Brockhaus, "The Effect of Job Dissatisfaction on the Decision to Start a Business," *Journal of Small Business Management* 18 (January 1980), pp. 37–43.

[4]J. Donald Weinrauch, "The Second Time Around: Entreprenuership as a Mid-Career Alternative," *Journal of Small Business Management* 18 (January 1980), pp. 25–32.

[5]"Choosing a Second Career," *Business Week* (19 September 1977), p. 23.

[6]David L. Hull, John J. Bosley, and Gerald G. Udell, "Renewing the Hunt for the Heffalump: Identifying Potential Entrepreneurs by Personality Characteristics," *Journal of Small Business Management* 18 (January 1980), p. 18.

[7]James Donald Powell and Charles F. Bimmerle, "A Model of Entrepreneurship: Moving toward Precision and Complexity," *Journal of Small Business Management* 18 (January 1980), pp. 33–36. For more insight into this and other aspects of entrepreneurship, see: James F. DeCarlo and Paul R. Lyons, "Toward a Contingency Theory of Entrepreneurship," *Journal of Small Business Management* 18 (July 1980), pp. 37–42.

[8]Alvin D. Star and Michael Z. Massel, "Survival Rates for Retailers," *Journal of Retailing* 57 (Summer 1981), pp. 87–99.

[9]James Kennedy, Janice Loutzenhiser, and John Chaney, "Problems of Small Business Firms: An Analysis of the SBI Consulting Program," *Journal of Small Business Management* 17 (January 1979), pp. 7–14.

[10]Dillard B. Tinsley and Danny R. Arnold, "Small Retailers in Small Towns: Is Marketing the Key?" *Journal of Small Business Management* 16 (January 1978), pp. 7–12.

[11]Irving Burstiner, "The Small Retailer and His Problems," *Journal of Business Education* 51 (March 1975), pp. 243–45.

[12]"The 50 Largest Retailing Companies Ranked by Sales," *Fortune* 109 (11 June 1984), pp. 186–87.

[13]U.S. Department of Commerce, Bureau of the Census, *Statistical Abstract of the United States, 1983–84,* 104th ed. (Washington, D.C.: U.S. Government Printing Office, 1983), p. 798.

[14]Committee on Definitions, *Marketing Definitions: A Glossary of Marketing Terms* (Chicago: American Marketing Association, 1960), p. 21.

[15]See the section on population characteristics in Chapter 3.

[16]For a more extensive discussion of these attributes of service offerings and suggestions for retail strategy, see: Richard M. Bessom and Donald W. Jackson, Jr., "Service Retailing: A Strategic Marketing Approach," *Journal of Retailing* 51 (Summer 1975), pp. 75–86; William R. George, "The Retailing of Services—A Challenging Future," *Journal of Retailing* 53 (Fall 1977), pp. 85–98; Gregory D. Upah, "Mass Marketing in Service Retailing: A Review and Synthesis of Major Methods," *Journal of Retailing* 56 (Fall 1980), pp. 59–76.

[17]Upah, "Mass Marketing," pp. 60–61.

[18]Bessom and Jackson, "Service Retailing," pp. 75–76. See also: Duane L. Davis, Joseph P. Guiltinan, and Wesley H. Jones, "Service Characteristics, Consumer Search, and the Classification of Retail Services," *Journal of Retailing* 55 (Fall 1979), pp. 3–23.

[19]George, "Retailing of Services," p. 90.

[20]Theodore Levitt, "The Industrialization of Service," *Harvard Business Review* 54 (September–October 1976), p. 66; George, "Retailing of Services," p. 95; Upah, "Mass Marketing," pp. 66–67.

[21]J. Patrick Kelly and William R. George, "Strategic Management Issues for the Retailing of Services," *Journal of Retailing* 58 (Summer 1982), p. 39.

[22]"Dentists Leave 'Elm Street' for Malls," *New York Times* (21 April 1982), p. D4; "Moving the Dentist's Chair to Retail Stores," *Business Week* (19 January 1981), pp. 56–57.

[23]J. C. Penney Seeks Bank," *New York Times* (28 April 1983), p. D4.

[24]William R. Davidson and Alice Rodgers, "Non-store Retailing: Its Importance to and Impact on Merchandise Suppliers and Competitive Channels," *The Growth of Non-store Retailing: Implications for Retailers, Manufacturers, and Public Policy Makers* (New York: Institute of Retail Management, New York University, 12 January 1979), p. 23.

[25]For some insights into street vending and a taxonomy of vendor types, see: Jerome Greenberg et al., "The Itinerant Street Vendor: A Form of Nonstore Retailing," *Journal of Retailing* 56 (Summer 1980), pp. 66–80.

[26]Marvin A. Jolson, "Causes of and Cures for Direct Sellers' Problems," *Akron Business and Economic Review* 4 (Summer 1973), p. 5.

[27]Marvin A. Jolson, "Direct Selling: Consumer vs. Salesman," *Business Horizons* 15 (October 1972), p. 88.

[28]Richard Greene, "A Boutique in Your Living Room," *Forbes* (7 May 1984), p. 86.

[29]Paul Muchnick, "Selling by Mail Order," *Small Business Bibliography No. 3* (Washington, D.C.: Small Business Administration, revised September 1977), p. 2.

[30]Larry J. Rosenberg and Elizabeth C. Hirschman, "Retailing without Stores," *Harvard Business Review* 58 (July–August 1980), p. 110.

[31]John A. Quelch and Hirotaka Takeuchi, "Nonstore Marketing: Fast Track or Slow?" *Harvard Business Review* 59 (July–August 1981), pp. 82–83.

[32]Irving Burstiner, *Mail Order Selling: How to Market Almost Anything by Mail* (Englewood Cliffs, N.J.: Prentice-Hall, 1982), p. 5.

[33]John Jennings, "Mail-order Insurance Passes the $5 Billion Mark," *Direct Marketing* 46 (March 1984), pp. 24ff.

[34]Stanley Hollander and J. J. Boddewyn, "Retailing and Public Policy: An International Overview," *Journal of Retailing* 50 (Spring 1974), p. 55.

[35]Bruce J. Walker and Michael J. Etzel, "The Internationalization of U.S. Franchise Systems: Progress and Procedures," *Journal of Marketing* 37 (April 1973), pp. 38–46.

[36]"Radio Shack for Europe," *Business Week* (31 August 1974), pp. 75–76.

[37]"Top Two Franchisors Walk Different Merchandise Paths," *Chain Store Age* 55 (November 1979), pp. 91–92.

[38]"F. W. Woolworth Co.," *Barron's* 61 (March 1982), p. 68.

[39]"World Trade Unit Formed by K Mart," *New York Times* (16 April 1983), p. 30.

[40]"Toys Are for World's Children," *Chain Store Age, General Merchandise Division* 60 (February 1984), p. 9.

[41]Robert Ball, "Europe's U.S. Shopping Spree," *Fortune* 102 (1 December 1980), p. 82.

[42]William R. Davidson and Alice L. Rodgers, "Changes and Challenges in Retailing," *Business Horizons* 24 (January–February 1981), pp. 82–83.

[43]"Canada Drugstore Chain Plans U.S. Drive: Shoppers Drug Set to Open 200 Stores in 1980s," *New York Times* (14 October 1980), p. D4.

[44]Isadore Barmash, "BATUS: A Mixed Record in Retailing," *New York Times* (18 March 1982), p. D4.

Courtesy Sears, Roebuck & Co., Chicago

THE ENVIRONMENTS OF RETAILING

Your Study Objectives

After you have studied this chapter, you will understand:

1. Significant demographic data and present trends that relate to the American consumer population.
2. Some aspects of the retailer's sociological, technological, and legal environments.
3. The consumerism movement and how retailers are reacting to it.

Essential to the success of an organization is a realistic and thorough understanding of its external environment. Retail executives can direct only those facets of an operation that are under their control. These include obtaining and deploying company assets, providing goods and services for resale, pricing, locating and decorating the store, personal selling, and promoting the business. Many outside factors lie beyond management's control. These impinge on and can constrain a firm's activities. Economic and social variables, for example, are in a continual state of flux. Yet they delineate the arena companies must operate in, in good times or bad.

Retail firms are no exception. These uncontrollable factors shape and constrain their activities.

The Changing Socioeconomic Environment

Plagued by changes in the world environment, today's business enterprise finds that the costs of energy, capital, and labor are all at record or near-record levels. To complicate the situation further, many raw materials required by manufacturers are in short supply.[1] There has been a steady erosion of confidence in government at all levels and in other institutions. Protest over government intervention is commonplace. Successive bouts of inflation and recession have buffeted the consumer as well as industry and commerce. The individual's tax burden is oppressive. Discretionary income has been curtailed. Housing starts are down, and home sales depressed. The price of a new residence has moved beyond the reach of the average family. Similarly, the cost of a new car remains frustratingly high to many consumers.

In this chapter, we first offer considerable demographic information regarding the 230-plus million residents of the United States. Implications for retail companies are provided. A discussion of the technological environment follows. We mention interactive communications and other new developments. We provide insight about the rise of consumerism, the concept of social responsibility for business organizations, the ecological concerns of consumers, and some details about the legal environment that are pertinent to retailers.

Demographic Details of the Population

In this section, we give information about trends in the birth, death, marriage, and divorce rates. You will learn of the surprisingly rapid growth in numbers of households, how consumers are concentrated in the country's urbanized areas, the extent of adults' educational preparation, the gradual aging of America, and rising household incomes.

A Growing Population

Figure 3.1 presents census statistics for the 20th century. It took 124 years from the signing of the Declaration of Independence for our

Figure 3.1   Population of the United States, 1900–1980

Year	Population	Growth
1900	76.0 million	
1910	92.0 million	+21.0%
1920	105.7 million	+14.9%
1930	122.8 million	+16.1%
1940	131.7 million	+7.2%
1950	150.7 million	+14.5%
1960	178.5 million	+18.4%
1970	203.3 million	+13.9%
1980	226.6 million	+11.4%

* Population figures to 1960 do not include Alaska or Hawaii.

Source: U.S. Department of Commerce, Bureau of the Census, *Statistical Abstract of the United States, 1984–85*, 105th ed. (Washington, D.C.: U.S. Government Printing Office, 1984), p. 6.

country to reach, in 1900, a population of about 76 million. Over the next 50 years, this figure doubled. Another 75.8 million consumers were added to our ranks between 1950 and 1980. Even now, despite a long-term trend toward smaller families and a tapering off of our growth rate, our numbers continue to increase at the rate of over 1 percent each year.

Established and new retailers alike will be called on to supply the needs and wants of these additional millions. Enormous quantities of food, clothing, appliances, household furnishings, and dwellings must be provided. Continued expansion of the retail sector is thus assured.

Two factors account for most population growth: (1) the net of immigration over emigration and (2) the number of births each year in excess of the number of deaths. A third significant factor is longevity: people are living longer. Along with a low incidence of emigration from the United States, we have witnessed an almost continuous influx of immigrants during the 1970s and early 1980s. Large numbers of Koreans, Vietnamese, Mexicans, Haitians, and other nationalities have been admitted to our shores. By far the greater contributor to national growth, however, has been the disparity between birth and death rates.

Births and Deaths The federal government keeps track of these and other occurrences in terms of a common denominator: per 1,000 population.

Figure 3.2
Birth and death rates,
1940 to 1980

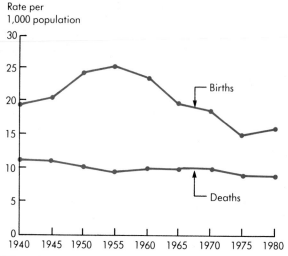

Source: U.S. Department of Commerce, Bureau of the Census, *Statistical Abstract of the United States, 1984–85,* 105th ed. (Washington, D.C.: U.S. Government Printing Office, 1984), p. 57.

Tallies since 1940, registered at five-year intervals, are shown in Figure 3.2. Rising from a low of 19.4 births per 1,000, the rate peaked at 25 per 1,000 in the baby boom year of 1955. By 1975, it had dropped to only 14.8. Often offered as contributing factors to the declining birthrate of the 60s and early 70s are improved methods of contraception, a rising divorce rate, changing societal values, the women's liberation movement, and the high cost of raising children.

Since 1975, however, a small but definite upturn can be noted in the graph. The fact that the pendulum appears to be swinging back suggests continuing sales growth for retailers of diapers, baby food, medicines and baby oils, infants' clothing, nursery furniture, and the like. It also holds promise for many other types of stores as these infants grow older.

According to the chart, the death rate has not changed very much from one five-year period to the next. If, however, we compare the 1980 low of 8.7 per 1,000 with 10.8 in 1940, we realize that a welcome drop has taken place over the four decades. Even so, we still face an excess of births over deaths for the foreseeable future. In 1975, where we can see the narrowest divergence between the two sets of statistics, the net difference still yields six more births than deaths per 1,000. Zero population growth, then, appears to remain in the realm of pure speculation.

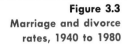

Figure 3.3
Marriage and divorce
rates, 1940 to 1980

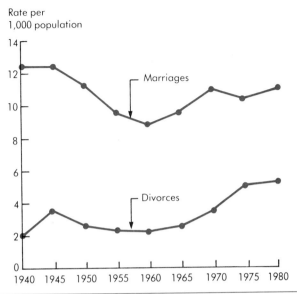

Source: U.S. Department of Commerce, Bureau of the Census, *Statistical Abstract of the United States, 1984–85,* 105th ed. (Washington, D.C.: U.S. Government Printing Office, 1984), p. 57.

Marriages and Divorces Although their influence on national growth is more indirect, marriage and divorce rates have an impact on population statistics. Their patterns since 1940 may be compared in Figure 3.3. Over the long term, the marriage rate has stood up rather well. This is evident when we compare current rates with the approximately 10 per 1,000 rate we had at the beginning of the 20th century. The graph would seem to suggest that the institution of marriage, although possibly somewhat battered, has not been affected all that much by cultural change over the past 80 years.

On the other hand, the divorce rate shows a strikingly different picture. Back in 1900, fewer than 1 divorce per 1,000 population occurred in American society. By 1940, the rate had doubled. By 1975, it reached more than 5 per 1,000. The healthy marriage rate and the increasing incidence of divorce contribute to stronger sales activity in many lines of retailing. Every year, millions of consumers must furnish and equip their new households. They buy appliances, food, clothing, household supplies, and other necessities.

An Acceleration in
Household Formation

As indicated in Figure 3.4, the Census Bureau counted 52.8 million households in 1960. By 1984, the figure had reached 85.4 million. This record growth of over 61 percent in 24 years inflated purchases

Figure 3.4   Household characteristics: 1960–1980 and 1984

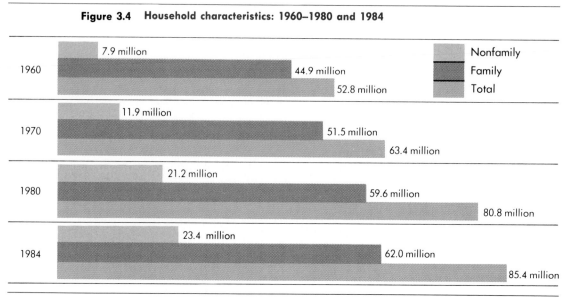

Source: U.S. Department of Commerce, Bureau of the Census, *Statistical Abstract of the United States, 1984–85,* 105th ed. (Washington, D.C.: U.S. Government Printing Office, 1984), p. 40; *Statistical Abstract, 1982–83,* p. 43.

of residences, furniture, bedding, floor coverings, home furnishings of every type and description, major appliances, and other goods.

Average household size declined more than 18 percent over the same period. One logical explanation is that couples nowadays are having fewer children. Another reason is the explosion of nonfamily households. In a typical family household, two or more members of the same family reside. This type accounts for nearly three out of every four households in the country. The balance, about 23.4 million in 1984, are categorized as the nonfamily type. While the number of family households rose by more than one third between 1960 and 1984, the ranks of their nonfamily counterparts swelled by a phenomenal 196.5 percent. This unusual disparity is a clear indication of changing lifestyles, as well as a higher divorce rate and increased longevity. At the beginning of the 1980s, 17.8 million people were living alone. Of this group, there were 1.4 million men and 5.7 million women in the 65-and-over age bracket.[2]

An Urbanized and Concentrated Population

A century ago, nearly three out of every four Americans lived in rural settings. Since then, an almost complete reversal has taken place. By 1980, 167 million consumers lived in urban or suburban areas. We have also become a geographically concentrated people. For years, the federal government recorded and issued statistical information for heavily populated areas labeled Standard Metropolitan Statistical Areas (SMSAs). In time, the list of SMSAs grew to well over 300. Then, in June 1983, the U.S. Office of Management and Budget revised the criteria for these areas and redesignated them Metropolitan Statistical Areas (MSAs).[3] Without specifying the precise criteria, the general idea was to apply the term to areas that contained a large population nucleus and adjacent communities which have a high degree of economic and social integration with that nucleus.

An even larger unit is the Primary Metropolitan Statistical Area (PMSA), defined as a component of a metropolitan area of 1 million or more population. An area that contains PMSAs is designated a Consolidated Metropolitan Statistical Area (CMSA). As of July 1, 1983, 257 MSAs and 23 CMSAs were identified. Figure 3.5A reveals that in 1983 over 45 million people lived in one of the top 10 PMSAs. That same year, according to Figure 3.5B, the six largest CMSAs contained more than one out of every five American consumers.

Such intense concentrations of people demand adequate numbers of retail enterprises, sufficiently stocked to cater to their needs. No wonder, then, that our MSAs and CMSAs contain quantities of central

Figure 3.5A **Top 10 primary metropolitan statistical areas (PMSAs), 1983**

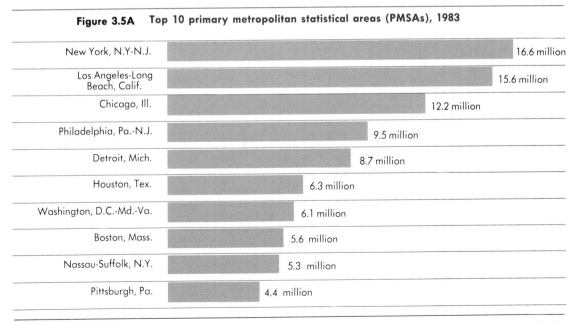

New York, N.Y.-N.J.	16.6 million
Los Angeles-Long Beach, Calif.	15.6 million
Chicago, Ill.	12.2 million
Philadelphia, Pa.-N.J.	9.5 million
Detroit, Mich.	8.7 million
Houston, Tex.	6.3 million
Washington, D.C.-Md.-Va.	6.1 million
Boston, Mass.	5.6 million
Nassau-Suffolk, N.Y.	5.3 million
Pittsburgh, Pa.	4.4 million

Source: U.S. Department of Commerce, Bureau of the Census, *Statistical Abstract of the United States, 1984–85,* 105th ed. (Washington, D.C.: U.S. Government Printing Office, 1984), pp. 876–82.

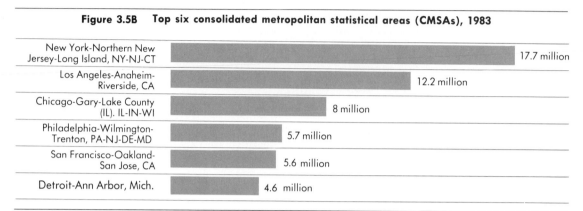

Figure 3.5B   Top six consolidated metropolitan statistical areas (CMSAs), 1983

New York-Northern New Jersey-Long Island, NY-NJ-CT	17.7 million
Los Angeles-Anaheim-Riverside, CA	12.2 million
Chicago-Gary-Lake County (IL). IL-IN-WI	8 million
Philadelphia-Wilmington-Trenton, PA-NJ-DE-MD	5.7 million
San Francisco-Oakland-San Jose, CA	5.6 million
Detroit-Ann Arbor, Mich.	4.6 million

Source: U.S. Department of Commerce, Bureau of the Census, *Statistical Abstract of the United States, 1984–85,* 105th ed. (Washington, D.C.: U.S. Government Printing Office, 1984), pp. 876–82.

and secondary business districts, suburban retail areas, and shopping centers of all sizes. (See Chapter 7 for more on store location.)

A Mobile Population   On the average, one of every five Americans moves each year. Some move to another address in the same neighborhood or to another city in the same state. Others relocate to another, often distant, state. Over the past 50 years, millions fled the downtown sections of our nation's cities and settled in suburban areas. Substantial numbers migrated from the Middle Atlantic and North Central regions to the West and South. Indeed, one forecast suggests that by the year 2000, people on the Pacific Coast and Southerners will constitute the majority of our more than 267 million people.[4] Figure 3.6 illustrates the interregional shifts that took place between the 1970 and 1980 censuses. During that 10-year interval, the population of the Mountain states increased by 37.1 percent. The West South Central region grew by 22.9 percent; and residents of the South Atlantic region increased 20.4 percent. During the same period, our overall population increase came to 11.4 percent. If we subtract the national growth percentage from these three regional changes, we have the following above-average figures:

Region	Total Growth	Net Percentage Change
Mountain	37.1%	25.7%
West South Central	22.9	11.5
South Atlantic	20.4	9.0

Figure 3.6   **Regions ranked by population growth, 1970–1980**

Region	Growth
Mountain	+37.1%
West South Central	+22.9%
South Atlantic	+20.4%
Pacific	+19.8%
East South Central	+14.5%
New England	+4.2%
West North Central	+0.05%
East North Central	+0.03%
Middle Atlantic	−0.1%

Source: U.S. Department of Commerce, Bureau of the Census, *Statistical Abstract of the United States, 1981*, 102d ed. (Washington, D.C.: U.S. Government Printing Office, 1981), p. 9.

Some states saw phenomenal growth over the same period:

State	Growth	Gain over National Growth
Nevada	63.5%	52.1%
Arizona	53.1	41.7
Florida	43.4	32.0
Wyoming	41.6	30.2
Utah	37.9	28.5

A Rising Level of Education

Americans are among the world's best educated consumers. As Table 3.1 shows, the median number of years of education completed by adults in 1983 was 12.6 years. High school graduation had been attained by 7 out of every 10; the proportion who had finished college rose to 18.8 percent.

Typically, the educated consumer is better informed and more sophisticated in choosing among brands, stores, and services. Today's shoppers are more alert to price, quality, packaging, and advertised claims. They are likely to demand better products and services, honest advertising and promotions, attractive stores, fair and cordial treatment by salespeople, and retailers who demonstrate social responsibility.

Table 3.1 Levels of education: adults, 25 years of age and older			
	Percentages of Total Adult Population*		
Year	**High School Graduation and Over**	**Four Years of College and Over**	**Median Number of Years Completed**
1940	24.5%	4.6%	8.6
1950	34.3	6.2	9.3
1960	41.1	7.7	10.6
1970	52.3	10.7	12.1
1980	66.5	16.2	12.5
1983	72.1	18.8	12.6

* 25 years of age and older.

Source: U.S. Department of Commerce, Bureau of the Census, *Statistical Abstract of the United States, 1984–85*, 105th ed. (Washington, D.C.: U.S. Government Printing Office, 1984), p. 134.

A Maturing Population and a Changing Age Mix

We are living longer. In 1800, the median age of our population was a mere 16 years. By 1900, it had reached 22.9 years. The 1980 census revealed a median age of 30—and, at the same time, that more than one third of the total population were 21 years of age or younger. Another third fell between the ages of 22 and 44, and the balance, above 44.[5]

Today's shoppers demand attractive stores.

Courtesy Sears, Roebuck & Co., Chicago

Figure 3.7   **Population change by age groups, 1960–1980**

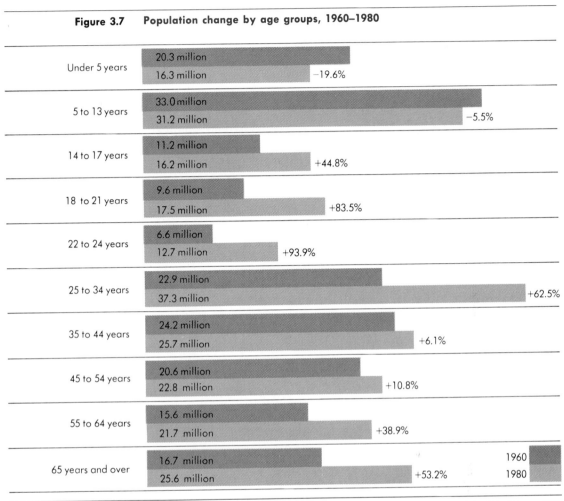

Under 5 years	20.3 million	
	16.3 million	−19.6%
5 to 13 years	33.0 million	
	31.2 million	−5.5%
14 to 17 years	11.2 million	
	16.2 million	+44.8%
18 to 21 years	9.6 million	
	17.5 million	+83.5%
22 to 24 years	6.6 million	
	12.7 million	+93.9%
25 to 34 years	22.9 million	
	37.3 million	+62.5%
35 to 44 years	24.2 million	
	25.7 million	+6.1%
45 to 54 years	20.6 million	
	22.8 million	+10.8%
55 to 64 years	15.6 million	
	21.7 million	+38.9%
65 years and over	16.7 million	1960
	25.6 million	+53.2% 1980

Source: U.S. Department of Commerce, Bureau of the Census, *Statistical Abstract of the United States, 1981,* 102d ed. (Washington, D.C.: U.S. Government Printing Office, 1981), p. 27.

Age Groups From 1960 to 1980, the age bracket that registered the sharpest growth was that between ages 18 and 34. Their numbers rose from 39 to 67.5 million, for a gain of nearly 73 percent. During the same 20 years, the number of senior citizens (ages 65 and over) grew by 53 percent—to more than 25 million. (See Figure 3.7.) By the end of the century, this group may account for 15 percent of the total population.[6] Thus, the senior citizen market represents an extraordinary opportunity for retailers over the next several decades. Other challenges are also evident. According to the last census, more than 37 million people were in their late 20s or early 30s. By 1990, these millions will have begun to swell the ranks of the next older age group: the 35- to 44-year-olds. That category already includes millions of people in the "moving bulge"—that shifting of post–World War II babies toward middle age.[7] Consumers in this age bracket enjoy higher earnings and have more discretionary income than younger people. Their spending behavior will have a significant impact on the sales of private homes and quality furnishings, better cars, more expensive apparel, college education for their children, major appliances and other durables, recreation, and travel.

Meanwhile, relatively fewer teenagers will be coming up in the next decade as the smaller-than-usual number of youngsters tallied in the last census begin to enter the 1990s. Fewer people will therefore be entering the work force toward the end of the century.

Rising Levels of Income   By 1983, American consumers were earning nearly three times as much as they earned in 1967. Consider the following figures:[8]

Year	Median Household Income
1967	$ 7,143
1970	8,734
1975	11,800
1980	17,710
1983	20,885

The picture is, however, not all that positive. Over the same period, the purchasing power of the dollar declined sharply. In terms of consumer prices, the 1967 dollar had slipped to 36.7 cents by May of 1981.[9] Table 3.2 reveals the wide distribution of income levels among all households. In 1967, 7 out of every 10 households received annual incomes of under $10,000. At the other end of the scale, fewer than 4 percent brought in $20,000. By 1983, however, this relatively insignificant proportion had swelled to over 50 percent. Median household income that same year reached $20,885.

A Changing Female Population   In 1920, there were 104.1 males for every 100 females in the country. By 1948, the proportion of males to females had decreased to 100.7. The 1980 census revealed only 94.5 males for every 100 females. If we segment the 1980 census data by age groups, we note these interesting proportions:[10]

Table 3.2		Percentages of Households with Incomes of:			
Household income, selected years	Number of Households (millions)	Under $10,000	$10,000 to $19,999	$20,000 to $34,999	Over $35,000
Year					
1967	60.8	70.5%	25.7%	3.2%	0.6%
1970	64.8	57.7	34.4	6.5	1.4
1974	71.2	44.2	37.0	15.5	3.3
1978	77.3	33.1	31.9	26.0	9.0
1983	85.4	22.9	25.0	27.8	24.3

Source: U.S. Department of Commerce, Bureau of the Census, *Statistical Abstract of the United States, 1984–85,* 105th ed. (Washington, D.C.: U.S. Government Printing Office, 1984), p. 442.

Age Group	Ratio of Males to Females
0 to 14 years	104.6
15 to 24 years	101.7
25 to 44 years	97.4
45 to 64 years	90.7
65 years and over	67.6

As you can deduce from the above, women live longer than men. Moreover, the female population has been aging. At the turn of the century, the median age for women was 22.4 years. It is now over 30 and may well reach some point between the ages of 33.1 and 38.2 by the year 2000.[11]

Although they still earn substantially less than men, women today are better educated and have higher incomes than ever before. As Figure 3.8 indicates, nearly half of all married women were holding jobs before the 1980s. They have shown some movement into the professions and into management ranks.[12] Today, we perceive such trends among women as increasing individualism and independence, more affluence, more education, and convenience replacing price as a critical factor in their shopping attitudes.[13] An illustration of this last trend is the popularity of packaged prepared foods and microwave ovens.

From a marketing standpoint, it would be too simplistic to characterize women as either housewives or working women. Both categories can be broken down further into distinct segments at which a company might target its efforts. Each group may reflect differences in attitudes, interests, motivations, and shopping behavior.[14]

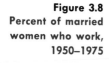

**Figure 3.8
Percent of married
women who work,
1950–1975**

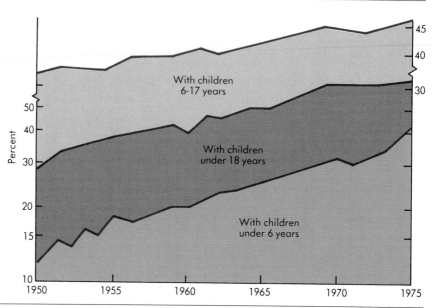

Source: Rena Bartos, "The Moving Target: The Impact of Women's Employment on Consumer Behavior," *Journal of Marketing* 41 (July 1977), p. 32. Reprinted with permission from the American Marketing Association.

Technology and Its Contributions

In recent years, the character of American retailing has been changed by technological developments. *Technology* is a term that embraces all the practical applications of scientific knowledge.

As an illustration, consider the TV. We have seen an astonishing array of refinements in this nearly universally owned appliance over the past few decades. From black-and-white screens, we have graduated to full, lifelike color. Miniature solid-state electronic circuits have replaced the vacuum tube. We have remote control and zoom gadgetry, models with 45-inch screens, tiny hand-held TVs, and easy adaptation to computer games.

We have grown accustomed to supersonic aircraft like the Concorde, spaceships departing our solar system, astronauts floating alongside their shuttle craft, talk of space stations, and the like. Each year, more robots show up on the nation's assembly lines. The new science of *biotechnology* (genetic engineering) holds great promise for the future.[15] Genetically created microorganisms have already been put to work consuming oil spills on the ocean surface. Others have been manufactured that eat toxic pollution. We have new growth hormones to treat abnormally small children. The future of this science may hold new ways to produce energy, extract minerals, breed animals, and raise crops. Even medicines and drugs may eventually be produced through genetically engineered fermentation methods.[16]

Innovative technology is all around us. We wear clothing made of synthetic fibers. We buy aseptically packaged milk and fruit juices that require no refrigeration. Millions of cordless telephones are in use. Laser-beam technology speeds up front-end checkouts in supermarkets by scanning the printed codes marked on packages. The laser beam also benefits humanity in surgery. Desk-top computers are now available that perform far faster than the giant vacuum-tube data processors of the 1950s or the transistor-fortified models of the 1960s.

A technological innovation that may revolutionize the retailing world is the exciting field of **interactive communications.**[17] The term applies to computer-assisted two-way communication, for example, by Videotex. Videotex brings information into the home. Systems such as Viewdata are relatively new in the United States, although similar systems have been used elsewhere since the 1970s. France, for example, has its *Antiope,* and Germany, its *Bildschirmtext.* In 1977, Warner Communications launched its own QUBE program in more than 30,000 households in Columbus, Ohio. In the fall of 1983, Knight-Ridder Newspapers initiated a videotex service called Viewtron in the Miami area. Similar services, initiated by other organizations, are available in Chicago and California. Viewtron does not require the use of a home computer. Subscribers purchase a terminal called Sceptre and pay a monthly service fee and a nominal hourly rate for the use

Chemical's Pronto Home Bank Service enables subscribers to have banking services at their fingertips.

Courtesy Chemical Bank, New York City

of telephone lines.[18] Made available are restaurant menus and prices, consumer reports, classified ads, home banking, late stock prices, electronic shopping, and much more. Even a database like the Dow Jones News/Retrieval Service or CompuServe can be accessed.

In the New York City area, the Chemical Bank offers the Pronto Home Banking service. Using home computers, subscribers can pay their bills, transfer funds, and enjoy other bank services at their fingertips.[19] Comp-U-Card is a computerized mail-order shopping service that offers consumers 60,000 brand name products. Members order merchandise via a toll free number. They save up to 40 percent off the retail prices.[20] By 1983, Comp-U-Card had 2 million members. The company calls its electronic in-home shopping system Telestore.

Computers in Retailing   By the mid-1960s, some chains and department stores had begun to switch over from manual inventory control methods to computer systems. In addition to reduced clerical costs, these early adopters experienced other benefits. Among them were a higher rate of inventory turnover, improved sales forecasting and merchandise planning, better control of branch stocks, more profitable space management, and sales increases.[21] Computers are valuable assets to today's retail organizations. They save time and expense. As a quick example, druggists can spend as much as 40 percent of their time on paperwork (filling out government forms, insurance billings, and the like). SupeRx, a 500-store subsidiary of the Kroger Company, acknowledged saving up to $300,000 annually *on price changes alone* because of the computer.[22]

Many smaller retail enterprises benefit from the availability of low-priced microcomputers.[23] Payroll, accounts receivable and accounts payable, inventory, correspondence, and record-keeping can be handled more efficiently and at lower cost. Rather than purchase their own equipment, retailers may contract with a computer service to handle their needs. The bureau charges a one-time fee for designing a program as well as a monthly data-processing charge. Or the firm can contract with a time-sharing service. In this case, the retailer rents time from a company that owns a computer. Data are processed by means of a terminal linked with the service firm by telephone. Time sharing or the use of service bureaus will most likely continue to decline, however, as the cost of computer capability spirals ever downward.[24]

Understanding the Terminology Given the rapid spread of mini- and microcomputers throughout industry, it would be useful to understand the more common computer-related terms. **Hardware,** for example, refers to the cabinet, electronic circuits, electromechanical devices, and other components that perform the essential functions: input, manipulation, and retrieval of data. With microcomputers, the input device (part of the hardware) is typically a keyboard.

The **central processing unit,** or **CPU,** executes program instructions, compares and controls the data flow, performs calculations, and so on. The memory or storage area for data is readily accessible to the CPU. Data may be stored on disks, diskettes, or magnetic tape.[25] The **output device** is usually some kind of printer. *Dot matrix printers* are available for internal reports. *Daisy wheel* and other types of printers are used for correspondence and other documents that require letter-quality printing.

Software is an all-embracing term that denotes sets of programs and instructions that tell the hardware how to operate. Software is available for hundreds of tasks: accounts receivable, payroll, balance sheets and income statements, inventory control, and the like. Special software translates programs into machine language that the CPU can execute.

Benefits of Computerization Sooner or later, an increasing workload and a pressing need for speedier information processing will lead retail management to consider computerization. Whether the question is finally resolved through use of a service bureau, time sharing, installation of a mainframe, or purchase of a microcomputer, a number of benefits may be expected.[26] Typically, the company can look forward to:

more efficient bookkeeping
easier billing of charge customers and collection of outstanding balances
speedier buying procedures and purchase order processing
faster customer checkout
reduction of cashier errors through the keying of retail prices and price changes into the system
better inventory management and control
identification of best-selling and slow-moving merchandise and red flagging of potential out-of-stocks
improved distribution of goods among store branches
considerable savings in clerical expense
speedier information gathering and retrieval
reduction in credit department costs
improvements in space utilization
more sophisticated sales forecasting
improved scheduling of employees, maintenance, displays, and other aspects of operations

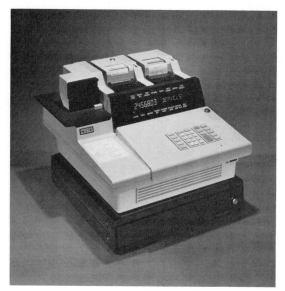

Photos courtesy NCR Corporation

Left, the NCR 2152 Retail Terminal System used by department stores and specialty stores. Right, *the NCR 1255 Retail Checkout Terminal used by supermarkets and discount stores.*

Computer-related Innovations Two familiar innovations that evolved from computers are bar coding and the electronic checkout. By processing the waiting line faster, the **electronic checkout** generates increased sales revenues, reduces labor costs, and provides better customer service.[27] Nowadays, we see electronic point-of-sale (POS) equipment in operation at many department stores, discount houses, drug chains, supermarkets, and other retail types. Input into the system may be provided by the Optical Character Recognition (OCR) method. Letters and numerals on price tags are printed in a special typescript, OCR-A.[28] Usually, the cashier rubs a light pen across the type to scan the information. Scanning equipment has also found its way into libraries, hospitals, the United States Postal Service, airlines (to sort baggage), and other organizations. Supermarket items now carry information registered in Universal Product Code (UPC) on their wrappers or containers. This **bar coding** consists of lines of different thicknesses. "Black bars absorb the light, white ones reflect it back in the scanner. The scanner then transforms the patterns of light and dark into electrical impulses that are measured by a decoder and translated into binary digits for transmission into the computer."[29]

To speed checkout time, many supermarkets are already equipped with scanning windows. The equipment not only provides the consumer with a detailed receipt tape but also yields data essential to the retailer's merchandise information system:

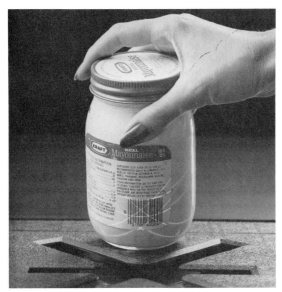 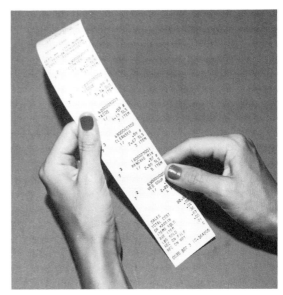

Courtesy NCR Corporation

Many supermarkets use UPC (bar code) scanners to speed checkout time, provide the customer with a detailed receipt, and to help track inventory and other merchandise information.

When the cashier passes the UPC symbol over the scanning window, a laser beam is activated which reads the bar code several times, decodes and verifies accuracy of the read, and queries the computer's disk memory for price and eligibility information. This information is then transmitted to the checkstand to be printed on the receipt tape and flashed on an alphanumeric display unit.[30]

Other exciting computer innovations are already on the market. Colorful charts and graphs, for example, can be produced quite easily with some of today's desk-top computers. These useful aids enable managers to spot trends more readily, leading to more efficient decision making.[31] In 1983, Hewlett Packard introduced the touch-screen computer.[32] This electronic innovation permits users to perform tasks by touching words, boxes, or pictures on the screen, rather than having to type commands. As early as 1981, talking scanners were being tested in some supermarkets including units of Safeway, Kroger, and Albertson's.[33] In these installations, speech synthesizers are used to announce item prices to shoppers at the checkout stand.

Visitors to the 6½ acre Royal Hawaiian Shopping Center in Waikiki are aided and pleased by Info-Vision. This convenient installation is a laser disc–based information retrieval system that provides interactive 19-inch TV screens at three separate stations. Consumers touch buttons on the keyboard to call up details regarding any of the more than 100 shops, restaurants, and service facilities. They can make dinner reservations, arrange to rent a car, obtain directions, or call up specific

In Waikiki's Royal Hawaiian Shopping Center, Info-Vision provides shoppers with orientation and direction.

Courtesy Royal Hawaiian Shopping Center, Inc.

information about apparel, jewelry, financial services, and other categories of goods and services.

Consumerism   Battered in the past by inflation and recession, many of today's consumers are skeptical of the intentions of American business.[34] Some feel they are being taken advantage of, and that companies are often not responsive to their needs. Manufactured goods seem to be made of poorer quality than those of yesteryear, even as their numbers, styles, and models proliferate. At the retail level, shoppers deplore the deteriorating quality of services offered and complain about the unsatisfactory handling of their complaints. Without singling out the retail sector, it should be pointed out that a number of consumer criticisms of marketing activity are commonly heard.[35] We cite below a few examples.

1. Some companies fail to provide enough information about their products and services for shoppers to be able to make sensible purchase decisions.
2. Many firms spend excessively on advertising and promotion. Because of this, consumers are compelled to pay higher prices for merchandise.

3. Competitors promote products that are essentially similar, yet each one attempts to convince the public that its products differ from those of the others.
4. Many goods in the marketplace are deficient; some are downright hazardous.
5. Some companies resort to misleading advertising, deception in packaging, bait-and-switch tactics, unethical pricing, or other shady and illegal business practices.
6. Manufacturers deliberately build obsolescence into their products so that consumers must replace them often.

The New Consumerism Movement

Consumerism has been described as "a social movement seeking to augment the rights and power of buyers in relation to sellers."[36] It is not a new phenomenon.[37] There have been two earlier consumer movements—one in the early 1900s, the other during the Great Depression. These waves of consumerism resulted in the passage of such landmark legislation as the Federal Trade Commission Act, the Clayton Act, and the Robinson-Patman Act.[38]

Figure 3.9 may shed some light on the different groups who are active in consumerism.

Retailers began to feel the effects of the present movement early in the 1960s.[39] In 1962, President John F. Kennedy lent impetus to the movement by formulating the Four Basic Rights of consumers: right to safety, right to be informed, right to choose, and right to be

Figure 3.9
Major groups in the consumer movement

1. *The Adaptationists,* who emphasize educating the consumers to avoid fraud and deception and seek to prepare him to deal intelligently with the market as it is. This group sees little need for new consumer protection legislation and gets along comfortably with consumer service specialists in industry and business and trade association representatives. Many consumer educators fall into this category.
2. *The Protectionists,* whose primary concern is with health and safety issues involving the possibility of physical harm to the individual. This group includes scientists, physicians, nutritionists, and other professionals.
3. *The Reformers,* who, like the adaptationists, want to improve consumer education and who, like the protectionists, want to ensure the individual's health and safety, and who, moreover, seek to increase the consumer's voice in government and the amount of product information available to him. This group consists chiefly of political liberals with a variety of professional affiliations.

Source: Robert O. Hermann, "Consumerism: Its Goals, Organizations and Future," *Journal of Marketing* 34 (October 1970), p. 57. Reprinted with permission from the American Marketing Association.

heard. In response to this third wave, more and more companies began viewing the movement in a positive sense. Many have chosen to regard it not as a threat, but, more properly, as a valuable marketing opportunity.[40]

Government's interest in consumer affairs is clear. Table 3.3 summa-

	Year	Legislation	Nature of the Legislation
Table 3.3 **Consumer protection** **legislation**	1906	Pure Food and Drug Act	Prohibited the adulteration or misbranding of foods and drugs sold in interstate commerce. Created the Food and Drug Adminstration (FDA).
	1907	Federal Meat Inspection Act	Authorized the U.S. Department of Agriculture to inspect slaughtering houses and meat-packing plants if these firms engaged in interstate commerce.
	1938	Food, Drug, and Cosmetics Act	Strengthened the authority of the FDA. Broadened the scope of the Pure Food and Drug Act to include cosmetics and therapeutic devices.
	1938	Wheeler-Lea Act	Gave the FTC jurisdiction over cases involving false or misleading advertising. Prohibited deceptive packaging and labeling practices.
	1939	Wool Products Labeling Act	Required the proper disclosure of the types and percentages of wool used in wool products.
	1951	Fur Products Labeling Act	Mandated that fur products bear explicit labels that disclose the kind of fur used, whether or not it has been dyed, the country of origin, and other details.
	1953	Flammable Fabrics Act	Barred the shipment, in interstate commerce, of clothing made of flammable goods. Subsequently amended to include materials, fabrics, and home furnishings.
	1957	Poultry Products Inspection Act	Provided for federal inspection of poultry products shipped between states.
	1958	Automobile Information Disclosure Act	Mandated that car dealers fully disclose information pertinent to new-car sales, including the posting of the manufacturer's suggested retail price.
	1958	Textile Fiber Products Identification Act	Mandated the proper indentification of fibers used in manufactured goods.
	1960	Hazardous Substances Labeling Act	Required that appropriate warning notices be affixed to all household products that contain poisonous, corrosive, or other dangerous substances.
	1966	Fair Packaging and Labeling Act	Mandated that manufacturers disclose an accurate and detailed listing of the ingredients in many packaged products.

Table 3.3 *(concluded)*	Year	Legislation	Nature of the Legislation
	1966	National Traffic and Motor Vehicle Act	Mandated initial safety standards for cars.
	1968	Consumer Credit Protection Act (Truth in Lending)	Required the full disclosure of interest charges and terms on purchases made on credit.
	1968	Radiation Control Act	Empowered the FDA to establish safe radiation levels for certain products.
	1969	Child Protection and Toy Safety Act	Barred dangerous and harmful toys from the marketplace.
	1970	Fair Credit Reporting Act	Attempted to halt credit reporting abuses; mandated accurate record-keeping by credit bureaus.
	1970	Poison Prevention Packaging Act	Mandated the use of safety packages for products that contain ingredients which can harm children.
	1970	Public Health Smoking Act	Required that cigarette makers advise of the dangers of smoking via warnings on the packages that read: "Warning: The Surgeon General Has Determined That Cigarette Smoking Is Dangerous to Your Health." Notice must also appear on ads.
	1972	Consumer Product Safety Act	Established the Consumer Product Safety Commission, authorizing that body to set safety standards for consumer products. Bars the manufacture or sale of unsafe articles.
	1975	Consumer Goods Pricing Act	Repealed earlier federal legislation which facilitated resale price maintenance (fair trade) in many states.
	1975	Equal Credit Opportunity Act	Prohibited discrimination against credit applicants because of sex or marital status. Later extended to include other bases for discrimination, such as race, age, religion, and national origin.
	1975	Fair Credit Billing Act	Enacted to protect consumers against billing errors and unfair credit practices; established a procedure for consumer query regarding billing entries.
	1975	Magnuson-Moss Warranty Act	Attempted to reform the warranty practices of manufacturers and distributors. Mandates the detailed disclosure of warranty terms in simple language.
	1976	Consumer Leasing Act	Required that firms leasing cars and other property fully disclose leasing terms.
	1977	Fair Debt Collection Practices Act	Aimed at barring unreasonable and abusive collection practices. Prohibited harassment, deception, and other unfair methods of collecting outstanding accounts.

rizes the highlights of the major federal consumer legislation. In the business world, many companies have set up internal consumer affairs departments.[41] J. C. Penney, Montgomery Ward, and other mass merchandising organizations actively promote consumer education. They make available information and publications through field programs, teacher participation, and other efforts. Along similar lines, retail management should monitor changing consumer needs. They should provide more information about product attributes and uses through good labeling, package inserts, and the like; conduct pretesting of merchandise; and install an effective complaint-handling system.[42] Retail researchers are now paying closer attention to shopper dissatisfaction.[43] They realize that some consumer discontent can stem from unrealistic expectations generated by promotional exaggeration.[44] Perhaps retail firms, more than manufacturers, need to install a satisfaction program. After all, "the retailer is seller, renderer, and servicer, and therefore becomes the first scapegoat of the consumer's wrath."[45]

Seldom do dissatisfied customers voice their complaints, other than to family and friends. A helpful suggestion is for management to set up an assistance center or hot lines to facilitate shopper feedback.[46]

Social Responsiveness and Ethical Considerations

Consider the situation of a successful nationwide chain with annual sales of hundreds of millions of dollars. Its management believes that the company adequately serves the needs of consumers by offering good merchandise and services at fair prices. Obviously, the organization contributes to the economy. For one thing, it buys goods from many sources, thus maintaining the health of its suppliers. For another, it provides a livelihood for hundreds, if not thousands, of employees. It also pays substantial sums to various levels of government in real estate, sales, and income taxes. Along the way, the firm manages to earn some profit, producing a satisfactory return on investment for the stockholders.

Does such an organization owe society more? Company managements have always been concerned with obligations to customers, stockholders, and employees. They are committed to pursuing profit and growth objectives. They have always felt that they were good citizens who contribute to the general good. Should the business sector ponder—and devote time, effort, and money to—the problems of our society? Should companies take steps to right racial injustice, protect the environment for future generations, help the poverty-stricken, work toward preserving our natural resources, and other pressing social needs?

Many marketers now subscribe to the belief that the modern business organization should stress social responsibility along with its day-to-

From *The Wall Street Journal*, with permission of Cartoon Features Syndicate.

"About this 101 Tips for Consumers *I bought—there are only 97 tips in it."*

day activities. Companies that have adopted this posture take positive action in various ways: attempting to cut down on pollution, hiring and training the disadvantaged, participating in community improvement projects, encouraging consumers to voice complaints and acting promptly to satisfy them, and so on.[47]

Social Responsibility in the Retail Sector

Social responsibility is difficult to define. Among small independent retailers, there seems to be some confusion over the term. Many tend to equate the words with *profitability.*[48] Even large retail companies are frequently "more concerned with increasing profit than with their role as a socially responsible institution."[49]

It might be appropriate for retailers to think of social responsibility as good neighborliness. As two educators have put it: "The concept involves two phases. On one hand, it means not doing things that spoil the neighborhood. On the other, it may be expressed as the voluntary assumption of the obligation to help solve neighborhood problems."[50]

Table 3.4 displays the results of a survey of socially responsible activities engaged in by a sample of large corporations.

Concern over the Ecology[51]

All of us are aware of the contamination of the earth's ecology. Smog, injurious to our health, covers some of our largest cities. Along with

Table 3.4
Socially responsible
activities of large
corporations

Activity	Percent Practicing
Contributions to education	86
Ecology	78
Minority hiring	78
Minority training	68
Contributions to the arts	68
Hard core hiring	58
Hard core training	55
Civil rights	53
Urban renewal	53
Consumer complaints	46
Understandable accounting statements	42
Truth in advertising	42
Product defects	36
Guarantees and warranties	32
Consumer-oriented label changes	24

Source: Henry Eilbirt and I. Robert Parket, "The Current Status of Corporate Social Responsibility," *Business Horizons* 16 (August 1973), p. 9. Copyright © 1973, by the Foundation for the School of Business at Indiana University. Reprinted by permission.

the many by-products of the nation's factories, gasoline exhaust fumes pollute the atmosphere. Rivers and lakes are contaminated with chemical wastes and sewage that seep through the ground, poisoning our water tables. Oil spills in the oceans kill fish. The federal government has demonstrated its concern by enacting a number of major environmental laws; these are listed in Table 3.5. During the 1980s, the government may spend as much as $680 million in its continuing struggle against environmental threats. We are not, of course, alone in the battle to protect the ecology. In self-defense, most nations have set up their own environmental protection agencies.[52] As concerned citizens, retailers can participate in community efforts to keep the environment clean and refuse to sell products that are not biodegradable.

Ethical and Moral Dimensions

Ethics are standards of behavior in a society. *Morals* relate to the principles behind conduct: what is right and what is wrong, what is good and what is evil. Any single organization, be it a business enterprise or a not-for-profit entity, is part of the whole society. Good business sense dictates ethical and moral conduct by management in all its actions. Questions of right and wrong must be addressed and answered according to acceptable societal standards. This applies not only to a company's promotional activities (where questionable deeds

Table 3.5
Federal environmental legislation

Year	Legislation
1963	Clean Air Act
1965	Solid Waste Disposal Act
	Water Quality Act
1967	Air Quality Act
1970	Clean Air Act
	National Environmental Policy Act
	Occupational Safety and Health Act
	Resource Recovery Act
	Water Quality and Improvement Act
1972	Coastal Zone Management Act
	Water Pollution Act
	Noise Control Act
	Pesticide Control Act
1974	Water Resources Act
1975	Energy Conservation Act
1976	Resource Conservation and Recovery Act
	Toxic Substances Control Act

are easily perceived) but also in financial management, purchasing, and every other aspect of the business. Ethical behavior ought to characterize the firm's relationships with all groups: stockholders, customers, suppliers, employees, competitors and other companies, and so on.[53] Owners and executives should exemplify such conduct in word and deed.

Figure 3.10 indicates some positive steps that retail firms can take.

Additional Legal Aspects of Retailing

Earlier, we mentioned the environmental and consumer protection legislation under which business organizations must operate. In this final section of the chapter, some additional aspects of the legal environment are introduced.

Legal Forms of Business

An early decision that new business owners face is the choice of a **legal form of business:** sole proprietorship, partnership, or corporation. Each has its advantages and drawbacks; these are presented in Table 3.6.

Most owners who opt for sole proprietorship or partnership select an assumed, or fictitious, name for their enterprise. They are required

Figure 3.10
Positive steps retailers
can take

Many possibilities are open to retailers who accept and want to actively promote social responsibility. Listed below are a few useful thoughts:

1. Demonstrate good neighborliness by keeping the premises clean, uncluttered, and attractive.
2. Know your clientele. Offer the kinds of merchandise and/or services they expect you to carry.
3. Institute a want-slip program to record consumer requests.
4. Maintain enough inventory on hand to avoid frequent out-of-stocks.
5. Refuse to sell shoddy or inferior merchandise.
6. To keep your costs and retail prices down, run an efficient operation.
7. Institute a fair system for merchandise returns.
8. Take special pains to avoid questionable promotional pricing techniques.
9. Be scrupulously honest and aboveboard in your media advertising.
10. Customer satisfaction builds company loyalty; handle complaints and criticisms effectively.
11. Do not carry products that may contribute to pollution.
12. Provide consumers with complete information about your merchandise and/or services.
13. Offer some form of consumer credit.
14. Join the local chamber of commerce and cooperate with neighborhood retailers.
15. Train salespeople to point out an item's limitations as well as its positive features.
16. Seek ways to promote good community relations in your trading area and participate in community affairs.
17. Hire and train members of minority groups.

to register that name with the city or county clerk. In some areas, the law requires the publication in a local newspaper of intent to run a business under a fictitious name. Permission to operate a corporation must be requested from the particular state in which the corporation's principal offices are to be located.

**Local and State Laws
and Regulations**

Businesses are subject to laws and regulations at all levels of government. At the local level, management must conform to zoning ordinances, building and construction codes, safety and health regulations, and so on. Occupancy permits must be obtained. Licenses are often required for specific types of retailing. Many places, for example, require the licensing of bowling alleys, movie theaters, and other places of amusement; hotels, motels, and garages; restaurants and luncheonettes; auctioneers, peddlers, and other retailers. State governments usually mandate the licensing of physicians, dentists, psychologists, pharmacists, optometrists, and other professionals. Licenses are also frequently needed by electricians, plumbers, beauticians, real estate brokers, insurance agents, and other occupational types.

Table 3.6 Legal forms of business ownership: advantages and disadvantages	Advantages	Disadvantages
	Sole Proprietorship	
	Easy to initiate or terminate	Unlimited personal liability for business debts
	Least expensive legal form to set up	Difficult to raise new capital for expansion
	Owner makes all decisions	Business is terminated upon owner's death
	Owner keeps all rewards	For taxation purposes, business income is added to owner's other income
	Owner can offset business losses against other income	Business skills limited to those possessed by owner
	Least amount of government regulation and paperwork	
	Partnership	
	Relatively simple to initiate	Unlimited personal liability for business debts
	Inexpensive to set up	Must share profits with partner(s)
	Usually more capital available (from one or more partners)	Each partner liable for decisions/commitments of other(s)
	Possible to attract additional capital	Problems in getting along with partner(s)
	Work load is shared	Divided authority
	Additional skills brought into the business	Business is terminated on the death of any partner
	Little record-keeping required for government purposes	Need for a partnership agreement including a buy-sell clause
	Can offset business losses against other income	
	Corporation	
	Exists as an independent legal entity	Most expensive business form to initiate
	Does not terminate on the death of a principal	Double taxation—both corporate and individual income tax
	Best form for attracting new capital and securing loans	Closely regulated by (state) government
	Liability limited to amount of investment	Considerable paperwork required
	Ownership easily sold or transferred	Need to hold stockholders' meetings, keep minutes

Tax responsibilities are another phase of the business operation. Not only must retailers pay income taxes and, in many cases, real estate tax, but they are also required to collect sales tax on most merchandise they sell. They must remit the monies collected to the state and, occasionally, local governments. Many states also maintain unfair practices statutes on their books that are designed to protect free competition. Sales below cost are expressly forbidden in some states, usually in connection with specific kinds of merchandise.

Important Federal Legislation Affecting Business

In addition to the various laws mentioned, several vital pieces of legislation strongly influence the business climate. The earliest federal statute to declare as public policy the notion of open, unrestricted competition

was the Sherman Antitrust Act of 1890. It was enacted to combat
the monopolistic behavior of the powerful giant trusts then existing
in industries such as oil and railroad transportation. The Sherman
Act declared the illegality of monopolizing, or attempting to monopo-
lize, interstate commerce.

In 1914, two important laws were passed: the Clayton Act and
the Federal Trade Commission Act. The first strengthened the Sherman Act's antimonopoly stance. It named specific illegal practices.
Among these were discriminating in price among buyers of commodities, the misuse of promotional allowances not made available to all
buyers, tying agreements, and exclusive dealing. The Federal Trade
Commission Act prohibited deception, fraud, and other unfair methods
of competition in interstate commerce. It also created a new federal
agency, the Federal Trade Commission (FTC). The agency's purpose
was to oversee business activity and to enforce proper behavior on
the part of business organizations.[54]

To aid thousands of independent retailers, especially those in the
grocery business at the time, Congress passed the Robinson-Patman
Act in 1936. Its aim was to put an end to the questionable buying
practices of the national chains. Thus, it constituted an important
rescue attempt for the small business sector during the difficult years
of the Great Depression. The Robinson-Patman Act declared that
discriminations in price, where such practice would tend to injure
or to lessen competition, were illegal. It also prohibited the granting
of price differentials that were not based on cost savings. For the
first time ever, the *buyer* could be held liable—for receiving a discriminatory price. The FTC is likely to proceed against any buyer for a
retail company who seeks discriminatory prices in the negotiation
process.[55]

Summary   Retailers can work only with factors within their control: the facility, other company assets, goods, services, pricing, promotion, and the like. Yet outside factors control, shape, and constrain its activities. These include the socioeconomic, technological, and legal environments. In these areas, change is constant. When we consider American demographics, a number of trends are evident. Among these are continued population growth, more divorces, concentrations of people in urban centers, the relocating of large numbers of people to the West and South, and a high level of education. Not only are we living longer, but the median age of our population has been rising. Still other trends include changes in the proportions of people in different age groups, rising affluence, and more married women who work.

Signs of innovative technology are all about us: in the clothes we wear, product packaging, electronic checkouts and bar coding, the spreading use of computers, and the growth of interactive communications.

Consumerism is a social movement. Present-day consumerism is not a new phenomenon, having been preceded by two earlier movements.

In response to consumer pressures, some large retailers have set up internal departments to handle consumer relations. Many others participate in field programs, publish and distribute useful information, and take pains to encourage consumer suggestions. As a rule, retail firms should furnish complete information about the merchandise and services they offer, label goods clearly, and handle customer complaints promptly and satisfactorily.

Modern-day retail organizations want to be regarded as good neighbors. Their managers believe in their responsibilities to the public. They evidence high ethical and moral behavior. Among the many positive actions a firm can take to be socially responsible are hiring and training the disadvantaged, instituting an effective customer complaint program, and working with others to help solve community problems.

The retailer operates under one of the three legal forms of business: sole proprietorship, partnership, or corporation. All three have their advantages and disadvantages. Whatever the form, every firm is subject to laws and regulations at all three levels of government: local, state, and federal.

Key Terms

interactive communications
hardware
central processing unit (CPU)
output device
software

electronic checkout
bar coding or Universal Product Code (UPC)
consumerism
legal form of business

1. Enumerate and briefly comment on at least six characteristics of the American consumer population.

2. How does the federal government keep track of such population statistics as the birth and marriage rates?

3. Explain the meaning of *urbanized* and *concentrated* in connection with population data.

4. What does the acronym *MSA* signify?

5. What three regions experienced the greatest population growth between 1970 and 1980?

6. Briefly describe the field of interactive communications. Furnish three examples of its application.

7. Distinguish between the computer-related terms *hardware* and *software*.

8. Identify six or more benefits that retail management might expect to obtain through computerization.

9. Identify and briefly describe each of the following:
   a. Videotex. *d.* OCR-A.
   b. Comp-U-Card. *e.* CPU.
   c. UPC.

10. What are the advantages for the small retail firm of using a computer service bureau? What are the disadvantages?

11. What are the Four Basic Rights of the consumer?

12. Identify four major consumer protection laws and specify the basic thrust of each.

13. Suggest five actions that socially responsible independent retailers might take.

14. List the advantages and drawbacks of the three basic legal forms of business ownership.

15. Comment on the primary thrust of each of the following:
   a. Sherman Antitrust Act.
   b. Clayton Act.
   c. Robinson-Patman Act.

1. Speculate about the possible appearance of several new types of retailers that might be able to capitalize on the rising divorce rate.

2. Suppose the proportion of employed versus nonemployed wives continues to rise. What are some implications for store merchants? Explain your reasoning.

3. Discuss the significance of technological innovations to the retailing sector.

4. Explain the term *biotechnology.* Briefly describe your own attitude, pro or con, toward this new science. Then, play the devil's advocate: outline several points in support of the opposite position.

5. What are the merits of the talking scanner in the supermarket? Do you think this innovation could be of value in a department store? Why or why not?

6. Try to recall a recent instance when you were not entirely satisfied with a purchase. Why were you discontent? What did you do about your dissatisfaction?

Notes [1]Rajan Chandran, Don Desalvia, and Allan Young, "The Impact of Current Economic Forces on Small Business," *Journal of Small Business Management* 15 (January 1977), pp. 30–36; Stephen W. Brown, Zohrab S. Demirdjian, and Sandra E. McKay, "The Consumer in an Era of Shortages," *MSU Business Topics* 25 (Spring 1977), pp. 49–53.

[2]U.S. Department of Commerce, Bureau of the Census, *Statistical Abstract of the United States, 1981,* 102d ed. (Washington, D.C.: U.S. Government Printing Office, 1981), p. 49.

[3]U.S. Department of Commerce, Bureau of the Census, *Statistical Abstract of the United States, 1984–85,* 105th ed. (Washington, D.C.: U.S. Government Printing Office, 1984), p. 873.

[4]"Prediction: Sunny Side Up," *Time* (19 December 1983), p. 28.

[5]*Statistical Abstract, 1981,* p. 25.

[6]Betsy D. Gelb, "Exploring the Gray market Segment," *MSU Business Topics* 26 (Spring 1978), pp. 41–46.

[7]"How the Changing Age Mix Changes Markets," *Business Week* (12 January 1976), pp. 74–78.

[8]*Statistical Abstract, 1984–85,* p. 873.

[9]*Statistical Abstract, 1981,* p. 458.

[10]Ibid., p. 25.

[11]William Lazer and John E. Smallwood, "The Changing Demographics of Women," *Journal of Marketing* 41 (July 1977), p. 14.

[12]Ibid., pp. 14–22.

[13]Suzanne H. McCall, "Meet the 'Workwife'," *Journal of Marketing* 41 (July 1977), pp. 55–64.

[14]Rena Bartos, "What Every Marketer Should Know about Women," *Harvard Business Review* 56 (May–June 1978), pp. 73–85; Fred D. Wells, "The Modern Feminine Life Style," *Journal of Marketing* 41 (July 1977), pp. 37–45.

[15]Jim Mintz, "Bio Technology," *Venture* 6 (February 1984), pp. 38–39.

[16]"The Biological Frontiers: Industries of the Next Decade," *Venture* 6 (February 1984), pp. 50–52.

[17]William R. Davidson and Alice L. Rodgers, "Changes and Challenges in Retailing," *Business Horizons* 24 (February 1981), p. 84.

[18]"The Big Rush to Videotex—and Its Big Risks," U.S. News & World Report (13 February 1984), pp. BC3–4.

[19]Anthony Brook, "Multiuse Videotex Systems Around the World," *Direct Marketing* 47 (January 1984), pp. 96–97.

[20]"Comp-U-Card Helps 1.5 Million Shop by Phone," *Business Week* (10 September 1979), p. 58; "Super VISA Package Increases Members for Comp-U-Card," *Direct Marketing* 46 (November 1983), pp. 32*ff.*

[21]David McConaughy, "An Appraisal of Computers in Department Store Inventory Control," *Journal of Retailing* 46 (Spring 1970), pp. 3–19; Spencer B. Smith, "Automated Inventory Management for Staples," *Journal of Retailing* 47 (Spring 1971), pp. 55–62; Raymond F. Barker, "Space and Inventory Management by Computer Simulation," *Journal of Retailing* 45 (Winter 1969–70), pp. 19–29.

[22]"Saving Druggists in a Paper Storm," *Business Week* (2 June 1980), p. 86.

[23]For information about computerization for the small business owner, see: Paul H. Cheney, "Selecting, Acquiring, and Coping with Your First Computer," *Journal of Small Business Management* 17 (January 1979), pp. 43–50; Frank Greenwood, "The Ten Commandments of Small Business Computerization," *Journal of Small Business Management* 19 (April 1981), pp. 61–67; Leo L. Pipino and Charles R. Necco, "A Systematic Approach to the Small Organization's Computer Decision," *Journal of Small Business Management* 19 (July 1981), pp. 8–16; James A. Senn and Virginia R. Gibson, "Risks of Investment in Microcomputers for Small Business Management," *Journal of Small Business Management* 19 (July 1981), pp. 24–34.

[24]Timothy J. Heintz, "On Acquiring Computer Services for a Small Business," *Journal of Small Business Management* 19 (July 1981), p. 4.

[25]Edward C. Cramer, "Can You Use a Microcomputer?" *Management Aids No. 250* (Washington, D.C.: Small Business Administration, 1979), p. 4.

[26]The choice of a computer may run from as low as several thousand dollars for a small portable to $1 million and more for a large installation. The IBM 3083, for example, has storage capacity for millions of characters and can operate at speeds in excess of several million instructions per second. See: Andrew Pollack, "IBM Introduces 3 Large Computers," *New York Times* (1 April 1982), p. D5.

[27]Michael A. McGinnis and Leland L. Gardner, "Electronic Checkout and Supermarket Sales Volume: Some Evidence," *Akron Business and Economic Review* 7 (Summer 1976), pp. 31–34.

[28]Peter McNulty, "The Bar-Coding of America," *Fortune* (27 December 1982), pp. 98–101.

[29]Ibid., p. 98.

[30]Michael D. Pommer, Eric N. Berkowitz, and John R. Walton, "UPC Scanning: An Assessment of Shopper Response to Technological Change," *Journal of Retailing* 56 (Summer 1980), p. 28.

[31]"The Spurt in Computer Graphics," *Business Week* (16 June 1980), pp. 104*ff.*

[32]Andrew Pollack, "Touch Screen: Views Mixed," *New York Times* (6 October 1983), p. D2.

[33]Isadore Barmash, "Talking Scanner to Be Tried," *New York Times* (10 November 1981), p. D5.

[34]"America's Growing Antibusiness Mood," *Business Week* (17 June 1972), pp. 100–103; Hiram C. Barksdale and William R. Darden, "Consumer Attitudes toward Marketing and Consumerism," *Journal of Marketing* 36 (October 1972), p. 29.

[35]See: James E. Haefner, "Indexing Consumer Issues through the Mass Media," *Journal of Consumer Affairs* 9 (Summer 1975), pp. 81–88; Gregory M. Gazda and David R. Gourley, "Attitudes of Businessmen, Consumers, and Consumerists toward Consumerism," *Journal of Consumer Affairs* 9 (Winter 1975), pp. 176–86.

[36]Philip Kotler, "What Consumerism Means for Marketers," *Harvard Business Review* 50 (May–June 1972), p. 49.

[37]For a cogent review of objectives pursued by consumer groups back to the turn of the century, see: Stanley C. Hollander, "Consumerism and Retailing: A Historical Perspective," *Journal of Retailing* 48 (Winter 1972–73), pp. 6–21; Robert O. Hermann, "Consumerism: Its Goals, Organizations and Future," *Journal of Marketing* 34 (October 1970), pp. 55–60.

[38]These laws are treated in a later section of this chapter.

[39]For insights into the evolving consumer movement, see: George S. Day and David A. Aaker, "A Guide to Consumerism," *Journal of Marketing* 34 (July 1970), pp. 12–19; Richard H. Buskirk and James T. Rothe, "Consumerism—An Interpretation," *Journal of Marketing* 34 (October 1970), pp. 61–65; Norman Kangun et al., "Consumerism and Marketing Management," *Journal of Marketing* 39 (April 1975), pp. 3–10; Leonard L. Berry, "The Future of Consumerism in Retailing," *Journal of Retailing* 53 (Fall 1977), pp. 99–112.

[40]Borris W. Becker, "Consumerism: A Challenge or a Threat?" *Journal of Retailing* 48 (Summer 1972), pp. 16–28; Stephen A. Greyser and Steven L. Diamond, "Business Is Adapting to Consumerism," *Harvard Business Review* 52 (September–October 1974), pp. 39–40*ff;* Esther Peterson, "Consumerism As a Retailer's Asset," *Harvard Business Review* 52 (May–June 1974), pp. 91–101; Zarrel V. Lambert, "Consumer Alienation, General Dissatisfaction, and Consumerism Issues: Conceptual and Managerial Perspectives," *Journal of Retailing* 56 (Summer 1980), pp. 3–24.

[41]For the functions of such a department, see: David A. Aaker and George S. Day, "Corporate Responses to Consumerism Pressures," *Harvard Business Review* 50 (November–December 1972), pp. 116–17.

[42]Paul N. Bloom and Mark J. Silver, "Consumer Education: Marketers Take Heed," *Harvard Business Review* 54 (January–February 1976), pp. 32–34*ff;* Leonard L. Berry, James S. Hensel, and Marian C. Burke, "Improving Retailer Capability for Effective Consumerism Response," *Journal of Retailing* 52 (Fall 1976), pp. 3–14*ff.*

[43]Kenneth L. Bernhardt, "Consumer Problems and Complaint Actions of Older Americans: A National View," *Journal of Retailing* 57 (Fall 1981), pp. 107–23; Ralph L. Day, "Prescription for the Marketplace: Everyone Listen Better!" *Business Horizons* 19 (December 1976), pp. 57–64; Ralph L. Day et al., "The Hidden Agenda of Consumer Complaints," *Journal of Retailing* 57 (Fall 1981), pp. 86–106.

[44]Rolph E. Anderson, "Consumer Dissatisfaction: The Effect of Disconfirmed Expectancy on Perceived Product Performance," *Journal of Marketing Research* 10 (February 1973), pp. 38–44; John A. Miller, "Store Satisfaction and Aspiration Theory: A Conceptual Basis for Studying Consumer Discontent," *Journal of Retailing* 52 (Fall 1976), pp. 65–84.

[45]Richard L. Oliver, "Measurment and Evaluation of Satisfaction Processes in Retail Settings," *Journal of Retailing* 57 (Fall 1981), p. 43.

[46]Betty J. Diener and Stephen A. Greyser, "Consumer Views of Redress Needs," *Journal of Marketing* 42 (October 1978), pp. 21–27; Michael J. Etzel and Bernard I. Silverman, "A Managerial Perspective on Directions for Retail Customer Dissatisfaction Research," *Journal of Retailing* 57 (Fall 1981), pp. 124–36.

[47]Robert J. Lavidge, "The Growing Responsibilities of Marketing," *Journal of Marketing* 34 (January 1970), pp. 25–28.

[48]Erika Wilson, "Social Responsibility of Business: What Are the Small Business Perspectives?" *Journal of Small Business Management* 18 (July 1980), p. 23.

[49]Ronald J. Dornoff and Clint B. Tankersley, "Do Retailers Practice Social Responsibility?" *Journal of Retailing* 51 (Winter 1975–76), p. 38.

[50]Henry Eilbirt and I. Robert Parket, "The Current State of Corporate Social Responsibility," *Business Horizons* 16 (August 1973), p. 7.

[51]Robert L. Thornton and Donald C. King, "Ecology—The Fear Appeal in the Public Sector," *MSU Business Topics* 20 (Winter 1972), pp. 35–38. See also: Peter M. Ginter and Jack M. Starling, "Reverse Distribution Channels for Recycling," *California Management Review* 20 (Spring 1978), pp. 72–83; Carl D. McDaniel, Jr., "The Social Costs of Disposable Packaging," *Business Horizons* 14 (February 1971), pp. 46–48; Edward M. Syring, "Realizing Recycling's Potential," *Nation's Business* (February 1976), pp. 68*ff.*

[52]"U.S. Is Not Alone," *U.S. News & World Report* (18 July 1983), pp. 39–40.

[53]See, for example: Earl A. Clasen, "Marketing Ethics and the Consumer," *Harvard Business Review* 45 (January–February 1967), pp. 79–86; Walter P. Gorman, "The Frightened Consumer?" *Journal of Retailing* 51 (Summer 1975), pp. 31–37*ff;* Lynn J. Loudenback and John W. Goebel, "Marketing in the Age of Strict Liability," *Journal of Marketing* 38 (January 1974), pp. 62–66.

[54]For insights into the workings of the FTC, see: Michael T. Brand and Ivan L. Preston, "The Federal Trade Commission's Use of Evidence to Determine Deception," *Journal of Marketing* 41 (January 1977), pp. 54–62; Dorothy Cohen, "The Concept of Unfairness as It Relates to Advertising Legislation," *Journal of Marketing* 38 (July 1974), pp. 8–13.

[55]Lawrence X. Tarpey, Sr., "Buyer Liability under the Robinson-Patman Act: A Current Appraisal," *Journal of Marketing* 36 (January 1972), pp. 38–42.

Eleanore Snow

SELECTED RETAIL INSTITUTIONS

Your Study Objectives

After you have studied this chapter, you will understand:

1. The traditional department store: its offerings, strengths, weaknesses, and problems.
2. What chain store organizations are like.
3. How today's supermarkets cope with low profit margins, energy and labor problems, and intense competition.
4. How to differentiate among discount stores, mass merchandisers, and off-price retailers.
5. The significance of retail franchising to the economy and its advantages and disadvantages for both franchisor and franchisee.

The first three chapters of this book introduced you to the fascinating world of the retail enterprise. In Chapters 1 and 2, you were made aware of the variety of settings where retailing can take place. You learned of its significance to the economy. We then traced the evolution of this sphere of business from colonial days to the present. You became acquainted with some of the major retail types and classifications: general merchandisers, specialty retailers, vertical marketing systems, and others. You discovered that most retailers are independents and were advised about the advantages and disadvantages of starting your own business.

We discussed the strong growth of service retailing in recent decades. We provided information about several characteristics of services that differentiate them from merchandise offerings. You became familiar with the nonstore retailers: direct selling companies, vending machine operators, and mail-order houses. Finally, you were advised of some aspects of retailing on an international scale.

In Chapter 3, you learned that retail organizations do not operate in a vacuum. Rather, they are subject to constraining external forces such as the socioeconomic, technological, and legal environments. You were presented with demographic data about the American consumer. We also addressed three important concerns of many business managements: consumerism, social responsibility, and ecology.

In this chapter, we expand further on some specific retail institutions: the traditional department store, the supermarket, the discount house and other mass merchandisers, the off-price outlet, and the franchising operation.

The Traditional Department Store

Department stores are large retail institutions that offer a variety of merchandise lines and are organized by departments. Characteristically, three major categories of goods are present: (1) apparel for the entire family, (2) appliances, home furnishings, and furniture, and (3) household linens and dry goods. Many additional lines are offered; jewelry, cosmetics, sporting goods, and toys are some examples. Because each department store presents the equivalent of many individual shops under a single roof, its drawing power is strong. Shoppers, mostly women, come from near and far. Annual sales of these large stores are typically in excess of $5 million. Some take in more than $100 million.

Department Store Strengths and Weaknesses

From management's point of view, the department store organization has a number of advantages. Because of its size and financial strength, it can purchase goods in large quantities at low prices. It is able to hire specialists in buying, merchandising, store design, real estate, sales

Figure 4.1   Gross margin percentages of sales in department stores: selected departments, 1983

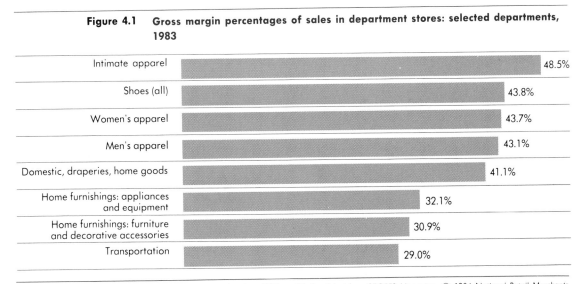

Intimate apparel	48.5%
Shoes (all)	43.8%
Women's apparel	43.7%
Men's apparel	43.1%
Domestic, draperies, home goods	41.1%
Home furnishings: appliances and equipment	32.1%
Home furnishings: furniture and decorative accessories	30.9%
Transportation	29.0%

Source: *Stores* 66 (October 1984), p. 26. Reprinted from STORES Magazine. © 1984 National Retail Merchants Association.

promotion, and other areas. It is capable of securing and promoting its own privately branded goods. On the other hand, the costs of operating such a giant enterprise are considerable. Large numbers of employees are needed to conduct business. Moreover, consumers expect these stores to provide many services. Thus, department stores, more than other retailers, must work on a higher **gross margin:** the difference between the cost of an item and its retail selling price. Retail firms rely on the gross dollars earned by selling merchandise to pay for their operating expenses and to earn a bit of profit. Because their retail prices are higher, department stores are particularly vulnerable to discount houses, catalog showrooms, and other stores that operate on lower gross margins.

As you can see in Figure 4.1, the gross margin percentages of sales earned by individual departments vary considerably. Nowadays, a typical storewide average might run 42 to 43 percent.

Here are a few well-known organizations, along with the locations of their main stores:

Burdine's (Miami)
Dayton's (Minneapolis)
Dillard's (Little Rock)
Emporium-Capwell (San Francisco)
Famous-Barr (St. Louis)
Hecht's (Washington)
Jordan Marsh (Boston)

Joske's (Houston)
Joslin's (Denver)
Lazarus (Columbus)
Marshall Field (Chicago)
Rich's (Atlanta)
Robinson's (Los Angeles)
The Bon (Seattle)

Among department stores there are some notable large chains or associations. Members of the Allied Stores group, for example, include Jordan Marsh, Stern's (Paramus, N.J.), Maas Brothers (Tampa), Donaldson's (Minneapolis), and others. Among those belonging to the Federated Department Stores organization are Bloomingdale's (New York City), Foley's (Houston), Burdines, Bullock's (Los Angeles), Rich's, Shillito's (Cincinnati), and Abraham and Straus (Brooklyn). Marshall Field and Gimbels–New York are members of the Associated Dry Goods group.

Problems of Department Stores

Ever since their introduction, department stores were in the vanguard among retailers. However, soon after the end of World War II, their main downtown units began to decline in sales. As more and more middle-class families relocated to the suburbs, less economically advantaged consumers replaced them. The companies were compelled to follow the trend by opening smaller branch stores in the rapidly growing suburban areas. In recent years, department stores have faced intensifying competition—from discount houses, quality clothing chains, general merchandisers, catalog houses, off-price apparel stores, and other retail types.[1] To meet the competitive challenge, some firms have diversified by launching their own specialty stores. Federated Department Stores, for example, has been expanding its Children's Place/Children's Outlet apparel chain.[2] Dayton-Hudson owns Target Stores, a national discount chain, and Mervyn's, a promotionally priced apparel chain.[3]

In recent years, department stores have faced increasing competition from many types of retail outlets.

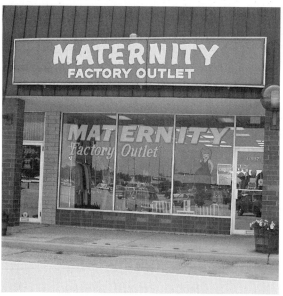

Eleanore Snow

Launching additional branch stores remains an appealing tactic for some organizations. In the early 1980s, for example, Boston's Filene's opened units in New Hampshire and Flushing, New York.[4] Bloomingdale's appeared in Dallas and Miami. Macy's New York division established branches in Florida and Texas.

Chain Stores

A **chain store organization** owns and operates two or more outlets that carry essentially the same merchandise. As a rule, the individual stores closely resemble each other. Storefront, signing, interior layout and decor, and other elements are almost exact copies of each other.[5] Identical operating systems and procedures are also used. Typically, tight administrative controls are in place; the management and the buying function are centralized.

Advantages and Disadvantages of the Chain Store

A major advantage of this type of organization is its buying power. Because the company buys in quantity for a number of outlets, it can obtain better prices and terms than can small independent retailers. Large chains are also able to effect economies of scale. They can, for example, shift merchandise that is overstocked in one store to other units that can sell it or sell it more quickly. They can afford to pay for top management talent and for specialists such as merchandise managers, professional buyers, advertising and sales promotion experts, window trimmers, and so on. They have the financial means for conducting market research, testing new products and services, experimenting with different retail prices for goods, trying out varia-

Courtesy Parisian, Birmingham, AL/Ed Malles photos

The Electronic ShowBoard and high-tech merchandising characterize Parisian, Alabama's largest retail chain.

tions in department layout, and the like. Advertising costs can be spread over the entire chain. Only a fraction of these costs, or, for that matter, of total company overhead, is allocated to any one store.

The chain organization also faces some disadvantages. Lack of flexibility is often a problem, mostly because the units are directed from the central office. Changes in systems and/or procedures progress slowly, and company-wide communications may be impeded. An individual store may not be able to respond quickly enough to the moves of a local competitor. Managers and other personnel must be found to staff the organization. To ensure a reservoir of capable workers to fill openings in the company, attention must be devoted to training and development. Effective supervision is needed to direct and motivate employees.

Types of Chains   Today, chain organizations dominate most of the retailing sector. There are small local chains of two, five, and eight units and regional firms that operate as many as 40 or 50 stores or more. Some huge national companies count their outlets in the hundreds or even thousands. There are food, apparel, drug, shoe, home furnishings, variety and general merchandise chains, and many other types of chains. There are also chains that sell services. Supermarkets, fast-food restaurants of many kinds, department stores, hardware stores, discount stores, beauty salons, and dry cleaning establishments are among the more highly visible operations.

General Merchandise Chains   The **general merchandise retailer** carries an extensive variety of lines: apparel for the family, accessories, home furnishings, appliances, hardware, household items, health and beauty aids, and other types of goods. The leading general merchandise chain in 1984 was Sears, Roebuck & Co.

Back in the mid-1970s, Sears was confronted with increasing costs of operation and plummeting profits. At the time, the company had some 900 stores and 1,700 catalog outlets, 124 warehouses, and 13 distribution centers. To improve its position, management created a corporate planning department, lowered prices, increased the promotion budget, and began to emphasize smaller stores.[6] Later on, Sears expanded its financial services. By 1983, financial centers were in operation in over 100 stores.[7] That same year, the company announced plans for a five-year modernization program that would include refurbishing more than 600 stores and opening over 60 new units.[8] In 1983, their 813 stores and 2,388 catalog centers brought in more than $20 billion in sales.[9]

K mart, with main offices in Troy, Michigan, is the nation's second largest retailer. The company targets at moderate-income adults be-

K mart is upgrading its image by carrying new upscale items and by grouping related merchandise into "centers" like the Homecare Center above.

Courtesy K mart Corporation. K MART and ACCENTS are service marks of K mart Corporation, Troy, MI

tween the ages of 25 and 44. It has been attempting to upgrade its image by adding new departments such as gold jewelry and books, and by consolidating paint, hardware, and lumber sections into home centers.[10] Pharmacies and optical centers have been introduced into some stores. K mart has also been experimenting with box stores—groceries that sell from cartons at discount prices. Among other novel approaches, K mart planned to launch a chain of freestanding home improvement centers in 1984.[11] The company owns other retail businesses, among them the Designer Depot off-price apparel chain and cafeteria chains such as Furr's and Bishop Buffets.

Some years ago, another giant general merchandiser, J. C. Penney, decided to change its image as an old-fashioned store aimed at the lower classes. They upgraded by emphasizing fashion merchandise and by deemphasizing price as a major element in their strategy.[12] Early in 1983, they announced plans to spend $1 billion over a five-year period to increase sales of apparel and related merchandise. They also began to close down their automotive centers and sharply curtail such lines as garden equipment, paints, hardware, and household appliances.[13]

Specialty Chains Radio Shack, owned by Tandy Corporation, of Fort Worth, Texas, is a huge specialty chain with more than 4,000 outlets. Among them

Unit of a successful electronics chain.

Courtesy of Radio Shack, a Division of Tandy Corporation

are domestic franchised and company-owned units as well as many stores in foreign countries. Tandy also owns other specialty chains. Among these are craft shops, garden centers, and stores that sell floor tiles.[14] By early 1980, the Radio Shack chain had already sold over 200,000 units of their TRS 80 microcomputers—a figure that accounted for at least one half of the market at the time.[15]

One of the newer, more rapidly growing specialty chains is The Foot Locker, with over 300 stores in operation by early 1982. These athletic shoe retailers are operated by the Kinney Shoe Corporation (which, in turn, is part of the F. W. Woolworth Company's portfolio). First tested in the South, The Foot Locker produced $200 million in sales in 1981.[16] St. Louis-based Edison Brothers Shoe Stores is one of the largest footwear chains. Among other organizations, they own and operate Bakers and Chandlers.

There are many apparel chains. Neiman-Marcus, Lerners, and Saks Fifth Avenue are among the better-known. Also popular today are the "toy supermarket" specialty chains. These facilities are usually large and freestanding. Their "wide aisles, shelves to the ceiling jam-packed with merchandise, and supermarket shopping wagons are hallmarks. Services are at a minimum, the atmosphere is impersonal, but the prices are low."[17] Representative chains include Toys "R" Us, based in Saddle Brook, New Jersey, and Child World, with headquarters in Avon, Massachusetts. Toys "R" Us was originally a small chain of juvenile furniture and toy stores in the state of Washington.[18]

Another new type of fast-growing specialty retailer is the computer chain. Computerland is one such organization. A franchise operation, the company launched its first store in 1977.[19] More recently, computer repair shops have begun to crop up to service the millions of home and small office computers already in the field. An example is Sorbus Service, a firm that opened outlets in Los Angeles, Chicago, and Philadelphia in September of 1982.[20]

As a final example of strong specialty chain growth, there in Merle Norman Cosmetics, with some 2,700 studios primarily in the South and Southwest, and in Canada. In 1981, the company expected its sales to exceed $130 million and announced plans to open studios in Europe.[21]

Supermarketing

Modern **supermarkets** are large, multiline, departmentized stores. They offer wide assortments of groceries, dairy products, fruits and vegetables, meats, detergents, paper goods, and other household supplies. They also carry many other nonfood and convenience items. The stores enjoy high shopper traffic, typically producing annual sales in excess of $1 million. For the most part, they operate on self-service. Supermarkets work on high volume and low margin for many of the lines carried. Profits are traditionally low, often no more than 1 or 2 percent of sales. To produce more gross margin dollars, these stores offer additional product lines on which the gross margin percentage earned is higher than the normally tight margins available, for example, on canned goods and other groceries. The concept is called **scrambled merchandising:** a policy of adding other profitable merchandise lines to a store's overall variety.

Today's supermarkets stock somewhere in the neighborhood of 10,000 different items. Chains dominate the field. Safeway, Winn-Dixie, the A&P, and Kroger are some well-known examples.

Background of the Modern Supermarket[22]

There seem to be five somewhat distinct stages in the development of the supermarket.

1. The pre-1930 food industry.
2. The revolutionary birth of the supermarket, 1930–1935.
3. Acceptance and growth, 1936–1941.
4. The war years, 1942–1945.
5. Postwar growth, 1946–present.[23]

Although checkouts had been introduced years earlier in some groceries, and self-service was no longer a novelty, it was not until the 1930s that the supermarket concept first took hold. Today's supermarket's originated in the neighborhood grocery and the food fairs or emporiums of the Depression years. The fairs were large stores, inexpensively furnished and situated in low-rent areas. They offered hundreds of items at low prices. With promotion-minded managements, they advertised heavily. Among these early supermarkets were the King Kullen and Big Bear stores.[24]

Supermarketing Today   Food retailing is highly competitive and beset with problems. In recent years, supermarket managements not only have had to struggle with more and stronger competition but also with spiraling costs of labor, energy, capital, and taxation. They have attempted to meet these challenges by instituting advances in electronics, automation, warehousing, and packaging. However, the costs of implementing these technological advances have been exorbitant.[25]

Seeking additional avenues out of their difficulties, some companies have experimented with new approaches. There is, for instance, a decided trend toward opening smaller outlets at a much lower cost than that required for a traditional unit. Although they stock many of the products that consumers regularly shop for, these smaller limited-line stores carry no produce or meats. They require fewer employees, offer no services, and sell some merchandise at discount prices. Kroger's Lo stores, Jewel's T Discount stores, and the A&P LoLo units are examples.[26]

Another trend, diametrically opposed, is to open much larger stores and offer for sale general merchandise in addition to the usual supermarket fare. The warehouse-sized food marts and combination stores are examples; eventually, hypermarkets may start to appear.[27]

Supermarket operators have also begun to realize they have been losing a substantial share of the consumer's food dollar to restaurants. Each year, consumers spend more than one third of our total food bill to eat out. Supermarkets have tried to combat this growing threat by introducing food specialties, snack bars, take-home foods, and other innovations into their stores.[28] Many chains have already introduced new service operations for their patrons' convenience. Safeway units in California and Publix Stores in Florida, for example, have added automated teller machines so that consumers can secure ready cash for shopping or make bank deposits.[29]

Generic Goods   **Generics** is the accepted name for those unbranded, plainly packaged no-frill items on today's supermarket shelves. Most of these products come in white packages with bold black print, although several chains have been experimenting with improving the stark packaging by affixing colored labels.

The concept is a European import. Generic merchandise appeared in the French Carrefour stores during the mid-1970s. In the United

POTATO CHIPS

ENGLEMAN

From *The Wall Street Journal*, with permission of Cartoon Features Syndicate.

"Where are the silicon chips?"

States, the Midwest's Jewel supermarket chain was first to offer the goods. By 1978, large numbers of consumers had already tried them. Many were well satisfied and continued to buy them regularly. Apparently, better-educated consumers and shoppers with large families are more apt to purchase generic products.[30] Most consumers perceive differences between these items and their national- or store-brand counterparts. On the whole, generic goods are looked on as generally inferior to the other types. National brands are considered superior in reliability, prestige, quality, and other characteristics. Shoppers feel that private, or store, brands are positioned between the two and usually represent particularly good value.[31]

Among the more popular generic items are canned vegetables and fruits, tea bags, preserves, soft drinks, juices, and household supplies (paper toweling, napkins, aluminum foil, trash bags, and so on). The prices of generic merchandise generally average around 30 percent lower than those of competitive brands—and about 15 percent below prices of private-label goods.[32]

One of the newer merchandising ideas in the supermarket is an extension of the generics concept. No-name, no-package bulk foods are offered for sale in sanitized liners with clear plastic tops. Shoppers may purchase sugar, spaghetti, flour, dried beans, spices, and other merchandise by the pound. Among the companies now selling bulk food items are Loblaws in New England and Canada, Safeway and Ralph's on the West Coast, and Pick-n-Pay in the midcentral states.[33]

One of the newer supermarket merchandising concepts: a bulk foods section, where shoppers may purchase baking items, pastas, dried foods, and other merchandise by the pound.

Courtesy Vons Grocery Co., Los Angeles, CA

Discount Stores and Other Mass Merchandisers

Discount houses first appeared on the American scene right after World War II. Promoting aggressively, these new retail merchants advertised popular, nationally branded goods at below customary market prices. Sales were mostly in household goods: appliances and other hard lines. The early outlets were housed in large, rented premises. Store fixtures were practical and basic, and the stores themselves not particularly attractive. They operated on self-service, with few salespeople and even fewer service offerings. A few discounters employed the private club concept: shoppers were admitted only with a membership card.

In the 1950s and 1960s, discounters gradually started adding other lines to their basic merchandise assortment. In essence, they were attempting to trade up. This trend has continued to the point where more and more discount operations are beginning to resemble small department stores. Today, most of the more successful firms prefer the label mass merchandiser.

Mass Merchandisers

The A. C. Nielsen Company defines **mass merchandisers** as "outlets presenting a discount image, handling at least three merchandise lines, and having a floor space of at least 10,000 square feet."[34] Nielsen also advises that more than 7,000 such stores were in operation at the end of 1982—despite the closing of the Fed-Mart and Kings chains and hundreds of others. In 1983, F. W. Woolworth abandoned its Woolco operation.

*K mart, the nation's second-
largest retailer, was launched
in 1962.*

Eleanore Snow

Chain organizations dominate the field. K mart, Zayre, Caldor, and Wal-Mart are some better-known mass merchandisers.

K mart The S. S. Kresge Company launched its first K mart unit in Garden City, Michigan in 1962. The budding chain has grown rapidly. It is now the second largest retailer in the country, behind Sears, Roebuck & Co. The typical K mart store contains some 48 departments. Newer outlets are being opened in several sizes. These run from 40,000 to 95,000 square feet, according to management's judgment as to how large a store can be supported by a community's demographics.[35]

Major competitors began to chip away at K mart's share of the market. Among these were Caldor in New England, the Target Stores in the Midwest, and Wal-Mart in the South. In the 1980s, the company shifted its strategy. It decided to put reins on its explosive expansion rate and devote time and effort to remodeling existing units. Management also committed itself to stock a broader range of more fashionable merchandise and to try to raise productivity.[36]

Off-price Stores One of the most exciting new developments has been the rapid and still accelerating growth of the **off-price retailers.** These firms offer popular, name-brand merchandise at prices considerably below those found at department stores and specialty shops. They are able to undersell traditional retailers because of lower and tightly controlled operating expenses. Many are set up on a self-selection and checkout basis, like supermarkets. More importantly, perhaps, they pay less than other retailers for the goods they purchase for resale. Instead of ordering months in advance, their buyers frequently place their orders at the start or end of a season. Unusually good buys can be made in this fashion.

The off-price store differs from the mass merchandiser in that it usually specializes in only one basic merchandise line such as clothing, shoes, or linens. Off-price stores are also generally smaller than the mass merchandising outlets.

In addition to both large and small chains, many independent retailers are found in the field. The largest chain of all is Marshall's, with units in Los Angeles, Kansas City, Chicago, Atlanta, and other cities. A subsidiary of the Melville Corporation, Marshall's stores are laid out in supermarket fashion and have a basic decor.[37] Two other off-price operations, growing rapidly, are the Zayre Corporation's T. J. Maxx apparel chain and its Hit or Miss stores. Zayre plans to have about 800 outlets by 1986.[38]

With sales totaling approximately $3 billion in 1979, off-price apparel and shoe retailers had doubled their volume by early 1982.[39] Industry sales are expected to keep mounting. More and more full-price retailers have been entering the field. The Dayton-Hudson Corporation is a notable example. In its portfolio are Waldenbooks, the Carter Hawley Hale stores, Contempo Casuals, and other chains. It is also the parent company of the Target Stores discount chain, Plums–The Elegant Discounter, and Mervyn's family apparel stores. Sales at Mervyn's alone reached $1 billion in 1981.[40] Another large corporation with off-price holdings is U.S. Shoe. Among these are the Crackers chain of children's clothing stores, the T. H. Mandy women's apparel shops, the Banister Shoe Outlets, and the Merchants Linen Warehouse chain.[41] Other divisions of U.S. Shoe include Casual Corner, Ups 'n' Downs, Caren Charles, and J. Riggins.

Until the early 1980s, most off-price chains were apparel or shoe retailers. Since then, other types have been attracted to the field. Linens outlets, such as the New Jersey–based Linens 'n Things (owned by the Melville Company) and the Merchants Linen Warehouse stores, are illustrations in point. Because these chains offer a far wider selection of goods, they have been cutting into department store sales. To counter the growing competition, department stores have been extending their white sales past the traditional time. They are also running promotions more often.[42]

In line with the rapid expansion of off-price retailing, new shopping centers devoted entirely to this activity are springing up around the country. By 1983, about 100 such centers were in operation.[43] One of the largest thus far is the 350,000 square foot Factory Outlet Mall in Orlando, Florida. It boasts 67 stores and 13 kiosks, all selling merchandise at below regular retail prices. Figure 4.2 shows the layout of this mall.

Opportunities in Franchising

The most dynamic growth area in retailing in recent years has been the franchising field. More often than not, franchising offers a safer route to entering the business arena than starting a brand-new venture. It has proven successful for thousands of people. For all its popularity, though, franchising is by no means a new idea. The concept has been around since the turn of the century. Long before the first franchised specialty stores began to appear, gasoline service station and car dealership franchises were well established.

In franchised fast-food restaurants, most of us have indulged in a variety of treats: hamburgers, pizza, tacos, fried chicken, doughnuts and coffee, seafood, and charcoal-broiled steaks. Motel franchises like Howard Johnson and Holiday Inn are familiar. Many of us have also shopped at franchised convenience stores, paint-and-wallpaper shops, hardware stores, car rental agencies, apparel stores, and so on. Perhaps some of us have even visited agencies that prepare income tax forms, such as H&R Block.

Retail Franchising Today

Franchising is "a system of distribution under which an individually owned business is operated as though it were part of a large chain, complete with trademarks, uniform symbols, design, equipment, and standardized services or products."[44] A company that offers this method of distribution to others is known as a **franchisor.** An individual or firm that contracts with the parent company, or franchisor, to operate a unit is called a **franchisee.**

The Department of Commerce distinguishes between **product or tradename franchising** and **business format franchising.** It describes the first as the kind engaged in, for example, by bottlers of soft drinks, car dealers, and gasoline stations. Far more common is the second type. Baskin-Robbins, Burger King, Kampgrounds of America, Kentucky Fried Chicken, and Ramada Inns are examples of business format franchising. This type is:

> characterized by an ongoing business relationship between franchisor and franchisee that includes not only the product, service, and trademark, but the entire business format itself—a marketing strategy and plan, operating manuals and standards, quality control, and continuing two-way communications. Restaurants, nonfood retailing, personal and business services, rental services, real estate services, and a long list of other service businesses fall into the category. . . . Business format franchising has been responsible for much of the growth of franchising in the United States since 1950.[45]

Figure 4.2 Factory Outlet Mall in Orlando, Florida

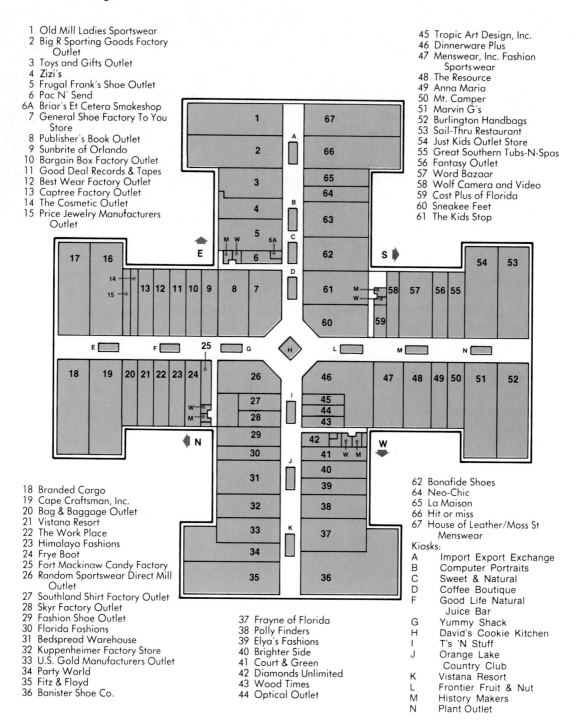

1 Old Mill Ladies Sportswear
2 Big R Sporting Goods Factory Outlet
3 Toys and Gifts Outlet
4 Zizi's
5 Frugal Frank's Shoe Outlet
6 Pac N' Send
6A Briar's Et Cetera Smokeshop
7 General Shoe Factory To You Store
8 Publisher's Book Outlet
9 Sunbrite of Orlando
10 Bargain Box Factory Outlet
11 Good Deal Records & Tapes
12 Best Wear Factory Outlet
13 Captree Factory Outlet
14 The Cosmetic Outlet
15 Price Jewelry Manufacturers Outlet

45 Tropic Art Design, Inc.
46 Dinnerware Plus
47 Menswear, Inc. Fashion Sportswear
48 The Resource
49 Anna Maria
50 Mt. Camper
51 Marvin G's
52 Burlington Handbags
53 Sail-Thru Restaurant
54 Just Kids Outlet Store
55 Great Southern Tubs-N-Spas
56 Fantasy Outlet
57 Word Bazaar
58 Wolf Camera and Video
59 Cost Plus of Florida
60 Sneakee Feet
61 The Kids Stop

18 Branded Cargo
19 Cape Craftsman, Inc.
20 Bag & Baggage Outlet
21 Vistana Resort
22 The Work Place
23 Himalaya Fashions
24 Frye Boot
25 Fort Mackinaw Candy Factory
26 Random Sportswear Direct Mill Outlet
27 Southland Shirt Factory Outlet
28 Skyr Factory Outlet
29 Fashion Shoe Outlet
30 Florida Fashions
31 Bedspread Warehouse
32 Kuppenheimer Factory Store
33 U.S. Gold Manufacturers Outlet
34 Party World
35 Fitz & Floyd
36 Banister Shoe Co.

37 Frayne of Florida
38 Polly Finders
39 Elya's Fashions
40 Brighter Side
41 Court & Green
42 Diamonds Unlimited
43 Wood Times
44 Optical Outlet

62 Bonafide Shoes
64 Neo-Chic
65 La Maison
66 Hit or miss
67 House of Leather/Moss St Menswear

Kiosks:
A Import Export Exchange
B Computer Portraits
C Sweet & Natural
D Coffee Boutique
F Good Life Natural Juice Bar
G Yummy Shack
H David's Cookie Kitchen
I T's 'N Stuff
J Orange Lake Country Club
K Vistana Resort
L Frontier Fruit & Nut
M History Makers
N Plant Outlet

Source: Eric Peterson, "Off-Price," Stores 65 (May 1983), p. 29. Reprinted from STORES Magazine © 1983 National Retail Merchants Association.

Ice cream franchises are popular examples of business-format franchising.

Courtesy Baskin-Robbins Ice Cream, Burbank, CA

Of growing interest today is still another kind: **conversion franchising,** defined as the conversion of an independent business to a franchise. Conversions appear to be an emerging trend in franchising, as is also the entry of women, in numbers larger than ever before, both as franchisors and franchisees.[46]

Figure 4.3 (page 107) underscores the rapid growth of retail franchising. The number of franchised restaurants more than doubled in the 13 years between 1970 and 1983. In the same time, convenience stores increased by more than 96 percent and nonfood retailers by over 30 percent. Total sales for retail franchises of all types amounted to $368 billion in 1983. This figure reportedly accounted for 88 percent of all franchising revenues in the country. In 1984, the sales volume of retail operations was expected to pass the $400 billion mark, slightly more than 30 percent of total retail sales.[47]

Often, the popularity of a franchise organization is a function of two marketing tactics: expanding the number of outlets and advertising more frequently than competitors. This is so only if the basic product line and/or services and the overall presentation are good. There are giant national operations with thousands of units: the 7-Eleven convenience chain, McDonald's (and their Golden Arches), Kentucky Fried Chicken, Baskin-Robbins, and so on. The majority of retail franchises, however, number their stores in the hundreds, not thousands. Many have fewer than one hundred. Table 4.1 offers information regarding selected franchising firms: company names, home cities, type of retailing involved, and approximate number of franchisees as of early 1983.

Table 4.1
Selected retail franchising companies

Franchisor (Home Offices)	Number of Franchisees	Type of Retailing
Athletic Attic Marketing, Inc. (Gainesville, Fla.)	198	Sporting goods
Baskin-Robbins, Inc. (Glendale, Calif.)	2,800+	Ice cream
Ben Franklin Division, Household Merchandising, Inc. (Des Plaines, Ill.)	146	General merchandise
Bonanza International, Inc. (Dallas, Tex.)	600+	Restaurants
Computerland Corporation (Hayward, Calif.)	400	Computers
Davis Paint Company (No. Kansas City, Mo.)	75	Paint and wallpaper
Dunkin' Donuts of America, Inc. (Randolph, Mass.)	1,184	Coffee and doughnut shops
Edie Adams Cut & Curl (Jericho, N.Y.)	297	Full-service beauty salons
Flowerama of America, Inc. (Waterloo, Iowa)	78	Flowers and plants
Great Earth Vitamin Stores (Santa Ana, Calif.)	150	Vitamin products
Hardee's Food Systems, Inc. (Rocky Mount, N.C.)	1,657	Fast-food restaurants
Hickory Farms of Ohio (Maumee, Ohio)	548	Specialty foods
International House of Pancakes Restaurants (No. Hollywood, Calif.)	472	Full-service family restaurants
Jo-Ann's Nut House, Inc. (Aberdeen, N.J.)	136	Retail candy and nuts
Just Pants (Chicago, Ill.)	52	Jeans, slacks, and accessories
Kampgrounds of America, Inc. (Billings, Mont.)	706	Campgrounds for recreational vehicles
Long John Silver's, Inc. (Lexington, Ky.)	531	Fast-food restaurants
Manpower, Inc. (Milwaukee, Wis.)	474	Temporary help services
Medicine Shoppes International, Inc. (St. Louis, Mo.)	435	Prescription and health care centers
Nutri/System, Inc. (Jenkintown, Pa.)	521	Weight loss centers
Pearle Vision Centers (Dallas, Tex.)	300	Full-service optical centers
Popeyes Famous Fried Chicken, Inc. (Jefferson, La.)	350	Fast-food operation

Table 4.1 (concluded)	Franchisor (Home Offices)	Number of Franchisees	Type of Retailing
	Ramada Inns, Inc. (Phoenix, Ariz.)	630	Hotels and motels
	The Ringgold Corporation (Houston, Tex.)	146	Picture frames, art
	Sir Speedy, Inc. (Newport Beach, Calif.)	450	Printing centers
	The Southland Corporation (Dallas, Tex.)	2,537	Convenience groceries (7-Eleven)
	Spring Crest Company (Brea, Calif.)	275	Drapery centers
	Wicks 'n' Sticks, Inc. (Houston, Tex.)	200	Candles and accessories

Source: Bureau of Industrial Economics and Minority Business Development Agency, U.S. Department of Commerce, *Franchise Opportunities Handbook* (Washington, D.C.: U.S. Government Printing Office, September 1983).

The biggest retail food franchise operation of them all, international in scope, is McDonald's. By 1977, the company directed about 4,100 restaurants and could boast of selling several billion hamburgers annually. In addition to their franchised units, the firm has company-owned stores.[48] A major competitor is Burger King, a subsidiary of the Pillsbury Company. Among other popular food franchises are ice cream stores and coffee and doughnut shops. In 1983, Baskin-Robbins outlets numbered more than 2,800, and Dunkin' Donuts, nearly 1,200.

Attractions and Drawbacks of the Franchise System

The franchise system of distribution has a unique advantage. It offers the parent company an opportunity for rapid expansion: the chance to open additional outlets that are financed by other people's money. A successful franchisor can quickly build a chain and come to enjoy the economies of scale and other benefits that accrue to chain operations. Channel management over all phases is thus assured.[49]

Provided that the franchising company is successful and well-established, the arrangement carries attractive potential for a would-be retailer. Typically, chances for success are higher than those involved in initiating a brand-new enterprise or, for that matter, buying a going business. The investor in a franchise is able to capitalize on a tried-and-proven business package. The known and respected company name captures public attention and goodwill. It also has instant pulling power. Moreover, in the majority of cases, the franchisee can expect able assistance in most of the following areas:

initial training	management counseling
site selection	opening promotion
store design, layout, and decor	ongoing promotional support
operating systems and procedures	employee training programs
merchandise selection	field supervision
setting up internal record-keeping	possible financial aid

Disadvantages of Franchising The headaches of starting up a franchise are considerable. A program of expansion via this route must be conceived, organized, and set into motion. Sales costs incurred in securing leads and converting them into franchised units mount up rapidly. Legal services must be paid for. Finding suitable candidates as franchisees is difficult.[50] One essential is financial soundness. In addition, franchisors look for people with some college education or at the very least, a high school diploma. They want people in good health with abundant energy, a cheerful personality, and a cooperative nature. Once the franchised outlet has opened for business, the parent company must provide supervision designed to maintain chainwide operating standards.

There are disadvantages for the franchisee as well. Franchisees soon discover that they have relinquished a considerable degree of control over both their business activity and their future. Never fully independent, they are required to follow the policies and procedures mandated by the franchisor. They are unable to expand their product/service offerings beyond those dictated. They may be restricted to a specified

Many franchisors provide site selection, store decor, and merchandise selection in addition to a complete operating system.

Courtesy Confectionery Square Corp., Morganville, NJ

Figure 4.3   Selected retail franchises: Number of establishments, 1970 and 1983

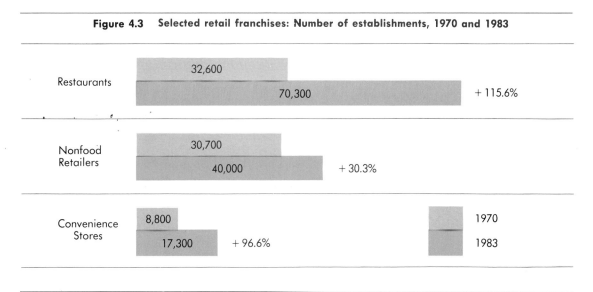

Source: U.S. Department of Commerce, Bureau of the Census, *Statistical Abstract of the United States, 1983–84,* 104th ed. (Washington, D.C.: U.S. Government Printing Office, 1983), p. 806.

territory. They must bow to franchisor supervision and worry about the possibility of losing the franchise. Heaviest of all burdens, however, is the required payment of royalties throughout the life of the contract. Usually these are an ongoing percentage of the firm's *gross* sales, payable monthly.

The Franchise Contract[51] The franchise applicant should proceed with caution and always with the support and advice of both attorney and accountant. Obviously, the contract to be signed will favor the party who draws it up—that is to say, the franchisor.

The contract is a legal document, an investment agreement. At the same time, it is a license to operate a business under the parent company's name and trademark. Listed in the agreement are the duties, responsibilities, and contributions to be made by both parties to the contract. Also covered are specifics regarding the required investment, initial fees and continuing royalties, contributions toward advertising and promotion, territorial limitations, methods and procedures, conditions for renewal or termination, and so on.

To protect investors from misrepresentations by franchisors, many states have enacted **full disclosure laws.** Among other requirements, these laws mandate disclosure of the background of the franchisor principals, a recent financial statement, franchise fees, royalties, termination provisions, and any requirement to purchase supplies from the franchisor.[52] **Fair-practice laws** also exist at the state level that generally prohibit franchisors from terminating or failing to renew a franchise without "good cause."

Summary   Department stores are large operations that combine a variety of merchandise lines under one roof. Major offerings include family apparel, furniture, home furnishings, household linens, and dry goods. Their size and financial strength enable these retailers to purchase merchandise at better prices, put the specialization of labor principle to good use, and offer private (store) brands. Because their operating costs are high, these institutions must work on higher gross margins than other types of stores. Consequently, they have been facing serious competition from discount houses, general merchandise stores, off-price apparel chains, and other retail types. In attempting to meet the competitive challenge, some companies attempt to diversify and/or add branches.

Chain store organizations own and operate two or more outlets that carry essentially the same merchandise and resemble each other. Usually, chains can obtain better prices and terms on goods for resale than can most independent retailers. They are also able to effect economies of scale, hire specialists, conduct research, and spread advertising costs over the entire chain. Among the disadvantages of the chain store organization are a lack of flexibility; the need to locate, hire, and train many employees; and the need for effective supervision. General merchandise chains like Sears, Roebuck & Co. and K mart offer a wide variety of types of goods: clothing, home furnishings, appliances, housewares, health and beauty aids, and so on. Radio Shack, Mervyn's, and Toys "R" Us are among the largest specialty chains.

Supermarkets are large, multiline, departmentized food stores that also sell household products, health and beauty aids, and many other nonfood items. Profits are traditionally low. To raise the gross margin dollars earned, these firms rely heavily on scrambled merchandising. Supermarkets have also faced problems with rising energy and labor costs and with keen competition. Some firms have experimented with opening smaller, limited-line food stores. Others have sought to expand by opening large combination stores.

Discount stores sell popular brand goods at below their customary market prices. Most of today's more successful discounters prefer the label *mass merchandiser*. Chains like K mart, Zayre, Caldor, and Wal-Mart are some of the better-known names in the field. Off-price stores represent a new breed of merchant who specializes in one or several merchandise lines. Lower operating expenses and distinctive buying practices enable these retailers to offer popular merchandise at prices well below those found at traditional department and specialty stores. Examples of off-price companies include Marshall's, T. J. Maxx, and Merchants Linen Warehouse stores.

Franchising is a popular avenue to business ownership. It offers a company the opportunity to build a chain organization by using other people's money. Franchisees are able to capitalize on a proven business package. They can expect assistance in site selection, layout and design of the premises, operating systems, training, and other aspects of business operation. Among the disadvantages to the franchisee are the relinquishing of some independence, restrictions imposed by the franchisor, and royalties on sales throughout the life of the franchise contract. Full disclosure laws exist in many states to protect would-be franchisees.

Key Terms	department stores	off-price retailers
	gross margin	franchisor
	chain store organization	franchisee
	general merchandise retailer	product or tradename franchising
	supermarkets	business format franchising
	scrambled merchandising	conversion franchising
	generics	full disclosure laws
	mass merchandisers	fair-practice laws

Review Questions

1. Offer a concise description of the traditional department store. Identify the three basic merchandise categories offered by these retailers.

2. List three advantages and three disadvantages of the *(a)* department store organization and *(b)* chain store organization.

3. Clearly distinguish between the general merchandise chain and the specialty chain.

4. Briefly describe each of the following types of retail companies: *(a)* discount house, *(b)* limited-line retailer, and *(c)* combination store.

5. What is meant by *scrambled merchandising*?

6. To hold down operating costs and gain competitive advantage, some supermarket organizations have experimented with new approaches. Identify and comment briefly on three or four of these.

7. What are generic goods? Cite four product types frequently stocked by supermarkets.

8. Today's discount operations are quite different from the discount houses of the early 1950s. In what ways do they differ?

9. What are mass merchandisers? Name at least three major chain organizations that fall into this category.

10. Comment on the rapid growth of off-price retailing. Offer your opinion about why these retailers are able to undersell both department stores and specialty shops.

11. Explain the following terms: *(a)* business format franchising *(b)* conversion franchising.

12. Summarize the attractions and drawbacks of the franchise method of distribution from the points of view of both franchisor and franchisee.

13. Review some of the major aspects covered in a typical franchise contract.

14. What is the significance of full disclosure laws to potential franchisees?

1. Visit a department store in your area. Record the names of six or more departments through which you pass and your estimate of the number of square feet devoted to each. Then, compare the largest and smallest departments on your list. Suggest several reasons why so much more space is assigned to the larger of the two.

2. Restaurants have been garnering an increasingly larger share of the consumer's food budget. Outline at least four steps that a supermarket chain might take to recover some of these lost dollars.

3. Research the generics section in your local supermarket. Select five products similar in size and content to branded items you use regularly at home. Record the prices of the items you customarily purchase and those of their generic counterparts. Calculate the average price differential percentage for all five sets of products.

4. Public receptivity to generic goods has been growing ever since their introduction in the 1970s. Do you think their popularity will increase even more in the next decade? Why or why not?

5. Give your assessment of the growth possibilities of off-price shopping centers over the next twenty-five years. What socioeconomic trends can you point to that would seem to support your view?

6. Offer three reasons why franchising may be considered a safer route to self-employment than starting a brand new venture.

Notes   [1]Eleanor G. May and Malcolm P. McNair, "Department Stores Face Stiff Challenge in Next Decade," *Journal of Retailing* 53 (Fall 1977), p. 56.

[2]David P. Schulz, "Expansion," *Stores* 65 (August 1983), p. 30.

[3]"Dayton-Hudson's Hard Push for National Clout," *Business Week* (8 September 1980), pp. 96*ff*.

[4]Schulz, "Expansion," p. 37.

[5]From time to time, a chain may experiment with a newer store prototype. If successful, this becomes the model for future units.

[6]"Sears' Identity Crisis," *Business Week* (8 December 1975), pp. 52–56*ff*.

[7]"New Look for the Top Retailer," *Time* (5 December 1983), pp. 66–68.

[8]Isadore Barmash, "$1.7 Billion Sears Modernization Due," *New York Times* (9 November 1983), p. D1.

[9]"Sears, Penney, Ward: Re-positioning at Work," *Stores* 66 (July 1984), p. 34.

[10]"Where K mart Goes Next Now that It's No. 2," *Business Week* (2 June 1980), pp. 109–110*ff*; Edward S. Dubbs, "Retail Expansion," *Stores* 61 (August 1979), pp. 23–26.

[11]"K mart Plans Home Center Test Units," *Chain Store Age, General Merchandise Division* 60 (February 1984), p. 16.

[12]"J. C. Penney's Fashion Gamble," *Business Week* (16 January 1978), p. 66.

[13]"Penney Plans $1 Billion Change-Over," *New York Times* (1 February 1983), p. D1*ff*.

[14]"Radio Shack for Europe," *Business Week* (31 August 1974), pp. 75–76.

[15]"Tandy's Next Big Drive into Home Electronics," *Business Week* (1 June 1980), p. 31*ff*.

[16]"The Foot Locker Chain's Rapid Rise," *New York Times* (25 March 1982), p. D4.

[17]Doreen Mangan, "The Toy Marts, *Stores* 61 (February 1979), p. 6.

[18]"Strong Growth Is Predicted at Wal-Mart and Toys 'R' Us," *New York Times* (2 March 1982), p. D5.

[19]Gene Bylinsky, "The Computer Stores Have Arrived," *Fortune* 97 (24 April 1978), pp. 52–55.

[20]Andrew Pollack, "Repairing a Computer," *New York Times* (23 September 1982), p. D2.

[21]"Makeup Chain Seeks Wider Awareness," *New York Times* (31 March 1981), p. D4.

[22]For more information on the evolution of the food retailing industry, see: Gene Arlin German, "The Dynamics of Food Retailing 1900–1975," Ph.D. dissertation, Cornell University, 1978.

[23]David Appel, "The Supermarket: Early Development of an Institutional Innovation," *Journal of Retailing* 48 (Spring 1972), p. 40.

[24]Arieh Goldman, "Stages in the Development of the Supermarket," *Journal of Retailing* 51 (Winter 1975–76), p. 56.

[25]Louis P. Bucklin, "Technological Change and Store Operations: The Supermarket Case," *Journal of Retailing* 56 (Spring 1980), pp. 3–15; Michael A. McGinnis and Leland L. Gardner, "Electronic Checkout and Supermarket Sales Volume: Some Evidence," *Akron Business and Economic Review* 7 (Summer 1976), pp. 31–34.

[26]"Grocers See New Hope in Limited-line Stores," *Business Week* (4 December 1978), pp. 29–30.

[27]"Warehouse Style Discount Supers for U.S.?" *Chain Store Age, Executive Edition* 49 (September 1973), pp. E30–31.

[28]N. Howard, "The Supermarkets Fight Back," *Dun's Review* 110 (October 1977), pp. 108–10.

[29]"Citicorp in the Supermarket: Teller Units Offer Cash," *New York Times* (29 November 1983), pp. D1*ff.*

[30]See: Patrick E. Murphy and Gene R. Laczniak, "Generic Supermarket Items: A Product and Consumer Analysis," *Journal of Retailing* 55 (Summer 1979), p. 13.

[31]Joseph A. Bellizzi et al., "Consumer Perceptions of National, Private, and Generic Brands," *Journal of Retailing* 57 (Winter 1981), pp. 56–70.

[32]J. L. Parks, *Generics in Supermarkets: Myth or Magic?* (Northbrook, Ill.: A. C. Nielsen Company, 1981), p. 14.

[33]"Buying in Bulk," *Time* (25 July 1983), p. 58.

[34]"Shifting Patterns Among Mass Merchandisers," *The Nielsen Researcher,* no. 2, 1983 (Northbrook, Ill.: A. C. Nielsen Company, 1983), pp. 14–18.

[35]"The Orchestrated Growth of S. S. Kresge," *Dun's Review* 108 (December 1975), pp. 46–49.

[36]Jeremy Main, "K mart's Plan to Be Born Again, Again," *Fortune* 104 (21 September 1981), pp. 74–76*ff.*

[37]Isadore Barmash, "How They're Selling Name Brands," *Stores* 63 (March 1981), pp. 9–14*ff.*

[38]"The 'Off-Price' Retailing Boom," *New York Times* (5 April 1983), pp. D1*ff;* "A Chain Whose Time Has Come," *Financial World* 150 (1 February 1981), pp. 35–36.

[39]Howard Rudnitsky with Jay Gissen, "Profits from Outlets," *Forbes* 129 (7 June 1982), pp. 128*ff.*

[40]"Dayton-Hudson's Hard Push for National Clout," *Business Week* (8 September 1980), pp. 96*ff;* Rudnitsky, "Profits from Outlets," p. 130; "'Off-price' Boom," pp. D1*ff.*

[41]Schulz, "Expansion," pp. 30*ff.*

[42]Penny Gill, "Hitting Home: Off-price Linens," *Stores* 65 (May 1983), pp. 56*ff.*

[43]Eric Peterson, "Off-price," *Stores* 65 (May 1983), pp. 28–30.

[44]A. L. Tunick, "Are You Ready for Franchising?" *Small Marketers Aids No. 114* (Washington, D.C.: Small Business Administration, reprinted January 1974), p. 1.

[45]Bureau of Industrial Economics, U.S. Department of Commerce, *Franchising in the Economy: 1982–1984* (Washington, D.C.: U.S. Government Printing Office, January 1984), pp. 1–3.

[46]Ibid., p. 4.

[47]Bureau of Industrial Economics, *Franchising,* p. 13.

[48]"There's More to Fast Food than Big Mac and Chicken," *Fortune* 95 (March 1977), pp. 213–15*ff.*

[49]For an interesting case history of one successful franchising organization, Wicks 'n' Sticks, see: "The House of Wax," *Forbes* (10 November 1980), pp. 100*ff.*

[50]Frank N. Edens, Donald R. Self, and Douglas T. Grider, Jr., "Franchisors Describe the Ideal Franchisee," *Journal of Small Business Management* 14 (July 1976), pp. 39–47.

[51]For a discussion of the problems and pitfalls in franchise contracts, see: Shelby D. Hunt, "Franchising: Promises, Problems, Prospects," *Journal of Retailing* 53 (Fall 1977), pp. 71–84; Pat Burr, Richard Burr, and Paul Bartlett, "Franchising and the Ominous 'Buy-Back' Clause," *Journal of Small Business Management* 13 (October 1975), pp. 39–41.

[52]Hunt, "Franchising," p. 78.

CHAPTER 5

Courtesy Levi Strauss & Co.

RETAIL STRATEGY

Your Study Objectives

After you have studied this chapter, you will understand:

1. How retailers analyze opportunities, develop strategies, and position their companies.
2. The need for planning and the methods that retailers use to forecast sales.
3. The role of retail research in aiding management problem solving and decision making and representative types of formal studies.
4. The use of survey, observation, and experimentation as methods of gathering primary data.

Analyzing Opportunities in Retailing

The new retail entrepreneur tries, first of all, to secure a foothold in the marketplace. He or she must then strive to develop a viable business by acquiring, over time, a regular and loyal clientele. Later on, even while continuing to pursue profitability, the store owner may seek further growth.

Established companies monitor the environment, scouting for attractive market opportunities. These may be found wherever there is sufficient demand for the firm's products and services. Other factors necessarily enhance or detract from the quality of an opportunity: whether the neighborhood under consideration is building up or deteriorating, the number of stores already in the area, the number and caliber of competitive outlets, and so on.

Most often, retail companies grow by adding store units. Some expand horizontally by acquiring additional firms in the same line of retailing. Others integrate backwards, setting up their own wholesaling operations to enjoy the benefits of quantity buying. A few may even establish their own manufacturing facility.

Portfolio building is another route to expansion and growth. Not only may some retail companies try to acquire other types of stores, but they may also diversify into different industries. Thus, we see a department store organization such as the Dayton-Hudson Company owning the B. Dalton bookstore chain; Sears, Roebuck & Co. holding Allstate Insurance; F. W. Woolworth as the parent of Anderson's Little Clothing Stores; K mart with its Designer Depots; Zayre with its T. J. Maxx and Hit or Miss specialty chains; and so on.[1]

Retailers may also be acquired by nonretailing companies. As an example, W. R. Grace and Company's portfolio holds a number of successful retail chains including the Channel Stores' Home Improvement Centers and Herman's World of Sporting Goods.

Markets consist of prospective customers who need and are inclined to purchase goods—and who have the financial ability to do so. Goods and services retailers alike realize that their businesses depend on serving these prospects adequately and at a profit. At the heart of **opportunity analysis,** then, must lie a careful evaluation of market demand.[2] Only an alert management, unafraid of taking risks, will investigate market opportunities. Careful analysis of internal and external environments will precede decision making. Even in large corporations, however, not all operating executives are sufficiently innovative or willing to take risks.[3]

Strategy in Retail Management

Many factors have diminished the role of strategy in retailing. Among them are changes in patterns of demand and supply; increased costs of capital, energy, and construction; and rapid copying of innovations by competitors.[4]

Planning company strategy necessitates some major decisions:

an analysis of the marketing environment to identify opportunities and constraints; a market opportunity analysis to select target markets; and the design, implementation, and control of marketing strategy to accomplish objectives in target markets.[5]

Retail firms need to develop strategies and tactics for both survival and growth. The development process involves a number of steps:

1. Ascertain the company's purpose or mission: what kind of business it is in, or wants to be in.
2. Develop a set of company objectives that are realistic, specific, and attainable.
3. Outline marketing goals that are consistent with these company objectives.
4. Select prospective customer groups and study their characteristics, needs, and wants.
5. Devise effective marketing programs to reach these consumers.
6. Implement the programs.

The Marketing Concept Prior to the 1950s, production occupied much of the attention of American manufacturers. Management devoted effort and time to turning out the product and improving plant efficiency. Factories produced what management believed consumers could use. This *production orientation* slowly gave way to another, distinctly different view. The new *marketing orientation* held that activities ought to center around the customer. It called for intensive study of the characteristics, needs, and preferences of the targeted consumers. This would increase a company's sensitivity to its environment and lead to its manufacturing products with greater likelihood of sale. To adopt the **marketing concept,** a firm would need to conduct research, elevate the marketing function in the organizational structure, and infuse salespeople with the idea that the consumer is indeed king.[6]

Retailers have always been closer to the marketing concept than have manufacturers because of their proximity to the public. By meeting and satisfying their customers' needs, they may be expected to prosper.

During the 1970s, articles challenging the widespread interest in the marketing concept began to appear in both academic journals and the general business press. One suggested that, nowadays, the concept may have little practical value.[7] Another maintained that companies may find it more profitable to concentrate instead on staying abreast of technological development.[8] Still others have called for a revision of the concept to build more social responsibility into the picture.[9]

Market Positioning The term **market positioning** has become a catchword among marketers. Manufacturers may use a positioning strategy to carve out a unique niche for their products in the marketplace. They employ segmentation methods to target at specific customer groups, then seek to persuade those consumers that their products are different and more desirable than those offered by competitors. Advertising, sales promotion, packaging, branding, and other elements of the marketing mix accomplish this purpose. A product's market position denotes the location it occupies in the public's mind in relation to similar, competitive products.

Although the retailing sector has demonstrated some interest in positioning, comparatively few companies have used it.[10] Among those that have, are: Pier I, a California firm that targets the under-35 market; Byerly's, a small chain of supermarkets in the Minneapolis area which targets the upscale grocery shopper; and The Limited, a chain that offers fashion apparel aimed at the 18-to-35-year-old shopper who is style- and fashion-conscious and "willing to pay moderately high prices to satisfy her desire for tasteful apparel."[11]

Retailers who seek to position their firms attempt to develop a unique store personality or image built around product/service delivery capabilities.[12] An article in *Stores,* a publication of the National Retail Merchants Association, provides a few insights into positioning by such large companies as Hudson's Bay, Oshman's, Bamberger's, and K mart.[13] K mart, for example, is positioned to attract a mass middle-income market.

Positioning a retail company requires attention to the following aspects of the enterprise:

1. Merchandise diversity.
2. Size of store and range of customers served.
3. Fashion distinctiveness.
4. Price competitiveness.
5. Convenience.
6. Service quality.
7. Innovativeness.
8. Lifestyle awareness.
9. Dependability.
10. Community identification.[14]

Planning

Planning is an integral part of modern retailing. Management must work up plans to provide direction for buying merchandise and for promoting goods and services. Companies must arrange for paying creditors, opening new stores, refurbishing older units, anticipating needs for additional personnel, and so on.

Plans are proposed schemes: schedules of methods for accomplishing future actions or states. Planning, then, necessarily goes two ways. One course leaps forward to foretell what the future period will be like. The other path begins with an analysis of the current state of

Retailers who seek to position their firms in the marketplace attempt to build a unique store personality or image built around their products or services.

Courtesy Docktor Pet Centers, Inc., Wilmington, MA

events and devises the strategies and tactics necessary to bring about the future situation.

The following illustration is offered to clarify the concept:

The owner of a camera shop wants to expand to a five-unit chain over the next three years. An immense amount of planning must be done. The proprietor will start by visualizing when four additional stores will have opened for business. Then he or she will work out all the components needed to reach that goal: finding the right locations, designing the units, choosing fixtures and equipment, putting up signing, choosing merchandise lines, ordering opening stock, hiring and training employees, and so on. Not the least of the budding chain's problems will be securing the financing required to build the company. Obviously, a schedule must be worked out, in advance, so that the planned program will result in the desired goals.

Plans may be strategic or tactical. **Strategic plans** outline the rationale for the firm's operation and overall company objectives. They provide guidance over the long term and format the tactics to be employed to meet those objectives. **Tactical plans** stem from the company's strategic plans. These have to do with the setting of short-range goals in the overall strategy and with the effective allocation of company resources.[15]

In planning, retail management establishes objectives in line with the company's mission. Usually, a vital element in planning is the sales forecast. To make reasonably accurate forecasts, management must:

study historical as well as current information

discern trends and anticipate changes in the economy

guess at the strategies and tactics competitors might employ between now and then

project what the attitudes and opinions of consumers will be at that future date

use one or more forecasting approaches to arrive at an estimate of sales for that future period

Many assumptions have to be made. Alternative courses of action are conceived of; these should be carefully weighed before making decisions. Planning and control go hand in hand. Once plans are put into operation, evaluations of performance should be conducted. Deviations from plan must be noted, analyzed, and corrected.

Management should study both the company and its external environment. It must take into consideration all aspects: its financial resources, marketing efforts, organizational resources, and the like. Opportunities and possible pitfalls must be visualized, and a sensible risk-taking attitude should prevail. Thorough planning increases the retail firm's chances for success. Unfortunately, though, it requires large blocks of time and effort. Many small business owners feel that it is an activity they can ill afford.[16] Even large retailers are not immune from this attitude. Their executives are often reluctant to engage in the process and "skeptical of its applicability and value."[17]

Because they are typically limited with regard to executive talent and finances, smaller retail firms should build a great deal of flexibility into their planning. Owners must often react quickly to abrupt changes. Among the useful techniques they might consider are leasing (instead of buying), staggering company debt, and ploughing profits back into the company's growth.[18]

Forecasting

Planning and forecasting are practically two sides of the same coin. A **forecast** is a prediction, an anticipation of what is to come. In retailing, forecasts of future sales volume depend, in the main, on estimates of consumer demand. As you already know, the term *demand* implies the consumers' desire to buy and having the means to pay for the merchandise. Yet demand is much more than just these two aspects. Many variables affect or modify demand. Some are within the consumer, others in the product or service itself. Examples of the latter include style, packaging, and price.

How Store Merchants Arrive at Their Sales Forecasts

Many retailers forecast sales by the **top-down method.** Management first appraises the state of the economy, then moves to the retail sector for an evaluation. The process is narrowed down even further to the particular industry to which the firm belongs. To discern trends, both past and present company performance are analyzed. Finally, having considered most angles, the retailer prepares the sales projections.

An alternate forecasting approach also has appeal. The **bottom-up method,** or **build-up method,** is based on a simple rationale: those who are most familiar with the store, its clientele, and the trading area are most likely to come up with more accurate forecasts. Where this method is used, top management delegates the responsibility for preparing projections to individual executives. In a chain store organization, for instance, the store managers would forecast sales for their respective units. In a department store, the responsibility might be assigned to the merchandise managers or to the department heads and/or buyers. The individual forecasts are collected and forwarded to company headquarters. There they are combined and reviewed by top management.

Using both approaches generally refines the process and is preferred. The two sets of projections can be reconciled through discussion of the more obvious differences.

Forecasting Methods[19]

The preparation of sales forecasts becomes a challenge for new business owners because historical data are not yet available. Unfortunately, too, few entrepreneurs have knowledge of forecasting techniques.[20]

Most sales forecasting methods fall into one of two categories: (1) qualitative, or judgmental, approaches or (2) quantitative methods that require the use and analysis of historical and other information. The former are often referred to as naive, or simple, techniques; the latter, as sophisticated methods, because statistical treatment is employed.

Qualitative Methods A number of techniques rely on qualitative or judgmental approaches. Some of these are briefly discussed below:

The **jury of executive opinion** calls for a meeting of company executives in order to draw from a fertile mix of different attitudes, knowledges, and experiences. An extremely popular technique, those invited in the retail organization might include the store manager, buyers, merchandise managers, company controller, and sales managers.

The **Delphi method** is a modification of the jury of executive opinion. Here, the executives prepare their estimates individually, instead of in a jury or committee format. Results submitted are returned to the executives for reconsideration. Several successive rounds take place. After the completion of the final round, a decision is made.

The **sales force composite method** is commonly seen in both industry and direct marketing, where personal selling is a crucial component of the promotion mix. The underlying thought is that a company's sales representatives are likely to be most knowledgeable about customer needs. They may therefore be expected to come up with realistic appraisals of future sales volume. This approach is seldom used in the retail sector, at least in connection with sales forecasting. However, the knowledge and experience of salespeople can be gainfully tapped on occasion to acquire information needed for other kinds of decisions.

Similarly, surveys of customer intentions are popular in industry. Variations of the technique are used by retailers, who often refer to them as shopper surveys or consumer surveys. They are generally not used in preparing sales forecasts, although they may be employed as a research tool.

Quantitative Methods Even though judgmental approaches are commonly used, retailers are conditioned to examine last year's sales records before projecting next year's sales. Indeed, the constant challenge most always appears to be bettering the prior year's figures. Internal records are studied in the hope of uncovering usable guidelines and discerning trends. In **trend analysis,** the retailer may review results for several preceding years. If records indicate an upward trend of, say, 6 percent, the merchant will probably add that percentage to last year's sales to come up with estimates for the coming year. More likely, however, the merchant will add another one or two points in the hope of doing even better.

Trend analysis and **time series extrapolation** methods may be used to forecast sales. In using time series approaches, historical sales information forms the base for projections. In the moving averages method, figures for two or more years are averaged. Each year is weighted equally with the other(s). To illustrate, let us suppose that a company's management is setting its sales objective for 1987. They tally actual sales results for the years 1983 to 1986, then divide the sum by four to arrive at the firm's average sales volume. Or the firm may choose to employ *exponential smoothing*—a technique that allots greater weight to the more recent years' figures and employs a constant to smooth out the sales curve so that projections may be made.

Correlation techniques relate company sales to other independent variables in the environment. Consumer income and plant productivity measures are two examples. Often, these are economic indicators that many kinds of companies make use of in their planning. Such indicators are termed *leading* if their movement (higher or lower) anticipates, or precedes, changes in sales activity. If both the indicator and actual sales are found to change at about the same time, the adjective *coincident* is used instead. *Lagging* indicators follow on the heels of sales movement.[21]

Leading indicators are used "to forecast the turning points of business cycles as well as assess the magnitude of rising or declining economic activity."[22] Among examples of these are productivity, money policy, and consumer spending. The Gross National Product and corporate profits are coincident indicators; two lagging indicators are the prime rate and inventory-to-sales ratios.[23]

Retail Research

To compete successfully in today's dynamic marketplace, the large marketing organization must devise and implement an effective **management information system,** or **MIS.** Large retail companies are no exception. According to marketing scholar Philip Kotler, the effective MIS contains four vital components:[24]

an *internal accounting system* that supplies information about sales, merchandise inventories, accounts payable, and so on
a *marketing intelligence system* to monitor the environment and keep management abreast of changing conditions
a *marketing research system* that makes surveys and conducts experiments and other studies to derive information needed for deciding marketing strategies and tactics
a *marketing management–science system* that uses scientific methods to improve organizational operations

The oldest system, and one that is already firmly in place in enterprises of every description, is the internal accounting system. Most companies also maintain at least a rudimentary intelligence-gathering activity, though by no stretch of the imagination can it be referred to as systematic. Furthermore, the majority of firms are small or medium-sized organizations with limited treasuries and other assets. Consequently, comparatively few possess more than a doubtful capability for conducting either operations or marketing research.

Yet marketing research often plays an essential role in the formation, initial success, and growth of an enterprise. Marketing research may be defined as "the systematic investigation of marketing activities carried out in order to discover new information and relationships as well as to expand existing knowledge."[25] An alternate definition, perhaps more specific, follows:

> Marketing research links the organization with its market environment. It involves the specification, gathering, analyzing, and interpreting of information to help management understand that environment, identify problems and opportunities, and develop and evaluate alternative courses of marketing action.[26]

Retail research is marketing research by retail firms. It involves the purposeful and orderly collection of facts, followed by careful analysis and interpretation. It assists management in solving problems and in making sensible business decisions.

Informal Study Activity

A distinction should be made between informal study and the formal research project. Throughout each year, retailers examine situations of all descriptions to improve their operations. They gather useful data on which to base decisions in informal ways. Informal study activity would typically be used to answer such questions as:

How should we allocate selling space to maximize sales revenues or gross margin dollars?

What merchandise should be displayed this week inside the store? Featured in the show window(s)?

Are this season's sales running ahead, falling behind, or about level with those of the same season last year?

Which items are our slow movers? Best sellers?

What is the better (best) media buy?

Can we locate a substitute supplier for this merchandise category— one who will give us better service or faster delivery?

What would be the most effective traffic-generating message we could place on this window banner?

How does our newspaper advertising compare with that of our main competitor(s)?

Most problems that confront retail companies crop up time and again. Somehow, each merchant manages to devise procedures and methods for handling recurrent situations. Usually this happens through trial and error. Only an occasional thorny situation resists ordinary problem solving. When a problem is perceived as being suffi-

A retailer may conduct informal studies to determine allocation of selling space and what merchandise to display in order to maximize sales revenues.

Courtesy K mart Corporation. K MART and ACCENTS are service marks of K mart Corporation, Troy, MI

ciently important—and the potential payoff much greater than the time, effort, and expense to be invested—the firm may initiate a major research project.

Formal Research

Some large retailers conduct several formal projects each year, especially when they maintain specialists on the payroll. Most merchants, however, cannot afford to employ research personnel. When faced with a major problem, some enlist the services of outside research agencies. Of course, many organizations do have their own location specialists who perform site studies periodically. Other retailers engage in research activity by setting up consumer advisory and other panels. An overall research capability, however, is found only in some of the largest department, specialty, and discount store chains.

Most formal research in retailing can be categorized under one of five types: market studies, promotion and sales research, product/service mix studies, personnel studies, and miscellaneous corporate research. Examples of the kinds of studies in these categories may be seen in Figure 5.1.

Stages in Retail Research

As we indicated earlier, most problems are ordinarily resolved without ever reaching the formal research project stage. Figure 5.2 displays the sequence of steps involved. The process begins with *problem recognition*—the realization that a problem exists. An initial *fact-gathering* stage follows—a preliminary search for pertinent information. As a result of this investigation, the formerly fuzzy problem is reduced to its most basic elements and is clearly delineated in the *problem clarification* stage. In the fourth stage of the research process, a *stop/go* decision must be made. If the data acquired up to this point are sufficient for management to reach a conclusion or make a decision, the problem is resolved and the process ended. If otherwise, a formal study may be indicated.

Having made the commitment to formal research, the *study design* must be formulated. This stage calls for a sequence of activities: ascertaining the nature of the information to be collected, choosing a method for gathering primary data, preparing and pretesting a questionnaire (if one is to be used), and selecting both the population to be sampled and the sample itself.

Data collection represents the next stage in the process. Information can be gathered by interviewers or observers in the field, by mail, or by telephone. After the completion of this step, the information is processed and subjected to *data analysis and interpretation:* facts are tabulated and cross-tabulated and statistical methods applied.

To communicate the study's findings to management and other interested parties, the *research report* is prepared. In the *action sequel,*

Figure 5.1
Types of retail research

Market Research:
Community analyses (demographics, life-style studies, and so on)
Competitor studies
Consumer motivation research
Consumer preference studies
Identification of market segments
Observational studies of shopping behavior
Site analysis
Store image surveys
Surveys of shoppers' attitudes, opinions, and so on
Trading area measurement

Promotion/Sales Research:
Appraisals of promotional effectiveness
Copy testing
Evaluations of effects of store layout changes
Evaluations of effectiveness of ads
Measuring effectiveness of personal selling activity
Media comparisons
Recall/recognition studies
Sales analyses (departmental, entire store)
Space utilization research
Testing of alternative direct-mail pieces

Product/Service Mix Research:
Analyses of alternative pricing strategies
Brand comparisons
Comparison shopping

Inventory movement studies
Markdown analyses
Merchandising research
Product testing
Returned-goods analyses
Studies of effectiveness of store services
Vendor rating and analysis

Personnel Research:
Assessments of impact of organizational change
Forecasts of future personnel requirements
Morale surveys
Performance evaluations
Productivity studies
Studies of alternative compensation plans
Studies of employee attitudes, opinions, and so on
Training program evaluations

Miscellaneous Corporate Research:
Analyses of business opportunities
Expense analyses
Lease or buy comparisons
Operations research
Sales cost analyses
Studies of alternative investment strategies
Systems research
Trend projections
Warehouse location studies

recommendations made as a result of the research are submitted to management and, after approval, are put into effect.

How Information May Be Classified

From management's viewpoint, information (or *data,* to use the researcher's term) may be regarded as internal or external. Internal data are facts that can be found in the company itself. Examples include the extensive information in the firm's sales records and analyses, purchasing records, personnel files, and the like. External data are facts that are available from sources outside the organization.

Data may also be classified as *primary* or *secondary,* according to their source(s). Facts that have been researched, organized, and issued

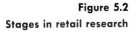

Figure 5.2
Stages in retail research

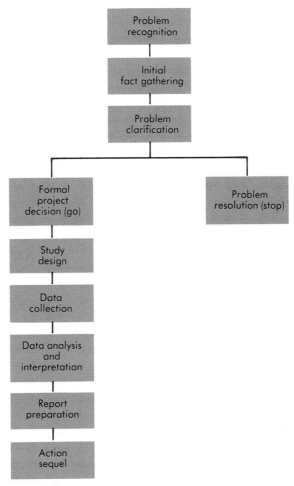

by other organizations and individuals are referred to as **secondary data.** This classification also includes the firm's earlier studies on file. The term **primary data** describes original information that researchers must gather, simply because it does not yet exist elsewhere. Both categories of data are discussed in the next two sections.

Secondary Data More information already exists somewhere than any single organization can ever hope to generate by itself. Outside sources of secondary data fall into three major classes: government sources, outside organizational sources, and personal sources. Secondary information is attractive to the business because time, energy, and money can be saved by using available data. A potential problem with such information is that it has been gathered, analyzed, and reported on by others for their own purposes. Thus, the reliability of the source may be in question. Another drawback is that a great deal of the information may be outdated. People, situations, and actions could have changed radically since the facts were first collected. A third disadvantage is that the information available may not be directly related to the problem under investigation.

Internal Sources Secondary data may be located both outside and inside the company. Among the retail firm's internal sources are all types of records and files, for example:

accounts payable	mail orders
accounts receivable	operating statements (store,
balance sheets	departmental)
budgets (former and current)	past research reports
cash-flow analyses	payroll
charge accounts	personnel files
customer complaints, returns,	sales analyses
and adjustments	shipping records
interstore transfers	telephone orders
of merchandise	vendor analyses
invoices	

External Sources Federal, state, and local governments; businesses and other organizations; and individuals produce all kinds of information of possible value to management in solving problems and making decisions. Most businesspeople soon discover that, for most purposes, the federal government is the biggest supplier of facts. It issues a steady stream of data concerning industry, commerce, and labor. It provides countless details about the American public: where and how we live, how much we spend and for what, the kinds of work we do, and so on. As might be expected, the U.S. Department of Commerce is the government's most prolific publisher and principal supplier of demographic and other statistical information. Its Bureau of the Census issues voluminous material each year of intense interest to the business world.[27]

Perhaps the most useful publication for retailers is the *Census of Population*. Last taken in 1980, the next one is not scheduled until 1990. This decennial census counts the inhabitants of all 50 states and gathers many other types of data. It analyzes and tabulates a host of consumer demographics: their ages, income levels, race, occupation, education, and so on. An accompanying *Census of Housing* counts the types and condition of residences as well as their value, type of heating, and other characteristics. *Census tracts* are valuable aids for retailers in search of new store locations. These are small-area statistics obtained by dividing cities and their surrounding areas into small sections. A typical tract encompasses a few city blocks, housing 4,000 to 5,000 residents. Also available are *block statistics*. These report on housing characteristics as well as residents. Local maps are included with both census tracts and block statistics.

The *Census of Business* and the *Census of Manufactures* are taken at five-year intervals. The first provides data relative to the retail and wholesale trades and selected services. Information is organized by state, county, metropolitan area, and city. Store types are identified by number in business, kind of outlet, sales receipts, employment figures, and the like. The *Census of Manufactures* gives information about American manufacturing companies. Data is organized by type, number, and size of firm, value of goods produced, size of company payroll, and so on.

A convenient Census Bureau publication is the annual *Statistical Abstract of the United States*. This valuable source work is a handy, thick volume reminiscent in shape and size of the *World Almanac*. It can be found in most public library branches or purchased from the Superintendent of Documents in Washington, D.C. The *Statistical Abstract* offers summary statistics from government agencies and various commercial and other sources. Statistics are furnished on the population, including details on income, housing, and education. It also contains substantial amounts of data regarding the economy: employment and unemployment, the distributive trades, manufacturing, agriculture, international trade, and so on.

Every few years, the Census Bureau issues the *County and City Data Book*. This is a reservoir of facts about agriculture, population characteristics, housing, bank deposits, and many other aspects of our economy. It presents details for all counties, cities, and unincorporated areas of over 25,000 residents. A sample page from this publication is shown in Figure 5.3. The Department of Commerce issues the monthly *Survey of Current Business*. This publication summarizes facts about inventories and revenues of manufacturing companies and presents information and articles on industry and commerce. The *Monthly Retail Trade* furnishes estimated store sales for different retail lines by regions and metropolitan areas.[28]

The Department of Labor, the Department of Agriculture, and other government agencies also publish useful reports periodically. Reports of many types are also forthcoming from state governments and many counties and municipalities.

Reference Works Public, college, and university libraries contain many reference sources.[29] Among the many reference works to be found in these institutions are indexes such as the *New York Times Index, The Wall Street Journal Index,* the *Business Periodicals Index,* and

Figure 5.3   **An excerpt from the *County and City Data Book***

Table B. Counties — **Wholesale Trade, Retail Trade, and Selected Service Industries**

County	Wholesale trade, 1977—Con. Paid employees	Annual payroll (Mil. dol.)	Establishments Number	With payroll (Percent)	Sales All establishments Total ($1,000)	Per capita (Dol.)	Establishments with payroll (Percent)	General merchandise group stores	Eating and drinking places	Establishments with payroll Paid employees	Annual payroll (Mil. dol.)	Establishments Number	With payroll (Percent)	Receipts All establishments ($1,000)	Establishments with payroll (Percent)
	171	172	173	174	175	176	177	178	179	180	181	182	183	184	185
CALIFORNIA—Con.															
Mono	D	D	157	73.9	29 629	4 039	94.9	D	22.6	867	3.9	162	41.4	13 793	88.7
Monterey	3 883	54.8	2 589	75.4	951 602	3 380	97.3	9.2	11.0	17 194	126.4	2 418	43.1	236 763	91.8
Napa	500	5.8	853	72.7	303 470	3 144	97.0	8.2	9.4	4 966	35.7	785	39.5	45 305	87.7
Nevada	91	.9	506	67.2	146 254	3 608	95.8	D	10.1	2 212	16.5	459	34.9	21 679	80.5
Orange	33 428	463.0	15 266	66.8	7 377 949	4 071	97.3	14.3	10.1	129 823	933.6	20 647	35.4	2 282 583	90.7
Placer	802	9.3	1 094	66.4	390 190	3 919	96.4	D	11.3	6 179	43.3	968	38.2	49 706	80.8
Plumas	43	.3	275	64.0	57 156	3 791	92.7	17.1	9.6	895	5.7	203	31.0	7 304	70.7
Riverside	6 475	75.8	4 878	69.8	2 098 656	3 631	97.1	12.1	9.3	35 055	248.5	5 127	35.0	390 292	87.2
Sacramento	12 613	176.3	5 662	73.8	2 881 986	3 961	98.0	16.7	9.0	49 823	361.5	6 884	39.6	573 064	90.6
San Benito	226	1.7	202	72.3	62 232	2 735	97.4	1.6	5.8	1 048	7.8	152	30.3	6 388	82.0
San Bernardino	7 362	88.6	6 075	69.9	2 482 813	3 226	97.1	15.9	9.0	42 600	296.2	5 601	36.9	412 676	88.1
San Diego	20 344	257.2	13 064	70.6	5 895 121	3 436	97.6	15.7	9.8	100 874	724.1	16 449	38.2	1 550 019	90.8
San Francisco	26 095	406.7	8 220	68.1	2 849 566	4 194	95.0	11.9	17.2	53 699	445.7	11 272	43.7	2 358 343	95.2
San Joaquin	6 396	86.5	2 798	68.8	1 115 368	3 476	96.5	12.2	8.8	18 209	133.1	2 380	41.3	167 117	86.9
San Luis Obispo	1 400	13.6	1 572	69.8	469 966	3 390	96.9	5.6	12.3	8 901	56.7	1 481	38.0	91 480	86.7
San Mateo	20 666	329.0	4 574	70.3	2 356 850	4 051	97.6	14.6	9.9	37 548	306.1	6 418	36.6	820 896	92.2
Santa Barbara	3 524	40.8	2 997	73.6	1 112 619	3 832	97.5	9.8	12.6	21 867	142.4	3 232	40.7	304 832	90.8
Santa Clara	21 295	322.5	9 210	72.3	4 920 896	3 995	97.8	14.5	8.6	82 426	624.0	13 594	35.6	1 670 318	92.7
Santa Cruz	1 661	19.7	1 842	68.9	653 672	3 732	96.8	D	10.1	11 756	81.1	1 819	32.2	97 481	82.9
Shasta	1 728	23.5	1 172	71.2	435 968	4 353	96.5	8.6	7.2	6 622	48.6	1 096	35.7	71 295	86.6
Sierra	–	–	43	51.2	4 295	1 482	78.1	D	17.0	84	.4	43	27.9	826	61.0
Siskiyou	376	3.4	489	72.8	114 424	3 128	94.3	D	11.1	2 011	11.7	398	32.7	14 627	78.2
Solano	1 318	18.3	1 422	76.6	636 112	3 107	97.9	11.6	11.0	10 706	79.7	1 349	42.5	84 916	89.2
Sonoma	3 185	41.6	2 640	68.6	1 009 728	3 696	97.1	10.5	8.6	16 011	121.5	2 810	35.1	154 509	85.3
Stanislaus	4 120	47.0	2 090	73.2	871 937	3 530	97.1	13.2	7.3	14 828	104.9	1 703	44.7	122 132	86.9
Sutter	814	10.9	381	69.8	164 518	3 325	96.7	D	7.3	2 501	18.0	393	37.2	24 627	85.3
Tehama	204	1.7	338	69.5	113 679	3 295	95.5	3.7	7.6	1 529	11.2	280	37.9	12 738	81.0
Trinity	12	.1	122	63.9	17 081	1 625	90.3	9.7	13.2	292	1.8	109	35.8	2 728	72.0
Tulare	4 332	38.4	1 894	72.1	731 206	3 237	96.7	11.6	6.5	11 609	81.6	1 596	36.3	82 394	83.2
Tuolumne	146	1.4	411	65.9	102 042	3 588	95.2	D	10.6	1 661	11.2	348	37.4	17 307	78.3
Ventura	5 331	58.0	3 389	69.5	1 511 465	3 157	97.6	12.8	8.3	24 895	179.5	4 091	34.1	280 403	86.9
Yolo	2 193	29.3	772	78.1	329 467	3 111	98.0	D	10.2	5 700	39.1	918	33.7	58 298	88.0
Yuba	414	6.3	428	72.0	129 725	2 732	95.8	7.8	9.6	2 321	15.6	313	36.7	18 731	87.1
COLORADO	60 824	790.8	25 675	70.6	9 824 594	3 644	97.2	12.3	9.8	189 776	1 225.6	30 112	39.0	2 480 983	90.5
Adams	5 962	80.6	1 613	71.4	803 612	3 527	97.9	17.0	7.5	13 615	93.4	1 768	35.9	138 528	90.5
Alamosa	D	D	168	69.0	48 897	4 216	94.8	14.3	D	1 103	8.0	117	54.7	6 889	85.7
Arapahoe	5 653	78.3	2 101	72.5	1 199 646	4 947	98.3	17.6	7.4	20 692	143.2	2 574	37.1	227 621	91.2
Archuleta	22	.2	56	73.2	9 820	2 960	93.1	D	8.5	176	.9	36	38.9	1 483	73.9
Baca	22	1.1	88	61.4	14 066	2 529	92.1	5.4	5.0	240	1.3	81	29.6	1 924	64.4
Bent	36	.3	48	72.9	12 673	2 055	96.1	5.4	4.7	221	1.3	48	16.7	639	41.2
Boulder	2 505	27.7	1 655	69.9	662 971	3 722	97.6	7.5	9.3	12 623	82.6	2 261	33.8	129 445	87.3
Chaffee	90	.8	244	61.5	48 234	3 839	94.0	5.1	8.7	892	4.9	171	40.4	17 847	93.4
Cheyenne	32	.4	40	50.0	5 856	2 837	87.0		9.3	110	.9	33	33.3	774	84.9
Clear Creek	18	.2	123	61.0	16 980	2 738	90.2	D	23.5	462	2.2	80	43.8	4 595	89.3
Conejos	87	.5	85	34.1	9 227	1 159	74.0	D	4.3	134	.8	43	37.2	977	70.9
Costilla	73	.2	37	37.8	2 645	834	59.5	D	13.0	41	.2	9	22.2	99	D
Crowley		.1		81.5	3 565	1 129	89.0	D		66		17			

Source: U.S. Department of Commerce, *County and City Data Book, 1983* (Washington, D.C.: U.S. Government Printing Office, 1983), p. 71.

so on. Also available are encyclopedias, almanacs, the latest copies of *Books in Print*, Dun & Bradstreet's directories, Thomas' *Register of American Manufacturers*, and many other helpful aids.

Other Sources Many retailers join trade associations. To mention just a few, there are the National Association of Retail Druggists, the Retail Jewelers of America, the National Retail Hardware Association, the National Association of Retail Grocers of the United States, and the Menswear Retailers of America.[30] This last association, for example, provides summary statistics every year about their member stores' operating results. They also send out monthly reports on trends in menswear sales and merchandising. In addition, they offer services like sales training seminars and management institutes, personnel policy manuals, fashion reports, EDP services, and group insurance plans.

There are also organizations that offer commercial data and syndicated reports. They include the A. C. Nielsen Corporation of America and SAMI (Selling Areas Marketing, Inc.). Newspapers, radio stations, TV stations, and magazines are able to furnish retailers with information about their audiences and about retail trading areas. Each year, *Sales and Marketing Management* publishes its *Survey of Buying Power*. This contains a great deal of data regarding retail sales around the country and information on households, incomes, and consumer purchasing power.

Primary Data Frequently, available secondary data may not yield enough information, or enough of the right kinds of information, to provide precise direction for management. A firm may need new, or primary, data relative to the problem under investigation. To collect such information, retail companies can choose from among three distinct approaches: (1) surveys, (2) observational methods, or (3) experimentation. Each technique is discussed in the following paragraphs.

Surveys The most widely used technique is the **survey method.** It is flexible enough to apply to many different kinds of problems. Surveys are used to determine customer preferences and dislikes, ascertain opinions and attitudes, obtain demographic and lifestyle information, probe consumers' reactions to print media ads or TV or radio commercials, and so on. These studies may be conducted through personal interviews, by mail, or by telephone.

Personal interviews generally yield the most information. People can be queried for longer periods than can be accomplished over the telephone or by mail. Respondents' replies can be probed more thoroughly. Interviewers have an opportunity to add their personal observations to the data volunteered by interviewees. The technique is not, however, without its drawbacks. Costs can be considerable, for only well-trained interviewers should be sent out into the field. Gathering information in this manner is often a slow, painstaking process. Several hundred people may have to be interviewed, yet a single session can require anywhere from a few minutes to an hour or more. If the individuals to be questioned are scattered geographically, the entire process may be extremely expensive. Moreover, the data collected may be biased due to interviewer errors. Interviewers can make mistakes in selecting respondents, in their interpretation of observed behavior, in the way they pose questions, and so on. Even variables such as the sex and age of the interviewer may affect the data gathering.[31]

Some of these problems can be avoided by using the mail survey. Mailing questionnaires to individuals is far less costly. This especially holds true when the target population is located in different sections of the country. Some people respond more readily to a mail questionnaire than to a time-consuming personal interview. Another advantage is that those who reply to mail questionnaires usually spend more time on their answers. The data furnished are often more accurate and detailed. Finally, because no field personnel are used, the possibility of interviewer bias can be ruled out.

A disadvantage of the mail survey is that a sizable proportion of those who are contacted can be expected not to respond at all. This phenomenon of nonrespondent bias detracts from the validity of the information gathered. Other drawbacks include the lengthy time that may transpire before all returns are in and that when the addressee fills out the questionnaire no interviewer is present to help clarify any questions.

To increase the number of usable returns, researchers often send out reminder letters. These are sent along with second and sometimes third copies of the questionnaire. Other techniques frequently used to increase the rate of return include monetary incentives, advance notification by telephone, the enclosure of prepaid return envelopes, and the like.[32]

The use of telephone surveys has accelerated in recent years, especially because of the availability of WATS lines (Wide Area Telecommunications Service). The method's most attractive virtue is the speed with which information can be collected. Time and money are saved by not having to print up questionnaires, address envelopes, stuff enclosures into them, and arrange for the post office to deliver the letters. Data gathered by telephone are comparable to those produced by either personal interviews or the mail questionnaire.[33] The development of computerized telephone interviewing technology has made this technique even more attractive to market researchers.[34]

There are a few problems with the telephone survey. Not everyone is a subscriber; invariably, some people are left out of the survey universe. Further, perhaps 15 to 20 percent of all subscribers have unlisted numbers. Even the telephone directory itself is a source for concern. Because consumers move on the average of once every five years, each new phone book is partially outdated right after its publication. Random dialing, however, may help to improve the situation.

Survey Instruments At the heart of the survey method is the questionnaire. This instrument may be disguised or undisguised. In the first type, both the study's purpose and the name of the sponsoring company are concealed from respondents to avoid the possibility of biased answers. In the second, purpose and sponsor are made known to interviewees. Questions must be clear and unambiguous. One common type of question requires a simple Yes or No response—perhaps room for a Don't Know or a Maybe. Researchers also use multiple-choice items and open-ended questions that permit respondents to formulate their own replies. Usually, the simpler and less personal questions are placed first so as not to discourage the interviewee from continuing to respond. Careful attention to question sequence is essential to the instrument's effectiveness.

A simple and popular alternate format is the **semantic differential** instrument. A sample of this type appears in Figure 5.4.[35] Instead of appearing in interrogatory form, questions are couched in individual scales. Each scale consists of a pair of opposite, or polar, words or short phrases. Space is marked off between the two for respondents to indicate their replies along a spectrum. As an illustration, let us consider this single scale:

High-quality   Shoddy
merchandise ____ ____ ____ ____ ____ merchandise

Shoppers are asked to rate the merchandise offered by Store X by checking off one of the blank spaces between the phrases. If they feel that Store X offers merchandise of extremely high quality, they check the first blank—the one nearest to that phrase on the scale. The next blank would be used by the shopper who deemed the merchandise to be of good quality, the third blank (a middle position) by people unable to make up their minds about which of the polar phrases was more applicable, and the fourth by someone who believed the merchandise was somewhat shoddy. Responses from many shoppers can be tallied, producing a composite picture of their opinions or attitudes.

Observation Techniques Useful information can also be gathered by watching people and noting what they do. **Observation methods** can be conducted in a natural setting or in an artificial environment. Individuals trained to record what they see and hear may do the observing. Mechanical or electronic devices may also serve the same purpose. Among others, these aids include cameras, tape recorders, TV monitors, psychogalvanometers, tachistoscopes, and audimeters.

A sometimes serious disadvantage of these approaches is that observations of behavior provide no insight into the attitudes, values, or motivations of the subjects being investigated. Inferences may, of course, be drawn from actions observed.

Experimental Methods A third way of collecting data, useful when neither surveys nor observational techniques will yield the needed information,

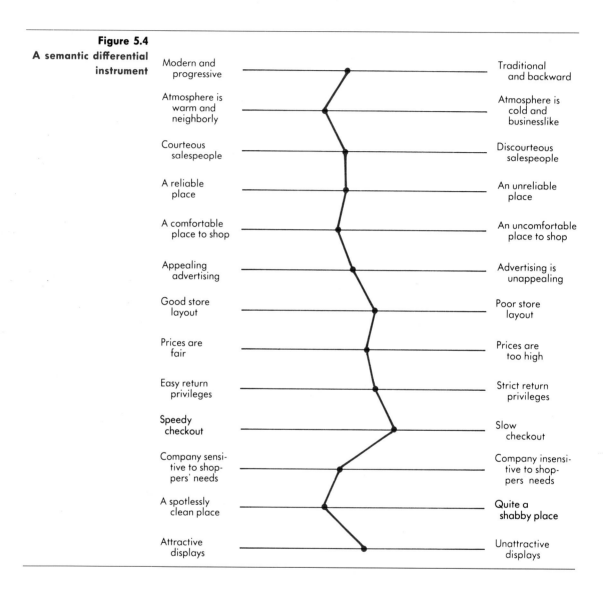

Figure 5.4
A semantic differential instrument

is the **experimental method.** This involves setting up one or more experiments to test some aspect or variable. *Treatments* are then applied to determine their effects on that variable. As an example, the management of a chain of discount stores wishes to decide which of two proposed retail prices should be placed on a new, small household appliance. The rationale behind the experiment is to determine at which price the company will enjoy a higher sales volume or more gross margin dollars. Management selects two similar groups of five store units. Each contains a mix of stores that are alike in type of location, size, and annual sales. All stores in the test are stocked

Observational studies of shoppers in a natural setting is one method of collecting primary data for retail research.

Courtesy Carter Hawley Hale Stores, Inc., Los Angeles, CA

with a substantial inventory of the appliance. Displays of the product are set up in all 10 locations on the same day. These are similar—with one exception. The accompanying poster features one price in the first group of stores and a higher price in the units in the second group. In brief, management tries to hold constant as many variables that might conceivably affect the outcome as possible.

Sales of the appliance are recorded for the two- or three-week trial period, and differences between the two groups of stores are noted. The more favorable price is then selected for the entire chain.

Of course, there are many other ways to set up experiments besides the simple procedure outlined above. Further discussion of such techniques, however, is beyond the scope of this book. For more information, we encourage you to refer to one of the many excellent texts on marketing research.

Experimental methods can be applied to most phases of store operation. A few examples of possible applications are given below:

to determine whether music in the store will increase employee productivity

to measure the outcomes of various training methods

to evaluate the recall power of different newspaper ads

to determine the effects on sales volume of changing the location of merchandise in a department (or expanding or contracting entire departments)

to ascertain the effectiveness of displays or signing

Summary   Forward-looking retailers remain alert to market opportunities. They seek to expand their operations in several ways: by adding store units, by integrating backward, or by acquiring other companies. Opportunity analysis requires management's careful evaluation of market demand and thorough appraisals of both the firm and its environment.

The steps of strategy development range from a determination of the organization's mission through goal setting and the selection of target customer groups to the devising and implementation of effective programs. Strategic positioning develops a unique niche in the market-place for the company.

Planning is future-oriented and present-based activity that requires time and effort. It calls for setting objectives and devising methods and procedures that will accomplish those goals. An essential element in much retail planning is sales forecasting. Both judgmental and statistical approaches are used to forecast sales.

Retail research is collecting, analyzing, and interpreting information to assist management in problem solving and decision making. Most study activity in the retail sector is informal. Formal studies can be classified into five types: market, promotion/sales, product-service mix, personnel, or miscellaneous corporate research. The stages in formal research are study design, data collection, data analysis and interpretation, report preparation, and action sequel.

Data can be classified as primary or secondary. Information that has already been reported and is available to the investigator is labeled secondary data. Primary data are facts that are not yet available and therefore must be gathered by the researcher. To secure primary data, retailers can use three basic methods: surveys, observational techniques, and experimentation. Most popular of the three is the survey method.

Key Terms

portfolio building	sales force composite method
opportunity analysis	trend analysis
marketing concept	time series extrapolation
market positioning	correlation techniques
plans	management information system (MIS)
strategic plans	retail research
tactical plans	secondary data
forecast	primary data
top-down planning	survey method
bottom-up (build-up) planning	semantic differential
jury of executive opinion	observation method
Delphi method	experimental method

Review Questions

1. Identify three methods of retail expansion.

2. How are planning and forecasting related?

3. Distinguish between strategic and tactical planning.

4. Define the term *market positioning* and cite four examples of retail companies that use this strategy.

5. Specify the four components of an effective management information system.

6. In which two categories can most sales forecasting techniques be placed?

7. Give five examples of each of the following types of studies in retailing: *(a)* product/service mix research and *(b)* promotion/sales research.

8. Name and briefly discuss two judgmental methods that retail merchants may use in forecasting sales.

9. Identify three quantitative methods used in forecasting sales.

10. In the formal research project, what is meant by *study design?* What is involved in the process?

11. Explain the terms *initial fact gathering* and *action sequel.*

12. Cite at least seven kinds of internal records from which retailers may be able to extract useful secondary data.

13. Give the titles of four reference works useful to retailers that can be found at many public libraries.

14. Suggest three techniques which can be used to increase the rate of return in a mail survey.

15. In your own words, offer a description of the semantic differential.

16. What is the most serious disadvantage of observation methods?

Discussion Questions

1. In positioning a new retail enterprise, management must give attention to quality of service and fashion distinctiveness, among other aspects of the operation. In your own words, indicate what is meant by these two phrases.

2. Outline how the owners of a small variety store chain should forecast sales for the coming fall-winter season. What kinds of information would they need to have?

3. Monetary incentives are one of the measures that researchers take to increase the number of returns on mail questionnaires. Can you suggest three alternative, *nonmonetary* incentives that may be used to accomplish the same result?

4. Prepare a short semantic differential instrument for use in exploring shoppers' attitudes toward a small card and gift shop. Among the elements to be rated are store attractiveness, merchandise, prices, and sales personnel.

5. Suggest three phases of store operations in which experimental methods can help uncover useful information.

Notes

[1] Bert Rosenbloom, "Strategic Planning in Retailing: Prospects and Problems," *Journal of Retailing* 56 (Spring 1980), p. 113. See also: David P. Schulz, "Expansion, " *Stores* 65 (August 1983), pp. 30*ff.*

[2] Robert B. Woodruff, "A Systematic Approach to Market Opportunity Analyses," *Business Horizons* 19 (August 1976), pp. 55–65.

[3] Frederick E. Webster, Jr., "Top Management's Concern about Marketing: Issues for the 1980s," *Journal of Marketing* 45 (Summer 1981), p. 16.

[4]Albert D. Bates, "The Troubled Future of Retailing," *Business Horizons* 19 (August 1976), p. 24.

[5]David W. Cravens, "Marketing Strategy Positioning," *Business Horizons* 18 (December 1975), pp. 53–61.

[6]Eugene H. Fram, "Application of the Marketing Concept to Retailing," *Journal of Retailing* 41 (Summer 1965), pp. 19–26.

[7]William S. Sachs and George Benson, "Is It Time to Discard the Marketing Concept?" *Business Horizons* 21 (August 1978), pp. 68–74.

[8]Roger C. Bennett and Robert G. Cooper, "Beyond the Marketing Concept," *Business Horizons* 22 (June 1979), pp. 76–83.

[9]Martin L. Bell and C. William Emory, "The Faltering Marketing Concept," *Journal of Marketing* 35 (October 1971), pp. 37–42.

[10]Bates, "Troubled Future," p. 27.

[11]Ibid., pp. 27–28.

[12]Charles W. King and Lawrence J. Ring, "Market Positioning across Retail Fashion Institutions: A Comparative Analysis of Store Types," *Journal of Retailing* 56 (Spring 1980), pp. 37–55.

[13]"Market Positioning to Maintain Momentum," *Stores* 61 (February 1979), pp. 33–34.

[14]Ibid., p. 33.

[15]For insight into the planning activities of the May Company, Federated Department Stores, and other large-scale retailers, see: Isadore Barmash, "How They Plan," *Stores* 65 (September 1983), pp. 7–9ff.

[16]Richard B. Robinson, Jr., and William F. Littlejohn, "Important Contingencies in Small Firm Planning," *Journal of Small Business Management* 19 (July 1981), p. 48; Jacob Naor, "How to Make Strategic Planning Work for Small Businesses," *S.A.M. Advanced Management Journal* 45 (Winter 1980), pp. 35–39.

[17]Rosenbloom, "Strategic Planning," p. 110.

[18]Charles P. Edmonds III, "Management for Flexibility," *Journal of Small Business Management* 15 (July 1977), pp. 15–18.

[19]For more details about forecasting approaches, see: W. W. Claycombe and William G. Sullivan, "Current Forecasting Techniques," *Journal of Systems Management* 29 (September 1978), pp. 18–20; Spyros Makridakis and Steven C. Wheelwright, "Forecasting: Issues and Challenges for Marketing Management," *Journal of Marketing* 41 (October 1977), pp. 24–38; Richard Robinson, "Forecasting and Small Business: A Study of the Strategic Planning Process," *Journal of Small Business Management* 17 (July 1979), pp. 19–27; John G. Wacker and Jane S. Cromartie, "Adapting Forecasting Methods to the Small Firm," *Journal of Small Business Management* 17 (July 1979), pp. 1–7.

[20]Earl H. Anderson, "Probabilistic Forecasting for the Small Business," *Journal of Small Business Management* 17 (June 1979), pp. 8–13.

[21]For an excellent overview of forecasting methods and concise descriptions of economic indicators, see: Robert S. Sobek, "A Manager's Primer on Forecasting," *Harvard Business Review* 51 (May–June 1973), pp. 6–28; Douglas J. Dalrymple, "Sales Forecasting Methods and Accuracy," *Business Horizons* 18 (December 1975), pp. 69–72.

[22]Sobek, "Manager's Primer," p. 6.

[23]Ibid., pp. 6–7.

[24]See: Philip Kotler, *Marketing Management: Analysis, Planning, and Control,* 4th ed. (Englewood Cliffs, N.J.: Prentice-Hall, 1980), pp. 601–27.

[25]George Kress, *Marketing Research,* 2d ed. (Reston, Va.: Reston Publishing, 1982), p. 4.

[26]David A. Aaker and George S. Day, *Marketing Research: Private and Public Sector Decisions* (New York: John Wiley & Sons, 1960), p. 1.

[27]For suggestions for small business owners about data sources, research basics, and information on how to use census reports, see: Michael F. D'Amico, "Marketing Research for Small Businesses," *Journal of Small Business Management* 16 (January 1978), pp. 41–49; Robert T. Justis and Bill Jackson, "Marketing Research for Dynamic Small Businesses," *Journal of Small Business Management* 16 (October 1978), pp. 10–20; Joseph G. Van Matre and Darrel R. Hankins, "Census Data: A Primer for Business Applications," *Journal of Small Business Management* 18 (July 1980), pp. 8–16.

[28]For a discussion of the reliability of available sales estimates such as those in the *Monthly Retail Trade* and other Census Bureau reports, see: Robert Ferber, William J. Hawkes, Jr., and Manuel D. Plotkin, "How Reliable Are National Retail Sales Estimates?" *Journal of Marketing* 40 (October 1976), pp. 13–22.

[29]Additional information for the small independent retailer may be found in: "Basic Library Reference Sources," *Small Business Bibliography No. 18* (Washington, D.C.: Small Business Administration, 1970); "National Directories for Use in Marketing," *Small Business Bibliography No. 13* (Washington, D.C.: Small Business Administration, 1971).

[30]An *Encyclopedia of Associations* is available at some libraries. This is published by Gale Research Company, Book Tower, Detroit, MI 48226.

[31]John Freeman and Edgar Butler, "Some Sources of Interviewer Variance in Surveys," *Public Opinion Quarterly* 40 (Spring 1976), pp. 79–81.

[32]Marvin A. Jolson, "How to Double or Triple Mail Survey Response Rates," *Journal of Marketing* 41 (October 1977), pp. 78–81.

[33]Theresa F. Rogers, "Interviews by Telephone and In Person: Quality of Responses and Field Performance," *Public Opinion Quarterly* 40 (Spring 1976), pp. 51–65; John J. Wheatley, "Self-Administered Written Questionnaires or Telephone Interviews?" *Journal of Marketing Research* 10 (February 1973), pp. 94–96.

[34]Tyzoon Tyebjee, "Telephone Survey Methods: The State of the Art," *Journal of Marketing* 43 (Summer 1979), pp. 68–78.

[35]Barnett A. Greenberg, Jac L. Goldstucker, and Danny N. Bellenger, "What Techniques Are Used by Marketing Researchers in Business?" *Journal of Marketing* 41 (April 1977), pp. 62–68.

Courtesy Shakey's Incorporated, Irving, TX

FINANCIAL ASPECTS OF RETAILING

Your Study Objectives

After you have studied this chapter, you will understand:

1. The purposes and use of two essential accounting documents: the balance sheet and the operating statement.
2. Ratio analysis as an aid to management decision making.
3. Retailer approaches to the classification of operating expenses.
4. Cash flow projections and other aspects of financial management.
5. Approaches to handling risk and the kinds of insurance retail firms buy.
6. Security problems in retailing.

In the preceding chapters, we explored the realm of modern retailing. By now you are aware of retailing's scope and complexity, its socioeconomic, technological, and legal environments, and the place of strategy in this sphere.

Like all other organizations, retail enterprises need money to operate. Proper management of the financial end of a business is crucial to its success.

In this chapter, you will come to understand and appreciate the significance of two essential accounting statements that organizations rely on in conducting their affairs. You will learn about ratio analysis and how it can be of value in evaluating any business operation. We will show you how retail companies manage and control their operating expenses and the approaches they take in assigning these expenses internally. You will be introduced to both cash flow analysis and capital budgeting. We discuss risk management and the ways retailers insure their firms against potential hazards. Finally, you will learn about the kinds of security problems that retailers face.

The Major Accounting Statements

Consumers who consider purchasing shares of corporate stock through their broker or bank can benefit by a firm understanding of the corporation's financial standing. Similarly, people who are interested in setting up their own business or buying an established business should be thoroughly familiar with two basic accounting documents. These are the balance sheet and the operating statement.

The Balance Sheet

The **balance sheet** is an accounting statement that describes the financial condition of a business at a given point. Companies of all kinds prepare such statements at least once annually, at the close of the calendar or fiscal year. Many organizations prefer to work up balance sheets each quarter. Others prepare them monthly. In this fashion, management can be kept apprised of the firm's status at all times. Executives are then able to make appropriate decisions more quickly. Moreover, before taking positive action on a company's loan application, the lender will most likely want to see a copy of its latest balance sheet and other documentation.

Typically, the balance sheet consists of a single page that is divided down the middle. An example of a simplified balance sheet for a small retail store owned by a sole proprietor may be seen in Figure 6.1. Entries on the left-hand side show and sum up the dollar value of various company assets. Indicated on the right-hand side are the firm's liabilities and net worth. Totals at the bottom of both parts of the statement must balance; that is, they must be identical.

Figure 6.1 A retailer's balance sheet

SHIRLEY'S FASHION BOUTIQUE
Balance Sheet
For the Year Ending December 31, 1985

Assets

Current assets:

Cash on hand	$ 350	
Cash in bank	14,625	
Securities	2,700	
Accounts receivable (less		
allowance for bad debts) . .	3,260	
Merchandise inventory . . .	65,530	
Inventory of supplies . . .	2,180	
Total current assets . . .		$ 88,645

Fixed assets:

Fixtures (less depreciation) . .	12,250	
Equipment (less depreciation) . .	6,470	
Leasehold improvements . . .	2,300	
Delivery truck (less depreciation) . .	6,740	
Total fixed assets		27,760
Total assets		$116,405

Liabilities

Current liabilities:

Accounts payable	$ 9,485	
Note payable 1986 . . .	4,500	
Accrued payroll taxes . . .	1,265	
Total current liabilities . .		$ 15,250

Long-term liabilities:

Loan payable 1989 . . .	23,200	
Loan payable 1991 . . .	14,000	
Total long-term liabilities . .		37,200
Total liabilities		$ 52,450

Net Worth

Owner's Equity, December 31, 1985 . .		$ 63,955
Total liabilities and net worth . .		$116,405

Understanding Balance Sheet Terms Assets are the physical resources the company owns. Included are such items as cash, securities (stocks and bonds which can readily be converted into cash), **accounts receivable** (monies due from charge customers), inventories, equipment, and so on. **Current assets** are those that may be relied on, or actively used, in operating the business during the coming year. **Fixed assets** are resources the firm will use over the years to come: buildings, vehicles, machinery, equipment, and the like. All assets, other than land, drop in value, or **depreciate,** in time. The amount of depreciation is deducted from the asset's original value before posting its current value on the balance sheet. In a somewhat similar process, the accounts receivable figure is adjusted by deducting some percentage of the total as an allowance for bad debts. This results in a more accurate valuation.

Liabilities are obligations or debts that the company must repay. Examples include bank loans, promissory notes, outstanding balances owed to suppliers, accrued taxes, and so on. **Current liabilities** are the more pressing; these are debts the organization will need to pay within the year following the balance sheet date. **Long-term liabilities** are those obligations which are to be repaid in the more distant future.

Often called the **owners' equity,** the **net worth** of a business is the amount that remains if all the firm's liabilities were to be paid out of total assets. The balance sheet itself is based on a simple accounting formula that demonstrates the fact:

$$\text{Assets} = \text{Liabilities} + \text{Net worth}$$

To ascertain a company's net worth, we simpy rearrange the terms in the basic formula:

$$\text{Net Worth} = \text{Assets} - \text{Liabilities}$$

If the firm has been incorporated, the term **capital** is usually substituted for net worth or owners' equity. The corporation's outstanding capital stock is listed in this section, along with any profits retained (not distributed to shareholders).

The Operating Statement

Also vital to the proper financial management of an enterprise is another accounting document, the **operating statement.** Other popular names for this form are *income statement* and *profit-and-loss statement,* or *P&L.* The operating statement reveals how profitable or unprofitable the business operation has been for a stated time. A shortsighted management team may permit a full year to elapse before working up a P&L. This could be dangerous: it may be too late, some 12 months after the fact, to identify and correct a deteriorating situation. Healthy business organizations generate operating statements at least quarterly and preferably once every month. Much time and reflection are devoted to analyzing results. Useful insights may be gained that will lead to changes in tactics and strategy.

Figure 6.2 illustrates one month's P&L for a small independent toy retailer.

Operating Statement Details The opening entry on the retailer's P&L is the **gross sales** figure. This represents the total of all monies collected during the time frame for merchandise sold. Sales taxes are omitted. Next, the retail value of all goods that have been returned by customers and special allowances the retailer may have granted are deducted from the gross sales amount. This yields the merchant's **net sales** for the period.

The following formula summarizes the computations:

$$\text{Gross Sales} - \text{Returns and allowances} = \text{Net sales}$$

Then the total cost of all merchandise sold during the period must be calculated. The procedure involves determining, first of all, the value of the store's inventory at the beginning of the period. To this amount, the cost of additional purchases of stock for resale during the period is added. So are any freight costs incurred. Thus, the value of all *merchandise made available for sale* is taken into account. From this total, the retailer deducts the value of all inventory at the end of the period to ascertain the **cost of goods sold,** or **COG sold.**

The retailer then subtracts the cost of goods sold from the net sales entry to obtain the **gross margin** earned by the business. Firms need sufficient gross margin to cover all expenses incurred, pay income tax, and end up with some profit. In the next section of the operating statement, all **operating expenses** are categorized and totaled. The sum is then subtracted from the gross margin figure to show the amount of **operating profit** generated by store operation. Income from other sources, such as interest on a bank account, is added to the operating profit to provide the entry total income before taxes. A provision for income tax is then entered. When this last entry is subtracted from total income, we reach the bottom line of the statement—the net income, or perhaps net loss, for the period.

We summarize the calculations in the following formula:

$$\text{Gross margin} - \text{Operating expenses} + \text{Other income} - \text{Provision for income tax} = \text{Net income (or loss)}$$

Ratio Analysis: Essential Management Tool

Entries on both major financial statements are valuable in that management can derive a variety of ratios from them for comparison. Current results can be compared to those of previous years to uncover trends. Since trade associations often collect and disseminate summary operating data among their members, retailers can compare their own ratio

Figure 6.2
A retailer's operating
statement (P&L)

THE KIDDIE TOY MART
Income Statement
September 1985

Gross sales	$20,670	
Less returns and allowances	530	
Net sales		$20,140
Less cost of goods sold:		
Merchandise inventory, September 1	39,230	
Purchases during month	5,885	
Freight paid	95	
Total merchandise available	45,210	
Less inventory, September 30	33,575	
Cost of goods sold		11,635
Gross margin		8,505
Less operating expenses:		
Salaries and wages	3,680	
Rent	725	
Electricity	310	
Telephone	220	
Repairs and maintenance	460	
Supplies	110	
Insurance	320	
Advertising	100	
Displays	245	
Dues and contributions	70	
Professional services	85	
Delivery expense	260	
Interest expense	70	
Depreciation	870	
Travel and entertainment	85	
Bad debts	70	
Miscellaneous expenses	90	
Total operating expenses		7,770
Operating profit		735
Other Income:		
Dividends on stock	155	
Interest on bank account	70	
Total other income		225
Total income before taxes		960
Less provision for taxes		200
Net income (or loss)		760

"Another successful year, gentlemen. We broke even on operations and pulled a net profit on accounting procedures."

results with those of stores of the same type and size. These ratios are usually expressed as percentages.

Assume, for example, that Store A pays an annual rent of $10,000, and that net sales for the year amount to $150,000. A rent-to-sales ratio may be worked out as follows:

$$\text{Rent-to-sales ratio} = \frac{\$10,000}{\$150,000} \times 100\%$$

$$= .067 \times 100\%$$

$$= 6.7\%$$

Should Store A's management discover, from trade association data, that the average rent-to-sales ratio of competitive stores is 8.5 percent, it can draw one of two conclusions: (1) compared to similar outlets, the firm enjoys a low rent and is saving nearly 2 percent of sales on rental expense or (2) sales are above average for this store.

To demonstrate another ratio possibility, let us refer again to Figure 6.2. We will calculate the Kiddie Toy Mart's gross margin-to-sales ratio in the following manner:

$$\text{Gross margin-to-sales ratio} = \frac{\text{Gross margin}}{\text{Sales}} \times 100\%$$

$$= \frac{\$8,505}{\$20,140} \times 100\%$$

$$= .422 \times 100\%$$

$$= 42.2\%$$

For the month of September, the Kiddie Toy Mart operation yielded approximately 42.2 cents in gross margin for every dollar taken in. Earned gross margin dollars then covered $7,770 in operating expenses and still produced a small operating profit of $735. Should the owners wish to increase their operating profit, they need to either: (1) buy better—obtaining merchandise at lower cost or (2) raise the selling prices of some goods while still trying to maintain the same sales volume. Both scenarios are, of course, predicated on the assumption that operating expenses will remain constant.

Liquidity and Profitability Ratios

Among the most important financial ratios for management decision making are the firm's liquidity and profitability ratios. **Liquidity ratios** measure how capable the business is of paying off all obligations. **Profitability ratios** describe the profits earned by the operation. Management monitors and evaluates both types of ratios. They are also studied by suppliers and by potential lenders to gauge a client company's creditworthiness.

Two significant liquidity measures, both derived from balance-sheet information, are the **current ratio** and the **quick,** or **acid-test ratio.** To understand how these are computed, let us refer to the balance sheet for Shirley's Fashion Boutique, shown in Figure 6.1:

$$\text{Current ratio} = \frac{\text{Current assets}}{\text{Current liabilities}}$$

$$= \frac{\$88,645}{\$15,250}$$

$$= 5.81$$

Our interpretation of the resulting ratio is that the boutique finished the year with current assets valued at nearly six times the amount of its outstanding short-term debt. This liquidity position is extremely favorable. If required, the firm would be able to pay off its current liabilities with little difficulty. Inventories, however, are not so easily liquidated at their full valuation. The acid-test ratio is a more exacting measure of a company's ability to satisfy current debts. To determine this ratio, the retailer uses a variation of the same formula. It is adjusted by dropping inventory values from the fraction's numerator. In the following calculations, we work out the firm's acid-test ratio:

$$\text{Acid-test ratio} = \frac{\text{Cash} + \text{Securities} + \text{Accounts receivable}}{\text{Current liabilities}}$$

$$= \frac{\$14,975 + \$2,700 + \$3,260}{\$15,250}$$

$$= 1.37$$

The acid-test ratio, 1.37, indicates that current obligations can be repaid readily without having to sell off inventory.

Profitability Ratios Among the more useful profitability ratios that managements traditionally calculate are profit-to-sales, return-on-assets, and return-on-equity. Let us assume that Shirley's Fashion Boutique's end-of-year operating statement (not shown) indicates net sales of $92,000, and a bottom line (net profit after taxes) of $6,000. Here is the way the owner will compute her profit-to-sales ratio:

$$\text{Profit-to-sales ratio} = \frac{\text{Net profit (after taxes)}}{\text{Net sales}}$$

$$= \frac{\$6,000}{\$92,000}$$

$$= 6.5\%$$

To calculate her store's return on assets, she divides the net profit of $6,000 by the sum for total store assets shown on the balance sheet (Figure 6.1):

$$\text{Return on assets} = \frac{\text{Net profit (after taxes)}}{\text{Total assets}}$$

$$= \frac{\$6,000}{\$116,405}$$

$$= 5.15\%$$

We find the boutique's return on equity in this manner:

$$\text{Return on equity} = \frac{\text{Net profit (after taxes)}}{\text{Owner's equity}}$$

$$= \frac{\$6,000}{\$63,955}$$

$$= 9.38\%$$

Every item on the operating statement can be linked to the net sales figure to provide management with useful information. By relating the labor expense (salaries and wages) in Figure 6.2 to net sales for the month, we find that it amounts to about 18.1 percent of sales. Suppose that operating results for the same month the year before show a significantly smaller figure of, say, 16.1 percent. Management would then be made aware of the rise in labor costs (in relation to sales volume), and take appropriate steps. A corresponding reduction in salaries and wages may not, of course, be the final answer. To make up for the deficit, the retailer may decide to cut down on some other expense category instead.

In similar fashion, an increase in the cost-of-goods-to-sales ratio of, say, 42.2 percent during the previous year to 44.8 percent this year would alert management to the need for quick action.

Some useful financial ratios are shown in Figure 6.3.

Figure 6.3
Useful financial ratios

Liquidity Ratios

$$\text{Current Ratio} = \frac{\text{Current assets}}{\text{Current liabilities}}$$

$$\text{Acid-test (quick) ratio} = \frac{\text{Cash} + \text{Securities} + \text{Accounts receivable}}{\text{Current liabilities}}$$

$$\text{Debt-to-assets ratio} = \frac{\text{Total debt}}{\text{Total assets}}$$

$$\frac{\text{Debt-to-net}}{\text{worth ratio}} = \frac{\text{Total debt}}{\text{Net worth}}$$

Profitability Ratios

$$\frac{\text{Cost-of-goods-to-}}{\text{sales ratio}} = \frac{\text{Cost of goods}}{\text{Net sales}}$$

$$\frac{\text{Gross-margin-to-}}{\text{sales ratio}} = \frac{\text{Gross margin}}{\text{Net sales}}$$

$$\frac{\text{Net profit-to-}}{\text{sales ratio}} = \frac{\text{Net profit (after taxes)}}{\text{Net sales}}$$

$$\frac{\text{Operating expenses-to-}}{\text{sales ratio}} = \frac{\text{Operating expenses}}{\text{Net sales}}$$

$$\text{Return on assets ratio} = \frac{\text{Net profit (after taxes)}}{\text{Total assets}}$$

$$\frac{\text{Return-on-}}{\text{equity ratio}} = \frac{\text{Net profit (after taxes)}}{\text{Owners' equity}}$$

Activity Ratios

$$\frac{\text{Rate of}}{\text{inventory turnover}} = \frac{\text{Net sales}}{\text{Average inventory}}$$

$$\text{Asset turnover} = \frac{\text{Net sales}}{\text{Total assets}}$$

$$\text{Capital turnover} = \frac{\text{Net sales}}{\text{Working capital}}$$

Breakeven Analysis

When planning new stores, retailers often try to determine how much in sales they will need in order to break even. The point at which all necessary expenses are covered and neither profit nor loss is earned is called the **breakeven point.** To calculate this point, they conduct breakeven analysis.

As you will recall, we need to subtract the cost of goods sold from net sales to determine the gross margin dollars earned. Retailers rely on those dollars to pay for all their operating expenses and to produce some profit. Clearly, then, breakeven would occur at the point where the gross margin dollars equal all expenses (both fixed and variable).

By way of demonstration, let us consider two partners who are planning to launch a small home-appliance store. They prepare, in advance, an operating statement for their first year. In it, they project $108,200 in fixed expenses and variable expenses that total $21,600. The two entrepreneurs also anticipate that they should be able to maintain a gross margin percentage of sales of 29 percent for the year. Here is how they can calculate their breakeven point:

$$\text{Breakeven point} = \frac{\text{Fixed expenses} + \text{Variable expenses}}{\text{Gross margin percentage of sales}}$$

$$= \frac{\$108,200 + \$21,600}{.29}$$

$$= \frac{\$129,800}{.29}$$

$$= \$447,586$$

The store should break even when net sales reach $447,586.

Records Retention[1]

A continuing administrative concern is the problem of how long different kinds of internal records should be kept by the retail firm. Although laws vary from one state to the next, the following suggestions provide a rough guide to records retention:

1. *Hold for a minimum of three years:* billing records, cancelled payroll checks, petty cash vouchers, purchase orders, receiving records, sales records, sales tax records.
2. *Hold for at least seven years:* accounts payable and accounts receivable records, all cancelled checks other than payroll checks, cash disbursements and cash receipts journals, expired contracts and leases, income tax returns and supporting documents, payroll records, records of lawsuits against the company.
3. *Keep indefinitely:* active contracts, copyrights and trademark registrations, corporate records (bylaws, minutes of stockholders' meetings, annual reports, and the like), deeds, depreciation schedules, easement records, financial statements, general ledgers, leases.

Expense Management

Expense management is a significant phase of business management. In their search for profits, in these days of stiff competition and tight gross margins, retailers need to monitor this and all other phases of their businesses. One useful approach is to prepare budgets for those phases. Budgets are plans—estimates of future conditions. They are forecasts that are tied to a predetermined period. In retailing, budgets are often prepared for three-month periods or six-month seasons. They can serve as both targets to shoot at and a means by which to gauge the efficiency of an operation. Results can be compared from one accounting period to the next, to historical data, and to trade statistics. Proper budgeting can lead to greater profitability for the firm.

As you will see in a later chapter, retailers budget sales for upcoming seasons in order to plan their merchandise inventories. They prepare budgets for advertising, display, personnel, and so on. These are consolidated to arrive at the company's overall operating budget.

Unfortunately, not too many of the one-million-plus independent retailers prepare detailed budgets. Most of these entrepreneurs are not well trained in the financial aspects of business. Moreover, they prefer to devote their time and energy to other activities, such as buying and selling.

Expense Budgets   A helpful tool in planning and controlling operating costs is the **expense budget.** This document details projected operating expenses for a specific period of time. Like all other plans, expense budgets should be realistic and flexible.

Types of Expenses In expense management, both direct and indirect expenses must be accounted for. Direct expenses are operational costs incurred by a specific department, function, or profit center. To a large degree, these may be regarded as controllable expenses. That is to say, they lie within the control of the manager of that department, function, or profit center. Indirect expenses are costs that are incurred outside of the specific selling unit or function. From the standpoint of that department or area, these are considered uncontrollable expenses.

How Retailers Classify **Operating Expenses**   Before the first expense budget can be prepared, management must decide how to classify expenditures. Accounting procedures require that all costs be identified. Once classified, they can be placed into specific accounts, or records, and kept track of for budgeting and control.

Retail companies use one of three approaches in expense classification: the natural, function, and expense center methods.

Most popular and favored by most retail operations is the older, **natural expenses** classification method. Expenses are identified by the commonly accepted categories, such as those outlined in the income statement for the Kiddie Toy Mart in Figure 6.2. For your information, several of these accounts are repeated below:

salaries and wages
rent
electricity
telephone

repairs and maintenance
supplies
insurance
advertising
displays

The **functional expenses** classification approach is used by larger retail companies when management wants more detailed information about the sources of its costs. Expenses are organized according to the particular business functions in which they are incurred. Thus, we see such expense categories as occupancy, sales promotion, buying, merchandising, sales promotion, and so on. Each of these groupings can be further subdivided into more specific accounts. For example, sales promotion can be broken down into display, media advertising, and other subcategories. Even further refinement is possible; for example, media advertising will encompass newspaper, radio, direct mail, and other media.

Department stores and other large departmentized operations prefer **expense center** classification. This approach enables management to appraise each type of activity (whether selling or nonselling) as a separate business, or expense center. Expenses are first identified by the natural classification method, then assigned to the various expense centers: accounting, credit, sales promotion, management, personnel, selling, property and equipment, and so on.

Approaches to Expense Allocation

A decision must be made about the most meaningful way to allocate expenses in the company. Such allocation can be done for the entire store or by selling departments or sections. In this regard, retailers use one of three basic approaches: the contribution, net profit, and combination plans.

Under the **net profit method,** management charges each selling department with all expenses it incurs and a proportionate share of indirect costs such as rent, maintenance, utilities, and other overhead expenses. Indirect costs may be assigned by sales volume, square footage of space in the department, or some other criterion. Many retailers like this approach, since it enables them to determine departmental profitability. It is also useful for appraising the performance of department managers. One drawback is that it is difficult to decide on a method of expense allocation that these executives will consider fair. Department managers know that indirect costs are beyond their control.

When the simpler **contribution method** is used, only direct expenses—those costs that lie within the manager's control—are charged to the department.

Some firms use the **combination method,** an approach that combines the net profit and contribution plans.

Managing the Cash Flow

Occasionally, the retailer may have cash flow problems. The firm may be temporarily short of funds with which to pay its bills. The **cash flow budget,** such as the one shown in Table 6.1, is a helpful device for managing a company's finances. Retailers may prepare the budget on an annual, semiannual, or quarterly basis. Budget preparation begins with a forecast of the firm's projected cash balance at the beginning of the first budget month. To this figure, expected receipts are added: cash sales, monies collected from accounts receivable, and other income. The retailer then deducts total estimated expenses to be paid during the month, thus providing an end-of-month cash balance. This last figure becomes the beginning-of-the-month cash balance for the following month. Once these details have been planned and placed on paper, management can ascertain those periods when it may need additional financing.

Capital Budgeting

From time to time, an organization must weigh the merits of purchasing equipment, installations, or other substantial property. As in other aspects of a business, budgetary approaches can help in this area. In

Table 6.1
Simplified cash budget forecast

	January		February	
	Est.	Actual	Est.	Actual
(1) Cash in bank (start of month)	$1,400	$1,400*	$1,850	$2,090*
(2) Cash in register (start of month)	100	100	150	70
(3) Total cash [add (1) and (2)]	$1,500	$1,500	$2,000	$2,160
(4) Expected cash sales	1,200	1,420	900	
(5) Expected collections	400	380	350	
(6) Other money expected	100	52	50	
(7) Total receipts [add (4), (5) and (6)]	$1,700	$1,852	$1,300	
(8) Total cash and receipts [add (3) and (7)]	$3,200	$3,352	$3,300	
(9) All disbursements (for month)	1,200	1,192	1,000	
(10) Cash balance at end of month in bank account and register [subtract (9) from (8)]	$2,000	$2,160	$2,300	

* The owner-manager writes in these figures as they become available.

Source: John F. Murphy, "Sound Cash Management and Borrowing," *Small Marketers Aids No. 147* (Washington, D.C.: Small Business Administration, 1977), p. 6.

Capital budgeting is one approach to determining the merits of purchasing installations and other items of substantial cost to the retail firm.

Courtesy Filene's, Boston, MA

capital budgeting, alternative budgets are constructed for decision making. The thought behind this activity is that management should be able to provide the greatest possible return on its investment. Costs and potential profits for each alternative are examined. Most retailers use one of two capital budgeting procedures: the *payback period method* and the *net present value method.* The first takes into account the number of years required for the invested amount (or outgo) to be repaid in full through income. The net present value method adjusts the expected income for the time value of money. Value tables are used in which money is discounted over the expected payback years at a certain rate. This approach recognizes the fact that the dollar next year and future years will be worth less than the dollar today.

Handling Risk and Insurance

Because the future is always unpredictable, every business must consider the implications of certain kinds of misfortunes that may befall the firm. A major fire, for example, can completely wipe out a long-established retail operation in an hour. When management's negligence results in a serious personal injury, an ensuing legal action may end in a settlement that forces the company into bankruptcy.

The proper handling of risk is a vital management responsibility. It is useful to distinguish between two types of risk: speculative and pure. **Speculative risk** prevails when the possibility of gain, as well as loss, is present. The purchase of 100 shares of corporate stock, buying a ticket in a lottery, or betting on a football game are all situations that involve speculative risk. **Pure risk,** however, carries only the possibility of loss. There is no promise of gain. Such situations merit the retailer's serious concern.

Approaches to Risk Management   In anticipating and handling pure risk, a retailer may select any of the following avenues:

1. Ignore the risk.
2. Accept full responsibility for the risk.
3. Reduce the likelihood of the risk's occurrence by establishing loss-prevention programs.
4. Transfer the risk to others.

Ignoring Risk It does not pay for a company to buy insurance against every possible contingency. When a potential loss would be minor enough to not appreciably tax the firm's resources, management would probably choose to ignore the risk. This is referred to as **noninsurance.** For example, insuring glass shelves or interior mirrors against breakage is considered relatively unnecessary.

Accepting Responsibility Another tactic would be for the company to absorb possible losses by setting up a separate internal fund designed to cover such eventualities. As an example, a firm that does a sizable mail-order business may avoid paying insurance fees to the U.S Postal Service on packages it sends out. In this case, the company treasury is reimbursed from the fund for the value of the small percentage of packages that are lost in the mail. This approach is called **self-insurance.**

Reducing Risk Retailers can also take steps to lower the chances of a loss. Installing a sprinkler system and placing fire extinguishers around the premises are examples of measures that can be taken. Instituting a loss-prevention program often leads to reduced insurance costs. Some suggestions for reducing risks are outlined in Figures 6.4 and 6.5.

Figure 6.4
Spotting hazards   Look for the following kinds of danger spots when you check your store for hazards which can cause accidents.

Falls

Highly polished floors
A single stairstep in an unexpected location
Dark stairs

Figure 6.4
(concluded)

Unanchored or torn rugs
Wet or slippery floors
Unused display fixtures
Projecting objects, such as open drawers behind counters
Wastebaskets, stock cartons, and ladders
Loose wires

Stockroom Hazards

Check for improper storage or improper use of papercutters, scissors, and razor blades. (Be sure that employees use proper knife for opening cartons.)

Dollies, carts, and other material-handling equipment
Goods improperly stacked, especially on high shelves
Ladders in bad repair

Aisles

Narrow or crowded aisles are dangerous, especially when employees are in a hurry. For one-way traffic, an aisle should be two feet wider than your widest stockcart. For two-way traffic, the aisle should be three feet wider than twice the width of your widest cart. Eliminate wherever possible sharp inclines, narrow passageways, and low ceilings. Even when you have taken these precautions, you have to be on the lookout for the following hazards:

Obstruction in aisles
Protruding valves and pipes
Blind corners

Fire Hazards

Even though your local fire department may inspect retail stores periodically, include fire hazards in your check. Thus you can be sure that the recommendations of the fire department are in force. Look for the following:

Accumulations of waste paper, rags, and so on
Smoking in areas containing flammable materials
Insufficient ash trays for smokers
Unmarked fire exits
Blocked fire exits
Fire doors which need repairs
Wrong size electrical fuses
Frayed or exposed electrical wires
Fire hose which has been weakened by rot
Extinguishers which need recharging (A store should have one for paper fires and another for electrical fires.)

Miscellaneous Hazards

Loose overhead plaster
Loose overhead light fixtures
Elevators (If you have one, has it been inspected recently?)

Source: S. J. (Bob) Curtis, ''Preventing Accidents in Small Stores,'' *Small Marketers Aids No. 104* (Washington, D.C.: Small Business Administration, 1974), p. 2.

**Figure 6.5
Rules for avoiding
injuries in the store**

The best rules for preventing injuries are those which are specific. Keep in mind that employees are more willing to observe your rules when they know the reason behind them. Here are 15 rules that will apply to practically all small stores:

1. If you smoke, smoke only in authorized areas and use an ashtray. Don't throw matches or ashes into the wastebasket or into an empty carton.
2. Open doors slowly to avoid hitting anyone coming from the other side.
3. When moving tanks and carts, watch out for customers and fellow workers.
4. Don't stand in front of a closed door.
5. Clean up liquid spilled on the floor immediately.
6. Use handrails when going up or down stairs. Never carry anything so heavy or bulky that you don't have one hand free to hold the railing. Carry so you can see where you are going.
7. Don't run—walk.
8. Never indulge in horseplay.
9. Never stand on an open drawer or climb on stock shelves.
10. When using a ladder, make sure that it is steady.
11. Don't leave drawers or cabinet doors open.
12. Remove staples with a staple remover.
13. Open cartons with the proper tool.
14. Keep selling and nonselling areas neat at all times.
15. When a repairer is working in your area, move out of the way and warn customers.

Source: S. J. (Bob) Curtis, "Preventing Accidents in Small Stores," *Small Marketers Aids No. 104* (Washington, D.C.: Small Business Administration, 1974), p. 3.

Transferring Risk The most common avenue to risk reduction is to purchase insurance coverage from a commercial insurance company. The insurance policy is a signed contract in which the firm transfers one or more stated perils to the insurer, who willingly accepts the risk in return for a stated fee, or **premium.** It is also possible to transfer risk to other companies or to other people. Store management may insist on product liability coverage from its suppliers. A retail firm may lease its fixtures, instead of purchasing them outright. In this manner, the responsibility for safeguarding the fixtures is assumed by the lessor.

Major Types of Insurance Coverage Retailers should view insurance coverage as falling into two categories: those that are essential and those that may be desirable but are not essential.[2] Three major types are nearly mandatory for all kinds of retail firms: property, liability, and workers' compensation insurance.

Property Insurance An enlightened management will strive to protect its assets against unexpected perils that could reduce their value sharply

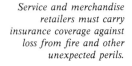

Service and merchandise retailers must carry insurance coverage against loss from fire and other unexpected perils.

Eleanore Snow

or destroy them totally. This holds true no matter how remote their chances of occurrence may be. Fire insurance is a prime requisite because a fire can rapidly ravage storefront, showcases, fixtures, interior decor, and the merchandise inventory. While the basic fire policy covers only the threats of fire and lightning, coverage may and should be extended to include damage from windstorm, hail, explosion, and other perils. By paying a small additional premium, the firm can obtain an extended policy.

Premiums for fire insurance vary. The individual policy takes into account the physical condition of the premises, the type of building, the store neighborhood, internal risk-reduction measures, and so on. For most types of retailers, goods for resale can also be covered by attaching a commercial property section to the fire insurance policy. Protection against vandalism can also be added. All-risk floater policies can be secured for jewelry shops, dry cleaning establishments, and other businesses with special needs.

Company cars, trucks, and other vehicles may be insured against physical damage (fire, collision) and theft. When computing the rate to charge for this protection, the insurance company considers and evaluates a number of factors. Among others, these include the type and size of the vehicle, its age, number of miles it is customarily driven each year, and where the vehicle will be driven. Retailers can hold their premium payments down by arranging for higher deductibles on trucks and cars. Management will also want to carry liability insurance on the firm's vehicles.

Liability Insurance Companies must protect their assets against the threat of legal action based on negligence. Retailers are particularly vulnerable to lawsuits because large numbers of consumers may enter and exit the premises every day. Whether they are shoppers, employees, or simply browsers, people injured while in the store often sue the firm. Even people who enter with an intent to rob, steal, or burglarize the premises have the right to institute legal action if they are accidentally hurt. Amounts awarded by juries in successful liability suits have escalated in recent years to the hundreds of thousands of dollars, and even more. Needless to say, having to pay that sizable an award from company funds can literally put the retailer out of business.

A comprehensive liability policy relieves management of a great deal of worry. The insurance company will defend the firm in liability lawsuits that are brought against it. It will also provide for medical treatment and needed surgery to injured persons. It will pay any sums awarded to plaintiffs. The size of the premium to be paid for the comprehensive policy depends on the size of the premises, geographical area in which the store is located, upper limits for coverage agreed on by the insured firm, and other factors.

Workers' Compensation Insurance Both legislation and common law demand that every company provide its employees with a safe working environment. This is a prime responsibility of an employer. However, despite all the safety measures and strict procedures that may be instituted, workers occasionally do have accidents while on the job. Employees may also fall ill, perhaps from an occupation-related disease. It is not uncommon for employees to bring suit against their companies. Workers who are compelled to remain at home should not have to suffer the loss of regular income. Nor should they have to bear the cost of medical treatment. By taking out workers' compensation insurance, both disability benefits and medical care can be provided for a company's employees.

In some states, this form of insurance protection is not mandated by law. Even when state legislation requires that companies carry it, firms that employ fewer than three or four people are usually exempted. Common sense would nevertheless dictate that even the small independent retail firm with one or two part- or full-time workers should secure workers' compensation coverage. Premiums depend, in the main, on the size of the firm's payroll and the types of jobs that employees perform.

Other Forms that May Be Desirable As we have seen, only three kinds of insurance are normally regarded as essential for most companies. A wide variety of other types can, of course, be obtained from commercial insurers. Figure 6.6 lists the more common varieties, in alphabetical order. From the viewpoint of the individual retail firm, many of them may be considered worthwhile.

Retailers need ample insurance protection—for example, this retailer may need workers' compensation, property, liability, business interruption, and other types of insurance coverage.

Courtesy Bresler's 33 Flavors Franchising Corporation, Chicago

Store Security

A perennial concern of retail management is the extent of its shrinkage. Merchants apply the term **shrinkage,** or **shrink,** to stock shortages. These are determined by discrepancies between book and actual inventory values. Although some percentage of these shortages may be due to faulty bookkeeping or errors in taking physical inventory, the greater proportion is usually ascribed to stealing. Both internal and external theft plague the retail trades.

To hold down shrinkage, management must set tight controls into place. Retailers measure their profits in mere pennies on each dollar. A net profit of between 2 and 4 percent of sales is typical for many stores. The loss of even 1 percent of sales because of shoplifting, employee theft, or other stealing can cut earnings by one third or more. As a case in point, the neighborhood shoestore that enjoys annual sales of $300,000 may normally look forward to $6,000–12,000 in end-of-year net profit. Yet an unexpected shrink figure of, say, 5 percent of sales would send the firm directly into the red.

Causes of Shrinkage: External Theft

Shrinkage may be due to both external and internal theft. In the first category are shoplifting, robbery, burglary, passing bad checks or counterfeit bills, buying merchandise with stolen credit cards, and other crimes. Losses due to internal theft are thought to be even greater. Perhaps the most damage is caused by employees who pilfer supplies and store merchandise or steal money from the register.

Some of the more common types of external crimes are discussed in the following section.

Figure 6.6
Additional types of
insurance

Boiler and machinery insurance: Covers damage due to an explosion and fire involving the store's heating plant.

Business interruption insurance: As a result of a fire or other catastrophe, a store operation may have to close down. Reimburses management for lost sales, utility bills, loan installments, and other obligations.

Crime insurance: Because their establishments are vulnerable to burglary and robbery, retailers often seek this kind of coverage. Rates depend on the type of business, area in which the store is located, and whatever loss prevention steps have been taken to reduce the likelihood that crimes will occur.

Fidelity bonds: These protect the firm from employee dishonesty. May be secured from bonding companies for personnel who have access to large sums of money.

Glass insurance: Covers breakage or damage to show windows, display cases, glass doors, mirrors, and the like. Even the cost of temporarily boarding up a broken window may be paid for.

Group insurance plans: Many retailers provide group policies for owners and employees at modest rates. Health, accident, hospitalization, and life insurance plans are available. In many situations, costs are shared by employer and employee according to some formula. In others, the company pays for this coverage completely. Some retailers go so far as to institute retirement income plans for their people.

Key-person insurance: The sudden loss of a company controller, vice president, store manager, or senior buyer can play havoc with operations. One likely result is a drop, however temporary, in revenues. Confusion in the ranks and adjustment problems are other probabilities.

Key-person insurance takes care of such troublesome concerns by paying for, among other things, the costs of locating, hiring, and training replacements for top people.

Life insurance: Entrepreneurs often secure business life policies when first starting up. They desire to protect themselves against the discontinuance of their operation, should they become ill or incapacitated, or die. This protection becomes especially important when partners are involved. Other owners defer taking out life insurance coverage until reasonably certain that the business can afford to pay the premiums involved.

Shoplifting Estimates of losses due to *shoplifting* are wide-ranging. Across industry, more than $40 billion may be lost each year through nonviolent crime.[3] Shoplifting may account for 5 percent or more of that figure. The National Coalition to Prevent Shoplifting, an organization that helps retailers in their loss prevention programs, estimated the value of merchandise stolen in 1979 alone at more than $16 billion.[4] Retailers must compensate for these extraordinary losses by raising the selling prices of their goods. An executive of one security systems firm related the appalling situation directly to the consumer's pocketbook, suggesting that retail thefts cost each American $150 a year.[5]

The magnitude of the problem sparked one investigation of high school and college students.[6] Nearly 20 percent of these young people admitted to having shoplifted once. Many were repeat offenders. Although most readily acknowledged that shoplifting was wrong, the students claimed they found this behavior exciting. They also claimed that, in most instances, store security was weak. In another study of young adults in Hawaii, more than one in four had stolen store merchandise. Moreover, among those who had shoplifted, 39.3 percent sold most of the stolen items; all of them had stores in which they preferred to shoplift; and 87.1 percent felt they had below average incomes.[7]

Current approaches to curbing this crime stress education and training, installation of appropriate systems and security measures, use of in-store signing to alert the public, deployment of trained security personnel, and prompt prosecution.[8] In 1974, the Illinois Retail Merchants Association launched an extensive educational campaign to combat shoplifting.[9] The campaign received wide coverage in the media. Among the activities were meetings with many groups of consumers; distribution of brochures, buttons, and posters; and the showing of films. As a direct consequence of these efforts, the state legislature passed a Retail Theft Act. Similar campaigns have since been waged in other areas across the nation.

Fortunately for the retailer, most shoplifters are amateurs. Well-trained store personnel remain alert to shoppers who behave suspiciously. Often, an employee will spot the thief in the act of palming an article or dropping it into a shopping bag. At times, a dishonest

Some retailers install electronic monitoring devices at exits to discourage shoplifting.

Courtesy 3M

shopper tries to remove the price ticket from an item in order to attach another ticket from a less expensive article. The professional shoplifter, however, relies more on special equipment such as clothing with slit pockets or booster boxes—small parcels that obviously are wrapped but are equipped with bottoms or sides that open easily.[10]

In addition to training their employees, retailers take any number of measures to reduce the problem. Valuable merchandise is placed in showcases or kept locked in a display case. Articles on countertops or tables are carefully tied down. Among other deterrents used are peepholes, closed-circuit TV monitors, convex and two-way mirrors, store detectives who pose as shoppers, magnetic detectors, and uniformed guards. Other suggestions for combating shoplifting are presented in Figure 6.7.

A device that aims at deterring, not catching, shoplifters is the electronic tag such as those manufactured by the Sensormatic Electronics Corporation. Retailers attach the tags to garments on the racks. Large, and made of white plastic, the tags are easily seen by store shoppers. They can only be removed by the retailer, with a device supplied by the producer. If a shopper leaves the premises with a garment without having the tag removed, an alarm sounds. The alarm is activated in a device set up on either side of the doorway. The device both transmits and receives high-frequency signals. It is triggered by a diode in the tag.[11]

There is developing concern that some shoppers may take offense at the protective measures that retailers take.[12] In this connection, Table 6.2 presents the results of a survey taken at a regional shopping center of consumer awareness and comfort with some of these techniques.

Robbery Retailers worry about being victimized by armed robbers. Technically, robbery is defined as "stealing or taking anything of value by force, or violence, or by use of fear."[13] Because they keep cash on the premises, in heavier amounts during holiday periods, stores hold a special attraction for the robber. Some establishments seem to be held up more often than others. This may be because conditions in these stores appeal to such criminals. The layout may be conducive to a holdup without the act being witnessed by store shoppers or other employees. A subway entrance may be nearby that the robber can quickly dart into. Or a confederate may be waiting outside in a car with its engine running.

In the mid-1970s, the Southland Corporation, parent company and franchisor of the 7-Eleven convenience stores, estimated that their thousands of units would be robbed on the average once each year. To reduce the expected number of holdups, management arranged for a few former armed robbers to visit and rate 159 of their stores in southern California on their attractiveness to this type of criminal.[14]

**Figure 6.7
Guides for reducing
losses from shoplifters**

1. Serve all customers as promptly as possible. Honest customers generally appreciate the quick service. The shoplifter does not want sales help and good, quick attention will generally motivate him to practice his trade elsewhere.

2. When another customer enters, the busy salesperson should acknowledge his presence by saying, "I'll be with you in a moment." Again, the good customer appreciates the service while the shoplifter knows he has been seen and is being thought of.

3. The salesperson should not turn his back on a customer. This is an open invitation to the shoplifter.

4. Keep an eye on people loitering around the entrances and exits of the store.

5. Never leave the store or department unattended.

6. Develop a warning system so that all employees can be alerted when the presence of shoplifters is suspected.

7. Lock up expensive merchandise that is attractive to shoplifters.

8. Do not stack merchandise so high on counters and in aisles that it blocks your view.

9. Do not arrange merchandise so that it can easily be pushed off counters into some type of container.

10. When merchandise is made up of pairs, display only one of the pair. A shoplifter does not want one earring, one shoe, or one glove.

11. Whenever possible, attach merchandise to displays so that it is not easily removed. Although a coat, for example, may look nice leisurely draped over a mannequin's arm, it is far more difficult for the shoplifter to take it if the mannequin's arms are in it.

12. Keep counters and tables neat and orderly.

13. Place telephones in such a way that salespeople can view their selling area when using the phone.

14. Examine your records to spot high shrinkage areas.

15. Return to stock any merchandise that was brought out for a customer's inspection but not sold.

16. Destroy discarded sales slips. Shoplifters may use them as evidence of purchase.

Source: Anthony J. Faria, "Minimizing Shoplifting Losses: Some Practical Guidelines," *Journal of Small Business Management* 15 (October 1977), p. 40.

Precautions against this ever-present threat are necessary. Retailers must set policy and instruct employees how to behave when faced with a robbery attempt. They need to recognize that human life is incalculably more valuable than any money that might be taken. Procedures to be followed should be outlined in advance. Generally, employees should be trained to:

remain as calm as possible under the circumstances
obey the robber's instructions, cooperating fully
make no sudden gestures or moves that could be misinterpreted as threatening by the criminal

Table 6.2
Awareness and comfort with shoplifting prevention methods

Method of Shoplifting Prevention	Percentage of Total Respondents Who Were Aware of Device	Percentage of Those Who Were Aware of the Device and Uncomfortable* with Its Use	Percentage of Those Who Were Aware of the Device and Comfortable† with Its Use
Locked display case	94.0	12.0	80.0
Mirrors	90.5	14.0	68.0
TV cameras	88.2	24.0	60.5
Rings and chains on merchandise	88.0	20.5	70.0
Floor walkers	79.0	24.0	59.0
Uniformed guards	79.0	27.0	55.0
Magnetic detector	77.0	18.0	70.0
Checkers in dressing rooms	74.0	35.0	52.0
Two-way mirrors	72.0	29.0	56.0
Observation tower	66.0	23.0	60.5

* As indicated by a score of 1 or 2 on a 5-point scale from "least comfortable" to "most comfortable."
† As indicated by a score of 4 or 5 on a 5-point scale from "least comfortable" to "most comfortable."
Source: Hugh J. Guffey, Jr., James R. Harris, and J. Ford Laumer, Jr., "Shopper Attitudes toward Shoplifting and Shoplifting Preventive Devices," *Journal of Retailing* 55 (Fall 1979), p. 82.

try to observe some of the intruder's physical characteristics: approximate height and weight, color of hair and eyes, details of clothing, and so on

after the robber has left and when it is perfectly safe to do so, notify the police

thereafter, cooperate fully with the authorities

Many measures can be taken to reduce the likelihood of occurrence of these crimes. A few suggestions are listed in Figure 6.8.

Burglary Less frightening to retail personnel than the armed robbery threat, though still a serious concern, is unlawful entry by a burglar. For the most part, these criminals work at night or over the weekend, when the premises are shut. Entrance may be gained through a rear door, basement window, skylight, or a broken show window. Experienced burglars, however, seldom use this last approach. They prefer to work under cover of darkness to avoid being spotted by a passing pedestrian or car.

Store merchants can also take positive steps to reduce the odds that favor burglars. Some are shown in Figure 6.8.

In many cities, there are companies that provide night patrol service for merchants in retail shopping areas. For a small monthly charge, retailers can have their front doors tried at least once each night to

Figure 6.8

Some crime-prevention measures retailers can take

Precautions against Robbery

1. Opening and closing times are particularly important; at least two employees should be present at both events.
2. Before locking up, the store, back room, basement, and washrooms should be thoroughly checked to make sure no one remains behind.
3. Registers should be cleared periodically of excess currency, and the bills promptly deposited in the safe.
4. Bank deposits should be made several times each day and taken to the bank by two people, not one.
5. Trips to the bank should never be made on a regular, scheduled basis. Instead, hours for making deposits should be varied, as should the routes taken to the bank.
6. Loiterers within or outside the store should be watched carefully. If there is suspicion that a robbery attempt may be made, the authorities should be called.

Precautions against Burglary

1. Front and rear doors should be secured with high-quality pin-tumbler locks. Installing a dead-bolt lock on the inside of the back door provides additional reinforcement.
2. Door frames should be firm and solid to discourage burglars from trying to jimmy them open.
3. Bars should be placed over skylights and basement windows.
4. At closing time, some lights should be left on so that passersby can see into the store.
5. To avoid possible damage to the machine(s), cash register drawers should be left open overnight.
6. Money should not be left in the till after the store has been closed. The store's daily bank should be carefully hidden in some spot where a thief would not ordinarily look.
7. If possible, a silent central alarm system should be installed to alert the authorities if the store is broken into.

see if they are well secured. Some larger retail firms keep a night watchman on duty. To prevent burglaries, a few companies have even resorted to trained guard dogs.

Other Forms of External Theft Stores are also prime targets for counterfeiters, bad-check passers, shoppers holding stolen credit cards, and people who are adept at deceiving and shortchanging cashiers. Employee training and effective supervision are the two most useful procedures a retailer can institute to help keep down losses associated with such crimes. In this connection, the NCR Corporation, of Dayton, Ohio, has been most helpful over the years to store merchants. Figures 6.9 and 6.10 contain brief excerpts from some of the valuable printed materials distributed to retailers by this organization.

Many approaches and devices are used to combat the bad-check problem, among them: camera systems, the issuance of identification cards to customers who plan to cash personal checks, dry thumb prints, check-guarantee programs, and computer linkups.[15]

Figure 6.9
Check acceptance
guidelines

ACCEPTING CHECKS

When presented with a check, insist on good indentification, such as:
- Driver's license.
- Auto registration.
- Employee identification card.
- Passport.

Do not accept:
- Social security cards.
- Selective service cards.
- Club or membership cards.

Follow your store's policy for accepting checks; and when a check is presented, examine it carefully to be sure:
- It is written in ink with no erasures or alterations on it.
- All blank lines are filled in.
- It has MICR encoding along the bottom of the check.
- It is neither more than 30 days old, nor dated ahead.
- The written and figure amounts agree.
- The signature is legible.
- The name of the person to whom the check is made, is legible.
- The name of the bank and its city and state are printed on the face of the check.
- All payroll checks have the firm name printed (not typed) on the face of the check. This also applies to other types of checks issued by businesses, governments, and commercial establishments.
- If the check is presented by anyone other than the orginator, it is endorsed (signed) on the back with the name of the person presenting it.
- The endorser signs his name exactly as it appears on the front of the check.
- If a check is made out to two people, both must endorse it before you can cash the check.
- It does not have a restrictive endorsement.

Follow any special rules your store may have for cashing Travelers' Checks or United States Postal Money Orders. Be careful, but not suspicious, in cashing checks. Most checks are good and the person who presents a check should be treated with as much courtesy as the person who presents cash.

Source: NCR Corporation.

Figure 6.10
Recognizing counterfeit
bills

RECOGNIZING BAD MONEY.

Be alert to recognize bad money. This may be authentic money that has been altered to increase its apparent value, or it may be counterfeit money.

Sometimes a large denomination bill will be split into two pieces. One half of the large denomination bill is pasted to the side of a real $1 bill, and the other half to another $1 bill. These bills are presented at a busy time with the large denomination side up. Another trick is to cut a large denomination bill in half and paste one half on one end of a $1 bill and the other half on the end of another. Each bill is then folded so only the large denomination end shows.

To prevent such swindles, make a habit of unfolding all paper money and looking at both sides of large bills.

To detect counterfeit currency, compare the suspected bill with a genuine bill of the same denomination.

FAULTS OF COUNTERFEIT MONEY

- The fine lines will be irregular, broken, and scratchy.
- The points on the rim of the printed seal may be broken and irregular.
- Portions of the designs may appear unusually white or dark and perhaps smudgy.
- Serial numbers probably will be unevenly spaced.
- There will be no tiny red and blue silk threads scattered about in the paper.

SECRET SERVICE SUGGESTIONS ARE:

- Do not return it.
- Telephone the police at once.
- Delay the passer under a pretext.
- Avoid argument; if necessary say that police will handle the matter.
- If the passer leaves, write down his description.
- Write down the license numbers of any cars involved.

Source: NCR Corporation.

Causes of Shrinkage: Internal Theft Employee stealing is pervasive throughout the economy, outpacing most other forms of theft. Each year, losses due to employee theft for all business organizations may reach as high as $40 billion.[16] The cost to the retailing sector may be five or six times greater than losses due to shoplifting.[17] Retailing is the most vulnerable of all industries to internal theft. Temptation is always present. Store employees work in an environment that holds many thousands of dollars' worth of merchandise. Many workers have ready access to the money being taken in all day long.

If we couple the unauthorized use/abuse of the employee discount privilege with other forms of internal theft, two out of three store employees are likely to steal.[18] Seldom do these workers look on these acts as real crimes; in fact, many would not report fellow workers they saw stealing.

Types of Internal Theft Among the misguided employee actions that plague retail organizations are:

abuse of the discount privilege
computer-related crimes
embezzlement
pilfering cash from the register
stealing store merchandise
time theft

Opportunities for criminal acts involving computers have increased dramatically with the growing use of point-of-sale terminals and electronic inventory control systems. To hide evidence of stealing, merchandise information can be manipulated. So can the firm's accounts payable or accounts receivable records. Charge account records can be tampered with and valuable customer lists stolen from computer tapes. People with access to the computer can create bogus accounts, issue duplicate payroll checks, or damage the company's electronic systems.[19] In realization of these potential problems, some retail organizations have set up off-site storage facilities to protect their computer data.[20]

Embezzlement differs from ordinary forms of internal theft. It is defined as "the fraudulent appropriation of property by a person to whom it has been entrusted." *Lapping* and *check-kiting* are but two examples of embezzlement.[21] The first term refers to temporarily holding back the deposit of cash receipts to cover shortages; the second applies to raising the amount on checks before cashing them.

Reducing Internal Theft Professionals in retailing and security agree on at least four significant preventive measures that should be taken to reduce the level of inside theft. These are the careful selection of new employees, proper training and motivation, good internal controls,

Figure 6.11
Some suggestions for
improving security

1. Review and carefully appraise the employee selection procedure. Make changes where needed.

2. Provide a store policy manual for the guidance of employees.

3. Emphasize honesty as a prime requirement for working in the company.

4. Provide for an open, two-way flow of internal communications.

5. Wherever possible, remove sources of temptation.

6. Reward outstanding performance.

7. Institute strict security measures at employee exits and entrances.

8. Set up procedures for the proper handling of cash and cash registers.

9. Closely supervise the employee discount program.

10. Occasionally audit payroll, accounts payable, receivables, and other financial data.

11. Install time clocks and monitor their use.

12. Employ a shopping service to check employees for honesty as well as courtesy and efficiency.

13. If theft is suspected, consider hiring a private detective to work in the store.

14. Exercise extra caution with regard to temporary employees, such as those hired for the Christmas holiday season.

and a tight security system.[22] A list of some specific measures retailers should explore when attempting to improve the security picture is given in Figure 6.11.[23] As an additional aid, the U.S. Government Printing Office offers an excellent handbook on store security.[24] It contains not only a detailed catalog of useful security techniques, but also information on how to design a retail security program.

An examination of cashier security problems at one chain (Target Stores) revealed that underringing at the registers and passing merchandise to friends or relatives accounted for the greater part of cashier theft.[25] Fraudulent refunds, check fraud, and the illegal use of employee discounts occurred less often. Impressive results were reportedly gained through the company-wide implementation of a Cashier Price Exception Report. Of course, not all misrings at the register are intentional. Cashier inaccuracy is related to such factors as the employee's length of experience in the position and the number of items in the sales transaction. It is known that the odds of a shopper being under- or overcharged varies from one type of store to another. According to one study, the odds in grocery stores are 1 in 5. In discount stores, they are 1 in 12 and in department stores, 1 in 55.[26]

Summary   Two major accounting statements are the balance sheet and the operating statement. The balance sheet summarizes the financial status of a business at a given time. It shows the company's assets, liabilities, and net worth. The operating, or income, statement reflects the results of operating the business for a stated period. Among other details, this statement includes information about sales, cost of goods sold, gross margin, operating expenses, operating profit, total income before taxes, and net income (or loss).

Useful ratios may be derived from both major financial statements. Management can evaluate these ratios by comparing present with past results or with ratios made available by trade associations or other industry sources. Among the most important ratios for management decision making are the liquidity and profitability ratios. Current and acid-test ratios are examples of the first type. Profit-to-sales and return on equity are among the useful profitability ratios.

Expense budgets are helpful tools in planning and controlling operating costs. To keep track of their expenses, retailers should choose a method by which these can be identified and classified. Most companies use the older, natural classification approach. Accounts are opened for such categories as salaries and wages, rent, electricity, telephone, repairs and maintenance, supplies, insurance, and so on. Some firms use the functional approach, classifying expenses by the type of activity they are tied to: administrative expense, selling expense, and the like. Department stores and many other large companies use expense center classification. This enables management to pinpoint responsibility and evaluate the performance of individual areas in the business. They first assign expenses to natural categories, then reassign them to specific expense centers in the organization. Examples include management, sales promotion, merchandising, buying, credit, and the like. To assign expenses to departments, retailers can choose from among three types of plans: net profit, contribution, and combination methods.

Cash flow budgets are valuable aids in forecasting cash needs. Capital budgeting techniques are used to evaluate and compare investment opportunities. Two common approaches used in this area are the payback period and the net present value method.

With regard to pure risk, four alternatives are available to retail management: (1) ignore the risk (noninsurance), (2) accept the responsibility (self-insurance), (3) reduce the likelihood of occurrence through loss-prevention programs, or (4) transfer the risk to others (buy insurance). Property, liability, and workers' compensation insurance are essential coverage for retail companies. Many other types of insurance are available.

Retailers are concerned about shrinkage. For the most part, inventory shortages are due to both external and internal theft. Companies attempt to combat shoplifting in a number of ways: by training their employees, by installing effective security measures, by using in-store signs, and by promptly prosecuting shoplifters. Other threats to the retail business include robbery, burglary, attempts to pass counterfeit bills or bad checks, and other types of criminal acts.

Losses from internal theft are considerable. Employees abuse the discount privilege, pilfer cash from the register, steal merchandise, and commit other crimes. To reduce such losses, retailers should have in place an efficient selection program for new employees, provide proper training and effective supervision, and establish tight internal controls.

Key Terms

balance sheet	profitability ratios
assets	current ratio
accounts receivable	quick (acid-test) ratio
current assets	breakeven point
fixed assets	expense budget
depreciate	natural expenses
liabilities	functional expenses
current liabilities	expense center method
long-term liabilities	net profit method
net worth (owners' equity)	contribution method
capital	combination method
operating statement	cash flow budget
gross sales	capital budgeting
net sales	speculative risk
cost of goods sold (COG sold)	pure risk
gross margin	noninsurance
operating expenses	self-insurance
operating profit	premium
liquidity ratios	shrinkage (shrink)

Review Questions

1. Name and briefly describe the two major accounting statements that companies must prepare at least once each year.

2. Define each of the following in one or two sentences:
   a. Accounts receivable.
   b. Fixed assets.
   c. Long-term liabilities.
   d. Net worth.

3. Explain the term *owners' equity*. What formula is used to calculate this amount?

4. Identify the major elements in an operating statement.

5. Distinguish between net sales and gross sales.

6. Demonstrate how retailers determine the cost-of-goods entry on their income statements.

7. Differentiate between liquidity and profitability ratios.

8. How is the current ratio determined? In what way does the acid-test ratio differ from the current ratio?

9. Show how the following ratios are calculated:
   a. Return on assets.
   b. Return on equity.
   c. Asset turnover.

10. What is meant by the break-even point?

11. Name three kinds of records that the retail firm should retain (a) for at least three years and (b) indefinitely.

12. Differentiate between direct and indirect expenses.

13. What is meant by the natural classification of expenses? How does this differ from a functional classification?

14. Contrast the net profit plan with the contribution plan.

15. Why is it important for the firm to prepare cash flow budgets for forthcoming periods?

16. Distinguish between speculative risk and pure risk.

17. Identify and briefly comment on the four approaches to risk management.

18. Cite the three most important kinds of insurance protection that retailers should buy.

19. What does *shrinkage* mean?

20. Specify four forms of antishoplifting equipment or devices.

21. Enumerate four types of internal theft that plague retail organizations.

22. What are (a) check-kiting and (b) lapping?

**Discussion
Questions**

1. Prepare an abbreviated operating statement from the following information:

Gross sales	$120,000
Returns and allowances	1,400
Cost of goods sold	72,500
Total operating expenses	39,800
Other income	900
Provision for income taxes	1,800

2. Based on the following information on a drugstore's balance sheet, calculate the retailer's (a) current ratio and (b) debt-to-assets ratio:

Current assets	$325,000
Fixed assets	47,000
Current liabilities	133,000
Long-term liabilities	71,000

3. Suggest four types of insurance, other than property and liability, that may be appropriate for some retail firms.

4. Propose five steps a merchant can take to lessen the odds of being burglarized.

5. What recommendations do you have for store personnel who are confronted by an armed robber?

6. Speculate on the possible reasons why employees may steal store merchandise.

7. Suggest at least six measures that retail management can take to cut down on theft by employees.

Notes

[1] A helpful information source is: Robert A. Shiff, "Records Retention: Normal and Disaster," *Management Aids No. 210* (Washington, D.C.: Small Business Administration, reprinted September 1973).

[2] See: Mark R. Greene, "Insurance Checklist for Small Business," *Small Marketers Aids No. 148* (Washington, D.C.: Small Business Administration, July 1971); Mark R. Greene, "Insurance and Risk Management for Small Business," *Small Business Management Series No. 30,* 2d ed. (Washington, D.C.: Small Business Administration, 1970).

[3] "In Hot Pursuit of Business Criminals," *U.S. News & World Report* (23 July 1979), pp. 59–60.

[4] "Self-service," *Forbes* (16 March 1981), p. 11.

[5] Addison H. Verrill, "Reducing Shoplifting Losses," *Management Aid 3.006* (Washington, D.C.: Small Business Administration, reprinted March 1981).

[6] Amin El-Dirghami, "Shoplifting among Students," *Journal of Retailing* 50 (Fall 1974), pp. 33–42.

[7] Michael D. Geurtz, Roman R. Andrus, and James Reinmuth, "Researching Shoplifting and Other Deviant Customer Behavior, Using the Randomized Response Research Design," *Journal of Retailing* 51 (Winter 1975–76), pp. 43–48.

[8] John A. Boyd and Jackson Harrell, "University Shoplifting Study," *Stores* 57 (September 1975), pp. 9*ff;* Francis J. D'addario, "Development of Security Self-sufficiency: Survival of the Urban Retailers," *Security Management* 21 (March 1977), pp. 18*ff;* Thomas J. Housel, "Finding Allies in the Fight Against Shoplifting," *Nation's Business* 65 (September 1977), pp. 64–66; David L. Steeno, "Retail Security Faces the External Threat," *Security Management* 22 (September 1978), pp. 46–50*ff.*

[9] Carol Messenger, "Anti-Shoplifting Campaign: Part II—State Programs Prove Successful," *Stores* 57 (November 1975), pp. 6–7*ff.*

[10] Anthony J. Faria, "Minimizing Shoplifting Losses: Some Practical Guidelines," *Journal of Small Business Management* 15 (October 1977), pp. 37–43.

[11] Peter Nulty, "Sensormatic Collars the Shoplifter," *Fortune* 101 (25 February 1980), pp. 114–16*ff;* "More Bad News for Shoplifters," *Dun's Business Monthly* 118 (September 1981), pp. 115–17.

[12] Hugh J. Guffey, Jr., James R. Harris, and J. Ford Laumer, Jr., "Shoppers' Attitudes toward Shoplifting and Shoplifting Preventive Devices," *Journal of Retailing* 55 (Fall 1979), pp. 75–89.

[13] S. J. Curtis, "Preventing Burglary and Robbery Loss," *Management Aid 3.007* (Washington, D.C.: Small Business Administration, reprinted July 1981), p. 4.

[14] "Holding Down the Hold-ups," *Business Week* (8 March 1976), p. 60.

[15] Anthony J. Faria, "Reducing Bad-check Losses: Some Practical Guidelines," *Journal of Small Business Management* 14 (January 1976), pp. 7–11; Leonard Kolodny, "Outwitting Bad-check Passers," *Management Aid No. 3.008* (Washington, D.C.: Small Business Administration, reprinted June 1974).

[16] "The High Cost of Employee Theft," *Dun's Business Monthly* 120 (October 1982), pp. 66–67*ff.*

[17] Mark Lipman, "What You Can Do About Employee Theft," *Nation's Business* 64 (May 1976), pp. 63–65.

[18] Ronald L. Tatham, "Employee Views on Theft in Retailing," *Journal of Retailing* 50 (Fall 1974), pp. 49–55.

[19] Charles Jackson, "Data Security—Key to Protecting Your Store's Assets," *Security Management* 22 (September 1978), pp. 68–72; Marian Burk Rothman, "The High Stakes in Computer Crimes," *Stores* 60 (February 1978), pp. 39–40*ff.*

[20] Rothman, "High Stakes," p. 40.

[21] Precautions that managements can take to reduce the likelihood of loss through embezzlement are outlined in: Christopher J. Moran, "Preventing Embezzlement," *Small Marketers Aids No. 151* (Washington, D.C.: Small Business Administration, reprinted June 1974).

[22] Joseph E. Bernstein, "How Improved Systems Can Control Theft and Fraud," *Stores* 58 (May 1976), pp. 34–35.

[23] For additional suggestions, see: Saul D. Aster, "Preventing Retail Theft," *Management Aid No. 3.004* (Washington, D.C.: Small Business Administration, reprinted March 1981); Edith M. Lynch, "Measures to Control Employee Theft," *Stores* 60 (May 1978), pp. 47–48; Marian Burk Rothman, "Measures to Trim Internal Theft," *Stores* 60 (November 1978), pp. 21–23; Steeno, "Retail Security," pp. 14–20.

[24] Eleanor Chelimsky et al., *Security and the Small Business Retailer* (Washington, D.C.: Law Enforcement Assistance Administration, U.S. Department of Justice, 1978).

[25] Charles M. Dancha, "Using Your Computer for Loss Prevention—One Retailer's Perspective," *Security Management* 24 (April 1980), pp. 43–46.

[26] Noel B. Zabriskie and Joe L. Welch, "Retail Cashier Accuracy: Misrings and Some Factors Related to Them," *Journal of Retailing* 54 (Spring 1978), pp. 43–50.

Case 1.1
Hope Studio

Betty Shannon had always had a strong desire to own her own business some day. For six years, she worked as a store manager for a greeting card chain. Her store was convenient to her large old frame house in Suffolk County, New York. An accomplished organist, she had been playing the quality instrument in her basement since childhood. In time, Betty managed to accumulate a few thousand dollars in savings. She decided to leave her job and begin earning her livelihood by giving organ lessons at her home. By advertising in the local weekly newspaper and by word of mouth, she acquired a small, steady clientele. Her students included older adults as well as young people. Although her income did not quite match the salary she received in her former position, she enjoyed the freedom and the challenge of being her own boss.

Two months ago, Betty was visited by Emma Alvarez, a close friend from her high school days. Emma was employed by a small private school as a ballet teacher. She had been attending a community college at night, studying business administration. Now that Emma had graduated, she was eager to put both her education and experience to work. Enthusiastically, she expressed her eagerness for self-employment to her friend. The two talked long into the night about the potential that a music-and-dance school might hold.

By the following week, Betty and Emma had decided to combine forces. They worked hard at developing a business plan for their new enterprise, Hope Studio. The curriculum would not be limited to organ and ballet lessons; Hope Studio would also offer instruction in piano, guitar, violin, and other musical instruments. Ballet would be only one of several dance forms in their repertoire. The owners would hire suitable part-time instructors on an hourly basis.

Subsequently, they found a two-story taxpayer building that seemed eminently suitable for the school. It was situated on a neighborhood shopping street in one of the better areas on Long Island. Betty and Emma were now ready to launch their new business.

Questions   1. What legal form of business would you suggest Betty and Emma choose for Hope Studio? What are the advantages of that form? What are its disadvantages?

2. What kinds of insurance coverage should they seek? Explain your reasoning.

Case 1.2
Ray's Children's
Place

Late in the summer of 1983, Ray Bailey resigned his position as store manager with a small chain of family clothing stores in the Baltimore-Washington area. Two months later, he launched his own children's clothing store in an active community shopping center in Virginia, less than 15 miles from Washington. Many community residents work in the capital city. The shopping center is anchored at one end by a junior department store and at the other by a large supermarket.

By February 1986, Ray had become quite concerned about the health of his enterprise. Sales, disappointing in 1985, had been relatively flat in January. Cash was tight. It was becoming more difficult to pay his bills on time. One night, he pored over his P&L statements, comparing results with the 1984 trade information that his accountant had obtained for him. In 1984, stores of approximately the same size and sales volume as Ray's managed to yield an average before-tax profit of 3.9 percent of sales. This was more than three times the amount of profit indicated on Ray's statement. Moreover, his 1985 profit percentage was far worse!

Ray mulled over the summary table he had prepared, trying to decide what to do next:

	1984 Results		1985 Results		Trade Data, 1985
	Sales	Percent of Sales	Sales	Percent of Sales	
Net sales	$175,000	100.0%	$187,400	100.0%	100.0%
Cost of goods sold	112,200	64.1	120,300	64.2	62.6
Gross margin	62,800	35.9	67,100	35.8	37.4
Operating expenses	60,700	34.7	66,270	35.4	33.5
Operating profit before taxes	2,100	1.2	830	0.4	3.9

Questions   1. What steps can Ray take to improve his picture for 1986?

2. Would a sizable increase in sales volume help? Why or why not?

3. What suggestions can you make to help bring about more sales?

**Case 1.3
R & J Apparel**

In little more than eight years, Rosemarie Shaw and Joanne Garten had successfully built up a six-store chain of family clothing stores in a major metropolitan area on the East Coast. All but one of the outlets were located in crowded lower- to middle-income neighborhoods. Last year, sales for R & J Apparel's five in-city outlets averaged $278,000 per unit. Sales at their sixth and largest store, situated in a suburban regional shopping center, were more than triple that figure. However, two years earlier, the two owners had been confronted with their first serious competitor: a large unit of a popular off-price apparel chain opened in the same shopping mall. Immediately, sales in their top store dropped by more than one third. By doubling their advertising budget and running more promotions, Rosemarie and Joanne eventually managed to gain back a portion of that drop. Sales, though, were still about 12 percent below those of their peak year.

Exhibit A

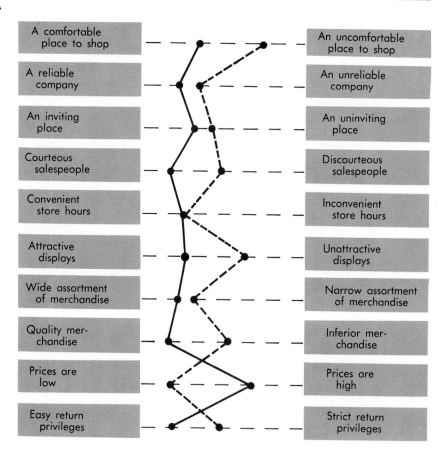

Joanne's niece, Michelle, was completing a master's degree in marketing at a local university. She suggested that it might be useful to conduct a study of mall shoppers to determine their attitudes toward the two competitive stores. After devising a semantic differential instrument, Michelle interviewed several hundred shoppers. She then prepared a summary chart of her findings (shown in Exhibit A).

Questions

1. What are R & J Apparel's more evident strengths as compared to the competitive firm?

2. What are its weaknesses?

3. What recommendations can you make that might help improve R & J's situation?

Case 1.4
The Dunbar
Furniture Company

Dick Dunbar and his brother-in-law Jim Senter established the Dunbar Furniture Company in 1980. Their store is located in a medium-sized town in the state of Oregon. They carry popularly priced name-brand furniture and a limited selection of better table lamps and other home furnishings. The company enjoys a well-earned reputation throughout the county for offering good quality merchandise at fair prices. Their sales are still quite modest, however. Few newly married couples live in this lower-middle-class area. For the most part, furniture is purchased by older families for replacement purposes.

Just this morning, Dick and Jim received a copy of their trade association's annual operations report for the preceding year. Using a pocket calculator, Jim calculated a few significant ratios from their own accounting statements. The two are now analyzing the results in light of the median ratios indicated in the report for similar stores of their type and size.

Ratio	Results	Association Figures
Current ratio	2.5	2.1
Acid-test ratio	0.7	1.0
Sales/Average inventory	1.3	2.7
Liabilities/Net worth	3.3	1.4
Return on assets	2.2	4.5
Return on equity	5.6	10.8

Questions

1. Obviously, the ratios of the Dunbar Furniture Company deviate considerably from those accumulated by the trade association. Interpret each of the ratios, in turn, for the two owners. What do they signify?

2. Is there any cause for concern? With which of the ratios? Why?

Courtesy Kroger, Inc.

Courtesy Sears, Roebuck & Co., Chicago

THE CUSTOMERS

Courtesy Jacobs, Visconsi & Jacobs Co., Cleveland, OH

THE RETAIL SHOPPER: PSYCHOLOGICAL ASPECTS

Your Study Objectives

After you have studied this chapter, you will understand:

1. The consumer decision-making process.
2. The significance of the role that motivation plays in our consumption behavior.
3. The five levels of basic human needs and how they affect our behavior.
4. The learning process, along with the more popular theories of learning.
5. What the self-concept, attitudes, and personality are and how they influence consumption behavior.
6. How new products, services, and other innovations diffuse through our society and the five stages in the consumer's adoption process.

Since the early 1950s, hundreds of researchers have probed that vast, challenging area known as **consumer behavior.** They have gleaned beneficial insights from the realms of anthropology, psychology, sociology, and other social sciences. They have analyzed human needs, wants, motivations, cognition, attitudes, personalities, and predispositions to behave. Today, numerous colleges of business offer a basic course on understanding the consumer. It is regarded as essential preparation for future marketing specialists. The textbooks used in the course generally carry the words *consumer behavior* somewhere in their titles.

Retailers need and want to know all they possibly can about what makes consumers buy—and what, when, why, where, and how they buy. They need a finely honed shopper orientation and a good working knowledge of consumer psychology. This is especially important for merchants who sell shopping and/or specialty goods and for service retailers. Their livelihoods depend on correctly interpreting and translating this knowledge into the right business decisions. They need to recognize and then buy the kinds and styles of merchandise that their customers want. They must know how to design effective promotions that will attract shoppers to their stores. They need to understand the effects of store design, layout, and overall atmosphere. They must know how to train their salespeople to cater to consumers with diverse perceptions, values, attitudes, and personalities.

Thus, retailers can benefit from insights into basic human needs, learned wants, motivation, the formation of attitudes, and the learning process itself. Retailers need to understand the self-concept and its significance in consumption behavior. They should be familiar with the process through which successful new concepts diffuse through society and the economy. And they need to know the stages individual consumers pass through in the process of adopting innovations.

Some Basic Definitions

We humans are exceedingly complex. And the ways we behave resist simplistic explanations. This is as true of our consumption behavior as it is of all our other behavior. We are affected by the physiological and mental forces within us and by forces in our environment.

Central to our understanding of behavior are needs. **Needs** are internal forces, conditions, or tensions that impel us toward some sort of action. We take action in order to maintain homeostasis—to keep our stability or balance. Needs may be innate, that is to say, born in us. Or they may be learned. **Wants** are needs that we learn. Each of our wants represents the knowledge that something is missing along with the simultaneous realization that we desire that something. Common wants that characterize our culture include the urge to acquire material possessions, the desire for prestige, and the need to be affiliated with groups. More urgent needs are called **drives.** These are strong forces or stimuli that induce compelling states of inner tension and drive us in the direction of their potential satisfaction.

The Consumer: Information Processor, Problem-Solver

Consumption behavior is essentially the outcome of an interplay among a number of variables. Some are internal, like needs, wants, and drives. Our emotions, beliefs, opinions, knowledge, and past experience may all play a part in our shopping behavior. Other influences stem from external sources: environmental stimuli, family relationships, norms, values, customs, and other social factors. We respond to situational variables as well. We are affected by our physical surroundings, our roles as shoppers, and our purchase intentions.[1]

Our shopping behavior also reflects an interpersonal dimension. In our actions, we tend to express our interpersonal response traits—the ways in which we normally respond to other people. We find ourselves being influenced by others. These others do not have to be physically present to affect our buying decisions.[2]

People take in and process information much as computers do. Stimuli assail our senses almost continually. They come from many directions and sources, both internal and external. Some we receive into our "systems." Others we manage to screen out. Those that gain admittance may be stored in our memories along with our past experiences. When faced with the need to solve a consumption problem,

Shoppers are affected by situational variables like their physical surroundings, their roles as shoppers, and their purchase intentions.

Courtesy The Taubman Company, Inc., Troy, MI

we can draw on these stored data and make our buying decision. Hence, we behave remarkably like electronic data processors—with input, processing, and output capabilities. We are also problem-solvers and decision makers.

Consumer Decision Making   Marketing theoreticians have devised various formal models of buying behavior based on a decision-making process. Typically, the models tie in the more significant internal and external variables believed to influence the process. Figure 7.1 depicts one model that has gained popular acceptance in the marketing literature. According to this, the Engel model, we receive all types of stimuli. Some of the information succeeds in penetrating our "system" and is then processed and stored in the memory. All sorts of influences are at work. Among these are cultural norms and values, reference group and family influences, and both anticipated and unanticipated circumstances. Such internalized environmental influences affect our motivation, attitudes, personalities, and shopping intentions, which in turn influence our shopping decision process.

In this model, purchase decisions consist of five successive stages:

1. Problem recognition.
2. Search.
3. Alternative evaluation.
4. Choice.
5. Outcomes.

Problem Recognition Problem recognition occurs when we realize the existence of a need or want. A cook runs out of ketchup for a recipe. A homeowner needs the roof repaired. A teenager wants a new pair of jeans. A car owner realizes that it is time to have the oil changed or to replace a tire. A New Englander requires a new coat or sweater for the coming winter.

Search Following the realization that something is indeed lacking, the consumer enters the second, or **search,** stage of the process. The search for information may be mental (internal) or external. The amount of time devoted to searching can be extensive, moderate, or inconsequential. A family may spend months searching for a new home. On the other hand, people spend little search time and effort on purchase decisions that involve most staple items. Food products such as butter, eggs, vegetables, and canned goods are examples. A question of trade-offs is involved in this stage. Shoppers strive to strike a balance between the importance and cost of the article or service and its value to them. Search time is also affected by the amount of risk consumers perceive. Retailers often attempt to reduce perceived risk by furnishing

Figure 7.1   Model of consumer behavior

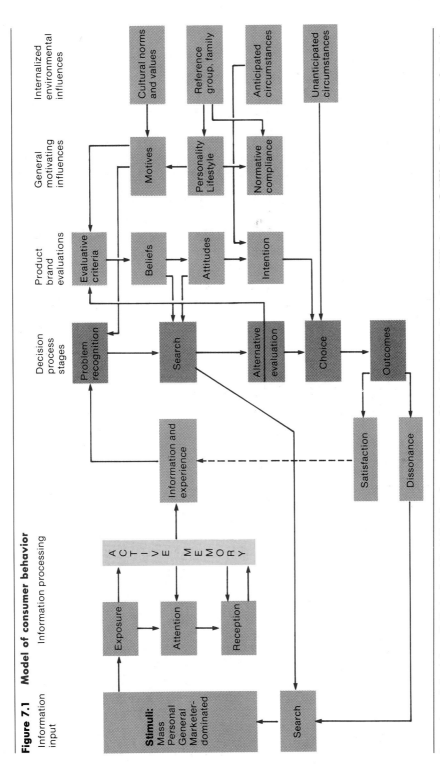

Source: James F. Engel, Roger D. Blackwell, and David T. Kollat, *Consumer Behavior*, 3d. ed. (Hinsdale, Ill.: Dryden Press, 1978) Copyright © 1978 by The Dryden Press. Reprinted by permission of CBS College Publishing.

detailed information about the merchandise and by using better, more informative advertising.[3]

Evaluation, Choice, and Outcomes The search process yields a number of possible selections. During the **alternative evaluation** stage, we weigh the various possibilities according to our own criteria. We evaluate, judge, and compare product and brand attributes, then enter the **choice** stage.

When any purchase is made, two **outcomes** are possible: satisfaction or dissonance. Consumer satisfaction appears to be the rule in most buying decisions. Dissonance is the exception. The term **dissonance,** also known as postpurchase or cognitive dissonance, refers to the kind of tension or anxiety that sometimes results after a consumer makes a purchase. When we have selected one of several, nearly as attractive, alternatives, we may doubt whether we made the right decision. This often occurs in connection with major purchases. Also, shoppers who do more comparative shopping apparently feel greater dissonance. That is, they consider more stores and more brands before making the decision to buy.[4]

Retailers may be able to reduce dissonance as well as other forms of shopper tension and frustration in several ways. They can clarify the company's image, offer merchandise that is directly relevant to their clientele's needs, and offer more information in their advertising and sales promotions. As simple a technique as mailing a letter to recent buyers of color TVs has been found to increase purchase satisfaction. It also produces customer recommendations to prospective buyers.[5]

Motivation and Human Behavior

Most, if not all, behavior results from the motives that operate within us. While behavior is of intrinsic interest to both psychologists and sociologists, businesspeople in commerce and industry are more concerned with *customer* behavior. They want to know just what moves an individual or an organization to buy. Each year, giant corporations like IBM, Dow Chemical, Exxon, and Texas Instruments spend enormous sums to keep abreast of trends in consumer demand. No less keen is the retail sphere's interest in consumer behavior. The more accurate its perceptions of shopper motivation, the more prepared retail management is to cater properly to customer needs. The executives of such companies as Bloomingdale's, Macy's, Bullock's, Toys "R" Us, Dart Drug, K mart, J. C. Penney, Safeway, and Woolworth try to keep in close, continuous touch with their clienteles. So do the smaller, more able independents. They monitor shopper likes and dislikes, preferences, attitudes, and purchase motives.

Retailers can reduce customer dissonance and increase customer satisfaction by sending follow-up letters such as this to recent purchasers of expensive items.

Van Drunen Ford Co.
"SOUTHERN COOK COUNTY'S OLDEST FORD DEALER"
3233 WEST 183RD STREET   Phone 798-1668
HOMEWOOD, ILLINOIS 60430
Parts Phone 798-4100

Dear Customer:

I want to personally say "Thank You" for your business. It is my wish that the vehicle you purchased from Van Drunen Ford will give you pleasure and good service. Below are the people of Van Drunen Ford able to help you if any problems should arise.

SERVICE MANAGER - FRANK GULICK
ASSISTANT MANAGER - DAVE DYKSTRA

Talk to Frank or Dave for mechanical repairs. We be lieve our service department is the best anywhere. Frank, Dave, and their staff will be happy to answer your service questions.

BODYSHOP MANAGER - JACK SWAN
ASSISTANT MANAGER - BOB JOHNSON

We hope you will never need our bodyshop, but accidents do happen. Jack and Bob will give you an accurate esti- mate of required repairs and follow through with the high- est quality workmanship available.

JUST IN CASE YOU DIDN'T KNOW...
We have expanded our facility, and we are now equipped to service most car makes. So, if you own a GM, Chrysler, or another brand car in addition to your Ford product, we can, in most cases, offer the same fine service and body repair which we have for over 50 years on Fords.

RENT-A-CAR - FRANKLIN VAN SOMEREN

Franklin will arrange for a new Ford Rent-A-Car at the most inexpensive rates available in the area. Rental by the day, week, and month can be arranged.

We value your business and want your experience with us to be a pleasant one. The people named above are experts in their fields.

Sincerely,

Marvin G. Van Drunen

MARVIN G. VAN DRUNEN
PRESIDENT

Business Goes Where it's Invited and Stays Where it is Well Treated.

Courtesy Van Drunen Ford Co.

What Motives Are Like   **Motives** are the needs, impulses, urges, or drives toward goals that occur in every one of us. They nudge us in one direction or another. The direction of thrust may be toward or away from a specific object: a concept; a person, organization, or store; a product or service; and so on. Motives impel us to act. When at work, motives build up states of inner tension. We find ourselves off balance, and we struggle to return to a more comfortable state by taking an action. If we are thirsty, for instance, this physiological want impels us toward seeking some liquid.

Motives are not only activated by bodily needs. They can also be triggered mentally or psychologically. The innumerable stimuli around us also have the power to arouse motives. Consider, for example, the odor of fresh-baked bread emanating from the neighborhood bakeshop, the sight of an attractive living-room suite in a store window, a radio announcement or TV commercial, or any of the hundreds of advertisements in the daily newspaper.

At any one time, several motives may be operating within us. We may be conscious of some, only partially aware of others, and completely unaware of even more. Our motives also vary in strength. The amount of force they exert ranges from very slight to exceedingly powerful. This force can be intensified or reinforced by a second and even a third motive pushing or pulling us in the same direction. Similarly, one motive can be weakened by a second that exerts energy in an opposite or a tangential direction. Motives at odds with each other may generate internal conflict.

Sometimes, people shop for personal or social reasons, and not just to obtain the goods and services they need or want.

Courtesy Jacobs, Visconsi & Jacobs Co., Cleveland, OH

Consumer Motivation It is frequently impossible to determine with any precision just which consumer motives are at work within a shopper. Generally, people shop to obtain the goods and services they need or want. Yet other motives may account at least in part for a person's shopping behavior. We shop for both personal and social reasons. We may feel a need for some temporary diversion from our day-to-day routines. Or we may simply have a desire to mingle with other people. We may regard walking through a shopping area as a pleasant alternative form of exercise. People go shopping to become acquainted with new fashions, to enjoy social experiences outside the home, for physical activity, and even to pass the time before dinner.[6]

Let us briefly consider several approaches to understanding the kinds of motives behind our behavior.

Rational and Emotional Motives Motives that induce us to purchase goods and services can be classified as either rational or emotional. **Rational motives** are prompted by logical thinking or good reasoning. If someone buys a car to get to and from work, the reasoning behind the purchase decision would appear to be sound. Similarly, it would be sensible for a homeowner to choose a room air conditioner that delivers the same number of Btu's as comparable brands but that consumes far less electricity than the others. Another rational move would be the decision to buy a particular make of vacuum cleaner because it may be relied on to provide a long, relatively trouble-free life of service.

Other rational motives for purchasing an article include an attractive cost in relation to the value the article provides, or substantial convenience, or easy and/or economical operation.

Frequently, we choose goods and services more as an outcome of our emotions than of due deliberation. Little, if any, rationality may be involved. **Emotional motives** outweigh logic. A young woman may purchase a gold chain because she feels it will enhance her appearance. Many shoppers buy clothes with designer labels by fashion notables like Givenchy, Yves St. Laurent, Oscar de la Renta and others to be in style or to emulate other people in their social circle. In their TV commercials, beer and soft-drink producers appeal not only to our physiological needs but also to our craving for companionship and peer participation. Thus, we see groups of people having fun together in attractive, even exciting surroundings.

Among the many motives that may be labeled more emotional than rational are affection, comfort, curiosity, emulation, fear, individuality, pride, recreation, sociability, and status.

A bit of reflection should convince you that much of our behavior in the marketplace results from motives containing elements that are both rational and emotional. In many instances, we may rationalize a particular purchase because of our emotions.

Primary and Selective Motives Another approach to classifying consumer motives is to break them down into primary and selective motives. Consider the situation of a young married couple discussing their need for a form of evening entertainment they can share at home. In their mid-20s, both are employed during the day. They have no children. Here is a *primary motive* at work. They can satisfy their urge with any of a number of choices: a video recorder, radio, stereo, or TV. Motives that can be satisfied by a variety of products are **primary motives.** In considering the pros and cons of each alternative, the two young people bear in mind their financial capability. Now the specifics must be attended to. Once they have decided to purchase, say, a TV set, *selective motives* begin to operate. The couple must decide on the specific type and brand of TV. They will base their final decision on their familiarity with the brands under consideration, what they have heard from other people, and information they have read. Or they may go shopping at one or more stores to gather additional details. The motives that impel them toward their final choice are **selective motives.** These include the reputation of the company behind the brand, durability, ease of operation, and warranty and service.

Patronage Motives Retailers are extremely interested in consumers' **patronage motives.** This is not an either/or classification. Patrons are the store's steady customers, those who shop there regularly and repeatedly. Shoppers patronize specific stores because of convenient location, courteous and helpful salespeople, fair and attractive pricing policies, selection and quality of the merchandise, the store's interior decor, and so on. Indeed, just about every aspect of the retail company that contributes toward its image may be thought of as a patronage appeal.[7]

Shopping Orientations   At this point, it may be worthwhile to review the findings of a classic study conducted in the Chicago area some decades ago. Shedding light on shopping orientations, Gregory P. Stone classified most women into one of four groups: economic, personalizing, ethical, or apathetic shoppers.[8]

Economic Shoppers About 33 percent of the women were classified as economic shoppers. The typical member of this largest group expressed a sense of responsibility for her household purchasing duties and was very sensitive to price, quality, and assortment of merchandise in the store. She demanded efficiency of the salespeople, regarding them as "merely the instruments of her purchase of goods."

Personalizing Shoppers Some 28 percent were labeled personalizing shoppers. These women preferred to shop in stores where they enjoyed personal relationships with the sales staff. Stone felt that this kind of relationship was crucial to these shoppers' patronage.

Ethical Shoppers About 18 percent of those surveyed fell into this category. They tended to judge stores by the quality of personal attention they received and by the warmth of the owner(s) and store personnel. They shied away from large retail companies; they felt these organizations were impersonal and cold. They preferred to deal with local, independent merchants. Often, they were willing to pay higher prices rather than shop at chain stores and other large retail institutions. They would even forgo wider assortments of merchandise.

Apathetic Shoppers Last, some 17 percent were of the apathetic variety. These women felt that shopping was a burdensome chore. Although they realized they needed to shop on occasion, they did not enjoy the task. They tended to shop at stores that were conveniently located.

The Basic Human Needs

An article in a psychological journal back in 1943 made a remarkable and lasting contribution to marketing thought.[9] Abraham H. Maslow proposed that people are continually motivated toward various, distinct sets of goals. In all, five sets of **basic human needs** may be discerned: physiological, safety, love and belongingness, esteem, and self-actualizing needs.[10] Conceptually, these sets of needs are arranged in a hierarchy—a rank order or ladder of needs. This can be seen in Figure 7.2. Needs on each succeeding lower rung of the ladder are more basic, and hence more prepotent, than the higher needs. This means that they are more powerful and take priority over those on the next higher step.

Figure 7.2
Maslow's hierarchy of needs

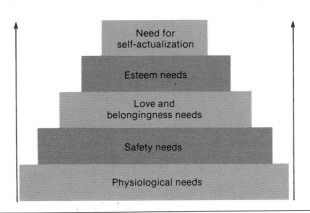

Need for self-actualization

Esteem needs

Love and belongingness needs

Safety needs

Physiological needs

All of us are continually trying to climb the ladder. As we manage to satisfy each lower set of needs, the next higher level begins to emerge within us, impelling us to seek new satisfactions.

Physiological Needs Easily the most powerful of our basic needs are those that relate to the proper functioning of our bodies—the **physiological needs.** Breathing fresh air, satisfying our hunger, resting and sleeping when tired—such acts as these are occasioned by bodily demands. If a person's physiological needs have not been satisfied to an appreciable degree, that individual will find it difficult, if not impossible, to respond to higher-level needs.

Safety Needs Once our lowest-order needs have been met, a new set of goals begins to motivate us—the **safety needs.** At this stage, we want to feel secure. We need to be shielded not only from physical threat but from emotional or psychological disturbance as well. We want to live in an orderly environment and in a comfortable dwelling protected from the vagaries of the elements: snow, rain, wind, cold, and heat.

In more advanced societies like ours, the vast majority of consumers find these two lower tiers of basic needs largely attended to. Thus, we find only occasional incidences of behavior associated with the satisfaction of our safety needs. Opening a savings account to provide some protection against future adversity is one example. Others include buying life insurance to safeguard the well-being of one's family or installing a burglar alarm system in one's home.

Love and Belongingness Needs As we largely satisfy these two lower sets of needs, we soon discover that a new array of goals begins to affect our behavior. These are the **love and belongingness needs.** At this point, we appear to be maturing. We push our self-interest into the background; we turn outward and look toward other people. At this level, we want to cater to others. We need to give and receive affection. We want to be loved, and we seek to express our love for others. We search out their company and comradeship. We need to form attachments—to belong to and be accepted by groups of people. This is our need for affiliation. Children look for the companionship of youngsters of the same sex. The adolescent is impelled toward persons of the opposite sex as well. The young adult not only seeks friends but begins searching for a sweetheart and eventually a mate.

Esteem Needs Satisfying these three levels of needs is still not enough for us. We soon begin to feel urges and impulses of an even higher order—the

esteem needs or ego needs. These are vital to our self-concept. We need to acquire and foster a healthy, rather high self-image. We want to be recognized and looked up to by other people. We wish to feel important and be respected in our chosen fields of endeavor. We look for status; we covet prestige.

Self-Actualization Needs

Some people succeed in attaining the fifth and highest level in Maslow's hierarchy of needs—**self-actualization.** Many never do. Even after we have satisfied our esteem needs, we continue in a wanting state. We want to be able to fulfill our individual potential, to be what we were destined to be and ought to be. Self-actualized persons do what they were born to do. Until we reach this stage of self-fulfillment, we cannot truly be satisfied.

Closing Comments

Products and services in abundance can satisfy the needs of consumers at whatever level in Maslow's hierarchy they find themselves. Retailers can target their customers' basic needs simply by working up the proper retailing mix of goods, services, promotion, and distribution. Thus, we see retail ads that carry appeals to consumers' physiological, safety, love and belongingness, esteem, or self-actualization needs. These appeals bring shoppers into stores.

Others have attempted to delineate and categorize human needs since Maslow first proposed his theory of motivation. As one example, the authors of a modern marketing textbook suggest:

In general, four types of goals, or drives, inspire consumers' motivations:

1. *Visceral drives,* such as hunger, thirst, breathing, sex, and temperature regulation.
2. *Activity drives,* such as exercise, rest, and novelty.
3. *Aesthetic drives,* such as color, tone, variety, and rhythm.
4. *Emotional drives,* such as fear, rage, disgust, and joy.[11]

Another typology of consumer needs proposes seven different types, each independent of the others. These are: physical safety, material security, material comfort, acceptance by others, recognition from others, influence over others, and personal growth.[12]

Perception

Perception has been defined as "the process by which an individual selects, organizes, and interprets stimuli into a meaningful and coherent picture of the world."[13] Each of us shapes our world the way it appears to us.

In and of itself a fascinating area of study, human perception is essential to learning. Retailers want consumers to perceive their stores

From *The Wall Street Journal*, with permission of Cartoon Features Syndicate.

"There's an energy shortage, crime is increasing, the inflation rate is at an all time high: this is no time to give up the life of a frog . . . !"

as attractive places to shop and to learn to shop there regularly. Shoppers' perceptions are strongly influenced by their needs, wants, and goals; their physiological and psychological makeup; the experiences they have as they go through life; and the external stimuli that constantly bombard them. Many stimuli succeed in penetrating our perceptual defenses, enter through one of our five senses, and cause awareness. Happily, far more are screened out. Otherwise, we would reel under the onslaught, incapable of any action.

Although three individuals may receive the same stimulus simultaneously, their perceptions are certain to differ. We are products of both environmental and hereditary factors. Because each of us is unique, no two persons' perceptions will be exactly alike.

Human perception is selective. We screen, filter out, turn off, or in some way modify any incoming information that disturbs us—or that is incompatible with our beliefs or opinions. This process of selection also appears to apply to our memory and to the learning process. We tend to retain information that supports our own viewpoints or is congruent with our interests, attitudes, and opinions. We tend to forget the things that conflict with these aspects of our personalities.

Learning   *Learning* is the process through which we acquire information, knowledge, skills, behavioral patterns, and the ability to discriminate. The following definitions may help clarify the meaning of learning:

The process that results in changes in behavior, immediate or expected, which come about from experience and practice or the conceptualization of that experience and practice in response to stimuli and/or situations.[14]

The result of a combination of motivation, strongly perceived experience, and repetition on behavioral tendencies in response to particular stimuli or situations.[15]

In consumer behavior, learning is the change, brought about by experience, in tendencies to perceive, think, or act in certain ways, with regard to brands, products, or services.[16]

A common thread is woven through the quotations above: the interaction of stimuli and other factors with the human organism. Situations, experience, and motivation are some of the factors.

Over time, consumers learn to select and use many different types of products and services. We learn to prefer certain brands over others and to maintain some degree of loyalty to those brands. We tend to shop at some stores, avoid others, and show loyalty to those we favor. We develop attitudes toward those objects, attitudes that contain cognitive, emotional, and behavioral components. Thus, more information about the learning process itself may be helpful at this point.

Theories of Learning[17] Some people still cling to the interesting but much discounted Freudian, or psychoanalytic, approach to understanding how people learn. They believe that biological factors lie behind much consumer behavior. For this reason some marketers resort to sexual appeals in promoting their products and services. Essentially, however, modern learning theories appear to fall into two categories: conditioning and cognitive learning.

Conditioning By far the simplest approach to understanding the learning process is **classical conditioning.** This had its roots in the well-known Pavlovian experiments and subsequent studies that involved dogs, mice, and other small animals. In these experiments, a buzzer or bell sounds at the same time that food is shown to the animal. The sight and odor of the food stimulate the animal's salivary glands. When the process has been repeated many times, the animal learns to associate the ringing or buzzing with the appearance of food. Thereafter, even if food is no longer displayed, the animal will start to salivate at the sound of the bell. It has learned to respond to a different but associated stimulus. A bond has been formed between the animal's behavior and the sound, or stimulus.

Because this response characteristically occurs, classical conditioning is frequently referred to as the **stimulus-response theory** of learning. A stimulus is something that stimulates, or arouses, an organism. Stimuli are also known as **cues.** The more generalized and rather strong stimuli within us are often called *drives,* a term we met earlier in the discussion of human motivation. Cues may be external as well

This retailer has provided an attractive, taste-tempting produce display to stimulate consumer purchase responses.

Courtesy D&W Food Centers, Inc., Grandville, MI

as internal. External cues emanate from sources in our environment: people, things, events around us, sights, sounds, odors, tastes, displays, advertisements, TV commercials, and so on. Responses are our reactions to stimuli—to cues and drives. They are the actions we take in response to stimuli.

As a theory of learning, classical conditioning is often frowned on. It appears too simplistic and mechanical. Opponents maintain that consumers cannot, and should not, be considered puppets to be manipulated or maneuvered like the animals in Pavlovian research. Humans are far too complex to be thought of merely as automatons that can be activated by external cues.

Supporters of **operant conditioning,** or instrumental learning, believe that the consumer participates more in learning than the stimulus-response pattern would indicate. We acquire and use information through repetition and reinforcement. *Reinforcement* is the strengthening of a response to one stimulus by another. When a shopper purchases an article of merchandise and has a satisfying experience with the item, reinforcement takes place. The resulting gratification enhances the probability that the shopper will buy the same article again. Positive reinforcement is crucial to repeat business. This fact applies both to retail enterprises and to products or brands. Thus, promotional and other marketing activity should aim at reinforcing the consumer's behavior.[18] The less the reinforcement and the less often information is repeated, the more rapidly shoppers will forget what they have learned.

Cognitive Learning Classical conditioning theory leans heavily on the formation and strengthening of bonds between stimuli and human responses. It regards learning as the natural outcome of a mechanical process. Repetition and association are thought to be essential elements, tools with which marketers can bring about desired responses in consumers. Operant conditioning goes further. It theorizes that people will learn if their behavior is rewarded or reinforced. Consumers work toward goals, look for satisfaction and rewards, and avoid punishment or unpleasantness.

In **cognitive learning theory,** a more complex and far more mature process is believed to be at work. The individual is seen to participate actively in the process. The learning process begins when stimuli penetrate our consciousness. Incoming information is then stored in our memory banks.[19] This knowledge, accumulated over time, aids in the formation of our beliefs, opinions, values, and attitudes. We are able to compare the known with the not-yet-known, develop judgment, learn to reason, and solve problems. Through association, we learn how to generalize—to transfer what we have learned in one situation to other, similar situations. We also learn to discriminate—to perceive differences among objects and persons. This cognitive or knowledge base enables shoppers to discriminate among stores, come to dislike some and enjoy shopping at others, and develop store loyalty.

The Self-Concept

One of the more fascinating aspects of the human personality for the retailer is the **self-concept** or self-image. Our self-image is vital to our well-being. It also plays an important role in influencing our consumption behavior.

We all have self-awareness—a mental picture of what we are like. Our perceptions of what and how we are may or may not be entirely realistic. Others may see us quite differently; their perceptions, too, may or may not be accurate. Nevertheless, we continually strive to protect and reinforce our own self-concepts.[20] The self-image is formed through interaction with parents, peers, teachers, and significant others in our lives. As consumers, we direct our behavior toward the furtherance and enhancement of our self-concepts. Moreover, the goods and services we buy often serve as social symbols, devices for communicating with other people.[21]

Marketing practitioners as well as psychologists often distinguish between the *real self* and the *ideal self.* The first term refers to the way people really are; the second, to the way they would like to be. Some psychologists go further, proposing no fewer than four facets within the self-concept. In addition to the two selves already mentioned, they detect a perceived self-image—the way we see ourselves, whether rightfully or wrongfully. The last facet is the mirror-image

In many situations, the visible goods and services people buy correlate with their ideal *(rather than their* actual*) self-concept.*

Courtesy BethCo Fragrances, Inc., New York City

or looking-glass self, which refers to how we believe other people view us.

Over the decades, many studies have attempted to link the self-image to consumption behavior. Such research, however, is still in its infancy stage.[22] We do know that people appear to prefer those products, brands, and stores that are congruous with their self-concepts.[23] Shoppers' preferences seem to be related more to their actual, rather than ideal, self-images. Of course, the two are positively related. In many situations, though, the goods and services people buy—as well as their purchase intentions—correlate more with the ideal self-concept. This is especially true when consumers purchase visible goods. These are products that are consumed in public: cars, clothing, and the like.[24]

The findings of a consumer survey published in 1982 underscore the significance of the self-image in apparel retailing. The study related consumer lifestyles to fashions in clothes. Significant differences in self-concept were revealed among seven distinct segments of the fashion spectrum of shoppers. The names of these groups are self-descriptive: (Fashion) Leaders, Independents, Followers, Neutrals, Uninvolveds, Negatives, and Rejectors. Both Fashion Leaders and Fashion Independents "saw themselves as more sophisticated, modern, different, chance-taking, confident, creative, and sociable, and as standing out in a crowd and having more complicated lifestyles than other segments."[25]

Attitudes

As we go through life, we manage to develop a bewildering array of *attitudes* toward innumerable objects. Among others, these objects are home, school, and the workplace; family, friends, neighbors, and strangers; and health, sickness, life, and death. We form attitudes, too, toward food, clothing, furniture, bicycles, automobiles, playing ball, swimming, jogging, and other activities. We hold attitudes toward other countries and other peoples around the globe as well as toward parts of our own country and other Americans.

No person is born with ready-made attitudes. We learn them over time. They form as we struggle to meet and satisfy our needs and wants. Our experiences affect them. So does our family, the social class to which we belong, and our group affiliations. Attitudes are also affected by and directly affect our perceptions, beliefs, values, personalities, and behavior.

An **attitude** can be described as "the way we think, feel, and act toward some aspect of the environment."[26] Each of these complex formations contains three major elements: (1) a cognitive component that encompasses the beliefs of the individual about the object; (2) an affective component, the emotions connected with the object; and (3) a conative or action element, all the behavioral readinesses associated with the attitude.[27]

Attitudes may serve one or more of four functions:

1. The *adjustive* function—associated with the satisfaction of needs. We tend to develop unfavorable attitudes toward those persons and objects that frustrate our needs and favorable ones toward those that give us satisfaction or pleasure. We seek to minimize punishment and maximize reward.
2. The *ego-defensive* function—which vies to protect our identities and shield our egos from hurt or attack.
3. The *value-expressive* function—essential to the maintenance and expression of our individual value systems and to the enhancement of our self-concept.
4. The *knowledge* function—which enables us to understand the meaning of things around us by organizing and integrating what we know. Thus, it provides frames of reference for making comparisons.[28]

Attitudes and Consumption Behavior

We can see attitudes at work in consumer shopping behavior in their choice of products, brands, services, and stores. Our own perceptions of and attitudes toward specific products and services are affected by how the people we know respond to them. We tend to favor those goods that others evaluate more favorably.[29] Our values and beliefs influence both our product/brand perceptions and our preferences.[30] In considering brand choice, we evaluate one or two in a positive fashion, regard others negatively, and omit still others from any consideration whatsoever.[31]

These reactions often override other factors. For example, the attitudes women have toward food preparation may influence their food shopping patterns more directly than their roles as working or nonworking women.[32]

Personality

Some acquaintance with the significance of the human personality is needed to help round off the retailer's understanding of consumer behavior.

Personality has been described as "the sum total of an individual's traits that makes that individual unique."[33] We readily recognize differences among people because of the complex trait patterns that individualize each person. Intricately woven into our personalities are needs, wants, motives, perceptions, beliefs, opinions, values, attitudes, self-concept, and ways of responding. Our personalities bear directly on our reactions to products and services, to other people, and to the shops we visit or avoid.

Differences in brand purchasing habits, for example, have been observed between consumers with more compliant personalities and those who score lower in compliance. Compliants want to feel needed and appreciated. They seek assurance that they are likable. Such persons have been found to be more inclined than noncompliants to use soap, deodorants, and mouthwash.[34] People who display more aggressive personalities want to be noticed, or to excel, or to be admired. They have been found to use cologne more frequently than those who are less aggressive. In a study of fashion shoppers' orientations, some 5,500 consumers were surveyed. The objective was to determine the kinds of personalities who purchase signature goods. These are products that bear the names or logotypes of famous designers, like Bill Blass, Louis Vuiton, and Calvin Klein. The researchers found that more active and more aggressive people were prone to buy more signature goods. They view these products as symbols of achievement.[35]

The Adoption of New Ideas

In *The Diffusion of Innovations,* a landmark work published in 1962, Everett M. Rogers described how new concepts diffuse through our society.[36] The term *diffusion* describes a spreading-out process, the dispersion of something through an environment. If, for example, we dip a tea bag into a cup of hot water, we can watch the tea diffuse through the liquid. Tinting the water an orange-brown, the tea produces a delectable drink. Or if we follow a searchlight beam through the night air, we see it widen and diffuse until it vanishes. To *innovate* means to create something new, to give birth to a new concept, method, product, or service. An innovation is that something which is newly introduced. The same term can also be applied to the process that produces that something.

In referring to the diffusion of innovations we mean the process whereby the adoption and use of an innovation spreads through our economy over time.

Not all innovations are completely new or unique. We can shed more light on the **diffusion process** by classifying innovative products, services, and the like according to the effects they have on consumer shopping behavior.

Innovations may be classified as (1) *continuous* innovations, (2) *dynamically continuous* innovations, and (3) *discontinuous* innovations.

1. A *continuous* innovation has the least disrupting influence on established patterns. Alterations of a product is involved, rather than the establishment of a new product. Examples: fluoride toothpaste; new-model automobile changeovers; menthol cigarettes.
2. A *dynamically continuous* innovation has more disrupting effects than a continuous innovation, although it still does not generally alter established patterns. It may involve the creation of a new product or the alteration of an existing product. Examples: electric toothbrushes; the Mustang automobile; Touch-Tone telephones.
3. A *discontinuous* innovation involves the establishment of a new product and the establishment of new behavior patterns. Examples: television; computers.[37]

We can view the diffusion process from two distinct vantage points. In the societal, or macro, view, we attempt to trace the new product gradually penetrating the American population as a whole. Working from a micro perspective, we try to understand how the typical consumer learns about, comes to try, and eventually adopts (or rejects) an innovation. Often, this second approach is referred to as the consumer's adoption process. It is discussed later in this chapter.

The Diffusion of Innovations: A Macro Perspective[38]

Some consumers will purchase and begin to use a new product or service regularly well in advance of the rest of us. Other people follow soon behind these early buyers. Still other segments of the population will neither try nor adopt/reject the innovation until much later.

Innovators First to buy and try the new product/service are the **Innovators** among us. Proportionately few in comparison to the mass of consumers, Innovators represent, at best, about 2.5 percent of Americans. What are Innovators like? Certainly, they seem more willing than most people to take risks, since they are first to test the innovation. Typically, they are younger people. They also appear to be better educated than most, participate in more activities, and belong to more groups. They demonstrate wide-ranging, cosmopolitan tastes and interests, are usually high in social standing, and enjoy well-above-average incomes.

People in this category, along with the next (and larger) group of consumers to purchase a new product or service, are believed to play a vital role in the innovation's success. It is also likely that such people use more of the product/service than later-adopting groups.[39] It is essential to point out, however, that someone who is classified as an Innovator with regard to one new item or service may fall into a later category with a second innovation. The first people to try a new food product, for example, may be later adopters of new apparel, home furnishings, or video games. The identical caution holds true for consumers who belong to the other groups yet to be described.

Innovators seem to learn about new things by reading about them in quality publications. They also learn of them from other innovators. These people also appear to be "disproportionately more exposed to the mass media than other groups—and more selective in their exposure.[40]

Early Adopters Large numbers of consumers soon begin to follow the Innovators' initiative. These **Early Adopters** constitute some 13.5 percent of the population. Although their incomes and levels of education are not as high as those of Innovators, Early Adopters are believed to be positioned well above the national average in both characteristics. As is true of the first group, they are relatively young people who move around quite a bit. They also maintain more social contacts than later adopting groups. They are more open to new ideas and to change and progress.

Some consumer goods manufacturers feel that new product success would be assured if they could clearly identify potential Innovators and Early Adopters. Then, by targeting their promotional efforts directly at these people, producers could gain almost instant acceptance for their new items. Eventually, large masses of other consumers would be influenced to try the product through contact with those two groups and by media advertising and salespeople. Word-of-mouth advertising alone could be counted on to produce substantial sales volume.

On occasion, marketers have sought to discover just which consumers represent the earliest adopters of an innovation. As we have already indicated, a major drawback is the certainty that Innovators and Early Adopters in one product category may not fall into the same classification for another product category. Firms need to consider other aspects: the cost of reaching such persons, the extent of influence they can be expected to exert on other consumers, who the heavy users of the new product will be, and so on.[41]

Early and Late Majorities Next to follow the first two groups in the diffusion process are the masses, representing about 68 percent of the population. We can divide these consumers into two equal groups: the **Early Majority** and the **Late Majority.** It is assumed that the population mean separates the two and that Early majority people probably qualify from average to somewhat above average in most of the traits mentioned in connection with Innovators and Early Adopters. Likewise, persons in the Late Majority are apt to range from average to somewhat below average in those same traits.

Laggards or Nonadopters So far we have assigned about 84 percent of all consumers to specific categories for purposes of understanding the diffusion process. The successful innovation continues to penetrate through society, eventually reaching still another, and final, segment. **Laggards** and **Nonadopters** are among the last to consider a new product or service. Some adopt it thereafter. Others reject it. Many will never try the innovation at all.

Most often, these individuals are at the lower end of society, both economically and statuswise. They tend to be tradition-bound persons who, because of their conservative nature, resist progress and change. Often, they are older people who work in low-status occupations. As shoppers, they are price-conscious, and they are usually far more brand loyal than Innovators and Early Adopters.[42]

The Micro View: The Consumer's Adoption Process

In the decison to buy, try, and finally adopt or reject a new concept, we apparently pass through a number of stages:

1. Awareness: A psychological state triggered when we first learn of the innovation's existence.[43]
2. Interest: A stage initiated only if we are motivated to seek out additional information regarding the innovation.
3. Evaluation: An internalized stage, where we think things through and decide whether to try the product or service.
4. Trial: The stage at which we purchase the innovation to explore its potential for need satisfaction (provided we reach a favorable decision in stage 3).
5. Adoption/Rejection: If results are satisfactory, the stage at which we decide to adopt, or continue to use, the product/service; if results are unsatisfactory, the stage at which we reject it for future use.

Summary

To be successful, retailers need a good working knowledge of human psychology. They need to learn how consumers find out about goods and services and where they can purchase them. Understanding shopper motivation, perception, learning, attitudes, personality, and the self-concept helps merchants devise ways to build loyal followings.

The consumer's purchase decision process has five stages: problem recognition, search, alternative evaluation, choice, and the resultant outcome. Like all other behavior, buying behavior results from the interaction of human motives. Motives are forces that move people to act. Three popular approaches to the classification of shoppers' motives are: rational or emotional, primary or selective, and the patronage motives that induce consumers to patronize specific stores. A well-known theory of motivation holds that people continually strive to satisfy their needs. These exist on five levels. Lowest and prepotent are the physiological needs. Once these have been largely satisfied, there emerge, in order, the safety, love and belongingness, esteem, and self-actualization needs.

Learning theories try to explain how consumers acquire information and knowledge, skills, behavioral patterns, and the ability to discriminate. Among the major learning theories are classical conditioning, operant conditioning, and cognitive learning.

Attitudes are complex, object-oriented mechanisms within us that influence our actions. They have belief, feeling, and action tendency components. Our behavior is also affected by the personality, that group of characteristics that makes each one of us unique.

The process whereby new products, services, or concepts are accepted and adopted for use can be regarded from either a macro or a micro perspective. On the larger, or societal, scale, the process is known as the diffusion of innovations. From the individual consumer's point of view, it is called the adoption process.

Key Terms

consumer behavior	patronage motives
needs	basic human needs
wants	physiological needs
drives	safety needs
problem recognition	love and belongingness needs
search	esteem needs
alternative evaluation	self-actualization needs
choice	perception
outcomes	classical conditioning
dissonance	stimulus-response theory
motives	cues
rational motives	operant conditioning
emotional motives	cognitive learning theory
primary motives	self-concept
selective motives	attitudes

personality   Early Majority
diffusion process   Late Majority
Innovators   Laggards
Early Adopters   Nonadopters

Review Questions

1. Contrast the terms *needs* and *drives.*

2. Why can it be said that the consumer is both an information processor and a problem-solver?

3. Identify and briefly describe the five steps in the consumer decision process.

4. Comment on the nature, strength, and direction of human motives.

5. Distinguish between emotional and rational motives, and give at least four illustrations of each type.

6. List two appeals to consumers' patronage motives that each of the following types of retailers might gainfully use:
   a. A women's sportswear shop.
   b. A fast-food hamburger restaurant.
   c. A supermarket.
   d. A store that sells expensive furniture.

7. The classic Stone study found four major shopping orientations among consumers. Name and briefly describe each of the four.

8. How do personalizing shoppers differ from apathetic shoppers?

9. Explain the use of the term *prepotency* in connection with Maslow's theory of human needs.

10. Differentiate among physiological, safety, and love and belongingness needs.

11. What is meant by "selective perception"?

12. Contrast the classical conditioning and cognitive theories of learning.

13. Explain each of the following terms: *real self, ideal self, looking-glass self.*

14. What is meant by the affective component of an attitude? The conative component?

15. Specify the four functions that attitudes may serve.

16. In your own words, define the term *personality.*

17. Describe how new products and other innovations are diffused through our society.

18. Contrast the characteristics of Innovators with those of people in the Late Majority.

19. List the five stages in the consumer's adoption process.

Discussion Questions

1. Discuss three selective motives that might induce a consumer to purchase a General Electric Toast-R-Oven.

2. Discuss the significance of patronage motives to retail merchants.

3. Suggest some ways in which a giftwares retailer might be able to attract more customers by using the findings of the Stone study.

4. What stage of Maslow's hierarchy of needs are you in? Why?

5. Changing consumer attitudes appears to be a most difficult task. Why do you think this is so?

6. When it comes to the purchase of a new type of household appliance, which of the five groups in the diffusion of innovations scheme do you belong to? Are you a much earlier adopter in some other product group?

Notes

[1]Russell W. Belk, "Situational Variables and Consumer Behavior," *Journal of Consumer Research* 2 (December 1975), pp. 157–64.

[2]Joel B. Cohen, "An Interpersonal Orientation to the Study of Consumer Behavior," *Journal of Marketing Research* 4 (August 1967), pp. 270–78.

[3]For a comprehensive theory of consumer risk taking, see: James W. Taylor, "The Role of Risk in Consumer Behavior," *Journal of Marketing* 38 (April 1974), pp. 54–60.

[4]Michael B. Menasco and Del I. Hawkins, "A Field Test of the Relationship between Cognitive Dissonance and State Anxiety," *Journal of Marketing Research* 15 (November 1976), pp. 650–54.

[5]Eldon M. Wirtz and Kenneth E. Miller, "The Effect of Postpurchase Communication on Consumer Satisfaction and on Consumer Recommendation of the Retailer," *Journal of Retailing* 53 (Summer 1977), pp. 39–46.

[6]Edward M. Tauber, "Why Do People Shop?" *Journal of Marketing* 36 (October 1972), pp. 46–49.

[7]For a review of the significance of some attributes of store image, see: Jay D. Lindquist, "Meaning of Image: A Survey of Empirical and Hypothetical Evidence," *Journal of Retailing* 50 (Winter 1974–75), pp. 29–38ff.

[8]Gregory P. Stone, "City and Urban Identification: Observations on the Social Psychology of City Life," *American Journal of Sociology* 60 (July 1954), pp. 39–40. University of Chicago, publisher. Copyright 1954 by the University of Chicago.

[9]A. H. Maslow, "A Theory of Human Motivation," *Psychological Review* 50 (1943), pp. 370–96.

[10]See also: Abraham H. Maslow, *Motivation and Personality* (New York: Harper & Row, 1954), pp. 80–106.

[11]William Lazer and James D. Culley, *Marketing Management: Foundations and Practices* (Boston: Houghton Mifflin, 1983), p. 359.

[12]Janice Gail Hanna, "A Consumer Needs Typology: An Exploratory Investigation," Ph.D. dissertation, University of Illinois at Urbana–Champaign, 1978.

[13]Leon G. Schiffman and Leslie Lazar Kanuk, *Consumer Behavior* (Englewood Cliffs, N.J.: Prentice-Hall, 1978), p. 95.

[14]Del I. Hawkins, Kenneth A. Coney, and Robert J. Best, *Consumer Behavior: Implications for Marketing Strategy* (Plano, Tex.: Business Publications, 1980), p. 271.

[15]Schiffman and Kanuk, *Consumer Behavior,* p. 95.

[16]Ibid.

[17]For cogent insights into consumer learning, see: Schiffman and Kanuk, *Consumer Behavior,* pp. 94–112, and Hawkins et al., *Consumer Behavior,* pp. 276–85.

[18]Michael L. Rothschild and William C. Gaidis, "Behavioral Learning Theory: Its Relevance to Marketing and Promotion," *Journal of Marketing* 45 (Spring 1981), pp. 70–78.

[19]James R. Bettman, "Memory Factors in Consumer Choice: A Review," *Journal of Marketing* 43 (Spring 1979), pp. 37–53.

[20]For a thorough description of the self-concept, see: Carl Rogers, Chap. 11, "A Theory of Personality and Behavior," in *Client-Centered Therapy: Its Current Practice, Implications, and Theory* (Boston: Houghton Mifflin, 1951), pp. 481–533.

[21]Edward L. Grubb and Harrison L. Grathwohl, "Consumer Self-Concept, Symbolism and Market Behavior: A Theoretical Approach," *Journal of Marketing* 31 (October 1967), pp. 22–27.

[22]M. Joseph Sirgy, "Self-Concept in Consumer Behavior: A Critical Review," *Journal of Consumer Research* 9 (December 1982), pp. 287–300.

[23]Ivan Ross, "Self-Concept and Brand Preference," *Journal of Business* 44 (January 1971), pp. 38–50; Bruce L. Stern, Ronald F. Bush, and Joseph F. Hair, Jr., "The Self Image/Store Image Matching Process: An Empirical Test," *Journal of Business* 50 (January 1977), pp. 63–69.

[24]R. Eugene Hughes, "Self-Concept and Brand Preference: A Partial Replication," *Journal of Business* 49 (1976), pp. 530–40; E. Laird Landon, Jr., "Self-Concept, Ideal Self-Concept, and Consumer Purchase Intentions," *Journal of Consumer Research* 1 (September 1974), pp. 44–45ff; Terrence V. O'Brien, Humberto S. Tapia, and Thomas L. Brown, "The Self-Concept in Buyer Behavior," *Business Horizons* 20 (October 1977), pp. 65–71.

[25]Jonathan Gutman and Michael K. Mills, "Fashion Life Style, Self-Concept, Shopping Orientation, and Store Patronage: An Integrative Analysis," *Journal of Retailing* 58 (Summer 1982), pp. 64–86.

[26]Hawkins et al., *Consumer Behavior,* p. 354.

[27]David Krech, Richard S. Crutchfield, and Egerton L. Ballachey, *Individual in Society: A Textbook of Social Psychology* (New York: McGraw-Hill, 1962), pp. 140–41.

[28]Reprinted by permission of Elsevier Science Publishing Co., Inc., from "The Functional Approach to the Study of Attitudes," by Daniel Katz. *Public Opinion Quarterly* 24, pp. 163–204. Copyright 1960 by The Trustees of Columbia University.

[29]Robert E. Burnkrant and Alain Cousineau, "Informational and Normative Social Influence in Buyer Behavior," *Journal of Consumer Behavior* 2 (December 1975), pp. 206–15.

[30]Donald E. Vinson, Jerome E. Scott, and Lawrence M. Lamot, "The Role of Personal Values in Marketing and Consumer Behavior," *Journal of Marketing* 41 (April 1977), pp. 44–50; V. Parker Lessig, "A Measurement of Dependencies between Values and Other Levels of the Consumer's Belief Space," *Journal of Business Research* 3 (July 1975), pp. 227–40.

[31]Chem L. Narayana and Rom J. Markin, "Consumer Behavior and Product Performance: An Alternative Conceptualization," *Journal of Marketing* 39 (October 1975), pp. 1–6.

[32]Mary Lou Roberts and Lawrence Wortzel, "New Life-Style Determinants of Women's Food Shopping Behavior," *Journal of Marketing* 43 (Summer 1979), pp. 28–39.

[33]Joel R. Evans and Barry Berman, *Marketing* (New York: Macmillan, 1982), p. 119.

[34]Cohen, "An Interpersonal Orientation," pp. 270–78.

[35]Marvin A. Jolson, Rolph E. Anderson, and Nancy J. Leber, "Profiles of Signature Goods Consumers and Avoiders," *Journal of Retailing* 57 (Winter 1981), pp. 19–38.

[36]Everett M. Rogers, *The Diffusion of Innovations* (New York: Free Press, 1962), pp. 281–86. See also: Everett M. Rogers, "New Product Adoption and Diffusion," *Journal of Consumer Research* 2 (March 1976), pp. 290–301.

[37]Thomas S. Robertson, "The Process of Innovation and the Diffusion of Innovation," *Journal of Marketing* 31 (January 1967), pp. 15–16.

[38]Much of the material in this section is based on the work of Everett M. Rogers and subsequent studies made by other researchers.

[39]Fred W. Morgan, Jr., "Are Early Triers Heavy Users?" *Journal of Business* 52 (July 1979), pp. 429–34.

[40]John O. Summers, "Media Exposure Patterns of Consumer Innovators," *Journal of Marketing* 36 (January 1972), pp. 43–49.

[41]Philip Kotler and Gerald Daltman, "Targeting Prospects for A New Product," *Journal of Advertising Research* 16 (February 1976), p. 16.

[42]Kenneth Uhl, Roman Andrus, and Lance Poulsen, "How Are Laggards Different? An Empirical Inquiry," *Journal of Marketing Research* 7 (February 1970), pp. 51–54.

[43]The importance of impersonal sources (television and other mass media) in furthering public awareness of new products cannot be overemphasized. See: William V. Muse and Robert J. Kegerreis, "New Product Awareness and Purchasing Behavior," *Marquette Business Review* 16 (Spring 1972), pp. 19–27.

CHAPTER 8

BUYER BEHAVIOR: ADDITIONAL INSIGHTS

Your Study Objectives

After you have studied this chapter, you will understand:

1. The meaning of culture and its significance with regard to consumer behavior.
2. The social class structure in the United States.
3. What subcultures are and some characteristics of several major American subcultures.
4. The influence of reference groups on the individual.
5. The stages of the family life cycle along with their implications for retailers.
6. Some useful methods for segmenting consumer markets.

In Chapter 7, you were introduced to the psychology of the American consumer. Insights were provided into Maslow's hierarchy of human needs, and several theories of learning were explained. You learned how to distinguish among rational, emotional, and other types of motives. We identified the various functions served by human attitudes. You were shown how new products and new ideas *diffuse* through our society and how people come to adopt these innovations. We also discussed the significance of the individual's self-concept.

This chapter will further your knowledge of consumers. You will learn the meaning of *culture* and how it affects our behavior. Some of the fundamental values that permeate our society will be described. You will be given insights into the lifestyles and consumption behavior of families and persons in each of six social classes along with implications for retail companies. The concept of American *subcultures* is introduced. You will learn about the pervasive influences exerted on our behavior by family, friends, and other *reference groups*. Details will be provided regarding the stages that a typical American family goes through during its *life cycle*. You will learn how companies select specific consumer *segments* at which to target their marketing activities. Finally, you will be introduced to a number of useful segmentation techniques.

Cultural Influences on Buyer Behavior

Each of us comes into this world preprogrammed, as it were, with a wide, individualized spectrum of traits and capacities for development. We enter equipped with inherited characteristics and propensities. We are then affected by our environment. We are all products of the culture in which we are reared. We learn beliefs, opinions, attitudes, and values. Most of our day-to-day behavior is also learned, including our shopping behavior.

Culture has been defined as "the complex of values, ideas, attitudes, and other meaningful symbols created by people to shape human behavior and the artifacts of that behavior, transmitted from one generation to the next."[1] We are strongly influenced by our customs and ways of doing things, the many norms of society, laws and regulations, and family, schools, religions, and other societal institutions. When we eat our meals, the kinds of foods we eat, the kinds of clothes we wear, and our methods of transportation are all part and parcel of our American culture. So are the apartments or homes we live in, the newspapers and magazines we read, the televisions and radios we listen to, the buildings where we work or attend school, and countless more artifacts.

Our culture decrees our common tongue, our political structure, and our competitive system of free enterprise. It also establishes limits, or boundaries, within which nearly all of us think and act.[2]

Part of our American culture.

Courtesy Popeyes Famous Fried Chicken and Biscuits, Inc., Jefferson (New Orleans), LA

Some Basic American Values

Apparently, a number of fundamental values are held by a majority of consumers in the United States.[3] A few of these are mentioned below:

1. Freedom appears to be an essential component of the American mystique. We must feel free to practice whatever religion we choose and to say what we wish to say. We want to make up our own minds about where we will live, work, shop, or play. We want to wear the kinds of clothes we prefer. We are convinced that we possess an inherent right to life, liberty, and the pursuit of happiness.
2. Equality is a value we hold dear and one that is almost a corollary of the first. We accept the equality of all persons in the eyes of government, the law, institutions, and other people.
3. Materialism prompts us to seek to acquire luxuries in addition to necessities. We buy products and services that enhance our self-image. We equate comfort and success with material possessions, especially those that we believe reflect our accomplishments. Hand in hand with this outlook goes a fascination with technology and new products.
4. Hedonism, a search for pleasure and the good life, characterizes much of the population. We want immediate gratification and rewards and are reluctant to defer satisfaction until some future date. We assign a high priority to our leisure time.
5. Work itself, in our eyes, carries its own reward. We value the work we do and we covet job success.

6. Our religiousness leads most of us to maintain strong moral and ethical qualities and to believe in a Supreme Being.
7. An infatuation with youth pervades the nation. TV programs and commercials, print advertising, movies, and published fiction stress youthfulness, rather than age. Consumers seek products that demonstrate their affinity with youth and that show they are "in" with the crowd. They buy items that enhance their appearances and enable them to follow more relaxed, natural lifestyles. They try to balance exercise and rest, follow a proper diet, and generally maintain their physical well-being.

Social Class   Most societies are stratified into relatively large groups of individuals and families whose members tend to think, live, and behave rather similarly. Persons in each group, or **social class,** regard those who belong to other groups as being of higher or lower **status,** a term applied to rank or position within the entire social system. Ordinarily, members of one class do not move easily into another, and interaction between members of different classes is often restricted. Social classes are "relatively permanent and homogeneous divisions in a society into which individuals sharing similar values, lifestyles, interests, and behavior can be categorized."[4] Persons of the same social class tend to hold similar attitudes and interests. They are also inclined to behave in much the same manner. This applies to their shopping orientations

Today's consumers seek to keep physically fit.

Courtesy Elaine Powers Figure Salons, Inc., Milwaukee, WI

and behavior as well.[5] Product and brand preferences and even consumers' choice of stores to patronize may be influenced by their social class backgrounds.[6]

Perceivable differences in shopping behavior that may be attributed to social status are of interest to retailers as well as to other marketers. Store organizations can put such knowledge to use in devising their own retailing mix. People of lower status, for example, often patronize stores where credit is readily available or shop at discount houses and off-price outlets. Higher-status individuals prefer to visit specialty stores of better reputation and quality department stores. Members of one social class may purchase homes, furniture, draperies, household appliances, clothing, cars, and many other products of a higher or lower quality than those bought by persons from another class background.

Warner's Social Class Structure

Perhaps the best-known analysis of our society is by W. Lloyd Warner. In his study of the modern community, the famed sociologist described six social classes. These are listed below with his estimate of the percentage of the population falling into each class.

Class	Percentage of Community
Upper-Upper	1.44%
Lower-Upper	1.56
Upper-Middle	10.22
Lower-Middle	28.12
Upper-Lower	32.60
Lower-Lower	25.22

Warner could not place about 0.84 percent of the people in any specific class. He noted, however, that these unknowns were definitely not in the two upper classes.[7]

Table 8.1 describes some of the characteristics of people in each of the six classes and gives current estimates of their respective membership totals.

Subcultures in America

Large numbers of American consumers share reasonably similar beliefs, opinions, values, attitudes, and even behavioral tendencies. Such persons may be regarded as belonging to specific subgroups, or **subcultures,** within the larger society. These subcultures may be based on demographic differences like race, nationality, age, or religion. Or they may have evolved simply because of regional differences, that is to say, because of variations in climate and other environmental factors.

Higher-status consumers usually prefer to shop at better stores.

Courtesy Neiman-Marcus, Dallas, TX

Table 8.1 The American social class structure				
Class Designation	**Estimated Percentage of Population**	**Representative Members**	**Distinguishing Lifestyle Characteristics**	**Insights into Shopping Behavior**
Upper-Upper	0.3% to 0.5%	Socially prominent persons, people with inherited wealth and highest community status, members of Social Register.	Live in large, expensive homes in exclusive areas. May own two or more homes. Homes are furnished with expensive furniture, antiques, and art objects. Well educated at the best schools and universities, these people live graciously. They demonstrate community leadership in civic, charitable, and cultural affairs. Many are art patrons. Conscious of their breeding, they protect and uphold their families' reputations.	Upper-Uppers shop at the best stores, wear fine though conservative clothes, buy jewelry, antiques, paintings, and other art. With little need to be concerned over costs, they may travel extensively and vacation often.

Table 8.1   *(continued)*

Class Designation	Estimated Percentage of Population	Representative Members	Distinguishing Lifestyle Characteristics	Insights into Shopping Behavior
Lower-Upper	1.5% to 2%	Newly rich families and persons who have acquired considerable wealth, owners of large businesses, top corporation executives.	Reside in fine homes in better neighborhoods. Home decor and furnishings reflect conspicuous use of wealth. Active both socially and in civic affairs. Characterized by a strong drive for success in their careers. They covet higher social status.	Lower-Uppers shop at the better stores, buying expensive merchandise like designer clothing originals, jewelry, fine silverware. They are most apt to purchase luxury cars, swimming pools, small planes, yachts, and other publicly consumed or socially visible luxuries.
Upper-Middle	10% to 12%	Owners of medium-sized enterprises; high income–earning lawyers, architects, physicians, and other professionals; star sales producers; young executives on their way to the top of large corporations.	Live in good homes in good areas. These are home- and child-centered people. They are oriented toward the future, have a strong interest in higher education, and work toward accumulating more wealth. They have broad interests, are civic-minded, and attend symphonies, concerts, and the theater. Frequently, they belong to golf or country clubs.	An excellent market for many expensive status symbols and higher-priced automobiles. They buy quality clothing, invest in securities, spend more on appliances and furniture, and save for college educations for their children.
Lower-Middle	29% to 33%	Store and other small business owners; white-collar workers: office employees, technicians, teachers, civil service workers, and so on; factory supervisors and skilled factory employees.	Occupy modest homes in nice neighborhoods and try to keep these residences clean and in good order. These people are good citizens who work hard at living respectably. They are conservative, churchgoing, and tradition oriented.	Along with members of the next class, they constitute the mass market for most goods and services. They buy at stores with wide appeal. Careful when shopping to compare prices and quality. Purchase good clothes and nondesigner furniture.
Upper-Lower	40% to 44%	Blue-collar or working-class, persons: construction workers, bus drivers, train conductors, semiskilled factory workers, retail	Reside in less expensive areas in rented apartments or small houses, some of which may be in need of repair. These persons are not as likely as those	Shop more than higher classes at discount houses and promotional department stores. Spend less than middle-class people on clothing,

Class Designation	Estimated Percentage of Population	Representative Members	Distinguishing Lifestyle Characteristics	Insights into Shopping Behavior
		store employees, union workers, service workers.	of higher classes to prepare for their children's college education. Nor are they much interested in keeping up with the Joneses. They try to enjoy life and its comforts day by day, although they strive for security. Many are sports enthusiasts. They join fraternal organizations, go bowling, play cards, and enjoy watching TV.	travel, higher education, and services. Active market for sporting goods and equipment. They purchase national brands and use credit extensively.
Lower-Lower	17% to 20%	Migrant farm workers, domestics, dishwashers, laborers, and other unskilled workers; welfare families, the sporadically unemployed, unassimilated ethnic group members.	Live in small apartments in poorer areas, often in slums. Their residences are poorly furnished and frequently not well maintained. These persons are below average in number of years of schooling. Living from one day to the next, they lack drive or ambition. Usually, they hold a fatalistic attitude toward life.	Purchase few luxury products. Most of their income goes for food, clothing, rent, utilities, and other necessities of life. Purchase second-hand cars, used furniture (or new furniture on the installment plan), and less expensive clothes.

Sources: This discussion based on and expanded from: W. Lloyd Warner and Paul S. Lunt, *The Social Life of a Modern Community* (New Haven, Conn.: Yale University Press, 1941); Leon Schiffman and Leslie Lazar Kanuk, *Consumer Behavior* (Englewood Cliffs, N.J.: Prentice-Hall, 1978), pp. 310–14; James F. Engel, Roger D. Blackwell, and David T. Kollat, *Consumer Behavior*, 3d ed. (Hinsdale, Ill.: Dryden Press, 1978), pp. 125–37; Pierre D. Martineau, "Social Classes and Spending Behavior," *Journal of Marketing* 23 (October 1958), pp. 121–30; W. Lloyd Warner, Marchia Meeker, and Kenneth Eels, *Social Class in America* (Chicago: Science Research Associates, 1949), pp. 11–21.

Thus, we recognize differences among the black, Oriental, and Native American subcultures. We observe distinctions in communal outlooks among those of Latin-American descent, Italians, Greeks, Polish, and other nationality groups. Cultural values vary, too, among Protestants, Roman Catholics, and Jews.

Subcultures have been more than amply documented in the sociologi-

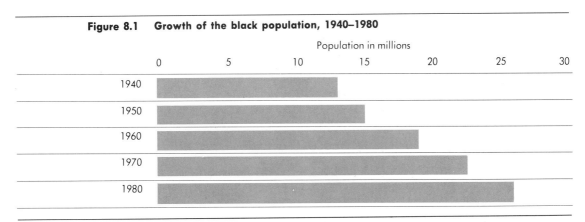

Figure 8.1   Growth of the black population, 1940–1980

Note: Figures through 1960 exclude Alaska and Hawaii.
Source: U.S. Department of Commerce, Bureau of the Census, *Statistical Abstract of the United States, 1984,* 104th ed. (Washington, D.C.: U.S. Government Printing Office, 1983), p. 32.

cal and business literatures. Consequently, only a few are briefly considered here because of their possible interest to some retailing companies.

The Black Subculture   Population statistics regarding the nation's largest ethnic group appear in Figure 8.1. The 26.5 million black residents in 1980 constituted nearly 12 percent of our population. Their growth rate is substantially higher than that of the general population. Blacks account for nearly one half (or more) of the residents of such major cities as Newark, Baltimore, Atlanta, and Washington.

In recent years, the education gap between blacks and other Americans appears to be closing more rapidly. As indicated in Figure 8.2, slightly more than 7 out of every 100 black adults age 25 or older possessed high school diplomas in 1940. This represented less than one third of the rate enjoyed by the population at large. By 1980, the picture was far more favorable—the percentage of black graduates had increased more than sevenfold. Blacks have also made strides in higher education, although the picture here is not quite as rosy. In 1980, only 7.9 percent of black adults had completed four years of college or more, less than half the rate of the overall population.

Figure 8.3 shows median household income statistics for a few selected years. In 1982, the median income for black households came to $11,968, a frustrating 43 percent below that of their white counterparts and only about four fifths of the median income of households headed by persons of Hispanic origin.

Research has yielded a number of interesting insights into black shopping and consumption behavior. Research seems to contradict the belief held by some investigators that race is not a viable way to

Figure 8.2   Levels of educational attainment among adults 25 years of age and older

A. Percentages of adult population who have completed high school

Year	Black adults	All adults
1940	7.3%	24.5%
1950	12.9%	34.3%
1960	20.1%	41.1%
1970	31.4%	52.3%
1980	51.2%	68.6%

B. Percentages of adult population with four years of college and more

Year	Black adults	All adults
1940	1.3%	4.6%
1950	2.1%	6.2%
1960	3.1%	7.7%
1970	4.4%	10.7%
1980	7.9%	17.0%

Black adults
All adults

Source: U.S. Department of Commerce, Bureau of the Census, *Statistical Abstract of the United States, 1984,* 104th ed. (Washington, D.C.: U.S. Government Printing Office, 1983), p. 144.

segment markets for some product classes or to segment consumers by their brand choice or shopping behavior.[8] Several findings are listed below:

1. Blacks are more innovative with respect to apparel, and black women are more fashion conscious.[9]
2. When compared to their white counterparts, black consumers spend proportionately more on clothing, personal care, home furnishings, tobacco, alcohol, and socially visible items—and proportionately less on food, medical care, and transportation.[10]

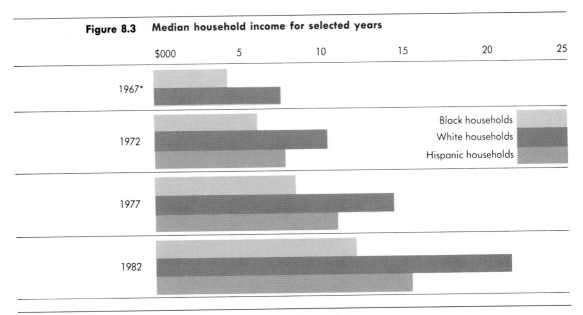

Figure 8.3   Median household income for selected years

* Median income of Hispanic households not available.
Source: U.S. Department of Commerce, Bureau of the Census, *Statistical Abstract of the United States, 1984,* 104th ed. (Washington, D.C.: U.S. Government Printing Office, 1983), p. 459.

3. Price levels are important to the store patronage decisions of college-age blacks. Such operating characteristics of retail firms as local newspaper and radio advertising, credit availability, nationally advertised brands, and black employees also significantly influence black patronage.[11]
4. A greater proportion of blacks visit discount houses more often than department stores.[12]

The Spanish Subculture   Second largest of the minorities after the black population, the Spanish subculture is comprised of more than 14 million people. It is our largest subculture based on nationality. Included are about 8.7 million persons of Mexican heritage, 2 million of Puerto Rican origin, .8 million Cubans, and another 3 million from other Latin-American countries and Spain. These consumers are concentrated geographically, and their numbers grow each year by approximately 1 million. As you can see in Table 8.2, Mexicans constitute the largest percentage. Over 6 million reside in California and Texas. Puerto Ricans are heavily concentrated in New York, and nearly 500,000 Cubans live in Florida.

Differences in the national distribution of income levels that same year among white, black, and Hispanic households are shown in Figure 8.4.

| Table 8.2 States with largest concentrations of persons of Hispanic heritage | Total Hispanic Population (000) | Country of Heritage | | | |
State		Mexico (000)	Puerto Rico (000)	Cuba (000)	All Others (000)
California	4,544	3,637	93	61	753
Texas	2,986	2,752	23	14	196
New York	1,659	39	986	77	557
Florida	858	79	95	470	214

Source: U.S. Department of Commerce, Bureau of the Census, *Statistical Abstract of the United States, 1984,* 104th ed. (Washington, D.C.: U.S. Government Printing Office, 1983), p. 40.

Subcultures Based on Age

Marketing practitioners frequently regard consumers who belong to different age categories as members of distinct subcultures. Examples include teenagers, young adults, and senior citizens. The young adult category may be broken down into two groups: young, single persons and young marrieds. Teenagers have their own particular culture. Much has been written about the characteristics of this group and its potential for the marketing of certain goods and services.[13]

Figure 8.4   National distribution of household incomes, 1982

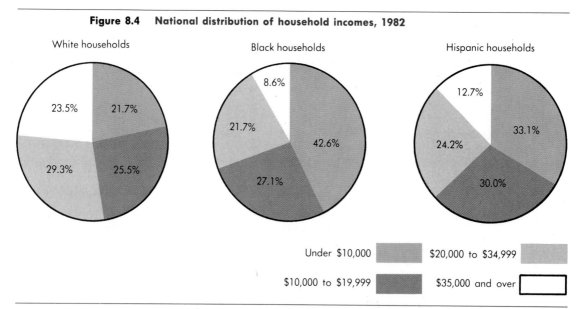

Source: Adapted from U.S. Department of Commerce, Bureau of the Census, *Statistical Abstract of the United States, 1984,* 104th ed. (Washington, D.C.: U.S. Government Printing Office, 1983), p. 460.

Some retailers can market successfully to all age subcultures.

Courtesy Baskin-Robbins Ice Cream, Burbank, CA

The Senior Citizen Subculture

To date, retailers have not reacted emphatically enough to the sales potential of the senior citizen market. Some have made tentative overtures to the over-65 age group by offering discounts on merchandise. Such discounts may be offered at all times or on one day a week.

In 1960, 16.7 million seniors were living in the United States. By 1980, the total had reached 25.5 million. Their ranks are expected to swell over the next several decades and the business sector will increasingly feel their demands.[14] Although the majority of seniors are retired and living on lowered incomes, they still represent an attractive market. People in this age bracket purchase a wide range of products and services in addition to the basic food, clothing, and shelter. They may also spend proportionately more than other age groups on health care and medicines and on travel and recreation.

Retailers can appeal more strongly to senior citizens by offering discounts on merchandise and services, having salespeople treat such shoppers attentively and patiently, providing assistance in locating merchandise, delivering goods to customers' homes, and enlarging print on price tags.[15] Larger stores can provide rest areas or lounges, expand and promote telephone shopping, and sponsor free or low-cost bus transportation.[16]

The complex senior citizen market is worthy of close study by retailers. Seniors cannot be treated as a single, homogeneous market. As an example, different social classes may be represented in this population.[17] Similarly, different lifestyles can be found. As a case in point, an analysis of elderly consumers in upstate New York revealed three different groupings: (1) Traditionalists—conservative people who resist rapid change and hold strong moral and religious beliefs, (2) Outgoers—socially active people who are concerned about their community and who travel extensively, and (3) isolationists—often unhappy seniors who appear to be withdrawn.[18]

Reference Groups

We do not live in a vacuum. From infancy on, all of us wend our way through the social maturation process under the influence of the many people we come in contact with. These include parents, siblings, aunts, uncles, cousins, neighbors, friends, schoolmates, teachers, and those with whom we work and play. Also included are members of the church we attend, the political party to which we subscribe, our social organizations, and so on. These **reference groups** we belong to as we travel through life serve as frames of reference that condition our ways of thinking and behaving. They play a significant role in attitude formation, the development of value systems, and the molding of opinions and beliefs. Small or large, such groups maintain norms and standards for their members. In turn, these normalize and standardize our own behavior.[19]

Groups we must deal with face to face are **primary groups.** They can have a profound effect on our behavior including our shopping behavior. From these primary groups we receive information and support. They influence us in our choice of clothing, home furnishings, leisure time activities, and the like. They exercise considerable direction on our consumer decision making.

The Family

In the process of acculturation, the family is the most powerful of all primary reference groups. The family household represents a controlled environment. Our parents are the predominant force in shaping not only how we determine right from wrong but our very ways of thinking and doing. From them and other members of our immediate, or nuclear, family we learn rules and guidelines, constraints and actions permitted, likes and dislikes. The family's pervasive influence conditions our eventual consumption behavior.[20]

The family, long recognized as an earning unit, is also a buying unit. For the young family, the bulk of purchasing activity is typically accomplished by the wife. Some buying decisions are made by both spouses acting in concert; others are made by either one independently. Still others involve input from the children. Some evidence exists that the changing female role in the United States is associated with changing buyer behavior. The husbands of more liberal women participate less frequently in purchase decisions than do those of conservative women.[21]

The Family Life Cycle

Sociologists and marketing analysts alike have long been entranced by the changes in consumption behavior that take place over the lifetime of the family unit. As the nuclear family undergoes major transformations household needs also change. Events such as the young adult moving out of the household, marriage, childbearing, and widowhood cause distinct changes in shopping orientation and behavior. The **family life cycle** is a generalization of the several phases of a typical American family. A popular conceptualization of this cycle is presented in Table 8.3.

**Table 8.3
The family life cycle**

Stage	Characteristics and Implications
Single Stage	In what is actually a prefamily stage, the young single person leaves home and family to take up residence elsewhere. Most single people rent apartments or share a residence with one or more peers. Earnings are typically quite low. These consumers will purchase basic home furnishings, radios and television sets, and perhaps a stereo. Single people buy fashionable clothes, frequent both fast-food and sit-down restaurants, are active socially, and spend on recreation and dating activity. They may also buy a car.
Newly Married Stage	The single person marries, and the young couple moves into their own apartment or modest home. Because they are setting up housekeeping, these couples are excellent prospects for many types of merchandise: bedroom and living-room furniture; dishes, pots, pans, and silverware; curtains, drapes, and floor coverings; lamps, stereos, and other household furnishings; toasters, irons, vacuum cleaners, and other appliances; and perhaps a refrigerator, stove, dishwasher, or other major appliance. They may be expected to spend on apparel for both partners, purchase a car, and devote some of their earnings to leisure time activities and vacationing. Finances are often tight. Nowadays, though, both husband and wife may be employed so the household budget may not be as stringent as yesteryear's.
Full Nest I Stage	This early parenthood stage is initiated by the birth of the couple's first child. Usually it extends from 6 to 10 years or more, depending on how many children the couple has. Hospital costs and the substantial expense of raising children contribute to the financial pressures felt by the spouses. They may find their total income insufficient to manage well and may be unable to set money aside in a savings account. Frequently, one income is lost because the mother remains at home for the first few years after the baby arrives. Full Nest I families are in the market for many types of goods, among them: baby carriages, strollers, cribs, children's furniture, infants and children's apparel, baby food, diapers, toys, tricycles, and cough medicines. Because of home constraints, the spouses have less leisure time available. However, they will enjoy occasional

Table 8.3 **(continued)**	**Stage**	**Characteristics and Implications**
		outings and short trips. In addition to carrying car and homeowners' insurance, the couple may purchase life insurance to protect the family against untoward loss. Often, too, they will put a down payment on a house, moving into it from their first apartment.
	Full Nest II Stage	When the youngest child reaches the age of six the family progresses automatically into the second full nest phase. By this time, one or more of the children may have reached adolescence. Since the children are for the most part able to take care of themselves, many of the mothers in this stage go back to work. Finances continue to improve, and more disposable income is available. Typically, these families begin to replace some furniture, old appliances, and TV sets with newer models. They buy food, laundry detergents, and other household supplies in larger, family-sized packages. They spend considerable sums on both children's and adults' apparel, bicycles, dance or music lessons, dental braces, and so on. The couple may send one or more of the youngsters to summer camp or enroll them in parochial or private schools. They set money aside to pay for their children's higher education. Some Full Nest II families purchase a larger house because the children are old enough to require separate rooms.
	Full Nest III Stage	Now the parents are older—in their late 30s or early 40s. While one or more dependent children may remain at home, others may be away at college or may have already left the household. The couple's earnings are approaching their peak, and their financial situation is usually excellent. The children may earn money baby-sitting, delivering newspapers, or working after school in a local store. During this stage, home improvements may be made. The spouses purchase more luxury goods: jewelry, more expensive furniture, better clothing, a higher-priced car, and perhaps a boat. They spend more on longer vacations and travel.
	Empty Nest I Stage	This stage is triggered when the last child leaves the household. For the first time in many years, the couple find themselves alone in an empty nest. By now the two may have reached their late 40s or early 50s. Family earnings are typically at their highest in this postparenthood phase. More disposable funds are available, and the two are able to save a larger proportion of their income than ever before. They may contribute to charitable organizations, entertain and seek to be entertained, spend considerable sums on recreation, take longer vacations, and travel more extensively. As the years pass, the two will express more interest in maintaining physical and mental well-being. Watching their weight, exercising, and trying to balance work and play become important concerns. In addition to purchasing more luxury products, the spouses may be in the market for appropriate apparel for vacationing and travel, exercise bikes and similar equipment, vitamin supplements, and a higher-priced car.

Table 8.3 (concluded)	Stage	Characteristics and Implications
	Empty Nest II Stage	The retirement of the household head marks the start of the Empty Nest II stage. As couples push through their 50s into their sixth decade, they become even more concerned about their health. Natural physical changes can be expected. More income may have to be diverted to health care, drugs and medicines, and perhaps medical appliances. With retirement, family income drops sharply, and the two attempt to adhere to a more stringent budget than they have lived with for many years. They spend proportionately less on clothing, entertainment, and travel. They buy food and household supplies in smaller packages. They purchase products that aid digestion and sleep. Some are better off financially, having already paid off their home mortgage. Others, who no longer desire to maintain a large house, sell the property to recover their equity. They may rent an apartment, buy a smaller home, or purchase a cooperative residence or condominium. Many elect to move to a warmer climate. These major moves necessitate new furniture, home furnishings, lighter clothing, and changes in leisure time activities.
		Of course, not all household heads retire at the customary retirement age of 65. Some continue working well into their 70s and even beyond. In such situations, the couple continues an extended Empty Nest I existence, enjoying a relatively good income.
	Solitary Survivor Stage	Inevitably one spouse dies, leaving the other alone in the household. This stage may be broken down still further into the Solitary Survivor, Employed and Solitary Survivor, Retired stages. Those who still work find that they can manage their affairs quite well so long as they remain physically and mentally able. Retired survivors, however, must frequently find ways of living adequately well below their customary standards. If income is still produced, the survivor may spend on handicrafts and hobby supplies, more sedentary forms of recreation, and occasional travel. Because they need to buy for only one person, their shopping patterns change considerably. They take advantage of senior citizen discounts where offered and continue to provide for their health needs.

Source: This discussion based on and expanded from: William D. Wells and George Gubar, "Life Cycle Concept in Marketing Research," *Journal of Marketing Research* 3 (November 1966), pp. 355–63. Reprinted with permission from the American Marketing Association.

An Alternate Profile   Although the majority of families appear to conform to the life-cycle pattern described in Table 8.3, millions of other people deviate from the pattern. Divorced people of all ages are an example. So are unmarried people, younger widows and widowers, married couples that remain childless, and others.[22]

Alternate life-cycle approaches have been proposed that take into consideration the changing dynamics of the American family: the rising divorce rate, couples divorcing at younger ages, the millions of unmarried people who live together, and so on. One fairly recent attempt at embracing these divergent situations is the modernized family life cycle proposed by Murphy and Staples.[23] They suggest a cycle containing five distinct stages. These are listed below, along with their estimates of the percentage of the total population that fall into each stage:

Stage of Life Cycle	Estimated Percentage
Young single persons	8.2%
Young married persons, no children	2.9
Other young persons	19.1
Middle-aged persons	45.4
Older persons	7.2
All other persons	17.2
Total population	100.2%

Murphy and Staples identify the young single persons phase as beginning at about the time of high school graduation or at age 18. They subdivide the other young persons designation into divorced without children, divorced with children, and married persons with children. Under the all other persons label are grouped all adults and children not accounted for by the family life-cycle stages.

Market Segmentation: Selecting Consumer Targets

American consumers now number in excess of 230 million, with their ranks increasing by several million each year. Fulfilling their needs and wants requires the studied attention of manufacturers, distributors, and service organizations. These companies must select appropriate strategies and tactics. To be able to enter the marketplace, survive, and grow, every firm that sells to consumers needs to select an overall operational strategy. In our economy, a company generally resorts to one of three distinct strategic approaches: (1) undifferentiated, (2) concentrated, or (3) differentiated marketing.

The firm that chooses an **undifferentiated marketing** approach regards the entire consumer market as holding sales potential. It seeks to market products and/or services that the vast majority of consumers can use or will buy. It makes no attempt to pinpoint specific subgroups at which to target its marketing activity. Manufacturers of such products as table salt, electric light bulbs, antifreeze, or laundry bleach follow an undifferentiated strategy. Few retail organizations do. Most retailers realize that they cannot sell their merchandise and/or services to all consumers. A grocery store is an example of a retailer that follows the undifferentiated approach.

A diametrically opposed strategy is **concentrated marketing.** Here, the firm takes aim at only one part, or segment, of the 230-million-strong consumer market. The company will research the segment in depth to discover all it can about the members. Following the study phase, it then creates a marketing mix to effectively reach those persons or organizations and accomplish sales at a profit. Among the types of retail firms that employ a concentrated strategy are ski shops in mountain resorts, ladies' dress outlets that offer half sizes, and mail order specialty firms.

Finally, companies that choose **differentiated marketing** seek out two or more large groups of potential buyers. They then prepare suitable marketing mixes to satisfy these buyers' demands. Essentially both differentiated and concentrated marketing are forms of **market segmentation.** The only difference between the two is that, under the latter approach, only a single target market is selected. Segmentation strategies are quite common in the retail sector. They are used by retailers of family apparel, sporting goods outlets, department stores, and many other types.

Segmenting Markets A viable segment, or target group, is readily identifiable, has the money to buy, and has the potential for appreciable sales volume. Moreover, the firm should be able to reach and market to that segment easily. Segmentation approaches give a company a clear concept of just who the potential buyers are and what they are like.

Markets can be segmented in various ways. A common approach is to identify the characteristics of prospective customers by analyzing available population data by specific categories. Where consumers are located, their sex, age group, income level, what social class or subculture they belong to, and many other categories may be employed. Or segmentation can be accomplished by using product-related variables: the benefits people look for when they purchase particular merchandise, the extent to which they use a product, the appeal of certain brands, and so on.[24]

Geographic Segmentation Perhaps the earliest approach of all, **geographic segmentation,** involves targeting groups of prospects in one of more specific areas of the country. A manufacturer of room air conditioners, for example, might concentrate on marketing only to households in the southern half of the nation, where the climate is more conducive to the use of such equipment. A hardware store located in southern California, Louisiana, or Florida would not be expected to carry snow throwers in its line

Americans who live in one region of the United States often display consumption behavior that is quite distinct from that of people who reside in other areas. For example, a large proportion of West Coast residents take their coffee black, while those who live on the East Coast prefer milk in their coffee. Southerners "spend the most of all regions on personal care, home operation, and utilities as well as a higher proportion on home furnishings and equipment." They "also consume more cereals, fats and oils, and dried fruits and pork" while Westerners "eat less starches and sweets, and less poultry."[25]

Here are some additional examples of regional differences among consumers:

1. Easterners are more likely than persons of most regions to go bowling and least likely to be thinking of buying life insurance.
2. Southerners are most likely to own a freezer, to drink iced tea, and to use mouthwash and cologne.
3. Westerners report the highest level of consumption of cottage cheese and yogurt, vitamin tablets, domestic wines (frequently with dinner), and regular but not instant coffee.
4. Southwesterners share with their Western neighbors a penchant for time-saving appliances (dishwashers and disposals) and bank credit cards. . . . They exceed the Westerners' dislike for instant coffee.[26]

Demographic Segmentation Most frequently used of all segmenting approaches by marketers is **demographic segmentation.** The term *demography* refers to the study of population statistics in terms of sex, age, marital status, income, occupation, family size, educational level, and the like. All of these factors may be related to consumption behavior. (We presented some demographic data in Chapter 3.) Large quantities of such information are made available by the U.S. Bureau of the Census and other government agencies and by businesses and other organizations.

You may recall a time when you purchased some type of appliance: a toaster oven, radio, steam iron, videocassette recorder, or home computer. Enclosed in the carton was a warranty card to be completed by the buyer and returned to the manufacturer. This registers the purchase and renders the warranty effective. A typical card asks not only for information about the purchase but also requests demographic data, such as the buyer's sex, age, and income. The producer tabulates and analyzes all information collected on the cards to better understand the kinds of people who are most apt to use the particular product.

In recent years, some firms have experimented with an interesting new segmenting technique that combines both geographic and demographic information. Known as geodemography, the method can furnish companies with "more precise information about their target markets and how best to reach them."[27] Census data and ZIP codes are used. The approach works well because people with similiar demographics and lifestyles tend to cluster in similar neighborhoods.

Benefit Segmentation A classic study during the 1960s segmented toothpaste buyers according to the benefits they sought in purchasing the product.[28] Using **benefit segmentation,** four distinct consumer target groups were identified: (1) Sensories—persons who principally looked for flavor, (2) Sociables—those who sought bright, or white, teeth, (3) Worriers—individuals who used toothpaste to prevent cavities, and (4) Independents—those who selected the product mainly for its price. Demographic and behavioral characteristics for members of each of the four segments can be seen in Table 8.4. The study's findings held significant implications for the toothpaste industry. They provided direction for media selection as well as other facets of promotion such as advertising, copywriting, and packaging.

Value Segmentation A close relative of the benefit approach is **value segmentation,** the targeting of sizable market segments according to the values that buyers hold with regard to the products or services they desire. In the early 1960s, Timex made a thorough investigation of the domestic watch market. The company then proceeded to carve out—and successfully sell to—two major segments that competitive watch manufacturers had been largely ignoring. One segment consisted of consumers who valued watches for their quality and durability; the other was comprised of people interested in purchasing a reliable and serviceable timepiece at a reasonable price.[29]

Value segmentation has been applied to products such as hair care items, adding machines, perfumes, cars, and many others. With regard to soft goods retailing to women, the market breaks down into four groups according to the conceptions of value that women hold:

Table 8.4   Segmenting the toothpaste market

Segment Name / Characteristics	The Sensories	The Sociables	The Worriers	The Independents
Principal benefit sought	Flavor, product appearance	Brightness of teeth	Decay prevention	Price
Demographic strengths	Children	Teens, young people	Large families	Men
Special behavioral characteristics	Users of spearmint flavored toothpaste	Smokers	Heavy users	Heavy users
Brands disproportionately favored	Colgate, Stripe	Macleans, Plus White, Ultra Brite	Crest	Brands on sale
Personality characteristics	High self-involvement	High sociability	High hypochon-driasis	High autonomy
Lifestyle characteristics	Hedonistic	Active	Conservative	Value-oriented

Source: Russell I. Haley, "Benefit Segmentation: A Decision-Oriented Research Tool," *Journal of Marketing* 32 (July 1968), p. 33. Reprinted with permission from the American Marketing Association.

1. A willingness to pay a little more for quality.
2. Merchandise on sale.
3. Value in terms of the lowest possible price.
4. Seconds or discounted merchandise.[30]

An unusual variation of the technique suggests that markets can be segmented by regional, rather than national, values since values are culturally or socially learned. This might be of importance to manufacturers in positioning their products, in selecting brand names or designs for packages, and in promoting products.[31]

Combining two or more segmentation approaches often defines the target market more clearly. A combination of demographic and benefit or value segmentation can frequently be productive. Combinations may also be accomplished with still other segmentation approaches, such as psychographics or usage segmentation.[32]

Psychographic Segmentation Early in the 1970s, experimentation with an array of psychologically based segmentation technique created a stir in marketing circles. Researchers investigated personality characteristics like independence, extroversion, and aggressiveness. They looked into various facets of consumer lifestyles, attitudes, interests, and opinions. The entire area under investigation was labeled psychographics. **Psychographics** has been defined as "quantitative research intended to place consumers on psychological—as distinguished from demographic—dimensions."[33] For several years, the methods remained relatively unknown not only within the corporate world but even among creative supervisors in large advertising agencies.[34]

A much-discussed psychographic method is **lifestyle segmentation.** Most often, it requires the use of a lengthy list of AIO statements. The initials stand for Activities, Interests, Opinions. Examples of the lifestyle dimensions explored are shown in Table 8.5. Respondents are asked to indicate their agreement or disagreement with the statements. The method has proved useful in furnishing portraits of consumer groups to be targeted for marketing purposes.[35] In one application, women shopping for an apparel item were segmented into five different groups according to their lifestyles: fashionable, conservative, brand-conscious, outgoing, and home-price oriented shoppers.[36]

Other Approaches Other useful possibilities are available for segmenting consumer markets. For example, there is the popular **usage-rate segmentation.** The procedure is based on the likelihood that, in any packaged consumer product market, a relatively small percentage of buyers consume a large share of the product.[37] For example, proportionately few beer drinkers are responsible for a large percentage of the beer purchased in this country. In using this approach, marketers assign consumers to categories based on their rate of product usage: heavy,

Consumption behavior changes as the family life cycle evolves, enabling this service retailer to market to several lifestyle segments.

Courtesy Kampgrounds of America, Inc.

moderate, light, or nonusers. The technique has been used in conjunction with psychographic segmentation to measure homemaker shopping orientations.[38]

Consumer loyalty, whether to products, brands, or stores, is yet another variable that shows promise. Groups can be segmented on the basis of the strength of their loyalty or lack of it.[39]

Outshoppers An unusual segmentation possibility for retailers involves people called **outshoppers.** In contrast to Inshoppers, outshoppers prefer to go out

Table 8.5
Lifestyle dimensions

Activities	Interests	Opinions	Demographics
Work	Family	Themselves	Age
Hobbies	Home	Social issues	Education
Social events	Job	Politics	Income
Vacation	Community	Business	Occupation
Entertainment	Recreation	Economics	Family size
Club membership	Fashion	Education	Dwelling
Community	Food	Products	Geography
Shopping	Media	Future	City size
Sports	Achievements	Culture	Stage in life cycle

Source: Joseph T. Plummer, "The Concept and Application of Life Style Segmentation," *Journal of Marketing* 38 (January 1974), p. 34. Reprinted with permission from the American Marketing Association.

of their local trade areas to do their buying. Outshopping is a function of the overall attitude toward existing shopping facilities. The more dissatisfied customers are, the more likely they are to outshop.[40] Heavy outshoppers, defined as people who shop out of town 75 percent or more of the time, are likely to be younger than light outshoppers. They are also more apt to have higher incomes and be more dissatisfied with local stores' merchandise selection, quality, price, and service.[41] Personality and lifestyle measures such as self-confidence, fashion-consciousness, and financial optimism have been found to be related to outshopping behavior.[42]

Among the outshopping public there are big-ticket outshoppers. These people buy expensive home products outside their local trade areas while purchasing other merchandise in stores that are close by. There are other product-specific outshopping types—for example, appearance outshoppers who prefer to buy apparel and jewelry out of town.[43] Local retailers lose sales to out-of-town stores. People outshop because of dissatisfaction with local facilities. Retail firms have a choice: relocate to facilities with larger trading areas or find and correct their weaknesses.[44] They can combat the outshopping problem by improving facilities, widening assortments, offering goods of better quality, and instituting liberal credit terms.

Summary

A useful understanding of behavior requires more than a familiarity with needs, wants, drives, motives, attitudes, and other aspects of the human personality. Our actions result from the interplay of many forces that lie both within and outside us. All people are affected by and respond to the culture in which they live. The term *culture* embraces all the values, ideas, attitudes, symbols, artifacts, and other characteristics of a civilization that are transmitted from generation to generation. Culture has a profound influence on our lives. It shapes our thinking and conditions our behavior. Among the values commonly held by Americans are freedom, equality, materialism, hedonism, esteem for work, religiousness, and an accent on youthfulness.

According to W. Lloyd Warner, six distinct classes form the social structure of the United States. There are two upper, two middle, and two lower classes. People and families in each class display characteristics and lifestyles that differ from those of people in the other classes. Our country is a melting pot that embraces people of different backgrounds, races, religions, and the like. Subcultures are large numbers of people who share similar attitudes, values, and consumption patterns by virtue of their backgrounds. Blacks comprise the largest of all our ethnic subcultures and the largest minority group. Second largest of the minorities is the Hispanic subculture. There are also subcultures based on age. Examples include the teenage and senior citizen groups.

The reference groups to which we belong also play a significant role in both attitude formation and the development of value systems. They function as frames of reference, help mold opinions and attitudes, and affect shopping behavior. Primary groups are the most influential. These consist of the people we interact with face to face. Of all primary groups, the family exerts the most influence. As both an earning and a buying unit, the family is of special importance to retail firms. An understanding of the needs and characteristics of consumers at each stage in the family life cycle is beneficial to retailers.

A company may choose any one of three basic marketing strategies to follow: undifferentiated, concentrated, or differentiated. The first regards all consumers as basically alike. The second targets only one segment of the population, and the last targets two or more segments. Both concentrated and differentiated strategies are forms of market segmentation. A number of segmentation techniques are available. Among these are geographic, demographic, benefit, value, psychographic/lifestyle, and usage-rate segmentation. These may be used alone or in combination.

Key Terms

culture	primary groups
social class	family life cycle
status	undifferentiated marketing
subcultures	concentrated marketing
reference groups	differentiated marketing

market segmentation   psychographics
geographic segmentation   lifestyle segmentation
demographic segmentation   usage-rate segmentation
benefit segmentation   outshoppers
value segmentation

Review Questions

1. Define the term *culture* and give a brief overview of its importance with respect to understanding consumer behavior.

2. List at least five fundamental values commonly held by American consumers.

3. Differentiate among the six social classes in the United States, outlining some of the characteristics of the members of each class.

4. Name three occupational types you believe are representative of each of the following social classes: *(a)* Upper-Middle, *(b)* Upper-Lower, and *(c)* Lower-Lower.

5. Present some useful details regarding: *(a)* the black subculture and *(b)* the Spanish subculture.

6. Why should today's retailer show more interest in the senior citizen market?

7. Identify the stages of the typical family life cycle and discuss the implications of each for retailers.

8. For shoppers in each of the following stages of the family life cycle, suggest three or more types of goods and/or services they are likely to buy: *(a)* Newly Married, *(b)* Full Nest I, *(c)* Empty Nest I, and *(d)* Solitary Survivor.

9. Specify and differentiate among three approaches to marketing strategy.

10. Define market segmentation. Explain the value of this approach to a retail company.

11. Identify at least five useful segmentation methods and furnish illustrations of products for which these approaches seem to be suitable.

12. What is geodemography?

13. Cite at least six of the many variables used in segmenting populations demographically.

14. Briefly describe the rationale behind each of the following segmentation possibilities: *(a)* benefit, *(b)* lifestyle, and *(c)* usage-rate.

15. Contrast the concentrated and undifferentiated marketing strategies and suggest two products that, in your judgment, are now being marketed according to each approach.

16. In what segmentation technique are AIO questions used? What do the initials stand for?

17. What are outshoppers? Why should retail firms be concerned about them?

Discussion Questions

1. Clip and bring in to class three magazine or newspaper advertisements that appeal to our infatuation with youthfulness.

2. Discuss the role that reference groups play in a person's life.

3. Prepare a chart in which you contrast several features of the teenage and senior citizen subcultures.

4. Discounts, large print on price tickets, water fountains, and lounges are among the steps many stores have already taken to appeal more strongly to older consumers. Can you thing of four or five additional creative ideas for retailers to use?

5. Speculate about some benefits that consumers might look for in considering the purchase of a home computer.

6. Prepare a list of suggestions about how local retailers can discourage consumers in the area from outshopping.

Notes

[1]James F. Engel, Roger D. Blackwell, and David T. Kollat, *Consumer Behavior,* 3d ed. (Hinsdale, Ill.: Dryden Press, 1978), p. 65.

[2]Del I. Hawkins, Kenneth A. Coney, and Roger J. Best, *Consumer Behavior: Implications for Marketing Strategy* (Plano, Tex.: Business Publications, 1980), p. 66.

[3]For a valid overview of the central, or core, values in our society, see: David L. Loudon and Albert J. Della Bitta, *Consumer Behavior: Concepts and Applications* (New York: McGraw-Hill, 1979), pp. 125–30; Leon Schiffman and Leslie Lazar Kanuk, *Consumer Behavior* (Englewood Cliffs, N.J.: Prentice-Hall, 1978), pp. 342–59.

[4]Engel, Blackwell, and Kollat, *Consumer Behavior,* p. 109.

[5]Pierre Martineau, "Social Classes and Spending Behavior," *Journal of Marketing* 23 (October 1958), pp. 121–30; Roy Daniel Howell, "A Multivariate Examination of a Patronage Model: The Impact of Values and Life Style on Shopping Orientations," Ph.D. dissertation, University of Arkansas, 1979.

[6]Philip Kotler, *Marketing Management: Analysis, Planning and Control,* 4th ed. (Englewood Cliffs, N.J.: Prentice-Hall, 1980), p. 140.

[7]W. Lloyd Warner and Paul S. Lunt, *The Social Life of a Modern Community* (New Haven, Conn.: Yale University Press, 1941), p. 203.

[8]Andrew Allen Brogowicz, "Race as a Basis for Market Segmentation: An Exploratory Analysis," Ph.D. dissertation, Michigan State University, 1977; Bobbye Kitchens Dunlap, "A Psychographic Analysis of New Automobile Purchase Behavior among Black and White Consumers in Selected SMSA's in the State of North Carolina," Ph.D. dissertation, Louisiana Tech University, 1978; James R. Smith, "Alternative Bases for Market Segmentation: An Empirical Investigation of Low and Middle Income Black and White Consumers of Clothing Items," Ph.D. dissertation, University of Tennessee, 1980.

[9]Donald E. Sexton, "Black Buyer Behavior," *Journal of Marketing* 36 (October 1972), pp. 36–39.

[10]Ibid. See also: Raymond A. Bauer and Scott M. Cunningham, "The Negro Market," *Journal of Advertising Research* 10 (April 1970), pp. 3–13.

[11]James Charles Carroll, "Patronage Decisions of College-Age Negroes: The Influence of Certain Operating Characteristics of Selected Kinds of Retail Stores," Ph.D. dissertation, University of Alabama, 1968.

[12]Sexton, "Black Buyer Behavior," p. 37.

[13]See: Dennis W. Tootelian and H. Nicholas Wineleshausen, "The Teen-age Market: A Comparative Analysis, 1964–1974," *Journal of Retailing* 52 (Summer 1976), pp. 51–60; George P. Moschis, Roy L. Moore, and Lowndes F. Stephens, "Purchasing Patterns of Adolescent Consumers," *Journal of Retailing* 53 (Spring 1977), pp. 17–26; George W. Schiele, "How to Reach the Young Consumer," *Harvard Business Review* 52 (March–April 1974), pp. 77–86.

[14]Zarrel V. Lambert, "An Investigation of Older Consumers' Unmet Needs and Wants at the Retail Level," *Journal of Retailing* 55 (Winter 1979), p. 35; Betsy D. Gelb, "Gray Power: Next Challenge to Business?" *Business Horizons* 20 (April 1977), pp. 38–45.

[15]Lambert, "An Investigation," p. 43. See also: James R. Lumpkin and Barnett A. Greenberg, "Apparel-Shopping Patterns of the Elderly Consumer," *Journal of Retailing* 58 (Winter 1982), p. 85.

[16]John A. Reinecke, "Supermarkets, Shopping Centers, and the Senior Shopper," *Marquette Business Review* 19 (Fall 1975), pp. 105–7.

[17]George Bernard Glisan, "An Investigation of Social Class as a Criterion for Deriving Market Segments among an Elderly Population," Ph.D. dissertation, University of Arkansas, 1981.

[18]Leonard John Fela, "The Elderly Consumer Market: A Psychographic Segmentation Study," Ph.D. dissertation, Syracuse University, 1977.

[19]William O. Bearden and Michael J. Etzel, "Reference Group Influence on Product and Brand Purchase Decisions," *Journal of Consumer Research* 9 (September 1982), pp. 183–94; George P. Moschis, "Social Comparison and Informal Group Influence," *Journal of Marketing Research* 13 (August 1976), pp. 237–44.

[20]For an introductory overview of family role structure and decision making, see: Harry L. Davis, "Measurement of Husband-Wife Influence in Consumer Purchase Decisions," *Journal of Marketing Research* 8 (August 1971), pp. 305–12; Harry L. Davis, "Decision Making within the Household," *Journal of Consumer Research* 3 (March 1976), pp. 241–60.

[21]Robert T. Green and Isabella C. M. Cunningham, "Feminine Role Perception and Family Purchasing Decisions," *Journal of Marketing Research* 12 (August 1975), pp. 325–32.

[22]See: Leon G. Schiffman and Leslie Lazar Kanuk, *Consumer Behavior,* (Englewood Cliffs, N.J.: Prentice-Hall, 1978), pp. 250–51.

[23]Adapted from Patrick E. Murphy and William A. Staples, "A Modernized Family Life Cycle," *Journal of Consumer Research* 6 (June 1979), p. 16. Reprinted with permission from the American Marketing Association.

[24]See: Daniel Yankelovich, "New Criteria for Market Segmentation," *Harvard Business Review* 42 (March–April 1964), pp. 83–90; Yoram Wind, "Issues and Advances in Segmentation Research," *Journal of Marketing Research* 15 (August 1978), pp. 317–37.

[25]Chester R. Wasson, Frederick D. Sturdivant, and David H. McConaughy, *Competition and Human Behavior* (New York: Appleton-Century-Crofts, 1968), p. 128.

[26]Fred D. Reynolds and William D. Wells, *Consumer Behavior* (New York: McGraw-Hill, 1977), pp. 210, 213, 214, 215.

[27]Sandra Salmans, "Technology: A New 'Rifle' for Marketers," *New York Times,* 19 November 1981, p. D2.

[28]Russell I. Haley, "Benefit Segmentation: A Decision-Oriented Research Tool," *Journal of Marketing* 32 (July 1968), pp. 30–35.

[29]Yankelovich, "New Criteria," p. 85.

[30]Ibid., p. 88.

[31]Donald E. Vinson, Jerome E. Scott, and Lawrence M. Lamont, "The Role of Personal Values in Marketing and Consumer Behavior," *Journal of Marketing* 41 (April 1977), pp. 44–50.

[32]See, for example: Jose Valentim Sartarelli, "A Market Segmentation Study of Single (1-Person) Householders by Demographic and Life Style Characteristics," Ph.D. dissertation, Michigan State University, 1979; William O. Bearden, Jesse E. Teel, Jr., and Richard M. Durand, "Media Usage, Psychographic, and Demographic Dimensions of Retail Shoppers," *Journal of Retailing* 54 (Spring 1978), pp. 65–74.

[33]W. D. Wells, "Psychographics: A Critical Review," *Journal of Marketing Research* 12 (May 1975), p. 197.

[34]Edward Winter and John T. Russell, "Psychographics and Creativity," *Journal of Advertising* (1973, no. 2), pp. 32–35; Peter W. Bernstein, "Psychographics Is Still an Issue on Madison Avenue," *Fortune* (16 January 1978), pp. 78–81.

[35]William D. Wells and Douglas J. Tigert, "Activities, Interests, and Opinions," *Journal of Advertising Research* 11 (August 1971), pp. 27–35. See also: Joseph T. Plummer, "The Concept and Application of Life Style Segmentation," *Journal of Marketing* 38 (January 1974), pp. 33–37; William R. Darden and Dub Ashton, "Psychographic Profiles of Patronage Preference Groups," *Journal of Retailing* 50 (Winter 1974–75), pp. 99–112; Nariman K. Dhalla and Winston H. Mahatoo, "Expanding the Scope of Segmentation Research," *Journal of Marketing* 40 (April 1976), pp. 34–41; Susan P. Douglas and Christine D. Urban, "Life-style Analysis to Profile Women in International Markets," *Journal of Marketing* 41 (July 1977), pp. 46–56.

[36]Elizabeth A. Richards and Stephen S. Sturman, "Life-style Segmentation in Apparel Marketing," *Journal of Marketing* 41 (October 1977), pp. 89–91.

[37]Stephen M. Barker and John F. Trost, "Cultivate the High-volume Consumers," *Harvard Business Review* 51 (March–April 1973), p. 122.

[38]William R. Darden and Fred D. Reynolds, "Shopping Orientations and Product Usage Rates," *Journal of Marketing Research* 8 (November 1971), pp. 505–8.

[39]James M. Carman, "Correlates of Brand Loyalty: Some Positive Results," *Journal of Marketing Research* 17 (February 1970), pp. 67–76; Ben M. Enis and Gordon W. Paul, "Store Loyalty as a Basis for Market Segmentation," *Journal of Retailing* 46 (Fall 1970), pp. 42–56; Kenneth E. Miller and Kent L. Granzin, "Simultaneous Loyalty and Benefit Segmentation of Retail Store Customers," *Journal of Retailing* 55 (Spring 1979), pp. 47–60.

[40]A. Coskun Samli and Ernest B. Uhr, "The Outshopping Spectrum: Key for Analyzing Intermarket Leakages," *Journal of Retailing* 50 (Summer 1974), p. 75.

[41]N. G. Papadopoulos, "Consumer Outshopping Research: Review and Extensions," *Journal of Retailing* 56 (Winter 1970), pp. 41–58.

[42]William R. Darden and William D. Perreault, Jr., "Identifying Interurban Shoppers: Multiproduct Purchase Patterns and Segmentation Profiles," *Journal of Marketing Research* 13 (February 1976), pp. 51–60; see also: Fred D. Reynolds and William R. Darden, "Intermarket Patronage: A Psychographic Study of Consumer Outshoppers," *Journal of Marketing* 36 (October 1972), pp. 50–54.

[43]Papadopoulos, "Consumer Outshopping," pp. 41–58.

[44]A. Coskun Samli, Glen Riecken, and Ugur Yavas, "Intermarket Shopping Behavior and the Small Community: Problems and Prospects of a Widespread Phenomenon," *Journal of the Academy of Marketing Science* 11 (Winter 1983), pp. 1–14.

Case 2.1
Janine's

Located in an upper-middle-class suburb of Chicago, Janine's is a specialty retailer of designer clothes for the sophisticated woman. The area is considered highly desirable. Physicians, lawyers, architects, and other professionals—as well as corporation presidents and business owners—reside in the community. Homes there are valued at $500,000 and over.

Among the other tenants of the new, U-shaped neighborhood shopping center where Janine's is situated are a large drugstore, a florist, an Italian restaurant, a bakery, a menswear shop, and two women's shoestores. The center is about a mile from a large community hospital and a public high school.

The storefront is of marble; the entrance is arch-shaped. The interior decor has an exquisite contemporary decor, with plush peach-colored carpeting and a free-flow layout. The ceiling is high, and the store is well illuminated with both in-ceiling and track lighting. Spacious, mirrored dressing rooms, an attractive sitting area where shoppers can sip a beverage in living-room comfort, and courteous, well-trained salespeople all project an air of quality and refinement. Free services offered include expert alterations, delivery, and gift wrapping.

Janine's runs no sales or specials. Four times a year, the owner mails out invitations to her regular customers to come in for a look at the new season's fashions. The clientele comes from as far as an hour's drive away.

Questions

1. Identify the patronage motives that most likely draw shoppers to Janine's.

2. What part does a person's self-concept play in influencing store patronage?

Case 2.2
Scenic Park Estates

Scenic Park Estates, Inc., is a land developer and builder operating in Pennsylvania's Pocono Mountains. With two successful leisure communities already behind it, the company has just initiated a third.

They have bulldozed roads through the property, subdivided the land, and begun to sell wooded homesites at low pre-development prices. An impressive central clubhouse is under construction. Plans call for, among other things, the installation of tennis courts, an Olympic-sized swimming pool, a lake stocked with trout, and a boathouse. Six different models are available for vacation, year-round, or retirement homes.

The company's sales operation is unusual and complex. It involves three distinct sales forces:

1. *Telephone solicitors* who, over WATS lines, canvass households throughout a tri-state area (New York, New Jersey, and Pennsylvania). Their objective is to set up appointments with consumers for a company representative to make a presentation in their homes.
2. *Sales representatives* who keep those appointments, present slides of the property and models, answer questions, and try to persuade the consumers to visit the property the following weekend.
3. *Property directors* who greet the prospects when they arrive at the Pocono development, take them on a tour of the property, and try to end up with a signed contract.

Telephone solicitors, sales representatives, and property directors all stress the following selling points:

1. A healthy environment for young and old: aesthetically pleasing, free of pollution, and without the frantic hustle and bustle of urban living.
2. Implied long-term capital gain. ("Land usually rises in value over time. When you buy land at 'pre-development' prices, you are buying it cheaply.")
3. Low taxes.
4. An active lifestyle: year-round sports ranging from swimming, boating, and horseback-riding to ice-skating and snowmobiling.
5. A clubhouse with meeting rooms and a hall for social events arranged by residents of the community.

Questions
1. At what specific consumer motives do the company's promotional efforts appear to be aimed?
2. In canvassing households indiscriminately throughout the tri-state area, Scenic Park Estates seems to be following an undifferentiated marketing strategy. In your opinion, what other segmentation approaches might prove of value to the firm? Explain your reasoning.

Courtesy J. C. Penney Company, Inc.

THE RETAIL FACILITY

STORE LOCATION

Your Study Objectives

After you have studied this chapter, you will understand:

1. What the older, in-city retail shopping areas are like.
2. The major types of planned shopping centers.
3. The trading area concept.
4. The more important factors to be considered in arriving at site location decisions.
5. The advantages and disadvantages of three avenues to store occupancy.

For most types of store retailing, the right location is often the single most essential element contributing to the firm's success. Implied in that term *right location* is a good-to-excellent match between the company's offerings and the needs and desires of the shoppers in the area. There are other essential components, of course: the firm's goods and services mix, its promotional efforts, the drawing power of the surrounding stores, the strength of the competition, and other environmental factors.

When searching for a promising location, most independent retailers appear to rely more on intuition than on careful study. Oddly enough, many choose locations that are close to their homes or locations that are situated in an area they would like to live in. Fortunately, some are sensible enough to at least take **traffic counts** at the site. They try to determine how many people pass by the location during different hours of the day and on different days of the week. They often clock vehicular traffic as well. With such information, they are able to estimate the level of sales that the location ought to generate.

Some go further, attempting to judge the quality of the passersby to decide if they are the kinds of shoppers who will buy the store's merchandise. A retailer of teenagers' jeans, for example, would want to open a store in a section where young people who are potential jeans buyers live or shop.

Department stores, chains, and other large retail organizations approach the location problem with more sophistication. Some maintain real estate departments. These are staffed with experienced analysts whose judgment has been refined and honed to the point where location decisions enjoy a moderate-to-high success rate. Many such companies develop lists of strict criteria and useful rating instruments for making such judgments. Some use computer models that build in a large number of factors pertinent to the location problem. These may take probabilities into account as well.

In this chapter, we discuss the diverse types of shopping areas where retailers situate their outlets. You will learn of the trading area concept and its significance in location selection. We will show how retailers approach the problem, discuss which aspects need to be considered when evaluating possible locations, and present some details regarding store occupancy.

Retail Shopping Areas

Location analysts find it convenient to distinguish between two broad categories of retail shopping areas in towns and cities: (1) the older, largely unplanned in-city sections and (2) the newer, planned shopping centers.

In-city Retail Shopping Sections

A ride through almost any city reveals a few distinct kinds of long-established shopping areas. The three major types are the central business district, the secondary business district, and the neighborhood shopping street. Other types include the retail cluster and the freestanding store.

The Central Business District Generally referred to by consumers as downtown, or center city, the **central business district,** or **CBD,** is the oldest shopping section in town. Often, the main thoroughfare in the area is named Main Street or Broadway. Located here are office buildings, banks, restaurants, theaters, one or more department stores, large units of regional or national chain stores, and independent retailers. We also find service retailers and occasional wholesale operations. Public transportation brings people into the area to work and to shop—and out again to their homes or apartments in the outer sections of the city. Hundreds of consumers may reside within walking distance of the area. Traffic, both pedestrian and vehicular, is more congested here than elsewhere in town. Parking space is limited. Real estate in the district commands premium prices. Rentals are often so high as to discourage most small merchants from locating here.

Retail sales in most CBDs have been declining for many years as middle-class families relocate to the suburbs and are replaced by less economically advantaged consumers. Other factors have accelerated the decline: aging building structures, a rising incidence of crime, deteriorating city services, higher tax rates, and so on. The trend among retailers to follow their customers to the suburbs has also contributed to the slow demise of the CBD.

The central business district, the oldest shopping area in town, serves consumers who live and work nearby and those who use public transportation to come in to work and to shop and then leave again. This is the central business district of Dallas in 1925.

Library of Congress

Efforts have been made and are still being made to rebuild and/ or revitalize these downtown sections. Some degree of success is occasionally noted. Whether such efforts will lead to permanent, long-term gains is debatable. The very nature of consumer shopping has been changed by the spread of planned shopping centers.

Some examples of urban renewal and revitalization projects are the Vermont-Slausson Shopping Center (Los Angeles), East Winston Shopping Center (Winston-Salem, North Carolina), Courthouse Center (Columbus, Indiana), Lafayette Place (Boston), and Hawthorne Plaza (Los Angeles).[1]

Warehouses, terminals, factories, and other buildings have been converted into shopping areas in some cities, often with historical overtones and wide consumer appeal. Boston's Faneuil Hall Marketplace, New York's South Street Seaport, and Baltimore's Harborplace are examples of such conversions.[2]

One of the most interesting developments in recent years has been the construction of both *multi-use facilities* and *mixed-use complexes.* Most are located in the older downtown sections. A **multi-use project** involves renovating and remodeling an old building (or several that are adjacent to each other) to provide stores and offices. Peter's Landing in Huntington Beach, California, is an example. **Mixed-use complexes** are usually much larger, involving a number of buildings. In addition to offices and stores, hotels, recreational facilities, places of entertainment, and even cultural facilities are included. Among others, Copley Place and Faneuil Hall Marketplace in Boston, New Orleans' Canal Place, and the Galleria in Atlanta (and in Houston) are examples of mixed-use complexes.[3]

In 1985, Manhattan's first multi-level shopping center will open— in thoroughly renovated premises formerly occupied by E. J. Korvettes. Located across from Macy's–34th Street, the striking glass-covered building is to house some 200 stores in a total of about 300,000 square feet of space. Different levels in the building will each represent a well-known part of New York: Greenwich Village, Fifth Avenue, the United Nations, Radio City, Broadway, and so on.[4]

Secondary Business Districts As the city's core expands over the decades, new shopping areas gradually develop. Usually these **secondary business districts** follow along the main roads that lead out of the downtown section toward the city's expanding boundaries. Most cities contain no more than one or two of these districts. A metropolitan area, however, may have as many as a half dozen or more.

These are energetic shopping districts that attract consumers from as far away as 10 to 20 minutes by car. For the most part, the retail outlets here resemble those in the CBD: a mix of apparel, shoe, furniture, and many other store types. Banks, movie houses, beauty parlors, and other service retailers are also represented. The stores are generally

*Herald Center, Manhattan's
multi-level, 200-store
shopping center that opened
in 1985 in renovated premises
formerly occupied by E. J.
Korvette. Each different level
in the building represents a
well-known part of
New York.*

Courtesy Herald Center, a development project of The New York Land Company

smaller in size than their counterparts downtown, and more independent retailers can be found among them. Here, too, are small office
and professional buildings, some wholesale establishments, and perhaps
a few small manufacturers.

Although traffic here is not as heavy as downtown, it is still quite
brisk. Merchants in the area enjoy a favorable sales volume. Vacant
stores are seldom available. Rents, although lower than those in the
CBD, are still high compared to those in neighborhood shopping areas.

Neighborhood Shopping Streets Typically, there are more **neighborhood
shopping streets** in a city than both central and secondary districts
combined. Chicago, New York, San Francisco, Greater Miami, and
other metropolitan centers may contain scores of these areas. Entire
blocks of stores, situated on both sides of a busy thoroughfare, may
extend through the section for as much as a half mile or more. Rows
of stores are nestled between blocks of apartment houses and/or private
residences. Retailers draw strongly from people living in the neighborhood. Representative types of firms include independently owned pharmacies, bakeries, butcher shops, fruit-and-vegetable stands, hardware
stores, groceries, superettes, bars, pizza parlors and other fast-food
places, and stationery stores. Services are also well represented: beauty
parlors, barber shops, laundromats, dry-cleaning establishments, shoe
repair shops, TV service outlets, and so on.

Neighborhood shopping streets often present the most attractive
opportunities for the new retailer. Rentals here are more moderate
and locations occasionally become available.

Other In-city Types Here and there in residential areas of the city, you will see a row of perhaps three to six stores. Vehicular traffic in front of these **retail clusters** is usually light. The stores are at the corner of a block of apartment houses or private dwellings and extend some 50 or more feet into the block. They may occupy one-story structures, or they may form part of two-story taxpayers—small buildings with one or more stores on the street floor and apartments above.

Frequently found alongside a busy highway or thoroughfare is the **freestanding store.** It consists of a single building, usually surrounded by ample parking space. Discount stores, restaurants, and other retailers often use this approach.

Shopping Centers The new **planned shopping centers** are a relatively recent retailing innovation. Only a few decades ago, in 1949, there were no more than 75 of such centers across the country. By the early 1970s, over 12,000 were actively catering to consumer shopping needs.[5]

The shopping center is a preplanned merchandising unit composed of a deliberately sought mix of retail stores. Designed to provide the convenience of one-stop shopping for the consumer, it is erected on a site accessible to motorists. It offers ample parking facilities. People drive to the center from home or workplace, park their cars, and then walk to the stores. Over and above the appeal of the individual stores, the layout and decor of the shopping center itself has considerable drawing power.[6]

There are three major types of planned centers: regional, community, and neighborhood.

Regional Centers Largest of all planned centers is the **regional shopping center.** Often, it occupies a site that extends from 30 to 50 acres, although there are some double that in size. Leasable space within a regional center may run from 300,000 to as many as 1 million square feet, with room for well over 100 stores. These giant merchandising arenas are designed to serve populations upwards of 100,000 to 200,000 shoppers, many of whom will come from as far away as 40 minutes by car.

Department stores are the center's major attractions. There may be as few as one or two or as many as five or more on the site. Today, almost all regional centers are enclosed, offering year-round climate control for their patrons' comfort. The stores are extremely varied. There are drugstores; apparel shops for men, women, and children; beauty parlors; jewelry stores; restaurants and snack bars; kiosks (freestanding shops) that sell candy, plants, gifts, and other merchandise; supermarkets; and a host of other types. There are also banks,

Department stores are the major attractions in regional shopping centers.

Courtesy University Towne Centre, a project of Ernest W. Hahn, Inc., San Diego, CA

theaters, travel agencies, optometrists, dental clinics, medical offices, and even an occasional motel, bowling alley, or office building.

Community Centers A more modest replica of the larger regional center, the **community shopping center** typically occupies about 10 acres and houses some 150,000 square feet of leasable space. It caters to between 30,000 and 150,000 consumers, most of whom live in nearby towns and villages up to a 20-minute drive away. The principal tenant, or **anchor store,** may be a large variety or junior department store. Examples of anchor stores include K mart, J. C. Penney, and Sears, Roebuck.

Neighborhood Centers Smallest of the planned centers is the **neighborhood shopping center.** It is often called a strip center because it is generally erected as a strip of some 10 to 20 stores that occupy a site of between four and five acres. There is parking space for 30 to 50 or more cars in front, and sometimes in back, of the buildings. Leasable space usually ranges between 35,000 and 75,000 square feet. Some neighborhood shopping centers have been constructed as a single straight row of stores; others are L- or U-shaped in design.

Shoppers come from the immediate vicinity and from up to 10 minutes away by car. These centers may serve as few as 5,000 to as many as 35,000 or more people. Traffic is largely generated by an anchor store, most often a large drugstore or supermarket. Often, other outlets include a luncheonette or pizza parlor, laundromat, beauty salon, women's sportswear shop, shoestore, hardware store, bakery, and similar types.

Evaluating Trading Areas

A trade area, or **trading area,** is the field or geographical territory from which a store (or a grouping of stores) draws most of its customers. Every store has its own trading area extending outward from its location. So does every conceivable kind of retail shopping area: central or secondary business district, neighborhood shopping street, store cluster, and any type of planned shopping center. As it radiates outward from the central site, each trading area can be theoretically divided into several zones. Well over half of a store's (or area's) customers can be expected to come from the closest, or primary, zone. Perhaps another 20 or 25 percent will be drawn from the next area, while no more than a small percentage of those in the furthest zone can be expected to shop at the store.

Extent of the Trading Area

Clearly, the closer to a store consumers live or work, the greater the probability that they will shop at that store. The more distant shoppers are from the site, the fewer the number who can be expected to trade there. When considering a proposed location, the retail firm first tries to ascertain the probable size of its trading area. It will then try to find out all it can about the consumers in the area to learn whether their characteristics match those of their intended target customers.

Geography plays an important role in determining the trading area. A riverbank, hill, lake, park, or other topographical feature may interfere with the normal traffic flow from north, south, east, or west. A major highway, bridge crossing, or railroad tracks can also eliminate one or more sections of territory that would otherwise lie within the store's trading area.

The trading area of a secondary business district may encompass many city blocks. However, if we were to study the drawing power of any three adjacent stores within the district, we would discover that their individual trading areas are dissimilar. Differences in store size may be partly responsible. Generally, the larger the outlet, the larger the trading area will be. Trading area size also depends on the kinds of merchandise offered for sale, the quality and exclusivity of the goods, the store's construction and decor, and other factors. The variety store on a neighborhood shopping street may attract most of its customers from within a three- to five-block radius. On the other hand, a freestanding discount house adjacent to a main highway may draw shoppers from miles away. A furniture store will attract consumers from greater distances than a grocery. An upscale apparel

Every store has its own trading area that radiates outward from its location. Retailers expect well over half of their customers to come from the store's closest, or primary, geographical zone.

Eleanore Snow

firm that carries on an extensive mail-order business may bring in sales from the suburbs and from neighboring towns. The trading area of a regional shopping center may extend in all directions to as far away as 15 or 20 miles.

Gravitational Models in Trading Area Estimation

In the 1920s, William J. Reilly drew a parallel between Sir Isaac Newton's Law of Gravitation and the capacity of towns and cities to attract shoppers. Newton theorized that the masses of celestial bodies exert a natural force, gravitation, that draws other bodies toward them. The greater the mass, the stronger the pull. Reilly concluded that, in the main, the drawing power of towns and cities stems from the interaction of two variables: population and distance. The larger a town's population, the greater its drawing power. The farther away the town is from a consumer, the less the likelihood of that person going there to shop. In time, this contribution became known as **Reilly's Law of Retail Gravitation.**[7]

Later investigators revised Reilly's original work. In the 1940s, for example, Paul D. Converse modified Reilly's formulas.[8] A popular version of the change is demonstrated in the following section, along with an illustration of its application.

The Breaking-point Formula Assume that two cities, A and B, are 15 miles apart. Consumers who reside in the territory between them may choose

Special events like this create excitement at regional shopping centers.

Courtesy Palm Beach Mall, West Palm Beach, FL

to shop in either A or B. City A has a population of 140,000; City B has only 20,000 residents. We are interested in learning what the *breaking point* between the two is. In short, at what distance from City B will City A begin to attract shoppers more strongly than City B?

Here is how to calculate the breaking point:

$$\text{Breaking point} = \frac{\text{Distance}_{A-B}}{1 + \sqrt{\dfrac{\text{Population}_A}{\text{Population}_B}}}$$

Substituting the known facts, we have:

$$\text{Breaking point} = \frac{15}{1 + \sqrt{\dfrac{140{,}000}{20{,}000}}}$$

$$\text{Breaking point} = \frac{15}{1 + \sqrt{7}}$$

$$= \frac{15}{1 + 2.65}$$

$$= 4.1 \text{ miles}$$

According to the calculations, then, the trading area of City B should extend outward approximately 4.1 miles in the direction of City A. Conversely, we can assume that A, the larger city, will draw persons as far away as 15 − 4.1, or 10.9 miles.

An underlying assumption of early gravitational models was that population size can substitute as an indicator of the number (and quality) of the retail stores in that city. This, of course, is not necessarily true. Moreover, consumers are willing to travel greater distances to shop for many kinds of merchandise. Furniture, major appliances, fine clothing, and floor coverings are just a few examples.

David L. Huff improved on Reilly's work. He developed models that are useful in analyzing trading areas for shopping centers and even individual stores as well as for towns or cities.[9] Subsequent studies have confirmed the value of these investigations. They have also pointed up the effects on trading area size of distance, store image, competitive stores, and other factors.[10]

Nongravitational Approaches

Gravity models are not the only techniques retailers have used to select sites. Usually they rely on simpler, judgmental methods. They depend on a good deal of demographic data and frequently a checklist of factors that management deems important.

On the whole, operations research activity is seen far less often in retailing than in the industrial sector. Nevertheless, management science is occasionally applied to location problems. Much work has already been done in developing different types of decision models.[11] As an example, one model is capable of predicting annual sales for a number of supermarket locations.[12] Another, known as MULTILOC, is useful for solving multiple-store location problems.[13] Further discussion of model development is beyond the scope of this book.

Finding and Evaluating New Locations

We have seen how retail shopping areas can be categorized into older, in-city types and newer, planned shopping centers. In searching for store locations, it has been suggested that retail management consider the city's traffic circulatory system. According to one analyst, retail sites can be classified into five distinct types:[14]

1. Internal—within the central business district.
2. Axial—along the major roads leading out of the CBD.
3. Pivotal—where two or more main thoroughfares meet.
4. Peripheral—along the community's outer edges.
5. External—along a busy highway between communities.

Growth Areas for Retailers

For the balance of this century, the so-called middle markets appear to hold promise for many retail firms. These are rather loosely defined as areas that contain smaller cities of between 10,000 and 50,000 residents with good-sized trading areas. Shopping malls, the suburbs of

Main entrance to Wausau Center, a 467,000-square-foot downtown redevelopment project in Wausau, Wisconsin. Revitalized CBDs are often promising locations for retail firms.

Courtesy Jacobs, Visconsi & Jacobs Co., Cleveland, OH

many cities, and revitalized CBDs also have appeal. Another attractive possibility is the infill location. The term includes metropolitan areas that were never used before for retailing, stores in planned centers that require modernization, and similar locations.[15]

Information Sources for Location Analysis

Retailers can draw on a variety of data sources. Most of these have already been described in Chapter 5. You will recall the various censuses issued by the Department of Commerce: the *County and City Data Book,* the *Statistical Abstract of the United States,* the "Survey of Buying Power," and so on. As a reminder, a firm interested in a specific location can obtain block statistics from the Bureau of the Census. A few such block statistics can be combined to derive a graphic and useful description of the population residing in the proposed store's trading area.

Another valuable aid not yet mentioned is the annual *Editor & Publisher Market Guide.* An excerpt from this publication may be seen in Figure 9.1. The report provides, in summary form, many descriptive details regarding states, counties, and cities. Included are facts on the number of households, income statistics, local industry, types of stores (by name and number), climate, central business districts and large shopping centers, the local daily newspaper, and the like.

Metropolitan newspapers and many smaller dailies conduct surveys

Figure 9.1
Excerpt from *Editor &*
Publisher Market Guide

II-380 Wisconsin

9 - PRINCIPAL INDUSTRIES: Industry, Number of Wage Earners (Av. Wkly. Wage)-Construction 1,262 ($358); Metal Mfg. 3,990 ($355); Food Prod. 2,003 ($269); Wood Prod. 344 ($286); Shoes 400 ($210).

10 - CLIMATE: Min. & Max. Temp.-Spring 20-80; Summer 40-96; Fall 20-72; Winter 20-40.

11 - TAP WATER: Soft. Water treatment & iron removal plant, fluoridated.

12 - RETAILING:
Nearby Shopping Centers

Name (No. of stores)	Miles from Downtown	Principal Stores
Beaver Mall(32)	1	Herbergers, J.C. Penney, Woolco, Lewis Drug
Park Plaza Mall(10)	1	Shop Ko, Piggly Wiggly, Montgomwery Ward

Principal Shopping Days-Mon., Thurs., Fri., Sat. **Stores Open Sundays**-Food, Drug and Dept; Beaver Mall; Shop Ko.

13 - RETAIL OUTLETS: Department Stores-J.C. Penney, Sears; Montgomery Ward, Shop Ko; Woolco; K mart, Fleet Farm; Herbergers; Spurgeons. **Variety Stores**-Schultz Bros **Chain Supermarkets**-Piggly Wiggly; Lauer's; Shop-Rite, Super Valu; Sentry, United Foods. **Other Chain Stores**-Elliots Model, Lewis Drug; Desmonds; Musicland; Jo Ann Fabrics; Tradehome Shoes, Wardrobe, Kinney Shoes; The Plum Tree; Tadio Shack, Walden Books, Zales, Copper Rivet; Kaybee Toys; Stevesons; Sterling Optical, Regis Hairstylists.

14 - NEWSPAPERS: CITIZEN (e) 10,020; sworn Mar. 31, 1982.
Local Contact for Advertising and Merchandising Data: Dick McDermott, Adv. Mgr. CITIZEN, 805 Park Ave., Beaver Dam, WI 53916; Tel. (414) 887-0321.
National Representative: None.

BELOIT, WI-SOUTH BELOIT-ROCKTON, IL

1 - LOCATION: Beloit in Rock County, WI (In Janesville-Beloit SMSA). E&P Map C-5. Beloit and Rockton in Winnebago County, IL. Educational ctr. On the banks of Rock River, 50 mi. S of Madison; 18 mi. N of Rockford; 90 mi. NW of Chicago; 75 mi. SW of Milwaukee. On U.S. Hwys. I-19 & 51, WI Hwys. 13, 21, 15, IL Hwys. 2, 75, 190.

2 - TRANSPORTATION: Railroads-Chicago, Milwaukee & Pacific; Chicago & North Western. **Motor Freight Carriers**-19. **Intercity Bus Lines**-Greyhound; Peoria-Rockford. **Airlines**-Republic, Mississippi Valley Airways.

POPULATION:

12 - RETAILING: Downtown Shopping Centers-6 blocks on Grand Ave., 4 on State St.; 3 on Broad St., 3 on Pleasant St., 1 on 4th St.; on Cranston Rd., Food Fair Center.
Regional Shopping Centers-Beloit Plaza, 38 stores at Riverside Dr. & Henry Ave.
Neighborhood Shopping Centers-1 block at Park & White; 1 at Grand & 8th; 1 at Brooks & St. Lawrence; 2 at Liberty & Madison Rd.; 1 at W. Grand & Town Line; 1 at Wisconsin & Woodward.

Nearby Shopping Centers

Name (No. of stores)	Miles from Downtown	Principal Stores
Beloit Plz.(41)	0	J.C. Penney, Sears, Weise
Westgate(3)	NA	Woodman Mkt.
Prairie Ave.(2)	NA	K mart, Sentry

Principal Shopping Days-Mon., Thu., Fri., Sat. **Stores Open Evenings**-Food nightly, others Mon., Fri. & Sun.; Beloit Plaza Mon. to Sat.

13 - RETAIL OUTLETS: Department Stores-J.C. Penney, McNeany, Stewarts; Sears; Weise's. **Variety Stores**-Woolworth. **Discount Stores**-Jupiter; K mart. **Chain Drug Stores**-Walgreen; May's. **Chain Supermarkets**-Eagle Foods 2; Fox 2; Crystal 3; Woodman's, Kohls; Sentry. **Other Chain Stores**-Singler Co.; Firestone; Leath (furn.); Sears; Montgomery Ward (catalog); Diane Shop, Nobil Shoes; Neumode; Father & Son Shoes; Stewarts; Schiff Shoes, Jupiter, Goodyear.

14 - NEWSPAPERS: NEWS (e) 19,563; sworn Sept. 1, 1981.
Local Contact for Advertising and Merchandising Data: Larry Brown, Adv. Dir., NEWS, 149 State St., Beloit, WI 53511, Tel (608) 365-8811.
National Representative: Landon Associates.

CHIPPEWA FALLS

1 - LOCATION: Chippewa County (In Eau Claire SMSA) E&P Map B-3. On Chippewa River, near Lake Wissota, 92 mi. N of LaCrosse, 90 miles E of Minneapolis-St. Paul; 10 mi. N of Eau Claire. In the NW part of the State. On U.S. Hwy. 53, State-WI Hwys. 29 & 178 & 124.

2 - TRANSPORTATION: Railroads-CM, St.; P&P; Soo and C St. PM&O (C&NW). **Motor Freight Carriers**-2. **Intercity Bus Lines**-Greyhound, Motor; North Central; B U S. City Bus with service to & from Eau Claire, Wis. **Airlines**-Republic.

3 - POPULATION:
Corp. City 80 Cen. 11,845; Loc. Est. 11,782
CZ-ABC. (70) 13,770; (82) 13,600
RTZ-ABC. (70) 39,505; (82) 45,700
County 80 Cen. 51,702; Loc. Est. 53,125
SMSA 80 Cen. 130,507; Loc. Est. 135,406
City & RTZ ABC   275; (82) 59,300

to-Coast; Spurgeon's; Mary's; Hardware Hank; PrangeWay; OK Hardware, Shop Ko.
Variety Stores-Woolworth; Schulz Bros.; Ben Franklin.
Chain Drug Stores-Badger Walgreen; Medicine Shop; Snyder.
Chain Supermarkets-Chippewa Super Valu; Red Owl; I.G.A., National Foods.

14 - NEWSPAPERS: HERALD-TELEGRAM (e) 9,158; Mar. 31, 1982 ABC.
Local Contact for Advertising and Merchandising Data: Peter Pritchard, Adv. Mgr., HERALD-TELEGRAM, 22 W. Central, Chippewa Falls, WI 54729; Tel. (715) 723-5515.
National Representative: None.

EAU CLAIRE

1 - LOCATION: Chippewa and Eau Claire Counties (SMSA). E&P Map B-4. 90 mi. E of St. Paul, MN; 225 mi. NW of Milwaukee. Junction Eau Claire and Chippewa Rivers. On U.S. Hwys. I-94, 12, 53; State Hwys. 93, 85 & 37.

2 - TRANSPORTATION: Railroads-Chicago & North Western, The Milwaukee Road; Soo Line. **Motor Freight Carriers**-18. **Intercity Bus Lines**-5 lines, 82 buses per day. Northland Greyhound; Stewart; Wis. Northern; North Central; La-Claire. **Airlines Serving City**-Republic; Mid State.

3 - POPULATION:
Corp. City 80 Cen. 51,509; Loc. Est. 53,589
CZ-ABC. (70) 51,000; (82) 60,900
RTZ-ABC. (70) 147,357; (82) 169,100
Counties/SMSA 80 Cen. 130,507; Loc. Est. 135,406
   Chippewa Falls 80 Cen. 51,702; Loc. Est. 53,125
   Eau Claire 80 Cen. 78,805; Loc. Est. 82,281
City & RTZ-ABC. (70) 198,357; (82) 230,000

4 - HOUSEHOLDS:
Corp. City 80 Cen. 18,359; Loc. Est. 19,444
CZ-ABC. (70) 15,621, (82) 21,900
RTZ-ABC. (70) 42,912; (82) 57,000
Counties/SMSA 80 Cen. 44,592; 47,677
   Chippewa Falls 80 Cen. 17,262; Loc. Est. 18,270
   Eau Claire 80 Cen. 27,330; Loc Est. 29,407
City & RTZ-ABC. (70) 58,533; (82) 79,800

5 - BANKS:

	NUMBER	EST. DEP.
Commercial	5	$473,000,000
Savings & Loan	4	$182,100,000
Credit Unions	8	$21,200,000

6 - PASSENGER AUTOS: Counties: Chippwea Falls 24,640; Eau Claire 40,800

7 - ELECTRIC METERS: 18,581

8 - GAS METERS: 8,350

9 - PRINCIPAL INDUSTRIES: Tire Plant; Paper Mill; Meat Packing; Machine Shops; Computer Co.; Printing & Publishing. Total 8,105 Wage Earners ($298 avg. wkly. wage).

Source: *Editor & Publisher Market Guide, 1983,* Section II, p. 380.

of their circulation areas from time to time. They make this information available to merchants, who use it to learn more about the consumers in their trading areas. Retailers can also secure information from local Chambers of Commerce, banks, public utility companies, city planning commissions, and shopping center developers.

Factors to Consider when Evaluating Locations

Many internal factors and management decisions affect the eventual success or failure of any one location. To illustrate this point, consider the physical attractiveness of storefronts and signs, interior decor and layout, kinds and quality of merchandise available, pricing approaches, credit and returned-goods policies, services, and similar aspects. All of these contribute to both the store's image and its trading area. So do all advertising and other promotional efforts.

Shopping areas themselves contain image-creating characteristics. Three of the more essential are:[16]

1. Assortment: the variety of stores in the area, quality of the outlets and of the merchandise they carry, special sales offered, and so on.
2. Facilities: overall layout, parking facilities, availability of refreshments, and so on.
3. Market Posture: general price level, store personnel, and so on.

External factors are also important to the retail firm. These include accessibility to the site, compatibility of adjacent stores, competitors, convenience of the location, and the store's business hours.[17]

In searching for good locations, the retailer needs to investigate on three levels: (1) the city or town where the store is situated, (2) the vicinity of the store, and (3) the exact site itself.

Factors to Check in the Larger Community

The store location decision is a serious one. At risk is a sizable, long-term financial commitment by the retailer. It is thus essential to consider, first of all, the potential rewards in the light of necessary costs.

In their quest for locations, most retailers take pains to check into three sets of variables that pertain to the city or town in question: (1) characteristics of the population, (2) economic factors, and (3) factors that contribute to the quality of life for those who live or work in the area. Some of the factors to be examined are listed below:

Population Characteristics:

> distribution of age groups
> level of education
> percentage of homeowners (as against renters)
> political attitudes
> rate of population growth (or decline)
> sex
> social classes
> subcultures (nationalities represented, racial composition)

Economic Factors:

> availability of labor (for larger retail organizations)
> disposable income of population

distribution of purchasing power
extent of employment (and unemployment rate)
seasonal inflows of visitors
taxation burden
types of businesses in town
total retail sales (and total retail potential)

Quality of Life Factors:

availability of public transportation
civic groups
climate
fraternal organizations
houses of worship
leisure time pursuits
parks and other recreation areas
public schools
quality of police and fire protection services
roads
theaters

The Store's Neighborhood and the Site Itself

Retailers need to study the surrounding neighborhood as well as the exact site. Some of the aspects of the shopping area that merit review are the:

overall attractiveness and general appeal
size of its trading area
adequacy of parking facilities
traffic that passes through (pedestrian and vehicular)
number, kind, size, quality, and effectiveness of stores that carry competitive merchandise
local ordinances and zoning regulations

As for the site, the following factors should be examined:

accessibility to the premises
location on the "right" (busier) side of the street
compatibility of neighboring stores
corner location (in preference to an in-block location)
condition of the storefront and building
costs (of building, renting, buying, renovating)
possibilities for expansion at the site
quantity (and quality) of passersby
sales potential of location

Location Research

Because of severe budgetary constraints, small independent retailers will seldom research store locations extensively. This is not true of

From *The Wall Street Journal*, with permission of Cartoon Features Syndicate.

"Before I sign this peace treaty, what's this small print about 'zoning laws'!?"

larger retail companies. Long-established firms often conduct their own research using computer models that involve 20 or more variables. Masses of external data and information from internal records are built into the program. Nevertheless, even small organizations can come up with one or more inexpensive approaches to location decisions. **License plate analysis,** for example, is a helpful and quick method for evaluating a particular location. The license numbers of several hundred cars parked nearby are recorded. These are later checked against motor vehicle bureau records to determine their owners' addresses.[18] The addresses are then pinpointed on an area map. When the job has been completed, the map will reveal the site's approximate trading area. It will also indicate from which neighborhoods the retailer can expect to draw the majority of shoppers.

Retailers can derive similar information through interviews either by telephone or in person with shoppers in the area. Maps are also used in connection with this technique. First, concentric circles that fan out from the location are traced on the map. Then, information about where the interviewed consumers reside and shop is plotted.[19] In the same way, department stores and other large retailers with many charge customers can analyze records for valuable insights into the geographic distribution of customers' homes.

The Index of Retail Saturation Because it describes the sales volume per square foot of selling space within a given area for specific products, manufacturers find the **Index of Retail Saturation** quite useful. Many retail chains also use the index to help make decisions about promising markets in which to expand.[20] The firm will first research the number of consumers in the area who are likely to buy the kinds of merchandise it sells. Next, it determines how much the individual will spend, on average, for those goods. Finally, the retail company calculates the total amount of space in the area that stores devote to the sale of such merchandise.

The index is calculated with a formula similar to the one below:

$$IRS = \frac{(P)(A.E.)}{S}$$

The symbols are interpreted as follows:

IRS = Index of Retail Saturation (for a specific area).
P = The number of people in the area who are likely customers for the particular line(s) of merchandise.
A.E. = The average per capita expenditure for these goods.
S = The total space devoted to selling these goods in *all* stores in the section (in square feet).

Assume, for example, that we contemplate opening a store in Community X. We estimate that 10,000 residents are likely to buy the kinds of merchandise we sell. An individual typically spends $25. In the area there are 12 other stores that carry similar goods. All together, about 5,000 square feet of selling space is devoted to this merchandise. We plug these figures into the formula:

$$IRS = \frac{(10,000)(\$25)}{5,000}$$

$$= \frac{\$250,000}{5,000}$$

$$= \underline{\$50}$$

The resulting Index of Retail Saturation of $50 indicates that the community has the potential to generate $50 per square foot for our merchandise. If we normally need to earn $35 per square foot of selling space to net a profit, then there is room in the community for our store. In other words, the area is understored. On the other hand, if the index shows a low figure of, say, $20, we assume there would not be enough business in the area for a 13th store selling the same type of merchandise. In our judgment, Community X would be overstored.

A major conceptual problem with the index is that it assumes that retail sales are a function of environmental variables. Marketing decisions made by a firm can strongly influence consumer expenditures. For example, merchandise assortment and service level can have substantial impact on how much the public will buy.[21]

Store Occupancy

The retail firm can choose from three approaches to store occupancy. It can: (1) buy a site on which to erect a new building, (2) buy an existing store, or (3) rent property. Each avenue has its advantages and disadvantages.

Building a Store

If finances are no problem, the best choice may well be to buy land and construct a new store building. The premises can be designed with all the space desired according to the firm's exact needs. Thereafter, the retailer can maintain this enviable position with no fear of rent increases or of losing the location some day to another tenant. Both of these situations are distinct possibilities when merchants rent stores. Management benefits in still other ways. A sizable depreciation allowance is available to help reduce income taxes. Should the company find itself in a tight cash position, the property can be mortgaged. If the premises are eventually sold, there is the prospect of capital gain. Further, the firm is able to carry whatever merchandise lines it wishes without restrictions by a landlord.

Owning the premises does have its drawbacks. Usually, it requires the largest capital investment of the three approaches. It may also be a painfully slow way for a retailer to get into a location; many months may go by before the store opens its doors to the public. The owners must secure the services of both a capable architect and a reputable builder. Local construction codes must be followed and permits obtained. As a property owner, the retailer is liable for real estate taxes, various types of insurance coverage, and upkeep of the premises.

The **sale-and-leaseback arrangement** is increasingly popular among larger organizations to avoid such headaches. The retail company builds the store to its own specifications then sells it to a realty firm. The REALTORS® then lease the store back to the retailer.

Buying a Store

The initial investment is less stringent if the company contracts to purchase a store occupied by another, often similar type of retailer. These situations carry many of the same benefits and disadvantages of new construction. However, extensive renovation or modernization of the premises may be required. Naturally, the space is purchased as is; it may be too small or too large for the new retailer's needs.

A redeeming feature of this approach is that records will show how the location has been performing for the previous occupant.

Renting a Store

The least burdensome and most popular avenue is leasing an empty store from a building owner. It is also the quickest way to enter a location and begin selling merchandise. If the tenant is able to negotiate a favorable lease, the initial investment may be confined to redecorating the interior, installing fixtures, and stocking the place with merchandise. In some cases, improvements have to be made to the ceiling, lighting, air conditioning, heating, and so on.

By renting, the company avoids paying property taxes. It can rely on the landlord to maintain the building. On the other hand, the firm holds no equity in the property, so long-term financial gain is out of the question. Once the lease expires there is the threat of a substantial boost in rent. Increases of 200 to 300 percent are not uncommon today. Nonrenewal is also a possibility. The landlord may wish to replace the present occupant with another tenant. If this happens, the retail firm will have to give up the location where, over a period of years, it successfully built up a large and loyal clientele.

Leases When renting, retail management must sign a lease with the property owner. A **lease** is a legal contract whose terms and conditions have been discussed and agreed to by both parties. It spells out the names of both landlord and tenant, location of the premises, how long the lease will be in effect, rent to be paid and terms of payment, and other details about default, abandonment, reentry by owner, subletting, repairs, and the like. It grants the lessee the use of the premises for a specific purpose and for a certain period. Both owner and tenant sign the lease. As with all contracts, the retail company should have legal representation.

Property owners may offer store leases under one of several basic arrangements. Because it calls for the smallest outlay of capital, the **turnkey lease** is preferred by many retailers. Under this arrangement, the landlord provides all necessary construction and turns over to the tenant a store that is basically finished. Walls, ceiling, flooring, electrical work, doors, windows, and air conditioning and heating equipment are all in place. The store is ready to be opened; hence the term *turnkey*. Sometimes the landlord will build the store unit in accordance with the lessee's specifications. The tenant only needs to be concerned with decorating the interior, installing signs and fixtures, and putting in stock.

At the opposite end of the spectrum is the **shell-and-allowance lease.** This type of contract calls for only the barest effort from the property owner. Little more is offered than the walls and roof, or *shell,* of the store. In addition, the landlord will provide an *allowance*—a token contribution toward the expenses the retailer will incur in finishing off the premises. The allowance is usually tied to the total square footage of leased space, perhaps $5 or $6 per square foot.

In some new construction (for example, when a property owner puts up a row of stores), a **building standards lease** may be offered. All the stores are constructed with identical storefronts, heating systems, restrooms, and so on. It is then up to the tenants to complete their stores' installations.

Retailers may rent their premises for a specific purpose for a specific period of time under conditions spelled out in a lease.

Courtesy Jacobs, Visconsi & Jacobs, Cleveland, OH

Rental Arrangements Lessors offer a variety of rental arrangements. Three of the more common are the fixed, percentage, and percentage-with-minimum-guarantee leases. The **fixed rental lease** requires the retailer to pay a stated sum every month or every year. For example, a merchant may be asked to pay $800 in rent each month, or $9,600 annually. The rental amount is constant regardless of whether the retail firm realizes or exceeds its expected sales volume. Thus, rent becomes a fixed expense item in the firm's budget. This is not the case, however, with the **percentage lease.** Under this arrangement, the company agrees to pay the lessor a stated percentage of gross sales in lieu of a fixed amount. Rent is treated as a variable expense. Frequently, building owners try to protect themselves against the possibility of low store sales by establishing a minimum rental figure. This type of lease is known as a **percentage lease with minimum guarantee.** Realizing that merchants may worry about excessive rental costs, many lessors will set a maximum figure as well. Another approach is to specify a sliding scale, such as 5 percent on the first $500,000 in sales, 4 percent on the next $500,000, and 3 percent on sales exceeding $1 million.

Summary

Within the typical city's retail structure, there are two broad categories of shopping areas. There are the older, in-city retail sections and the newer, planned shopping centers. In-city types include the central business district, secondary business districts, and neighborhood shopping streets. There are also occasional retail clusters and freestanding stores. Planned shopping centers are complex merchandising units that contain a number of stores and provide convenient, one-stop shopping for the consumer. Among these are regional, community, and neighborhood centers.

The territory surrounding a store (or group of stores), from which most of its customers are drawn, is its trading area. The closer consumers are to the retail location, the greater the probability that they will shop there. Trading area size is affected by surrounding geography, store size, design, decor, kinds of merchandise carried, quality (and exclusivity) of the goods, and so on.

Retail analysts have developed gravitational models to estimate trading area size and the drawing power of stores and retail shopping areas. Other types of decision models have also been developed. Most retailers, however, rely more on the careful evaluation of demographic data and on checklists than on the use of available models.

Before choosing a location, the firm must study the larger community, the neighborhood of the site, and the location itself. With regard to the city or town, the retailer must look into population characteristics, economic factors, and quality-of-life factors. Trading area size, its general attractiveness, and competitive stores must be checked with regard to the neighborhood. Important aspects of the site itself include accessibility, compatibility of neighboring stores, cost factors, and sales potential.

There are three basic ways for a retail company to open up at a location: by erecting its own building, by buying existing premises, or by renting a store. Each avenue has its advantages and disadvantages. The most common approach is to rent. Among the different leases that property owners may offer are the turnkey, shell-and-allowance, and building standards lease. Rental arrangements may be made according to a fixed rental lease or some kind of percentage lease.

Key Terms

traffic counts
central business district (CBD)
multi-use project
mixed-use complexes
secondary business districts
neighborhood shopping streets
retail clusters
freestanding store
planned shopping centers
regional shopping center

community shopping center
anchor store
neighborhood shopping center
trading area
Reilly's Law of Retail Gravitation
license plate analysis
Index of Retail Saturation
sale-and-leaseback arrangement
lease
turnkey lease

shell-and-allowance lease   percentage lease
building standards lease   percentage lease with minimum guarantee
fixed rental lease

**Review
Questions**

1. Identify and briefly describe the three major types of older, in-city shopping areas.

2. What is a retail cluster?

3. Contrast the central business district and the secondary business district.

4. Explain why retail sales in the nation's CBDs have been declining for decades.

5. Why do locations in neighborhood shopping streets often represent more attractive opportunities for new retailers than those in central and secondary business districts?

6. Specify and differentiate among three major types of planned shopping centers.

7. Name the characteristics of a regional shopping center. List a minimum of eight different types of stores that are often found in them.

8. Explain the trading area concept. What is its significance to the retailer?

9. Cite at least five factors that affect trading area size.

10. What is Reilly's Law of Retail Gravitation?

11. Specify some information sources for store location problems.

12. List a minimum of eight population and economic factors that should be taken into account in retail site selection.

13. Identify and comment briefly on some of the quality-of-life factors that merit consideration in selecting a particular city for a retail business.

14. Explain the meaning of each of the following terms.
    a. Axial site.
    b. Middle market.
    c. Infill locations.
    d. Index of Retail Saturation.

15. Contrast the three approaches to store occupancy.

16. What advantages are there for the retailer in building a store rather than renting? What are the disadvantages?

17. Differentiate between the turnkey lease and the shell-and-allowance lease.

**Discussion
Questions**

1. In your opinion, what socioeconomic factors most likely accounted for the spectacular growth of planned shopping centers since the 1950s?

2. Suggest at least two store types that you feel would be compatible with each of the following:
   a. Women's shoestore.
   b. Hardware store.
   c. Home furnishings store.
   d. Bookstore.

3. Locate a retail cluster in or near your home community. Draw a chart, to approximate scale, of the stores that make up the cluster. Fill in the names of the different store types. Does any outlet seem out of place in this group?

4. Why would a retailer prefer to sign a percentage lease with a guaranteed minimum rather than a fixed rental arrangement?

Notes

[1] See: Barbara Bryan, "Urban Renewal," *Stores* 66 (July 1984), pp. 47–49; Lewis A. Spalding, "Some Proof There Is Life after Death Downtown," *Stores* 63 (October 1981), pp. 59–64.

[2] Eric Peterson, "Conversions," *Stores* 66 (July 1984), pp. 35–36*ff.*

[3] Eric C. Peterson, "Multi- and Mixed-Use Projects," *Stores* 65 (January 1983), pp. 52*ff;* Eric C. Peterson, "Multi-Use," *Stores* 65 (March 1983), pp. 40*ff.*

[4] "Going Up! New York's First Multi-Level Theme Retail Project, Herald Center," *Stores* 65 (January 1983), pp. 50–51.

[5] For helpful information regarding shopping centers from the Small Business Administration, see: J. Ross McKeever, "Factors in Considering a Shopping Center Location," *Small Marketers Aids No. 143* (May 1970); Dr. Robert H. Myers, "Suburban Shopping Centers," *Small Business Bibliography No. 27* (January 1974); James R. Lowry, "Using a Traffic Study to Select a Retail Site," *Small Marketers Aids No. 152* (May 1973).

[6] Randall Craig Nevils, "A Study of Retail Shopping Center Atmospherics as a Buying Influence" (Ph.D. diss., University of Arkansas, 1977).

[7] William J. Reilly, "Methods for the Study of Retail Relationships," *Research Monograph No. 4* (Austin, Tex.: Bureau of Business Research, University of Texas, 1929).

[8] Paul D. Converse, "New Laws of Retail Gravitation," *Journal of Marketing* 14 (October 1949), pp. 379–84.

[9] David L. Huff, "Defining and Estimating a Trading Area," *Journal of Marketing* 28 (July 1964), pp. 34–38.

[10] For example, see: Thomas J. Stanley and Murphy A. Sewall, "Image Inputs to a Probabilistic Model: Predicting Retail Potential," *Journal of Marketing* 40 (July 1976), pp. 48–53; John R. Nevins and Michael J. Houston, "Image as a Component of Attraction to Interurban Shopping Areas," *Journal of Retailing* 56 (Spring 1980), pp. 77–93; Melvin R. Crask, "A Simulation Model of Patronage Behavior within Shopping Centers," *Decision Sciences* 10 (January 1979), pp. 1–13.

[11] For a summary table of some approaches to location analysis, see: Louis W. Stern and Adel I. El-Ansary, *Marketing Channels*, 2d ed. (Englewood Cliffs, N.J.: Prentice-Hall, 1981), p. 60. See also: William Applebaum, "Methods for Determining Store Trade Areas, Market Penetrations, and Potential Sales," *Journal of Marketing Research* 3 (May 1966), pp. 127–41; David B. MacKay, "A Microanalytic Approach to Store Location Analysis," *Journal of Marketing Research* 9 (May 1972), pp. 134–40; William R. Kinney, Jr., "Separating Environmental Factor Effects for Location and Facility Decisions," *Journal of Retailing* 48 (Spring 1972), pp. 67–71; C. Samuel Craig, Avijit Ghosh, and Sara McLafferty, "Models of the Retail Location Process: A Review," *Journal of Retailing* 60 (Spring 1984), pp. 5–36.

[12] L. A. White and J. B. Ellis, "A Systems Construct for Evaluating Retail Market Locations," *Journal of Marketing Research* 8 (February 1971), pp. 43–46.

[13] Dale D. Achabal, Wilpen L. Gorr, and Vijay Mahajan, "MULTILOC: A Multiple Store Location Decision Model," *Journal of Retailing* 58 (Summer 1982), pp. 5–25.

[14] John E. Mertes, "A Retail Structural Theory for Site Analysis," *Journal of Retailing* 40 (Summer 1964), pp. 19–30*ff.*

[15] Morton S. Stark, "Where Retailing Will Expand," *Stores* 62 (January 1980), pp. 50*ff.*

[16] Nevins and Houston, "Image as a Component," pp. 87–88.

[17] Herbert H. Hand, John S. Dunkelberg, and W. Palmer Sineath, "Economic Feasibility Analysis for Retail Locations," *Journal of Small Business Management* 17 (July 1979), pp. 28–35.

[18] "Citing a Superior Retail Site," *Stores* 62 (February 1980), p. 65.

[19] Edward M. Mazze, "Determining Shopper Movement Patterns by Cognitive Maps," *Journal of Retailing* 50 (Fall 1974), pp. 43–48.

[20] See: Bernard J. LaLonde, "The Logistics of Retail Locations," in William D. Stevens, ed., *The Social Responsibilities of Marketing* (Chicago: American Marketing Association, 1961), pp. 567–73.

[21] Charles A. Ingene and Robert F. Lusch, "Market Selection Decisions for Department Stores," *Journal of Retailing* 56 (Fall 1980), pp. 21–40.

Courtesy Sears, Roebuck & Co., Chicago

DESIGNING THE STORE

Your Study Objectives

After you have studied this chapter, you will understand:

1. The importance of the retail store's exterior in attracting shoppers and creating company image.
2. The details of interior design and decor.
3. Popular store layout arrangements.
4. The retailer's concern with productivity and how it affects space allocation.

In Chapter 9 we reviewed the methods retail management uses to select store locations. You learned how to recognize and differentiate among the various types of retail locations. You were introduced to the trading area and discovered which factors merit serious consideration in site analysis. You were given information about store occupancy.

In this chapter we discuss the elements of store construction and design. First we consider the outer physical structure: the storefront (or facade), signing, show window(s), entrance(s), and other aspects of the store exterior. Next we move inside the premises. We show how today's retailers treat walls, floors, ceilings, and lighting to create an attractive shopping environment. We describe distinct patterns of store layout. You will learn why and how retailers try to maximize their use of space and use proper fixtures and equipment. Figure 10.1 outlines these elements and their interrelationships.

Store Construction

In setting up shopkeeping in a new location, management faces two choices: (1) erect a building or (2) remodel and/or refurbish an existing structure.

During the 1960s and early 1970s, many supermarket, drug, and specialty store chains sought rapid expansion by adding large numbers of units. A significant percentage of these stores were new construction. The new outlets were often larger. A deteriorating economy in the early 1980s led to a new spirit of conservatism. Escalating costs of land, materials and labor, and high interest rates on borrowed capital have forced retailers to pay closer attention to their return on investment (ROI).[1] Retailers have been curtailing their investment costs by constructing smaller stores and by economizing on fixtures and decor.[2] More and more firms are gravitating toward **second-use facilities.** These are premises originally built for and occupied by other tenants.[3] Remodeling an existing store requires far less capital than new store construction.

Consider Green Acres, a major shopping center located in Valley Stream, New York. A Gimbel's branch is at one end of the enclosed mall. At the opposite end stands another large store. It was once occupied by S. Klein, a department store chain that went out of business in the 1970s. Subsequently, the building was taken over by the E. J. Korvettes discount chain. In 1980, Korvettes began liquidating its holdings and vacated the premises. Since that time, the building has been occupied by branches of two other department store chains.

The Store as a Machine

A major book on store planning points out that "stores are machines designed to display, house, and sell merchandise."[4] This is a realistic

Figure 10.1
Elements considered in
designing the store

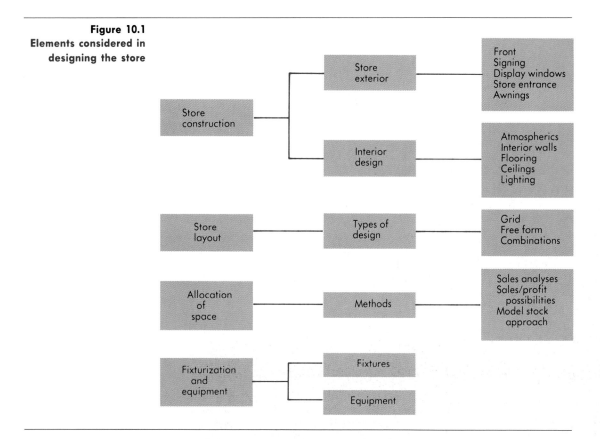

and pragmatic view. It suggests the need for careful planning and studied attention to purposes, functions, design, and form. It conjures up visions of gears, cogs, flywheels, wiring, and other machine parts. In a store these parts translate to the exterior, the interior (both structure and contents), selling and nonselling personnel, systems and procedures, and so on. Like a well-built machine, the higher the quality of its components, the better the output.

Different types of stores require different treatments, for each is a distinct kind of machine. The composition of the treatment depends on a variety of factors: kind of merchandise, quality level, prices, size of store, and type of shopping area where it is located. A neighborhood bar differs strongly from a liquor store, although both sell alcoholic beverages. The florist's shop, grocery, bakery, pharmacy, and women's ready-to-wear boutique all need to create distinct shopping environments for their patrons.

For assistance in store layout and decor, large retail companies often maintain a staff of architects, store designers, and engineers.

Small independents may need to secure aid from outside professionals. They can also obtain information from their trade association, from suppliers, or by visiting other stores of the same type.

The Store Exterior

In and of itself, the *storefront* is a major form of sales promotion for the retail company. It functions as the interface between the company's image and the community.[5] It promotes the firm day and night, seven days a week, all year round—year after year! Compare it, if you will, to advertising. Newspaper advertisers are concerned about the number of impressions made on readers. How productive is a storefront with regard to the total number of impressions made over many years? Or the number of people impressed? A storefront's advertising cost is likely far lower than the cost of a continuous year-long advertising campaign!

Think of the storefront as a three-dimensional advertisement.[6] It projects both the type and character of the retail firm. It must capture the pedestrian's attention within seconds. Passersby must quickly grasp the kind of store it is—and how it differs from the surrounding stores; the type of merchandise it carries; and an idea of the kind of atmosphere to be expected inside.

Many kinds of building and surfacing materials are used in constructing storefronts. Brick, concrete, fieldstone, granite, marble, metals (bronze, aluminum, and others), stucco, and tile are some examples. Consideration is given not only to the cost of the materials but also to their resistance to extreme weather conditions, durability, attractiveness, cost of maintenance, and so on.

Other aspects of the store exterior include the signing, windows, and entrances. Many retail stores also have awnings.

Signing

Signs are effective communication media. As the Small Business Administration points out: "Signs help people find you; they reach people who are passing by your establishment; they present an image of your business. In short, signs tell people who you are and what you are selling."[7]

Retailers find that it pays to invest in good signing because of its value in promotion. The store sign is generally placed above the show window(s) to catch the eyes of shoppers across the street. Typically, this overhead sign is laid flat against the building. It may also be set up to project outward if local ordinances do not ban this position. Projecting signs are frequently two sided and occasionally three sided so they may be readily seen by people walking in both directions.

Besides identifying the name and type of business, the sign should fit in with the image the retailer intends to convey to the public.

Signs are effective communication media.

Courtesy Orange Julius of America, Santa Monica, CA

Signs may be illuminated or nonilluminated. Many are box-like and contain light fixtures over which is placed a cover sheet of translucent plastic. Molded letters form the firm's name and perhaps several words identifying what is being sold inside. Or instead of the sign box, cutout letters may be superimposed over a light source. The letters may be of wood, metal, or plastic and are indirectly illuminated from behind. Sometimes simple neon tubing is used, the glass tubing forming the logo, or signature, of the retail company.

Before ordering their overhead signs, retailers need to check with local authorities about signing regulations.

Many stores also have their firm names lettered on the window glass. Others suspend illuminated signs inside the windows. Freestanding outlets often install large signs on posts or pillars in front of their premises. This permits shoppers traveling by car to see them easily and from a distance.

Display Windows
The major purpose of a display window, or **show window,** is to attract the attention of passersby. The window tells consumers about the store and its offerings. It suggests the quality and prices of merchandise. It imparts a first impression, along with the storefront, of the firm's image. The merchandise and display technique employed in the window induce some people to enter the store.

Sometimes the overhead sign takes the form of the company's logo.

Courtesy D&L Venture Corporation, New Britain, CT

For many stores the display window is a significant sales generator. Like the colorful wrapping and fancy bow on a packaged gift, it suggests the excitement that may be found within. A store may have one, two, three, or more show windows. Some merchants prefer the **open front;** many of the shops in enclosed malls are of this type. An open storefront encourages those who are strolling past to come in and look around. No barrier exists between the shoppers and the store.

Many stores have more than two windows.

Courtesy Hess Shoes, Baltimore, MD/Betsy H. Hess photo

An arcade front generates increased shopper attention.

Courtesy Streicher's, San Diego, CA

Oversized panes of glass close up the fronts of some stores, and there are no display windows. Supermarkets are typically built this way. So are many discount, variety, and drug outlets that are organized for self-service. Frequently, these retailers tape large posters, banners, or blowups of newspaper advertisements to the glass to call attention to special promotions.

Window Construction Although the typical show window is rectangular, other shapes are possible. In a row of stores, most windows are aligned. An occasional window may be set back at an angle from the street line or recessed so that a lobby, or arcade, is formed. Variations like these in a row of stores tend to generate increased shopper attention.

The window base is generally a wooden platform. Its surface may be left unpainted or it may be tiled, painted, or covered with linoleum. Many materials may be used to cover the window floor to create distinct settings and themes. Burlap, netting, satin, grass, cloth, wood shavings, mirrors, and felt are a few of the possibilities.

Selected merchandise is arranged at different heights and in groups with the aid of such props as pedestals, easels, ladders, stands, and the like. (See Chapter 20 for a more detailed discussion of the retail display area.) Windows should be well lighted so that consumers can see the merchandise and signs easily. The right type of illumination is needed to show the goods on display in their true colors and to their best advantage.

Window Backs Most display windows are enclosed on the sides by glass panes or walls. Window backs may be completely closed, partially closed, or completely open. With an **open-back window,** passersby can see inside. The store itself becomes part of the grand display. This arrangement is often valuable if a store's layout and decor, the displayed merchandise, and even the shoppers inside create a more attractive atmosphere. The open back may, however, pose a problem. What shoppers are able to view inside tends to merge and even conflict with their perceptions of the window features.

With the **closed-back window,** we have a totally different situation. The retailer can give full rein to the imagination and talent of the decorator. Interference from the store interior is avoided, so picture postcard-like settings can be created in the window. An almost infinite number of background scenes, floor coverings, props, dummies, and other materials and equipment can be brought into play. Different moods can be established. The height of displays is limited only by the window ceiling. The display windows that encircle Macy's–34th Street in Manhattan—and many downtown department stores around the country—are of this type.

The partially closed back aims at securing the advantages of the other types. It provides the passing consumer with a glimpse of an interesting interior. At the same time, it fences off the window display, thus rendering it more effective. Usually the window back in these cases rises to about eye level or slightly above.

Store Entrances Most stores have a single entrance, often located to the right of the display window. In the two-window store, the entrance is typically found between the windows. A corner location may have windows and doors on both main and side streets or a single entryway at the corner. In the latter case, a pillar is needed for building support; shoppers enter and exit by passing on either side of the pillar. Outlets located in shopping centers may have two customer entrances: the main entrance inside the mall and another providing access from the parking lot. Department stores, discount houses, and other large retailers may have multiple entrances. These are located on several or all sides of their buildings. Some allocate one side of the structure to the receiving department. Often there is a customer-service area, too. This is where shoppers go to pick up their purchases of large bulky goods such as garden furniture, TV sets, and the like.

The small store often has a back entrance for back-door deliveries and for use as an emergency fire exit. These doors are not used by shoppers. They are generally kept well secured with deadbolt and/ or pin-tumbler locks.

Doors of solid glass or of glass framed by wood or metal are popular. These enable shoppers to see easily into the store. Merchants often

Open storefronts encourage mall shoppers to come in.

Courtesy
Paul Harris Stores, Inc.,
Indianapolis, IN

place designs or store-hours signs on the glass to prevent people from accidentally walking into the door. Doorless open-front stores are commonly seen in shopping centers. These may be closed overnight by gates that are drawn down from overhead or pulled closed along a horizontal track from one or both sides.

Awnings Stores located in enclosed shopping centers do not need awnings. An occasional retailer will use an awning or perhaps a canopy for decorative purposes. Elsewhere, many merchants use awnings to shield window merchandise and materials from the sun and from reflected glare. They are also used to protect pedestrians who stand in front of the window during inclement weather.

Interior Design and Decor A major purpose of the storefront is to initiate retail sales. It calls attention to the location and arouses shopper curiosity to the extent that some will enter. Creating an effective selling environment from the space inside is a challenge to the store designer's expertise and creativity. All essential elements and activities must be anticipated and coordinated into a unified and pleasing whole.

Both functional and aesthetic considerations govern interior design;

they are intertwined and inseparable. The designer must devote thought to the construction and decor of space boundaries: walls, floors, and ceilings. The area must be illuminated and the space maintained at comfortable temperatures while the store is open for business. Electrical fixtures and wiring, conduits and equipment for heating and air conditioning, pipes, and plumbing fixtures must be installed. The space must be partitioned into selling and nonselling areas. Depending on the nature and size of the store, accommodations are made for storerooms, an employee lounge, a customer-service desk, receiving and marking sections, dressing rooms, restrooms, offices, and so on. Main and secondary aisles are mapped out. These facilitate customer traffic. Behind-the-counter passageways for sales personnel are planned. Fixtures are positioned properly and display areas designated.

Atmospherics Each of the following retail types has its own special atmosphere, or ambience: an Oriental restaurant, a high-fashion women's dress boutique, a sporting goods store, and an old-fashioned ice cream parlor. Choice of wall coverings, flooring, ceiling type, lighting fixtures, and the use of color all contribute to the total effect.

Marketing scholar Philip Kotler suggested that many retailers have neglected the use of *atmospherics* as a marketing tool. He defined **atmospherics** as "the effort to design buying environments to produce specific emotional effects in the buyer that enhance his purchase probability."[8] Retailers can evoke desired emotional reactions in consumers by appealing to their senses. Wafting perfume through a cosmetics department or arranging for chamber music to emanate from hidden speakers in a fine furniture outlet are examples of what can be done. A quality restaurant could use high-backed chairs covered with rich brown or purple velour.

The use of atmospherics becomes more relevant for retailers as the number of competitors increases, where product and/or price differences are small, and when goods are aimed at specific social classes or lifestyle groups.[9]

Interior Walls Interior walls are used to segment store space and to partition selling areas from nonselling sections such as stockrooms, workrooms, lounges, and the like. In the past, walls were permanently fixed, but the current trend is toward flexibility in space utilization. Increasingly, retailers use movable partitions, room dividers, and portable walls. These enable management to introduce new merchandise lines, expand and contract sections, and install or eliminate entire departments within a short time.[10] Seasonal changes especially require dynamic approaches: the expansion of a toy department before the Christmas season, the phasing out of a swimwear section in August, and so on.

An attractive wall covering and signing enhance this section of a Sears Women's Contemporary Shop.

Courtesy Sears, Roebuck & Co., Chicago

Wall Construction Panels and other dividers are made of many different materials. Wood, pressed board, plastics, metal, and mirrored glass in metal frames are some examples. Lightweight materials are preferred because they can be carried and stored easily. Dividers may be painted, decorated with wallpaper, or covered with cork, felt, vinyl, and other materials. To produce more engaging effects, murals may be put up. These can be panoramic photographic prints in full color or tastefully sketched artwork.

Flooring   A tile floor in a local supermarket would not evoke the slightest notice from a shopper. Yet similar flooring in a high-quality furniture store might jolt the sensitivities of a couple searching for a living-room suite. Rich plush carpeting would be more in line with the couple's image of the interior of such a specialty outlet.

Floor coverings are an integral part of a firm's atmosphere, but there is a utilitarian aspect to them as well. They must be safe to walk on and easy to keep clean, dry, and free from obstacles. They should bear up well, especially in heavy traffic locations. Because replacement is costly they should not be affected or damaged by cleaning compounds or equipment.

Ceilings   Ceilings also contribute to the overall atmosphere of the premises. A secondary purpose is to conceal electrical wiring, pipes, ductwork, and other necessary elements. Whether building a new facility or remodeling an older structure, retailers are concerned with ceiling costs in addition to function and compatibility with interior decor. Old-fashioned, cracked, or unseemly looking ceilings can be modernized by suspending false ceilings below them. Or they can be repainted or covered with a number of surfacing materials. Lighting fixtures can be installed flush with the ceiling surface or suspended from it and can be concealed from public view by eggcrates or sheets of translucent plastic. Walls, flooring, ceilings, and lighting designs may be integrated to produce dramatic effects or to highlight merchandise displays. Instances of effective integration may be seen in Shillito's in Louisville and in Saks Fifth Avenue and Costa Mesa stores.[11]

Ceiling Height A low ceiling can create a more intimate atmosphere in the store. It may, however, impart a discomforting, closed-in feeling to some shoppers. This often occurs if a store is overcrowded with fixtures, displays, and people. Yet low ceilings can reduce energy costs. Because the volume of air inside the store is reduced, less heat is needed for the winter months and less air conditioning is used in warm weather. As a case in point, the Detroit-based K mart corporation decided to lower their standard ceilings in future stores to cut energy expense. They also planned smaller stores. Prior store size for the company had run about 84,000 square feet; newer units were to range between 40,000 and 73,000 square feet.[12]

A high ceiling creates a more spacious environment. Often, however, this is interpreted by consumers as a more impersonal, even cold, atmosphere. Increased lighting, heating, and air-conditioning costs can be expected. Some retailers may be able to take advantage of natural illumination if there are skylights in the building. An interesting example is Bullock's at Oakridge Mall in San Jose. This department store installed a light-emitting roof that consists of two layers of Fiberglas

Spotlights bring out the sparkle and luster of china and glassware in an ACCENTS branch.

Courtesy K mart Corporation. K MART and ACCENTS are service marks of K mart Corporation, Troy, MI

fabric separated by air space. The result is an open, airy environment. The roof is protected with a Teflon coating and is automatically cleaned when it rains. Further, the double layer of Fiberglas reduces the transfer of heat, cutting energy costs.[13]

Lighting Appropriate interior lighting is needed so shoppers feel comfortable as they walk around and so they can see the merchandise on display. Displays need additional illumination to attract consumer attention. They also need a type of lighting that reflects the true colors of the goods displayed. Glare, taxing to the viewer's eyes, can be avoided by using indirect lighting. In designing store interiors, retailers consult with lighting engineers and architects. They may also seek advice from manufacturers of lighting fixtures and from their local electric utility.[14]

Store illumination is measured in terms of *footcandles*. One footcandle represents the amount of light thrown by a standard candle on a flat surface, every point of which is one foot distant from the candle. Merchandise displays usually call for two to five times as much illumination as overall store lighting.

Retail firms are concerned about the high cost of electricity and the replacement cost of worn-out bulbs, or lamps. Two types of lighting are generally available: incandescent and fluorescent. The latter is by far the more cost efficient. For example, a four-foot, 50-watt fluorescent

**Figure 10.2
Use store lighting to
enhance merchandise**

Proper lighting can make common merchandise appear more attractive. For example, the vertical surfaces can be shown to the best advantage by using incident light on a display of opaque merchandise. Incident light is a beam of light falling on a surface. Aim the beam at an oblique angle. If the lower shelves stick out farther than upper shelves, they will intercept the light beam more readily.

Glassware, small appliances, and similar items look better when free of distracting shadows. Shadows can be cut out by lighting each open shelf individually. Use thin fluorescent lamps with shields and locate them just under the front edge of each shelf. A more elaborate method would be to use double translucent glass shelves. Between the two panes of glass there is a thin strip-type lighting fixture which is shielded by a narrow, semiopaque front pane.

Emphasizing the decoration and glazing on china increases its appeal. Do it with vertical fluorescent strips in front of the display case. As part of the room lights in a china department, decorative incandescent fixtures can, for example, simulate lighting in the shopper's home.

The attractiveness of merchandise can also be increased by lighting which brings out its true color. Lamps with complete light energy spectrum and tinted light help do it.

In addition, color-tinted sources can be used to create various atmospheres. For example, pale pink lamps glamorize lingerie, and moonlight blue lamps enhance summer evening wear.

Dramatic displays can be made with color-tinted lamps casting black, grey, or colored shadows. For example, a display of trench coats can be dramatized by the use of shadows to suggest intrigue and identification with the character of spy thriller movies or private-eye television shows.

However, a word of caution on the use of colored lights. Make sure that the customer can examine the merchandise under a light which brings out the true color of the item. Lipsticks provide an example. Suppose you display them under a pink fluorescent light to suggest a romantic evening. Your customer is apt to get the wrong shade if she picks a lipstick. The reason: she usually sees the lipstick under the incandescent lights of her home or in the sunlight.

Mirror lighting is important because a shopper rejects or accepts a frock depending on how it looks on her. Mirror lights should illuminate the figure from head to toe. The angle of the light beams is critical. The wrong angle throws long shadows which emphasize both wrinkled apparel and complexions. If you want to make older people look younger, supplement directional light with a generous amount of diffused lighting.

Fluorescent lamps, which flatter skin tones, incandescent or tungsten-halogen lamps are good for lighting mirrors. Keep in mind also that the light on mirrors should show the true color of merchandise so the customer will not be disappointed when she gets the garment home.

Source: Charles B. Elliott, "Pointers on Display Lighting," *Small Marketers Aid No. 125* (Washington, D.C.: Small Business Administration, 1967), pp. 4–5.

lamp produces the same number of footcandles as a 150-watt incandescent lamp. The cost of using the fluorescent would, therefore, amount to only one third of the other lamp. Incandescent lamps also have a relatively short lifespan: 750 to 4,000 hours. The fluorescent lamp normally averages 18,000 or more hours.

Retailers generally use cool fluorescents to illuminate the store interior. The hotter incandescents are useful for highlighting or featuring merchandise on display. Spotlights, or spots, are reflector-type incandescent lamps used for accenting goods. Colored spots (amber, blue, green, red) may be used to produce special atmospheres and effects. Improved colored fluorescents are also available. Often seen in novelty and gift shops, for example, is the black light lamp that brings out glowing colors on posters, figures, and the like.

Some pointers on using store lighting to enhance merchandise can be found in Figures 10.2 and 10.3.

Figure 10.3
Lighting tips for specific merchandise

1. Use large area lighting fixtures plus incandescent downlighting to avoid heavy shadows when displaying major appliances and furniture.

2. Use general diffuse lighting, accented with point-type spotlights to emphasize the beauty of china, glass, home accessories, and giftware.

3. Bring out the sparkle and luster of hardware, toys, auto accessories, highly polished silver, and other metalware by using a blend of general light and concentrated light sources—spotlights.

4. Use concentrated beams of high-brightness incandescent sources to add brilliant highlights to jewelry, gold and silver, or cut glass.

5. Highlight the colors, patterns, and textures of rugs, carpets, upholstery, heavy drapes, and bedspreads by using oblique directional lighting plus general low-intensity overhead lighting.

6. Heighten the appeal of menswear by using a cool blend of fluorescent and incandescent—with fluorescent predominating.

7. Highlight womenswear—especially the bright, cheerful colors and patterns—by using Natural White fluorescents blended with tungsten-halogen.

8. Bring out the tempting colors of meats, fruits, and vegetables by using fluorescent lamps rich in red energy, including the deluxe cool white type. Cool reflector incandescent lamps may also be used for direct-type lighting.

Source: Charles B. Elliott, "Pointers on Display Lighting," *Small Marketers Aid No. 125* (Washington, D.C.: Small Business Administration, 1967), p. 5.

The stained glass dome in the San Francisco Union Square Neiman-Marcus department store admits light and enhances the elegant atmosphere.

Courtesy Neiman-Marcus, Dallas, TX

For best advantage, lighting fixtures must be spaced properly. The space between fixtures is usually less than the ceiling height. If, for instance, the ceiling is 12 feet high, the space between fluorescent fixtures should run about 9 or 10 feet. With incandescent lighting, fixtures should be placed even closer together.

Store Layout Patterns

Store layout planning must take into account the flow of shopper traffic, the arrangement of selling and nonselling areas, and the location of fixtures. Access to stockrooms and workrooms must be considered along with all other related activities that will be conducted on the premises.

Shoppers should be able to enter, move about unhurriedly, and see the merchandise on display. In a service operation, they expect to be served by salespeople. In a self-service department or store, they need to be able to pick up desired merchandise, pay for it, and exit at will. People are prone to spend more time in stores that are conducive to shopping and that project pleasing environments. The longer they remain, the higher the probability they will buy more. In the congested store, shoppers tend to become confused. They may overlook much of the merchandise on display and curtail their shopping time.[15]

The two basic approaches to store layout are the grid, or gridiron, design and the freeform design.

The Grid(iron) Layout By far the more popular arrangement is the **grid,** or **gridiron, layout.** As indicated in Figure 10.4, the most familiar instance of its use is in the supermarket. Inside the store, shoppers wheel their carts up one aisle, turn the corner, then turn again and proceed down the adjacent aisle in the opposite direction. The straight aisles and 90-degree turns compel consumers to move generally in the same direction and in sequence, much like vehicular traffic moves along city streets. This orderly progression calls to mind the straight-line principle that warehouse operators follow: To maximize efficiency and minimize cost, always move goods about in a straight line (the shortest distance between two points).

High vertical displays, or gondolas, maximize shopper exposure to merchandise and encourage impulse buying. Major departments such

Figure 10.4   A grid layout

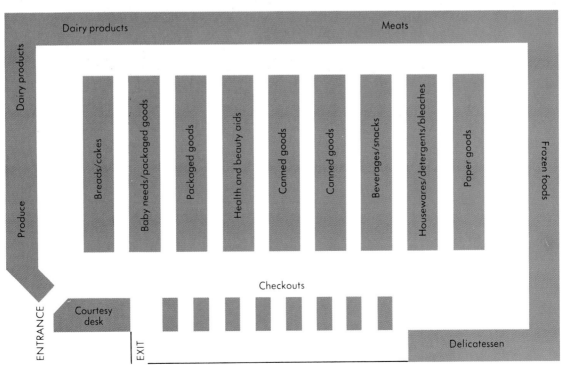

as the meat, delicatessen, and bakery sections are typically situated around the store's perimeter. These are busy sections where numbers of shoppers may congregate.

The grid layout is found in many other types of small and medium-sized stores and in large units of drug, discount, and variety chains. Indeed, it is preferable wherever self-service and self-selection are the major forms of sales presentation.

Some years ago, the Chicago-based National Tea Company designed an innovative departure from the traditional supermarket grid layout.[16] The new layout was based on a radial design that resembled an open fan. Gondolas were aligned so that the aisles between them radiated out from the front-end checkouts like the spokes of a wheel. Dairy, meat, and other counters ringed the circular back of the store. According to management, this variation of the grid layout both encourages impulse shopping and reduces shoplifting.

Freeform Layout   Even though it is a rigid and somewhat austere design, many retailers prefer the grid layout because it exposes shoppers to the most merchandise. Thus, they can maximize their selling area. Where the **freeform layout** is used, fewer goods can be displayed. Shoppers are not encouraged to follow a prearranged path through the store. Missing, too, are the rows of fixtures that typify the grid. Aisles and department boundaries curve around in graceful arcs and irregular shapes that please the eye. People can walk in any direction without restriction. Shoppers are able to stand in front of merchandise on display and examine it leisurely. (See Figure 10.5.)

The freeform design is becoming increasingly popular among retailers of specialty and shopping goods.

Combinations   Traditional and junior department stores, as well as large departmentized apparel and specialty shops, often incorporate elements of both grid and freeform designs. So do better discount houses and other general merchandise outlets. The net effect is a stimulating, more enjoyable shopping environment for the consumer. The combination approach caters to leisurely shoppers who wish to compare merchandise for quality, price, brand, and so on. It also appeals to consumers in a hurry.

In the **boutique layout,** selling departments are remodeled to form attractive individual shops. Each offers a variety of related merchandise. Fixtures, merchandise, and displays are arranged more creatively. Backgrounds and props are added to help project the overall ambience of a small, unique specialty store. A notable, though somewhat extreme, example is The Cellar at Macy's–34th Street. Instead of a basement-

Figure 10.5   A freeform layout

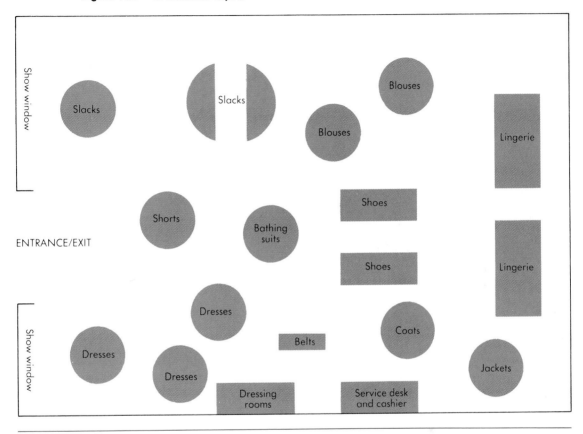

store atmosphere, there are a number of delightful specialty shops. (See Figure 10.6.)

Allocating Space for Greater Productivity

Merchandise retailers realize that space is costly. They can easily calculate its cost by dividing the amount of rent paid by the number of square feet in the store. As an illustration, consider a small store that is 15 by 60 feet. These dimensions yield 900 square feet of space. At a yearly rental of, say, $10,000, the merchant pays $11.11 annually for each square foot. Retailers not only seek to recover their costs but also try to maximize their investment. They assign the greater portion of the space to the true productive end of their business—the selling area. As little space as necessary is devoted to the nonselling

Figure 10.6   A boutique layout

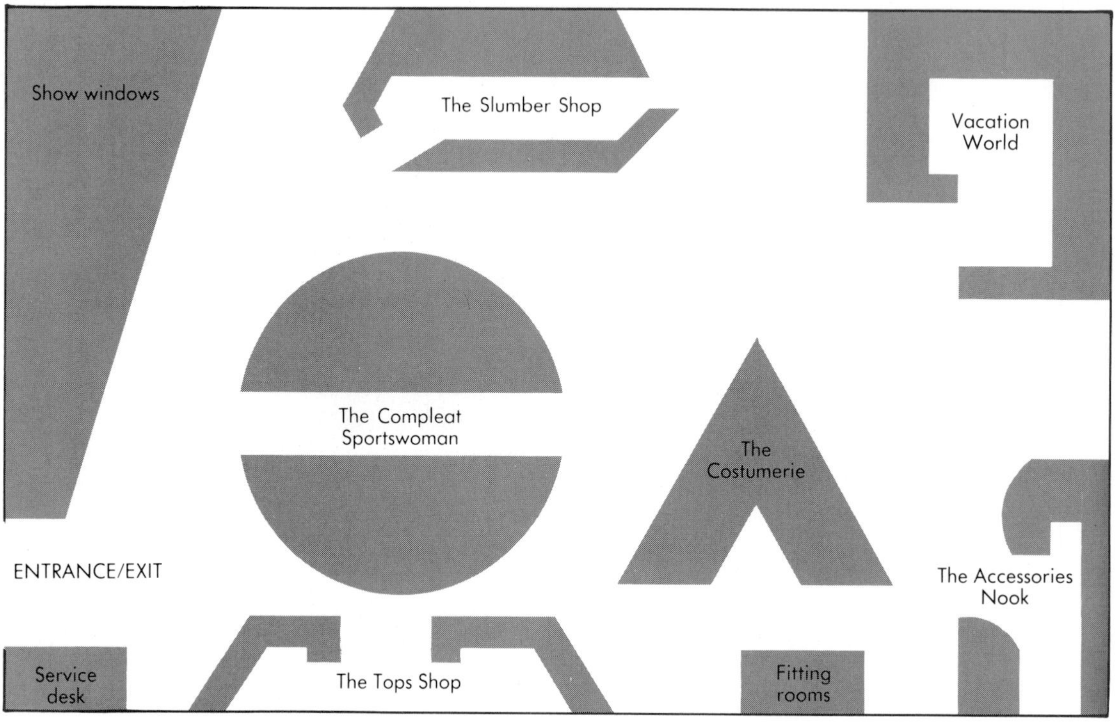

activities required to support sales. Toward the rear of the small store, then, a partition or wall usually sections off a back room. This is a combination of workroom and storeroom. Typically, the selling area occupies 70 to 80 percent of the total square footage, although this depends on the type of store.

Larger retailers face the same problem: how best to separate selling from nonselling space. Obviously, more of the latter is needed to support the greater volume of business such firms do. In some cases, the merchant must make room for customer service, receiving and marking, alterations, fitting rooms, restrooms, employee lounges, and so on. Nonselling space for such activities may be assigned to the store's perimeter and to upper floors in multilevel structures.

Concern over Productivity   Today's retail management is greatly concerned with productivity. Retailers want to increase productivity through the wiser use of space and through improved visual merchandising.[17] It has been suggested that "too frequently, store design and space utilization are not well

Retailers allocate space wisely to increase productivity.

Courtesy K mart Corporation. K MART and ACCENTS are service marks of K mart Corporation, Troy, MI

integrated into the overall merchandising plan."[18] In *Retailing and its Environment,* Albert Bates noted the decline of sales per square foot in virtually every major line of retail trade between 1966 and 1978. He attributed this phenomenon to three developments: overstoring (rapid growth in the number of stores and their aggregate square footage), the expanding number of merchandise items, and management inattention to proper use of space.[19]

As mentioned earlier in the chapter, there has been a decided trend toward smaller stores since the mid-1970s. The typical Lerner Stores outlet, for example, once averaged 11,000 square feet; more recent units are more than one third smaller.[20] New J. C. Penney stores are 20 or 25 percent smaller than older units. Edison Brothers has cut back new store size by 40 percent. Despite the reductions in size, both J. C. Penney and Edison Brothers expect to maintain sales levels in the smaller units by improving merchandising techniques and using taller, high-density fixtures.[21]

Approaches to Selling-Space Allocation

Retailers use a number of approaches to improve the productivity of their selling areas. They may allocate selling space based on sales analyses made according to merchandise categories. They can also increase the size of departments that show greater sales potential or yield more gross profit per square foot. Or they can assign space as needed for their planned model stocks.

Sales Analyses Many retail companies analyze their sales for the previous year by merchandise categories. The resulting information serves as a guide for space allocation. Assume, for the sake of illustration, that a small menswear store measures 20 by 100 feet, of which 1,500 square feet are devoted to selling space. Last year, net sales totaled $600,000. Inventory records show the following statistics for four merchandise categories: sport jackets—$75,600, topcoats—$53,000, shirts—$38,600, and neckties—$17,400. With the aid of a pocket calculator, the merchant can easily compute the approximate percentage of store sales earned in each classification and the amount of square footage that ought to be allocated to each section.

Table 10.1 illustrates this situation.

This procedure might appear sound and capable of providing rough guidelines for space allocation. Yet there are several complications here. For one thing, topcoat sales in late spring and summer are practically nil. Evidently, the 132 square feet must be drastically curtailed during the warmer months and expanded when the weather turns colder. For another, neckties may not require 43 square feet of selling space. A wall display that occupies half that amount of space may suffice to produce the $17,400 in sales indicated for the category. So may four or five counter-top racks. Then, too, topcoats and sport jackets are bulky items. More space may be needed for them than the areas calculated for the two classifications in terms of the percentage of sales each represents. To do $75,600 worth of business in jackets, for example, the retailer has to display a wide assortment of sizes, styles, colors and materials on the store's racks. Much more than 189 square feet would most likely be required to attain that much sales volume in this category.

The logic behind this method does have a flaw. It tends to accent sales as the cause, rather than the effect, of displaying merchandise.

Sales and Profit Possibilities It does make sense to assign more space to departments that can produce more sales or more gross profit dollars. However, the retailer needs to temper this approach with good judgment. Some articles (furniture and major appliances, for example) require more space than others.

Often, trade associations collect data from their member companies so that they can supply operating results for the previous year to all. Along with typical, or median, balance sheets and income statements, these organizations may provide beginning-of-the-month inventory ratios, stock turnover rates, expenditures for advertising and display, and so on. **Space productivity ratios** may also be given. These show the typical dollar sales per square foot of selling space for different merchandise classifications.

Variety and drug chains, discount houses, department stores, and other large-scale retailers generally pay close attention to productivity

Table 10.1 Calculating space allocation by sales analysis — Merchandise Category	Prior Year's Sales	Percent of Store Sales	Selling Area (in square feet)
Sport jackets	$75,600	12.6%	189
Topcoats	53,000	8.8	132
Shirts	38,600	6.4	96
Neckties	17,400	2.9	43

ratios. They use them to apportion interior space and to make decisions aimed at improving the bottom line on their income statements. Many smaller chain-store organizations and independent merchants do the same. They compare results regularly with available industry averages or trends to find out how much better, or how much poorer, their own firms are faring. Retailers continually search for ways to bring in additional sales dollars, or more gross margin dollars, from the same space. Supermarket operators think in terms of sales or gross margin per *linear* foot of shelf space—and with frozen foods, in terms of sales per cubic foot of freezer space.

Assigning Space for the Model Stock Some retailers allocate department and general store space according to their planned model stocks. They plan in advance the complete assortment needed to satisfy customer demand for a specific season. They decide on the breadth and depth of the assortment mix, choosing the quantities of every item to be stocked in each classification. (These and other terms related to merchandise inventory are explained in Chapter 13.) They estimate the total amount of room needed to house the merchandise and the space required for display and selling. They select the types and number of fixtures to be assigned to the model stock, calculate the area that these will require, allow room for customer and salesclerk aisles, and so on. In this bottom-up, or build-up, approach, the requirements for all stock, fixtures, displays, and activities are then totaled to provide guidelines for space allocation.

Fixtures and Equipment

Your neighborhood bakery shop may contain two or three rather long, glass-topped showcases. These are aligned so that each touches the next. While you wait for service the cakes, breads, and buns on display are certain to tantalize your appetite. The posh interiors of many jewelry stores hold smaller display cases. Generally, these are well illuminated and lined with velvet to enhance the gold and diamond pieces within. An array of gondolas, line after line of them, greets the supermarket shopper. The womenswear store contains rack after rack of blouses, dresses, and other garments. In the low-priced variety store, the walls may be covered with pegboards. From the many holes extend metal hooks holding a wide assortment of goods.

Fixtures Showcases, small display cases, gondolas, racks, and pegboard display-ers are examples of **store fixtures.** Traditionally, the term *fixture* has been applied to articles or accessories that are attached to other things, or to structures. Thus, electrical and plumbing fixtures are called fix-tures because they become a permanent part of the premises in which they are installed. In modern retailing practice, the term encompasses even those items that shoppers think of as the store's furniture—all those accessory goods that enable the merchant to store, protect, dis-play, or otherwise help to sell goods. In addition to those already mentioned, here are some other store fixtures:

aisle tables	floor stands
barrels	islands
baskets	racks
bins	shadow boxes
buckets	shelves
counters	tubs
counter-top displayers	wall cases
end-of-aisle racks	wrapping desks

As you know, many of these are not necessarily fixed permanently in place. Indeed, a major characteristic of tóday's fixtures is flexibility. Another is adaptability. Retailers prefer fixtures that can be moved easily as needs dictate. They like modular units that can be grouped together or taken apart to form larger or smaller sections in the store. Such modules are commonly available in a number of standard sizes.

Equipment The retail enterprise also needs other kinds of store equipment to carry on necessary support (nonselling) activities and to facilitate store traffic. Here are some examples of the types found in many establish-ments:

air conditioners	copiers
bookkeeping machines	desk calculators
brooms	dollies
call system	electronic scanners
carts	elevators
cash registers	escalators
computer	floor-waxing machines
conveyors	heating equipment

labeling machines   tape machines
mops   time clocks
scales   tools
sewing machines   trucks
skids   typewriters
stapling machines   wrapping machines

Summary   The outer physical structure, or store exterior, is the consumer's first exposure to the retail firm. Storefront, signing, show window(s), and entrance(s) all combine to promote the company and help to create the store image. The storefront tells the public the kind of store it is and how it differs from neighboring stores. It suggests the atmosphere to be expected inside. The major purpose of show windows is to attract the attention of passersby. Show windows also advertise the quality and price levels of the merchandise carried. Thus, they generate sales for many types of retail companies.

Both functional and aesthetic considerations govern interior store design. Walls, floors, ceilings, and lighting can create an attractive shopping environment. By using well-designed atmospherics, retailers can evoke desired emotional reactions in shoppers. In planning the store layout, the merchant needs to consider the flow of shopper traffic, arrangement of both selling and nonselling areas, location of fixtures, access to stockrooms and workrooms, and other factors. The most popular layout arrangement is the grid(iron). Its straight aisles and 90-degree turns compel consumers to move generally in the same direction, much like vehicular traffic. Where a freeform layout is used, fewer goods can be displayed. Aisles and department boundaries are curved and irregular, not straight. Shoppers do not follow a prearranged path through the store. To add more interest, combinations of grid and freeform are often used.

Space is always at a premium. Retailers strive to allocate store space sensibly in order to produce more sales. Showcases, gondolas, racks, and other fixtures display and help sell merchandise. Retailers also need equipment of various types to carry on their business activities.

Key Terms

second-use facilities	grid(iron) layout
show window	freeform layout
open front	boutique layout
open-back window	space productivity ratios
closed-back window	store fixtures
atmospherics	

Review Questions

1. What purposes is a storefront designed to accomplish?

2. Comment on the retailer's need for proper signing and windows.

3. Contrast open- and closed-back show windows.

4. What is atmospherics? Explain its significance in modern retailing.

5. What specific recommendations do you have regarding the use of atmospherics in the following outlets:
   a. A restaurant that specializes in Italian food.
   b. A sporting goods store.

    c. A music store.

    d. An off-price children's clothing outlet.

6. How does ceiling height affect store shoppers?

7. What are the advantages and disadvantages for the retailer of using *(a)* incandescent, and *(b)* fluorescent lighting?

8. Distinguish between the gridiron and freeform patterns of store layout.

9. How do space productivity ratios for department stores differ from those used by supermarkets?

10. List at least six different kinds of store fixtures.

11. Name 10 common examples of equipment that retailers use.

Discussion Questions

1. Why are many chain-store organizations cutting back on the size of their new units? Is it realistic for management to expect that the smaller stores will enjoy the same sales volume as their larger predecessors? Why or why not?

2. Can you think of any disadvantages to retailers from second-use facilities?

3. Admittedly, display windows are sales generators. Yet many stores, especially in shopping malls, have no show windows at all. How would sales be affected if display windows were erected in these stores?

4. Some merchants change their windows only once each season. One reason they give is that they cannot afford to pay a professional window trimmer more often. What are your thoughts on this?

5. The backs of show windows may be closed, semiclosed, or completely open. For each of the following stores, which type would you recommend? Why?

    a. A florist's shop.

    b. A neighborhood retail bakery.

    c. A women's sportswear boutique.

    d. A corner drugstore.

    e. A junior department store.

6. The ceilings of many supermarkets are quite high. In your judgment, what would be the effects if their ceilings were lowered to, say, eight feet?

7. Select a store in your community that has a boutique layout. Draw a complete floor plan showing departments, fixtures, aisles, wall displays, and show windows.

Notes

[1]Edward S. Dubbs, "Retail Expansion," *Stores* 61 (August 1979), pp. 23–26; Lawrence J. Israel, "Design for Today's and Tomorrow's New Stores," *Stores* 58 (June 1976), pp. 2–3.

[2]Albert D. Bates, "The Troubled Future of Retailing," *Business Horizons* 19 (August 1976), pp. 26–27.

[3]Leonard J. Berry and Ian H. Wilson, "Retailing: The Next Ten Years," *Journal of Retailing* 53 (Fall 1977), pp. 22–23.

[4]Adolph Novak, *Store Planning and Design* (New York: Lebhar-Friedman Books, 1977), p. 1.

[5]Israel, "Design for Today's," p. 2.

[6]Charles S. Telchin and Seymour Helfant, *Planning Your Store for Maximum Sales and Profit* (New York: National Retail Merchants Association, 1969), p. 50.

[7]Karen E. Claus and R. J. Claus, "Signs and Your Business," *Small Marketers Aids No. 161* (Washington, D.C.: Small Business Administration, 1977), p. 2.

[8]Philip Kotler, "Atmospherics As a Marketing Tool," *Journal of Retailing* 49 (Winter 1973–74), p. 50.

294 PART 3 THE RETAIL FACILITY

[9]Ibid., pp. 52–53.

[10]Frank S. Kelly, "Flexibility in Store Design," *Stores* 56 (November 1974), pp. 12–13*ff.*

[11]Photographs of these may be seen in: Lawrence J. Israel, "Store Design," *Stores* 62 (December 1980), p. 32.

[12]"Where K mart Goes Next Now that It's No. 2," *Business Week* (June 2, 1980), pp. 109–110*ff.*

[13]"Let There Be Light! Bullock's New Roof," *Stores* 61 (March 1979), p. 30.

[14]Much of the information in this section is based on two useful publications by the Small Business Administration: Herbert Berman, "Efficient Lighting in Small Stores," *Small Marketers Aids No. 157* (1976); Charles B. Elliott, "Pointers on Display Lighting," *Small Marketers Aids No. 125* (1967).

[15]Gilbert D. Harrell and Michael D. Hunt, "Crowding in Retail Stores," *MSU Business Topics* 24 (Winter 1976), pp. 33–39.

[16]"Radical Radial Store Layout Tops Sales Goals," *Chain Store Age* (September 1972), pp. E66–67.

[17]Edward S. Dubbs, "Upping Productivity: A Major Goal," *Stores* 62 (May 1980), pp. 62–63.

[18]Rom J. Markin, Charles M. Lillis, and Chem L. Narayana, "Social-Psychological Significance of Store Space," *Journal of Retailing* 52 (Spring 1976), p. 44.

[19]Albert D. Bates, *Retailing and Its Environment* (New York: Van Nostrand Reinhold, 1979), pp. 116–18.

[20]Lewis A. Spalding, "Specialty Chains," *Stores* 62 (March 1980), pp. 23–25*ff.*

[21]Albert D. Bates, "Ahead—The Retrenchment Era," *Journal of Retailing* 53 (Fall 1977), p. 40.

Case 3.1
The Children's Store

Peter Barash has operated a children's furnishings store in a busy New Jersey suburb for six years. The area has been growing rapidly as more and more young families move into the area. The Children's Store is a large, brightly illuminated outlet with attractive decor, wide aisles, and colorful signs suspended from the ceiling that identify the various departments and sections. In addition to cribs, bassinets, playpens, strollers, and the like, he carries wide assortments of infants' and children's wear and a limited line of gifts and toys. All merchandise is above average in quality and priced accordingly. Business continues to be brisk.

During the past four months, Peter searched within a 45-mile radius of The Children's Store for a second location. He managed to accumulate a wealth of information about the sites he visited and liked from sources such as the *County and City Data Book, Editor and Publisher Market Guide,* and others. He also ordered census tracts from Washington. Eventually he reduced the list of possibilities to two locations, A and B. Both are in high-traffic community shopping centers. Also, the monthly rent asked for both stores is about the same.

To help make his decision, Peter set down on paper all the facts he had been able to gather. (See Exhibit A.)

Questions

1. Based on available facts, which location should prove more profitable for Peter Barash, A or B? Explain your decision.

2. Suggest three or four other points of information that Peter should try to obtain before making his choice.

Case 3.2
Fred's Mens Shop

Since 1980, Fred Francisco has owned and operated a small menswear store in downtown Tulsa, Oklahoma. Despite cramped quarters, he has succeeded in building his annual sales volume up to over $400,000. This summer, he plans to open a second, much larger unit in a large shopping mall a 45-minute drive from his present location. For more than a year, Fred has been training his young, college-educated assis-

Exhibit A

	Location A	Location B
Space available (in square feet)	3,600	3,000
Number of windows	3	2
Number of households in trading area	17,674	22,121
Persons per household	3.3	2.7
Median household income	$24,730	$19,660
Population growth, 1970–1980	+8.8%	+1.1%
Median years of education, adults	13.3	12.2
Homeowners	38.5%	44.2%
Renters	61.5%	55.8%
Number of private automobiles	51,022	48,769
Percentage of population between ages 21 and 34	20.2%	16.3%
Number of competitive stores in area	3	4

tant, Bob Reiter, to take over as manager of the older unit once the new store has opened.

The two are discussing the new store's layout. Bob is convinced that space ought to be allocated to the five major merchandise classifications they carry in strict accordance with the percentage of overall sales that each contributes. He shows Fred his analysis of the previous year's sales:

Classification	Percentage of Total Sales
Men's clothing	46%
Men's sportswear	27
Men's furnishings	18
Boys' and teens' apparel	5
Shoes (boys' and men's)	4
Total sales	100%

Fred, on the other hand, has a different concept in mind. He feels that a large proportion of the consumers who visit major shopping centers are women and children. Because of this, he believes that demand at the new location should be much higher for boys' and teenagers' apparel and shoes than at his older store. He visualizes a spacious, open-front store with more of a boutique arrangement inside.

He would like to set up two special areas: a separate Teenagers' Corner and a Footwear Nook. He explains to Bob that, in the long run, this approach is bound to pay off. Satisfied teenage customers would become men and continue their patronage of his store. In addition, he is thinking of adding a small women's sportswear department, something he was unable to do at his first store because of space limitations. This would bring him new business.

Questions 1. Carefully consider and evaluate both approaches.
2. Which of the two do you prefer? Why? Defend your position.

The Bettmann Archive, Inc.

Courtesy W. R. Grace & Co.

THE RETAIL EMPLOYEE

Courtesy NCR Corporation

MANAGING HUMAN RESOURCES IN RETAILING

Your Study Objectives

After you have studied this chapter, you will understand:

1. The critical importance of the employee in successful retailing.
2. The basic management principles used in organizing companies.
3. The staffing process and commonly used tools and techniques.
4. Employee compensation plans in the retail sector.
5. The different kinds of training and development activities that retailers use.
6. How and why retail firms evaluate employee performance.

Human Resources: An Introduction

Top management has always underscored the need for conserving and shrewdly allocating its company resources: capital, machinery, inventory, plant, and other assets. Only in recent years have some business leaders expanded this traditional outlook to include an organization's most vital asset: its *human* resources. Many executives still assign a lesser status to the care and nurture of employees. Yet, these are the people who perform the activities necessary to a company's continued viability and growth.

Retail Stores Are Powered by People

In the retail sector, managing human resources is a major challenge. Retailing is highly labor intensive. In all but the smallest firms, labor costs represent the single largest operating expense other than the cost of goods.

Like most small business owners, independent retailers often complain about the difficulty of hiring and retaining competent help. Yet they often show only a modest concern for other aspects of personnel administration. Small retailers prefer to concentrate on the buying, selling, and financial functions.[1] Part of the explanation is that the neighborhood grocery, variety store, or hardware outlet typically hires only salesclerks and stockpersons. These entry-level positions require little in the way of educational background or prior experience.

Larger retailers face more intricate problems. Department stores, drug chains, discount houses, and other large-scale operations need

Department store managers must locate and hire merchandise buyers and planners and many other kinds of behind-the-scenes workers in addition to the salespeople their customers see.

Courtesy NCR Corporation

many kinds of specialized personnel. Organizations like Macy's, Dillard's, Sears, K mart, and J. C. Penney employ thousands of people. In reality, the department store is a one-stop shopping center that may contain a hundred or more departments. To produce annual sales in the millions of dollars requires a sizable personnel contingent. Department store management must locate and hire: buyers, merchandise planners, department and floor managers, typists, stenographers, file clerks, engineers, mechanics, maintenance workers, computer experts, switchboard operators, porters, cafeteria help, lawyers, real estate experts, display personnel, nurses, and other workers. It must indoctrinate and train these personnel and motivate them to maintain adequate levels of performance. Management must also adjust employee complaints and settle grievances, develop managers and supervisors, and conduct many other activities.

Certain characteristics contribute to the difficulty of people management in retailing:

1. The large number of workers.
2. The high rate of employee turnover.
3. The continuous demand for managers at all levels.
4. The need to provide store coverage for daytime, evening, weekend, and holiday shopping.
5. The need to cater to so many different types of employees.

Employees Are Critical to Store Success

As many of us can readily attest, retail salespeople can attract and build a loyal clientele. They can also drive customers away. Research supports this notion. According to one study, more than two out of every three lost customers stopped buying at the store because of employee indifference.[2] Not only can the quality, expertise, and credibility of salespeople strongly influence a store's image, but they can also have a powerful effect on sales.[3]

Personnel Administration in Transition

Large companies have a personnel department that oversees all of the following functions: job analyses and job specifications; the staffing process (recruitment, selection, induction); employee training and development; wage and salary administration; employee maintenance and welfare; performance appraisal; conformance with labor regulations; industrial/union relations; and maintenance of personnel files.

More details regarding the activities of a personnel department may be observed in Figure 11.1.

Over the past several decades, the personnel area itself has been slowly maturing.[4] It has been expanding in the direction of a more participatory role in business administration. Interest in the human aspects of enterprise accelerated strongly during the 1970s. Such concepts as human resource planning (HRP) and organization develop-

Figure 11.1   Functions of personnel administration

Personnel Relations Director
1. To plan, organize, and control personnel relations program
2. To assist in collective bargaining
3. To assist in formulation of personnel policies
4. To maintain close liaison with the line organizations
5. To keep all management current on personnel relations matters

Research and Standards

1. Job analysis
2. Job descriptions
3. Job specifications
4. Job evaluation
5. Job grading
6. Wage analysis
7. Labor market surveys
8. Organizational planning
9. Design of records and reports
10. Manuals and forms
11. Personnel audit

Employment

1. Recruitment
2. Interviewing
3. Testing
4. Induction
5. Placement
6. Changes of status
7. Merit rating
8. Counseling
9. Separation interviews
10. Employment records

Education and Training

1. Education and training standards
2. Economic education
3. Libraries and reading rooms
4. Company schools
5. Training plans
   Operative training
   Supervisory training
   Executive training
6. Training materials
7. Visual aids
8. Records and statistics

Medical

1. Health standards
2. Sanitation control
3. Physical examinations
4. Personal hygiene
5. Professional medical services
6. First aid rooms, hospitals and dispensaries
7. Case histories and other records and reports
8. Health education

Safety

1. Safety standards
2. Safety inspections
3. Safety publicity
4. Mechanical safeguards
5. Safety engineering
6. Safety contests
7. Safety education
8. Accident investigation
9. Safety rules
10. Records and statistics

Employee Service

1. Recreation plans
2. Group insurance
3. Pensions
4. Profit sharing
5. Credit unions
6. Employees association
7. Cafeteria
8. Miscellaneous services
9. Legal assistance
10. Records and statistics

Employee Relations

1. Collective bargaining
2. Wage and salary administration
3. Grievance systems
4. Suggestion systems
5. Morale studies
6. Governmental, public, and union relations
7. Hours and work conditions
8. Integration of group interests
9. Records and statistics

Source: Michael J. Jucius, *Personnel Management,* 9th ed. (Homewood, Ill.: Richard D. Irwin, 1979), p. 76.

ment (OD) came into prominence both in the business press and in discussions among personnel administrators. Specialists applied techniques like modeling and systems thinking in order to understand and interpret what the mission of a modern personnel department should be. (See Figure 11.2 for an example of a systems approach drawn from a personnel textbook.)

Human resource planning is "a process by which an organization assures that it has the right number and kinds of people, at the right

Figure 11.2   The human resource system

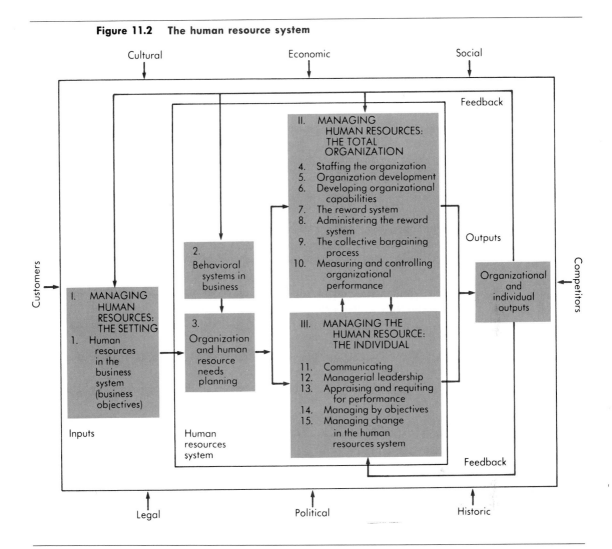

Source: Lawrence A. Klatt, Robert G. Murdick, and Fred E. Schuster, *Human Resources Management: A Behavioral Systems Approach* (Homewood, Ill.: Richard D. Irwin, 1978), p. 13.

places, at the right time, capable of effectively and efficiently completing those tasks that will aid the organization in achieving its overall objectives."[5] HRP programs have moved from the theoretical and discussion stage into the workaday world. Programs have been instituted in a wide range of organizations: industrial, professional, and government.[6] In essence, the process of human resource planning encompasses the following steps:

1. Determine present organization needs.
2. Anticipate and list future requirements.

3. Take inventory of current human resources.
4. Match this assessment of current resources against future needs.
5. Plan and institute training and development programs to attain objectives.
6. Set up a control system to ensure that goals will be reached.

The subject of intensive discussion by scores of writers in the human resource field, **organization development** involves applying behavioral science techniques to induce change in an organization to improve its effectiveness.[7]

Organizing the Retail Company

The proper operation of most goods retailing, no matter how small the firm may be, calls for the diligent performance of three major functions. Merchandise must be purchased for resale, selling must take place, and the financial end of the business must be adequately managed. Subsidiary functions are added as needs dictate. To discharge all functions, an organization is required.

Organization

An administrative function, organizing calls for management to oversee the arrangement of all parts of the company into a unified structure. First, the retailer needs to set objectives and then identify the tasks to be done in the light of these goals. Activities must be arranged into sensible groupings. Thereafter, management must delegate tasks, assign authority, and otherwise arrange personnel resources efficiently. The resulting internal arrangement is the **organization:** the *framework* comprising the positions and persons structured into a company. The term *organization* is also commonly used to mean the *administrative process* of structuring a firm.

Organizational Charts These depict, on paper, the formal structure of a company at precise times: the jobs and relationships among those who fill the jobs. **Organizational charts** are useful for providing guidance to new employees. They serve, too, as points of departure for needed organizational change. Many retailers also rely on company manuals to help indoctrinate new personnel. Typically, the manuals provide a brief history of the firm, outline policies and regulations, show how the firm is organized, and the like.

Basic Principles of Management

Company operations call for following a few fundamental management principles. Basics such as the specialization of work, delegation of responsibility and authority, unity of command, and others are briefly explained below:

Specialization of Work Activities in a business organization are extremely varied. The **specialization of work principle** calls for breaking down the total workload into groupings of activities. By assigning these groupings to specific persons, work is performed more efficiently. Many positions therefore call for specialists with appropriate skills.

The Scalar Principle Under the **scalar principle,** duties, responsibilities, and authority are assigned to positions within the company in a vertical structure, or hierarchy. Decisions are made and promptly carried out. All employees are expected to fulfill their duties without hesitation. **Authority** implies power, the wielding of influence over others. It implies the enforcement of decisions and control over other workers' activities. The other side of the coin is **responsibility.** This refers to the obligation of employees to perform assigned duties to the best of their ability. **Accountability** is also involved; employees are answerable to their supervisors.

Line and Staff Most management jobs in a retail company are **line positions.** People who fill these slots have both the responsibility and the authority to make decisions. They pass these decisions down to others in the hierarchy because they have been delegated the power to give instructions and orders. Other employees hold **staff positions.** Staff personnel are advisers of some sort, technical personnel, or specialists. These individuals exercise little or no line authority other than over their own staffs of assistants and typists, for example. Staff employees in the large retail company might include, among others: store planners and designers, window display specialists, managers and workers in the security and maintenance sections, and the advertising/promotion director.

Unity of Command A long-supported management tenet is that no employee should work under the supervision of more than one person. The logic behind this **unity of command principle** is understandable. If a worker must report to two (or more) bosses, instructions and orders will occasionally conflict. This can only confuse the employee.

Span of Control The **span of control,** or **span of authority, principle** challenges a manager's capability to direct effectively more than a few subordinates. It holds that the number of people who report to a manager has to be limited. Of course, the number can vary somewhat depending on three factors: (1) the caliber of the manager, (2) the caliber of the subordinates, and (3) the nature of the work. A supervisor on some factory production belt might easily oversee 15 to 20 people. Yet the national sales manager of a large chain of sporting goods stores might find it difficult to adequately supervise and motivate half that many regional sales managers.

Departmentizing makes it easier for shoppers to locate merchandise.

Courtesy K mart Corporation. K MART and ACCENTS are service marks of K mart Corporation, Troy, MI

Departmentizing   A common practice among retailers is that of **departmentizing.** To make shopping easier for its clientele, even a small, independent store will organize its merchandise assortment into groupings, or departments. Thus, supermarket shoppers can readily locate canned vegetables, meats, produce, dairy products, health and beauty aids (HBA), and pet foods. The department store houses many departments under one roof: domestics, draperies and home goods, women's apparel, toys, cosmetics, and so on.

Departmentizing enables many types of retailers to run their organizations more efficiently. Service retailers are no exception. Banks, airlines, restaurants, hotels, and other types benefit from organizing in this manner.

In large retail operations, departments are typically well defined. Each may be placed under the direction of a department manager. Or, to hold down payroll costs, one manager may be assigned to supervise two or even three departments. Each department can keep track of sales, costs, and other details. This enables management to treat each department as a separate profit center. Departmental operating statements can then be prepared periodically.

Here are some of the advantages of departmentizing:

1. Makes it easier for shoppers to locate merchandise.
2. Helps the retailer identify fast- and slow-moving merchandise.

3. Enables the company to employ the principle of labor specialization to good advantage. Capable salespeople can be assigned to departments that call for selling skills, such as cosmetics, floor coverings, and furniture.
4. Allows each department to be evaluated periodically against past performance and/or total store performance.
5. Permits complete departmental responsibility to be assigned to a specific manager, who is held accountable.
6. Often increases sales by grouping similar items together.
7. Aids in curbing shrinkage—the loss of merchandise through shoplifting or other means.
8. Allows the size of departments to be expanded or contracted at will.
9. Permits departments to be relocated to increase sales or gross margin income.

Small Store Organization

The small, independent firm requires an extremely simple organizational structure. The owner takes complete charge of all major facets of the business: buying, selling, store operations, and finance. The grocer, for example, will handle the buying of merchandise for resale as well as the purchasing of fixtures, equipment, supplies, and other necessary materials. Small-scale retailers cannot afford to employ specialists any more than they can afford more than a modest advertising budget. Often, the entire personnel component will consist of the proprietor and one or two employees. Frequently, too, these are members of the owner's family who work part or full time. Responsibilities are delegated by the proprietor.

As the enterprise prospers, the merchant may hire additional people to handle an increasing workload. Typically, the new hires are cashiers, salespersons, stockpersons, and other relatively unspecialized workers. At this juncture, the company's organization may resemble the chart shown in Figure 11.3. As revenues continue to increase, the retailer may eventually place one or more specialists on the payroll. A part- or full-time bookkeeper, buyer, or display person are possibilities.

Large Store Organization

Larger retail companies may employ 15 to 20 people. Many have hundreds of employees; large chains may need thousands. The larger the size of the organization, the more desirable it becomes to follow the specialization of labor principle. As the firm expands, different levels, or layers, of management are added. In the large corporation, the president and vice presidents form the top management group. These officials determine long-range objectives. They establish a framework of policies within which lower levels will operate. It is the responsibility of middle management, the next level, to follow through by

Figure 11.3 **The small store organization**

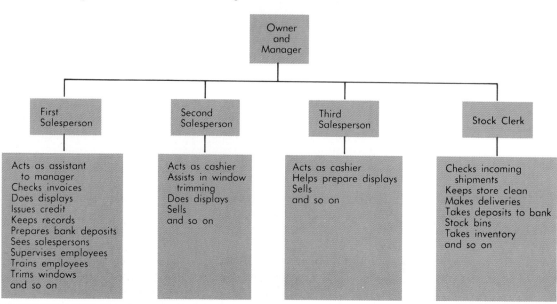

Owner can now devote more time to the *buying* and *control* functions. In addition, owner must now *oversee all* employees. Owner begins to rely more heavily on the first employee to train and supervise the others.

Source: From the book, *The Small Business Handbook* by Irving Burstiner. © 1979 by Prentice-Hall, Inc. Published by Prentice-Hall, Inc., Englewood Cliffs, NJ 07632.

developing and implementing programs designed to attain the firm's objectives. Finally, lower management is given the authority to carry out these programs by directing the activities of their subordinates.

The department store serves as an excellent illustration of large-store organization practice. Well over half a century ago, Paul Mazur proposed an organizational chart that department stores could beneficially use to administer the four basic functions: financial, merchandise, publicity, and store management.[8] With some modifications, the majority of department stores have since modeled their organizations in accordance with the Mazur four-function plan. A popular variation today is the five-function organization, which elevates the personnel function to a par with the other four.

Bookkeeping, credit management, budgets, and other financial affairs are now handled by the company controller. The merchandise manager is responsible for such activities as merchandise planning and budgeting, buying, inventory control, and selling. The publicity manager, nowadays more often called the advertising (or promotion) director, directs both media and in-store advertising, publicity, sales promotion, and public relations. The store manager oversees store operations.

Among other duties and responsibilities, this executive sees to it that the store opens and closes as scheduled and that it is properly staffed; supervises all maintenance and store upkeep; is responsible for incoming deliveries and outgoing shipments; oversees the satisfaction of customer complaints; and directs the operation of all departments, as well as dressing rooms, restrooms, employee lockers, lounges, and other nonselling areas.

Stock and sales employees are supervised by department managers and buyers. In turn, these employees are under the jurisdiction of merchandise managers and division heads.

Staffing the Retail Enterprise

The **staffing function** involves locating, screening, and selecting personnel for job vacancies in the organization. Good judgment must be exercised at every stage of the staffing process. This has become increasingly important since the 1960s with the passage of the Equal Pay Act and the Civil Rights Act. Caution became even more imperative with the passage, in 1972, of the Equal Employment Opportunity Act. (See Table 11.1.) Today employers may not discriminate against individuals in any aspect of personnel administration because of age, sex, color, race, religion, or country of origin. A federal agency, the Equal Employment Opportunity Commission (EEOC), published guidelines for employers to follow. Companies were encouraged to develop affirmative action programs to demonstrate their acceptance of and compliance with the principles embodied in the legislation.

Table 11.1
Federal labor legislation

Year Enacted	Statute	Significant Aspects
1935	National Labor Relations Act (Wagner Act)	Prohibits unfair practices by employers and labor unions. Gives employees the right to organize and engage in collective bargaining. Established the National Labor Relations Board.
1938	Fair Labor Standards Act (Federal Wages and Hours Law)	Established the minimum hourly wage. Set conditions for working minors. Regulates wages and hours; provides for overtime pay. Amended over the years to include small, independent retailers.
1947	Labor-Management Relations Act (Taft-Hartley Act)	Established the Federal Mediation and Conciliation Service. Outlawed the closed shop. Provides for the postponement of strikes which endanger the national safety.

Table 11.1
(concluded)

Year Enacted	Statute	Significant Aspects
1959	Labor-Management Reporting and Disclosure Act (Landrum-Griffin Act)	Prohibited employers from restraining the right of employees to organize or engage in collective bargaining. Restricted unfair union practices. Regulates the internal affairs of unions.
1963	Equal Pay Act	Prohibited employers from discriminating against employees because of sex. Calls for equal pay for men and women doing the same work.
1964	Civil Rights Act	Prohibited discrimination in hiring practices because of race, color, religion, sex, or national origin. Created the Equal Employment Opportunity Commission.
1967	Age Discrimination in Employment Act	Prohibited discrimination in employment practices against persons from 40 to 65 years of age (to age 70, as amended in 1978).
1970	Occupational Safety and Health Act	Ensured a safe work environment for employees. Businesses are subject to unannounced visits by government inspectors.
1972	Equal Employment Opportunity Act	Amended the Civil Rights Act to include all private employers of 15 or more people, state and local governments, labor unions, and other organizations. Empowered the Equal Employment Opportunity Commission to bring suit against firms in violation of the statute.
1974	Employee Retirement Income Security Act	Protects the pension rights of employees, including vesting rights and accrual of benefits. Requires companies to file reports with government.

Rather than considering them constraints, personnel administrators should construe the EEOC guidelines as worthwhile suggestions for good management practice. Qualifications established for all positions in an organization must be demonstrably relevant to on-the-job performance. The same attitude prevails with regard to methods and devices used to gather information about job applicants: employment application, interview, reference checking, and testing.[9]

Personnel Sources   Retail companies, especially the larger organizations, need to cultivate all possible sources of personnel. Walk-ins and recommendations are the two internal sources most frequently tapped. Referrals from suppliers are another possibility. If openings are few, a Salesperson Wanted sign in the show window or on the door often will do the job. Outside sources include:

Local high schools, especially distributive education students
Business, technical, and trade schools
Classified advertising in newspapers
State employment offices
Private employment agencies
Placement offices of colleges and universities
On-campus recruitment
Trade associations
Professional organizations
Independent buying offices

Classified ads in newspapers are one outside source retailers use to recruit sales personnel.

Table 11.2
Information sources in
the selection process

Technique	Exempt Employees*	Full-Time Nonexempt Employees	Part-Time Nonexempt Employees
Interview	82.3	95.2	93.4
Application blank	77.8	92.3	90.2
Business references	70.4	74.9	66.4
Personal references	55.6	62.4	58.5
Credit report	33.3	27.0	19.6
Police check	19.0	21.7	19.8
Physical examination	13.8	14.0	9.5
Testing	9.0	16.4	13.5
Polygraph	4.5	7.1	5.8
Assessment center	3.4	1.3	0.3
Handwriting analysis	0.0	1.1	1.1

* Executives and others not required to sign a timesheet.

Source: Charles J. Hollon and Myron Gable, "Information Sources in Retail Employment Decision-making Process," *Journal of Retailing* 55 (Fall 1979), p. 62.

Aids in Selection   Among the tools available to help retailers make hiring decisions are job specifications, employment applications, interviews, reference checking, and testing. Credit reports, police checks, and other less traditional aids are occasionally used. In this regard, Table 11.2 summarizes the findings of a survey of several hundred retail companies.

Job Specifications A single job vacancy may attract a number of applicants. If there are specifications for the job on hand, applicants can be matched against the organization's requirements. Job specs are also useful for orienting new employees, assisting supervisors, and evaluating current employees. Yet the majority of retail firms maintain no written specifications on file despite recommendations to the contrary by personnel professionals.

Developing these specifications entails a three-step procedure:

1. Management first reviews all positions in the company. Employees are asked to help with this **job analysis.** Examined are the kind of work being done, conditions under which the work is performed, knowledge and skills required for suitable performance, organizational relationships, and the like.
2. A **job description** for each position is then prepared from the results of the analyses. As can be seen in Figure 11.4, this form not only defines the job but also lists the duties, responsibilities, limits placed on authority, working relationships and conditions, and other details.

3. Finally, the individual **job specifications** are prepared. These summarize each job to be done and specify the skills, abilities, educational background, and other attributes the jobholder must possess.

The Employment Application To gather information about the applicant, the firm uses an **employment application.** In addition to name, address, telephone number, and social security number, the form has room for the applicant's educational background, employment history, personal data, and other information. Employment applications are sometimes used to assess applicants' writing skills as well, or their ability to follow instructions. A more unusual purpose might be to try to predict the likelihood of an applicant's success in the new job. Some details on application forms have been found to correlate with on-the-job success.[10]

The Short Application Form An abbreviated application blank is often used by larger companies. The morning after an opening has been advertised, the firm's reception area may be swamped with jobseekers. To save time a short form is given out. The form has room for only a few of the more pertinent details called for in the job specifications. It can be filled out in three or four minutes. The reception clerk can quickly review the completed forms and dismiss those applicants who are clearly not qualified. The others are then asked to complete the regular full-length application and stay to be interviewed. Some retailers hold the unqualified short forms on file for future openings that may call for lesser qualifications.

The Weighted Application Blank In attempts to improve the staffing process, some large companies have experimented with weighted application forms. This relatively simple procedure involves selecting two separate batches of past applications from the personnel files. One represents better employees; the other is composed of poorer workers. Item analysis is then used to determine those personal history items that discriminate between good and poor workers. Weights are then developed for the items.[11]

The Employment Interview The most universally used of all selection techniques is the **employment interview.** Even the smallest store owner will question prospective employees thoroughly before making the decision to hire or reject. Regardless of the size of the firm, an appropriate interchange ought to take place. Some independents feel that only an informal procedure is needed because their companies are small. Such an attitude may create problems later on if the firm should prosper and grow.

The completed application form becomes a script for the retailer to follow in interviewing a job applicant. During the interview, the retailer seeks additional information that cannot be found in the application, such as an assessment, however rough, of the jobseeker's ability to communicate. The applicant's appearance, posture, level of enthusiasm, self-control, and other personality aspects are also considered. The merchant will probe into reasons for having left earlier positions, duties performed in those jobs, work attitudes, and so on. Ideally, the interview should represent a two-way exchange. The employer obtains the facts essential to the hiring decision, and the applicant receives information about the job and the company.

Number of Interviews Retailers often grant only a single interview to an applicant, especially for entry-level positions. It may last no more

Figure 11.4
Sample job descriptions: Sales associate and department manager

D&L

Job Title: Sales Associate

Title of Immediate Supervisor: Department Manager
Store Manager

General Nature, Scope, and Purpose of Work

1. Responsible for dressing professionally and for personal hygiene. Responsible for being punctual and dependable.

2. Responsible for approaching customers in a professional manner; for handling customer problems properly, treating each customer courteously, whether a sale or return; and remembering you are the D&L ambassador of goodwill. May be required to Intersell.

3. Responsible for receiving product information from your Department Manager, the location of merchandise in your department(s); knowing what merchandise is new; what's being advertised and its location.

4. Communicates with Department Manager and Store Management and is aware of the "Open Door Policy."

5. Performs stockkeeping and housekeeping functions—cleaning fitting rooms, fixtures, mirrors, and using proper hangers.

6. Responsible for knowing proper procedures in handling security problems; being alert in your department and neighboring department(s).

7. Understands and implements D&L Policies and Procedures in paperwork, terminal procedures, and servicing the customer. Understands our Return Policy, Customer and Sale Adjustment Policy, Proper Telephone Usage, and Special Orders. Understands and implements our procedures for ISI's, Price Changes, Key Recs, Holds, and Layaways.

8. Performs with a positive attitude toward your job and its responsibilities and realizing your importance to the company. Readily accepts challenges and constructive criticisms.

Figure 11.4
(concluded)

D&L

Job Title: Department Manager

Title of Immediate Supervisor: Store Manager

General Nature, Scope, and Purpose of Work

1. Responsible for setting daily goals. Prioritizes daily list of duties.

2. Communicates with other company staff members. Reports to the Store Management for guidance when problems arise. Requests and provides information relating to company operations to salespeople. Delegates responsibilities for day's accomplishments to salespeople on day off. Sets leadership example for salespeople to follow. Communicates with management and buying staff when aware of best sellers and poor sellers.

3. Understands and has a thorough knowledge of:

   Receiving Key Rec's   Receiving/Writing ISI's
   Writing Debit Invoices   Doing Price Changes
   Handling "Holds"   Handling Damaged Merchandise
   Writing Debit Invoices   Handling "Alterations for Stock" and
   Handling Special Orders   "Customers Own Goods"
   Security System   Handling "Marked out of Stock"
   Departmental Coverage   merchandise
   Policy of Importance of Authorizing
      Signature
   Opening/Closing Procedures for Terminal (including cash wrap, paper supplies, adequate cash funds)

4. Coordinates proper placement of merchandise and displays on a daily basis. Understands the proper usage of fixtures and signs.

5. Makes commitments to meet daily goals. Conducts proper follow through of daily priorities.

6. Responsible for dressing professionally and for personal hygiene. Performs job responsibilities with a positive attitude and has leadership qualities. Shows courteousness to customers and fellow employees. Responsible for being punctual and proper notification to management of absenteeism.

7. Performs stockkeeping and housekeeping functions. Responsible for departmental organization, clean mirrors, floors, fitting rooms, fixtures, and cash wrap areas.

8. Trains employees in their departments on a continual basis on D&L Policies and Procedures, and merchandise knowledge. Communicates advertised merchandise and its location with salespeople. Understands that the customer is our first priority in any selling situation.

9. Responsible for the motivation of self and other people. Accepts and invites challenges in a daily working environment. Performs over and above the normal job responsibilities to get ahead.

10. Responsible for approaching customers in a professional manner; for handling customer problems properly, treating each customer courteously, whether a sale or return; and remembering you are the D&L ambassador of goodwill.

Source: Reprinted courtesy D&L, New Britain, Connecticut.

From The Wall Street Journal, with permission of Cartoon Features Syndicate.

"I can remember when all we needed was someone who could carve and someone who could sew."

than 10 to 15 minutes. This is hardly enough time to evaluate anyone's potential, let alone to fill that person in on job duties and company background. Happily, though, many retail companies offer two interviews. A few conduct three. The initial interview may be held by a representative of the personnel department; the second, by a buyer, department head, merchandise manager, or other executive. Usually, this second individual represents the section to which the new hire will be assigned.

Types of Interviews Seldom does the small business owner follow a set interviewing procedure. The dialogue is conducted in an informal manner. Many large firms follow a somewhat similar approach, relying on an open, **nondirected interview.** Some companies employ a more structured, or **patterned interview,** procedure. Here, the interviewer follows a set of questions that have been planned and placed in logical sequence well in advance. Whatever the type of interview, many retailers employ an interview rating form such as that shown in Figure 11.5. This makes the entire process more objective. It also helps to reduce the possibility of personal bias or halo effects creeping in.

Knock-out Factors During an interview, certain information about the applicant may come to light which will cause the interviewer to reject that person at once. Among the **knock-out factors** listed in Table 11.3 are poor communicative ability, excessive job-hopping, unex-

Figure 11.5
An interview rating form

DUCKWALL/ALCO

APPLICANT SCREENING PROFILE

Name _____ Date _____

Address _____ Telephone _____

Applying For Job As_____ Date Available _____

Present Job _____ Education _____

PERSONAL GROOMING	Unkempt; noticeable lack of neatness 1	No special care in dress or appearance 2	Neat and clean 3	Pays special attention to personal details 4	Immaculately dressed and groomed 5
VOICE QUALITY	Harsh, irritating 1	Indistinct, difficult to understand 2	Pleasant tone and voice 3	Clear, understandable; good tone quality 4	Unusually expressive; excellent voice 5
PHYSICAL APPEARANCE	Unpleasant, unhealthy appearance 1	Appears to lack energy, listless 2	Good physical condition; pleasant appearance 3	Appears fit, alert, energetic 4	Especially energetic, good carriage; appears in excellent condition 5
PERSONAL MANNER	Nervous, embarrassed; compulsive mannerisms 1	Stiff, uncomfortable; ill at ease 2	No unusual tension, comfortable, at ease 3	Appears alert, free of tension 4	Unusually self-possessed and composed 5
CONFIDENCE	Shy, retiring; arrogant, "cocky" 1	Submissive; argumentative 2	Reasonably self-assured; forthright 3	Shows self-confidence 4	Unusually self-assured; inspires confidence 5
EXPRESSION OF IDEAS	Unclear, illogical; speaks without thinking 1	Dwells on non-essentials; thoughts not well defined or expressed 2	Speaks clearly & logically, words have meaning 3	Convincing; thoughts developed logically 4	Unusual ability to express ideas logically 5
MENTAL ALERTNESS	Dull, slow to grasp ideas 1	Comprehends ideas but contributes little to discussion 2	Fairly attentive; expresses own thoughts 3	Quick-witted, alert; asks intelligent questions 4	Unusually quick thinker, keen mind; grasps complex ideas 5
MOTIVATION AND AMBITION	No drive, ambition limited 1	Little interest in development; seems satisfied 2	Interest and ambition fair; reasonable desire to work and develop 3	Definite future goals; wants to succeed and grow 4	Ambitions high, future well planned; evidence of personal development 5
EXPERIENCE AND EDUCATION	Education and experience unsuitable for the job 1	Education and experience not directly applicable, but helpful 2	Good educational and work background; experience fair 3	Education and experience fit job; above average qualifications 4	Background especially well suited; continues to study 5
PERSONALITY	Immature, impulsive; indecisive, unstable 1	Opinionated; difficulty in accepting others' ideas 2	Reasonable stability and maturity. 3	Stable, cooperative; accepts responsibilities 4	Very mature, a "self-starter"; outstanding personality 5

TOTAL _____

Remarks: _____

_____

Recommended For Further Consideration:_____ Not Recommended: _____

IBM # 965962 1/78 _____
Signature of Interviewer

Source: Reprinted courtesy Duckwall/Alco Stores, Inc., Abilene, Kansas.

plained omissions in the employment record, and poor emotional control.

Checking References Retail firms check the references supplied by an applicant. They also try to verify the accuracy of all other entries

Table 11.3   Procedures and techniques in the selection process: 58 department stores

Procedure/Technique	Number of Stores	Percent of Total	Procedure/Technique	Number of Stores	Percent of Total
Preliminary (screening) application			Estimated time, first interview		
Use	42	72.4%	Under 10 minutes	22	37.9
Do not use	16	27.6	10 to 20 minutes	27	46.6
Academic transcript			20 to 30 minutes	9	15.5
Require	2	3.4	Type of interview		
Do not require	56	96.6	Patterned	12	20.7
Minimum educational requirements			Nondirected	41	70.7
None	20	34.5	Combination	2	3.4
Elementary school graduate	1	1.7	(Not indicated)	3	5.2
Some high school	20	34.5	Knock-out factors used		
High school graduate	15	25.9	Poor communicative ability	48	82.8
Some college	2	3.4	Job-hopping	41	70.7
Minimum required experience			Unexplained gaps in employment record	36	62.1
None	48	82.8	Poor emotional control	32	55.2
Some retailing	6	10.3	Excessive indebtedness	15	25.9
One year or more in retailing	4	6.9	Too high a living standard	4	6.9
Checking of references			Others*	4	6.9
Do check	52	89.7	Interview rating form		
Do not check	6	10.3	Use	48	82.8
How references are checked			Do not use	8	13.8
By mail	8	13.8	(Not indicated)	2	3.4
By telephone	10	17.2	Testing of applicants		
By both mail and telephone	34	58.6	No testing at all	39	67.2
Usual number of interviews			Clerical ability†	14	24.1
One	24	41.4	Sales aptitude	7	12.1
Two	33	56.9	Mental ability	4	6.9
Three	1	1.7	Personality	3	5.2
(Not indicated)	2	3.4	Physical examination	2	3.4
			Mechanical ability	1	1.7

* Includes items such as penmanship, personal appearance, sales ability.

† Includes arithmetic tests and tests of mathematical ability.

Source: Irving Burstiner, "Current Personnel Practices in Department Stores," *Journal of Retailing* 51 (Winter 1975–76), p. 8–9.

on the application form. References are checked by mail, telephone, or a combination of the two. Telephone calls are sometimes more useful than contact by mail since many employers are reluctant to put in writing derogatory information about former employees. Over the telephone, a caller often can readily detect any hesitancy on the other person's part or sense emotionally tinged undercurrents. The other side of the coin, however, is that many people prefer not to discuss other people over the telephone.

Testing This has long served as a popular aid in screening applicants for many kinds of positions. Along with the advent of equal employment opportunity legislation, interest among personnel professionals in testing began to wane. Companies found it difficult to develop evidence that would support the validity of many of the tests then in vogue.

Certain tests are still used if both their validity and reliability are demonstrable. To avoid problems with the Equal Employment Opportunity Commission, test results must be correlated with successful on-the-job performance. Examples of appropriate tests would include a test of typing skill that measures speed and accuracy or a test of occupational knowledge for skilled workers. The various Short Occupational Knowledge Tests (for electricians, automobile mechanics, bookkeepers, office machine operators, plumbers, and other occupations) might be considered appropriate.[12]

Standardized tests available for personnel selection fall into four major categories: aptitude, performance/achievement, intelligence, and personality tests. Aptitude and performance/achievement tests measure either capacity for learning a particular occupation or skill or proficiency in that area. Because of validity problems, intelligence measures are used only infrequently and then usually in connection with clerical workers.[13] Personality tests may be used to select candidates for middle management and especially to screen out people with emotional problems. These tests attempt to assess various traits: initiative, sociability, dominance, self-confidence, anxiety, flexibility, and so on. Among the more popular ones are the Edwards Personality Inventory and the California Psychological Inventory.

Compensation: Paying Retail Employees

The majority of retailers neither have nor need much sophistication in wage and salary administration. Typically, they pay employees at rates prevailing in the community and on an hourly or weekly salary basis. In some instances, such as the sale of furniture, floor coverings, and automobiles, management encourages additional selling effort by paying employees a percentage of net sales, or commission.

In larger retail organizations, the area of **employee compensation** is of significant concern. The work force is sizable, and many different occupations may be represented. While the basic pay plan is the heart of a company's compensation program, other factors need to be considered. Employees require fair and impartial treatment, safe working conditions, and opportunity for advancement. They also seek other nonfinancial rewards, like security, recognition, and a sense of accomplishment.[14]

Characteristics of a Sound Pay Plan

A good pay program meets the needs of both management and labor. Retailers need a pay plan that:

attracts workers who enable the firm to progress toward its long-term goals
encourages employees to remain with the company
ensures an adequate level of productivity
prevents payroll costs from getting out of hand
provides a worthwhile return on investment

Employees need a pay plan that:

compensates them fairly for their work
gives them a sense of security
ensures a decent standard of living
provides some collateral benefits
leads to higher earnings over time

Setting up a Pay Plan

As a company grows, it becomes desirable for its management to institute a well-conceived compensation program that will help build the kind of organization it needs. A simple procedure for initiating a pay plan follows:

1. Define the jobs.
2. Evaluate the jobs.
3. Price the jobs.
4. Install the plan.
5. Communicate the plan to employees.
6. Appraise employee performance under the plan.[15]

Only the first three require brief comment. Step 1 comprises both job analysis and job description, each discussed earlier in this chapter. In Step 2, all existing positions are compared. These are then grouped into a number of levels according to scope, complexity, and level of responsibility. This involves a simple ranking process. Arriving at Step 3, management checks the going rates for similar work in the area where the company is located. The idea is to set up rates that are fair and competitive for each level, or job class. A **pay range** (minimum and maximum rates) is then established for each job class. This ensures that employees who continue to perform satisfactorily will earn more as time goes by.

Types of Pay Plans

Across industry, three basic approaches to compensating employees are found: the salary, commission, and combination plan.

The Salary Plan Under the **salary plan,** employees are paid a set amount of money, usually on a weekly basis. In all industries, most workers look forward to the feeling of security induced by a regular paycheck. A steady income enables them to budget their finances sensibly. Most retailers favor this pay approach because labor costs are known in advance and their own budgets can be planned accordingly. It is also the simplest plan for the bookkeeping section to handle. From management's vantage point, its most serious drawback is that labor costs remain fixed. Should sales decline, the percentage of sales allocated to labor will increase. A small shoestore, for instance, may show sales of $200,000 for the year and an outlay of $30,000 for labor. The cost of labor then represents 15 percent of sales. Should revenues drop the following year to, say, $150,000 and the payroll remain at the same $30,000, then the new cost-of-labor ratio increases to 20 percent. This would reduce the firm's operating profit before taxes. In the long run, such a situation can prove damaging to the financial health of the enterprise. However, the principle works two ways. Should sales increase, the labor-to-sales percentage would correspondingly drop, improving the financial picture.

A second disadvantage is that payroll costs will increase over time as employees are granted occasional raises. A final criticism, and one that may distress both worker and employer, is that the salary plan fails to reward extra effort. An evident rebuttal to this criticism is that good supervision ought to ensure an acceptable level of productivity. Improving supervision, though, may call for placing more supervisors on the payroll; in turn, this adds to total labor costs.

The Commission Plan For the most part, the **commission plan** is reserved for salespeople. Instead of a salary, the employee receives a *commission*—some percentage of the sales personally consummated. In industries other than retailing, the commission plan is a popular method for compensating sales representatives. It is also commonly used in the direct retailing of such products as cosmetics, vacuum cleaners, encyclopedias, home improvements, and the like.[16]

Often, a company will pay a modest training salary to sales recruits during their breaking-in period. Or it may offer a **drawing account (draw).** This is an advance against commission as yet unearned—a flat sum of, say, $250 or $300 advanced each week. Once the salesperson begins to make sales, the account is adjusted, usually once each month. Earned commissions are credited and advances debited to the account. Any overage at the end of the month is paid to the employee, often by separate check.

The commission plan provides maximum incentive. The salesperson's earnings are directly tied to personal effort, selling skill, and perseverance. Some retail companies prefer this plan because they can relate labor expense directly to sales volume. As variable costs, commissions fluctuate in direct proportion to the peaks and valleys in the firm's revenue charts. There is one possible negative aspect associated with paying commissions, however. In their eagerness to earn more, salespeople may use hard-sell tactics that can turn off the customer.

The Combination Plan A number of pay approaches are grouped together under the catch-all label **combination plan.** Some examples are the salary-and-commission, salary-plus-bonus, and quota-bonus plans. In store retailing, the preferred combination is the salary-and-commission plan. Salespeople receive a regular base salary to which a small commission is added. Typically, this is a percentage of net sales, perhaps ½ or 1 percent. The extra incentive stimulates employee interest in increasing sales volume. It also leads to faster, more efficient customer service. The salary-and-commission plan is found in stores of all sizes and in both discount and chain operations, especially where high-ticket merchandise is sold. Fur coats, furniture, and major appliances are examples. Combination plans may also be used to compensate lower- and middle-management personnel, such as store and department managers.

Supplemental Benefits   Other benefits are needed to round out the basic pay plan. These **supplemental benefits** can tack on an additional 28 to 30 cents to every dollar of wages paid by the company.[17]

Most Common Benefits Once considered fringe benefits, four pay practices are now found nearly universally in store retailing: (1) paid vacations, (2) holidays off with pay, (3) sick leave, and (4) employee discounts.

Paid Vacations One universally accepted practice is the paid vacation. The amount of time offered by a company usually depends on the employee's length of service in the organization. New employees with fewer than six months of service may be permitted several days off with (or without) pay. After six months on the job, they may be granted a three-day vacation with full pay. A one-week paid vacation is often extended to 1-year employees, while a 10-year retail worker may look forward to as many as four full weeks of paid vacation time. Typically, preference in vacation scheduling is accorded by seniority.

Holidays off with Pay Today's retail workers expect to be paid for certain holidays they are off. Unlike manufacturing plants and wholesale establishments, many stores remain open for business on holidays. Indeed, some holidays are excellent shopping days when retailers traditionally offer special sales events. Columbus Day, Washington's Birthday, and Labor Day are examples. Employees who work on these occasions may be paid at twice their regular rate or even at double and one half time.

Sick Leave Workers occasionally need to be absent because of illness. Good personnel relations dictate that they should not be penalized for being out sick. A common policy is to allow three days of sick pay for the six-month employee and a full week for the one-year employee. Workers with more longevity and managerial personnel may be granted additional sick leave.

Employee Discounts Most retailers offer their employees a set percentage, or discount, off the regular list prices of store merchandise they buy. Depending on management policy, the discount ranges from 5 to 10 percent to as high as 25 to 35 percent. Merchandise on sale is generally exempted or offered at a lesser discount. Retailers try to minimize abuses of the privilege by limiting the discount to employees and members of their immediate families.

Miscellaneous Benefits. Many retail firms provide group hospitalization and medical plans for their personnel. In some cases, costs are shared by management and employees. Group life insurance programs are also popular. The amount of coverage is usually a function of the employee's age, length of employment, and salary level.

Other benefits may be offered, such as:

bonuses
employee pension plan
profit-sharing plan
company cars for supervisors and executives
credit union
employee cafeteria or lunchroom
loans for emergencies
reimbursement for travel expenses
social and recreational activities

Training and Development

Training is a vital phase of human resources management. New employees require **initial training** so that they quickly become familiar with their jobs and with company policy. Salespeople need to know the merchandise, prices, company systems and procedures, and what the clientele is like. Workers can profit by **follow-up training** to reinforce their skills. Further along the way, they may be exposed to **developmental training** that contributes to on-the-job growth. Finally, **management development programs** enable them to reach their fullest potential. Such programs give the firm a great deal of flexibility as well as the continuing supply of managers it needs to prosper and grow.

Many small independents feel that employee training is too costly for them and that it is more appropriate for the large organization. They are mistaken. Good training is essential in organizations of any size. In fact, the smaller the company, the greater the potential effect of the interaction between the firm's salespeople and its customers.

Why Retailers Train Employees

Among the more common training objectives pursued by retail companies are to:

increase sales
lower costs
increase profits
lower the rate of employee turnover
reduce errors
upgrade skill levels
improve job performance
instill healthy work attitudes
maintain good morale
motivate employees
make employees more productive

Designing Training Programs

To aid in the design of an effective training program, the following steps should be considered:

1. Assess training needs.
2. Define behavioral objectives (what the learner should be able to do as a result of the training).
3. Define the abilities, interests, and attitudes of the prospective learners.
4. Select the appropriate personnel and methods for presenting the training.
5. Make the presentation.
6. Evaluate the effectiveness of the training effort.[18]

The Small Business Administration offers a valuable eight-page checklist on training program development.[19] It is divided into categories, each containing sets of questions designed to stimulate management thinking. It is too long to reproduce here in its entirety. However, the section headings are worth mentioning and are displayed in Figure 11.6. They are provocative and give an overview of the kind of preparation that is needed.

Training Methods

Instructional techniques available to the retail operation include both in-store (in-house) and outside methods. Among the more common approaches are on-the-job training, coaching, classroom instruction, and job rotation.

Figure 11.6
Developing the training program: some major questions

What is the goal of the training?

What does the employee need to learn?

What type of training?

What method of instruction?

What audiovisual aids will you use?

What physical facilities will you need?

What about the timing?

Who will be selected as instructor?

Who should be selected [for training]?

What will the program cost?

What checks or controls will you use?

How should the program be publicized?

Source: Leonard J. Smith, "Checklist for Developing a Training Program," *Management Aids No. 186* (Washington, D.C.: Small Business Administration, 1977).

Most popular of all instructional methods in retailing is on-the-job training. A probable reason is that 9 out of 10 retail firms in the country are small operations. They have neither the funds nor the expertise available for other techniques. Following a brief orientation, new employees are simply set to work. They are expected to learn their duties and responsibilities on the job. To accelerate the process, the company may use **coaching** or the **sponsor method.** A new employee is assigned to an experienced worker. The coach, or sponsor, assists the trainee by answering questions, demonstrating procedures, and the like.

The larger company often equips an area for formal classroom training. An entire model store might be set up, complete with counters, merchandise, bins, displays, cash register, and even a dummy show window. Chains and department stores use the classroom facility for orientation and initial training. Topics covered in the curriculum for salespeople, for example, typically include company background, employee rules and regulations, merchandise information, knowledge of the customer, register and systems operations, and sales training. Oddly enough, less time is often devoted to this last area than to most of the other subjects. One study of department store personnel practices revealed a median time allotment during initial training of only one hour to the art of selling.[20]

As part of their ongoing education, employees may be shifted to different positions within the company. This is **job rotation,** a method frequently used in management development programs. Other instructional approaches include small group discussions, demonstrations, role playing, slide and filmstrip presentations, movies, in-basket exercises, case studies, and sensitivity training. Some of these methods

The "Penney Idea"—the philosophy of operation adopted in 1913 when the Golden Rule stores incorporated as the J. C. Penney Company—still guides management decision making today.

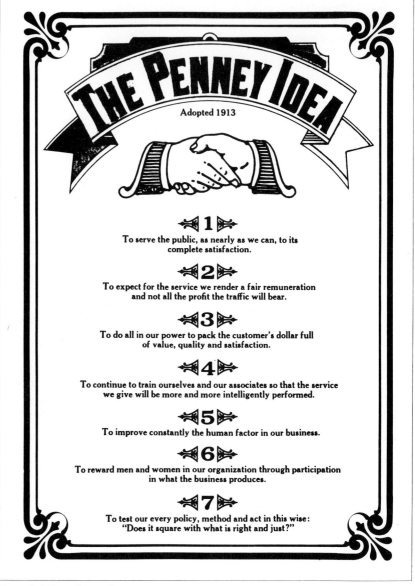

THE PENNEY IDEA

Adopted 1913

1
To serve the public, as nearly as we can, to its complete satisfaction.

2
To expect for the service we render a fair remuneration and not all the profit the traffic will bear.

3
To do all in our power to pack the customer's dollar full of value, quality and satisfaction.

4
To continue to train ourselves and our associates so that the service we give will be more and more intelligently performed.

5
To improve constantly the human factor in our business.

6
To reward men and women in our organization through participation in what the business produces.

7
To test our every policy, method and act in this wise: "Does it square with what is right and just?"

Courtesy J. C. Penney Company, Inc.

may be reserved for employees in line for promotion, such as the recent college graduate who is hired as a management trainee.

Off-premises methods are also used. These include courses and seminars at local colleges, lectures and presentations offered by trade associations, programmed instruction, and others.

**Management
Development**

Sizable retail companies must be able to draw from a reservoir of potential managers. If the system is to work at all, the firm's top executives should be strongly committed to an intensive training and development effort. In addition to the instructional methods already mentioned, the use of the **assessment center** in connection with management development has been growing in popularity. The basic thrust of the method is that of identifying employees' work-related strengths and weaknesses in order to devise training plans for their long-term development.[21] As early as 1971, more than 100 companies in different fields were relying on assessment centers for this purpose. Among them were AT&T, Kodak, IBM, Ford, and J. C. Penney.[22]

**Evaluating
Employee
Performance**

Because of the intimacy of the store environment, small retailers generally experience little difficulty in judging employee performance. Appraisal becomes a continuous, one-to-one process. On the other hand, more formal approaches to employee evaluation are required in the larger organization. A sensible **performance evaluation program** calls for periodic and objective appraisals of each worker's performance. Weaknesses and strengths are first determined. These form the basis for guidance and further training and for pinpointing candidates for promotion. The program contributes toward improved work attitudes as well as performance.[23] Employees may be evaluated quarterly, semiannually, or annually. Evaluations are made more often during an employee's first year with the company. To avoid problems related to equal employment opportunity legislation, the program "should be formulized, standardized, and made as objective as possible."[24]

**Rating Forms in
Employee Evaluation**

Large retail companies commonly use internally developed rating forms in appraising employee performance. The intent is to stress objectivity while improving validity by using a variety of criteria. Some firms try to avoid personal bias by insisting that two or more evaluators complete the form.

Rating devices contain both objective and subjective measures. Typically, a different form is used for salespeople than for managers. Among the subjective items that often appear on evaluation forms are:

appearance
cooperation
courtesy
dependability
evaluation skills
follows policy
initiative
knowledge of good human relations

job knowledge
judgment
leadership ability
loyalty
personality
quality of performance
resourcefulness
self-confidence
supportive of subordinates
willingness to assume responsibility

Some commonly used objective measures are:

customer complaints (numerical count)
earnings as a percentage of sales
number of transactions per hour
production records
record of attendance, punctuality
returns by customers
sales volume per number of hours worked

A simple rating form for department managers appears in Figure 11.7.

Figure 11.7
Rating form for store department managers

1. Rate the person being reviewed by checking the appropriate space after each item:

How well does the person—	Poorly	Ade-quately	Excel-lent	Not observed
Plan a broad program for the division (or store)?				
Carry out the current program?				
Make wise and prompt decisions?				
Delegate authority to subordinates?				
Personally supervise subordinates?				
Review and evaluate work of subordinates?				
Make contacts with outside organizations?				
Manage sales growth?				
Handle inventory and expense control?				

2. In your estimation, which of the following best describes the person's attitude toward his organization:

_____Dedicated to helping it reach its objectives, with personal ambitions subordinated to this goal.

_____Wants to establish a secure position with the organization.

_____Wants to use this position as a stepping stone to a major position elsewhere.

3. Do you feel that the person has the capacity to grow in case the store expands in size and activity?

_____Yes.   _____No.   _____Doubtful.

Source: John W. Wingate and Seymour Helfant, "Small Store Planning for Growth," *Small Business Management Series No. 33,* 2d ed. (Washington, D.C.: Small Business Administration, 1977), p. 34.

Summary   To a large extent, the success of any business depends on the effectiveness of its employees in helping management achieve its goals. In retailing, labor expenses are a relatively large portion of the company's operating budget. Thus, the proper management of a firm's human resources represents both a challenge and an opportunity for its executives. It demands their thoughtful and continuous attention.

Each company must devise the kind of organization that will enable management to attain its objectives. Building a viable organization calls for incorporating some basic principles of management, like the specialization of work, delegation of responsibility, line and staff assignments, unity of command, and span of control. As the company grows larger, the organization grows more complex.

Among the more critical phases of human resources management are staffing, training, supervising, and motivating employees. The staffing function involves locating and selecting personnel for positions in the organization. Among the aids commonly used in the selection process are job specifications, employment applications, personal interviews, reference checking, and testing.

An effective program for compensating employees for their work is a necessity. The pay plan should be designed to meet the needs of both labor and management. In the retail sector, three different types of pay plans are used: salary, commission, and combination. Most favored is the salary plan. Supplemental benefits are also offered. Among the more common benefits are vacation pay, holidays off with pay (or extra compensation for working on holidays), sick benefits, and employee discounts on store merchandise. However, financial rewards alone are not enough to constitute an effective compensation program. Retailers also need to consider the nonfinancial incentives they may be able to provide. They need to cater to their employees' needs for security, recognition, sense of accomplishment, and so on.

Training and development are integral elements in modern human resources management. Training aims at a variety of goals: to increase sales, lower costs, maintain morale, lower the employee turnover rate, motivate personnel, and others. While the most common method is on-the-job training, other techniques are frequently used. Some examples are: classroom training, small group discussions, job rotation, demonstrations, role playing, audiovisual aids, case studies, courses at local colleges, programmed instruction, and sensitivity training. Management development also calls for many of these techniques. Some retail companies make use of the assessment center in training their future managers.

Performance evaluations, conducted periodically, enable retail firms to determine the strengths, weaknesses, and contributions of their employees. Both subjective and objective measures may be used to develop these individual assessments. Results serve as guides for further training and development.

Key Terms

human resource planning
organization development
organization
organizational charts
specialization of work principle
scalar principle
authority
responsibility
accountability
line positions
staff positions
unity of command principle
span of control (span of authority) principle
departmentizing
staffing function
job analysis
job description
job specifications
employment application

employment interview
nondirected interview
patterned interview
knock-out factors
employee compensation
pay range
salary plan
commission plan
drawing account (draw)
combination plan
supplemental benefits
initial training
follow-up training
developmental training
management development programs
coaching (sponsor method)
job rotation
assessment center
performance evaluation program

Review Questions

1. What aspects of store retailing make human resources management a difficult task?

2. Discuss the human resources function in both small and large retail companies.

3. Define each of the following terms: (1) organization, (2) organizational charts, and (3) organization development.

4. Cite six benefits to the merchant of departmentizing a store.

5. Describe the four-function Mazur plan for department store organization.

6. What tools are commonly used in the selection process?

7. Describe the procedure by which management arrives at written job specifications.

8. Prepare a list of six questions that you believe would be useful in structured interviews with prospective supermarket managers.

9. Identify at least four knock-out factors used by personnel interviewers.

10. Outline a procedure for installing a formal pay plan in a growing organization.

11. Specify the advantages and drawbacks of the salary plan from store management's viewpoint. Contrast them with those of the commission plan.

12. Cite five fringe benefits frequently offered to retail employees.

13. Specify eight criteria that might be useful in appraising the performance of department managers in a traditional department store.

14. Propose four training methods that a small retailer of greeting cards may profitably use for sales personnel.

Discussion Questions

1. Prepare an organizational chart for a small bakery with four employees in addition to the baker.

2. Salesperson indifference can induce customers to shop elsewhere. Cite two examples from your experience where you were turned off by store salespeople.

3. Retailers seem to stress honesty and dependability above all other qualities in their sales personnel. Evaluate this position.

4. One study revealed the following unsought characteristics in the recruitment of salespeople by department stores: independent, outspoken, practical, self-reliant. Can you offer an opinion as to why management might not look for these traits?

5. Comment on this statement: "We should hold employee discounts to a minimum. They cost us a great deal of money."

6. Prepare a brief job description for the position of assistant manager in a 10-unit chain of sporting goods stores.

7. Give and defend your opinion on the use of the polygraph, or lie detector, in the selection process.

8. As the CEO (chief executive officer) of a regional chain of women's dress shops, you are interested in setting up a management development program. How would you proceed?

Notes   [1]See: Irving Burstiner, "The Small Retailer and His Problems," *Journal of Business Education* 50 (March 1975), pp. 243–45; Kenneth E. Rindt, "Small-Firm Personnel Problems and Management Assistance," *Journal of Small Business Management* 13 (July 1975), pp. 13–17; Kamal E. Said and J. Keith Hughey, "Managerial Problems of the Small Firm," *Journal of Small Business Management* 15 (January 1977), p. 42.

[2]P. L Pfeiffer, "Where Do Your Customers Go?" *Stores* 55 (February 1973), p. 30.

[3]See: Leonard J. Berry, "The Components of Department Store Image: A Theoretical and Empirical Analysis," *Journal of Retailing* 45 (Spring 1969), pp. 3–20; John O'Shaughnessy, "Selling as an Interpersonal Influence Process," *Journal of Retailing* 47 (Winter 1971–72), pp. 32–46; Richard W. Olshavsky, "Customer-Salesman Interaction in Appliance Retailing," *Journal of Marketing Research* 10 (May 1973), pp. 208–12.

[4]See: Fred K. Foulkes, "The Expanding Role of the Personnel Function," *Harvard Business Review* 53 (March–April 1975), pp. 71–84; Elmer H. Burack and Edwin L. Miller, "The Personnel Function in Transition," *California Management Review* 18 (Spring 1976), pp. 32–38; Paul C. Gorden, " 'Magnetic' Management: The Real Role of Personnel," *Personnel Journal* 59 (June 1980), pp. 485–87*ff.*

[5]Stephen P. Robbins, *Personnel: The Management of Human Resources* (Englewood Cliffs, N.J.: Prentice-Hall, 1978), p. 53.

[6]See: Douglas M. Reid, "Human Resource Planning: A Tool for People Development," *Personnel* 54 (March–April 1977), pp. 15–25; Jackson F. Gillespie, Wayne E. Leininger, and Harvey Kahalas, "A Human Resource Planning and Validation Model," *Academy of Management Journal* 9 (December 1976), pp. 650–56; Albert C. Hyde and Jay M. Shafritz, "HRIS: Introduction to Tomorrow's System for Managing Human Resources," *Public Personnel Management* 6 (March–April 1977), pp. 70–77.

[7]For further reading, see: Newton Margulies and Anthony P. Raia, *Conceptual Foundations of Organizational Development* (New York: McGraw-Hill, 1978); Wendell L. French and Cecil H. Bell, Jr., *Organization Development: Behavioral Science Interventions for Organization Improvement,* 2d ed. (Englewood Cliffs, N.J.: Prentice-Hall, 1978).

[8]Paul M. Mazur, *Principles of Organization Applied to Modern Retailing* (New York: Harper & Row, 1927).

[9]W. Austin Spivey, J. Michael Munson, and William B. Locander, "Meeting Retail Staffing Needs Via Improved Selection," *Journal of Retailing* 55 (Winter 1979), p. 4; Clemn C. Kessler, III and George J. Gibbs, "Getting the Most from Application Blanks and References," *Personnel* 51 (January–February 1975), p. 54; Arthur A. Witkin, "Commonly Overlooked Dimensions of Employee Selection," *Personnel Journal* 59 (July 1980), pp. 573–75*ff.*

[10]Kessler and Gibbs, "Application Blanks," p. 56. See also: Charles N. Weaver, "An Empirical Study to Aid in the Selection of Retail Salesclerks," *Journal of Retailing* 45 (Fall 1969), p. 82.

[11]Robert F. Hartley, "The Weighted Application Blank Can Improve Retail Employee Selection," *Journal of Retailing* 46 (Spring 1970), pp. 32–40.

[12]For more information on these and other tests, consult the following reference work: Oscar Krisen Buros, ed., *The Eighth Mental Measurements Yearbook* (Highland Park, N.J.: Gryphon Press, 1978).

[13]However, see: Charles Bahn, "Can Intelligence Tests Predict Executive Competence?" *Personnel* 56 (July–August 1979), pp. 52–58.

[14]See: Charles N. Weaver, "What Workers Want Most from Their Jobs," *Personnel* 53 (May–June 1976), pp. 48–54; Sherman Tingey, "Managing Supermarket Managers," *Journal of Retailing* 45 (Spring 1969), p. 69.

[15]Gene F. Scollard, "Setting Up a Pay System," *Management Aids No. 241* (Washington, D.C.: Small Business Administration, 1979), pp. 2–3.

[16]Michael Granfield and Alfred Nichols, "Economic and Marketing Aspects of the Direct Selling Industry," *Journal of Retailing* 51 (Spring 1975), pp. 33–50*ff.*

[17]Ralph L. Harris, "Let's Take the 'Fringe' Out of Fringe Benefits," *Personnel Journal* 54 (February 1975), pp. 86–89.

[18]Elmer H. Burack and Robert D. Smith, *Personnel Management: A Human Resource Systems Approach* (St. Paul, Minn.: West Publishing, 1977), p. 235.

[19]Leonard J. Smith, "Checklist for Developing a Training Program," *Management Aids No. 186* (Washington, D.C.: Small Business Administration, 1977).

[20]Irving Burstiner, "Current Personnel Practices in Department Stores," *Journal of Retailing* 51 (Winter 1975–76), p. 11.

[21]Barry M. Cohen, "The Assessment Center: Whom to Develop," *Training in Business and Industry* 11 (February 1974), p. 19; Louis Olivas, "Using Assessment Centers for Individual and Organization Development," *Personnel* 57 (May–June 1980), pp. 63–67.

[22]William C. Byham, "The Assessment Center As an Aid in Management Development," *Training and Development Journal* 25 (December 1971), p. 10.

[23]Robert A. Zawacki and Robert L. Taylor, "A View of Performance Appraisal from Organizations Using It," *Personnel Journal* 55 (June 1976), p. 299.

[24]Gary L. Lubben, Duane E. Thompson, and Charles R. Klassor, "Performance Appraisal: The Legal Implications of Title VII," *Personnel* 57 (May–June 1980), p. 20.

Gary Csuk

DIRECTING RETAIL EMPLOYEES

Your Study Objectives

After you have studied this chapter, you will understand:

1. The basic managerial functions.
2. Communication and its role in business management.
3. The meaning of leadership and the various leadership styles.
4. The importance of employee productivity and good organizational morale.
5. Some approaches to motivation theory.

Managerial Leadership

For an enterprise to attain its goals, the necessary tasks and activities must be arranged and structured into a unified, coordinated mechanism. The right people must be slotted into positions in the structure. There, they can conduct their assignments and progress toward common objectives. Managers are needed to direct segments of this organization and to coordinate activities. Whatever their levels in the hierarchy, managers are people who work with others to get things done.

Much of the managerial job involves accomplishing assigned tasks. Because they work with subordinates as well as with peers and superiors, managers must spend much time and effort on what sociologists label *consideration behavior.* This is the kind of behavior needed to work in harmony with other people. Leading and directing are only two of the action verbs used to describe a manager's dealings with subordinates. Others are guiding, coaching, training, counseling, advising, encouraging, and so on.

To perform effectively, managers require specific skills in "developing peer relationships, carrying out negotiations, motivating subordinates, resolving conflicts, establishing information networks and subsequently disseminating information, making decisions in conditions of extreme ambiguity, and allocating resources."[1] Better managers in large corporations have been found to enjoy their work, have a keen sense of justice, and place the organization before their own self-interest.[2] In the retail setting, successful managers appear to display a good balance between their task-oriented behavior and their handling of people.[3]

The Basic Managerial Functions

When we examine the activities of managers closely, we find that they fall into one of four distinct classifications. Store managers, company presidents, merchandisers, advertising directors, vice presidents, buyers, department heads, and other managers all plan, organize, direct, and control.[4] These basic **managerial functions** are shown in Figure 12.1.

Planning The complexities of **planning** involve forward thinking: forecasting situations and conditions, formulating objectives, setting appropriate policies, devising procedures, and making decisions. If the time frame is an extended one, long-range planning is necessary. If the situation is near, short-range plans must be devised. Usually, top management monitors the long-range planning; short-range planning is the work of middle and lower managers.

Planning answers the basic questions:

1. Where are we now?
2. Where do we want to be?
3. How can we get there from here?[5]

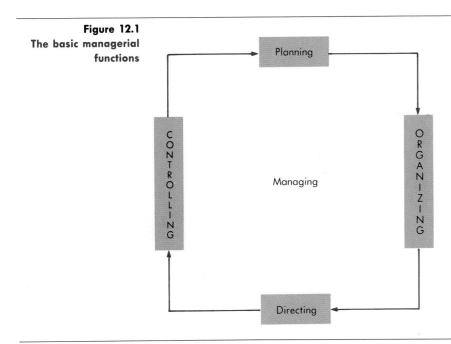

Figure 12.1
The basic managerial functions

Organizing Once plans have been formulated, **organizing** proceeds. All elements essential to their implementation must then be selected and set into place. Employees, premises, work assignments, activities and events, equipment and machines, the requisite finances, methods, and other components must be coordinated before plans can be activated. Authority relations, too, must be clarified and arrangements made to delegate responsibilities.[6]

Directing After these first two tasks have been accomplished, the manager is ready to initiate the plan. The group, directed by its leader, begins to work the plan. It is in this **directing** phase that a manager's interpersonal skills are tested. Although all four basic managerial functions call for considerable skill in communication, it is particularly vital in leading subordinates.[7] Managers give instructions, guide, train, present ideas to, and supervise their people.

Controlling All along the way, managers need to monitor all aspects of working plans. The **controlling** function involves an ongoing evaluation of operational methods, behaviors, and outcomes. Deviations from plan call for quick action. Steps are taken to correct these deviations by initiating fine adjustments in one or more plan elements.

Good supervisors see to it that salespeople are well trained.

Courtesy Dress Barn, Inc., Stamford, CT

Communication in Management

Managers get work done by communicating with other people. Effective business administration depends on effective communications. Effective managers are skilled communicators.

Communication itself has been defined as interaction, and as "all those processes in which there is an interchange of facts, ideas, feelings, and courses of action by which people influence one another."[8] The author of a helpful guide to business communication suggests these fundamental truths regarding the communication process:

1. Communication is imperfect.
2. When we communicate, we communicate about ourselves.
3. Meaning is in the mind, not in the symbols used.[9]

In the healthy business organization, communication is an open, rapid, three-directional process. Messages continually pass down from higher management through to the lowest echelons of the enterprise. They also flow upward through the various levels to top management. A good internal system facilitates horizontal communication among people on the same level. In addition to this formal structure, an informal communications network is present in every company. Employees talk with each other, discussing not only all sorts of personal matters but also the business and operational details. All kinds of information, especially gossip and rumors, can sweep quickly through the organization via the grapevine. Good managers learn how to tap this informal channel with good results.

Types of Communications

Messages may be communicated to others orally or visually using words, symbols, charts, or body language. Quickest and most effective are those transmitted orally, delivered to others in person.[10] In face-to-face contact, the manager can explain new policies in depth, give specific and detailed instructions, ask questions, listen to suggestions, and clarify misunderstandings.[11]

Methods used by managers in business organizations include, among others:

bulletin boards	drawings	newsletters
bulletins	films	photographs
cassettes	graphs	reports
chalkboards	house organs	slides
charts	manuals	transparencies
correspondence	memoranda	

Nonverbal Communication It has been said that a photograph in a newspaper is worth a thousand words. So, too, is body language. Managers need to learn to interpret the significance of gestures and body movements. They will observe how employees maintain distance between themselves and others and how they commonly react to their surroundings during the work day. A frown, smile, raised eyebrow, grimace, or other nonverbal communication often conveys more meaning and clearer intent than the spoken or written word. Understanding these signs can benefit a firm "in establishing favorable company-management-employee-public relationships."[12]

Problems in Communicating

People frequently have difficulty communicating with others. Communication problems stem from the very nature of individual differences. People's backgrounds differ, and their life experiences vary. So do their perceptions, attitudes, value systems, personalities, ways of responding, and so on. Moreover, poor listening habits alone can play a significant role in erecting barriers to understanding.[13] Indeed, the importance of good listening skills cannot be overemphasized.

Leadership Basics

Leadership has been written about, discussed, examined, praised, and censured down through the ages and in all sorts of environments. Many sources have defined leadership in the business enterprise; only two are quoted below to spark reader insights:

A process of influencing the activities of either formal or informal work groups in their tasks of goal setting and goal achievement.[14]

The ability of management to induce subordinates to work toward group goals with confidence and enthusiasm.[15]

Leadership, then, may be described as a process and as an ability or set of skills. It may also be described in terms of leader behavior on the job.

Certain concepts about leadership have been accepted. It is now conceded, for example, that the leadership process involves three interrelated dimensions: the leader, the members of the group, and the specific situation in which the process takes place. That leaders are born, not made, is an old idea that has now been shelved. People develop into leaders over time. Early studies of leadership tried, without much success, to identify traits that could be used to separate leader types from nonleaders. No single set of personal qualities seems to adequately describe the true leader. Employees, however, often feel they can readily isolate many of the characteristics that effective managers or supervisors ought to possess. They believe leaders should be:

adaptable	fair	patient
capable	friendly	reasonable
considerate	honest	self-motivated
consistent	impartial	tactful
dependable	knowledgeable	tolerant
diplomatic	mature	understanding
empathetic	open	
enthusiastic	optimistic	

It is true that the more effective managers/leaders seem to be self-motivated, enthusiastic people. They set goals, create an open atmosphere at work, give praise when deserved, and do not lose their perspectives under strain.[16] In retailing, high-performing store managers were found to be more popular in group situations than low-performers.[17] They also viewed their occupational status as higher. It has been suggested that retail companies have traditionally hired people for management that fit the SDC syndrome. The initials stand for *sincere, dedicated,* and *conscientious.* Nowadays, these traits are just not enough. Managers not only need to possess leadership skills; they must be flexible, sensitive to problems, imaginative, and able to demonstrate other characteristics frequently identified with the creative personality.[18]

Styles of Leadership   The behavior styles used by managers are blends of their own personalities, those of the people in their groups, and the particular circumstances. These approaches range from the autocratic to the laissez-faire style, with the democrat's operating methods somewhere near the midpoint between the two.[19]

Autocratic Leaders The classic autocrat has a tough, domineering, and demanding personality. **Autocratic leaders** rule their subordinates through fear. They insist on complete subservience to their whims and fancies. Orders issued must be carried out precisely as mandated, under threat of harsh discipline.

Some small-store independents are autocratic leaders. However, department store and other large retail organizations generally frown on this behavior in their managers. They are dependent on and need to show concern for their human resources. Yet, even here, instances of authoritarian rule may occasionally be found, sometimes at the very top of an organization.[20] This style of management can lead to undesirable conduct by group members. Instead of a cooperative spirit, it fosters competition. It encourages members to try to curry the boss' favor. It makes for internal friction and attempts at backbiting.

Yet, especially under stressful conditions, the autocratic style of leadership can produce temporary increases in productivity.[21]

Democratic Leaders Managers in this category demonstrate a high degree of respect for the individual. **Democratic leaders** encourage group members to communicate freely with one another and share thoughts, opinions, and suggestions in an open atmosphere. They seek member participation in all phases of the work. This ranges from the mutual setting of objectives to the development of procedures for reaching the common goals. For this reason, they are often referred to as partici-pative leaders. They try to help their subordinates develop to their fullest potential.

Among large corporations, those managers who were deemed better as adjudged by their subordinates' morale were found to display a more democratic style.[22]

Laissez-faire Leaders Seldom found in the retail sector is this relatively rare type. Upper management holds managers responsible for the output of their groups, and the well-monitored environment characteristic of large store organizations works against the existence of this behavior for any length of time. Roughly translated, the French term *laissez-faire* means "let the others do it." **Laissez-faire leaders** provide little or no direction to the members of their groups. Nor are encouragement, guidance, assistance, or training ordinarily forthcoming from these managers. Peculiarly enough, some believe themselves to be democratic because they: *(a)* readily hand over work to their subordinates, and *(b)* permit them to proceed entirely on their own. This, whether they stand or fall.

The most important steps in a leader's decision-making process is to clearly define the problem.

Gary Csuk

Finally, we need to emphasize the fact that no leader adheres to a single type of behavior 100 percent of the time. Since leadership activity also depends on the particular situation, there are occasions when democratic, autocratic, or laissez-faire behavior are not only possible but desirable.

Leader Decision Making

Managers make decisions every day, many of them on the spot. At times, however, problems must be solved before decisions become feasible. Better leaders learn not only how to solve problems at work but also how to find them in the first place.[23] Decision trees, linear programming, simulation, and PERT/Cost are a few of the more sophisticated problem-solving methods available for the more demanding or intricate problems. However, most operating decisions are made without using such techniques. Leader judgment and needed information are brought to bear on the problem.

Perhaps the most important step in the **decision-making process** is the first one—clearly defining the problem. Often, this means breaking the problem down into more manageable parts. The resulting subproblems can then be worked on one by one. After completing the problem definition stage, the process continues. Pertinent information is obtained, and a number of alternative solutions are developed. These tentative findings are then evaluated according to specific criteria, and the better solutions are selected.

**Motivating
Employees and
Improving
Productivity**

Motives are internal drives that impel us in one direction or another. They cause us to take action. Most human behavior results from responding to these forces. Motives disturb our equilibrium, compelling us to move to regain our balance. When we are hungry or thirsty, we are motivated to find and consume food or drink. When our supervisors at work give us instructions, we move to carry them out. At times, there are conflicting motives working in us. They may pull us in opposite directions, causing temporary indecision or confusion, until the stronger of the two wins out. Motives may also be complementary. By working together, they lend more strength to the impulse to act in a certain way.

Motives are generated by many things—our basic needs and wants, urges and drives, aspirations, beliefs, opinions, and attitudes. Even an individual's value system plays a significant role in both motivation and on-the-job productivity.[24]

Highly motivated employees are more enthusiastic than their less motivated counterparts. They also pour more energy into their work and make better use of their time.[25] Thus, they are more productive people. Knowing this, managers continually seek ways of fostering enthusiastic behavior in their subordinates. They quickly learn to view motivation from two separate and distinct standpoints: **intrinsic motivation**—within the workers and **extrinsic motivation**—outside forces that motivate. Supervisors recognize that a worker may be self-motivated to do a job well and that the same person may also be motivated by others.

Inducing employees to become more highly motivated is, of course, usually held to be a prime responsibility of their immediate supervisors. Often, management is quite content to set into place little more than a suitable salary schedule and acceptable work surroundings. Vacations with pay, group medical insurance, and perhaps one or two other incentives are added to round off their motivational package. This is, however, a vital responsibility that must begin with top management. When displayed by a company's top executives, enthusiasm and drive are contagious.

Unfortunately, it has been suggested that "Despite all the rhetoric, most organizations do little that is constructive to motivate all but the highest levels of employees."[26] Moreover, one human resources consultant contends that, while most new employees are motivated at first, they gradually become demotivated. This happens through thoughtlessness and neglect, particularly on the part of their *immediate supervisors.*[27]

Some motivational suggestions are shown in Figures 12.2 and 12.3.

Organizational Morale **Morale** is a term that bears many connotations. It is used to describe the psychological state of individuals and of entire groups of people

Figure 12.2

Tips for getting ahead:

1. Be optimistic.

2. Strengthen your human relations skills.

3. Work toward better communication.

4. Learn to listen.

5. Adopt a questioning attitude.

6. Develop creative thinking abilities.

7. Set high standards.

8. Increase your overall knowledge.

9. To become a leader, get involved.

10. Adopt the "Owner attitude."

11. Use the "hat-switching" technique.

Source: "Moving Up: Guidelines for Aspiring Executives," by Irving Burstiner, copyright December 1974. Reprinted with the permission of *Personnel Journal,* Costa Mesa, California; all rights reserved.

Figure 12.3
Suggestions for
motivating yourself and
others

How do you learn to motivate others? And motivate yourself? A few suggestions are:

Have a naive appearance and attitude but a sophisticated mind.

Keep your name in "soft lights" before others at all levels.

Learn and use a new word or phrase each week. Do you know right now what "Pareto's Law," "Phillip's Curve," "managerial grid," "S curve and overlapping S curve," and "black holes" mean?

Use simple words to express your thoughts.

Set aside a certain period of time each day for serious reading. This will help give you a perspective on what you are working at.

Use positive and action words.

Whenever possible, avoid the telephone. Present your ideas in person.

Set goals for yourself; for each day (just jot down a short list of two or three things each day during coffee break), week, month, year, and for the future.

Each day, do something that you would really prefer not to do. Chances are it will be the most important thing you do that day.

Recharge your battery by becoming an *active* member of a management or professional society.

Source: Jack C. Staehle, "How to Motivate Others—Start by Motivating Yourself," *Administrative Management* 35 (May 1974), pp. 57–58. Excerpted from *Administrative Management,* © May 1974 by Geyer-McAllister Publications, Inc., New York.

who work together. It portrays a person's level of buoyancy of spirit and enthusiastic outlook. Involved are the intellect, emotions, and action tendencies. Applied to an organization, it signifies the group's collective spirit, or esprit de corps. This comprises, among other things, the positive attitudes that group members have toward each other

	Rank	Job Factor
Figure 12.4	1	Interesting work
What young people look	2	Wages
for in their retailing jobs	3	Pleasant working conditions
	4	Advancement possibilities
	5	People with whom they work
	6	Job security
	7	Recognition
	8	Training
	9	Job importance
	10	Discipline

Source: Burt K. Scanlan, ''Motivating Young Adults in Retailing,'' *Journal of Small Business Management* 14 (April 1976), pp. 46–54.

and toward their leader. Also involved are approval of mutual objectives, acceptance of responsibility, and a high level of satisfaction with their work and its progress.

Morale can be low or poor, satisfactory, or high. A perceptive observer can appraise a work group's approximate level of morale through such objective measures as the incidence of tardiness, rate of absenteeism, and turnover rate. Morale levels may also be assessed in day-to-day conversations with the employees or at meetings. From time to time, management may conduct attitude surveys among workers and supervisors to gain valuable insights from two different viewpoints.

As will be seen later on in this chapter, any number of factors can affect morale. These include, but are not by any means limited to: working conditions, company policies, pay scales, relationships with the supervisor and with other group members, opportunity for advancement, and recognition and rewards. (Figure 12.4 lists 10 important factors that young people seek in their retailing jobs.) Just fulfilling assigned responsibilities in an organization can give rise to serious fluctuations in a worker's morale level.

Job Factors Management theorists and behavioral scientists alike have speculated about relationships between employee productivity and various psychological aspects. Thus, we have seen research attempting to link productivity to morale, motivation, and job satisfaction/dissatisfaction. New terms have appeared in the literature such as *role conflict, role ambiguity,* and *role clarity.*

An employee may, from time to time, experience some degree of **role conflict.** This surfaces when superiors make conflicting demands on the employee. The salesperson in a housewares department who takes orders regularly from the department buyer may find that the

Preparation and training for assigned responsibilities and knowing what behavior is expected of them give retail employees a considerable degree of role clarity.

Sue Markson

merchandise manager will occasionally issue instructions to the contrary. Still a third position may be taken by the store manager, who looks at things differently.

When an employee has not been adequately trained or lacks knowledge or information about some job aspect then **role ambiguity** is present. This causes confusion in the worker's mind and, in turn, some degree of dissatisfaction. Preparation and training for assigned responsibilities and knowledge about the kinds of behavior expected of them give employees a considerable degree of **role clarity.**

These and other aspects concerning morale and job satisfaction were well researched during the 1960s and early 1970s in fields such as industrial sales, engineering, and accounting. Of more recent vintage are studies involving retail personnel. As an example, two researchers queried more than 200 salespeople employed by a midwestern chain of department stores. They found a significant inverse relationship between role conflict and ambiguity and job satisfaction, job performance, and organizational commitment.[28] Among the recommendations to management for reducing role conflict were: provide proper sales training for salespeople, communicate company policies clearly, and appraise employee performance periodically.

Another study confirmed essentially the same relationship between job satisfaction and both role conflict and ambiguity among chain store department managers.[29] Job satisfaction and several role dimensions have also been investigated at the store manager level. A trio of researchers gathered information from 179 store managers in a national chain that sells home improvement and leisure products. They discovered a significant correlation between job satisfaction and job tension. Both of these were also found to be related to role clarity.[30]

Raising the Morale Level Managements typically try to improve employee morale through a combination of approaches. These involve good human relations techniques, favorable working conditions, adequate pay, concern for employee health and safety, and nonfinancial rewards. This is as common a practice in retailing as in all other industries. Perhaps this is so because, as one writer has claimed, "You can't motivate people. That door is locked from the inside. You can create a climate in which most of your people will motivate themselves to help the company to reach its objectives."[31]

To meet their employees' needs and increase job satisfaction, management may use a variety of nonfinancial rewards and incentives. Among others, these include:

enlarging and enriching jobs and redesigning work
encouraging employee participation in goal setting and decision making
recognizing and publicizing achievement
assigning titles to enhance personal status
promoting from within
facilitating and improving internal communications
training supervisory personnel in the areas of human relations and
    worker motivation[32]

Role of the Supervisor Often, the layperson regards the supervisory position as an intermediate one between management and the rank and file. In actuality, supervisors represent the first rung of the management ladder.[33] They are the company's noncommissioned officers, its corporals and sergeants. To their subordinates, they are the firm's formal representatives. Higher management regards them as small group leaders and as conduits for communication with the workers in those groups.

> Effective supervisors are supportive toward their subordinates, facilitate the work, set challenging performance goals, exhibit upward influence in the hierarchy, develop strong peer relations and participation, and concentrate upon management functions.[34]

Only part of the supervisor's responsibility is issuing and following up on orders and instructions. Supervisors explain company policy, coach and instruct workers, enforce rules and regulations, apply disciplinary measures when necessary, motivate their subordinates, sustain morale, and build teams. (See Figures 12.5 and 12.6 for suggestions regarding the motivation of employees.)

Organizational behaviorists have long recognized that supervisory conduct and workers' perceptions of their immediate supervisors have

Figure 12.5

Motivating and building employee morale

Arrange time to talk with your people.
Find ways to restructure jobs.
Rotate jobs among people.
Look for opportunities to offer people more challenging—and interesting—assignments.
Praise people for work well done.
Give people the opportunity to participate in decisions affecting them.
Show genuine personal interest in—and respect for—your people.
Give people opportunities for special training and personal growth.
Explain the importance of each person's job.
Encourage a friendly group atmosphere.
Appeal to personal and/or professional pride.
Ensure good physical work conditions.
Give your people clear and reasonable goals.

Source: Reprinted, by permission of the publisher, from "You Can Lift Morale—and Productivity," by James Owens, *Supervisory Management,* July 1974, pp. 36–38. © 1974 by AMACOM, a division of American Management Associations, New York. All rights reserved.

Figure 12.6

Human relations techniques that motivate employees

How can it be that management *still* has to ask the question "How can people be motivated?" Some techniques of good human relations which appeal to the basic needs of people, and therefore prove to be good motivators, are summarized here. These techniques must of course be accompanied by appropriate supervisory styles.

Motivation

Based on needs of people, which are:
recognition
opportunity
security
belonging

Recognition

Call people by name when you speak to them.
Treat them with the friendly politeness that you do a friend.
Show interest in their family and other things they are particularly interested in.
Listen to what they have to say.
Watch for anything they do well and compliment them on it. (Sometimes compliment them when others can hear.)
Compliment them on *specific* things, not just generalities.
Notice things that other people don't notice and compliment them on these *unexpected* things. Above all, the compliment must be genuine and sincere.
Smile!

Opportunity

Encourage employees to look for new and better ways of doing work. Expand work by enrichment.
Listen to any new idea anyone has. (Use it if it's sound. If you can't use it, explain why you can't and urge them to develop another one.)
Give employees as much freedom as they can handle.

**Figure 12.6
(concluded)**

Encourage them to feel responsible for seeing that their work is carried out well.

Give them full credit for anything good they have done when you talk to their supervisors.

If they are good workers, help them get a promotion.

Belonging

Explain to new workers their job, the section, and the company.

Take them around and introduce them to other employees, explaining who each one is and what their jobs are.

Try to make each person feel needed by the company.

Get someone to buddy with a new employee while learning the ropes.

Explain to employees *why* their job is important and *how* it fits into the big operation, so they will be *proud* of their job.

Encourage social and recreational get-togethers for all the people under you and their families.

Encourage your people to eat, talk, play together.

Never, never blame "the company" for things your people don't like. Set an example of loyalty!

Security

Keep them as well informed as you can about what is going on in the company. Help them feel that they are "in the know." (This cuts down rumors.)

Especially, tell them when there are going to be *changes,* and explain why and what the effect will be.

Be *consistent yourself!* Don't be one way today, another tomorrow.

When you have to reprimand someone, end it with some encouragement that they *can* be successful.

Suggest a better procedure, whenever possible, instead of criticizing a poor one.

Source: "Motivation—The State of the Art" by Haluk Bekiroglu and Turan Gonen, *Personnel Journal,* November 1977. Reprinted with the permission of *Personnel Journal,* Costa Mesa, California; all rights reserved.

a strong impact on job satisfaction and morale. One survey of department store salespeople revealed a higher level of satisfaction among those who were more "closely supervised in terms of high leader consideration and initiation of structure."[35] If supervisors employ appropriate rewards in dealing with subordinates, employee role conflict decreases and the degree of job satisfaction rises. So does satisfaction with the supervisor.[36]

Training Supervisory Personnel

Because of the critical relationship of the front-line supervisor to the motivation/productivity problem, companies try to improve their supervisors' capabilities through advanced training techniques. Older management training methods such as role playing and sensitivity training are being shelved in favor of newer techniques. Currently in vogue are **behavior modification** and **modeling** approaches. As is explained in Figure 12.7, modeling largely involves learning through imitation. An interesting illustration of a behavior modification tech-

Figure 12.7
Learning through
modeling

The theory of imitative learning, more accurately called modeling, is not new. Studies date back to 1896. Modeling theory is very useful in explaining the learning process of complex behavioral patterns, and is so normal a procedure that we seldom even realize that we are involved in it. If we want our children to sharpen their own pencils, we get their attention (!), show them how to use the sharpener, let them try it, and then say "Good work! See, you can do it on your own. Aren't you grown-up!" We first acted as a model, and then reinforced the desired behavior that the tyke exhibited. This is a complex behavioral pattern: consider the difficulty involved in the process of waiting for Junior to randomly sharpen a pencil so that we could reward pencil-sharpening behavior!

Learning through modeling occurs constantly, all around us. Consider some of the imitative behaviors you have witnessed in children who are heavy television viewers. How does one learn to eat a lobster? By observing others. Drive a truck? Operate complex equipment? Shoot a bow and arrow? By observing others. Observational learning can add totally new behaviors to our repertoire and, when the model is punished or rewarded, can result in inhibitory or disinhibitory behavior as well.

Source: "How Training through Behavior Modeling Works," by Stephen B. Wehrenberg and Robert Kuhnie, copyright, July 1980. Reprinted with the permission of *Personnel Journal*, Costa Mesa, California; all rights reserved.

nique is positive management (PM). PM is a system that deals with observable behavior and emphasizes the positive aspects of job performance. It stresses learning rather than motivation. Holding that desirable acts should be promptly reinforced, it employs performance shaping. This is defined as the systematic reinforcement of successively close approximations to a specific target behavior.[37]

Motivation Theory: A Brief Review

In classical management theory, money was long held to be the worker's prime motivator. This attitude existed prior to the Industrial Revolution and all the way to the first few decades of this century. The latter years of the 19th century witnessed growing interest among business managers, engineers, and others in evolving a true science of management. Delving avidly into the work environment, they studied operations in minute detail. They sought to uncover basic principles and to devise methods and procedures that could be used to improve plant and worker efficiency.

The efforts of Frederic W. Taylor lent a major impetus to this new scientific management movement. Taylor's major work, *Principles of Scientific Management,* was published in 1911. He stressed the need for management to define job tasks with the utmost clarity. Taylor called for the setting of work standards and the institution of performance controls. He maintained that worker productivity should be measured and employees rewarded for their output.

Among other well-known members of this new school of management thinking were Henry L. Gantt, who devised methods of planning

From *The Wall Street Journal,* with permission of Cartoon Features Syndicate.

"I'm giving up spells and going into behavior modification."

and control; Frank Gilbreth, the contributor of motion study techniques to industry; and Harrington Emerson, famous for his principles of efficiency.

The Human Relations Era Frequent accusations against the concepts of scientific management held that its supporters viewed people purely as resources to be managed and manipulated by the company. Its approaches were considered impersonal and mechanical. By the 1930s, social scientists and behavioral psychologists had already been drawn into the ranks of concerned managers and theorists in the arena of the workplace. Diligently, they hunted for new insights into the personal dimensions of employees: attitudes, satisfaction or dissatisfaction with job or firm, and behavioral tendencies. Also investigated were the relationships of workers with one another and with supervisors and company administration; group behavior; symptoms and causes of morale; and so on. During these years the ancient saw about money being the principal element in motivation came under serious challenge. In the now-famous Hawthorne Studies, conducted at a Western Electric plant in the 1940s, Elton Mayo confirmed that such aspects as cooperation among workers and the manager's role are essential to both productivity and morale.

The Ladder of Needs Around the same time, an article in a psychological journal profoundly influenced modern motivational thought. It represented the contribution, by Abraham Maslow, of a proposed theory of human motivation.[38] Many hundreds of articles that dealt with this theory subsequently appeared in print.[39]

Let us review Maslow's needs theory, which we met in an earlier chapter. Maslow suggested that we are perennially needy beings. He proposed a five-tier ladder, or hierarchy, of human needs. Beginning with the lowest level of needs, each set must be fairly well satisfied before we are able to proceed to the next higher set. Most basic (and most powerful) of all are the physiological needs: our bodies' demands for food, drink, rest, and other physical necessities. Once we have largely answered these, a new set will emerge—the safety needs. We want to feel secure both inside and outside our homes. We need shelter against the elements. Applied to workers, meeting these needs suggests safe working conditions, job security, life and health insurance, and other such concepts. As we continue to climb this ladder, we next must satisfy our social needs for love, affection, and affiliation with groups. Fourth-tier needs have to do with our self-esteem and ego satisfaction. We want to be recognized and respected by others. Finally, even if we successfully meet these and all lower needs, still another major level begins to function. This, the highest level of all, is the need for self-actualization. Those comparatively few who finally reach this top-of-the-ladder position succeed in becoming the kind of people they were destined to be. They attain their fullest potential.

Theories X and Y Impressed by Maslow's theory of human motivation, Douglas McGregor concluded that managements, in practice, pay scant attention to any but the lowest levels of human needs. He codified into a few sentences what he perceived to be the typical management attitude toward workers. This approach he titled **Theory X.** He also suggested an alternative, **Theory Y.** Details of both attitudes are given below:

Theory X:

1. The average human being has an inherent dislike of work and will avoid it if he can.
2. Because of this human characteristic of dislike of work, most people must be coerced, controlled, directed, threatened with punishment to get them to put forth adequate effort toward the achievement of organizational objectives.
3. The average human being prefers to be directed, wishes to avoid responsibility, has relatively little ambition, wants security above all.

Theory Y:

1. The expenditure of physical and mental effort in work is as natural as play or rest.
2. Man will exercise self-direction and self-control in the service of objectives to which he is committed.

3. Commitment to objectives is a function of the rewards associated with their achievement.
4. The average human being learns, under proper conditions, not only to accept but to seek responsibility.
5. The capacity to exercise a relatively high degree of imagination, ingenuity, and creativity in the solution of organizational problems is widely, not narrowly, distributed in the population.
6. Under the conditions of modern industrial life, the intellectual potentialities of the average human being are only partially utilized.[40]

The Dual-Factor Theory Frederick Herzberg investigated motivational aspects among engineers and accountants in Pennsylvania. From his research, he evolved his **dual-factor theory.** He suggested that the work environment contains two sets of factors that affect workers' outlooks: motivators and hygiene factors.[41] Among others, the latter include company policy, work conditions, relations with supervisors, and salary. Herzberg labeled these factors *dissatisfiers,* holding that they aim at fulfilling only the more basic needs and do not motivate employees.

In a 1968 article in the *Harvard Business Review,* Herzberg described the findings of a dozen studies. He concluded that hygiene factors constitute the primary cause of unhappiness on the job.[42] Satisfying employees' hygiene needs does little more than remove the specter of dissatisfaction. Motivators (or *satisfiers*), on the other hand, appeal to the higher human needs and are the primary cause of satisfaction. Factors such as achievement, recognition, advancement, growth, responsibility, and the work itself are motivators.

Newer Insights In more recent years, management theorists have contributed additional insights into motivation and leadership. **Expectancy theory,** for example, holds that worker motivation is a function of (a) individual expectancies of reward for effort, and (b) the value of specific rewards as perceived by the employee. If workers believe that job performance will lead to highly valued rewards, then they will work harder and be more satisfied at work.

Still emerging is the path-goal theory of leadership, related to expectancy theory. It "suggests that a leader's behavior is motivating or satisfying to the degree that the behavior increases subordinate goal attainment and clarifies the paths to these goals."[43]

Even more recent is William Ouchi's contribution regarding Japanese approaches to management and productivity.[44] In his best-selling *Theory Z,* Ouchi outlined many of the major characteristics of Japanese business organizations. Among the attributes he found were: trust, coordination, egalitarian relationships among workers, and collective decision making.

Summary   Managers direct and coordinate the activities that need to be performed in an organization. Planning, organizing, directing, and controlling are the four basic managerial functions.

In the effective organization, communications flow smoothly in three directions: from the top down, from the bottom up, and horizontally. Managers perform their functions, getting the required work done by communicating with others. Messages can be conveyed orally or in writing. Thoughts may also be expressed by gesture or facial expression and by body language. Good listening skills form an integral part of the manager's communication capabilities. Problems in communicating stem from individual differences among the participants: different backgrounds, experiences, perceptions, personalities, and the like.

Managers must lead. Leaders are not born; they are made. Leadership itself is both a process and a set of skills. As a process, leadership is situationally based. The leader, the members of the group, and the individual situation all influence the outcome. Leaders may display autocratic, democratic, or laissez-faire behavior.

Employee motivation and the improvement of productivity are essential elements in modern retail management. The morale and contributions of workers are affected by many aspects of the business. To mention a few, there are the working conditions, company policies, the basic pay plan and other supplementary financial benefits, supervision, and nonfinancial rewards.

The conduct of the supervisor directly influences job satisfaction and morale. Today's retailers emphasize better and more advanced training for supervisors. In addition to established methods, behavior modification and modeling are among the newer techniques being used to train supervisory personnel.

The human relations era ushered in new approaches to management thinking. The influences of Maslow, McGregor, Herzberg, and others have served to form modern motivational theory. An understanding of their contributions helps managers to cope better with problems in the complex area of human resources management.

Key Terms

managerial functions	intrinsic motivation
planning	extrinsic motivation
organizing	morale
directing	role conflict
controlling	role ambiguity
communication	role clarity
leadership	behavior modification
autocratic leaders	modeling
democratic leaders	Theories X and Y
laissez-faire leaders	dual-factor theory
decision-making process	expectancy theory

Review Questions

1. Name and describe the four basic managerial functions.

2. Discuss the role and significance of communication in an organization.

3. Identify at least five possible sources of communication difficulties in an organization.

4. Prepare a list of traits that workers would like to find in their supervisors.

5. Differentiate among three different styles of leadership.

6. Outline the major steps in the decision-making process.

7. Explain the terms *role conflict* and *role ambiguity*. Discuss their relationship to job satisfaction and employee morale.

8. Give six or more examples of nonfinancial incentives and rewards that managements use to motivate employees.

9. Explain the concept of *modeling*. Show how it may be used to improve the effectiveness of supervisors.

10. Specify and explain in your own words three different theories of worker motivation.

11. Distinguish between motivators and hygiene factors.

Discussion Questions

1. With your partner-to-be, you are making plans to launch a boys' clothing store in your neighborhood within the next six months. Make a list of the major aspects of the business for which the two of you will need to plan.

2. Define the SDC syndrome. Why do you believe stores in the past looked for managers who possessed these qualities? What reasoning lies behind the demand for people with imagination and creativity? Explain.

3. As the new manager of a home furnishings store, suggest ways you can attempt to satisfy the social and esteem needs of your eight employees.

4. Give an opinion about what can cause role ambiguity in a position. What measures can be taken to improve role clarity?

5. Explain the reasoning outlined in Theory X. Do you believe this is a realistic view for the foreman of a construction gang to adhere to? Give reasons for your answer.

6. What actions might management take to motivate stockroom employees? Department managers?

7. Contrast Theories X and Y with the Japanese approaches outlined in William Ouchi's *Theory Z*.

Notes

[1]Henry Mintzberg, "The Manager's Job: Folklore and Fact," *Harvard Business Review* 53 (July–August 1975), p. 61.

[2]David C. McClelland and David H. Burnham, "Power is the Great Motivator," *Harvard Business Review* 54 (March–April 1976), pp. 100–110.

[3]Leslie Kanuk, "Leadership Effectiveness of Department Managers in a Department Store Chain: A Contingency Analysis," *Journal of Retailing* 52 (Spring 1976), pp. 9–16*ff.*

[4]For early suggestions that management involves forecasting and planning, organizing, command, coordination, and control, see: Henri Fayol, *General and Industrial Management* (London: Sir Isaac Pitman & Sons, 1949).

[5]Leslie W. Rue and Lloyd L. Byars, *Management: Theory and Application,* rev. ed. (Homewood, Ill.: Richard D. Irwin, 1980), p. 116.

[6]Robert C. Appleby with Irving Burstiner, *The Essential Guide to Management* (Englewood Cliffs, N.J.: Prentice-Hall, 1981), p 10.

[7]Ibid., p. 55.

[8]Leland Brown, *Communicating Facts and Ideas in Business* (Englewood Cliffs, N.J.: Prentice-Hall, 1982), p. 24.

[9]Raymond V. Lesikar, *Business Communication: Theory and Application,* 4th ed. (Homewood, Ill.: Richard D. Irwin, 1980), pp. 27–29.

[10]Leonard R. Sayles and George Strauss, *Managing Human Resources,* 2d ed. (Englewood CLiffs, N.J.: Prentice-Hall, 1981), p. 103.

[11]W. F. Coventry and Irving Burstiner, *Management: A Basic Handbook* (Englewood Cliffs, N.J.: Prentice-Hall, 1977), p. 117.

[12]Brown, *Communicating Facts,* p. 46.

[13]Rue and Byars, *Management,* p. 265.

[14]Ibid., p. 339.

[15]Appleby with Burstiner, *Essential Guide,* p. 49.

[16]Raymond L. Hilgert, "The Manager's Guide to Influencing Others," *Personnel Journal* 53 (November 1974), pp. 832–35.

[17]Jan P. Muczyk, T. H. Matthiess, and Myron Gable, "Predicting Success of Store Managers," *Journal of Retailing* 50 (Summer 1974), pp. 43–49*ff.*

[18]Bernard L. Rosenbaum, "Changing Psychological Profile of the Successful Retailer," *Stores* 55 (May 1973), pp. 25*ff.*

[19]For informative capsulized descriptions of five leadership styles (autocratic, bureaucratic, diplomatic, participative, and free rein), see: James Owens, "The Uses of Leadership Theory," *Michigan Business Review* 25 (January 1973), pp. 13–19.

[20]See: Howard Rudnitsky, "Retailing through Intimidation," *Forbes* 126 (November 9, 1981), pp. 50*ff.*

[21]Leonard L. Rosenbaum and William B. Rosenbaum, "Morale and Productivity Consequences of Group Leadership Style, Stress, and Type of Task," *Journal of Applied Psychology* 55, no. 4 (1971), pp. 343–48.

[22]McClelland and Burnham, "Power," p. 105.

[23]For an interesting discussion of a model of cognitive style that reviews the ways in which managers approach problem solving and decision making, see: James L. McKenney and Peter G. W. Keen, "How Managers' Minds Work," *Harvard Business Review* 52 (May–June 1974), pp. 79–90.

[24]Albert W. Mankoff, "Values—Not Attitudes—Are the Real Key to Motivation," *Management Review* 63 (December 1974), pp. 23–29; Martha A. Brown, "Values—A Necessary but Neglected Ingredient of Motivation on the Job," *Academy of Management Review* 1 (October 1976), pp. 15–23; Niles Howard, "How Good Is Values Analysis?" *Dun's Review* 117 (March 1981), pp. 118–120*ff.*

[25]Harold Mack, "Some Lessons in Motivation," *Supervisory Management* 21 (August 1976), pp. 2–7.

[26]Edward J. Giblin, "Motivating Employees: A Closer Look," *Personnel Journal* 55 (February 1976), p. 70.

[27]Mary Coeli Meyer, "Six States of Demotivation," *International Management* 32 (April 1977), pp. 14–17.

[28]Alan J. Dubinsky and Bruce E. Mattson, "Consequences of Role Conflict and Ambiguity Experienced by Retail Salespeople," *Journal of Retailing* 55 (Winter 1979), pp. 70–86.

[29]Richard L. Oliver and Arthur P. Brief, "Determinants and Consequences of Role Conflict and Ambiguity among Retail Sales Managers," *Journal of Retailing* 53 (Winter 1977–78), pp. 47–58*ff.*

[30]J. Patrick Kelly, Myron Gable, and Richard T. Hise, "Conflict, Clarity, Tension, and Satisfaction in Chain Store Manager Roles," *Journal of Retailing* 57 (Spring 1981), pp. 27–42.

[31]Kenneth A. Kovach, "Improving Employee Motivation in Today's Business Environment," *MSU Business Topics* 24 (Autumn 1976), p. 12.

[32]For more information on these and other techniques designed to motivate employees, see: Ernest W. Ward, "Elements of an Employee Motivation Program," *Personnel Journal* 53 (March 1974), pp. 205–8; R. Minicucci, "Motivating Employees in a Down Economy," *Administrative Management* 36 (June 1975), pp. 20–21*ff;* Giblin, "Motivating Employees," pp. 68–71*ff;* Edward E. Lawler III, "Developing a Motivating Work Climate," *Management Review* 66 (July 1977), pp. 25–28*ff.*

[33]Lester R. Bittell, *What Every Supervisor Should Know: The Basics of Supervisory Management,* 4th ed. (New York: McGraw-Hill, 1980), p. 3.

[34]Dale S. Beach, *Personnel: The Management of People at Work,* 4th ed. (New York: Macmillan, 1980), p. 495.

[35]R. Kenneth Teas, "A Test of a Model of Department Store Salespeople's Job Satisfaction," *Journal of Retailing* 57 (Spring 1981), pp. 3–25.

[36]Robert T. Keller and Andrew D. Szilagyi, "Employee Reactions to Leader Reward Behavior," *Academy of Management Journal* 19 (December 1976), pp. 619–27.

[37]Robert Kreitner, "PM—A New Method of Behavior Change," *Business Horizons* 18 (December 1975), pp. 79–86.

[38]A. H. Maslow, "A Theory of Human Motivation," *Psychological Review* 50 (1943), pp. 370–96.

[39]For an extended treatment of the subject, see: Abraham H. Maslow, *Motivation and Personality,* 2d ed. (New York: Harper & Row, 1970).

[40]Douglas McGregor, *The Human Side of Enterprise* (New York: McGraw-Hill, 1960), pp. 31–44, 47–48.

[41]Frederick Herzberg, *Work and the Nature of Man* (New York: Thomas Y. Crowell, 1966), pp. 71–91.

[42]Frederick Herzberg, "One More Time: How Do You Motivate Employees?" *Harvard Business Review* 46 (January–February 1968), pp. 53–62.

[43]Robert J. House and Terence R. Mitchell, "Path-Goal Theory of Leadership," *Journal of Contemporary Business* 3 (Autumn 1974), pp. 81–97.

[44]See: William Ouchi, *Theory Z* (Reading, Mass.: Addison-Wesley, 1981).

Case 4.1
E-Z Automotive

Todd Reynolds is the 28-year-old owner of E-Z Automotive, a closely held corporate chain of three automotive supply stores in the state of Washington. His father founded the business in 1966 in a large store, still the busiest in the chain, situated in a medium-sized town south of Seattle. At the time his father passed away, rather suddenly, Todd was the West Coast sales representative for a national distributor of office furniture. An only son, he immediately left his job to take over the management of the family business. That was three years ago. Last year, company sales exceeded $1 million for the first time.

Like their competitors, the E-Z stores carry a wide assortment of replacement parts for most car makes. They sell motor oil; antifreeze; brake, power steering, and other fluids; batteries; distributor caps and cables; car mats and seat coverings; hoses and belts; and many other accessories.

Todd has just completed an exciting financial arrangement with Dr. Edmund Dilgard, a wealthy physician and close friend of the family. In exchange for a one-third interest in the company, Dr. Dilgard has invested $200,000 in seed money. Their idea is to increase the number of stores to 10 within two years and then convert E-Z to a franchising organization. Their ultimate goal is rapid regional expansion. They are aware that one or two franchisors are already operating successfully in the automotive supply field.

Todd knows he will no longer be able to oversee all aspects of the business. If he is to be busy finding locations for, and setting up, seven additional outlets, he will need an effective organization behind him. Up to this time, he has managed the main store himself and supervised the managers of the other two units as best he could. Todd does all the buying, with a clerk handling the attendant paperwork for him. A bookkeeper keeps his accounts and makes up the weekly payroll.

With paper and pencil, Todd is attempting to draw up an organizational chart for a 10-store chain. He realizes, of course, that he will need still another, more complex organization three years from today. However, franchising is still far down the road.

Questions   1. Prepare an appropriate organizational chart that would facilitate the operation of E-Z Automotive's planned 10-unit chain.

   2. How will the new organization change when the company begins to sell franchises?

Case 4.2
The Olympiad
Sports Shops

Bud King is the founder and president of The Olympiad Shops, a western regional chain of seven sporting-goods stores. A low-overhead operation, the company offers a wide assortment of merchandise at prices that are in line with those of Herman's World of Sporting Goods and similar competitive outlets. Customer services are minimal. While VISA, MasterCard, and other major cards are accepted, the stores offer no credit arrangements of their own.

From his home offices in Los Angeles, Bud oversees the buying and merchandising end of the business as well as the payroll and bookkeeping departments. From the firm's inception in the mid-1970s, he has emphasized decentralization of the personnel function. All store managers interview, hire, and train their employees. From the standpoint of overall financial control, each store is organized as a separate profit center. Bud personally evaluates manager performance twice each year by reviewing the individual store operating statements. Managers earn salaries that are slightly above the industry average. In addition, they are rewarded with semiannual bonuses: a small, set percentage of the profits they have earned. Consequently, these executives strive to keep their controllable costs down. In all units, new hires are started at the same hourly rate: 75 cents above minimum wage. Provided their work is satisfactory, they receive a raise of 50 cents an hour at the end of their one-month probationary period. All future increases and promotions are then left up to the manager.

Recently, Bud hired a bright young college graduate, Melissa Vamberry, with the intention of training her for the newly created post of assistant to the president. One afternoon, he told her how disturbed he was about the high rate of employee turnover that had plagued the firm over the past six months. "I'd like you to dig into this problem for me," he added. "I want to know why we've been losing people and what we can do about correcting the situation."

Thanking him for the assignment, Melissa replied that she would begin by visiting every store and getting to meet their staffs. From the payroll department, she secured a list of all current employees as well as those who had recently left the company. Over the following two weeks, she met and spoke with all managers and assistant managers in the chain—and with most cashiers, salesclerks, and stockpersons. In each area, too, she managed to contact one or two of Olympiad's former employees.

In her report to the president, Melissa stressed the following observations:

1. Three of the store managers could be characterized as autocratic leaders who rule through coercion and intimidation.
2. Managers and assistant managers alike demonstrate little concern for the feelings of their employees. For example, they frequently criticize or scold employees in front of their co-workers.
3. A common feeling among many of the workers is that the managers and even their assistants show favoritism to a select few.
4. Good work does not seem to be rewarded.
5. The typical worker's attitude is that top management is distant, impersonal, and uncaring.
6. Employees are doubtful about their long-term prospects with the company.

Questions
1. In your opinion, what facts may account for the obviously low state of morale among the employees of The Olympiad Sports Shops?
2. What immediate steps would you advise Bud King to take to improve his personnel situation in general and the turnover rate in particular?

The Bettmann Archive

Courtesy The Great Atlantic & Pacific Tea Company, Inc.

MERCHANDISE AND STORE SERVICES

Courtesy Sears, Roebuck & Co., Chicago

PLANNING THE MERCHANDISE MIX

Your Study Objectives

After you have studied this chapter, you will understand:

1. The areas in which retailers need to set policy with regard to their merchandise inventories.
2. How retail managements use gross margin return on investment and ABC analysis in store and merchandise management.
3. The variety of information sources, both internal and external, that store merchants consult to determine customer needs and wants.
4. How consumer products and services differ from industrial goods and some useful approaches to consumer goods classification.
5. The distinguishing characteristics of the various stages of the product life cycle and their implications for the retail buyer.
6. The procedures retailers follow in planning their inventories for staple merchandise and fashion goods.

The merchandise inventory is a store's life-support system. Only by reselling goods can the retailer produce the funds needed to support an operation and earn profit. In most retail lines, the cost of goods easily accounts for 50 to 60 cents of every sales dollar. In groceries, alcoholic beverages, major appliances, and some other lines, the cost-of-goods figure runs up to 70 percent and even more. Moreover, it is not at all unusual for the carrying costs associated with keeping the store well-stocked to reach 25 or 30 percent of the actual cost of the merchandise.

Thus, the retailer is continually challenged to maintain a sensible balance between inventory costs and potential profits. Too heavy an investment in merchandise needlessly ties up essential capital. Too small an investment can lead to stockouts, lost sales, and eventually, a shrinking customer base. To manage the flow of inventory, retailers need to effectively plan, coordinate, and control all elements relating to store merchandise. First of all, they need to determine and correctly interpret shoppers' needs and wants. They must then locate, select, and purchase in the correct quantities the right mix of goods to meet customer demand. Appropriate pricing techniques must also be applied. Retailers know where to find useful information about consumer needs and wants. They need to know how to choose merchandise for resale and to be aware of the implications of the product life cycle concept when purchasing goods. They need to know how to reorder staple products and how to merchandise fashion goods.

Some Basic Inventory Decisions

Difficult merchandising decisions confront the retailer who is first starting out in business. Typically, a store must present a representative assortment of the kinds of products that shoppers expect it to carry. Goods offered for sale contribute strongly to the formation of the firm's image. A high-fashion boutique will not remain in business for long if it offers its clientele shoddy merchandise. Nor can a cut-rate outlet successfully upgrade its image merely by adding a few quality items.

Merchandise Concerns of Retailers

Merchants must make decisions about these aspects of their merchandise inventories: (1) variety, (2) assortment, (3) breadth, and (4) depth.

Variety The number of different merchandise lines that the retail company offers shoppers is its **variety.** A neighborhood bakery, for example, may make available a variety of bread, rolls, cakes, pies, and cookies. Within each of these major categories, or merchandise groups, an assortment is offered. These items will differ from one another in size, shape, ingredients, price, or other characteristics. Collectively, the merchandise selection represents the store's variety.

A wide variety of merchandise characterizes this well-stocked Kitchen Korner.

Courtesy K mart Corporation. K MART and ACCENTS are service marks of K mart Corporation, Troy, MI

Assortment The term **assortment** applies to the number of different choices offered in a particular retail line. The bakery may carry four kinds of breads, seven types of pies, six varieties of cakes, and so on. As a further illustration, consider a typical menswear outlet. In addition to suits, coats, and slacks, the store offers other lines such as sportswear, men's furnishings, and shoes. In each of these major groups there is a good assortment of merchandise items differentiated by style, fabric, color, size, and other variants.

Breadth and Depth The **breadth,** or width, of a merchandise assortment is the number of different styles, colors, sizes, and other variants carried. The term **depth** is applied to the number of pieces stocked of these variants. Depending on the image they want to project, merchants may choose from four possible alternatives in stocking their stores: (1) broad and shallow, (2) broad and deep, (3) narrow and shallow, and (4) narrow and deep. A retailer who selects the first alternative may offer a wide array of, say 6 to 10 or more merchandise categories. However, the store will carry only the more popular articles in each category—with a narrow range of sizes, color choices, materials, and so on. Not stocked are items that shoppers request infrequently, like the end sizes. On the other hand, a retail firm may specialize in a narrow assortment of two or three categories, yet maintain substantial depth in them. Among other types, cheese shops, specialty bookstores, and jeans shops offer narrow and deep assortments.

Merchandise Classifications

For more efficient stock planning and control, many retailers arrange their inventory by **merchandise classifications.** Similar articles or goods that shoppers would normally expect to be located near each other in the store are arranged in a merchandise grouping. In the department store setting, examples include home furnishings, housewares, toys, men's apparel, domestics, and children's clothing. These basic groups are further refined by assigning the products to distinct categories. Each category contains a variety of merchandise from which shoppers can make their selections. In the men's sportswear category, for example, shoppers can find shirts, sweaters, and swimwear. Belts, handkerchiefs, and gloves would be found in men's accessories. Each category is, in turn, divided further into classifications and subclassifications. Sweaters, for example, may be broken down according to style (V necks, turtlenecks, and the like), and each style is further subclassified by material, colors, price lines, and so on.

In a good retail control system, every stock variant is assigned its own **stockkeeping unit (SKU)** number. SKU numbers are used to keep track of every article in the store and for reordering purposes.

Two Planning and Control Aids

Of value in merchandise planning and control are two interesting management aids: (1) gross margin return on investment, or GMROI, and (2) ABC analysis.

Gross Margin Return on Investment

A healthy return on investment—the monies a firm has placed into its assets—is a fundamental management objective in companies of all kinds. Many retail companies rely today on a somewhat similar approach to improving their merchandising results. A more significant indicator of performance than the traditional ROI, this is a planning and control formula that shows the firm's return on *inventory* investment. Known as **gross margin return on investment,** or more simply, **GMROI,** it combines the gross margin dollars earned from the sale of merchandise with the rate of stock turnover.[1] (Stock turnover is discussed in detail in Chapter 14.) The formula shows the product of two different ratios, as you can see below:

$$1. \text{ GMROI} = \frac{\text{Gross margin dollars}}{\text{Sales}} \times \frac{\text{Sales}}{\text{Average inventory}}$$

Note that the two Sales entries cancel out, producing the end result below:

$$2. \text{ GMROI} = \frac{\text{Gross margin dollars}}{\text{Average inventory}}$$

GMROI is useful because it demonstrates that inventory can generate a return in two ways: turnover and gross margin. Two items may vary considerably with regard to turnover or gross margin and yet be equally attractive overall. Lowering the gross margin to increase an item's turnover rate may be advantageous to a retailer.

ABC Analysis

There is a well-accepted axiom in marketing known as the **80–20 principle.** Based on a form of distribution called a Pareto curve, it serves as a useful guide. It suggests that roughly 80 percent of a manufacturer's sales volume can be accounted for by some 20 percent of the items in the firm's product line. Or, in the case of a field sales force, approximately one fifth of the sales representatives produce four fifths of the company's sales. If we apply the concept to a retail business, we would expect that about 80 percent of annual sales volume might be brought in by just 20 percent of the merchandise items carried.

ABC analysis makes use of the 80–20 principle. It is an inventory control technique that categorizes goods into three groups, according to their rate of movement. It suggests that the large number of products in a store's assortment that contribute little to the total sales should be strictly controlled.[2] A relatively simple procedure is involved. The sales generated by each article carried in stock are tracked for a season or an entire year. Then, all items are ranked from most to least, according to the revenue they produce. The goods are then assigned to one of three groups: (1) the A group, which usually accounts for some 50 percent of total sales, although they only represent about 10 percent of the items sold, (2) the B group, a larger number of items that collectively bring in another 25 percent of sales, and (3) the C group, the balance of the inventory. For the most part, the retailer concentrates on the A group, watching sales carefully and seeing to it that the store is kept well stocked with this merchandise.

Analyzing Shoppers' Needs

To be productive, retail merchandising practices need to be predicated on a thorough understanding of customer needs, wants, preferences, and patterns of shopping behavior. Many sources of information are available to assist the merchandising department in general and the buying staff in particular. For the sake of convenience, we can categorize these sources as either internal or external.

Internal Sources of Information

Readily available in most retail organizations are four valuable data sources: (1) the firm's records of cash sales, (2) the credit files, (3) records of customer returns and adjustments, and (4) store employees. Frequently, management will introduce one or more additional fact-

Retailers try to stock the right sizes, styles, and other product variants.

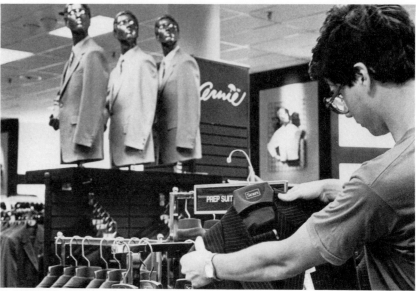

Courtesy Sears, Roebuck & Co., Chicago

gathering techniques. These may include an efficient want-slip system, comparison shopping, consumer panels, primary (experimental) research, and even computer simulation.

Sales Records Typically, these are the retailer's most valuable information source. Every merchant records the total sales dollars taken in each and every day the facility is open for business. Whether these totals are subsequently compiled on a quarterly, monthly, or weekly basis, sales records serve as essential guides in the preparation of forecasts. The comparison of current results with those of prior periods enables the retailer to detect both short- and long-term trends. These are taken into consideration when sales projections must be made. Planned sales for upcoming periods can be adjusted upward or downward in accordance with estimates of economic conditions. Other variables can be built in: changes in the local competitive situation, desired increases or cutbacks in the firm's promotional activities, and so on. In a chain store operation, potential problem units can be spotted early enough for management to take corrective action.

In addition to actual sales expressed in terms of dollar amounts, the modern firm can accumulate and process sales data in terms of the merchandise itself. Records of stock movement play a vital role in inventory planning. Retailers are able to calculate requirements, order, and maintain enough stock on hand to meet their needs all through the year. This can be done despite the peaks and valleys in sales activity expected around the calendar. They are able to ascertain the relative weakness or strength of consumer demand for every major classification and subclassification carried. They can determine the best sellers, what goods turn over at an average rate of speed, and the slow-moving items. This information is crucial to the reordering of goods. It enables merchandisers to stock the right sizes, styles, colors, materials, and other product variants in the correct proportions.

Credit Files The majority of our nation's retail companies readily extend some form of credit to regular customers. Credit has been a way of life among consumers for many years, and it is a way for the astute merchant to increase store sales.[3] Some firms offer open (regular) credit. Others sell merchandise on the installment plan or on a 90-day plan. Shoppers are encouraged to buy goods and/or services by charging their purchases to third-party cards such as VISA or MasterCard. Department stores and large chains may install and maintain their own store charge systems. In any event, a periodic investigation of all noncash, or charged, purchases can provide worthwhile insights into consumer behavior. Whether the goods have been charged through the mail, by telephone, or in person at the store, a review of the attendant paperwork yields a great deal of useful information. The retailer can determine the kinds of products that are more (or less) popular, shopper preferences for styles, materials, colors, and the like, and what seasonal merchandise sells or does not sell. If the firm has its own charge account system, an examination of the original credit applications will reveal valuable data about the clientele with regard to sex, occupation, income sources, and other demographic factors. By spotting the addresses of charge customers on an area map, management can determine both the shape and size of the store's trading area.

Customer Returns An occasional shopper will bring back merchandise to a store to exchange it for some other article or to obtain a refund. The shopper may be dissatisfied because the item was soiled or damaged, defective, poorly made, or did not perform as expected. Or the shopper may simply have had a change of heart and does not want the product. Retail companies typically establish a returns policy to handle such problems. In many stores, when articles are brought back, a complaint form is completed by the customer service section, department head, or store manager. The customer's name, address, and telephone number are filled in, as is the reason given for the return. Tallying up a batch of these forms and studying the information may uncover a number of problem areas. These may not only reflect on the merchandise, but they often also point up difficulties with store practices and policies. This internal research can lead to improved buying procedures, better quality goods, changes in suppliers, and the like.

Store Employees The retail sales force works directly on the firing line. Sales employees meet, greet, and communicate with shoppers one to one. These are the people who are the most knowledgeable about the customer. They know what shoppers look at, ask for, and comment on favorably or unfavorably. Store employees are also consumers, just like you and I. Both they and we learn of new products and services while watching TV and listening to the radio. We gather additional information by reading magazines and newspapers and by interacting with family members, friends, associates at work, and others.

An enlightened management encourages employee input regarding the merchandise inventory or, for that matter, any other phase of operations. Whether they be profit or nonprofit entities, organizations of all kinds often introduce a suggestion-box system as one vital component of a healthy personnel relations program. Retailers, too, reap the benefits of this system. The cost is insignificant; no frills are required. All that is needed to launch the program is a box, some paper forms, and clear communication of the concept to employees. The box itself can be of simple construction with a hinged cover secured by a small padlock and a slot cut into its top through which interested personnel can deposit their suggestions. It can be placed in the employees' rest area or near their entrance in the large store. The small store owner will keep it in the back room. The system is productive only if contributions are reviewed regularly by management or by someone authorized to read them. Prompt and courteous replies to contributors are an essential element. Payment of small amounts of

From *The Wall Street Journal*, with permission of Cartoon Features Syndicate.

cash, coupons, trading stamps, gifts, or other token awards to all whose suggestions are adopted helps to spark more excitement among employees.

Want-slip Program Frequently, shoppers ask for merchandise that the firm does not normally stock. Many merchants regard such requests as lost sales, dollars that could have been rung up at the register if only the right goods were carried. A simple, no-cost solution to this problem is the installation of a **want-slip program.** A sheet, or pad, of paper is positioned in a convenient place, perhaps behind the cash register or near the wrapping desk. Salespeople are instructed to enter on the sheet every call for an item not carried. Some retailers even expand the program to include customer comments, favorable or unfavorable, about any aspect of store operations. Periodically, the manager or buyer checks the want slips. If the demand for any particular item is heavy enough, a decision may be made to introduce it into the regular line.

Comparison Shopping Practically all retailers strive to keep abreast of competitors' offerings by **comparison shopping.** They check the window displays of their competition regularly. They want to know the kinds of goods displayed, which styles and varieties are featured, and at what prices the articles are being sold. Painstakingly, they study the newspaper advertisements for insights into competitors' promotional activities and for usable ideas for their own stores. Independent store owners often ask their employees to visit competitive stores to check window and interior displays and to find out what their salespeople are pushing and how they treat their customers.

The large retail organization does much the same, in a more professional manner. The firm may hire one or two comparison shoppers or staff an entire department with these specialists. Comparison shoppers visit many stores that offer similar goods. They may travel all over town, even out of town, reviewing not only merchandise lines, pricing approaches, and promotions, but also other phases of their operations. On their return, they report their findings to management.

Consumer Panels Department stores and other large retail companies frequently set up **consumer panels,** small groups of consumers who have been selected as representative of the kinds of people who shop at the store.[4] Management looks to panel members for assistance; their opinions, attitudes, and judgments are tapped for evaluations of store merchandise, policies, services, advertising, and other aspects. The panel comes up with helpful criticisms and suggestions about current fashions and soon-to-be-outmoded styles, new merchandise items or services under consideration, proposed store locations, and so on.

Other Internal Sources Retailers obtain facts on which to base merchandising decisions by researching shopper preferences and dislikes, conducting pricing studies, evaluating their advertising and sales promotion activities, and so on. To gather such information, they can draw upon survey techniques, observational methods, and even experimentation. In addition, the accelerated evolution of the computer has provided today's merchant with a marvelous tool for appraising inventory movement and customer demand. Some larger retailing organizations use computer simulation techniques to evaluate the impact of alternative merchandise assortments on department or store performance.

External Sources of Information Valuable information can be obtained from individuals and organizations external to the retail facility. Among these, the major sources are suppliers, trade and other publications, the buying office with which the firm may be affiliated, and the media in which it advertises.

Suppliers As a group, the wholesalers and manufacturers from which retailers buy goods for resale constitute a most valuable reservoir of information. Often, they are the prime source of news for the small store owner. Suppliers' sales representatives visit the firm periodically. Through personal contact, they can keep the merchant informed about current styles and fashions, trends in the industry, the better-selling items among their product offerings, news of competitor activity, and the like. Throughout the year, their companies supplement these personal visits by mailing bulletins, illustrated circulars, brochures, catalogs, and other printed materials to the retailer.

Publications For most retail lines, useful publications are available. Offered by trade associations and other interested organizations, they contain feature articles about successful retailers, new lines of merchandise and new products, sources of supply, shopping centers in the planning stage or under construction, efforts at revitalizing downtown business districts, offers of cooperative advertising, and so on. The publications also carry advertisements by manufacturers and wholesalers of consumer goods and display equipment, signing, fixtures, and supplies.

Here are a few representative examples:

American Druggist   *Merchandising Week*
Antiques Dealer   *Progressive Grocer*
Chain Store Age   *Restaurant Business*
Discount Store News   *Sporting Goods Business*
Drug Topics   *Stores*
Footwear News   *Supermarket News*
Hardware Age   *Women's Wear Daily*
Menswear

Information about fashions can also be gleaned from the various shelter magazines, such as *Better Homes and Gardens, House and Garden,* and *House Beautiful*—and from many other consumer publications. *Cosmopolitan, Glamour, Mademoiselle, Ladies Home Journal,* and *Vogue* are just a few examples.

Other External Sources of Information Another substantial resource is the independent buying office.[5] An apparel retailer located in the Midwest or South, far from such metropolitan centers as Chicago or New York, may well regard a contract with a resident buying service as the firm's lifeline to proper merchandising. The arrangement will bring a continuous flow of valuable information, knowledge that would ordinarily be too costly for the small company to acquire by itself.

Finally retailers can frequently obtain useful data from the newspapers and other media in which they advertise. Big-city dailies conduct surveys of their trade areas from time to time and offer demographic and other information to local firms. Many radio and TV stations do the same.

Classifying Products

For effective, profitable merchandise management, retailers need a clear understanding of what consumer products are and what they mean to both shoppers and the store. They also need to realize that consumers perceive different types of products in substantially different ways.

The author of a popular work on product management defines a *product* as an object of economic choice and consumption. He then elaborates as follows: "From the seller's point of view, products are a source of revenue. From the buyer-user's point of view, they represent potential consumption benefits."[6]

It has been suggested that a product should be looked at in a three-dimensional fashion since three sets of elements are combined in the one product: attributes, benefits, and support system.

1. *Product attributes* are associated with the core product itself and include such elements as ingredients, quality, style, brand, and package.
2. *Product benefits* are what the consumer perceives as meeting his or her needs—the "bundle of potential satisfaction" that a product represents.
3. The *product support system* includes all elements that the marketing organization provides in addition to the core product—for example, warranties, advertising, the sales force, delivery terms, service support, availability of parts, and the reputations of the manufacturing and marketing organizations.[7]

Industrial Goods A distinction must first be made between industrial and consumer products. Goods and services of the latter variety are destined for the ultimate consumer's personal use or family consumption. Food, clothing, furniture, household appliances, hair styling, education, and medical services are just a few examples. The **industrial goods** classification applies generally to products and services purchased by industrial, commercial, agricultural, and other types of organizations, including nonprofit groups and government agencies at all levels. These organizations need such products and services to conduct their day-to-day affairs.

An Illinois manufacturer of electrical equipment opens a second plant in West Virginia. The new factory and the machinery subsequently installed in it are examples of industrial goods. In a food distributor's warehouse in Oregon, conveyor belts, forklift trucks, and wheeled carts are used to move around the cases of foodstuffs. These, too, are industrial products. So are the office desks, file cabinets, computer terminal, and intercom system in the same warehouse. Retailers use cash registers, fixtures, display equipment, paper goods, and other types of industrial goods. Also falling into the same category are the hundreds of beds in a large metropolitan hospital, the CAT scanner and X-ray machines, all sorts of laboratory equipment, and even the chemicals and supplies needed to keep rooms and hallways spotlessly clean.

Major classifications within this category include:

1. Capital goods (plant, machinery).
2. Goods needed to produce other goods (raw materials, semifabricated goods, components).
3. Commercial goods (supplies, equipment).[8]

Consumer Goods The retailer is far more concerned with **consumer goods,** for these constitute the merchandise that store operations revolve around. Such products may be looked at in a number of different ways. Each view leads to useful insights for management decisions.

Nondurables and Durables Consumer products are frequently classified by the rapidity or slowness with which people consume them, or use them up. An apple or pear, a Pepsi, Coke, or 7UP, a Sunday night bingo game at the neighborhood church, a can of Budweiser, or a one-shot TV sitcom are all quickly consumed. Such products are referred to as **nondurables.** For the most part, nondurable goods are the more popular, faster-moving items that consumers purchase repeatedly throughout the year. Their price tags are usually low, although some articles are more moderately priced. On the other hand, **durables** are bought less often and are generally offered at high unit prices.

Durable goods last for long periods of time and continue to deliver satisfaction to consumers month after month and year after year.

Eleanore Snow

These are articles that last for a long time and that continue to deliver satisfaction to consumers month after month and year after year. Examples include washing machines, air conditioners, living-room suites, bedroom furniture, trucks, cars, storm windows, bicycles, wristwatches, and silverware.

Necessities and Luxuries Another approach to product classification takes into consideration both consumer attitudes and the effect that the purchase of a particular item will have on a person's income. Many products are thought of by most people as *must* purchases. Essentials like food, basic clothing, shelter, and household furniture are **necessities.** We need to provide these for ourselves, regardless of how low our income may be. Milk, eggs, and bread, for example, are staples that can be found in most American households. Pots to cook with, a bed to sleep in, shoes, a heavy jacket for protection against the cold, and a radio are among the numerous necessities of modern living. Many products are, however, looked on as frills or extras by large numbers of people, especially those with more limited incomes. Purchases of **luxury goods** must come out of the consumer's discretionary income—that portion left over after taxes and necessities have been taken care of. Not everyone needs, nor does everyone want, a videocassette recorder, home computer, Gucci wallet or handbag, sailboat, fishing tackle, or formalwear. Even a car may fall into the luxury goods category, despite the fact that many millions of consumers regard this as a necessity.

Therein lies the problem of trying to separate goods into the two categories. What one person may feel is a necessary article, another will believe to be a luxury item.

Convenience, Shopping, and Specialty Goods Perhaps the most important classification scheme for retailers to grasp is the one proposed well over half a century ago by Copeland.[9] It is based on the consumer's shopping behavior with regard to merchandise. There are some items that shoppers expend little effort in searching for and some for which they will want to compare values from one store to another. There are still other products for which consumers are willing to hunt longer and travel even greater distances to buy.

Items in that first category are called **convenience goods.** Generally, these are low-priced products that are available in many stores. Consumers purchase them often throughout the year, almost as if by habit.[10] The classification includes **impulse goods**—items purchased because they are seen by a shopper, who may not have had any prior intent to buy; **staple goods**—articles bought regularly as part of the consumer's merchandise used during the year; and **emergency goods**—purchased only when a need suddenly becomes pressing, as might be the case with an umbrella or snow shovel.

For many retail businesses, staple products constitute the major portion of the merchandise inventory. By displaying impulse items effectively, store merchants can add significantly to their sales. Interviews with about 1,600 customers at one department store in the Southeast revealed that nearly 40 percent of all purchases had been made on impulse.[11] Variables such as age, race, merchandise line, and the shopper's purpose for being in the area were found to be related to impulse buying. The results of another study suggest that unplanned buying may be more a function of situational variables (store-environment, product, and trip-specific variables) than of shopper characteristics.[12]

Consumers are willing to delay the decision to buy **shopping goods** until they have had the opportunity to compare values for the same article in several stores.[13] These products generally fall into a higher price class than most convenience goods. Often, they represent a major purchase for the household or individual such as washers, dryers, refrigerators, and other durables; fine jewelry or clothing, and the like. Comparisons from store to store may be made for some merchandise on the sole basis of price. On other articles, shoppers may also compare style, quality of materials, comfort, guarantee or warranty, and so on.

Even more time and effort are expended by consumers in purchasing merchandise that can be classified as **specialty goods.** The specialty product possesses one or more unique characteristics that so strongly attract consumers that they are unwilling to consider a substitute item. Shoppers will readily travel across town or out of town to visit a store that carries the item which interests them.[14] Among the many examples of such merchandise are famous-brand suits, better shoes, expensive perfumes and cosmetics, high-fashion gowns and dresses, special-label health foods, gourmet products, quality ski equipment, Electrolux vacuums, Porsche cars, and custom-made draperies.

Over the years, empirical studies have largely supported Copeland's goods-classification scheme and basic generalizations regarding consumer shopping behavior.[15] However, our buying habits have changed drastically since the 1920s—at least so far as the amount of time and/or effort today's shoppers are willing to expend. In at least one case, it was found that Copeland's classification may not accurately reflect the behavior patterns of both low income and more affluent customers.[16]

The Product Life Cycle

Given our fiercely competitive economic climate, forward-looking manufacturing companies usually try to maintain or enhance their market positions by investing time, effort, and money in developing new items.

Although a detailed review of the **new product development process** is well beyond the scope of this book, it might be helpful to list the seven stages of a new concept before it evolves into a product launched on the marketplace.

1. Idea generation.
2. Product screening.
3. Concept testing.
4. Business analysis.
5. Product development.
6. Test marketing.
7. Commercialization.[17]

The ratio of discarded ideas to those accepted and processed through to commercialization is high. For every new article that reaches the marketplace, dozens of other product ideas may have been conceived of, evaluated for their potential, and scrapped. Furthermore, perhaps no more than 2 or 3 out of every 10 new items that are distributed continue to sell well. The balance die out, some quickly, others at a much slower rate.[18]

What may be expected to happen with the successful product? Its sales history would, of course, be of major interest to the manufacturer. The more the producing firm can know about what to expect, the better able will its management be to evolve the right marketing tactics designed to ensure continued sales and profits.

For several decades, a relatively simple concept has been available to assist marketers: the **product life cycle, or PLC.**[19]

The PLC attempts to describe the probable sales history of a typical, newly launched item. The crux of the concept is the analogy it makes to the life cycle of an individual. A person is born and instantly begins to grow. In time, he or she passes through childhood into adolescence, becomes an adult, continues to age, and eventually dies. When we examine the behavior of a new product in the marketplace from a similar perspective, we see it pass through four recognizable stages: product introduction, growth, maturity, and decline.

Some marketing theorists interpose a fifth stage, saturation, between the third and fourth stages. They propose a PLC curve as shown in section A of Figure 13.1. Others believe that the maturity stage should be divided into two segments—maintenance and proliferation—with each segment requiring different marketing strategies on the manufacturer's part.[20] For the student of retailing, however, the four-stage process suffices to explain new-product behavior and its implications for retail merchandising decisions as well as for the producer.

Not all products follow all four stages so clearly.[21] Variations occur because the sales on which the PLC concept is based are composed of both initial purchases and repeat purchases. Many different life cycle patterns are theoretically possible. Fashion goods, for instance, show somewhat altered patterns. As you can see in Figure 13.1(B), so do fads. You may recall how items like pet rocks, leisure suits, and miniskirts were so popular for a time and then vanished from the marketplace.

The PLC concept has intrinsic, intuitive appeal. Because of its simplicity, however, criticisms have been advanced from many quarters ever since the idea first appeared in the literature.[22] Still, it continues to provoke the interest of marketing professionals, even on the international scene. Today, marketers feel that the PLC applies even to the gradual acceptance of fashion goods and that they can predict the movement of such merchandise to a fair degree.[23] Models of the PLC have been prepared, and it has been noted that product life cycles have been growing shorter.[24]

Summarized below are short descriptions of each stage of the PLC. Given, too, are their challenges for the innovative manufacturer and implications for retailer strategy.

Product Introduction Stage

If, through an error in management judgment, a manufacturing firm were to launch a new product without prior fanfare, it would soon discover that consumer demand was nonexistent, or insignificant at best. Most shoppers would not know of it. Nor would they know where to go to purchase the item. In the initial **product introduction stage,** two major challenges therefore confront the producer: (1) how best to create product awareness in the minds of consumers and (2)

**Figure 13.1
Types of product life
cycles**

A. The theoretical normal life cycle of a fashion or other new product

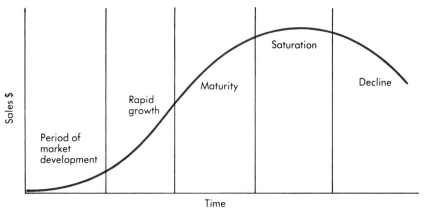

B. Usual trajectory of a fad

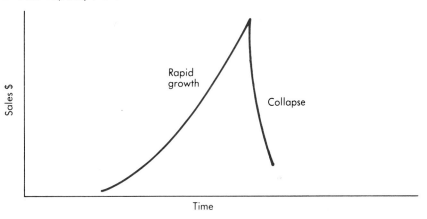

C. Apparent life cycle pattern of some new products for which the market seemed to be waiting

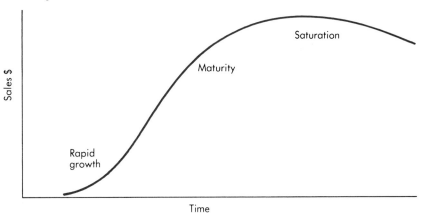

Source: Chester R. Wasson, "How Predictable Are Fashion and Other Product Cycles?" *Journal of Marketing* 32 (July 1968), p. 38. Reprinted with permission from the American Marketing Association.

how best to enlist the aid of distributors to help position the merchandise so that people might buy it.[25]

To meet the first challenge, substantial amounts of money must be invested in pioneering, or informative, advertising. Convincing wholesalers and/or retailers to stock the item requires additional funding for sales promotion and direct selling activities. To recover these extraordinary outlays (in addition to the initial costs of development), the manufacturer will most often place a relatively high selling price on the article. This assures the firm of a greater per unit return on its investment. Sometimes the producer will seek selective distribution, limiting the number of outlets permitted to offer the item. An occasional manufacturer may deliberately select a diametrically opposed approach. The firm will encourage wider, more intensive distribution and place a lower unit price on the product. In such cases, producers attempt to recoup their investments by earning less profit per unit but moving out a far greater volume.

If the product launch is successful, more and more consumers will purchase the item. Early shoppers will buy replacements as their original purchases are used up. Soon, the second stage of the PLC begins to manifest itself.

Implications for Retailers Few products submitted to retail firms each year are truly new. Store merchants exercise a great deal of caution in considering such goods. They understand that even though the new item may look promising, only minimal shopper demand is to be expected. To move such merchandise without supporting promotion, a store would need to rely almost totally on its displays and the selling staff. Consequently, retail buyers may insist on advertising support from the supplier, often requesting cooperative advertising assistance. They look for point-of-purchase materials and, possibly, PMs (push money—explained in Chapter 18) for the salespeople.

An astute buyer for a department store or other large retail organization may decide to take in the new merchandise only if accompanied by a promise of exclusivity. Most merchants will test an untried item gingerly, purchasing only a limited quantity at the outset. They will also take pains to make certain that the new resource is a responsible firm and in sound financial shape. They need to feel confident that, should demand start to expand rapidly, the supplier can produce ever-increasing quantities and deliver promptly. In this introductory stage, there is usually no alternate resource to turn to.

Growth Stage　Assuming a successful pattern of consumer acceptance, more revenue starts to flow into the manufacturer's treasury. Exposure to increasing numbers of shoppers accelerates word-of-mouth advertising, additional product trials, and repeat purchases. At some point (which resists precise determination) the new product enters the second phase of its PLC, the **growth stage.** As consumer requests continue to proliferate, additional distributors will want to carry the merchandise. This increases the number of outlets where shoppers can buy the item. In the meantime, the manufacturer makes further refinements in production methods that affect the budget. Unit costs fall and the company generally earns its highest profits during this stage of the PLC. Unfortunately, it is also during this period of sales growth and mounting profits that other manufacturers become interested in emulating the firm's apparent success. They begin to enter the market with their own versions of the product. This forces the original company to institute measures for countering the growing competitive onslaught. More promotion is typically needed, along with the continued expansion of distribution channels.

Implications for Retailers As consumer demand for the article increases, the retail buyer will begin to bring more inventory into the store. More sizes, colors, and other variants are ordered. The retailer may seek special promotional assistance from the supplier, request improved packaging, ask for better terms or for the goods to be prepriced, and so on. As competitors bring their own versions to the firms' attention, the buyer will begin to compare these offerings with the original item for quality, price, terms, and the like. Often, it is profitable to develop one or more alternative sources of supply.

Maturity Stage When the new product reaches the third, or **maturity stage,** of its life cycle, a number of competitors have established themselves firmly in the field. Each possesses some share of the total market. Each also promotes its own product version, stressing the unique benefits that differentiate it from others. Although total sales continue to build, the original manufacturer soon discovers that its sales curve is beginning to lose momentum. In the mix of competitors, each tries to improve its own sales picture by producing new designs, shapes, colors, sizes, or models to attract more consumers. Advertising and promotional efforts gather speed in this environment. Pricing is also frequently used as a weapon. Occasionally, this sets off intense price competition among the producers. Profits for the innovating company begin to slide as it tools up internally to counter the threat, all the while sustaining a good level of promotional activity and, perhaps, lowering its prices.

The vast majority of today's products are in the third stage of the PLC. The market for most items has already matured and may even be saturated. A number of firms supply essentially similar products. These may differ only slightly from one to the next. Milk, packaged white bread, toasters, clock radios, children's socks, men's shoes,

Products like these are in the maturity stage of their life cycle.

Courtesy Radio Shack, A Division of Tandy Corporation

pancake syrup, canned sardines, color TVs, cars, and shower curtains are among the thousands of products that have been squarely in the maturity stage for many years.

Implications for Retailers Competition among manufacturers for store shelf space and the consumer dollar works to the retailer's advantage. Buyers are spurred on to weed out marginal suppliers and stay with the few that can be counted on with regard to prices, terms, delivery, quality, extended warranties, and so on. Cooperative advertising funds can be sought successfully. Best-selling brands are stocked heavily. Poor sellers are sold off and discontinued. Price promotions become more frequent. Additional benefits such as premiums, giveaways, and point-of-purchase materials are provided by producers to prolong the maturity stage.[26]

Decline Stage Sooner or later, and despite all attempts by the manufacturer to move the product, the firm's sales curve will level off and begin to fall. The product enters the **decline stage.** Competitors also experience a drop-off in sales volume. Eventually, the original company must begin to anticipate a gradual cutback in manufacturing to the point where all production finally ceases. It must also think about phasing out remaining inventory, both in its own warehouse and in those of its distributors. Frequently, there is internal resistance to the elimination

Brands from many producers compete for a retailer's limited shelf space. The retailer stocks the best-selling brands heavily and buys from suppliers who often provide additional benefits like price promotions and premiums.

John Thoeming/Richard D. Irwin

of items from a company's product line. This is caused by lack of interest from top management, no formal policy for handling items in their decline stage, resistance by sales personnel, and sheer inertia in making decisions.[27] One survey of large manufacturers revealed that most had never developed a highly structured and sophisticated product elimination program.[28]

Some writers have protested that by adhering slavishly to the product life cycle concept, marketers may be depriving their companies of additional sales by giving up the ghost too soon.[29]

Several useful approaches are available for regenerating the sales of a declining product. The manufacturer may be able to reposition the item through advertising. Or the firm may be able to expand its consumer market base by targeting at previously untapped groups. Another possibility is to conceive of and actively promote one or more new uses for the ailing product.

Implications for Retailers Once the retailer recognizes that a particular item has entered the final, fatal phase of its PLC, some serious decision making is in order. For one thing, the buyer will curtail reorders and limit the inventory to only the most popular sizes, colors, and so on. To reduce the stock further, markdowns may be necessary. The merchant also must consider how best to phase out the merchandise in such a way as to minimize adverse reaction among customers. For example, a shopper in a china department may want to purchase one or two matching pieces of dinnerware to replace those that were broken or chipped. Or a consumer may look for an attachment or replacement part for an outmoded appliance. In situations like these, retailers prefer to keep enough stock on hand to satisfy their clienteles for some time after the articles have been largely dropped from regular inventory.

Length of the PLC   Based on their personal observations, some marketers have noted that the product life cycle has been getting shorter over the decades. In grocery products, for example, the life cycle of truly innovative items seems to run its course in no more than 18 months, and often in fewer.[30] Empirical evidence is available to support the gradual reduction of the length of the PLC, at least during the first two stages. Shipment data for 37 household appliances were analyzed. The time span was more than 50 years. The products introduced over that half century were separated into three time periods and their movement was tracked. Averages for the number of years of the items' introductory and growth stages are given below:[31]

Period	Years in Introductory Stage	Years in Growth Stage
1922–1944	12.5	33.8
1945–1964	7	19.5
1965–1979	2	6.8

Ordering Staple Merchandise

Except for a few shops that specialize in fashion merchandise, much of the retailer's inventory is in staple goods. Consumer demand for staples is fairly regular and predictable; possible exceptions are seasonal staples like Halloween costumes and holiday eggnog or fruitcake. Merchants need to make staple goods available throughout the year. For most inventory carried, then, the retailer is able to prepare a **basic stock plan.** This is usually done semiannually.

The Basic Stock Plan   In preparing the plan, the retailer spells out the entire inventory to be carried by the store. The inventory is broken down by categories and into classifications and subclassifications. In large retailing companies, SKU numbers are typically used. Listed are the exact quantities needed to meet sales projections by brands, materials, colors, sizes, and the like. To reorder staple merchandise, retailers rely on either a **minimum-maximum reorder point** approach or an **automatic replenishment,** or **fill-in system.** The first method calls for establishing both minimum and maximum inventory levels for every item in the assortment. Reorders are placed as the inventory level drops toward the minimum. The automatic replenishment approach requires the formula shown below:

$$Q = [T_1 + T_2] R - I$$

An explanation of the various symbols follows:

Q = the quantity to be reordered
T_1 = the number of weeks between regular inventory counts
T_2 = the number of weeks between order placement and receipt of the goods into stock
R = the article's average weekly rate of sale
I = the number of units currently in stock

To illustrate the method, let us assume that Item Z sells at an average rate of 45 pieces per week. The owner takes physical inventory at the end of each month (roughly interpreted as every four weeks). From experience, the retailer knows that about two weeks are required from the day an order for Item Z is sent to the supplier until the merchandise is received and placed in stock. At reordering time, 75 units are on hand.

We fill in the known facts and solve the equation:

$$Q = [4 + 2] 45 - 75$$
$$= 270 - 75$$
$$= 195$$

Safety Stock To nearly always prevent being out of stock, some retail firms resort to a modified formula that builds in some reserve or **safety stock.** The reserve is determined by: *(a)* adding T_1 and T_2, *(b)* multiplying the result by R, *(c)* working out the square root of this amount, and *(d)* multiplying the square root by 2.3.

Expressed algebraically, this is how it works:

$$\text{Safety stock} = 2.3 \sqrt{[T_1 + T_2] R}$$

In the Item Z illustration above, the safety stock works out to approximately 37 pieces:

$$\text{Safety stock} = 2.3 \sqrt{[T_1 + T_2] R}$$
$$= 2.3 \sqrt{[4 + 2] 45}$$
$$= 2.3 \times 16.4$$
$$= 37.02$$

Provided the retailer adds 37 pieces to the original reorder quantity of 195 (for a total of 232 units), approximately 95 percent of the chance fluctuations in Item Z's stock level will be covered. This reduces the likelihood of a stockout on the item to a probability of 5 percent or less.[32]

Merchandising Fashion Goods

Fashion merchandise cannot be treated in the same manner as staples. Consumer demand for fashion items is not very predictable, although some aspects can be predicted. One example is the distribution of sizes (or colors) that will sell in the store. Consequently, the basic stock plan method is unsuitable for reordering purposes. Planning and controlling fashion goods require complex managerial decisions. Both the automatic replenishment and minimum-maximum reorder point methods are out of the question. In their place, retailers prepare a model stock for each season of the year.

Model Stock

A **model stock** serves as a planning guide for the buyer for a specified period of time. A written record, it stipulates the precise assortment of goods to be carried in the store or department. Different model stocks are usually prepared from one season to the next. Indeed, given the accelerating rate of fashion cycles in recent years, an astute buyer may well prepare separate model stocks within a single season. Different assortments can, for example, be planned for the early- , mid- , and late-spring seasons.

Included in each model stock are the types and classifications of merchandise to be offered for sale and adequate quantities to meet shopper demand. The goods are organized according to styles and materials, by sizes and colors, by price lines, and by other selection factors. An element of flexibility is built into the entire process so the buyer can modify quantities and selection factors as the season progresses. Indeed, timing is an essential element in fashion buying.

Retailers prepare their buying plans according to the information set forth in the model stock.[33]

Fashion Merchandise

Fashions are styles or designs that large numbers of consumers accept and continue to use for some time. Buyers of fashion apparel monitor trends in styles to learn what is currently in vogue and what will soon be considered stylish. They are concerned with such factors as cut, silhouette, decoration, and other product attributes. A key factor in managing fashion goods for a firm is an effective merchandise information system.[34] This helps the buyer determine the better-selling and the slow-moving articles. It also aids in perceiving fashion trends so the buyer can buy into the trend.

Fashions evolve over time. They reflect changes that take place in our society. Such changes can be attributed to many different factors: economic conditions, technological advances, changes in lifestyles, TV and the movies, and so on.

The life cycle of a fashion good resembles those of other new products.[35] It passes through several stages, although typically with greater speed than most new items. **Fads** are fashion goods with relatively short life spans that may not go through all phases of a normal product life cycle. When a fad manages to catch the public's fancy, there is a period of rapid growth. Then, no matter how popular it becomes, eventually it suffers a sharp and swift decline in sales as the product falls out of favor among consumers. An approximation of a fad's life cycle can be seen in Figure 13.1 (B).

Early studies of how new fashions in garments and accessories originate and become stylish supported the **trickle-down theory.**[36] This holds that original designs are created for a relatively few, usually upper-class individuals. Others among their peers find some designs interesting and copy them for their own use. The growing popularity of the new fashion then attracts the attention of, or trickles down to, people lower on the social ladder. Still popular, this view visualizes the fashion life cycle as embracing four stages: (1) the item's distinctive introduction at a high price, (2) the copying, or emulation, stage, where a limited number of people try to copy and use the article, (3) its broad popularization as it is mass produced and sold, at much lower prices, and (4) the final, or decline, phase, where the item gradually disappears from public sight and favor.

A newer and contrary view perceives new styles and fashions as emanating from an entirely opposite social stratum.[37] Supporters of the **bottom-up theory** of fashion propose that innovative styles are born among lower-class consumers and often in subcultures such as the teenage and black subcultures. Upper-class consumers like them and begin to wear or use them. Their high status lends strong impetus to the fashion's popularization. The item is then adopted by large numbers of people in the middle classes. Believers in the bottom-up concept point to the introduction of such products as blue jeans and tank tops to underscore their conviction that new fashions flow upward, not downward.

Finally, there is the even more recent **trickle-across theory.** Today's fashion goods retailer considers this a more appropriate description of the diffusion of fashion innovations. It holds that persons in any social class can begin a new fashion. These persons are popular among their peers, who copy and adopt the fashion.

Summary

Retail operations revolve around buying and selling merchandise. Management strives to maintain a sensible balance between inventory costs and potential profits. Every firm needs to decide how extensive a variety of merchandise it will offer and its assortments, breadth, and depth. In managing their stores and controlling inventories, retailers can profitably use such techniques as gross margin return on investment and ABC analysis.

To determine shoppers' needs, retailers consult many sources. They obtain useful information from their records of cash and credit sales, from customer returns and adjustments, and from their employees. Other fruitful internal sources may include a want-slip system, comparison shopping, consumer panels, and primary research. Store merchants also benefit from sources outside the firm. Suppliers, trade and other publications, the buying office, and the advertising media are examples.

Most products and services can be classified as either industrial or consumer goods. Industrial goods are those purchased by all kinds of organizations for use in conducting their affairs. Major categories include capital goods, raw and semiprocessed goods and components, equipment, and supplies. Products and services that consumers buy and use are consumer goods. These can be classified as durables or nondurables, as necessities or luxuries, or as convenience, shopping, or specialty goods. Included in the convenience category are impulse, staple, and emergency products.

According to the product life cycle (PLC) concept, the market behavior of a newly launched item reflects a distinctive pattern over its selling lifetime. For most products, four stages of the PLC can be discerned: product introduction, growth, maturity, and decline. PLC patterns for fads and fashion goods appear to differ somewhat. Knowing what stages their merchandise currently falls into enables retailers to buy more effectively.

Typically, retailers plan their inventories carefully, using different procedures for staple goods and fashion merchandise. The basic stock plan is used for staples, the retailer choosing either a minimum-maximum reorder point approach or an automatic replenishment system. Because fashion goods, unlike staples, do not move at a predictable rate, the retailer prepares a distinct planning guide, the model stock.

Key Terms

variety	staple goods
assortment	emergency goods
breadth	shopping goods
depth	specialty goods
merchandise classifications	new product development process
stockkeeping unit (SKU)	product life cycle (PLC)
gross margin return on investment (GMROI)	product introduction stage
	growth stage

80–20 principle
ABC analysis
want-slip program
comparison shopping
consumer panels
industrial goods
consumer goods
nondurables
durables
necessities
luxury goods
convenience goods
impulse goods

maturity stage
decline stage
basic stock plan
minimum-maximum reorder point approach
automatic replenishment (fill-in) system
safety stock
model stock
fashions
fashions
trickle-down theory
bottom-up theory
trickle-across theory

Review Questions

1. Clearly differentiate among the following terms: *(a) assortment, (b) depth,* and *(c) width.*

2. Give a brief explanation of GMROI and its significance to the modern retailer.

3. What is meant by the 80–20 principle?

4. Specify four internal and three external sources of information about shoppers' needs that retailers can rely on.

5. Review the purpose and mechanics of a want-slip system.

6. Contrast the comparison shopping efforts of the large department store with those of the small, independent merchant.

7. Define the term *product.*

8. Identify and briefly describe three different approaches to classifying consumer products.

9. Many consumer goods can be called nondurables. Prepare a list of 10 products in this category.

10. Name and differentiate among three types of convenience goods.

11. Specify six nonfood products that are staples for most Americans.

12. Identify and briefly comment on the four stages of the product life cycle.

13. During which stage of the product life cycle do the innovating firm's profits usually peak? In which stage are profits typically poor or nonexistent?

14. Suggest two likely reasons why the life cycles of new products have been growing shorter over the past few decades.

15. Explain the trickle-down theory of fashion acceptance.

Discussion Questions

1. Visit several different types of stores in your area. Ask the merchants whether they belong to a trade association. Prepare a list of the names and addresses of at least three such associations.

2. Suggest five areas of retail operations in which a consumer advisory group can be helpful to a regional chain of apparel stores.

3. Could a product normally viewed by the majority of consumers as a luxury good be regarded by some as a necessity? Explain and give examples.

4. A department store buyer of health and beauty aids is offered a new kind of hair conditioner that has just been introduced into the marketplace. What advice would you give the buyer?

5. The housewares buyer at a large discount house is considering adding a small appliance to the line. It is evidently in the growth stage of its life cycle. Suggest several guidelines for the buyer.

Notes

[1] For more details of the GMROI approach, see: Daniel J. Sweeney, "Improving the Profitability of Retail Merchandising Decisions," *Journal of Marketing* 37 (January 1973), pp. 60–68.

[2] The technique is explained in: William L. Fuerst, "Small Businesses Get a New Look at ABC Analysis for Inventory Control," *Journal of Small Business Management* 19 (July 1981), pp. 39–44.

[3] See the section on credit in Chapter 17.

[4] For information about different types of consumer panels, see: John W. Wingate and Joseph S. Friedlander, *The Management of Retail Buying*, 2d ed. (Englewood Cliffs, NJ: Prentice-Hall, 1978), pp. 155–56.

[5] More on the services of the buying office can be found in Chapter 16.

[6] Edgar A. Pessemier, *Product Management: Strategy and Organization*, 2d ed. (New York: John Wiley & Sons, 1982), p. 12.

[7] William Lazer and James D. Culley, *Marketing Management: Foundations and Practices* (Boston: Houghton Mifflin, 1983), p. 444.

[8] David J. Rachman and Michael H. Mescon, *Business Today*, 2d ed. (New York: Random House, 1979), pp. 203–4.

[9] Melvin T. Copeland, "Relation of Consumers' Buying Habits to Marketing Methods," *Harvard Business Review* 1 (October 1922), pp. 282–89.

[10] Ibid., p. 282.

[11] Danny N. Bellenger, Dan H. Robertson, and Elizabeth C. Hirschman, "Impulse Buying Varies by Product," *Journal of Advertising Research* 18 (December 1978), pp. 15–18.

[12] V. Kanti Prasad, "Unplanned Buying in Two Retail Settings," *Journal of Retailing* 51 (Fall 1975), pp. 3–12

[13] Copeland, "Consumers' Buying Habits," p. 283.

[14] Ibid., p. 284.

[15] Arno K. Kleimenhagen, "Shopping, Specialty, or Convenience Goods?" *Journal of Retailing* 42 (Winter 1966–67), pp. 32–39; Louis P. Bucklin, "Retail Strategy and the Classification of Consumer Goods," *Journal of Marketing* 27 (January 1963), pp. 50–55; Henry Assael, "Product Classification and the Theory of Consumer Behavior," *Journal of the Academy of Marketing Science* 2 (Fall 1974), pp. 539–42.

[16] Joseph Barry Mason and Morris L. Mayer, "Empirical Observations of Consumer Behavior: As Related to Goods Classification and Retail Strategy," *Journal of Retailing* 48 (Fall 1972), pp. 17–31.

[17] Joel R. Evans and Barry Berman, *Marketing* (New York: Macmillan, 1982), pp. 246–47.

[18] C. Merle Crawford, "Marketing Research and the New-Product Failure Rate," *Journal of Marketing* 41 (April 1977), pp. 51–61.

[19] For an excellent treatment of the PLC and its significance in marketing planning, see: Theodore Levitt, "Exploit the Product Life Cycle," *Harvard Business Review* 43 (November–December 1965), pp. 81–94; John E. Smallwood, "The Product Life Cycle: A Key to Strategic Marketing Planning," *MSU Business Topics* 21 (Winter 1973), pp. 29–35; Bernard Catry and Michel Chevalier, "Market Share Strategy and the Product Life Cycle," *Journal of Marketing* 38 (October 1974), pp. 29–34.

[20] Ben M. Enis, Raymond LaGarce, and Arthur E. Prell, "Extending the Product Life Cycle," *Business Horizons* 20 (June 1977), pp. 46–56.

[21] David F. Midgley, "Toward a Theory of the Product Life Cycle: Explaining Diversity," *Journal of Marketing* 45 (Fall 1981), pp. 109–15.

[22] George S. Day, "The Product Life Cycle: Analysis & Applications Issues," *Journal of Marketing* 45 (Fall 1981), pp. 60–67; Igal Ayal, "International Product Life Cycle: A Reassessment and Product Policy Implications," *Journal of Marketing* 45 (Fall 1981), pp. 91–96.

[23] Chester R. Wasson, "How Predictable Are Fashion and Other Product Cycles?" *Journal of Marketing* 32 (July 1968), pp. 36–43.

[24] Stephen G. Harrell and Elmer D. Taylor, "Modeling the Product Life Cycle for Consumer Durables," *Journal of Marketing* 45 (Fall 1981), pp. 68–75. See also: Douglas Tigert and Behrooz Farivar, "The Bass New Product Growth Model: A Sensitivity Analysis for a High Technology Product," *Journal of Marketing* 45 (Fall 1981), pp. 81–90.

[25]See: William V. Muse and Robert J. Kegerreis, "New Product Awareness and Purchasing Behavior," *Marquette Business Review* 16 (Spring 1972), pp. 19–27.

[26]The story of nylon in our economy is an example of a life cycle that has been repeatedly and systematically extended. See: Levitt, "Exploit the Product Life Cycle," pp. 88–91.

[27]James T. Rothe, "The Product Elimination Decision," *MSU Business Topics* 18 (Autumn 1970), pp. 45–52; Philip Kotler, "Phasing Out Weak Products," *Harvard Business Review* 43 (March–April 1965), pp. 107–18.

[28]Richard T. Hise and Michael A. McGinnis, "Product Elimination: Practices, Policies, and Ethics," *Business Horizons* 18 (June 1975), pp. 25–32.

[29]See: Nariman K. Dhalla and Sonia Yuspech, "Forget the Product Life Cycle Concept," *Harvard Business Review* 54 (January–February 1976), pp. 102–12.

[30]E. Jerome McCarthy, *Essentials of Marketing,* rev. ed. (Homewood, Ill.: Richard D. Irwin, 1982), p. 221.

[31]William Qualls, Richard W. Olshavsky, and Ronald E. Michaels, "Shortening of the PLC—An Empirical Test," *Journal of Marketing* 45 (Fall 1981), pp. 76–80.

[32]The abbreviated formula used to calculate the safety stock is based on a form of distribution known as the Poisson curve.

[33]For more details on model stocks as well as insights into how buyers profile assortments, budget sales, scale colors and sizes, and other aspects, see: Wingate and Friedlander, Chapter 8, "The Merchandise Assortment: Quantitative Considerations for Fashion and Seasonal Goods," *Retail Buying,* pp. 196–220.

[34]Roger A. Dickinson, "Fashion Management: Ways & Means," *Stores* 56 (November 1974), pp. 8–9*ff.*

[35]Wasson, "How Predictable?" pp. 36–43.

[36]For more on fashion adoption theories, see: Mary D. Troxell and Elaine Stone, *Fashion Merchandising,* 3d ed. (New York: McGraw-Hill, 1981), pp. 58–62.

[37]Helena De Paola and Carol Stewart Mueller, *Marketing Today's Fashion* (Englewood Cliffs, N.J.: Prentice-Hall, 1980), p. 51.

CHAPTER 14

MERCHANDISE MANAGEMENT AND CONTROL

Your Study Objectives

After you have studied this chapter, you will understand:

1. The procedures that retail companies use in planning and controlling inventory.
2. The measurement and use of the inventory turnover rate (at retail or cost, and in units).
3. The process of merchandise budgeting and the four major methods of planning stock requirements.
4. The procedure for calculating projected purchases and the open-to-buy.
5. The benefits of instituting the retail method of inventory valuation and how it may be used to derive the cost of goods.
6. The inventory methods commonly available to the retailer.

In the preceding chapter, you were introduced to some basic under-standings that retailers need to manage their inventories effectively. You learned about the information sources that these firms consult to help determine shoppers' needs. You discovered that consumer products may be classified in different ways. We reviewed the four stages of the product life cycle and their implications for the store buyer.

In this chapter, you will learn how retailers control the flow of merchandise. You will become aware of the importance of inventory turnover and find out how sales goals can be established and translated into monthly objectives. You will be shown, step by step, the retail method of inventory valuation. We will explain terms like *perpetual inventory* and the *tickler method.* Not covered here are the funda-mentals of the buying function. These are treated in detail in Chap-ter 16.

Inventory Planning and Control

Retail companies need an inventory control system that provides infor-mation useful in decision making. The system must be able to separate better-selling merchandise from the slow movers. It must also deter-mine quantities of goods to be provided, hold markdowns to a mini-mum, avoid stockouts, and provide direction for the buying staff. The two basic approaches to inventory management are unit control and dollar control. Either approach may be based on the cost prices of the goods or on their retail selling prices. Both approaches are useful. A retailer might have enough money invested in inventory but the wrong merchandise assortment. Conversely, the assortment may be correct but insufficient inventory carried.

Unit Control

Of the two, **unit control** is by far the simpler approach. In using this method, the retailer keeps track of merchandise movement in terms of physical units. Unit control is especially suited to outlets that sell high-ticket goods and where the rate of inventory turnover is relatively slow. Car dealerships, furniture outlets, fine jewelry shops, and stores that sell major appliances all fall into this category. If a *perpetual inventory* system is in effect, a record is made of all goods as they are received. Other entries in the bookkeeping system are made as each piece, or unit, is sold. Control procedures involve collect-ing all sales slips (or stubs, if perforated tickets are used). At closing time each day, the slips are tallied to determine how many pieces of each type have been sold. The totals are then deducted from inventory records. The work is not necessarily done by hand. Perforated stubs are counted by machine in many stores. With the advent of the point-of-sale register, sales slips or stubs may be dispensed with entirely.

Sweda's user-friendly 9800 Retail Control System enables the retailer to customize point-of-sale needs.

Courtesy Sweda International, Inc.

Perpetual inventory control is not, of course, absolutely necessary. Many merchants simply take physical inventory periodically. Or a simple visual inspection (eyeball control) is used to determine stock movement—as well as when and how much to reorder.

Dollar Control   A more popular method, **dollar control,** involves tracking merchandise in terms of cost or retail prices instead of by units. Some firms that have instituted dollar control keep their records on a cost basis. These are usually stores that sell expensive goods and where sales are relatively few.

By and large, however, most companies with dollar control systems work with retail prices. They practice an accounting approach called the retail method of inventory valuation, discussed later in this chapter. The method requires a great deal of record-keeping: purchases, merchandise returns, markdowns, price increases, and so on. Records are maintained in terms of the selling prices of goods for the entire store or by departments, categories, classifications, and subclassifications of merchandise.

Because of the excessive paperwork, electronic data processing (EDP) becomes almost a necessity for firms using the retail method. In recent years, thousands of stores have installed point-of-sale terminals which feed data into the system instantaneously as sales are recorded. A few large retail companies began using computers for inventory control early in the 1960s. It was not until the last years of that decade that computer applications to the planning of merchandise inventories were initiated.[1] In department stores, EDP was being used in planning and controlling inventories, mostly for apparel and shoe departments.[2] Some positive results were noted: sales increases, more rapid stockturn rates, fewer stockouts, and lower clerical costs.

Today, EDP enjoys far wider applications in retailing than inventory management and control. Retailers use these systems to evaluate alternative capital investments, appraise the effectiveness of displays and promotions, determine optimum layout patterns, and so on.

Stock Turnover

Retailers find it extremely useful to monitor the rate of stock movement. Known as **inventory turnover,** it is defined as the number of times a store's average inventory is bought and sold in a defined period. Most often, this period is one year, although it may be calculated semiannually, seasonally, or even monthly, if desired.

Inventory turnover is often called, more popularly, **stockturn.** Knowing the precise stockturn rates, especially by department, goods classification, or individual item, is most helpful in planning merchandise budgets. The faster goods arrive; are sorted, priced, and placed in the selling stock; and are purchased by shoppers, the lower the odds of them becoming shopworn, damaged, or going out of style, in the case of fashion merchandise. For these and other reasons, a more rapid inventory turnover will result in fewer markdowns. A faster turnover also leads to more efficient use of the firm's capital. Moreover, it tends to cut down those expenses associated with maintaining inventory, such as storage and insurance costs. Holding costs for staple goods, for example, may run as high as one third of the retail price.[3] Inventory carrying costs rise when the turnover rate is low, and falls as the rate increases.

A healthy stockturn rate is usually due to efficient merchandise management. Efficiency involves setting realistic sales goals, careful inventory planning and selection, good buying practices, sensible pricing, and effective promotion. Turnover may be accelerated artificially by simply reducing the amount of inventory carried. "Hand-to-mouth" buying, that is, purchasing goods more often and in small amounts, frequently leads to just such a situation. This practice also increases the probability of **stockouts**—running out of some items and being unable to fulfill customer requests. When merchandise is out of stock, shoppers face a dilemma. They may decide to defer the purchase to a later date. Or they may buy right there and then, substituting a different brand, model, color, or size for the article they originally planned to purchase. Still another possibility is to shop at a competitor's

Figure 14.1   **A stockout model**

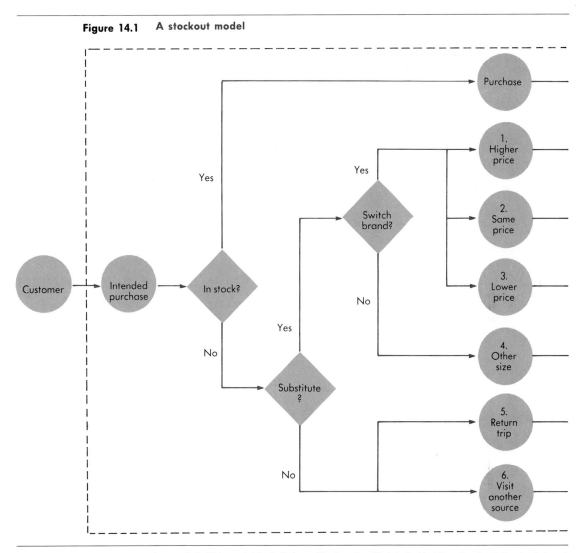

Source: C. K. Walter and John R. Grabner, "Stockout Cost Models: Empirical Tests in a Retail Situation," *Journal of Marketing* 39 (January 1975), p. 57. Reprinted with permission from the American Marketing Association.

store. In any event, some losses will accrue over time to the store.[4] A model of the stockout situation may be seen in Figure 14.1.

Retailers seek to maintain a proper balance between inventory costs and stocking out. Only in special cases can the retailer afford to have a 100 percent service level (by carrying sufficient "safety stock").

Turnover rates vary considerably for different types of stores and for different kinds of goods. As you can see in Figure 14.2, a typical jewelry store shows the relatively slow annual rate of 1.3 times. Apparel

Figure 14.2   Stock turnover rates for different store types, 1983

SIC	Rate	Store Type
5411	16.1*	Groceries, meats
5921	7.8	Liquor
5713	5.9	Floor coverings
5211	4.5	Lumber
5231	4.2	Paint, glass, wallpaper
5912	4.2	Drugs
5946	4.1	Cameras, photographic supplies
5722	3.9	Household appliances
5732	3.6	Radios, TVs, record players
5942	3.6	Books, stationery
5621	3.5	Women's ready-to- wear
5651	2.7	Family clothing
5251	2.6	Hardware
5712	2.5	Furniture
5611	2.4	Men's, boys' clothing
5941	2.4	Sporting goods, bicycles
5661	2.3	Shoes
5947(48)	2.3	Luggage, gifts
5733	2.1	Musical instruments, supplies
5944	1.3	Jewelry

* Median rate of stock turnover, based on the formula: Cost of Goods Sold/Inventory. Entries on the basic accounting statements were used to calculate the rates. Based on statement studies of firms with fiscal year—ends 6/30/82 through 3/31/83.

Note regarding interpetation of Statement Studies figures.

RMA cautions that the Studies be regarded only as a general guideline and not as an absolute industry norm. This is due to limited samples within categories, the categorization of companies by their primary Standard Industrial Classification (SIC) number only, and different methods of operations by companies within the same industry. For these reasons, RMA recommends that the figures be used only as general guidelines in addition to other methods of financial analysis.

Source: Adapted from Robert Morris Associates, '83 Annual Statement Studies (Philadelphia: Robert Morris Associates, 1983). Copyright 1983 by Robert Morris Associates. Used with permission.

outlets turn over their average stock at twice that rate. The median rate for liquor stores is more than seven times a year. Groceries show a hyperactive 16 turns annually. In departmentized stores, different rates prevail for each of the many classifications.

Retailers compare their current rates of inventory turnover to those obtained in prior periods. They also compare them to data provided for the industry by their trade associations. Table 14.1 for example, shows the stockturn rates for specific merchandise classifications in the menswear industry.

The Basic Stockturn Formula

Depending on management requirements, the inventory turnover rate can be calculated by retail dollars, in terms of costs, or by units of merchandise. The basic formula for all calculations is:

$$\text{Stockturn} = \frac{\text{Net sales}}{\text{Average inventory}}$$

All terms in the equation must be expressed on the same basis. Thus, in computing stockturn at retail, both the net sales and average inventory entries must be expressed in retail dollars. If the aim is to determine the rate on a cost basis, both the numerator and denominator of the fraction must reflect cost figures. And in calculating inventory movement in terms of units, the formula appears as:

$$\text{ST in units} = \frac{\text{Net sales in units}}{\text{Average inventory in units}}$$

Stockturn at Retail

Consider the following situation: The manager of the paint department in a discount store wants to determine the department's inventory turnover rate for the year just ended. Net sales for the year totalled $285,000. To calculate the rate, the manager must compute the average inventory, valued at retail. Physical inventory is taken four times a year, at the end of every quarter. Records show the following inventory valuations:

Date Inventory Taken	Value at Retail
March 31	$66,400
June 30	59,300
September 30	82,700
December 31	96,500

Let us ponder the problem at hand. If we follow our understanding of the averaging principle, we are tempted to total up the four listings and divide the resulting sum by four. Were we to do this, we would

Table 14.1   Stockturn rates for menswear, 1983

	All Firms (38 firms)		Firms Handling Menswear Only (20 firms)		Firms Handling Womenswear (18 firms)	
	Range of Common Experience	Median Firm	Range of Common Experience	Median Firm	Range of Common Experience	Median Firm
Men's Clothing						
*010 Men's suits	1.2–1.8	1.4	1.2–1.8	1.4	1.0–1.8	1.4
040 Men's coats	1.4–2.6	1.9	1.5–2.8	2.3	1.4–2.3	1.8
060 Sport coats	1.2–2.1	1.5	1.3–2.2	1.7	1.1–2.1	1.4
080 Dress slacks	1.6–2.7	2.0	1.7–3.0	2.2	1.5–2.7	2.0
Total men's clothing	1.3–2.1	1.6	1.3–2.2	1.6	1.2–2.1	1.6
Men's Sportswear						
100 Sport shirts	1.8–3.4	2.6	1.9–3.1	2.5	1.8–3.8	2.7
130 Sweaters	1.9–3.4	2.4	1.2–3.5	2.3	2.1–3.4	2.6
150 Actionwear	1.6–2.8	2.1	2.0–3.0	2.5	1.4–2.7	2.0
180 Casual slacks	1.7–3.1	2.6	1.7–3.1	2.5	1.8–3.1	2.6
200 Jeans	1.3–2.2	1.9	1.7–3.0	2.2	1.2–1.9	1.5
220 Jackets and heavy outerwear	1.6–3.1	2.1	1.2–3.1	2.2	1.8–3.1	2.0
240 Coordinated leisurewear	2.5–3.1	2.8	n.a.	n.a.	1.4–3.0	2.6
Total men's sportswear	1.7–2.8	2.3	1.6–3.0	2.4	1.8–2.7	2.3
Men's Furnishings						
260 Dress shirts	1.4–2.3	1.9	1.4–2.2	1.8	1.6–2.4	1.9
290 Neckwear	1.7–3.1	2.3	1.6–3.2	2.3	1.9–3.2	2.5
300 Hosiery	1.9–3.0	2.1	1.9–3.2	2.2	1.9–2.9	2.1
310 Men's belts	1.4–2.2	1.7	1.3–2.3	1.5	1.3–2.1	1.7
320 Men's accessories	1.3–2.2	1.5	1.2–2.3	1.5	1.3–2.1	1.5

340	Underwear	1.1–2.0	1.5	1.0–1.9	1.5	1.3–2.0	1.5
360	Sleepwear	1.1–2.1	1.7	1.0–1.8	1.6	1.3–2.3	1.9
380	Men's headwear	1.3–2.5	1.7	1.5–3.1	2.2	1.2–1.9	1.5
	Total men's furnishings	1.6–2.3	1.9	1.4–2.3	1.9	1.8–2.3	2.1
Boys' and Teens'							
400–440	Clothing	0.8–1.4	1.0	n.a.	n.a.	0.8–1.1	0.9
450–510	Sportswear	0.9–2.2	1.2	n.a.	n.a.	0.9–1.4	1.2
520–560	Furnishings	1.0–1.7	1.3	n.a.	n.a.	1.0–1.3	1.2
	Total boys' and teens'	1.1–2.7	1.3	n.a.	n.a.	1.1–2.0	1.2
Men's and Boys Shoes							
570–595		1.1–2.0	1.6	0.7–1.9	1.4	1.2–2.1	1.6
Womenswear							
600–699	Misses	2.1–2.6	2.3	n.a.	n.a.	2.1–2.6	2.3
700–799	Junior	n.a.	n.a.	n.a.	n.a.	n.a.	n.a.
	Total Women's Wear	1.9–2.6	2.3	n.a.	n.a.	1.9–2.6	2.3
Western Wear							
810–890		n.a.	n.a.	n.a.	n.a.	n.a.	n.a.
Overall total		1.4–2.3	1.9	1.3–2.4	1.9	1.5–2.2	2.0

* Classification numbers, 010, etc., are taken from the ''Menswear Basic Management Accounting Manual'' of the MRA Financial & Operations Group.

Note: For each merchandise classification, only those stores reporting that classification are included in the tabulation.

Inventory turnover is the number of times during a given period, in this case one year, that the average inventory on hand at retail has been sold and replaced. The rate of turnover is computed by dividing net sales by average retail inventory.

Source: Menswear Retailers of America, 1983 Annual Business Survey: Men's Store Operating Experiences (Washington: Menswear Retailers of America, 1984), p. 33.

be overlooking the time period that extends from January through March. To solve this problem correctly, we need to search through the records and locate the results of the physical inventory taken the prior year on December 31. This valuation then becomes the department's opening inventory for the year under discussion. It must be inserted as a fifth listing into the columns, as follows:

Date Inventory Taken	Value at Retail
December 31 (prior year)	$ 92,800
March 31	66,400
June 30	59,300
September 30	82,700
December 31	96,500
Totals for year	$397,700

The sum of these listings is divided by five to obtain an average inventory figure for the department of $79,540.

Reverting now to the basic formula, the manager can determine the department's stockturn rate at retail:

$$ST = \frac{\text{Net sales}}{\text{Average inventory}}$$

$$= \frac{\$285,000}{\$79,540}$$

$$= 3.6\times$$

A home electronics department in a large retail store. Under the retail method of accounting, operating results are often recorded by individual departments as well as for the entire store.

Courtesy K mart Corporation. K MART and ACCENTS are service marks of K mart Corporation, Troy, MI

As a final comment, note that *three* listings are needed when inventory is taken twice a year. Where the retailer takes count every month, *thirteen* listings are needed to calculate the average inventory maintained.

Calculating Stockturn for the Entire Store

Departmentized stores that follow the retail method of accounting often record operating results by departments or sections as well as for the entire store. Movement will differ from one section or department to the next. Yet an overall turnover rate can be computed quite readily.

To illustrate the procedure, let us assume that the following results have been recorded for four departments in a large hardware store:

Department	Net Sales for Year	Average Inventory	Stockturn Rate
A	$122,400	$ 55,700	2.2
B	55,800	32,200	1.7
C	52,700	17,500	3.0
D	37,300	10,400	3.6
Store	$268,200	$115,800	?

To determine the overall velocity of inventory turnover for the store, plug the totals for net sales and average inventory into the basic formula. Then solve the equation:

$$ST = \frac{\$268,200}{\$115,800}$$
$$= 2.3\times$$

Calculating Stockturn at Cost: An Illustration

Last year, a bookstore in a community shopping center enjoyed net sales amounting to $271,500. The employees take physical inventory only once each year, at cost prices. To calculate the stockturn rate, the retailer must also express sales in terms of costs, or the cost of goods sold. Reviewing the end-of-year income statement, the merchant determines that the cost of goods amounted to 58.5 percent of sales. Rounded off to the nearest dollar, 58.5 percent of $271,500 is $158,827.

The average inventory figure is still needed for the formula. You recall that to compute the average stock an opening inventory is always needed. Below are the retailer's inventory valuations:

Date of Inventory	Valuation at Cost
December 31, year before	$ 63,500
December 31, last year	101,300
Total listings	$164,800

By dividing the total by two, we obtain the value at cost of the store's average inventory: \$82,400. Applying the formula, we then show:

$$\text{Stockturn at cost} = \frac{\text{Sales at cost (COG sold)}}{\text{Average inventory at cost}}$$

$$= \frac{\$158,827}{\$82,400}$$

$$= 1.9\times$$

Turnover Expressed in Merchandise Units

The manager of a music shop would like to know the annual stockturn rate for a given line of electric guitars. Inventory is taken every six months, customarily in terms of units. Sales are recorded in the same manner. Company records indicate that 190 guitars were sold during the year. The inventory listings appear below:

Date of Inventory	Number of Guitars
December 31, year before	55
June 30	72
December 31, last year	47
Total listings	174

Dividing the sum of the listings by three, the manager obtains an average inventory of 58 units. Stockturn rate is then calculated as follows:

$$\text{Stockturn in units} = \frac{\text{Sales in units}}{\text{Average inventory in units}}$$

$$= \frac{190}{58}$$

$$= 3.3\times$$

Merchandise Budgeting

To plan their inventories, retailers usually prepare **merchandise budgets** for each season. As with any budget, some flexibility must be built in so needed adjustments can be made along the way. The merchandise budget is a planning and a control device. It shows forecasted sales, planned inventory levels, expected retail reductions, and purchases that will be needed. This plan also indicates the initial markup percentage, expected gross margin, inventory turnover rate, and other useful elements. Figure 14.3 shows a typical plan sheet for a department.

Figure 14.3
Sample worksheet for merchandise and sales planning

Department Name _Better Dresses_ Department No. ___47-16___

SIX MONTH MERCHANDISING PLAN			PLAN (This Year)	ACTUAL (Last Year)
		Stock Turnover	2.8%	2.7%
		Workroom Costs	1.2%	1.2%
		Etc.		

SPRING 19XX		FEB.	MAR.	APR.	MAY	JUNE	JULY	SEASON TOTAL
FALL 19—		AUG.	SEP.	OCT.	NOV.	DEC.	JAN.	
SALES	Last Year	1800	2700	2100	2100	2400	1100	12,200
	Plan	1890	2160	2730	2100	2520	1210	12,610
	Percent of Increase	5%	−20%	+30%	0%	5%	10%	3%
	Revised							
	Actual							
RETAIL STOCK (BOM)	Last Year	5100	6300	5200	4500	5100	4500	3600*
	Plan	5300	5700	6500	5400	4500	3800	3600*
	Revised							
	Actual							
MARKDOWNS	Last Year	170	240	330	230	320	300	1590
	Plan (dollars)	170	240	230	300	300	300	1540
	Plan (percent)	9%	11%	8%	14%	12%	17%	12%
	Revised							
	Actual							
RETAIL PURCHASES	Last Year	3170	1840	1730	2930	2120	500	12,290
	Plan	2460	3200	1860	1500	2120	1310	12,450
	Revised							
	Actual							
PERCENT OF INITIAL MARKON	Last Year	44%	44%	44.6%	44.8%	44.7%	44.2%	44.9%
	Plan	45%	45%	45%	45%	45%	45%	45%
	Revised							
	Actual							

Comments * Ending Stock

Merchandise Manager _J. C. Smith_   Buyer _L. T. Lewis_

Controller_____

Source: Reprinted by permission from _Retail Store System: Inventory Management Concepts._ © 1973 by International Business Machines Corporation, 2nd ed., 1978.

Forecasting Sales For each new planning period, the first decision the retailer faces is the **sales forecast**—an estimate or prediction of future sales volume.[5] All merchandise budgeting is based on the sales objectives established. Since forecasting approaches were discussed in some depth in Chapter 5, only a brief mention is made here. Forecasts are typically prepared some months in advance of each season. To help determine their sales objectives, retailers consider prior years' records first of all. They also review general economic conditions on all levels: national, regional, and local. They check for long-term and more recent trends, study the actions of competitors, and anticipate possible change in the areas where their facilities are located. Taken into account, too, are contemplated moves inside the store, enlarging or cutting back section size, relocating departments, and the like. Such actions will affect sales volume.

The overall total is then broken down into monthly figures by using percentages. Some retailers go even further, working up sales projections weekly.

Top-Down and Bottom-Up Planning Most often, sales planning is initiated and completed by management. Projections are then broken down into estimates for individual departments, merchandise groups, and classifications. In the case of a chain store organization, estimates for the individual store units are prepared as well. When top management determines overall revenue goals and then breaks them down into smaller segments or units, the procedure is called **top-down planning.** In **bottom-up planning,** management delegates the responsibility for generating sales projections to operating personnel. In a chain operation, for example, the individual store managers may be required to submit estimates for their respective outlets. Planning is often delegated even farther down the chain of command to department managers. The department heads are asked to forward their projections to the store manager. Following a review of the figures and some discussion, the store manager then sends the approved estimates to central management. At the home office, they are totaled to derive the company-wide sales objective for the period.

There is logic behind the bottom-up approach. Since they are really on the firing line, department and/or store managers are closer to the shopping public than are the executives who head the company. Lower-level managers have a better grasp of what is going on at the store level than central office executives. Human error may, however, enter the picture. In their eagerness to please superiors, employees may occasionally project unrealistically high sales figures. Overconfidence on a manager's part may also cause problems. So may a "lowball" estimate, furnished under the erroneous assumption that the manager will be regarded more favorably if the department or store ends up well over budgeted sales.

Accuracy is strengthened by combining both approaches: top-down and bottom-up. If the two sets of projections are far apart, differences can be reconciled through discussion.

Translating Sales Objectives into Monthly Projections

The targeted sales goal for the season is further broken down into monthly sales projections. Consider the following situation:

An independent shoe salon has been operating in a neighborhood shopping center for nearly three years. It caters to the entire family, *offering a broad selection of footwear. The two partners who manage the enterprise began planning, late in September, their merchandise budget for their fourth year of operation. First, they worked on their sales projections. They estimated that they would finish up the year with total net sales of $360,000. After analyzing past performance and appraising the current state of the local economy, the owners were convinced that next year's sales would show an increase of 12 percent. By multiplying $360,000 by 112 percent, they projected sales of $403,200 for the coming year.*

The partners knew that their sales curve was sure to show peaks and valleys: each month would bring in a different percentage of yearly sales. January was normally the slowest month of the year. Since they opened, it had averaged about 6.1 percent of annual sales. On the other hand, records for April indicated 10.3 percent. The partners prepared the following list of monthly sales projections:

Month	Percent of Year	Estimated Sales
January	6.1%	$ 24,595
February	6.3	25,402
March	9.8	39,514
April	10.3	41,530
May	9.0	36,288
June	7.0	28,224
First half:	48.5%	$175,553
July	6.4	25,805
August	7.9	31,853
September	10.2	41,126
October	9.8	39,514
November	7.6	30,643
December	9.6	38,707
Second half:	51.5%	$207,648

Having set their monthly figures, the partners were then in a position to continue with planning their merchandise.

An Alternate Example Large retail companies usually plan their merchandise budgets around six-month seasons, fall/winter and spring/summer. In deriving monthly sales projections, management in these organizations uses the six-month period as a base, rather than annual sales projections. Planned monthly sales figures are calculated as percentages based on 100 percent of the sales expected during the six months.

Let us assume, for example, that a toy department has planned

sales figures for the fall/winter season. This is how its monthly estimates might look:

Month	Percent of Season	Estimated Sales
August	9.5%	$ 41,800
September	11.3	49,720
October	13.7	60,280
November	20.4	89,760
December	34.5	151,800
January	10.6%	46,640
Fall/winter	100.0%	$440,000

Planning the Merchandise Inventory

After working up sales objectives, retailers tackle the problem of determining their inventory needs. They know that to take in x dollars
in sales they will have to stock far more inventory than merely the
x amount. This is true because stores carry many different items,
and these goods may come in various styles, colors, sizes, and other
variants. It would be impossible to sell all articles at equal stockturn
rates. Nor does the merchant want to wind up at the end of a period
with a completely depleted inventory. Shoppers need to be able to
make their selections from an assortment of merchandise.

When working up stock requirements for forthcoming periods, retailers can choose from among four distinct approaches. These are
the weeks' supply, basic stock, percentage variation, and stock-to-sales
ratio methods.

Weeks' Supply Method This is favored by some independent retailers of
staple merchandise and by a few departments in large stores that
carry similar goods. In the **weeks' supply method,** stock planning is
tied to the rate of inventory turnover. The retailer provides sufficient
inventory to cover several weeks of operation at the average weekly
sales rate expected. The procedure is relatively simple to install if
goods can be expected to move out at a fairly regular, predictable
pace. Suppose, for instance, that a store expects to average $2,500
per week during the months of June and July. Management wishes
to keep enough merchandise on hand to last for 3½ weeks. Obviously,
the firm will need 3.5 × $2,500, or $8,750 worth of goods at retail.

The decision about how many weeks' supply should be provided
is determined by the following equation:

$$\text{Weeks of supply needed} = \frac{\text{Total weeks in period}}{\text{Stockturn rate}}$$

Inventory must be sufficient to take care of expected sales.

Courtesy Western Auto Supply Company

To illustrate the computation, assume that a company anticipates a turnover rate of 4× for the next quarter. During that time, weekly sales should average $3,000:

$$\text{Weeks of supply needed} = \frac{\text{Total weeks in period}}{\text{Stockturn rate}}$$

$$= \frac{13}{4}$$

$$= 3.25 \text{ weeks}$$

We then work out the inventory needed to begin the season:

$$\text{Inventory needed} = \text{Number of weeks' supply needed} \times$$
$$\text{Expected weekly sales}$$
$$= 3.25 \times \$3,000$$
$$= \$9,750$$

There is one drawback to the weeks' supply method. It may lead to an understocked position during a busy time of year or an overstocked condition when sales are off.

Basic Stock Method More commonly seen is the **basic stock method.** It involves carrying a basic inventory throughout the period and adding sufficient merchandise to cover each month's expected sales. The technique is useful in departments and stores where the rate of inventory turnover is relatively slow. Typically, the rate is from less than one turn to as many as six over the year.

Assume, for example, that a luggage merchant wishes to maintain a minimum level of inventory all during the second quarter of the year, regardless of revenues. The retailer must add enough goods to this basic stock at the start of each month to take care of expected sales for that month. Planned sales for the three months are $36,100, $47,000, and $54,300 respectively. The *annual* inventory turnover rate for the store, computed from past records, is 5.6×. Here is how the merchant works out both the required basic stock and the additional merchandise needed to cover expected sales:

1. Calculate the average stock needed for the quarter:

   a. Average stock $= \dfrac{\text{Total sales for period}}{\text{Turnover rate for period}}$

   b. Total sales for period $= \$36,100 + \$47,000 + \$54,300$
   $$= \$137,400$$

   c. Turnover rate for period $= \dfrac{5.6}{4}$
   $$= 1.4\times$$

   d. Solving the equation:

   $$\text{Average stock} = \dfrac{\$137,400}{1.4}$$
   $$= \$98,143$$

2. Ascertain the average monthly sales during the period:

   a. Average monthly sales $= \dfrac{\text{Total sales for period}}{\text{Number of months in period}}$
   $$= \dfrac{\$137,400}{3}$$
   $$= \$45,800$$

3. Work up the basic stock figure:

   a. Basic stock $=$ Average stock $-$ Average monthly sales
   $$= \$98,143 - \$45,800$$
   $$= \$52,343$$

4. Determine the total inventory required at the beginning of the month (BOM):

   a. BOM stock needed $=$ Basic stock $+$ Expected sales for month

Month	Basic Stock	Expected Sales	Total BOM Stock Needed
1.	$52,343	$36,100	$ 88,443
2.	52,343	47,000	99,343
3.	52,343	54,300	106,643

Percentage Variation Method If the average inventory maintained by a retail company can be expected to move out rapidly, the **percentage variation method** is preferred. In these situations, the annual stockturn rate typically exceeds 6×. The retailer works entirely from average stock figures for the season, expected monthly sales, and average monthly sales. Beginning-of-the-month inventories become a function of the average stock and planned sales. The percentage variation method tends to dampen monthly changes in inventory when monthly sales vary significantly. Inventory changes only one half as much as sales. This makes it easier to adjust monthly inventories.

Consider the following:

A store owner is planning merchandise requirements for the first six months of next year. Past records indicate an annual stockturn rate of 10×. Planned sales for each month follow:

January	*$ 38,300*
February	*45,000*
March	*50,600*
April	*71,400*
May	*42,500*
June	*37,200*
Total	*$285,000*

Here is how the proprietor works up BOM inventory requirements for each month:

1. Calculate the average stock needed during the period:

   a. *Average stock* $= \dfrac{\text{Total sales for period}}{\text{Turnover rate for period}}$

   b. *Total sales for period* $= \$285,000$

   c. *Turnover rate for period* $= \dfrac{10}{2}$

   $= 5\times$

d. *Solving the equation:*

$$Average\ stock = \frac{\$285,000}{5}$$

$$= \$57,000$$

2. *Ascertain the average monthly sales during the period:*

a. *Average monthly sales* = $\dfrac{Total\ sales}{Number\ of\ months}$

$$= \frac{\$285,000}{6}$$

$$= \$47,500$$

3. *Compute the necessary BOM inventory for each month, using the formula below:*

$$BOM\ inventory = Average\ stock \times \tfrac{1}{2} \left(1 + \frac{Expected\ sales\ for\ month}{Average\ monthly\ sales} \right)$$

a. *Determine the BOM inventory for each month, as indicated below for January:*

$$January\ BOM\ stock = \$57,000 \times \tfrac{1}{2} \left(1 + \frac{\$38,300}{\$47,550} \right)$$

$$= \$57,000 \times \tfrac{1}{2}(1.81)$$
$$= \$57,000 \times 0.90$$
$$= \$51,300$$

b. *Here are the remaining calculations:*

BOM inventory for:

February	$= \$57,000 \times \tfrac{1}{2}(1.95) = \$57,000 \times 0.97 = \$55,290$
March	$= \$57,000 \times \tfrac{1}{2}(2.07) = \$57,000 \times 1.03 = \$58,710$
April	$= \$57,000 \times \tfrac{1}{2}(2.50) = \$57,000 \times 1.25 = \$71,250$
May	$= \$57,000 \times \tfrac{1}{2}(1.89) = \$57,000 \times 0.94 = \$53,580$
June	$= \$57,000 \times \tfrac{1}{2}(1.78) = \$57,000 \times 0.89 = \$50,730$

Stock-to-Sales Ratio Method A ratio can readily be developed that describes the relationship between the inventory on hand at the start of any given month and sales volume for the month. Retail companies arrive at such **stock-to-sales ratios** by analyzing internal records. Useful data concerning other stores' stock-to-sales ratios are frequently made available by the retailer's trade association. Table 14.2 contains just such data.

Table 14.2 BOM stock-to-sales ratios in the menswear industry, 1983

	Firms Handling Menswear Only				Firms Handling Womenswear			
	Distribution of Sales by Month (51 firms)		Beginning of the Month Stock-to-Sales Ratio (37 firms)		Distribution of Sales by Month (55 firms)		Beginning of the Month Stock-to-Sales Ratio (39 firms)	
	Range of Common Experience	Median Firm	Range of Common Experience	Median Firm	Range of Common Experience	Median Firm	Range of Common Experience	Median Firm
February	5.1– 6.7	5.9	6.0–11.5	7.6	5.0– 6.6	5.6	6.4–9.5	7.3
March	5.5– 7.2	6.1	5.5–11.6	6.9	5.4– 7.4	6.3	5.1–9.5	7.1
April	6.3– 7.8	7.0	5.7–10.8	8.1	5.7– 7.9	6.6	6.0–9.2	7.4
May	6.7– 8.0	7.2	5.8– 9.7	7.1	6.4– 8.0	7.4	5.6–9.2	6.5
June	7.8– 9.5	8.7	4.5– 8.5	6.1	6.7– 9.6	8.2	4.8–7.9	5.5
July	6.3– 8.8	7.5	5.4– 8.6	6.9	7.0– 9.2	7.8	4.1–7.7	5.9
August	5.2– 6.8	6.0	5.9–11.8	7.9	5.6– 7.6	6.3	6.0–9.2	7.5
September	5.8– 7.6	6.5	5.5–11.1	8.3	6.4– 8.5	7.2	5.3–9.5	6.6
October	7.0– 9.2	7.9	5.7– 9.8	7.6	7.3– 8.9	7.9	5.7–9.3	6.8
November	8.5–10.7	9.3	5.1– 8.6	7.4	8.5–10.4	9.0	4.8–8.2	6.5
December	16.1–20.7	18.6	2.7– 4.9	3.3	14.2–19.7	17.7	2.4–4.9	3.7
January	6.0– 9.0	7.7	5.3– 8.8	6.7	6.3– 9.4	7.4	4.9–7.8	5.7
Total	100.0%				100.0%			

Source: Menswear Retailers of America, *1983 Annual Business Survey: Men's Store Operating Experiences* (Washington: Menswear Retailers of America, 1984), p. 34.

Two formulas are needed to calculate BOM inventory requirements under this method:

1. $\text{BOM stock-to-sales ratio} = \dfrac{\text{BOM stock}}{\text{Sales for month}}$

2. BOM inventory needed = BOM stock-to-sales ratio × Expected sales for month

For example, a domestics buyer has arrived at these planned monthly sales:

Month	Planned Sales
May	$15,000
June	$12,800
July	$12,500

By checking sales figures for the same months the year before, the buyer first works out the BOM stock-to-sales ratios for May, June, and July:

Month	Actual Sales	BOM Stock	BOM Stock-to-Sales Ratio
May	$13,700	$42,500	3.1
June	$10,600	$27,900	2.6
July	$ 9,200	$30,400	3.3

The buyer then calculates the BOM inventory levels needed for the department in the following manner:

Month	Stock-to-Sales Ratio	Expected Sales	Total BOM Stock Needed
May	3.1	× $15,000 =	$46,500
June	2.6	× $12,800 =	$33,280
July	3.3	× $12,500 =	$41,250

Compensating for Inventory Reductions

Let us look in on two partners. They run a successful women's sportswear store in a western city of 80,000 people. They use stock-to-sales ratios in their merchandise planning. They have projected $25,000 in sales for this coming February. From prior records, they determine that February's stock-to-sales ratio should be 3.2. For the following month of March, with estimated sales of $32,000, a ratio of 3.4 is indicated. By multiplying the February sales target of $25,000 by 3.2, the partners plan for a BOM inventory valued at $80,000 in retail dollars. The end-of-month (EOM) inventory is to total $108,800 ($32,000 × 3.4).

With sales in February expected to reach $25,000, it is evident that far more than that amount in merchandise at retail must be purchased to end the month with an additional $28,800 in goods. The owners are certain that during February some **retail reductions** will take place. These will lower the inventory's valuation. Store policy, for instance, mandates a 20 percent discount off the retail selling price on all sales to employees. After reviewing their records, the two estimate that their employees are likely to purchase $1,500 worth of goods at retail. If this occurs, some $300 in sales will be missing from their projection (based on 20 percent of $1,500). In short, the retail valuation of the merchandise made available for sale will be reduced by $300.

They also anticipate that other types of retail reductions will take place: markdowns, customer discounts, and stock shortages. All such reductions decrease the value of the inventory. To attain their planned sales objective, the partners will need to provide additional merchandise to cover the total amount of deductions.

Projected Purchases | Once inventory requirements for a period have been determined, retailers need to work out the additional purchases needed to bring the inventory level into line. Naturally, preparations must also be made for having on hand the desired opening (BOP) and closing (EOP) inventories.

Consider this example:

The proprietor of a children's clothing outlet has projected net sales of $27,000 for May. Based on past experience, the merchant estimates the following retail reductions during May:

Reductions	*Percent of Sales**
Markdowns	6%
Employee discounts	3
Customer discounts	1
Stock shortages	1
Total deductions	11%

* Note that the owner has expressed the reductions in percentages of net sales. This is a customary practice in retailing.

The planned BOM stock for May 1 is $62,000. EOM stock projected for May 31 is set at $50,000. Additional goods that must be purchased to complete the store's needs for the month are calculated as follows:

$$\begin{aligned}
\textit{Projected purchases} &= \textit{Sales for month} + \textit{Deductions for month} + \\
&\quad \textit{EOM Stock} - \textit{BOM Stock} \\
&= \$27,000 + .11(\$27,000) + \$50,000 - \$62,000 \\
&= \$27,000 + \$2,970 + \$50,000 - \$62,000 \\
&= \$17,970
\end{aligned}$$

Calculating the Open-to-Buy

In the above illustration, an additional $17,970 worth of goods (at retail) will be needed. Let us assume it is now May 1. The store has already received $4,500 worth of merchandise ordered for May. Other orders totaling $8,050 have been placed with suppliers, and some shipments may already be on their way to the store. The proprietor wants to know *how many more dollars,* at retail, are available to complete May's inventory needs. In brief, how much remains **open-to-buy (OTB)?** A simple formula is used to calculate the OTB:

$$OTB = \text{Projected purchases} - \text{Stock on order} - \text{Stock already received}$$
$$= \$17,970 - \$8,050 - \$4,500$$
$$= \$5,420$$

Obviously, the retailer still needs to spend $5,420 to complete the store's requirements. Of course, results during May might not turn out exactly as planned. Sales may be higher or lower and so may the retail reductions. The remaining OTB dollars may need to be adjusted to compensate for deviations from budgeted figures.

Retail Method of Inventory Valuation

Many years ago, retail firms of all types and sizes kept track of the merchandise flowing in and out in terms of the prices they had to pay. Some merchants would manually maintain a continuous, or perpetual, book inventory. Each and every article introduced into stock would be duly recorded. The item's cost would usually be entered on the attached price tag along with the retail selling price. Because costs were always disguised in code, store shoppers were unable to determine how much the retailer had paid for the goods.

Under this cost method of accounting, retailers could not readily ascertain their cost of goods sold during any one period. Nor could they determine the gross profit earned unless they actually counted and tallied all of their stock. Because of the time, effort, and expense involved in taking inventory, most merchants saw fit to limit this activity to no more than once or twice each year. When the cost approach was used, it was also impossible to determine the correct valuation of merchandise that had been stolen by shoplifters or employees.

Nowadays, most large retail organizations (and a sizable proportion of medium-sized companies) use an alternate approach, the *retail method of inventory valuation.* Many small stores, however, still adhere to the cost method. They prefer the relatively simpler record-keeping to the more modern—and more complex—retail method. The older approach is also preferred by those who operate nondepartmentized stores or where the turnover rate is low and the prices of goods are high. Retailers of household furniture and major appliances are examples. The cost method is also commonly used if an element of expense attributable to manufacturing labor must be taken into account. Bakeries, prescription pharmacies, and restaurants often operate under the cost method.

Nature of the Retail Method

The **retail method of inventory valuation** is an accounting procedure based on the retail selling prices of merchandise. Cost figures appear neither on price tickets nor on inventory sheets or tags. Salespeople need to learn only current selling prices. Original costs are, however, in the company's record-keeping system with price changes, markdowns, discounts, and other pertinent information. When physical inventory must be taken, all goods are totaled at their retail values.

An outstanding advantage of the retail method is that management can determine operating results without having to take inventory. From the paperwork in the system, it can easily generate an appropriate valuation of the inventory in terms of original costs and retail prices. Both the cost of goods and the subsequent gross margin yield can be calculated almost at will for any period. This can be done for the entire year, a six-month season, quarterly, or monthly. Even a weekly profit-and-loss statement, if desired by management, is feasible. Application of the method is shown in Figure 14.4.

**Figure 14.4
Retail method of inventory valuation: an illustration**

A. Determine the value of merchandise inventory available for sale during the period, at both cost and retail prices:

Item	Cost	Retail
BOP inventory	$27,000	$44,100
Purchases made during period	15,000	25,400
Freight charges paid	375	—
Net additional markups	—	650
Total inventory available for sale	$42,375	$70,150

B. Total all reductions from inventory available for sale, at retail:

Item	Retail
Net sales	$30,500
Net markdowns	1,600
Employee discounts	1,100
Shrinkage	750
Total deductions	$33,950

C. Obtain EOP inventory valuation, at retail:

Total inventory available, at retail	$70,150
Less: total reductions, at retail	−33,950
Value of EOP stock, at retail	$36,200

**Figure 14.4
(concluded)**

D. Markup calculations:

1. Find the total markup in dollars on the inventory available for sale:

Available inventory, at retail $70,150
Less: available inventory,
    at cost   −42,375
      Total markup in dollars $27,775

2. Compute the cumulative markup percentage at retail on the inventory available for sale:

$$\text{Cum MU}\% = \frac{\text{Markup in dollars}}{\text{Total retail dollars}} \times 100\%$$

$$= \frac{\$27,775}{\$70,150} \times 100\%$$

$$= 39.6\%$$

3. Determine the cost percentage (complement of the markup):

$$\text{Cost }\% = 100\% - \text{Cum MU}\%$$
$$= 100\% - 39.6\%$$
$$= 60.4\%$$

E. Assess the valuation, at cost, of the EOP inventory:

EOP inventory,
    at cost   = (EOP inventory at retail)(cost percentage)
                = ($36,200)(60.4%)
                = $21,865

F. Finally, calculate the cost of goods sold. (This is the total amount of merchandise, valued at cost, that "moved out" of the store's inventory.):

COG = Total inventory available for sale − EOP inventory
     = $42,375 − $21,865
     = $20,510

There are other advantages as well. For example, should the premises suffer damage from a fire or other peril, an appraisal of the inventory loss can be prepared from the records. Much of the actual stock might have literally gone up in smoke! Accounting statements based on the retail method are acceptable, at tax time, to the Internal Revenue Service. Moreover, retailers who follow the method find they are able to ascertain the existence and the extent of shortages. They are even able to pinpoint the departments in which shrinkage has become a serious problem.

The retail method does have at least two drawbacks. First, the record-keeping is complicated and must be tightly controlled. All purchases of inventory, discounts given, price changes, and similar elements must be carefully monitored and properly fed into the system. Second, the derived figures are only an approximation. Costs are arrived at through computations with retail prices and averaging methods. Thus, it is entirely possible that the true value of an inventory (at cost) may be higher or lower at any time. For this reason, a physical inventory still needs to be taken occasionally.

Inventory Methods

The retail company must institute an adequate inventory control procedure for three reasons: (1) reordering, (2) securing appropriate information for management decisions, and (3) holding down its investment in store merchandise. Essential to the proper functioning of merchandise control is the method employed to determine the inventory on hand. Four approaches are commonly in use: physical inventory, perpetual inventory, observation, and the tickler method.

Physical Inventory

Every retail firm must take **physical inventory** at least once each year to close its books. For some merchants, this is a semiannual chore. For others, it is a quarterly activity. Many prefer doing it every month, especially if the stockturn rate is moderate or high. Of the four methods, physical inventory is the most accurate. It involves checking and counting every item of merchandise in the selling area, on display,

Physical inventory involves checking and counting every article of merchandise.

Courtesy Sears, Roebuck & Co., Chicago

in bins, on shelves, or in the back room or warehouse. Even goods en route to customers by delivery truck are included. As it is counted, all merchandise is inspected for breakage, damage, fading, and general salability. Often, two employees take the inventory. One inspects and counts the goods, calling out the amounts to the other, who enters the figures on an inventory sheet.

Retailers develop their own inventory forms that list all items carried in stock. Listings are sectioned off by major lines. The merchandise is itemized by prices, sizes, and the like. There are columns for retail prices, item descriptions, recording the amounts that are called out, and the extensions to be made by the bookkeeping section. An alternate approach to the inventory sheet is the tag method. As each bin, shelf, or other area is inspected and the goods they contain counted, the inventory clerk lists the contents on a tag. The tag is affixed to the merchandise. After all stock has been inventoried, the tags are collected and sent to bookkeeping for processing.

Perpetual Inventory The word *perpetual* means lasting forever. The company that maintains a **perpetual inventory** keeps continuous track of the stock—by hand, mechanically, or electronically. A perpetual inventory system is also known as a book inventory system because records are maintained of all transactions involving merchandise. These include sales, receipts of delivered goods into stock, transfers-out to other units in a chain store organization, and so on. Running balances are always available. A separate record is usually kept for each item carried in stock.

With today's modern equipment, the cashier or checkout clerk enters an item's classification, number, and other information into a computer merely by depressing the keys of a point-of-sale register. As you recall from Chapter 3, if articles bear UPC codes, optical scanners send the details directly to the computer. Store management may thus keep track of merchandise movement and stock balances at the close of each business day.

Observation This approach is characteristically used by independent retailers. Seldom do small store owners feel they can spare the time, let alone afford the expense, to take physical inventory more often than the mandatory once each year. They watch stock levels by the so-called eyeball control method—mere observation. Bins, back room, displays, and other areas are checked out visually from time to time to find out what items are running low and should be reordered. Little or no record-keeping is involved.

The Tickler Method Some retailers use the **tickler method,** an inventory approach fairly similar to the ABC technique discussed in Chapter 13. After studying

Stock rotation is important in retailing goods with a short shelf life.

Courtesy Swiss Colony Stores, Inc., Monroe, WI

stock movement patterns for some time, the retailer divides the inventory into three groups of items: best sellers, articles that sell at a moderate pace, and slow movers. Physical inventory is then taken fairly often on the first group, perhaps every two or three weeks. The second, and much larger, group of moderate sellers is checked every month or two. Slow-moving merchandise may be inventoried only once or twice yearly.

FIFO and LIFO

In determining the cost of goods sold, retail companies have two accounting options: (1) the customary first-in, first-out—or FIFO, and (2) the newer last-in, first-out—or LIFO. The former approach is still used by the vast majority of firms. In recent years, however, more and more retailers have become interested in switching to LIFO because of inflation.

The **FIFO** method appears to be a natural outgrowth of a long-standing tradition among store merchants of making absolutely certain that all stock is rotated. Retailers have always taught their stock clerks and salespeople how to fill in shelves and bins properly. This entails first removing the older goods, replacing them with newer stock, and then setting the older merchandise in front. This way, older goods are sold off first. This is especially important in bakeries, meat and fish stores, fruit-and-vegetable stands, confectionery shops, and to other retailers of products with relatively short shelf life.

With this philosophy, it was only natural for retailers to employ the first in, first out method of accounting, basing the inventory's value on the cost prices of the earliest goods to come into the store. In periods of inflation, however, valuing inventory by FIFO results in a somewhat lower cost-of-goods figure. As a consequence, the operating statement shows more gross margin dollars earned. This eventually translates down to more profits shown on the bottom line. Thus, the firm may be liable for higher income tax.

Under the **LIFO** approach, merchandise items purchased *last* are counted as the first ones sold.[6] This procedure has an opposite effect: The cost of goods sold is higher, the gross margin dollars fewer, and the operating profit reduced. The company therefore feels a lower income tax bite. At the same time, the use of LIFO results in an increase in the firm's cash position.

Let us suppose that a giftwares buyer purchased five statuettes four months ago at a cost of $150 each. Doubling the cost, the buyer priced the articles to sell at $300 each. Three were sold; two remained in stock. Recently, the wholesale price of the statuettes was raised by 10 percent, costing the firm $165 per unit for an additional three purchased. Under the old FIFO arrangement, the retailer can expect $150 in gross margin dollars for each one sold and a total of $750 if all five are sold. Under LIFO, each sale would bring only $135, or $675 in all. Assuming that expenses are held constant, the $75 overage under FIFO would show up in the operating profit of the income statement. This would compel the merchant to pay additional income tax. If LIFO had been used, less profit would be shown, and the tax required would be lower.

Summary

With an effective inventory planning and control system, the retailer can monitor stock movement, avoid stockouts, decide what merchandise to buy, and determine quantities needed. Unit and dollar control are approaches to inventory management. Either can be based on the cost or retail prices of goods. Some retailers use unit control, usually those who sell more expensive goods and merchandise that moves slowly. The more popular method is dollar control, an approach that keeps track of the movement of goods in terms of their prices, rather than by units.

A useful measure in merchandise management is the rate of inventory turnover, or stockturn. This is defined as the number of times the average inventory is bought and sold during a particular period, usually one year. Stockturn can be measured by retail or cost prices, or in units. It can be calculated for an entire company, individual store unit, department, classification, subclassification, or single item. The more rapid the rate of inventory turnover, the faster flow in the gross margin dollars earned by the firm. Typically, retailers compare their stockturn rates with those of prior periods and to available trade association data. Turnover rates vary for different types of stores and different kinds of merchandise.

Many retail firms prepare merchandise budgets well in advance of every season. Each budget outlines targeted sales, planned inventories, planned retail reductions, and additional purchases to be made. Often, it also shows the planned initial markup percentage, expected gross margin, and the stockturn. As is true with other internal budgets, flexibility is a necessary characteristic.

Forecasting procedures help in setting sales objectives for merchandise budgets. Among other things retailers take into account when forecasting are national, regional, and local economic conditions, market trends, the actions of competitors, anticipated changes in the community, and internal moves planned in the company itself.

In top-down planning, management sets overall objectives and plans and breaks the plans down into smaller segments. In bottom-up planning, the responsibility for establishing sales goals is delegated to operating personnel. More accurate plans result from combining the two approaches. Annual, semiannual, or seasonal sales objectives are translated into monthly projections, usually by applying percentages.

Four common approaches to determining inventory requirements are the weeks' supply, basic stock, percentage variation, and stock-to-sales ratio methods. When planning for their merchandise needs, retailers try to compensate for expected retail reductions such as markdowns, employee and customer discounts, and stock shortages. These lower the value of the inventory. Retailers also need to plan their projected purchases and open-to-buy.

Today, many retailers follow the retail method of inventory valuation. Based on the retail prices of goods, its advantages include a capability for generating operating statements whenever needed and for finding shortages. A major drawback is that it requires continuous and complicated record-keeping.

Inventory methods popular among retailers include physical inventory, perpetual inventory, observation, and the tickler method. Traditionally, retailers have based their inventory valuations on the FIFO (first in, first out) method. Under this approach, the goods received earliest are assumed to have been sold off first. The method results in a lower cost-of-goods figure during inflationary periods. Thus, more profits are made, and more income tax may have to be paid. Many retailers have switched to LIFO, where the merchandise purchased last is counted as the first sold. Under this arrangement, the cost of goods is higher, the gross margin (and profits) lower, and there is less tax liability.

Key Terms

unit control	percentage variation method
dollar control	stock-to-sales ratios
inventory turnover (stockturn)	retail reductions
stockouts	open-to-buy (OTB)
merchandise budgets	retail method of inventory valuation
sales forecast	physical inventory
top-down planning	perpetual inventory
bottom-up planning	tickler method
weeks' supply method	FIFO
basic stock method	LIFO

Review Questions

1. What are the consumer's alternatives when the item being shopped for is out of stock?

2. Specify the benefits to the retail company of a more rapid stock turnover rate.

3. A home improvements department shows sales of $327,000 for a six-month period. Inventory records reveal that, during that time, the department carried an average stock valued at $104,500 in retail dollars. What was the department's rate of stock turnover during the period?

4. Name two kinds of stores where the inventory typically averages at least six turns annually. Give three examples of stores with average rates lower than 3×.

5. A pharmacy takes inventory only once each year, at the close of business on January 31. The retail valuation of the closing inventory for the year just ended is $151,900. The opening inventory taken on the prior January 31 was valued at $168,400 at retail. The pharmacist has calculated the stockturn rate to be 4.8× for the year. Determine the net sales figure for the year just ended.

6. The manager of a health and beauty aids (HBA) department calculated the rate of stockturn for the fall-winter period to be 1.9×. The cost of goods sold for the six months amounted to $445,500. Determine the value of the average stock maintained in the department, in terms of cost prices.

7. Given the following data, determine the overall stockturn rate attained for the third quarter of the year:

Inventory Date	Retail Value	Sales for Month
August 1 (BOP)	$ 88,600	$ —
August 31	92,200	45,800
September 30	107,300	53,400
October 31	124,900	61,500

8. A jewelry store keeps track of a line of women's diamond watches by individual pieces. During the last six months of the year, the jeweler sold 143 units. The average stock maintained on the watches came to 112 pieces. Calculate the stockturn rate, in units, for the half-year period.

9. The proprietor of a busy camera shop has targeted some $396,000 in sales for the spring-summer season. Given the following percentages, work out the owner's projected sales figures for each month:

February	16%	May	17%
March	21%	June	14%
April	23%	July	9%

10. Distinguish between the weeks' supply and the basic stock methods of planning store inventory.

11. Describe the major features of the percentage variation method.

12. Demonstrate how stock-to-sales ratios are used by retailers.

13. Identify and briefly describe four types of retail inventory reductions.

14. Write out the formulas used to calculate: (a) projected purchases, and (b) open-to-buy.

15. List several advantages and disadvantages of employing the retail method of inventory valuation.

16. Explain what is meant by each of these terms: *(a) perpetual inventory, (b) tickler method, (c) physical inventory, (d) LIFO.*

Discussion Questions

1. Speculate about the reasons why some merchants buy goods hand to mouth. How may this affect the firm's sales volume?

2. Suggest three or four measures that a retail company can take to increase its rate of inventory turnover.

3. What can account for a lower than usual stockturn rate in a hardware store?

4. Distinguish between top-down and bottom-up planning and specify the advantages and disadvantages of each approach.

5. Why do furniture retailers and neighborhood bakeries often prefer to use the cost method over the retail method of inventory valuation?

Notes

[1]Leroy G. Olson and Richard H. Olson, "A Computerized Merchandise Budget for Use in Retailing," *Journal of Retailing* 46 (Summer 1970), pp. 3–17ff. See also: Raymond F. Barker, "Space and Inventory Management by Computer Simulation," *Journal of Retailing* 45 (Winter 1969–70), pp. 19–29.

[2]David McConaughy, "An Appraisal of Computers in Department Store Inventory Control," *Journal of Retailing* 46 (Spring 1970), pp. 3–19.

[3]Donald E. Edwards, "Is Your Sales Dollar Being Consumed by Inventory Holding Costs?" *Journal of Retailing* 45 (Fall 1969), pp. 55–68*ff.*

[4]See: Philip B. Schary and Martin Christopher, "The Anatomy of a Stock-out," *Journal of Retailing* 55 (Summer 1979), pp. 59–70; C. K. Walter and John R. Grabner, "Stockout Cost Models: Empirical Tests in a Retail Situation," *Journal of Marketing* 39 (July 1975), pp. 56–60.

[5]William A. Staples and Robert Swerdlow, "Planning and Budgeting for Effective Retail Merchandise Management," *Journal of Small Business Management* 16 (January 1976), p. 1.

[6]For some informal comments on the value of LIFO, see: "LIFO Saves," *Inc.* 3 (January 1981), pp. 52–54.

CHAPTER 15

PRICING THE MERCHANDISE

Your Study Objectives

After you have studied this chapter, you will understand:

1. The store factors and merchandise factors that influence pricing decisions.
2. The types of pricing policies that retailers may establish.
3. The various promotional pricing strategies that retail companies may employ.
4. The major kinds of markups and how they are calculated.
5. The causes of and reasons for taking price markdowns.
6. The types and uses of discounts in business.
7. The influence of federal legislation on retail pricing.

The Meaning of Price

Does this situation seem familiar? At the supermarket checkout, the clerk comes across an item among your selections that has not been price marked and loudly exclaims, "I need a price." Time goes by while someone on the floor checks the section from which the item has been taken. In the meantime, shoppers in line behind you stare impatiently. The clerk finally receives the information, then proceeds with ringing up the balance of your purchases. (Happily, this type of problem has nearly disappeared with the increasing use of scanning equipment and the universal product code!)

What is the meaning of a price to the consumer? At least in this instance, it would seem to be the amount of money we are asked to pay for an item. Or as a popular marketing textbook puts it: ". . . Price is what is charged for 'something.' *Any business transaction in our modern economy can be thought of as an exchange of money— the money being the Price—for Something.*"[1]

To regard price merely as the amount of money charged for a product or service is too simplistic. Were it so, we would not be compelled to make numerous judgments regarding fair prices, excessively high or outrageous prices, and bargain prices. Evidently, there are other ramifications, or connotations, that surround the price concept.

The economist holds that price is an expression, in monetary terms, of the exchange value of something. In turn, value can be construed as that something's usefulness, worth, want-satisfying characteristics, and the like. To the manufacturer, price is a composite mechanism, carefully formulated of (a) the cost of materials used in manufacturing the product, (b) attendant labor expenses, (c) a proportional share of overhead costs, and (d) desired profit. Prices are also the means by which companies secure revenues in order to exist and grow.

Factors that Influence Pricing Decisions

The manufacturer, for the most part, initiates the pricing structure on which intermediary institutions base their own prices. Because they purchase merchandise for resale to others, wholesalers and retailers alike look to their cost of goods as the point of departure in setting prices. In both types of establishments, price administration may be affected by a variety of factors: different costs, company policies, marketing tactics, environmental influences, and even the characteristics of the goods themselves.

Cost Factors in Retailing Other than the basic cost of goods, many cost elements bear directly on the determination of prices. Among others, these include:

advertising
customer discounts
customer returns and adjustments
delivery and other services

employee discounts
freight charges
net workroom expenses
pilferage
sales promotion
selling expenses
shoplifting

Company Policies Price setting by retail management may take into account the desired store image, psychological pricing methods, how sizable a return on investment is expected, promotional pricing approaches, and so on. Even the store's location and its decor may affect price decisions.

Other Factors Numerous other influences impinge on pricing procedure. Among them are the state of the economy, local competition, the legal environment, and management's business ethics. Merchandise characteristics also modify pricing behavior. These range from the more obvious, such as seasonality or perishability, to whether consumers consider the products to be staples or fashion items, or convenience, shopping, or specialty goods. In September, swimwear sold in the North typically carries reduced prices. In the supermarket, the head of lettuce that sells today at 89 cents may be offered the day after tomorrow at 49 cents because it has begun to deteriorate in appearance.

The Price-Quality Relationship In the minds of most shoppers, quality and price go hand in hand. Rightfully or not, higher prices usually signify higher quality. Research has confirmed this fact time and again. As an example, a study of over 10,000 brands in some 685 product categories revealed a sizable correlation between price and quality. The relationship held up over a fifteen year period.[2] It was stronger for durables than for nondurable goods.

Other investigators have found that this **price-quality relationship** may be affected by other factors, such as the consumer's income level or lack of information.[3] In forming an image of a product's quality, shoppers often use other stimuli as cues instead of or in addition to price. Among these stimuli are the retailer's reputation, the brand name, and physical attributes of the item, such as color.[4] In judging product quality, consumers in other countries may well use different cues than we do or use similar cues differently.[5]

For several years, the Great Atlantic & Pacific Tea Company promoted the Price and Pride theme. Their intention was to generate a strong price-quality image in the public's mind. In the late 1970s, they departed radically from this approach by opening their Plus Discount Food Stores. These were smaller stores that averaged between

5,000 and 12,000 square feet in size. They stocked fewer than one tenth the number of items carried in the larger A&P units. The Plus stores followed a no frills concept. Goods were not individually priced or shelved. Customers had to buy paper bags or bring their own to the store. No manufacturers' coupons were redeemed. Price alone was the chain's major attraction.[6]

Setting Prices

Planning for all aspects of an enterprise calls for the setting of objectives first, then organizing the activities needed to attain them. This procedure is as vital in the area of pricing as it is in all other facets of the business.

Manufacturers' Objectives in Pricing

The manufacturing company sets overall goals at the outset: a targeted return on their investment, a reasonable share of market, long-term growth, and the like. Producers who seek to assure themselves rapidly of a niche in the marketplace through intensive distribution may price their goods below those of competitors in a market penetration policy. Or they may elect to follow a skimming policy to recoup their investment in product development and to help defray the heavy costs of initial promotion and distribution. In this case, prices are set above the market. In effect, the seller attempts to skim the cream by targeting at only those consumers who are willing to pay a higher price. Either policy—market penetration or skimming—will affect public perceptions of product quality.

Manufacturers may also choose to pursue other objectives, such as gaining a larger market share, increasing return on their investment, growing, maximizing profit, improving the company's image, and so on.

Retailers' Objectives in Pricing

Most of the basic goals set by retailing companies, like an adequate return on investment or growth, parallel those of the manufacturer. There are differences, however. Because their markets are local, retail firms seldom try to maximize profit. They are also more sensitive to the policies and tactics of nearby competitors. In pricing merchandise, retail firms aim at increasing store traffic, raising sales volume, disposing of slow-moving items, and attracting shoppers who ordinarily buy at other stores. They think in terms of increasing their gross profit percentages. Figure 15.1 presents median gross profit percentages earned by different kinds of retailers in 1983.

Pricing Approaches

Most consumers understand the concepts of supply and demand. They know that the interplay of these two forces affects the prices of goods

Figure 15.1   Gross profit percentages for various retail types, 1983

Drinking place	59.8%
Fast-food restaurant	57.0
Restaurant	54.8
Cut flowers, growing plants	48.9
Jewelry	47.8
Luggage, gifts	45.9
Men's, boys' clothing	41.1
Shoes	41.1
Furniture	39.5
Women's ready-to-wear	39.5
Books, stationery	38.0
Infants' clothing	36.5
Department store	35.6
Hardware	33.7
Dry goods, general merchandise	33.2
Drugs	32.3
Household appliances	29.3
Groceries, meats	21.4
Liquor	21.3
Fuel oil	15.1

Based on statement studies of firms with fiscal year-ends 6/30/82 through 3/31/83.

Note above interpretation of Statement Studies figures:

    RMA cautions that the Studies be regarded only as a general guideline and not as an absolute industry norm. This is due to limited samples within categories, the categorization of companies by their primary Standard Industrial Classification (SIC) number only, and different methods of operations by companies within the same industry. For these reasons, RMA recommends that the figures be used only as general guidelines in addition to other methods of financial analysis.

Source: Adapted from Robert Morris Associates, *'83 Annual Statement Studies* (Philadelphia: Robert Morris Associates, 1983). Copyright 1983 by Robert Morris Associates. Used with permission.

and services. If demand for a popular product abruptly slackens while supplies remain plentiful, we expect the customary price of that item to fall. The converse is also true. We expect the prices of goods in demand to rise as they become scarcer. An allied concept, intuitively grasped by retailers as well as shoppers, is that of **price elasticity.** Most merchandise is price elastic; that is to say, more units are purchased as prices are reduced, and higher prices usually lead to decreases in sales volume. Of course, the size of the price reduction must be considered. Lowering the price of an article by a small percentage may bring only a small increase in sales or perhaps no increase at all.

Manufacturer Techniques In setting prices, manufacturers often embrace demand as a point of departure. In creating a series of demand schedules for a product, they estimate probable levels of demand at different selling prices. They select the one price that promises to yield the maximum in sales volume and/or profit. They may bring marginal analysis into play. This involves comparing revenues with costs to determine the point at which marginal cost will equal marginal revenue. *Marginal cost* is defined as the incremental cost of producing one more unit; *marginal revenue,* as the income received from the additional sale. Or they consider break-even analysis, a technique that aims at determining the exact quantity of a given product that must be sold at a given price to cover all production costs. This may be calculated either in units or in dollar sales volume.

In setting prices, producers consider many aspects: market factors (skimming, penetration pricing), competitive factors (at, above, below the going price of goods), and demand factors. Cost-based approaches are the norm. Most prices are set with an eye to covering all relevant costs and yielding some profit.[7]

Retailer Pricing Techniques Similar considerations govern pricing practices in the retail organization. Strategies may have a competitive, market, and/or demand orientation. To project a desired company image, management may set its price levels at, above, or below those in the marketplace. Consumers may be asked to pay more for upper floors in high-rise apartment houses or for first-class seats in an airplane. Discounted prices are offered to senior citizens at the movies and in many restaurants. Off-price retailers like Marshall's and T. J. Maxx are examples of companies that have selected the strategy of selling goods at below-market prices.

Typically, the manufacturer initiates price-setting in the channels of distribution. Wholesalers and retailers must work with the prices they pay for the merchandise they buy. To their cost of goods, they add some amount, or **markup,** designed to cover overhead expenses

The strategy of off-price retailers like T. J. Maxx is to sell goods at below-market prices.

Gary Csuk

and produce some profit. Cost-plus pricing is the norm among distributors as well as manufacturers.

Pricing Policies

As a prelude to profitable price administration, retailers need to examine and clarify their basic business philosophies. They need to determine the pricing practices that would most benefit the organization and set company policy to provide guidelines for pricing decisions. Among the pricing policies commonly considered are variable or fixed pricing, price lining, psychological pricing, and unit pricing.

Variable or Fixed Pricing

Most retailers in the United States maintain a fixed, or one price, policy. The prices of goods are set and all shoppers pay the same prices. Consequently, consumers can be confident that they will be treated no differently than other customers. **Fixed pricing,** however, does not rule out the use of markdowns or promotional pricing methods. Nor does it rule out granting discounts to specific groups of customers, such as employees, neighborhood merchants, and the clergy. Exceptions to fixed pricing are the practices of antique dealers, flea marketers, used car dealers, sellers of unpainted furniture, and other retail types. **Variable pricing** is also used by dealers in sculptures or paintings and other vendors of unique or high-priced articles for which potential buyers might find it difficult to estimate the selling price. Prices are flexible and bargaining between shopper and merchant becomes the order of the day. Variable price policies are commonplace in many parts of the globe, as the seasoned traveler can readily confirm.

Most retailers stoutly resist attempts by consumers to bargain. Some are occasionally willing to reduce the price of an item in order to save the sale. This is not a practice to be encouraged; news of such transactions spread rapidly by word of mouth. Regular customers are apt to become disgruntled on hearing the news.

Price Lining   Frequently, the retailer's merchandise reflects a wide range of prices. A menswear store, for example, may carry neckties that range from $5.95 to $25. The lowest-priced scarves in a women's accessories department may sell for $8.50 each; top of the line scarves may be priced as high as $39.95. House slippers displayed in a shoe department may carry price tags of $7.50, $12, or $20.

To simplify the choice for shoppers, retailers often adopt a **price lining** strategy. Similar goods are separated into several grades or groupings according to their quality, fabric, or cost. The several groups are offered at specific **price points.** Neckties, for example, may be displayed in four groups and sold at $5.95, $10.50, $16.95, and $24. The retailer selects these particular price points in the belief that they are the prices customers prefer to pay for the different grades.

Retail companies see additional benefits in price lining other than the fact that it makes shopper buying decisions easier. It enables salespeople to trade up some customers to the next higher price line and to satisfy others who seek less expensive merchandise. Inventory taking, bookkeeping, and store display are simplified. Price lining also makes it more convenient for management to mark down merchandise that moves too slowly.

Psychological Pricing   Retailers often employ price in a psychological manner. They appeal to shoppers' preferences and emotions, instead of relying on more rational factors to sell merchandise, such as quality, ease of operation, brand name, and durability. They attempt to "influence buying decisions by setting prices that are emotionally pleasing to buyers."[8]

Examples of **psychological pricing** include odd or even pricing, prestige pricing, and promotional pricing techniques such as leader pricing and comparative pricing (discussed in a later section). In essence, even price lining can be considered a form of psychological pricing. The price range and price points decided on are thought to be satisfying and attractive to prospective customers. Moreover, the differences promoted among the various price lines may be more apparent than real.

Some merchants use odd pricing in an attempt to influence consumers' buying decisions.

Courtesy Vons Grocery Co., Los Angeles, CA

Odd or Even Pricing Some merchants prefer prices that end in even figures like $2.50, $10, and $50. A much more common approach is to use odd-figure selling prices like $1.35, $9.99, and $49.95. If a firm's prices end in odd numbers, it is using **odd pricing.** Merchants who favor prices that end in even figures follow an **even pricing** policy.

Whether a store can sell more of an item at $2.98, $2.99, or $3 is a subject that can be debated endlessly. It is true that some shoppers, when asked how much they paid for an article, will say: "Four dollars and change," when, in reality, they may have paid $4.99 plus the sales tax. Studies of price endings have often proved inconclusive, and marketers stress the need for more and better research.[9] According to one interesting tabulation of prices for products advertised by super-markets in 23 metropolitan areas, 9 was the digit most frequently found in price endings.[10] This situation may still hold true today, at least in food retailing.

Prestige Pricing Retail companies that seek to project a high-quality image often adhere to a **prestige pricing** approach. Merchandise is priced to sell above the market in order to appeal to status-conscious shoppers and quality seekers. Often, the stores are located in better areas and are tastefully furnished and decorated. Retailers who use prestige pricing avoid odd price endings. They would prefer to sell an article at $90 rather than at $89.99.

Unit Pricing   During the 1960s, some supermarket chains began to experiment with **unit pricing.** They put up shelf tickets ("shelf talkers") that displayed not only the prices of items, but also the cost per pound, quart, or other unit of measurement. This enabled shoppers to compare packages of differing sizes and weights and choose the best buys. By the early 1970s, Massachusets, Connecticut, Maryland, and several other states had enacted legislation requiring supermarkets to institute unit pricing. Even though its installation was costly, supermarket managements soon agreed that the concept was of considerable value to consumers.[11] A substantial percentage of shoppers make profitable use of the information, although usage varies by product class.[12]

One of the curious side effects of unit pricing has been the pointing up of disparities in the pricing methods of some manufacturers. Consumers reasonably expect that medium-, large- and giant-sized packages should prove less costly, ounce for ounce of content, than smaller packages. One researcher probed this very situation by sampling grocery stores in New York State. He studied more than 2,000 brands in 12 popular product categories. Nearly one out of every five brands was found to carry a quantity surcharge. This meant that the unit price of a larger-sized package was actually higher than that of the smaller version, even though the packaging was essentially the same.[13]

In today's supermarkets, unit price information is given on shelf tickets below the product facings. Tomorrow's markets may carry printed lists of such data on the vertical supports of the shelving in each section. Posting such lists can significantly alter the usual purchasing patterns of consumers and result in price savings.[14]

Promotional Pricing Methods   To promote store traffic and increase sales, retailers draw upon a variety of techniques. These range from the perfectly acceptable leader pricing and sale pricing methods to more questionable, even illegal, practices.

Leader Pricing   A popular promotional technique designed to attract large numbers of consumers to a store is **leader pricing.** It is based on the theory that once the premises are crowded salespeople and interior displays can induce many shoppers to purchase additional merchandise. The retailer selects one or more leader items from inventory for the promotion. Usually these are popular articles, often branded, the customary prices of which are well known to consumers. A leader is advertised at a reduced price with the retailer taking only a short markup. Consumers readily perceive the offer as a bargain. Highly promotional discount, supermarket, and drug chains advertise leader items almost continuously.

Loss Leader Pricing A variant of leader pricing, this method is open to serious question. **Loss leaders** are goods that the firm sells at a loss, that is, below its cost. There are, of course, several legitimate reasons why a retailer may decide to cut prices sharply. The merchant may want to avoid potential losses on perishable products, clear out smoke-damaged inventory, or liquidate the business completely. Reducing selling prices to cost or below can, however, be construed as an unfair tactic by a firm's competitors. Indeed, some states carry laws that prohibit sales below cost or that establish a minimum markup percentage as a floor for retailers. Such legislation, however, has proven difficult to enforce.

Bait Pricing An essentially dishonest business practice occasionally tried by unethical merchants is **bait pricing.** The retailer promotes a popular article at a sharply reduced selling price. Often, the regular price of the item is lowered by 40 to 50 percent, or even more. By dangling the bait before the public, traffic is drawn to the store. Unfortunately for shoppers, the company has no intention of selling the product. Instead, customers are switched to another, more expensive substitute. Hence the often-heard term *bait and switch.* For example, an appliance retailer places a newspaper advertisement announcing a One-Day Sale. The ad will say that famous-brand 19-inch color TVs, regularly sold at $395, will be on sale the next day at only $199. Even the shoppers who arrive at the store precisely at opening time are told: "We sold out last night." Or "We have only two floor models left, but they need repair." The salesperson then attempts to sell the disappointed shopper a more expensive set, extolling its virtues and all the while criticizing the advertised model. Although retailers who employ deceptive methods leave themselves open to prosecution, they know that it is difficult to prove an intent to deceive.

Reputable companies maintain sufficient stock on hand to service most customers and readily issue rain checks to the rest.

Comparative Pricing Some retailers place signs in their windows or store interiors that advise shoppers to: "Compare our prices with those of our competitors." By itself, this kind of statement is relatively innocuous and acceptable to consumers. However, the **comparative pricing** technique can be used to mislead consumers. For example, a menswear retailer attaches a tag to a sport jacket that reads: "Our competitors sell this for $155; our price is $85." In this case, there may be some cause for concern for the shopper. The statement may be true; then again, it may not be.

In an occasional flagrant violation, no mention is made of the competition. Instead, the garment carries a price tag that shows two or even three retail prices. All but the last is crossed out; the final entry is, obviously, the current selling price. This leads consumers to believe that the merchandise represents an exceptional buy. It appears to have been marked down several times. Some unscrupulous merchants employ this technique to promote sales. Both the original and marked down prices are fictitious.

Trade-ins   A typewriter store advertises that it will allow you $50 on your twenty-year-old portable toward the purchase of a new electric machine. The automotive department in a discount store offers you $5 each for your old snow tires if you buy a new pair. A car dealer happily quotes a substantial trade-in price on your 1977 Chevrolet providing you order the latest model Oldsmobile. These and similar **trade-in allowances** are commonplace in retailing. The technique appeals to consumers. Shoppers benefit by purchasing goods, in effect, at reduced prices. Trade-ins have much the same effect as discounts. Although generally adjudged an acceptable method of promotion, abuses do occur. The consumer is cautioned to be wary of unwarranted trade-in allowances.

Markups   Buying and selling merchandise are the two core functions in store retailing. No retail firm can survive by offering goods for sale at their cost prices. How much above cost the selling price of an article should be depends on a variety of factors, as you have already seen. Whatever the excess over the cost charged to consumers, that amount must cover some fraction of the costs of operating the business. It must also earn a bit of profit.

As an illustration, the owner of a jewelry boutique purchases six pairs of gold leaf earrings from a vendor. Delivered cost is $85 per pair. As is common practice with many merchants, the proprietor decides to **keystone** the earrings. Keystoning means to set a selling price by doubling the cost of merchandise. The owner adds on another $85 to cost and displays the earrings in the showcase at a retail price of $170 a pair. The $85 earned when the earrings are sold is the **markup** on the item. The markup is the difference between the cost of an article and what it is sold for. Because this amount is marked on to the original cost, some retailers use the term **markon** instead. Markon is commonly used by manufacturers in pricing their goods. Markup and markon, however, mean essentially the same thing. Throughout this book, we will use *markup*.

Markups are valuable in planning and controlling the retail operation and in buying merchandise for resale.[15] Buyers need to know how much they should pay for the goods they purchase—and at what prices to sell them to cover expenses and generate desired profits. Working with markups helps the retailer maintain adequate sales volume and increase store profitability.[16]

Individual Markups In the earrings example, we saw that a markup of $85 was added to the cost to establish the retail selling price. We can easily translate this thinking into a useful basic formula:

$$\text{Cost} + \text{Markup} = \text{Retail price}$$

Or more simply:

$$C + MU = RP$$

From this basic formula, we can derive two other handy equations simply by shifting around the terms. As you may recall from elementary algebra, when shifting a term from one side of the equation to the other (around the equal sign), you change the signs in front of them. A *plus* becomes a *minus,* and vice versa.

1. How to calculate the *cost,* when both the markup and the retail price are known:

$$C = RP - MU$$

2. How to calculate the *markup,* when both cost and retail prices are given:

$$MU = RP - C$$

Now, practice using these formulas by working through the following two problems:

1. A home furnishings store offers consumers an end table at a price of $270. The retailer has placed a markup of $115 on the article. What was the store's cost for the table?

Solution:

$$
\begin{aligned}
C &= RP - MU \\
&= \$270 - \$115 \\
&= \$155
\end{aligned}
$$

2. A menswear department sells a line of wallets at a unit price of $22. Delivered cost to the store per wallet was $10.45. What markup did the buyer place on the wallets?

Solution:

$$
\begin{aligned}
MU &= RP - C \\
&= \$22 - \$10.45 \\
&= \$11.55
\end{aligned}
$$

Markup Percentages Thus far, markups have been expressed in dollars and cents. We can also express markups as percentages of either cost or retail price. Retailers can readily translate these percentages into dollars-and-cents figures for pricing and other decisions.

We calculate markup as a percentage of cost by dividing the amount of markup dollars by the cost and then multiplying the result by 100 percent:

$$MU\% \text{ on cost} = \frac{MU \ \$}{Cost} \times 100\%$$

In the earrings example given earlier, we would compute the markup percentage on cost in this manner:

$$MU\% \text{ on cost} = \frac{\$85}{\$85} \times 100\%$$
$$= 1 \times 100\%$$
$$= 100\%$$

In much the same fashion, markup percentages on retail are worked up by substituting the retail price in the fraction's denominator:

$$MU\% \text{ on retail} = \frac{MU \ \$}{Retail} \times 100\%$$
$$= \frac{\$85}{\$170} \times 100\%$$
$$= 50\%$$

Some retailers compute their markups on a cost basis. This is especially true of many small independents as well as firms that require some degree of production/manufacturing in their operation. Bakeries, upholstery shops, and appliance repair stores are examples. Like manufacturers, these retailers think in terms of the costs of materials and labor. To these costs, they add some percentage for overhead and profit. However, department stores, chain store organizations, discount houses, and many other retailers prefer a markup structure based on retail prices. This approach is necessary when the retail method of inventory valuation is followed.

Retailers can readily convert retail markup percentages to their cost equivalents and vice versa with the aid of conversion tables such as the abbreviated one shown in Table 15.1. If you refer to the table now, you will note that a 25% markup at retail equals a 33.3 percent markup on cost. Note, too, that a 300% markup on cost represents only a 75 percent markup at retail. As you see, retail markups may approach but can never quite reach 100 percent.

To take an extreme, though implausible, situation, suppose that a store owner were fortunate enough to find an item that costs only $1 and yet is readily salable at $100. On this article, the retail markup would work out to 99 percent, as you can see below:

$$MU\% = \frac{\$99}{\$100} \times 100\%$$
$$= 99\%$$

Table 15.1
Markup equivalents at retail and cost

Markup at Retail	Markup at Cost	Markup at Retail	Markup at Cost
10.0%	11.1%	46.0%	85.2%
15.0	17.6	47.0	88.7
20.0	25.0	48.0	92.3
25.0	33.3	49.0	96.1
30.0	42.9	50.0	100.0
35.0	53.8	55.0	122.2
36.0	56.3	60.0	150.0
37.0	58.7	65.0	185.7
38.0	61.3	70.0	233.3
39.0	63.9	75.0	300.0
40.0	66.7	80.0	400.0
41.0	69.5	85.0	566.7
42.0	72.4	90.0	900.0
43.0	75.4	95.0	1,900.0
44.0	78.6	99.0	9,900.0
45.0	81.8	99.9	99,900.0

Working with Both Percentages and Dollars-and-Cents Figures

Retailers must continually set retail selling prices for the merchandise they purchase throughout the year. They generally have an idea of the overall markup percentage they need to run a profitable store. They can readily work out selling prices by using the basic formula then converting the percentage to a dollars-and-cents figure. The illustration below shows how this is done:

Two partners operate a ski shop at a mountain resort in Colorado. They purchase a dozen pairs of skis at a cost per pair of $155. To maintain a quality image, the owners usually mark up all merchandise 55% on retail.

Here is their procedure for determining the retail price:

1. *Using the formula $RP = C + MU$, they fill in the known facts as shown below:*

$$RP = C + MU$$
$$= \$155 + 55\%$$

2. *The retail price of an item is equal to its cost plus the markup taken. The retail price itself represents 100% of the total. In this case, since the desired markup is 55% of the total, the cost price must be equivalent to 100% minus 55% of the retail, or 45%.*

Markups on supermarket merchandise lines vary considerably.

Courtesy D&W Food Centers, Inc., Grandville, MI

3. *Rewriting the equation above in accordance with this thinking, it turns out like this:*

$$RP \ (or \ 100\%) = \$155 \ (or \ 45\%) + 55\%$$

4. *Knowing that $155 represents 45% of the retail price, we can now determine what the retail should be. A simple approach is to create a new equation in which* x *represents the unknown retail price.*

Solution:

$$0.45\,x = \$155$$
$$45\,x = \$15,500$$
$$x = \$344.44$$

Note that we can work out this problem without resorting to algebra at all. Knowing both the cost and the cost percentage, we can divide the former by the latter, as follows:

$$\frac{\$155}{0.45} = \$344.44$$

5. *By subtracting the cost ($155) from the retail price ($344.14), we learn that the markup earned will be $189.44.*

6. However, $344.44 appears to be an unusual selling price. The partners decide to round off this odd figure by setting a retail price of $350 on the skis.

Average Markup Many retailers do not apply the same markup percentage to all products. Depending on the type of goods, some are marked up higher than others and some lower. For example, markups on merchandise lines in supermarkets vary considerably. Canned goods may carry a relatively low markup of 18 or 20 percent. Nonfood items such as housewares, women's hosiery, and men's shirts may be marked up as much as 40 to 50 percent. Calculating the **average markup** is particularly important because inventory is continually being replenished, often at different costs, and sold at the same or at different prices. Retailers can determine their average markups on merchandise lines, classifications, price lines, additional purchases, and so on.

Here is an illustration of the markup averaging procedure:

A men's furnishings department offers neckties at two different price points: $7.50 and $12. The department's buyer purchases the higher-priced neckties from suppliers A, B, and C. Given the following facts, let us calculate the average markup on the $12 line during the month of March:

Source	Number of Units	Total Cost
On hand March 1	85	$560
Expected from A	36	227
Expected from B	24	152
Expected from C	60	400

Solution:
1. Complete the table above, adding the computed retail value:

Source	Number of Units	Total Cost	Total Retail
On hand March 1	85	$ 560	$1,020
From A	36	227	432
From B	24	152	288
From C	60	400	720
Totals:	205	$1,339	$2,460

2. Total the markup dollars:

$$MU = R - C$$
$$= \$2,460 - \$1,339$$
$$= \$1,121$$

3. *Calculate the average markup percentage:*

$$Average\ MU = \frac{MU\ \$}{Retail} \times 100\%$$

$$= \frac{\$1,121}{\$2,460} \times 100\%$$

$$= 45.6\%$$

Here is another common type of average markup problem:

A women's accessories department is divided into sections A, B, and C. Goods in each section carry differing markups: A—38.5%, B—41%, and C—44%. The inventory in Section A totals $5,500 at retail; Section B carries $7,000 at retail; merchandise in Section C is valued at $4,000 at retail. Assuming that no additional orders will be received during the period, calculate the average markup for the department:

Solution:

Lay out the problem in table form as below, entering all known data. Use question marks where information is missing.

Section	Cost of Goods	Total Retail	Markup Dollars	Markup Percent
A	?	$5,500	?	38.5%
B	?	7,000	?	41
C	?	4,000	?	44
Totals	?	$16,500	?	?

Obviously, we cannot simply total the three markup percentages given to obtain an average because sections A, B, and C each stock different amounts of inventory. Just as obviously, if we determine the cost of goods section by section, we can ascertain the markup dollars involved. We can then total the columns and determine the average markup for the department.

To illustrate, let us consider Section A. Since the markup percentage here is 38.5 percent, the cost of goods in the section must amount to 100 − 38.5 percent, or 61.5 percent of the retail value. This works out to $3,382.50. By doing the same with the other sections, we find the cost valuations: Section B—$4,130; Section C—$2,240. We then subtract each section's cost from its retail value to obtain the markup in dollars. Finally, we enter all figures into the table, do the necessary computations, and end up with the following results:

Section	Cost of Goods	Total Retail	Markup Dollars	Markup Percent
A	$3,382.50	$ 5,500	$2,117.50	38.5%
B	4,130	7,000	2,870	41
C	2,240	4,000	1,760	44
Totals	$9,752.50	$16,500	$6,747.50	?

To arrive at the desired average markup (the last remaining question mark), proceed in this manner:

$$Average\ MU\% = \frac{MU\ \$}{Retail} \times 100\%$$

$$= \frac{\$\ 6,747.50}{\$16,500} \times 100\%$$

$$= 40.9\%$$

Cumulative Markup At times, retailers will want to determine the markup percentage on all merchandise handled in the store or department during a particular period. This **cumulative markup** actually represents the sum total of all markups placed on individual articles.

By way of illustration, consider the notions department in a large variety store.

The department's BOM inventory is priced to retail at $58,000. Total merchandise costs amount to $33,930. During the month, new purchases were received at a cost of $19,500; these goods were marked up to retail at $34,200. Delivery charges were an additional $340. What is the notion department's cumulative markup for the month?

Solution:

	Cost	Retail	MU $
BOM inventory	$33,930	$58,000	$24,070
Purchases	19,500	34,200	14,700
Freight charges	340	—	—
All stock handled	$53,770	$92,200	$38,770*

$$Cumulative\ MU\% = \frac{MU\ \$}{Retail} \times 100\%$$

$$= \frac{\$38,430}{\$92,200} \times 100\%$$

$$= 41.7\%$$

---

* Note that $340 goes to defray the freight charges paid, resulting in $38,430 in markup dollars.

Initial Markup   Most companies plan their merchandise inventories well in advance of each season. Thorough planners need more than a generalized understanding that markups must cover the cost of goods and contribute toward both overhead and profits. They realize that markups initially set on products when they first arrive will be affected (reduced) by various operating factors. Markdowns and stock shortages are two such factors. If all pertinent figures have been properly planned, the retailer will have specified, in writing, projected figures for sales, expenses, and reductions for the period. Even the estimated profit will have been planned. These amounts can then be introduced into a formula to calculate the **initial markup** percentage that should be placed on incoming merchandise. The formula appears below:

$$\text{Initial MU\%} = \frac{\text{Expenses} + \text{Profit} + \text{Reductions}}{\text{Net sales} + \text{Reductions}} \times 100\%$$

Consider the following details planned for a women's sportswear store:

Planned Figures		Expressed as Percentages of Net Sales
Net sales	$277,000	100.0%
Expenses	93,350	33.7
Profits	18,800	6.8
Reductions:		
Markdowns	10,000	3.6
Employee discounts	4,150	1.5
Stock shortages	2,500	0.9

Note that the reductions listed include markdowns, employee discounts, and stock shortages (shrinkage). These total 6.0 percent of net sales, or $16,650. Using the formula, we determine the initial markup percentage:

$$\begin{aligned}
\text{Initial MU\%} &= \frac{\text{Expenses} + \text{Profit} + \text{Reductions}}{\text{Net sales} + \text{Reductions}} \times 100\% \\
&= \frac{\$93,350 + \$18,800 + \$16,650}{\$277,000 + \$16,650} \times 100\% \\
&= \frac{\$128,800}{\$293,650} \times 100\% \\
&= 43.9\%
\end{aligned}$$

In light of this planning, the proprietor should place a 43.9 percent initial markup on all merchandise brought in. Of course, suggested prices derived from all markup calculations need to be rounded out so that they are appropriate as retail selling prices.

If percentages of sales have been calculated for each category, these may be used directly in the same formula to compute the desired initial markup:

$$Initial\ MU\% = \frac{Expenses + Profit + Reductions}{Net\ sales + Reductions} \times 100\%$$

$$= \frac{33.7 + 6.8 + 6.0}{100.0 + 6.0} \times 100\%$$

$$= \frac{46.5}{106.0} \times 100\%$$

$$= 43.9\%$$

Maintained Markup In planning for their departments or stores, buyers take into consideration important factors that affect the operating statement by working out the initial markup to be placed on incoming goods. In effect, however, that percentage is a goal-oriented guesstimate. The retailer knows that the markup percentage finally realized, or maintained, for the selling period will deviate from the planned figure. For this reason, the initial markup may be set a bit higher than planned figures would indicate to allow for additional reductions. The **maintained markup** can be defined as net sales less the gross cost of goods sold during the period:

$$Maintained\ MU = Net\ sales - Gross\ C.O.G.\ sold$$

Computing the maintained markup percentage is similar to calculating other types of markup percentages:

$$Maintained\ MU\% = \frac{MU\ \$}{Retail} \times 100\%$$

Note that the word *retail* in the fraction's denominator stands for net sales, rather than retail price. To illustrate the computation, let us take this situation:

The stationery department in the flagship store of a department store chain records $230,000 in net sales for the month. The gross cost of goods sold amounted to $126,000.

1. *Maintained MU* $= Net\ sales - Gross\ C.O.G.\ sold$
   $= \$230,000 - \$126,000$
   $= \$104,000$

$$2.\ \textit{Maintained MU\%} = \frac{MU\ \$}{Retail} \times 100\%$$

$$= \frac{\$104,000}{\$230,000} \times 100\%$$

$$= 45.2\%$$

Maintained Markup and Gross Margin

Frequently, firms using the retail method regard the *cost of goods* as being comprised of only two factors: the gross total of all invoices paid and freight charges paid. Cash discounts earned and alteration/workroom costs are left out. To arrive at a true gross margin figure, these omissions must be taken into account.

Earlier, we defined maintained markup as Net sales − Gross C.O.G. sold. Thus, the maintained markup only approximates the earned gross margin. Taking cash discounts for early payment of bills reduces the retailer's cost of goods, increasing gross margin. Some stores maintain a workroom for alterations, repairs, or refinishing. These services are sometimes offered free to shoppers. More often than not, however, the retailer charges modest fees. Workroom costs over and above what has been collected from customers increase the cost-of-goods amount and lower the gross margin.

To arrive at the true gross margin earned, we can use the following formulas:

Gross margin = Net sales − Gross C.O.G. sold
+ Cash discounts − Net workroom cost

Or:

Gross margin = Maintained markup + Cash discounts
− Net workroom cost

Or:

Gross margin = Net sales − Actual C.O.G. sold

Markdowns

To mark down an article of merchandise means to reduce its selling price. The retailer may mark down an item only once, say from $24.95 to $15.95. Or two or more markdowns may be taken over time until the item is sold. A **markdown,** then, is a reduction in the selling price of merchandise.

Merchants are often reluctant to take markdowns because they will realize fewer gross margin dollars. Generally, retailers try to hold down the percentage of markdowns on sales to a low level. Yet most understand that markdowns are essential to price administration.

Markdowns may be taken as a sales promotion to bring customers into the store—or as a result of the retail buyer's error or other factors outside of the buyer's control.

Gary Csuk

Knowledgeable executives estimate these percentages long in advance of each season and build them into their merchandise planning.

Markdowns are often taken for promotional purposes, for example, to attract more shoppers or increase revenues. In these situations, the firm may lower prices on one or a few popular items, an entire classification, or all merchandise. However, most markdowns are taken for other reasons.

Reasons for Taking Markdowns

Most markdowns can be attributed to (1) buying and selling errors; (2) their use for clearing out shopworn goods, meeting competition, and so on; and (3) sales promotion.[17] An even simpler alternate breakdown of the factors behind markdowns might be: (1) those largely outside the buyer's control and (2) those attributed directly to the buyer. The second category might include buyer inexperience, poor planning and forecasting techniques, insufficient knowledge of competitive offerings, inattention to trends, and so on.

Retailers may be compelled to reduce prices because of a downturn in the economy or because of local events that affect consumer purchasing power in the store's trading area. The closing of a large plant and subsequent loss of hundreds of jobs is an example. Adverse or inclement weather might be another reason. Still other possibilities include the initial overpricing of goods, poor stockkeeping practices, a weak inventory control system, poorly trained employees, and improper handling of merchandise by shoppers. In many cases, however, the buyer can effect improvements in pricing procedures, merchandise rotation, and sales personnel. Through diligent effort, the ratio of markdowns to sales can be reduced in the long run.

Buyer inefficiency may be responsible for a large proportion of the markdowns taken. Among the more common problems are:

1. Overzealousness: not buying according to plan, playing hunches, relying inordinately on intuition, over-ordering, and so on.
2. Failure to monitor stock movement closely: delay in recognizing fast- and slow-moving items and taking appropriate action.
3. Poor preparation: seldom visiting competitive outlets, not keeping up with trends by reading trade publications regularly, inattention to need-list information or records from the customer service department, and the like.
4. Poor timing: ordering heavily late in the season or bringing in goods long in advance of the season.
5. Stocking the department/store with too many classifications or in too much depth.
6. Errors of judgment in merchandise selection: buying the wrong sizes, colors, materials, fabrics, brands, and other selection factors.

Calculating Markdown Percentages

Retailers use markdown percentages in two ways: (1) to compute markdowns on individual items so that price reductions may be properly entered into the merchandise accounting procedure and (2) to determine the relationship of total markdowns to sales for a particular period.

Markdowns on Individual Items If, for example, an article that sells regularly for $20 is reduced to $15, a shopper would normally regard the $5 saved as representing a 25 percent discount off the original retail. Yet where the retail method of accounting is used, the markdown percentage is computed in a different manner. Under this method, the firm keeps track of its inventory by its retail value. Additional markups on the same item are entirely possible. In calculating the markdown percentage, the numerator of the fraction is the difference between original and new selling prices. However, the latest, or marked down, price becomes the denominator. This is shown below:

$$MD\% = \frac{MD\ \$}{Retail} \times 100\%$$

$$= \frac{\$20 - \$15}{\$15} \times 100\%$$

$$= 33.3\%$$

Total Markdowns as a Percentage of Sales In merchandise planning, markdowns must be taken into account along with markups, discounts, and other factors that affect operating results. Such elements are easily handled when expressed as percentages of sales. Deviations from planned figures can be noted from one season or year to the next. Management action can then be taken to correct deficiencies.

Assume, for example, that a department shows sales of $350,000 for the year. It has recorded $23,000 in markdowns. The markdown ratio, then, is approximately 6.6 percent. Whether this is too high, too low, or about right depends on what is considered typical for this kind of department or whether the figure represents an improvement over last year or a worsening of the situation.

Other Considerations How much to reduce selling prices is a decision retailers learn to make through trial and error. Intuition comes into play as much as judgment and experience. Naturally, the size of a markdown must be large enough to move out the merchandise within a reasonable period. If the markdown, however, is bigger than necessary, more gross profit is lost. Reducing the price of $85 radios to $79.95 may not accelerate sales enough to readily clear out stock, even though customers would save more than $5 per sale. The difference of a few dollars may not mean much when goods are high priced. Yet a price reduction of only 40 cents on a can of household cleanser, say from $1.39 to 99 cents, may well double or even triple the item's normal rate of sale.

Frequency and timing are two other important considerations. Some retail companies will mark merchandise down only two or three times during the year. Favored times are the post-Christmas holidays and before summer begins. Discount houses and many other stores promote price reductions year round. Some retailers avoid markdowns entirely, preferring to maintain a nonpromotional, high-level store image. Merchants who sell apparel and other fashion goods may mark down individual articles at any time of year, as needs dictate. Another approach is an automatic markdown policy: merchandise that has been in the selling stock for more than two or three weeks is automatically lowered in price by a set percentage. The new prices may be further reduced after another few weeks have gone by.

Markdowns on seasonal goods may be taken early in the season to leave room for additional markdowns that may be needed. Or they can be taken late in the season to clear out the inventory and make room for the next season's merchandise. A markdown may also be cancelled; when this is done, the previous retail price is restored.

Understanding Discounts A **discount** is a reduction from the selling, or list, price of merchandise. Discounts play a significant role in the pricing structure of our economy. Manufacturers set up trade discount arrangements for their products. Thus, channel members who help move the goods out to customers know their costs and are able to plan their own desired markups. Wholesalers and retailers alike need an understanding of discounts to administer their prices. Retailers often give discounts on merchandise to their employees and customers. Buyers need to know about both trade and quantity discounts and how to lower their costs by taking advantage of cash discounts and other allowances that may be available.

Trade Discounts　　**Trade discounts** are price reductions made available to channel members for performing those activities expected of them.

By way of illustration, consider the electrical goods distributor who orders 100 gross of 6-foot extension cords from a manufacturer. These electric extension cords are to be sold in hardware and variety stores at a suggested price to the consumer of $2.50 per unit. They come packaged in folding cartons suitable for counter-top display. Each carton contains three dozen cords. An attractive diecut sign is also included in the carton.

In the sales literature distributed by the producer to wholesalers across the country, a photograph of the display carton and its sign is shown. Listed, too, is the price: $90 per carton, less 42 percent, less 15 percent.

Here is how to interpret the pricing structure for this item:

Selling price ($2.50/unit $\times$ 36 pieces) = $90.00
Retailer's gross markup (@ 42%)　　 = $\underline{\ 37.80}$
　　Retailer pays wholesale price of:　　$52.20
Wholesaler's markup (@ 15%)　　 = $\underline{\ \ 7.33}$
　　Wholesaler pays manufacturer:　　$44.37

Note that if the manufacturer works through an agent, who receives a 5 percent commission for securing orders from wholesalers, the manufacturer will receive $44.37 *less 5 percent,* or $42.15, for each carton sold.

Cash Discounts　　As a general rule, most companies encourage the prompt payment of their receivables by offering **cash discounts.** Customers who pay their bills early are entitled to deduct a small, stated percentage of the amount they owe.

Assume, for example, that a home furnishings retailer purchases 10 table lamps at a total cost of $465. The invoice, dated April 5, shows the full amount the firm owes: $465. Terms on the invoice may read as follows: 2/10, net 30. The percentage indicated, *2 percent,* is the cash discount offered. The figure 10 represents the number of days from the date of the invoice that constitute the discount period. *If* the store pays before April 15, 2 percent may be deducted from the face amount of the bill. Thus, the retailer sends out a check for $455.70 instead of $465, retaining the difference of $9.30. If the invoice is paid after the expiration of the 10-day period, the net, or full, amount must be paid. Actually, *net* means free of all deductions. In any event, the supplier expects payment within 30 days of the invoice date. If the bill has not been paid by May 5, the outstanding amount is held to be overdue.

Retailers should take advantage of every cash discount, if possible. While the amount saved on a single invoice may not come to more than a few dollars, a firm that purchases $100,000 worth of merchandise over the year can easily earn from $2,000 to $5,000 in cash discounts. Taking these discounts lowers the cost of goods sold and, assuming that operating costs are held constant, substantially increases the net profits before taxes.

Quantity Discounts   A manufacturer of room air conditioners quotes retailers a price of $235 for a specific model. However, on orders placed for 10 or more units at one time, a **quantity discount** of 5 percent off invoice is available. Ordinarily, the retail firm would be billed for $2,350 for the 10 units—less, of course, any cash discount that is offered. By itself, the 5 percent quantity discount reduces the invoice total by $117.50, to $2,232.50.

This one-shot discount, involving a single large order, is called a **noncumulative quantity discount.** The discounted amount is deducted only from the one invoice. Because they save on billing and delivery costs, suppliers are able to justify lowering their regular, or list, prices. These savings are passed on to their customers. Suppliers also extend quantity discounts to encourage retail companies to buy from them, rather than from competitors. The **cumulative quantity discount** is granted to buyers for purchasing goods in quantity over time. For example, a manufacturer of boys' corduroy pants may offer a cumulative discount of 6 percent if purchases during the year amount to $2,000 or more. This encourages continued patronage by the retail accounts. All orders are then billed at their regular prices until the $2,000 figure is reached. At that point, the 6 percent discount is applied retroactively.

Sellers cannot readily justify granting cumulative discounts by claims of cost savings on billing and delivery. Consequently, they may be open to legal problems because of federal legislation such as the Robinson-Patman Act.

Retailers frequently grant noncumulative discounts to their customers who buy in quantity at one time.

Seasonal Discounts   Producers of seasonal goods often attempt to keep both machines and employees busy throughout the year by offering their customers

seasonal discounts. Garden furniture, ski and other winter sports equipment, bathing suits, and outerwear are a few examples of such products. Manufacturers may extend a discount of from 5 to 10 percent, and sometimes more, to companies that place orders in advance of the season. This type of offer is often labeled an **early-bird discount.** To build up inventory in anticipation of peak sales in December, for example, toy manufacturers begin producing quantities of goods early in the year. By midsummer, their warehouses may be bulging with accumulated stock. By encouraging distributors to buy early and advantageously (at a considerable savings), toy producers not only relieve the congestion in their warehouses but improve their cash positions as well.

Retailers, too, use seasonal discounts. Pre-holiday sales events and early-bird dinners are examples.

Special-Purpose Discounts

Introductory discounts are popular with manufacturers, wholesalers, and retailers alike. Promotional in nature, these discounts are deductions from the regular prices of articles of merchandise. They are offered to induce consumers (or organizations) to try new items. Retailers give **employee discounts** to their personnel on merchandise they buy from the store. **Customer discounts** may be offered to special groups: neighboring merchants, members of religious orders, students from local high schools or colleges (on displaying their ID cards), senior citizens, charities, and so on.

Allowances

While not discounts in the narrow sense of the word, **allowances,** such as those made for promotional purposes, have the force of reducing buying costs. Manufacturers, for example, often offer cooperative advertising allowances to encourage retail concerns to promote their products. They may contribute as much as 50 percent or more of the advertising expenses incurred by the retailer. Other approaches are also common: sending along one carton free of charge with every dozen cartons ordered, offering free point-of-purchase materials and displays, providing stores with demonstrators, giving an advertising allowance with merchandise orders, and so on.

Legal Considerations

Legislation aimed at fostering a free, competitive economy is in place at both state and national levels. Many states, for example, have laws against predatory pricing practices. Retailers are deterred from selling merchandise below cost if it is done to injure competition. Unfair trade practices laws generally place a floor under retail prices, mandating that goods must be sold at a small, specified markup above cost.

It is illegal for business organizations to conspire to fix prices. Instances of such collusion have not been confined to the manufacturing sector. In the mid-1970s, for example, several fashionable department stores in the New York metropolitan area were accused of conspiring to fix prices by the Federal Trade Commission.

Resale Price Maintenance For more than 40 years, retail prices in many states were governed by **fair trade laws.** Under such legislation, manufacturers could dictate the prices at which their products were to be sold by signing resale price maintenance agreements with retailers. Some states went even further by passing *nonsigner clauses.* If one retailer in the state signed up, then all other retailers in that state who offered the same merchandise were legally bound to follow the suggested prices. This was in apparent contradiction with the thrust of federal legislation such as the Sherman and Federal Trade Commission Acts. Yet even the federal government endorsed the fair trade concept in both the Miller-Tydings Act and the McGuire Act. Congress finally abandoned this tack in the mid-1970s, prohibiting fair trade in interstate commerce.

Pertinent Federal Legislation In Chapter 3, you learned about consumer protection laws and other aspects of the legal environment within which the retailer must operate. At this point, it might be helpful to review briefly the major legislation that affects pricing and other financial aspects of business operation:

The Sherman Antitrust Act (1890) Passed by Congress in reaction to the excessive power and abuses of the giant trusts, this was the federal government's first major step toward endorsement of the free enterprise system. A broadly drawn antimonopoly law, the Sherman Act held that contracts, combinations, trusts, and conspiracies in restraint of trade were illegal.

The Clayton Act (1914) This was designed to amend and strengthen the Sherman Act. It banned discrimination in prices among buyers if this lessens competition. It also prohibited the use of *tying contracts.* These were used by suppliers to force buyers to purchase additional, unwanted goods along with the products they originally wanted.

The Federal Trade Commission Act (1914) This law declared that competitive methods aimed at injuring competitors were illegal. In addition, it established the Federal Trade Commission, an agency empowered to oversee trade practices. Subsequent legislation, enacted in more recent years, further strengthened the government's antimonopolistic role. Mergers, for example, must be approved by the FTC. Companies considering such moves must inform the government of their intent. The

FTC monitors the economic environment with care and is ready and willing to prosecute offenders.

The Robinson-Patman Act (1936) This is probably the most important piece of federal legislation to affect pricing. Its origins lie in the rapid expansion of chain store organizations during the 1920s. Its intent was to curtail the growing number of abuses by large chains. It sought to abolish discriminatory pricing practices in interstate commerce. Declared unlawful were attempts by suppliers to charge buyers different prices for goods of like grade and quality, where such discrimination would substantially lessen or injure competition. It barred the selective use of promotional allowances. These must be available to all buyers on proportionately equal terms. Quantity discounts not justified by cost considerations or needed to meet competition were deemed illegal. It prohibited the granting of brokerage allowances where no real brokerage activities were conducted. And, for the first time, it made it unlawful for buyers to accept a discriminatory price.[18]

Summary   Pricing is an essential component of the retailer's product and services mix. The price of an article or service is its exchange value in terms of money. Many factors influence pricing decisions. Besides the cost of goods, there are other cost considerations: selling and other promotional expenses, losses due to shoplifting and employee pilferage, and so on. Retail firms also take other aspects into account: the state of the economy, competition, the legal environment, their philosophy of management, and the characteristics of the merchandise itself.

Before setting prices, modern retail companies establish clear-cut pricing objectives. Although such objectives vary widely, some of the more popular are to produce store traffic, increase sales, get rid of slow-moving merchandise, and attract shoppers from competitors. Depending on their primary orientation, retailers may set prices at, above, or below those in the marketplace.

New retail firms need to establish some major pricing policies at the outset. They must decide whether to follow variable or fixed pricing, end their selling prices with odd- or even-numbered digits, and use price lining for some goods. Established retailers make expert use of leader pricing and other promotional pricing techniques.

For effective merchandise management, retailers require a good working knowledge of markups. The markup on an item is the difference between its cost and its selling price. Markups may be expressed in terms of dollars and cents or as percentages of cost or retail prices. Retailers need some familiarity with the methods of calculating and applying markups of different types. Examples include individual, average, cumulative, initial, and maintained markups.

Markdowns are reductions in the selling price of goods. An item may be marked down once, twice, or even more often. Store merchants take markdowns to clear out shopworn goods, reduce inventory, increase sales, meet competition's prices, and for promotional purposes.

A discount is a deduction from the selling price of something. Trade discounts are extended to channel members to compensate them for performing their services. Cash discounts are offered to encourage the prompt payment of bills. Firms that buy merchandise in large quantities may earn quantity discounts. Also popular in retailing are seasonal discounts and such special-purpose types as introductory, employee, and customer discounts.

Many states have outlawed predatory pricing tactics. State legislation often prevents retail companies from selling merchandise below cost by establishing price floors. It is also illegal for companies to conspire to fix prices. Since the Sherman Antitrust Act of 1890, the thrust of federal legislation has been against monopolies and in favor of free enterprise and competition. Under the law, firms shall not employ methods aimed at injuring competitors.

Key Terms

price-quality relationship	average markup
price elasticity	cumulative markup
markup	initial markup
fixed pricing	maintained markup
variable pricing	markdown
price lining	discount
price points	trade discount
psychological pricing	cash discount
odd (even) pricing	quantity discount
prestige pricing	noncumulative quantity discount
unit pricing	cumulative quantity discount
leader pricing	seasonal discount
loss leader	early-bird discount
bait pricing	introductory discount
comparative pricing	employee discount
trade-in allowances	customer discount
keystone	allowances
markup (markon)	fair trade laws

Review Questions

1. What are some of the cost factors in retailing that influence price policies?

2. In an above-average income area, three partners launch a large store in which they plan to sell rugs and floor coverings. The owners decide to use a prestige pricing approach. Do you think they have made a wise decision? Why or why not?

3. Identify and briefly describe four different pricing policies retail companies can establish.

4. Comment on the usefulness of price lining to the retailer. Is this of benefit to shoppers? Explain your answer.

5. What is meant by psychological pricing? Give examples.

6. Contrast leader pricing with comparative pricing.

7. Would you propose a one-price policy for a retailer of antique furniture? Why or why not? Give reasons for your decision.

8. Under what conditions might selling merchandise below cost be justified?

9. Suggest six products that might be suitable for trade-in promotions.

10. A manufacturer of snack trays offers a large hardware retailer trade discounts of 40 and 15 if orders are placed in six dozen lots. The trays retail at $12 each. Provided the store orders 72 at a time, what will the cost per unit come to?

11. A line of stemware in the glassware section carries a markup on cost of 68.5 percent. What is the line's equivalent markup on retail?

12. A liquor store offers its customers a brand of imported cognac on sale at $16 a quart. This price gives the merchant a markup on retail of $4. What is the markup percent that has been placed on the item, both at retail and at cost?

13. The notions department in a departmentized specialty store has the following *planned* figures for the spring/summer season: Net sales—$132,000, profits—$8,500, expenses—$46,700, markdowns—$4,900, employee discounts—$3,500,

stock shortages—$1,100. Calculate the initial markup percentage that should be used by the department.

14. Name and briefly explain four different kinds of retail discounts.

Discussion Questions

1. Comment on the price-quality relationship and its significance to retail organizations.

2. Some merchants charge as much as they can get for items that are in demand. Is this good business practice? Why or why not?

3. Under what conditions might a sporting goods store deliberately price its merchandise below the market? Above the market?

4. Explain how bait-and-switch tactics might be employed by a home appliances department in a large discount store.

5. Should the identical markup percentage be applied to all items carried by a store? Give reasons for and against.

6. To clear out old merchandise in the toy department after Christmas, the buyer wants to mark down the stock. A choice is open: either mark down the goods a full 25 percent at once or use several successive and shorter markups spaced one or two weeks apart. Which choice would you make? Why? Defend your position.

7. Suggest some steps a buyer of junior sportswear can take to reduce excessive markdowns in the department.

Notes

[1] E. Jerome McCarthy and William D. Perreault, Jr., *Basic Marketing: A Managerial Approach,* 8th ed. (Homewood, Ill.: Richard D. Irwin, 1984), p. 555.

[2] Peter C. Riesz, "Price versus Quality in the Marketplace, 1961–75," *Journal of Retailing* 54 (Winter 1978), pp. 15–28.

[3] Norman D. French, William A. Chance, and John J. Williams, "A Shopping Experiment on Price-Quality Relationships," *Journal of Retailing* 48 (Fall 1972), pp. 3–17; Arch G. Woodside and J. Taylor Sims, "Retail Experiment in Pricing a New Product," *Journal of Retailing* 50 (Fall 1974), pp. 56–65.

[4] John J. Wheatley and John S. Y. Chiu, "The Effects of Price, Store Image, and Product and Respondent Characteristics on Perceptions of Quality," *Journal of Marketing Research* 14 (May 1977), 181–86; John J. Wheatley, John S. Y. Chiu, and Arieh Goldman, "Physical Quality, Price, and Perceptions of Product Quality: Implications for Retailers," *Journal of Retailing* 57 (Summer 1981), pp. 100–115.

[5] Robert A. Peterson and Alain J. P. Jolibert, "A Cross-National Investigation of Price and Brand as Determinants of Perceived Product Quality," *Journal of Applied Psychology* 61 (August 1976), pp. 533–36.

[6] "Price and Price," *Forbes* 124 (October 29, 1979), pp. 98*ff.*

[7] For a suggested simplified target return on investment model, see: Douglas G. Brooks, "Cost-oriented Pricing: A Realistic Solution to a Complicated Problem," *Journal of Marketing* 39 (April 1975), pp. 72–74.

[8] William F. Schoell and Thomas T. Ivy, *Marketing: Contemporary Concepts and Practices* (Boston: Allyn & Bacon, 1982), p. 641.

[9] Zarrel V. Lambert, "Perceived Prices as Related to Odd and Even Price Endings," *Journal of Retailing* 51 (Fall 1975), pp. 13–22*ff.*

[10] Dik Warren Twedt, "Does the '9 Fixation' in Retail Pricing Really Promote Sales?" *Journal of Marketing* 29 (October 1965), pp. 54–55.

[11] Kent B. Monroe and Peter J. LaPlaca, "What Are the Benefits of Unit Pricing?" *Journal of Marketing* 36 (July 1972), pp. 16–22.

[12] Bruce F. McElroy and David A. Aaker, "Unit Pricing Six Years after Introduction," *Journal of Retailing* 55 (Fall 1979), pp. 44–57.

[13]Stanley M. Wildrick, "Quantity Surcharge: A Pricing Practice among Grocery Store Items—Validation and Extension," *Journal of Retailing* 55 (Summer 1979), pp. 47–58.

[14]Edward Russo, Gene Krieser, and Sally Miyashita, "An Effective Display of Unit Price Information," *Journal of Marketing* 39 (April 1975), pp. 11–19.

[15]Roger Dickinson, "Markup in Department Store Management," *Journal of Marketing* 31 (January 1967), pp. 32–34.

[16]R. W. Pfouts, "Profit Maximization in Chain Retail Stores," *Journal of Industrial Economics* 27 (September 1978), pp. 69–83.

[17]Ralph D. Shipp, Jr., *Retail Merchandising: Principles and Applications* (Boston: Houghton Mifflin, 1976), pp. 92–93.

[18]For some valuable insights into buyer liability, see: Lawrence X. Tarpey, Sr., "Buyer Liability Under the Robinson-Patman Act: A Current Appraisal," *Journal of Marketing* 36 (Jaunary 1972), pp. 38–42.

RETAIL BUYING

Your Study Objectives

After you have studied this chapter, you will understand:

1. The role and significance of the retail buyer.
2. The different buying approaches of retail firms.
3. The useful sources of product/service information for the retail buyer.
4. The contributions of the manufacturer, wholesaler, agent, and broker in channeling consumer goods to retailers.
5. The major types and services of resident buying offices.
6. How retailers improve their buying practices through vendor analysis.
7. How incoming merchandise is received, handled, and marked.

At the core of retailing activity is the buying and selling of merchandise. You already know about some of the difficulties of planning and controlling the flow of goods in and out of a retail company. It is this flow that keeps the firm going and growing. You learned of different classification schemes for consumer products and saw that retail firms rely on unit or dollar control systems to keep track of inventory movement. You learned the significance of the inventory turnover rate and several ways to calculate stockturn. We also exposed you to top-down and bottom-up planning procedures, showed you how sales objectives are translated into monthly goals, taught you the importance of considering retail reductions, and explained the benefits of the retail method of inventory valuation.

We then discussed pricing and its significance to retailers. You learned how to establish selling prices, apply markups, and take markdowns.

In this chapter, you will learn the approaches retailers use to buy merchandise for resale to consumers. You will learn about the responsibilities and activities of the retail buyer and the buying process itself. You will become familiar with the major information sources that buyers consult. You will be introduced to different types of suppliers. You will learn how resident buying offices assist retailers in their buying.

Finally, you will see how incoming goods are received and marked before they are ready for sale.

Company Size and the Buying Function

More than 8 out of every 10 retail businesses in the country are small installations with a modest annual sales volume. Most have only one proprietor. Some enterprises operate as corporations; fewer still are run by partners. Independent merchants typically are too busy attending to their daily chores and waiting on customers to have much time to shop for merchandise for resale. Most are located far from Chicago, New York, and other market centers. A small percentage take an annual, expensive trip to a metropolitan area to visit showrooms in search of goods for their outlets. Others order stock from mail-order distributors. However, most of these retailers order merchandise from visiting sales representatives.

Independent store owners usually decide on purchases by themselves. Thus, the most common approach to retail buying on a small scale is **owner buying.** Most independents also buy hand to mouth. They buy only as they need goods, in small quantities, and frequently. As the small business grows, building its sales volume and adding personnel, the retailer begins to devote more time to the buying function. Business may eventually become brisk enough for the owner(s) to consider hiring a specialist, the retail buyer. Often, the firm's first buyer works part time.

Larger retail companies may maintain a number of buyers on their payrolls. The large drug or hardware chain may have ten or more buyers at its central offices, each knowledgeable about one or two specific merchandise lines. Large department stores may employ upward of 30 buyers: specialists in housewares, lingerie, junior dresses, health and beauty aids, men's shoes, and so on. Many buyers have assistants, among them merchandise controllers who monitor computer printouts on stock movement, allocate inventory to branch stores, and the like.

The Retail Buyer

Retail buyers differ somewhat from **purchasing agents,** their counterparts in industry, commerce, government, and nonprofit organizations. The major role of the industrial buyer is to ensure a steady flow of materials and supplies to the company at the lowest cost consistent with quality and service requirements.[1] Like purchasing agents, retail buyers are agents who represent their firms. Much of the necessary administrative detail—issuing purchase orders, keeping inventory records, locating suppliers, and so on—parallels the duties of the industrial purchasing agent. The retail buyer, though, is a distinct breed. Instead of ordering materials or components for fabrication or assembly at a plant, the retail buyer purchases finished goods to be resold to consumers. Rather than catering to the needs of the production facility, the retail buyer tries to fulfill the needs and wants of the firm's clientele.

Retail buyers must thoroughly know the product fields they operate in. But such knowledge alone does not make for success in this vocation. Buyers need to be familiar with changing consumer needs, desires, and preferences. Somehow, they have to stay abreast of popular styles and trends in the marketplace. By remaining alert and by reading trade journals and other publications, they become adept at spotting selling opportunities.[2]

The Buying Process

Buying can never be staid or cut and dried. The buying process is dynamic. It involves continuous activity that requires the buyer to pit knowledge, experience, judgment, interpersonal capability, and decision-making skill against the challenges of the environment. The following list of activities is not all-inclusive, but it illustrates enough of the retail buyer's responsibilities to serve as a useful guide:

1. Keeping up with market information and trends.
2. Forecasting sales for future periods.

The retail buyer must follow through with department managers and salespeople to be sure that goods are sold.

Courtesy Macy's

3. Ascertaining the needs and wants of customers.
4. Selecting the merchandise to satisfy those needs and wants.
5. Deciding on the quantities of goods needed to attain the projected sales figures.
6. Locating and developing resources to supply the merchandise.
7. Negotiating prices, terms, and conditions of sale.
8. Placing purchase orders with suppliers and arranging for shipment.
9. Following through with department managers and salespeople to ensure that goods are sold.
10. Maintaining adequate records and monitoring stock movement.
11. Continually evaluating results and making the necessary adjustments in plans.

Some suggestions for the future buyer are shown in Figure 16.1.

Buyers also try to maximize the productivity of the space allocated to their merchandise. A common measure of productivity is the **sales per square foot** figure. Buyers work this out by dividing the annual sales volume by the total square footage in the department or section. They compare these results from one year to the next to learn whether their productivity has increased or decreased. They may also compare the figures with available trade data, such as those that appeared in Chapter 4.

Other Buying Approaches   Once the retail company has expanded and hired specialists, it adopts **centralized buying.** Most chain store organizations use this approach.

1. Keep your finger on the consumer's pulse. Study purchase records, sales records, and want slips. Talk to sales personnel and to shoppers.

2. Visit supplier showrooms and factories regularly to familiarize yourself with their operations, strengths and weaknesses, and merchandise lines. Build friendly, long-term resource relationships.

3. Comparison shop: check competitors' merchandise, displays, promotions, and advertising.

4. Keep abreast of fashion trends and everything that is happening in your field. Read trade publications and general consumer magazines. Attend trade shows to scout for new merchandise and meet potential suppliers.

5. Buy new or innovative products only in small quantities until consumer acceptance has been determined.

6. Buy to budget, not by hunch or intuition.

7. Buy often and in small quantities for fresher goods and to keep markdowns to a minimum.

8. On seasonal or fashion merchandise, take your markdowns early, not late.

9. Watch colors, sizes, materials, brands, and other selection factors carefully.

10. Be open to offers of job lots or closeouts, but make certain your clientele will find the merchandise attractive.

11. To reduce your cost of goods, consider buying cooperatively with other retailers who sell your type of merchandise.

12. Train your sales staff in the Art of Selling. Teach them how to handle the merchandise you buy.

13. Maintain quality control by developing an effective vendor evaluation system. Use it to appraise supplier performance at least once a year.

14. Pay bills promptly and take all cash discounts.

Department, drug, discount, variety, and other chains locate their buying offices at corporate headquarters to maintain tight control over costs and production. A serious weakness of this approach, however, is that central buyers are often not thoroughly acquainted with consumer needs in their stores' trading areas. Few firms attempt to overcome this handicap by decentralizing, or delegating much of the buying responsibility to individual store managers.

Some retail firms employ **committee buying.** This is characteristic of the supermarket industry. Suppliers submit merchandise proposals to an executive of the firm, sometimes to the tune of several hundred different products monthly. The executive screens the proposals, submitting some at regular intervals to a buying committee for approval or disapproval. Typically, the committee is composed of the merchandise manager, promotion manager, sales manager, grocery manager, and several other specialists. It is usually advisable to include other members of the organization like the store manager.[3]

In such merchandise lines as hardware, drugs, foods, and some specialities, independents and/or small chains often band together to increase their purchasing power. This is called **group** or **cooperative buying.** Buying collectively, the retailers are able to place larger orders. Thus, they gain better discounts, terms of sale, and services. In the **retailer cooperative,** independent firms that sell similar merchandise contract to pool their resources. In effect, they integrate backwards in the marketing channel, forming their own wholesale operation. Associated Grocers is an example.

A similar cooperative arrangement is the **wholesaler-sponsored voluntary chain.** This voluntary marketing system is initiated by a large distributor. Better prices are usually the retailers' main reason for joining, but other benefits and services are normally offered by the sponsor. The wholesale firm is, of course, eager to help the member stores grow. It may provide advertising allowances, promotional help, and assistance in inventory management. Often the wholesaler also gives advice about new store locations, offers sales training for store employees, and other services. Examples include Western Auto and IGA (Independent Grocers Alliance).

Finally, there is **resident buying.** This approach involves maintaining specialists in major market centers. Because of its importance to many stores, a separate section is devoted to resident buying later in this chapter.

Information Sources

In their quest for merchandise, buyers draw on many sources of information. A convenient classification scheme is division into *internal* and *external* sources.

Internal Sources

In larger retail companies, the most fruitful source for new buyers is the preceding buyer's resource file. This file contains the names, addresses, and telephone numbers of suppliers, the names of the people to contact, merchandise item descriptions, trade and cash discounts, and other information. Today, many retailers formally evaluate their suppliers periodically, and rating results may be available as well.

Other internal records are also of value. In large organizations, the customer service department can usually furnish information about merchandise returns and adjustments. These records often explain why goods have been returned. Similarly, the buyer can study charge sales records to learn about customer preferences.

Store salespeople are another excellent source. These are the firms's front-line troops, in daily contact with shoppers. Other employees can also contribute; as consumers, they are also familiar with other stores.

External Sources There are many outside opportunities for learning about merchandise, resources, changes in fashions, new directions in promotion, and the like. We can categorize these broadly by the contact between retailer and resource:

1. Store visits by suppliers or their representatives.
2. Local trips by the buyer to showrooms and factories.
3. Lengthier buyer trips.
4. Mail and telephone contacts.

Visits by Suppliers The principal source of information for most retailers is the store visit. Sales representatives call regularly to show their merchandise lines, talk about upcoming promotions, and secure orders. Retail buyers need to maintain regular hours for seeing vendors.

Local Trips by the Buyer In many areas of the country, supply sources are nearby. Buyers visit manufacturing plants, distributors, and showrooms to look over their product lines. They try to establish good working relationships with the firms' principals. The professional buyer also comparison shops at local retail outlets that carry competitive merchandise.

Lengthier Trips Though infrequent because of cost, long-distance trips to major market centers like Chicago, New York, Dallas, or San Francisco are fruitful. Attending regional trade shows can also be productive. At these shows, buyers see new merchandise lines and new resources. They mingle with other buyers from all over the country. They can ask questions about fast-moving items and available promotions, and place orders.

If the firm carries merchandise purchased from overseas, trips may also be made to foreign markets.[4]

Mail and Telephone Contacts Buyers have a great deal of worthwhile information at their fingertips from telephone calls or by mail. Many retailers can become members of trade associations. These organizations work for the industry in general. They keep up with the changing environment and work toward legislation favorable to their industry. They furnish their member companies with industry news and trends, guidance in different facets of retail management, and special reports of interest. They collect operating information from member firms and make summary results available.

Examples of trade associations are the Menswear Retailers of America, the National Home Furnishings Association, the Shoe Retailers Association, and the National Association of Retail Grocers of the United States.

Trade associations of wholesalers also exist. These can be contacted by the individual retail firm for information about resources, new lines of merchandise, and so on. The Toy Wholesalers Association, the Toiletry Merchandisers Association, and the Pet Industry Distributors Association are examples. Trade directories are also available. Published each year, they contain names and addresses of resources in the particular trade, types of goods and brands offered, and other details. Another aid, valuable in ferreting out nearby suppliers, is the telephone directory's Yellow Pages. Here are just a few of the titles found by leafing through one small city's telephone book:

Draperies—Whol & Mfrs
Furniture—Whol
Jewelers—Whol & Mfrs
Linens—Whol
Men's Clothing & Furnishings—Whol & Mfrs
Women's Apparel—Whol & Mfrs

Usually buyers receive many catalogs and direct-mail pieces from present and prospective sources during the year. They also read general consumer magazines to keep up with popular preferences and tastes.

Sources of Merchandise

Retail buyers need to locate and develop resources they can rely on to provide them with the goods and services they need for their customers. Smaller retail firms might carry 100 or so different merchandise items. A supermarket may stock several thousand. A department store may carry well over 100,000. All through the year, then, larger companies need to purchase many types of goods. Retailers buy merchandise from producers and wholesalers, and through agents and brokers. Most producers are manufacturers, but the category also includes farmers, cattle ranchers, fishery owners, and others.

In our economy, goods reach us—the end users or consumers—by moving from their producers through one or more intermediary institutions. As an illustration, consider a common furniture item, dinette sets. A selling agent, who represents a manufacturer of dinette sets, secures orders from wholesale distributors around the country. In turn, these wholesalers sell the furniture to retail firms in their territories. At the stores consumers can see, examine, and purchase them. All the institutions that cooperate in bringing the goods to consumers—manufacturer, agent, wholesalers, and retailers—constitute a **marketing channel.** Other combinations, or marketing channels, are possible. Merchandise may travel from producer to wholesalers, bypassing the agent. Or the manufacturer may elect to sell directly to retailers instead of going through wholesaling firms. Some producers prefer to avoid intermediaries altogether, aiming their effort solely at the final consumer. Direct selling companies like Avon, Tupperware,

A short marketing channel: this producer/retailer sells his product without the aid of any intermediaries.

Chicago Tribune/Carl Hugare

and World Book are examples of this last, shortest channel arrangement.

Manufacturers   Far more numerous than wholesaling establishments are our nation's manufacturing companies. In their factories and plants, they convert raw and/or semiprocessed materials and components into useful products. Some change the form of the material they work on by cutting, stamping, molding, pressing, shaping, weaving, or other mechanical process. Other producers, like the glass manufacturers, synthesize materials into entirely new products. Some fabricate parts for use in the manufacture of other items. Others create goods by assembling parts.

Many manufacturing firms maintain their own sales forces. Others, especially the smaller organizations, call on agents, brokers, or wholesalers to market their goods. Retail firms frequently purchase merchandise directly from manufacturers to save the costs of intermediaries. Even small-scale merchants occasionally buy goods in this manner. This is fairly common in the areas of apparel, meat and dairy products, and jewelry.

Wholesalers   Fewer than 400,000 wholesaling companies of all types operate in the United States. Most are small enterprises with a limited number of employees. Yet these distributors play a vital role in the economy, accounting for over $1 trillion in sales transactions each year. Some

Most merchant wholesalers are small enterprises with a limited number of employees; they mainly serve the retail sector and play a vital role in the nation's economy.

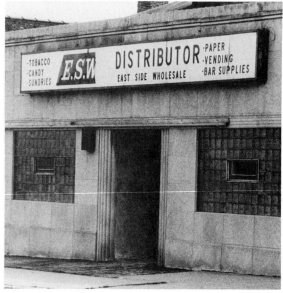

Gary Csuk

wholesalers stock a tremendous variety of merchandise to supply their retail accounts. An automotive distributor, for example, may carry as many as 25,000 different items.[5]

Merchant Wholesalers More than three quarters of all wholesaling establishments are **merchant wholesalers:** intermediaries between producers and the retailing and/or industrial sectors. They are more numerous in fields like machinery and equipment, groceries, cars, hardware, paper goods, chemicals, and general merchandise. Some companies deal only with industrial firms, government agencies, schools, hospitals, and other institutions. The majority of wholesalers, however, concentrate on the retail sector.

Most merchant wholesalers are **full-service wholesalers,** so named because they provide all the services that channel members expect of them. These services include buying and selling goods, warehousing, breaking bulk (breaking large quantities down into small orders), shipping, extending credit, and so on. As you can see in Figure 16.2, these distributors offer a variety of services to their accounts.

Full-service distributors are of three types. There are a few **general merchandise houses** that offer an extensive variety of merchandise lines. They sell to discount and drug stores, variety and general merchandise outlets, small department stores, and other retailers. General merchandise houses can be found in fields such as health and beauty aids, drugs, electrical supplies, and hardware. The **single-line wholesaler** stocks a complete assortment of goods within one major line

Figure 16.2
Wholesalers provide a
wide range of services

Wholesalers offer services that small retailers can use to strengthen their operations. In some instances, the helping hand concerns only sales. In others, it extends to advice and help on record-keeping, financing, administrative practices, location, insurance, and personnel.

*   *   *   *   *

The types of services and the extent to which they are available varies with wholesalers and lines of merchandise. . . .

1. **Promotion:** stock control system, point-of-sale promotional aids, window/counter/bin displays, cooperative advertising.

2. **Market information:** facts about consumer demand, prices (including competitive price information), market conditions which would affect supply, new methods/products/ideas.

3. **Financial aid:** assistance in keeping the retailer's inventory small (through prompt, frequent deliveries), trade credit, delayed billing.

4. **Accounting system.**

5. **Guidance/counsel on policy setting and methods.**

6. **Help with real estate:** tips on stores that are for rent or sale, evaluation of potential locations.

7. **Finance:** help with long-range financing, support at bank or insurance company (partial or full guarantee).

8. **Insurance counsel.**

9. **Assistance in finding qualified store personnel.**

Source: Richard M. Hill, "Profit by Your Wholesalers' Services," *Small Marketers Aids No. 140* (Washington, D.C.: Small Business Administration, January 1970), pp. 1–5.

of trade such as groceries, hardware, or drugs. Single-line retail stores are their customers. There are also **specialty wholesalers,** distributors who specialize in a narrow product range within a single merchandise line. Wholesalers of seafood, meats, spices, and Chinese food products fall into this category.

Limited-Service
Wholesalers

Not all merchant wholesalers perform all the functions characteristic of this channel institution. Some do not extend credit, requiring cash payment with each purchase. Others do not warehouse their goods. Some do not deliver goods or provide their customers with market information. Representing fewer than 1 in every 10 merchant wholesalers, these **limited-service wholesalers** include some interesting types.

Desk Jobbers Often one-person firms, **desk jobbers** maintain no inventory. Typically, they work at home or in small offices, needing little more than a desk, chair, and telephone. On securing orders from retail accounts, these distributors place them with manufacturers or other suppliers. They arrange for the merchandise to be shipped directly to the customer. The supplier bills the desk jobber at the factory price plus, perhaps, freight charges. In turn, the wholesaler bills the retail firm at the wholesale price.

Another name for the desk jobber is **drop-shipper.** These intermediaries operate in a few retail fields, most notably lumber, construction materials, gravel, and other bulky products.

Truck Jobbers Also known as wagon jobbers, **truck jobbers** make deliveries regularly to groceries, supermarkets, delicatessens, and other food stores. Covering a set route, they deliver perishable merchandise and impulse items: candy, potato chips, baked goods, dairy products, fruits, vegetables, and the like. The merchandise is usually sold on a cash basis.

Mail-Order Distributors These companies use the U.S. Postal Service and other agencies (such as United Parcel Service) to supply retail firms across the country. **Mail-order distributors** send out catalogs and direct-mail literature to prospective buyers. Thus, they give retailers the opportunity to select merchandise at leisure and place their orders by mail. Goods are shipped directly to the stores. Wholesaling by mail is common in many retail fields: jewelry, stationery, musical instruments and supplies, and so on.

Rack Merchandisers Many marketers consider this type of distributor to be full-function because of the considerable amount of service they perform. The name is descriptive: the **rack merchandiser,** or **rack jobber,** introduces floor stands or other display racks into stores at no charge to the retailers. The racks are then stocked with merchandise. Thereafter, the wholesaler visits the stores regularly to freshen up the display and replace the items that have been sold. The rack merchandiser collects from the retailer the wholesale cost of whatever has been sold. Payment is generally immediate; this jobber often does not extend credit.

Retailers enjoy this arrangement for two reasons: (1) space requirements are usually minimal and (2) the gross margin earned on the racked goods contributes toward the monthly rent without diminishing the sales of the retailer's regular merchandise assortment. Today, rack jobbers distribute many types of merchandise: hardware, household items, health aids, inexpensive novelties and toys, school supplies, paperback books, and other impulse and convenience goods.

Cash-and-Carry Wholesalers These are distributors who maintain ample stock in their warehouses to service area merchants. The **cash-and-carry wholesaler** normally does not extend credit. Retailers go there to buy and pick up needed goods. They pay in cash or by check for the merchandise they carry out. These wholesalers supply mostly staples: paper goods, institutional foods, canned and bottled soft drinks by the case, and so on. Local delicatessens, groceries, restaurants, and similar stores are their customers.

Other Types of Wholesaling Establishments

Although far fewer in number than the merchant wholesaler, other types of distributors play a significant role in some sections of the economy. They include manufacturers' sales branches and offices, petroleum bulk plants, and assemblers. Another category typically included by the government is that of agents and brokers. These two will be treated in a later section.

Manufacturers' Sales Branches/Sales Offices These are owned and operated by some producers in fields such as foodstuffs, clothing and apparel (men's, women's, children's), chemicals, agricultural equipment and supplies, and machinery. At **manufacturers' sales offices,** company products are displayed for visiting buyers. Orders are accepted for shipment from company warehouses; no inventory is maintained on the premises. Offering essentially the same service, **manufacturers' sales branches** have the additional advantage of being able to supply buyers' needs in the area directly from stock on hand.

Petroleum Bulk Plants For the most part, these distributors sell to gasoline stations and fuel oil dealers. **Petroleum bulk plants** must maintain storage tanks and other specialized equipment to handle the gasoline, oil, and other petroleum products they offer.

Assemblers The majority of **assemblers** deal in agricultural products, seafood, and a few other lines. At their production facilities, these firms assemble products they usually purchase from a number of sources. They box or can them and ready the goods for shipment to retail establishments or to warehouses.

Agents and Brokers

Because they are in an intermediate position between the country's producers and the final consumer, **agents** and **brokers** are often included under the wholesaling classification. In effect, though, many of these people and organizations deal exclusively with manufacturers and wholesalers, not with retailers. They act as representatives of either side, receiving commissions or fees for their services.

To avoid the costs and headaches associated with maintaining their own field sales force, many manufacturers choose to contract with a **selling agent** to represent them. This approach is common among small and medium-sized producers in fields like lumber, clothing, textiles, and electronics. With access to a number of wholesalers and/or large retail organizations, the agent is able to sell off the manufacturer's entire output. Because of the significance of their relationship, the manufacturer relies on the selling agent for advice on products, packaging, pricing, and other elements of the marketing mix. At times, manufacturers may even call on their agents for financial assistance. Selling agents earn commissions on the goods they sell.

Manufacturer's representatives are independent businesspeople or small firms that act as agents, under contract, for manufacturers. Like the selling agent, the manufacturer's representative is compensated by commission. A major distinction between the two is that while a manufacturing firm may have only one selling agent, it can employ a number of manufacturer's representatives. Each rep is generally assigned a portion of the factory's output to sell and a specific territory to sell it in. Consequently, these agents have little influence on the producer's product-line decisions, pricing approaches, terms of sale, and the like. Taking the entire package offered by the manufacturer, they try to sell it in their assigned territories. One person may represent several different, usually noncompeting, manufacturing companies. Thus, they offer retailers an opportunity to buy several merchandise lines at one time for their stores. Manufacturer's reps are found in fields ranging from apparel to household utensils, and from food products to office supplies, equipment, and machinery.

Brokers are intermediaries who buy or sell goods on behalf of their principals—the people or companies they represent. Their primary function is to bring together buyers and sellers. They do not take title to the goods. Brokers are active in real estate transactions, in the sale of securities and commodities, and in many merchandise lines. Retailing examples include women's and men's apparel and accessories, small appliances, foods, and agricultural products. A special type, the **auction company,** deals in transactions that involve cattle or other livestock, tobacco, fruits and vegetables, and other farm products. Some auction companies broker secondhand cars, furs, antiques, and other types of goods. These firms provide facilities where sellers can display their goods, and where potential buyers can inspect them leisurely. An auction company is authorized by sellers to dispose of the goods at any price obtainable above prearranged minimums. For its services, the company receives either a commission or a set fee.

A somewhat unique species of intermediary is the **commission merchant,** or **commission house.** Although some of these firms deal in livestock, dry goods, or groceries, most are involved in the distribution of agricultural products. The commission merchant acts as an agent selling for farmers, growers, and other, usually small, producers. Commission is earned on each sale. They differ from other agents in that they take in and store the goods until they have been sold.

Resident Buying Offices

Resident buying offices are firms in the business of buying merchandise for the retailers they represent. Such firms maintain offices in one or more of the major market centers: New York, Chicago, Los Angeles, Dallas, and several other metropolitan areas. These cities house the showrooms and sales offices of hundreds of manufacturers and wholesalers. Resident buyers can easily make contact, visit these suppliers, and keep abreast of what is going on in the marketplace.

Types of Buying Offices

Resident buying offices can be grouped into two main types. There are the **independent buying offices,** which exist to service their client retailers. There are also a much smaller number of resident buying organizations that act only for those retail companies they are intimately connected with. This category embraces several types. Relatively rare is the **private buying office,** owned and directed by a single large retailer. Neiman-Marcus Co. in Dallas and Marshall Field & Co. in Chicago are major retailers that manage private offices. More common are those set up to serve a group or association of retail firms, which manage the offices. These are the **associated** or **cooperative buying offices.** Frederick Atkins and the Associated Merchandising Corporation are among the better-known examples. Still a third type, with more authority and control over the member stores in merchandising and procedures, is the **syndicate buying office.** Examples include Allied Purchasing and Associated Dry Goods.

Independent Buying Offices

Independent buying offices far outnumber the store-connected types. They are found in many retail fields: apparel, soft goods, housewares, appliances, furniture, hardware, and so on. The majority of independents are located in New York City, with smaller numbers in other market centers. They range in size from small firms with fewer than 10 employees to large, multibranch companies with personnel in the hundreds. They maintain their own staffs of experienced, specialized buyers. They represent retailers across the country. The member firms enjoy the benefits of professional and thorough market coverage and a steady flow of information by mail. Retailers sign up annually with the buying office, agreeing to pay a service fee of around one half of one percent of yearly sales. If a merchant's sales volume is low, the buying office may require a minimum monthly retainer.

Services Offered The actual kinds and quality of services rendered by independent buying offices may vary from one organization to the next. See Figure 16.3 for an example of a visit to a buying office. A typical company also offers most of the following:[6]

1. Assists client retailers by maintaining a staff of experienced buyers. These specialists visit the local market regularly and search continuously for new merchandise and suppliers.

Figure 16.3
How the buying office
can help

As your good right arm in the market, your buying office eliminates unnecessary market trips. And when you do come to the market, say in January and June, it can shorten your trip and make it more profitable.

The experience of a dress buyer, Mrs. Jane Holter,* illustrates the timesaving service that a buying office provides. Look at the amount of work she accomplished on a typical day in New York.

Mrs. Holter wrote several weeks in advance of her trip and told her buying office that she wanted to visit certain manufacturers' showrooms to buy her new fall line. She also wanted to purchase dresses for a store anniversary sale.

On her arrival, she met with the buying office's dress buyer and together they planned what Mrs. Holter would need. Because appointments had already been made with certain manufacturers, her visits to their showrooms were made without wasting time. This gave her time in which to discuss with the buying office specialist how the merchandise might best be promoted.

When Mrs. Holter returned home, the buying office followed up. Had her orders been delivered? If not, why not? If incorrect merchandise had been delivered, returns were arranged, If reorders were necessary, they were expedited.

---

* All names in *Aids* are disguised.

Source: Ernest A. Miller, "How to Select a Resident Buying Office," *Small Marketers Aids No. 116* (Washington, D.C.: Small Business Administration, reprinted September 1976), p. 3.

2. Regularly forwards to member stores information and recommendations for products, merchandise lines, fashion trends, promotions, and other details of resource offerings.
3. On request, places orders for goods for member firms.
4. Follows up on orders placed and takes care of returns, adjustments, and other problems.
5. Provides promotional assistance to retail chains for new store openings.
6. Offers advice about inventory and merchandise control methods. May provide data-processing assistance for record-keeping.
7. When clients plan to visit the market center, informs suppliers and arranges appointments with their sales representatives.
8. Provides office and desk space and clerical help while the client is in town.
9. When requested, schedules visits to manufacturers' plants and showrooms. May send along an escort with the retailer on some of those visits.
10. Plans and sets up fashion clinics for members.
11. Often assists retailers in locating new merchandisers, store managers, buyers, and other retail executives.

An example of a large independent buying office is Merchants Buying Syndicate, with executive offices in Manhattan. The company maintains branch offices in Hong Kong, Korea, Japan, Germany, England,

Italy, and in several other countries. They are somewhat atypical in preferring that their member retailers write their own orders to vendors and in requiring payment of a fixed annual fee. Their clients run the gamut from variety chains and discount houses to department stores, supermarkets, drug stores, and automotive supply stores. Among the merchandise lines they handle are housewares, lamps, china, glassware, linens, domestics, hardware, sporting goods, toys and games, radios, TVs, and paper goods. One of MBS's major attractions is its frequent use of mail circulars that offer special deals.

Dealing with Vendors

Earlier in the chapter, we briefly mentioned the various distribution channels for consumer goods. Often, a large manufacturing company will try to set up the best possible channel arrangement for its products, then exercise leadership with the other channel members. This makes for more efficient distribution, better control, and higher profits.[7] In conventional channels (leaving aside contractual arrangements such as franchises and voluntary chains), producers rely mostly on product development, delivery, and product-related support activites in securing channel leadership.[8]

Retailers and wholesalers may also try to lead marketing channels. One common example is a powerful national chain that is being solicited by a small manufacturer or by a weak regional wholesaler. The retailer will be able to dictate terms and conditions to the hopeful, and somewhat hapless, vendor. Whoever tries to manage the channel system, the offer of specific incentives often helps to obtain compliance with the management policies. These can include advertising assistance, market information, management advice, and financial aid.[9]

Channel Conflict

Conflict among channel members seems unavoidable because of: (1) interdependency, (2) differences among roles in distribution, (3) differing sizes and financial strengths, and (4) differences in attitudes, interests, backgrounds, and so on. A few of the difficulties are accented in the following quotation:

> Manufacturers and wholesalers want retailers to pay for local advertising. Retailers want their suppliers to cover this cost. Retailers like exclusive distribution, where they have no nearby competitors. Manufacturers tend toward intensive distribution, which provides their products maximum consumer exposure and convenience of purchase. Manufacturers prefer their middlemen not to carry competing lines, but middlemen tend to handle competing lines.[10]

Channel conflict can be reduced by improving communications among the members.[11] Concern and cooperation among channel institutions appear to be more prevalent nowadays than in the past. Indeed, the entire problem area might be more academic than practical reality, according to one study.[12] The study found that retail personnel tend not to understand the distribution channel concept.

Buyer-Supplier Relations

Professional buyers search for resources that can provide the kinds of merchandise their clienteles desire. They want to purchase these goods in the right quantities, at fair prices, and under favorable terms and conditions of sale. They look for suppliers who are strong financially and who can be counted on to offer promotional aid, useful services, and occasional concessions. Buyers foster close, long-term associations with these sources. They are willing to concentrate their purchases with those they can comfortably work with.

Relationships must go two ways. Buyers also have obligations to their resources; both retailer and supplier need to work in partnership to satisfy consumer needs.[13] The buyer should:

> Be open to the offerings of all suppliers; even the most unlikely source should be received courteously for just as long as it takes to determine the value of the offering.
>
> Work hard to establish and maintain a preferred position with the most important resources in each merchandise category.
>
> Be as loyal to a good supplier as the supplier is expected to be to the buyer's company.
>
> Never cut off a good supplier without substantial cause and only after mutual discussion and criticism have failed to produce the desired results.
>
> Make all commitments definite—written, if possible—and require suppliers to be just as precise.[14]

Negotiations Buyers must have clear thoughts about what they want to accomplish *before* entering negotiations with their resources. Settling on prices and terms that are acceptable to both sides is only part of the process. Among the many details that must be agreed on are:

1. The method of delivery.
2. Who will pay for transporting the goods.
3. How returns are to be handled.
4. Guarantees and warranties.
5. Point-of-purchase materials and other selling aids.
6. Allowances for cooperative advertising.
7. Preticketing (if desired).

When a retail company requests changes in products according to its own specifications, this is known as **specification buying.** Retailers may also ask suppliers to send in goods on consignment or on memo.

In **consignment buying** the merchant acts as agent for the supplier, taking title and paying for only the merchandise that is sold. The remaining stock is returned to the vendor. **Memorandum buying** is somewhat similar, but the retailer owns the goods. What cannot be sold can, however, be returned for credit.

Dating of Invoices The terms of sale significantly affect the buying situation and resulting price decisions. **Dating** refers to how credit arrangements with accounts are handled. The extension of credit on purchases is tied to the invoice date. Thus, we have ordinary (or regular) dating, future dating, extra dating, and so on.

Suppliers have customary dating practices, although these can be modified during negotiations. In **ordinary dating,** no cash discount is offered. Terms such as *Net 30 days* or *Net 45 days* may be indicated on the invoice. In such cases, the purchaser has up to 30 or 45 days from the invoice date to pay the amount in full. (These terms may be abbreviated to *n30* or *n45.*) Failure to pay the bill in the designated period results in the account being overdue. If no terms have been shown on the invoice, the buyer generally assumes that 30 days of credit have been extended.

Cash discounts were discussed in an earlier chapter. As a reminder, a common example of dating that carries a cash discount offer is *2/10, n30.* This is interpreted as trade credit extended for 30 days and a discount from the vendor of 2 percent from the face amount of the bill *if* paid within 10 days of the invoice date. Suppliers are often willing to permit **anticipation** as well. This is an additional discount designed to encourage buyers to pay their bills *before* the cash discount period ends. Anticipation is based on the number of days left between payment and the termination of the discount period. Percentages offered by vendors fluctuate. When high interest rates prevail, they may range from 10 percent to as high as 18 percent. The size of the percentage is often worked out during buyer-seller negotiations.

Let us assume that we receive an invoice for $3,000. It has been dated July 10 and carries the terms *4/10, n30, 12% Anticipation.* We decide to pay the bill on July 13. If we do so, we would be entitled to seven days of anticipation. We first apply the 4 percent cash discount, deducting $120 from the face amount. We now owe $2,880. We then calculate our anticipation. At 12 percent annually, this additional discount works out to 1 percent per month. Seven days account for $7/30$ of 1 percent, or 0.233 percent. Multiplying the $2,880 by 0.233 percent, we find we can deduct another $6.71 from the invoice. Thus, we remit a check in the amount of $2,873.29 in full payment.

Other Datings A retailer in Oregon orders merchandise from a vendor in Massachusetts. On shipping the goods, the supplier mails out the invoice, which reaches the store in a few days. However, weeks go by before the merchandise is actually received by the retailer. In such cases, suppliers may use **ROG** or **AOG dating.** The initials stand for Receipt of Goods and Arrival of Goods. The terms are indicated on the invoice as, for example: *5/15, n45, ROG.* In this particular case, the customer has 15 days to obtain the 5 percent cash discount and 45 days to pay the invoice in full. The terms, however, do not apply until the merchandise has been received by the retailer.

The initials EOM may appear on an invoice. They stand for End of Month. If they appear, the payer knows that the terms apply *after* the last day of the month shown on the invoice.

Shipping Terms Among the more commonly used shipping terms are FOB, CIF, and COD. The first set of letters stands for Free on Board and is usually followed by the designation of a place, city, or point of departure. Examples include: FOB Factory (Plant, Warehouse) or FOB Store (City of Destination). Goods purchased under an FOB Factory arrangement become the property of the buyer the moment they leave the supplier's plant. Transportation costs thereafter are the purchaser's responsibility. CIF stands for Cost, Insurance, and Freight. COD signifies Cash on Delivery. This latter approach is often used by companies that sell to firms with doubtful credit backgrounds.

Rating Suppliers Buyers for department stores, supermarkets, large chains, discount outlets, and other mass merchandising operations may work with hundreds of vendors. Active resources are culled from among thousands of potential suppliers. Retailers should develop methods that are more objective than subjective for deciding which vendors are better to work with. The process is called **vendor analysis.** Its objective is to improve the quality of the retailer's buying practices.

A typical approach is to list a number of criteria on a rating form. A four- or five-point scale is used to rank all vendors on each. Some criteria are assigned more weight than others according to their importance as perceived by the retailer. More complicated rating forms may carry 10 to 15 criteria. Some criteria are obvious: prices and conditions of sale, consistency in merchandise quality, and promptness in delivery. Other criteria to be considered are product suitability for the store's clientele, exclusivity, promotional support, handling of returned goods, and the like.

Small independent retailers can institute supplier rating systems that are both simple and inexpensive. This can be done with fewer criteria weighted according to different purchase situations. An example of such an approach can be seen in Figure 16.4 and Table 16.1.

**Figure 16.4
Sample supplier
rating form**

VENDOR ....

ITEM ORDERED ....

PURCHASE ORDER NO. .... QUANTITY .... PURCHASE CLASS ....

ORDER DATE .... REQUESTED DELIVERY DATE ....

PROMISED DATE .... ACTUAL RECEIPT DATE ....

PERFORMANCE RATING

RATING CRITERIA	Relative* Weight (A)	Performance Rating** (B)	Weighted Score (A × B)
NET PRICE	8	3	24
QUALITY	5	2	10
DELIVERY	5	4	20
ATTITUDE	2	5	10
FINANCIAL STABILITY	0	0	0
TOTAL POINT SCORE			64

* The relative weights are chosen to reflect the purchasing situation as specified by the purchase class above.

** The following performance rating scale is associated with relative weights that total to 20 points.

Rating	Description	Rating	Description	Rating	Description
1	Unacceptable	3	Acceptable	4	Good
2	Poor			5	Excellent

INTERPRETATION OF TOTAL POINT SCORE

Range	Performance	Appropriate Purchasing Action
Less than 60	Unacceptable	Replace supplier at earliest opportunity.
60-70	Acceptable	Review performance with supplier.
70-85	Good	Optional review with supplier.
80-100	Excellent	Commend the supplier.

Source: C. David Wieters and Lonnie L. Ostrom, "Maintaining Effective Suppliers: A Small Business Approach," *Journal of Small Business Management* 15 (October 1977), p. 48.

Handling Incoming Merchandise

If we regard a retail operation as a money-making machine, then its engine is fueled by the merchandise brought in to be resold to consumers. Goods flow in constantly. As some are sold off, more merchandise must be purchased to replace those articles. Millions of dollars' worth of goods pass through a large department store each year. Coordinating the flow of incoming merchandise can be an awesome responsibility.

Rating Criteria	Economic Emphasis	Quality Emphasis	Delivery Emphasis	Single Source Emphasis
Net price	8	2	2	2
Consistent quality	5	9	5	4
Dependable delivery	5	5	9	4
Supplier attitude	2	2	2	6
Financial stability	0	2	2	4
Total points	20	20	20	20

* A distribution of 20 points is used to represent relative emphasis among criteria.

Source: Adapted from C. David Wieters and Lonnie L. Ostrom, "Maintaining Effective Suppliers: A Small Business Approach," *Journal of Small Business Management* 15 (October 1977), p. 47.

Although occasional sidewalk deliveries are made, merchandise ordered by most small independent retailers is delivered directly to the store. The shipments may be brought into the stockroom through the back door or delivered into the selling area through the front entrance. The cartons are moved from delivery truck to the premises by depositing them, a few at a time, on dollies. These are wooden platforms with wheels that can be pulled or pushed in any direction. Once inside, the shipment is checked for type, quantity, and often, quality of the merchandise. The cartons are opened, and the individual articles are marked with their selling price and, often, additional information. Following **marking,** the goods are distributed to their intended locations: department, selling area, or stockroom.

Many large retail companies maintain central warehouses. Trucks pull into truck bays—openings on the side or in the rear of the warehouse. The cartons or cases are unloaded onto a platform. Workers in the **receiving department** check off the goods. Later on, the merchandise is properly stored in the building and held to fill orders for the various store branches. As orders arrive, goods are picked from their locations and forwarded to the ready stocks area. Here they are prepared for outgoing shipment by the **shipping department.** This means that if retailers operate their own warehouses, receiving activities must be conducted twice: once at the facility and again at the individual store when the delivery comes in.

Receiving Merchandise   Incoming shipments are delivered to the receiving department. The delivery is checked against the accompanying packing slip or invoice to make certain that no cartons are damaged. A record is then made in the **receiving log** maintained by the department. The clerk enters the date and time the shipment was received, name of the carrier, supplier's name, number of pieces delivered, freight charges (if these are to be paid by the retailer), and department or section for which

If a retail operation is a money-making machine, then its engine is fueled by the merchandise brought in to be resold to consumers. The boxes (right) each containing 30 foam-plastic hats, are being delivered to a novelty shop in downtown Hartford, Connecticut.

Wide World Photos

the merchandise is destined. Later, the cartons are opened and their contents inspected. Worktables are often used to unpack, count, and mark the merchandise.

Methods of Checking Deliveries Retailers choose one of several methods for checking incoming goods. Among firms of all types and sizes, far and away the favored approach is the timesaving **direct check** method. The checker—store manager, salesperson, or stock clerk—works with the invoice or packing slip that accompanied the shipment or with a copy of the purchase order. First, a simple count verifies the number of cartons. The checker then reviews each carton's label or markings to make certain that its contents match with the information given on the document. If all appears in order, the checker signs for the receipt of the goods. Afterward, all cartons are opened and their contents checked before sending them to the marking section.

The direct check is favored because of its simplicity. Retailers prefer to get back as quickly as possible to serving their customers or to other necessary work. Yet this approach may encourage hasty, even careless checking. Checkers are occasionally observed signing delivery receipts without having verified the individual cartons. To avoid possible errors, some establishments employ a more painstaking approach, the **blind check.** In using this method, the checker must proceed without the aid of any document. Using a blank sheet of paper, the clerk records quantity and contents of the cartons delivered. In a variation of the technique, the **semiblind check,** the process is hastened by using a printed form which lists the names, but not the quantities, of all goods in the shipment. In both approaches, the paperwork is checked later on, usually by someone in the bookkeeping or receiving departments. Discrepancies are called to management's attention.

Special care must be exercised in verifying cartons of goods shipped in bulk, that is to say, not sold by units or pieces. Such cartons can vary considerably in weight. Examples include squash, eggplants, grapes, and other vegetables and fruits; candies and nutmeats; and supplies for various handicrafts. Bulk goods need to be weighed on a good scale, and the **tare** (weight of the carton itself) deducted from the total weight in order to determine the weight of the merchandise alone.

Marking

Marking is an important activity of store operation. The term refers to affixing prices and other details to items before they are forwarded to the selling or reserve stock areas. Marking is a necessity today because of the prevalence of self-selection and self-service. Shoppers want to know the prices of articles they examine. Especially with high-ticket merchandise, many consumers like to compare prices from one store to the next before making a purchase decision. Even within the same store, shoppers will often compare prices among different brands of the same basic product. They also need price information to decide if a particular item represents good value for the amount of money asked.

Salespeople must know the prices of merchandise so they can talk convincingly and persuade shoppers to buy. Cashiers need to know prices in order to record customer purchases at the register.

How Goods Are Marked Merchants mark their stock in various ways. Many small independents mark the selling prices on merchandise by hand, using a crayon or marking pen. This is simple, fast, and inexpensive. Grocery stores may use a handstamping machine that rapidly inks the price on the tops of cereal boxes, canned goods, jars, and other packages. With labeling machines, supermarket clerks can affix price labels on all 24 or 48 cans in a carton within a few seconds after opening the box.

Merchants also place labels on goods, affix price tickets, or attach price tags. For many clothing items, for example, pin, button, or string tickets are used. Pin tickets are pinned to vests, sweaters, scarves, jackets, and the like. Button tickets have openings in them that fit snugly around a button on men's shirts, women's blouses, coats, and so on. String tickets are attached to gloves, shoes, and other items normally sold in pairs.

Tickets can be written out, hand-lettered, or printed by machine so customers and employees can easily read them. Holes may be punched in them for machine reading; this is vital to some inventory control systems. Or packages can be preprinted with a code system such as the Universal Product Code used in supermarkets, to be interpreted by optical scanning equipment.

In large retail operations, price tickets generally carry much more information than simply the price. Among other data, the ticket shows the number of the department that stocks the item, merchandise classification, SKU number, style, size, vendor number, and even the article's cost. Chain organizations frequently add an identification number for the specific store unit where the item is sold.

Encoding Cost Prices Some retailers place the cost of an article on the price ticket. They do this for better inventory control, in anticipation of markdowns that may need to be taken, or because they have a variable pricing policy. Whatever the reason, they do not want shoppers to be aware of the cost. To conceal the information, they use a simple substitution code. Usually, the merchant selects a 10-letter word or phrase that is easy to remember. No letter can be repeated. Each becomes a substitute on the price ticket for one of 10 digits: 1 through 9, with 0 at the end of the list. Clothespin, broad lines, trampoline, corn flakes, and shrimp boat are words or phrases that meet the requirements.

For example, a proprietor has decided to use the first word as the store's pricing code. Printing the word on the sheet of paper, he or she fills in the 10 digits under the letters so the result looks like this:

$$C \quad L \quad O \quad T \quad H \quad E \quad S \quad P \quad I \quad N$$
$$1 \quad 2 \quad 3 \quad 4 \quad 5 \quad 6 \quad 7 \quad 8 \quad 9 \quad 0$$

An encoded cost of $6.40 would appear on the price ticket as ETN. Similary, the letters CHHP would represent a cost to the retailer of $15.58.

The Marking Section To ensure faster, more accurate marking, many larger companies maintain a separate marking section or department. The section's clerks are responsible not only for properly marking all incoming goods but also for occasional **remarking.** Remarking is required if the original price ticket has been torn off the article, if it is too worn to be read by shoppers, or when the retail price is raised or lowered.

To save time and expense, some retailers ask their suppliers to mark the merchandise at their plants or warehouses before shipment. This is known as **source marking.** Price tickets, labels or tags may be provided by either the retailer or the vendor.

Ordinarily, on receiving a shipment, the marking section tries to contact the buyer to obtain price information. Buyers are often not available. They are out scouting the marketplace for merchandise. For this reason, some firms **preretail** their goods. When preretailing is desired, the buyer types the selling price directly on the purchase order and the marking section works from a copy of the order.

Summary Owners buy the merchandise for most independent retailers. Larger companies maintain buying specialists on their payrolls. Most such firms use centralized buying. Committee buying is seen in the supermarket industry. Retailers of all sizes may also engage in cooperative buying.

Retail buyers aim at fulfilling the needs of their customers. These executives require a thorough knowledge of their markets and must keep abreast of trends. They make sales forecasts; these help determine merchandise requirements for future periods. Buyers also locate and develop sources of supply, negotiate prices and terms, issue purchase orders, instruct store salespeople and department managers, monitor inventory movement, and evaluate results.

Among the valuable internal sources of information available to retail buyers are the preceding buyer's resource files, customer service records, sales records, and store salespeople. External sources include visits by suppliers or their representatives, buyer trips, and mail and telephone contacts.

Marketing channels consist of one or more institutions engaged in cooperative effort to sell goods to consumers. Retailers purchase merchandise for resale from manufacturers and/or wholesalers. The major kinds of wholesaling establishments are merchant wholesalers, manufacturers' sales branches and offices, petroleum bulk plants, and assemblers. Merchant wholesalers are in the majority. Most are full-service operations. Limited-service wholesalers do not perform all the services normally expected of the wholesaler. The three basic types of full-service distributors are the general merchandise house, the single-line wholesaler, and the specialty wholesaler. Examples of limited-function distributors include the desk jobber, truck jobber, mail-order distributor, rack merchandiser, and cash-and-carry wholesaler.

Agents and brokers are intermediaries who act on behalf of buyers or sellers, generally without taking title to the goods. The selling agent contracts to sell a manufacturer's entire output. Manufacturer's representatives are responsible for selling part of a plant's production and are usually restricted to particular territories. Brokers operate in many lines of retailing.

Resident buying offices are in major market centers where they perform buying-related services for the retailers they represent. Some are store-connected; the majority are not. Independent buying offices serve their member companies by scouting the marketplace for new merchandise and suppliers, placing and following up on orders, offering promotional assistance, providing desk space for visiting retailers, and other services.

Conflict in marketing channels arises from the interdependency of the participants, the different roles they play, their disparate size and financial strength, and individual differences among the principals of their firms. Yet conflict can be held to a minimum through improved communication. Loyalty and mutual respect should characterize the buyer-vendor relationship. Many retail companies use vendor rating systems to help improve their buying practices.

Goods ordered by smaller retailers are usually delivered right to the store. Merchandise delivered to larger stores or their warehouses is taken in by the receiving section or department. Among the available methods of checking incoming goods are the direct, blind, and semi-blind checks. An important subsequent activity is marking—affixing prices and other information to the merchandise. Some retailers enter the cost prices on the goods, disguising them with a secret code.

Key Terms

owner buying	broker
purchasing agent	auction company
sales per square foot	commission merchant (house)
centralized buying	resident buying office
committee buying	independent buying office
group (cooperative) buying	private buying office
retailer cooperative	associated (cooperative) buying office
wholesaler-sponsored voluntary chain	syndicate buying office
resident buying	specification buying
marketing channel	consignment buying
merchant wholesaler	memorandum buying
full-service wholesaler	dating
general merchandise house	ordinary dating
single-line wholesaler	anticipation
specialty wholesaler	ROG and AOG dating
limited-service wholesaler	vendor analysis
desk jobber	marking
drop-shipper	receiving department
truck jobber	shipping department
mail-order distributor	receiving log
rack merchandiser (rack jobber)	direct check
cash-and-carry wholesaler	blind check
manufacturers' sales branches and offices	semiblind check
petroleum bulk plant	tare
assembler	marking
agent	remarking
selling agent	source marking
manufacturer's representatives	preretailing

Review Questions

1. Clearly differentiate among the following: *(a)* owner buying, *(b)* group buying, and *(c)* committee buying.

2. List four activities involved in the buying process.

3. Cite at least four internal and four external sources of information for retail buyers.

4. What are the advantages to a retail company of buying directly from the manufacturer? What, if any, are the drawbacks?

5. Contrast the role of the selling agent with that of the manufacturer's representative.

6. Identify and briefly describe three types of merchant wholesalers.

7. Explain the term *limited-service wholesaler* and name at least four examples of intermediaries that fall into this category.

8. Contrast the independent buying office with store-connected resident offices.

9. List five services typically offered by an independent buying office.

10. What contribution does the commission house make in the marketing channel?

11. What benefits may a hardware retailer look forward to when joining a wholesaler-sponsored voluntary chain?

12. Suggest the three most important criteria that a variety store chain might rate its suppliers by.

13. Explain the following terms: *(a)* FOB Factory, *(b)* COD, *(c)* ROG dating, and *(d)* future dating.

14. A music shop receives an invoice for $2,750. It is dated April 27, and the terms indicated are 3/10, 1/30, n45. The proprietor pays the bill on May 5. How much cash discount is the owner entitled to? If the bill were paid instead on May 21, how much would the discount be?

Discussion Questions

1. Today, most large retail organizations hire buyer trainees with a college education. They send the new recruits through an extended training program where they are exposed to a variety of positions. Actual selling on the floor is an important aspect of the training. In your opinion, is this procedure worthwhile? Why, or why not?

2. Why do you think some suppliers are willing to place their goods in stores on consignment?

3. The jewelry buyer for a large discount house finds that sales per square foot are considerably below the average for jewelry departments. Suggest four ways to improve results.

4. Since the manufacturer's rep often represents several different producers and cannot concentrate on any one product line, why do you suppose a small manufacturer may want to use reps?

5. You buy merchandise for a five-unit chain of camera and photographic supply stores. Devise your own rating form for evaluating your resources. Use at least six criteria and assign more weight to those you feel are more important to your firm.

Notes

[1]Stuart F. Heinritz and Paul V. Farrell, *Purchasing: Principles and Applications,* 6th ed. (Englewood Cliffs, N.J.: Prentice-Hall, 1981), p. 3.

[2]Murray Krieger, "Buying for Retail Stores," *Small Business Bibliography No. 37* (Washington, D.C.: Small Business Administration, revised April 1981), p. 4.

[3]Michael D. Hutt, "The Retail Buying Committee: A Look at Cohesiveness and Leadership," *Journal of Retailing* 55 (Winter 1979), pp. 87–97.

[4]William R. Cline, "Imports and Consumer Prices: A Survey Analysis," *Journal of Retailing* 55 (Spring 1979), p. 24.

[5]Darlene J. Forte, "Wholesaling," *Small Business Bibliography No. 55* (Washington, D.C.: Small Business Administration, revised September 1973).

[6]Much of this material is based on information supplied in: Ernest A. Miller, "How to Select a Resident Buying Office," *Small Marketers Aids No. 116* (Washington, D.C.: Small Business Administration, reprinted September 1976).

[7]See: Roy T. Shaw, Richard J. Seminik, and Robert H. Williams, *Marketing: An Integrated Analytical Approach* (Cincinnati: South-Western Publishing, 1981), pp. 256–60.

[8]Michael Etgar, "Differences in the Use of Manufacturer Power in Conventional and Contractual Channels," *Journal of Retailing* 54 (Winter 1978), pp. 49–62.

[9]M. Etgar, "Selection of an Effective Channel Control Mix," *Journal of Marketing* 42 (July 1978), pp. 53–58.

[10]Walter B. Wentz, *Marketing* (St. Paul, Minn.: West Publishing, 1979), p. 168.

[11]Michael Etgar, "Sources and Types of Intrachannel Conflict," *Journal of Retailing* 55 (Spring 1979), pp. 61–78.

[12]Thomas W. Speh and E. H. Bonfield, "The Control Process in Marketing Channels: An Exploratory Investigation," *Journal of Retailing* 54 (Spring 1978), pp. 13–26*ff.*

[13]For a discussion of 17 fundamentals valuable in cementing good vendor relations, see: Charles G. Taylor, "How to Work with Resources," in *The Buyer's Manual: The Merchandising Handbook for All Retailers* (New York: National Retail Merchants Association, 1965), pp. 65–67. See also: Maryanne Smith Bohlinger, *Merchandise Buying: Principles and Applications* (Dubuque, Iowa: Wm. C. Brown, 1977), pp. 468–69.

[14]Donald L. Belden, *The Role of the Buyer in Mass Merchandising* (New York: Lebhar-Friedman, Chain Store Age Books, 1972), pp. 22–23.

STORE SERVICES

Your Study Objectives

After you have studied this chapter, you will understand:

1. The variety of services offered by merchandise and service retailers.
2. The many worthwhile and low-cost services that even the small independent merchant can offer.
3. How the extension of consumer purchase credit benefits the retail firm and encourages shoppers to buy.
4. The procedures retailers follow in granting credit to consumers.
5. The more popular retailer credit plans.
6. The measures retailers take in billing and collecting their accounts receivable.
7. The major federal laws that deal with consumer credit.

Services are an integral part of the modern store's offerings. Merchandise alone may not suffice to sustain the long-term growth of a retail enterprise. Today's shoppers are mature and sophisticated. They have been conditioned to expect most establishments to provide them with certain amenities. They expect prompt, courteous attention from salespeople. They want their purchases to be neatly wrapped or bagged. They expect to be able to return articles they find unsatisfactory and have adjustments made without resistance. They feel their complaints should be heard by a sympathetic ear. They look for stores that are open at convenient times and they shy away from shopping at outlets that seem unresponsive to their needs. Consumers often, prefer to buy on credit, rather than pay cash, especially if high-priced goods are involved.

In the manufacturing sector of the economy, customer service has always commanded a high level of management interest. Producers have long recognized the significance of service in making sales and in keeping customers.[1] Many set service levels higher than those expected by their customers. Through careful analysis, however, manufacturers are often able to effect considerable savings while still improving service as the customer perceives it.[2]

Services in the Retail Sector

Traditionally, retailers have regarded services not only as necessary to the merchandise mix but also as valuable promotional tools. Services can be useful in distinguishing their firms from their competitors. This is difficult to do with goods alone because many stores carry essentially the same product lines and brands. Retailers try to use distinct decor, layout, displays, advertising, and personal selling. By choosing, instituting, and actively promoting one or more services that other retailers do not offer, the firm can engage in nonprice, though nonetheless effective, competitive strategy.

Service Retailers

There are many different types of service retailers. These companies do not necessarily use storefronts, although many do. Occasionally, they may offer merchandise for sale as well as the basic service they offer to bring in additional revenue. We have witnessed a surprisingly sharp and steady growth in service retailing for many years. For example, in the area of personal services alone, there are more than half a million firms now operating year round. Among them are beauty parlors, barber shops, dry cleaners, shoe repair shops, and laundries. Another 300,000 or so companies cater principally to business and industry: advertising agencies, public relations firms, equipment-leasing companies, consultants, research services, cleaning and maintenance firms, and so on. To these service categories, we can add thousands

A major service retailer: The Hilton at Walt Disney World Village.

Courtesy Hilton Hotels Corporation, Beverly Hills, CA

of motels, hotels, racetracks, stadiums, amusement parks, theaters, tennis courts, golf courses, all kinds of legal services, automotive and appliance repair shops, music, dance, and karate studios, and dozens of other types of service enterprises.

Services Offered by Merchandise Retailers

Small independent merchants are limited in their service offerings by little available space and small operating budgets. Many can afford only the most basic: convenient store hours, parcel wrap, proper lighting, comfortable air conditioning and heating, a telephone for local calls, check acceptance, and some granting of credit. In some instances, retailers should provide special equipment for their customers' needs: high chairs for tots in restaurants, carts for supermarket shoppers, and so on. Consumers also expect certain types of establishments to offer specialized services. Examples include the installation of carpeting and other floor coverings, furniture upholstering, watch and jewelry repair, and the installation of home security systems and TV antennas. Shoppers generally seek quality in services more than any other characteristic.[3]

Most large retail companies have both the space and the finances to introduce additional services. Many rely on these services to enhance their image, foster goodwill in the community, and draw their clientele closer to the firm. A common objective is to increase the prospects for one-stop shopping. Another is to attract new customers, who may then be expected to purchase other merchandise. Department and discount stores and variety chains often encourage consumers to spend

Courtesy MAACO Enterprises, Inc., King of Prussia, PA

Eleanore Snow

*Two of the many offerings in
the growing retail sector.*

more time shopping by making food service available. This can range from a small snack bar to a full-blown, quality restaurant. General merchandise chains may induce a savings bank to install branches in their stores. A post office substation, catalog sales department, rental service for power tools, and service contracts for durable goods are all worthwhile offerings.

Many retail firms have expanded their goods and services mix in recent years by introducing entirely new services designed to produce rental income or to generate profits directly. Indeed, the retailing of services sold apart from merchandise seems to hold promise for today's larger establishments. Travel agencies, optometry departments, the preparation of income tax forms, and homeowners' and automobile insurance policies were among the many innovations introduced in the late 1960s and early 1970s. Nowadays, we find even newer types being offered. Only a decade ago, few consumers ever dreamed of finding some of these in a retail environment. Already offered in many locations are legal services, podiatry, dental services, and a host of financial services. Long popularized by retailers such as J. C. Penney and Sears, Roebuck & Co., financial services are entering other retailing arenas. As an example, the Kroger Company, a giant chain of some 1,200 supermarkets and 500 pharmacies in 21 states set up a financial center in one of its markets in 1982. This was a joint venture with an insurance company. The center sells not only insurance but also mutual funds, IRAs (individual retirement accounts), and money market funds.[4]

**Customer
Satisfaction**

Retail organizations need and want to build satisfying, long-term relationships with consumers. Prompt, courteous service and fair treatment are the twin pathways to developing a steady, loyal clientele. The dissatisfied customer no longer is a loyal customer. Consequently, top management needs to set into place firm policy and procedure for satisfying shoppers.

Relatively few unhappy customers complain to retailers about discourtesy or improper handling by their salespeople. Complaints made are easily handled with an apology at the time, followed by improved employee training. Most complaints have to do with goods that customers bring back to the store. Some more commonly heard reasons for such returns are:

"The garment does not fit well."

"This article isn't wearing well."

"The merchandise is damaged (soiled, torn)."

"It's the wrong size."

"It doesn't work properly."

"I ordered this by mail and it arrived too late. I no longer want it."

"The wrong item was delivered to me."

"I received this as a gift and I cannot use it."

"I saw this at your competitor's store. Their price is much lower."

To keep their customers content, most firms make adjustments readily. Retailers are quick to understand that, in some situations, the company may be at fault. Mistakes may have been made in buying goods for resale. Merchandise on the racks may have been handled far too much. Salespeople may have sold some customers the wrong sizes or may have been too aggressive in persuading shoppers to buy. Experienced merchants know, too, that some consumers are more likely to complain than others. Among the many shopper variables that can affect the likelihood of complaint behavior are "personality, attitudes, motives, perceived value of time, information level, and sociodemographics."[5] It is also true that a small percentage of complaints have little merit. Indeed, an exploratory study in one suburban department store bore this out, suggesting that some consumer complaints are unreasonable and even fraudulent.[6]

Frequently Offered Services

Most retailers offer some services to their customers free or at a modest charge. Those services most often found are briefly described in this section.

Some Popular Services

Alterations Some retailers find that they need to maintain well-equipped and well-staffed workrooms. Here, trained employees touch up, polish, repair, or make **alterations** in merchandise for customers. Apparel shops are an example. Whether they sell men's, women's, or children's clothing, they must arrange for someone to tailor the garments to fit their patrons. Jackets, sleeves, and trousers frequently must be shortened or lengthened. Shoulders may have to be padded. Buttons may have to be moved on jackets or vests. Skilled tailors, usually well paid, are kept on the payroll to make the necessary changes. Some firms, especially those offering higher-priced clothing, provide this service free of charge. The more popular approach today is, however, to charge modest fees for alterations. These fees help retailers recover part or all of their costs.

Bulletin Boards As a community relations gesture, supermarkets, discount and variety stores, and other large operations often install a bulletin board at or near their store entrances. On these boards, neighborhood residents may tack up announcements of upcoming garage sales, baby-sitting help wanted, used typewriters, sewing machines, or bicycles for sale, and the like. Local community groups can post information about school plays or church-related events, fund-raising drives, civic meetings, and so on. The bulletin board has considerable impact and the cost is infinitesimal. Retailers realize that these boards must be carefully monitored. They must be kept neat, clean, and current. Outdated notices, unwanted or obscene material, and information that is incongruent with the firm's image must be removed.

Check Cashing This popular service is offered by most retailers. Typically, the merchant will cash personal checks for shoppers only in the amount of the merchandise purchased and up to a specified limit. Checks that have been altered or dated ahead and second-party checks are generally avoided. (See "Check Acceptance Guidelines" in Chapter 6.)

Coffee and Other Refreshments A relatively inexpensive and easily offered service from independent retailers is the free cup of coffee. Shoppers welcome this kind of attention, especially in chilly weather. Whether the coffee is brewed or instant, the customer's reaction is almost always one of pleasure. A jar of nondairy creamer, some sugar, stirrers, and a box of napkins complete the setup. Some stores vary the approach, offering instead hot chocolate, tea, or other warm drink. During the summer months, cool beverages may be enjoyed by shoppers.

Of course, the refreshment area should be kept spotless at all times and supplies should be refilled frequently.

Delivery Service Fried chicken outlets, pizza parlors, Chinese restaurants, and other food places frequently offer delivery service at a modest charge. Some groceries deliver free of charge in the immediate neighborhood. Deliveries may be made by truck, van, or car. This service is convenient and often leads to customers patronizing one store rather than another.[7] Several retailers in an area may band together and establish their own delivery service. Or they may use the services of an independent company for deliveries. The United Parcel Service (UPS) and the U.S. Postal Service are alternatives for small and large retailers alike. Chain store operations, department and departmentized specialty stores, and other large companies may deploy their own trucks, whether owned or rented. Some merchants rely on common carriers to deliver their goods. Large, freestanding discount houses and similar-sized outlets may set up a parcel pickup department at the rear of the building for the convenience of their patrons. Customers can drive up to the department and have their purchases deposited directly into their cars.

Because of steadily rising costs, most department stores no longer deliver merchandise free of charge.[8] Many set a minimum fee, regardless of package size or weight, of from $1 to $3 for deliveries to residences within a 25- to 50-mile radius. Charges for heavier goods such as major appliances and furniture, may range as high as $30 or $35.

Gift Certificates A convenient service for consumers who do not know what gifts to buy, **gift certificates** are a fine way for the retailer to bring in additional revenue. These are usually printed in several denominations, such as $5, $10, and $20. Upscale firms favor even larger face amounts.

Gift Wrapping Shoppers expect their purchases to be bagged or wrapped so they can carry them home comfortably. Many articles are purchased, however, as gifts for special occasions. The Christmas holiday season is the busiest period of all for gift wrapping, but this service is in demand throughout the year. Shoppers want merchandise gift wrapped for birthdays and anniversaries, Mother's and Father's Day, first communions, bar and bas mitzvahs, and so on. The larger stores often maintain departments where shoppers can take their purchases to be wrapped. Plain wrap may be free, or it may carry a modest charge of, say, 50 cents. Fancy boxes of various sizes and colors, ribbons, and bows are available at prices from $1 to $2.50 or more, depending on the customer's preference. Even the smallest independent store can offer this popular service to its clientele with no more than a modest investment in supplies.

Information and Instructions With some kinds of merchandise, shoppers need and expect assistance from the retailer. Examples include knitting wools and accessories, art supplies, ceramic wares, sporting goods, audio equipment, hardware, plumbing and electrical supplies, and the like. Help may be available in the form of technical advice from the salesperson, through printed instruction sheets, by holding classes on

Ample parking facilities encourage shopping.

Courtesy White Stores, Inc., Wichita Falls, TX

the premises to teach customers how to use or finish the articles they buy, and so on.

Music To enhance the shopping environment, malls and individual stores frequently arrange for pleasant, subdued music to be piped into them. At even less cost, retailers can provide background music for their customers with radio or tape player.

Parking Parking problems are seldom encountered in most of the planned shopping centers. In-city retailers, however, may find that their customers have difficulty parking, especially where metered spaces are few in number or nonexistent. Occasionally, merchants in a neighborhood will band together to press the local government to install meters. Retail firms may also be able to contract with a nearby facility for parking space for their customers.

Rain Checks During any advertised sales event, a firm may run out of featured merchandise. When this occurs, shoppers often request a **rain check.** A rain check is a form, or slip of paper, which entitles the shopper to buy the out-of-stock article at a future date and at the sale price. Some retailers go even further, providing postcards for the shopper to fill in and leave with the store. When the stock has been replenished, the postcards are mailed to inform shoppers so they can come in to purchase the item.

Courtesy Hess Shoes, Baltimore, MD/Betsy H. Hess

Richard D. Irwin, Inc./John Thoeming

Left, seating, a necessary service in a shoe store, can become an attractive part of the decor; right, store merchants realize that providing shopping carts is an expensive but necessary customer service.

Restrooms More than simply a convenience, restrooms for men and women become a necessity in stores where shoppers spend a great deal of time. Unfortunately, many retailers prefer not to make restrooms available to customers, even when labor regulations require their installation for employees. Some are afraid that they encourage shoplifting. Some companies control restroom doors with electric locks. Usually they also post signs that warn shoppers against taking store merchandise with them inside. Others fear they would prove too costly to maintain properly. In such cases, the retailer might prove penny wise, pound foolish.

Returns and Adjustments In the smaller store, returns and adjustments are handled by the owner or manager. In larger operations, a customer service department is often set up to take care of these problems. Usually, the merchandise must first be brought to the attention of the manager of the department where it was purchased. Here, the shopper secures a signed approval slip from the department head and proceeds to the customer service section where adjustment is made. The firm may offer to exchange the item for similar or other goods, issue a credit slip for the amount of the return, or make a cash refund.

A common policy is to refund the money if the register receipt accompanies the returned article and the merchandise is still salable. Often, time limits are posted near the cash register. In New York and some other states, there are laws on the books governing where and how store refund policies must be displayed.[9] The period during which returned goods are readily accepted may run from one to two

Taco Bell's customer services include extended store hours and a drive-up window for carry-out orders.

Courtesy Taco Bell, Irvine, CA

weeks and even up to a month after purchase. If items are returned after expiration of the time limit or without register receipts, many retailers will persuade the consumer to take a credit slip instead of a cash refund.

Seating Tired shoppers welcome being able to sit down, if only for a few minutes. In apparel stores, people waiting for friends or spouses to finish shopping are especially pleased if several chairs are available. Seats can be placed near the fitting room or on the side, where they do not interfere with store traffic.

Shopping Carts Shopping carts are seen in every supermarket. Similar wagons, smaller versions of the supermarket cart, are provided for the shopper's convenience in many discount and variety stores, meat markets, groceries, and the like. Some retailers avoid investing a considerable sum of money in wagons by purchasing relatively inexpensive carrying baskets for shoppers to use. These are usually light in weight, being made of heavy cloth reinforced with metal rods. Store merchants realize that carriers or carts are more a necessity than a service.

Store Hours In planned shopping centers, the stores are generally required to follow the opening and closing times specified by the tenants' association. For most in-city locations, retailers usually go along with the store hours set by other firms in the vicinity. In many cases, this means opening at 9 or 9:30 in the morning, closing some days at 5:30 or 6, and remaining open two or three nights during the week. Any retailer can, however, stay open longer or open up earlier than neighboring stores. These decisions should, of course, be made with shopper preferences in mind.

Telephones Shoppers appreciate being able to call home or summon a taxi from the store. Where there is ample space, retailers may have pay telephones installed. Other stores permit customers to use their business telephone for local calls.

Telephone Shopping Department stores, specialty goods chains, and some independent retailers encourage their clienteles to order goods by telephone. Frequently they promote this service in their newspaper advertising and by direct mail. Inserts, folders, and/or brochures are sent along with the monthly statements mailed to their charge customers. Trained telephone salespeople handle orders promptly and efficiently.

Managing Customer Credit

At the root of every credit transaction are trust and belief in the individual. When a company sells goods on credit, it does so with the expectation that the purchaser will make full payment within a reasonable period.

Consumer credit is of two types: loan and purchase. **Loan credit** has to do with a consumer borrowing an amount of money and promising to repay the lender at some future date or according to a set schedule. With the exception, perhaps, of loans from family members or friends, the borrower normally must pay interest on the loan. The term **purchase credit** applies to buying merchandise or a service without paying for it in full at the time of purchase. Interest charges may or may not apply, depending on the type of credit extended. Some retail companies offer their own credit plans. Others willingly accept bank credit cards (VISA and MasterCard, for example) or travel and entertainment cards such as American Express and Diner's Club.

Why Credit Is Offered

Today's shopper is extremely credit-oriented. Consumers like credit because it makes their shopping easier. They do not need to carry around large amounts of money to pay for the goods they buy. They can purchase merchandise today that they cannot yet afford and pay for it over time. Credit also makes ordering by mail or telephone simpler. Many people believe that stores accept returned merchandise more readily when it has been charged to their accounts. Some also feel that retail salespeople treat charge customers better than cash customers and adjust their complaints more quickly.[10]

Retailers extend credit to responsible patrons to increase sales revenue and as a way of differentiating their stores from others. According to one survey, women holding charge accounts bought more—both on credit and in cash—than cash-only shoppers.[11] Not only do charge customers buy more, they are also more store loyal. They prefer shopping at places that honor their credit cards or will extend credit on their own. Moreover, the list of charge customers developed by a retailer can be promoted by mail and/or telephone to bring in additional sales volume. Many firms enclose mailing pieces with their monthly statements or send out catalogs periodically.

Retailers try to build long-term, pleasant, and profitable relationships with their charge customers. They realize, too, that the extension of credit encourages the purchase of more expensive goods.

How Retail Credit Is Handled   If a company offers its own credit plan, the procedure by which consumers are granted this privilege typically involves the following steps:

1. The shopper fills out a credit application form such as the one shown in Figure 17.1.
2. All information submitted is checked, and a report on the shopper is obtained from a credit bureau.[12]
3. The decision is made to grant credit or reject the application.
4. A dollar limit is established for credit purchases by the approved applicant.
5. The account is thereafter monitored.

The typical charge application calls for the customer to indicate name, address, and telephone number; specify the length of residence at that address; provide details regarding current employment (where, how long in the position, earnings, and so on); furnish details as to prior residence and prior job; list bank accounts, outstanding loans and charge account balances due elsewhere; indicate sources of other income; give personal references; and other details.

In evaluating an application, retail companies usually employ their own numerical scoring system. This makes for more careful analysis of the information and also introduces objectivity into the process.[13] More weight is assigned to certain facts than to others. Weighted criteria are the applicant's earning level, number of years in residence at both present and prior addresses, whether the person owns or rents the premises, length of employment, and the like. During the evaluation process, the credit department attempts to determine the **three Cs of credit:** the character, capacity, and capital of the applicant.

A person's *character* is generally understood to be the personality—the set of qualities that makes that individual distinct from others. In the world of credit, the term has little to do with how we live or behave. Instead, it refers to an assessment of our past history or perfor-

Courtesy J. C. Penney Company, Inc.

mance in paying obligations and managing our financial affairs. To determine the credit applicant's *capacity,* a judgment must be rendered about that person's ability to pay back obligations. The question to be answered affirmatively is: Can the applicant afford to pay debts out of current income? Finally, the term *capital* refers to net worth—how much the applicant has left in assets after all present liabilities are subtracted.

It should be noted that credit must not be denied because of age, sex, religion, nationality, and the like. (See Table 17.1.) Nor can marital status be used to refuse credit. Indeed, lenders' reports to credit agencies must include the names of both spouses "if both use the account and if either requests the dual reporting."[14]

Table 17.1 **Federal consumer credit** **legislation**	**Year** **Enacted**	**Name of Law**	**Salient Details**
	1969	Consumer Credit Protection Act (Truth in Lending)	Mandates the full disclosure by sellers of credit costs and terms. Limits the liability of credit card holders.
	1970	Fair Credit Reporting Act	Regulates information reported by credit bureaus and other agencies. Ensures fair treatment and accuracy of data. Gives the consumer the right to have incorrect information investigated and to ascertain reasons for denial of credit.
	1975	Equal Credit Opportunity Act	Prohibits the retailer from discriminating against credit applicants on the basis of sex or marital status. Subsequently amended (1977) to include other characteristics: race, color, religion, national origin.
	1975	Fair Credit Billing Act	Amends the Consumer Credit Protection Act. Sets forth guidelines for billing charge customers. Establishes a procedure for resolving accounts in dispute. The customer must be informed of the retailer's procedure.
	1977	Fair Debt Collection Practices Act	Attempts to prevent customer harassment and abusive tactics by collection agencies. Prohibits the use of subterfuge, threats, and contacting people in debt at inconvenient times.

Credit Plans for Shoppers

Every retail firm must decide whether to extend credit to its customers or to run a cash-only operation. Once the decision to offer credit is made, retailers face three options: extend some form of store-based credit, rely on outside, or third-party plans, or combine both approaches. Today, both bank credit cards and travel/entertainment cards are so widely distributed that most credit-worthy individuals already possess them. This fact alone has encouraged many merchants to avoid risk by limiting credit sales to outside plans. Some larger companies still carry and actively promote their own plans. They feel that these weld a closer bond between customer and store and discourage consumers from shopping at a competitor.

Store credit plans include open-account, revolving, option-terms, and installment credit.

Open-account Credit Long before the advent of the bank credit card, there were innumerable instances where consumers lacked the cash needed to pay for merchandise they wished to buy. Rather than lose these sales, retailers would permit many of their regular customers to buy on credit. The shopkeeper would duly record each transaction. To keep alive their credit-worthiness, clients were expected to pay the balance owed in their accounts in a reasonable time. Eventually, custom dictated that 30 days following the date of purchase was a reasonable expectation for payment in full. No down payment was required, nor was any carrying charge added to the account. Of course, merchants would extend this privilege only to customers who appeared trustworthy and able to pay in time. Nevertheless, some accounts were never fully paid off. Debtors would occasionally move away, leaving behind their liabilities.

Known as **open-account,** or **regular, credit,** this type of service is still provided by many establishments. Today's high cost of money and the risk of incurring bad debts has led to retailers instituting tight policies and procedures for handling consumer credit applications.

Revolving Credit Under the **revolving credit** plan, a credit limit is set for each customer. Shoppers are permitted to buy up to the established amount, with all purchases charged to their accounts. As payment is made, the customer may buy additional merchandise, again up to the limit. There is a customary 30-day period after billing for clearing up all indebtedness with no penalty asked.

Option-terms Credit This is probably the most popular form of credit advanced today by department stores and chains. **Option-terms credit** combines open-account and revolving credit. Under this procedure, the charge customer may choose one of two options: (1) to pay the bill in full within 30 days or (2) to make a partial payment and then clear up the balance over a number of months. A minimum sum is usually required in each subsequent payment.

With the first choice, there is no additional charge. Finance charges are added in the event that the customer exercises the second option. These are calculated monthly on the balance that remains in the account.

Installment Credit The **installment credit plan** requires that the customer place a down payment on the article purchased. The buyer pays out

**Figure 17.2
An installment
agreement form**

Seller's Name: _____   Contract #_____

RETAIL INSTALLMENT CONTRACT AND SECURITY AGREEMENT

The undersigned (herein called Purchaser, whether one or more) purchases from _____ _____ (seller) and grants to _____ a security interest, in, subject to the terms and conditions hereof, the following described property.

QUANTITY	DESCRIPTION	AMOUNT

Description of Trade-In:

	Sales Tax	
	Total	

Insurance Agreement

The purchase of insurance coverage is voluntary and not required for credit. _____(Type of Ins.) Insurance coverage is available at a cost of $_____ for the term of credit.

  I desire insurance coverage

Signed _____ Date _____

  I do not desire insurance coverage

Signed _____ Date _____

PURCHASER'S NAME _____
PURCHASER'S ADDRESS _____
CITY _____ STATE _____ ZIP _____

1. CASH PRICE $_____
2. LESS: CASH DOWN
             PAYMENT $_____
3.   TRADE-IN   _____
4.   TOTAL DOWN
             PAYMENT   _____$_____

5. UNPAID BALANCE OF CASH
    PRICE $_____
6. OTHER CHARGES:

   _____ $_____
   _____ $_____
7. AMOUNT FINANCED $_____
8. FINANCE CHARGE $_____
9. TOTAL OF PAYMENTS $_____
10. DEFERRED PAYMENT PRICE
     (1+6+8) $_____
11. ANNUAL PERCENTAGE RATE _____%

Purchaser hereby agrees to pay to _____ _____ at their offices shown above the "TOTAL OF PAYMENTS" shown above in _____ monthly installments of $_____(final payment to be $_____) the first installment being payable _____ 19____, and all subsequent installments on the same day of each consecutive month until paid in full. The finance charge applies from __(Date)

Signed _____

Notice to Buyer: You are entitled to a copy of the contract you sign. You have the right to pay in advance the unpaid balance of this contract and obtain a partial refund of the finance charge based on the "Actuarial Method." [Any other method of computation may be so identified, for example, "Rule of 78's," "Sum of the Digits," etc.]

Source: Benny L. Kass, "Understanding Truth in Lending," *Small Marketers Aids No. 139* (Washington, D.C.: Small Business Administration, reprinted April 1974), p. 7.

the balance owed in a series of installments. The shopper is usually asked to sign a conditional sales contract. Even though the customer takes the merchandise away, the retailer continues to own it until it has been fully paid for. In some instances, ownership may be transferred to the buyer but secured by a chattel mortgage. A retail installment agreement is shown in Figure 17.2.

The customer may be issued a book that contains detachable cou-

"Can I put myself in until Christmas?"

pons, one to be submitted with each payment. Or the retail firm may simply send out statements each month to installment buyers. Should the customer default, that is to say, fail to make the payments as they become due, the merchandise may be repossessed by the retailer.

The Consumer Credit Protection Act of 1969, more popularly known as **Truth in Lending,** requires the retailer to make full disclosure of the details of every installment sale. This includes, among other information, the amount of the purchase, size of the down payment requested, finance charge to be added and annual rate of interest it reflects, and dates when additional payments are to be made. Every customer has the **right of rescission**—the right to cancel an order within three days after having signed a contract. Installment contracts are also regulated by law in many states. Of special interest to consumers as well as state legislators are interest rates and service charges. Indeed, many shoppers appear to be more sensitive to such rates than to the price of the article purchased.[15]

Layaway Plans Many merchants actively promote a **layaway plan** as a customer service. The technique is designed for shoppers who are unable to buy merchandise, usually expensive articles, outright. Consumers regard these plans as forms of credit extension, although in reality they are not. The retailer does not transfer ownership of the merchandise until the customer has paid for it in full. To secure an article in the first place, a down payment is required. The balance due must be paid out over a reasonable period. Often, this is accomplished in three equal monthly installments (the 90-day or three-month plan). Retailers who offer layaways must fully understand the need for keeping accurate records. Some consumers may renege on the agreement, failing to make the required payments. If this happens, the merchant returns the item to the selling stock. Sometimes the article may have to be marked down to assure its sale. This is often the case with fashion goods.

Outside Credit Card Plans

Retailers use credit widely to attract new shoppers and to encourage additional purchases from present customers. Surprisingly enough, a particular type of credit plan may not necessarily enhance a store's attractiveness to consumers. Indeed, the most widely accepted form of credit among shoppers appears to be the bank credit card plan.[16]

Bank cards such as MasterCard and VISA can bring in significant sales volume to smaller retailers. These firms generally lack the managerial or financial capability to maintain and promote their own charge account systems. The banks take care of the initial screening and approval of credit applications, as well as all record-keeping, billing, and collection of outstanding balances. In turn, the retailers receive their money promptly. Monies are not tied up in accounts receivable; revenue can be reinvested at once in goods for resale.

Outside plans, however, have several drawbacks. For one thing, the merchant must pay a small percentage of sales (perhaps 4 or 5 percent) for the service. This is not always a disadvantage. In recent years, more than a few large retail companies shelved their internal credit programs because of continually rising operating costs. They found that accepting bank credit cards actually saved them money. Another drawback is that the retailer loses an ongoing opportunity for additional sales volume by enclosing direct-mail pieces with the monthly statements mailed to charge customers. Finally, people who use bank credit cards rather than store charge plans are perfectly free to shop elsewhere. They are less prone to be store-loyal customers.

Gulf, Shell, Exxon, and other gasoline companies offer consumers their own credit cards. Depending on the individual plan, these may be used not only for oil and gasoline but also for car repairs, tires, lodging at hotels and motels, and other types of purchases. Diner's Club and American Express are well-known examples of credit card plans available for charging expenses for travel, dining out, and entertainment.

Recently, there has been a great deal of experimentation with electronic funds transferring (EFT) systems in connection with bank cards.

In one instance, both NCR Corporation and Iowa Transfer System, Inc. (a clearinghouse for statewide financial institutions) cooperated with Dahl's Foods, Inc., in Des Moines, Iowa, to set up a pilot program. Customers can pay for their groceries with their bank credit cards. The shopper "simply passes the plastic card through a magnetic-stripe reader built into a point-of-sale terminal that also functions as a cash register, punches in a personal identification number, and the amount of the tab is instantly transferred" from the account to that of the supermarket.[17]

Billing the Charge Customer

Retail companies that extend credit usually mail out statements to their charge account customers at the end of each month. A statement of the balance due may suffice for the small independent. Some organizations, however, carry so many names on file that their accounts receivable department cannot physically handle them in the few days preceding the first of the month. Large department store chains, for example, may have upward of 1 or 2 million charge account regulars. Such firms customarily bill in cycles. Different dates for outgoing statements are assigned to groups of customers according to the spelling of their last names (since the files are kept alphabetically). Charge customers whose last names begin, for example, with the letters *Aa* to *Ch* may be billed on the 10th of every month. Statements for those with surnames in the *Ci* to *Em* category will be dated on the 11th, and so on.

Billing Formats Larger companies tend to select one of two procedures: descriptive billing or country club billing. In **descriptive billing,** every transaction made during the period covered is entered with the date on the customer's statement. Also shown are the branch and department where the purchase was made, the amount of the purchase, any payments that have been received during the period, and all credits given for goods the customer may have returned. Debits and credits are then totaled and the balance due on the account is indicated. The statement also contains the shopper's account number, a reference telephone listing for making inquiries, the finance charge that has been added, and the minimum payment expected.

Some retail firms use **country club billing.** A monthly statement is mailed to charge customers; this carries much of the same information indicated in the descriptive billing approach. A notable difference is that original copies of sales slips for all transactions are enclosed with the statement. This makes it simpler for the buyer to check the slips against the copies picked up at the store when the purchases were made. Clearly, this is a more costly approach for the retailer in postage alone—not to mention the time and labor needed to handle, file, and assort the various sales slips. Still, country club billing does provide more shopper convenience.

Collecting Past-due Accounts

The NCR Corporation, with world headquarters in Dayton, Ohio, offers this advice to retail companies:

> Profits in a business depend upon the number of times a merchant can turn over his capital. Frequent turnovers can hardly be accomplished with slow collection. The longer an account is allowed to run, the harder it is to collect.

* * * * *

> The retailer can lose customers and suffer losses by allowing balances to increase beyond the danger line. People do not like to trade where they are deeply in debt, and so they do their buying elsewhere. It is highly important to keep customers open to buying by having them pay their accounts promptly.

> About 80 percent of all credit accounts become past due at some time during their life. About 20 percent of the amount becomes sufficiently delinquent to be put in the hands of collectors—IF they are not followed up closely. A good follow-up system not only reduces this materially, but also prevents accounts from becoming past due in the first place.[18]

The retailer's credit department must first institute an effective program for identifying and screening out people who are doubtful risks. No program yet devised can promise complete security, however. Thus, a second challenge is to design a procedure for monitoring outstanding receivables and minimizing the likelihood of accumulating bad debts. On the one hand, retail management dislikes losing a charge customer whose long-term contribution to sales and profits is likely to be much greater than that of the cash buyer. On the other hand, the firm needs to keep payments flowing in, in a respectable time frame for each and every account on the books. This becomes even more vital during times when the cost of borrowing capital increases.

An efficient debt-collection procedure holds outstanding balances to a minimum. It also reduces internal costs: for clerical help, stationery, postage, and telephone calls. Handling the delinquent account typically calls for dispatching, at first, a gently worded reminder. If no response is elicited from the customer, the credit department will begin to send out a series of letters spaced over a number of weeks. As suggested in Figure 17.3, each successive piece of correspondence becomes firmer in tone than the one preceding. If these fail, one or several telephone calls may be placed. Care must be exercised to conform to the tenor of the Fair Debt Collection Practices Act of 1977. Finally, the account may be turned over to an outside agency for collection. Unfortunately for the retail company, fees charged by collection agents may run as high as 40 or 50 percent of the amount owed. Retailers may also institute legal action against delinquent customers.

Figure 17.3
Personalized collection letters

One of the best methods to collect past-due accounts is through the use of personalized collection letters. Here, above all, tact must be used and the appeal varied because not everyone responds to the same appeal.

The first letter of the series should be a friendly reminder. There must be no hint of suspicion that the debtor does not fully intend to pay. In fact, willingness must be assumed, and the merchant must make the assumption evident. The debtor who is treated with suspicion responds in the same manner.

Pride is one of the strongest appeals to the debtor who has few or no tangible assets. The publicity accompanying suit . . . exposure of the fact that there are no assets . . . the humiliation of letting friends and neighbors know of nonpayment of debts . . . these may be used to good effect, but only after frank and friendly appeals have proved futile.

Future need is another strong appeal. Customers should be shown what it means to have the right to credit destroyed by not paying promptly. They should be told that they might require credit in the future and be unable to obtain it if the right is abused.

Merchants usually use a series of four or five collection letters. Each becomes slightly more firm and more urgent than the last. The final letter usually sets a time limit and warns that legal action will be taken without further notice unless payment is made. Threats should never be made unless all other means have failed. Then the merchant should do exactly what was promised.

These letters should be personal and written on the store's letterhead. They should be typed, not mimeographed, lithographed, or printed. Mailings that are 10 days to two weeks apart are preferred. They should be mailed so that the debtor receives them on a Wednesday or Thursday rather than the first or the last day of the week.

Source: NCR Corporation, *Credit and Collections.* Copyright 1981, NCR Corporation.

Summary

Services are an integral part of the retailing mix. They are also useful promotional tools and a form of nonprice competition. Merchandise retailers have always offered some services with their product offerings: wrapping and bagging, convenient store hours, salesclerk service, alterations or installation, and the like. Today, many offer additional, relatively new services. Some are tied to the purchase of goods. Others are sold independently of store merchandise. Retailers now provide the services of travel agencies, optometrists, podiatrists, and income tax preparers. Other retail offerings include dental clinics, insurance agencies, pharmacies, financial services, and so on.

In recent years, service retailing has been growing rapidly. There are now more than half a million service retailers. Among the older and more familiar types are beauty parlors, dry cleaning establishments, car-repair shops, hotels and motels, schools, and places of entertainment.

Whether dispensing goods, services, or both, retailers try to build customer satisfaction in the hopes of welding effective, long-term, and profitable relationships. Regardless of the size of their firms, most retailers stress consumer service. Many services are offered free of charge or at nominal cost to the shopper.

A major service is the extension of consumer purchase credit. Credit makes it easier for the consumer to shop. Store merchants who offer credit find that their sales volume goes up. They also succeed in distinguishing their stores from those of competitors who do not extend credit to consumers.

Credit privileges depend on the three Cs of credit: the applicant's character, capacity, and capital. The more popular retail credit plans include open-account, revolving, option-terms, and installment credit. Typically, the majority of retailers honor bank, travel and entertainment, and other major outside credit card plans.

Retailers bill charge customers monthly. Some do cycle billing because of large numbers of accounts. Statements may be in descriptive or country club billing format. To reduce costs and hold bad debts to a minimum, retailers must install an effective collection system for their charge customers.

Key Terms

alterations	option terms credit
gift certificates	installment credit plan
rain check	Truth in Lending Act
loan credit	right of rescission
purchase credit	layaway plan
three Cs of credit	descriptive billing
open-account (regular) credit	country club billing
revolving credit	

**Review
Questions**

1. Services are often referred to as forms of nonprice competition. Explain.

2. Customers occasionally return goods which were purchased by others and given to them as gifts. Should the retailer accept such merchandise willingly and make refunds if shoppers so desire? Why or why not?

3. Suggest a minimum of seven low-cost services that even the small store owner can provide.

4. Offer three reasons why retailers benefit by offering their customers credit.

5. In the credit management field, what is meant by an applicant's *character?*

6. How does ordinary credit differ from a revolving charge account?

7. Explain how a 90-day layaway plan works.

8. Differentiate between descriptive and country club billing.

9. What is the *right of rescission?*

10. What is meant by *truth in lending?*

11. Review the logical progression of steps to take in attempting to collect past-due accounts.

12. Briefly describe the thrust of each of the following federal laws: *(a)* Consumer Credit Protection Act, *(b)* Equal Credit Opportunity Act, and *(c)* Fair Debt Collection Practices Act.

**Discussion
Questions**

1. What are some of the benefits which would accrue to a regional discount store chain that offers such professional services as a dental clinic and legal services? Why might consumers use store-based services instead of visiting their own dentists or lawyers?

2. Interview the owners of a few shops in your neighborhood and ask them about their policy on returns and adjustments. Prepare a short report outlining your findings.

3. Visit a local supermarket that has a bulletin board for use by residents of the community. Make a list of the kinds of notices you find tacked to the board. Do you think the retailer's use of a community bulletin board is an effective public relations measure for the firm?

Notes

[1] Paul Harvey Zinszer, "Customer Service as an Element of the Marketing Mix: The Evaluation of a Descriptive Model of Customer Service," Ph.D. dissertation, Ohio State University, 1977.

[2] Robert E. Sabath, "How Much Service Do Customers Really Want?" *Business Horizons* 21 (April 1978), pp. 26–32.

[3] Lee Adler and James D. Hlavacek, "Key Repair Service Factors for Consumer Durable Goods," *Journal of Marketing Research* 15 (November 1978), pp. 634–38.

[4] "Ohio Supermarket Is Selling Insurance and Mutual Funds," *New York Times,* 28 September 1982, p. A13.

[5] Jacob Jacoby and James J. Jaccard, "The Source, Meaning, and Validity of Consumer Complaint Behavior: A Psychological Analysis," *Journal of Retailing* 57 (Fall 1981), pp. 4–24.

[6] Noel B. Zabriskie, "Fraud by Consumers," *Journal of Retailing* 48 (Winter 1972–73), pp. 22–27.

[7] A helpful guide for the independent retailer is: Gerald B. Halverson, "Can You Afford Delivery Service?" *Small Marketers Aids No. 133* (Washington, D.C.: Small Business Administration, reprinted September 1976).

[8] Ron Alexander, "Store Delivery Charges Cover Wide Range," *New York Times,* 4 September 1982, p. 18.

[9]Marian Burk Rothman, "New Guides for Handling Returns," *Stores* 60 (September 1978), p. 22.

[10]Robert D. Breth, "The Challenge of Charge Accounts to Discount Merchants," *Journal of Retailing* 40 (Winter 1964–65), pp. 11–16*ff.*

[11]Ibid., p. 12.

[12]There are more than 2,000 credit bureaus throughout the United States, Canada, and some other countries. All are members of the Associated Credit Bureaus of America, Inc., headquartered in Houston, Texas. See: W. Henry Blake, "Retail Credit and Collections," *Small Business Bibliography No. 31* (Washington, D.C.: Small Business Administration, reprinted April 1981), p. 3.

[13]Credit legislation since the late 1960s has resulted in more objectivity in decisions of credit officers. See: John R. Nevin and Gilbert A. Churchill, "The Equal Credit Opportunity Act: An Evaluation," *Journal of Marketing* 43 (Spring 1979), pp. 95–104.

[14]"Married Women Get a Credit Rating," *Business Week,* 6 June 1977, p. 28.

[15]Orville C. Walker, Jr. and Richard F. Sauter, "Consumer Preferences for Alternative Retail Credit Terms: A Concept Test of the Effects of Consumer Legislation," *Journal of Marketing Research* 11 (February 1974), pp. 70–78.

[16]Michael J. Etzel and James H. Donnelly, Jr., "Consumer Perceptions of Alternative Retail Credit Plans," *Journal of Retailing* 48 (Summer 1972), pp. 67–73.

[17]"Electronic Shopping Builds a Base," *Business Week,* 26 October 1981, pp. 125*ff.*

[18]NCR Corporation, *Credits and Collections.* Copyright 1981, NCR Corporation.

Case 5.1
Kirby's Department
Store

Randy Wyler is an executive trainee at the flagship store of Kirby's, a small department store chain with branches in two of the north central states. Midway through the merchandising training program, he is assigned to assist Louise Wallens, the senior menswear buyer. As part of his preparation, Ms. Wallens wants Randy to help plan her department's merchandise requirements for the upcoming fall/ winter season. As a preliminary project, she asks Randy to work up some information about her winter outerwear section.

Her instructions to Randy are as follows:

1. Given the following information, work out the winter outerwear section's sales goals for each of the six months:
   a. Projected outerwear sales for the season: $620,000.
   b. Expected monthly percentages of total season's sales are:

August	3%
September	5
October	8
November	19
December	42
January	23
Total	100%

2. Determine the BOM outerwear inventory needed at retail for each month by using the stock-to-sales-ratio approach. Last year's actuals are given below:

Month	Sales	BOM Stock
August	$ 17,050	$ 24,800
September	27,670	65,750
October	40,120	115,670
November	106,340	343,110
December	229,210	857,240
January	127,080	407,680

Question   1. Assume that you are in Randy's place and looking forward excitedly to a buying career at Kirby's. Demonstrate your grasp of the processes involved by working up the information Ms. Wallens has requested.

Case 5.2
Johnson & Smith's, Ltd.

Johnson & Smith's is a specialty apparel chain with stores throughout several mid-Atlantic states. Only two weeks ago, Harriet Gleason successfully completed her 16 months of management training with the company. She was rewarded with a promotion to the position of assistant buyer and assigned to the junior sportswear department. She is now in the throes of preparing her department's six-month plan for the spring/summer season. On her worksheet, Harriet has listed the following projections for the month of May:

Gross sales	$28,700
Customer returns	550
Expenses	10,480
Profit	1,435
Markdowns	1,150
Employee discounts	230
Stock shortages	240
Customer discounts	450

Questions   1. What initial markup percentage should Harriet plan to use?

2. If she had projected a total of $2,000 in markdowns, rather than $1,150, what would be the initial markup percentage required?

Case 5.3
Maison Dianne

Situated in a busy shopping center in Lincoln, Nebraska, Maison Dianne offers a variety of better dresses to middle-income women between the ages of 18 and 35. In less than two years, the owner, Dianne Coleman, succeeded in building a small but loyal clientele.

Three months after opening the store, she added limited assortments of higher-priced scarves, belts, and handbags. In both quality and price, these new lines were entirely in keeping with the store image she hoped to project. By featuring these accessory items in her secondary window, she quickly established a flourishing "second business." Maison Dianne's annual sales volume is now approaching $230,000. Accessories account for about 15 percent of sales.

Recently, Dianne has not been satisfied with her handbag sales.

Turnover has been low. It seems that, because of the high cost of a dress purchase, few shoppers buy an expensive handbag at the same time. In addition, Dianne carries only a few select styles and colors.

A wholesaler has offered Dianne an attractive and wide line of popularly priced handbags on consignment. They are designed to retail at $15 to $20, less than one third the retail price of the present bags. Intuitively, Dianne feels they will move out rapidly. She is also convinced that effective window treatments of the new merchandise will draw new customers into her store.

Still, she is concerned about the impact that introducing the less expensive line may have on her store's quality image. There is also the possibility that her regular customers will simply switch to lower-priced handbags in the future.

Questions
1. What are the advantages of taking in goods on consignment?
2. Should Dianne introduce the new line of handbags? Why or why not?

**Case 5.4
The Browns'
Country Store**

Not far from the Snake River and the Oregon border, in western Idaho, stands The Browns' Country Store. There it has stood, an oversized, barnlike structure, for nearly 40 years. Patrick Brown had worked in it as a youngster, alongside his parents and older brother. Fifteen years ago, his folks retired to California, leaving the place to him. He and his wife, Leona, both now in their early 50s, run the store. In addition to groceries, home-baked bread, eggs, milk, and dairy products, The Browns' Country Store carries kitchen utensils, blankets, towels, and other household goods, health and beauty aids, tools and hardware, farm implements and accessories, seed and fertilizer, and work clothing. The Browns are well liked by the villagers, who visit the place occasionally to enjoy the free coffee and homemade cookies and a little conversation. Last year, the store generated some $235,000 in sales.

The surrounding area encompasses both mountain terrain and fertile farmland. Potatoes, onions, and lettuce are among the more common crops. Lumber and mining are the local industries. There are a few cattle ranches in the county and a number of vacation resorts in the mountains. Many of the vacationers come to the village and, while there, stop at the Browns' Country Store.

For the first time, the Browns are considering the acceptance of VISA and other bank credit cards. They had never felt the need for this before. They had always regarded the charges that credit card companies would place on their sales as an unnecessary and unwarranted expense. Most of their customers paid cash for their purchases.

Traditionally, the Brown family always extended open credit to any of the local area residents who were temporarily out of work or otherwise short of funds. Often, these accounts were open for as long as six months and more. However, several families recently moved out of state, leaving behind sizable over-due accounts. New, younger families were also coming into the area; these newcomers were accustomed to paying by credit card. So were the vacationers who were visiting the store in increasing numbers.

Questions

1. Should the Browns make arrangements for the acceptance of bank credit cards? Explain your decision.

2. Should the couple continue its long-time policy of extending open credit to its regular customers? Why or why not?

3. What can they do about collecting the amounts still due from families who left town without paying their bills in full?

The Bettmann Archive, Inc.

PROMOTION
IN RETAILING

Courtesy Macy's California, San Francisco, CA

RETAIL PROMOTION: AN OVERVIEW

Your Study Objectives

After you have studied this chapter, you will understand:

1. The nature and role of promotion in retailing.
2. Sales promotion and the tools and techniques that are available.
3. Those aspects of a retail operation that contribute to the consumer's store image.
4. The retailer's need for, and characteristics of, a good public relations program.

Promotion in Action   Here are a few mini-scenarios depicting retail promotion at work:

For a full week, spot announcements on three local radio stations advertise "All the Pizza You Can Eat, at Only $3.99," on behalf of a freestanding pizza parlor. Signs atop the building flag passing motorists, reinforcing this theme.

A department store takes a full-page advertisement in the local newspaper on Tuesday, Wednesday, and Thursday to announce its forthcoming "Weekend Store-wide Sale." During the same week, banners throughout the store's interior alert shoppers to this event.

Pennants flying from the building and a flag-draped facade herald the grand opening of a unit of a popular drugstore chain. Prior to opening day, the local newspaper carried stories of the firm's history, store construction, merchandise lines carried, and the ribbon-cutting ceremony at which the mayor will preside. Radio and TV stations in the area described the planned gala, down to the clowns and kiddie rides that will be on the scene.

In a men's haberdashery, a salesperson writes up a sales ticket for a winter overcoat, then persuades the customer to buy a hat and a pair of gloves to go along with the coat.

On a Friday night, a skating rink awards prizes to six outstanding performers.

Large banners, printed in red and blue on white, proclaim "Double Coupon Days" on a supermarket window. Inside, two demonstrators wheel small tables around the store. The tables are covered with clean white tablecloths; on them lie platters of four different imported cheeses. The demonstrators give out free samples of thin, bite-sized slices of cheese to store shoppers.

At a local savings bank, consumers waiting in line leaf through printed materials available from a floor stand. Among other information, they read about the bank's IRA plans and long-term deposit accounts.

Immediately after the Thanksgiving weekend, the owners of a large toy and novelty store change the two show windows. They use red, white, and green materials to decorate the displays and hang fake icicles and huge foam candy canes from the ceiling eggcrates. Merchandise for Christmas gift giving is grouped attractively. The merchants also position a four-foot-tall, tastefully costumed Santa Claus directly in the center of the main window. Santa is an animated, mechanical figure. He moves his head from side to side and his hand beckons to passersby, inviting them into the store.

Significance of Retail   It is not enough for a retail firm to select a proper site, outfit the
Promotion   facility with an attractive decor and sensible fixtures, stock the place

with the right merchandise, and open the doors to the public. It also must convey information about the company, its offerings and prices, and the kinds of shoppers it plans to serve. The total product must be publicized so that consumers are encouraged to visit, look, and buy.

Promotion is goal-oriented communication. It aims at stimulating trade in the first place and consummating sales thereafter. Its overriding objective is to build repeat business and a loyal clientele. Promotion projects the company's image and strongly affects that image as well. It has been defined as "any form of communication used by a firm to inform, persuade, or remind people about its products, services, image, ideas, community involvement, or impact on society."[1]

We borrow from another source to shed a bit more light on the subject: "Promotion . . . seeks to (1) modify behavior and thoughts (e.g., get you to drink Pepsi rather than Coke) or (2) reinforce existing

Braniff's promotional strategy to meet stiff competition from other airline service retailers is to advertise their consistent, unrestricted, everyday low air fares.

Courtesy Braniff

behavior (e.g., get you to continue to drink Pepsi once you have converted."[2]

The Promotion Mix Promotion is a composite, or blend, of three distinct communication approaches: media advertising, personal selling, and sales promotion. Marketers see the first two components as contrasting ways to make strategic and tactical decisions. **Advertising** is a form of nonpersonal selling that aims at large numbers of potential buyers. **Personal selling** involves one or several salespeople making a presentation to an individual or small group. The third element in the promotion mix, **sales promotion,** encompasses a wide variety of promotional techniques used to complement and supplement advertising and personal selling.

Much like manufacturers and wholesalers, retailers employ all three approaches in various proportions to get their stories across to customers, both actual and potential. This point is illustrated in Figure 18.1. Typically, advertising is used primarily to inform consumers and induce them to visit stores. Once they arrive, sales promotion—in the form of an attractive storefront and window displays—enhances the company's appeal and invites shoppers to step inside. Interior displays and personal selling efforts persuade many shoppers to make purchases.

Objectives of Promotion
Manufacturers aim at promotion goals such as increased market share, better brand acceptance, or opening up new markets. At first blush, retailer goals seem to differ from those of producers. On examination retailer objectives are not altogether different, but retailing calls for a slightly altered perspective.

Among the many objectives that retail companies set are to:

bring shoppers to the store
build sales volume
contribute to the firm's image
cultivate store loyalty
differentiate the company from other retail firms
encourage repeat business
enhance the firm's reputation
extend the store's trading area
foster goodwill between the company and the community
gain acceptance for a new store unit
generate in-store traffic
increase the number of charge customers
induce passersby to enter the store
inform the public of new fashions
introduce new merchandise or new services
persuade shoppers to buy

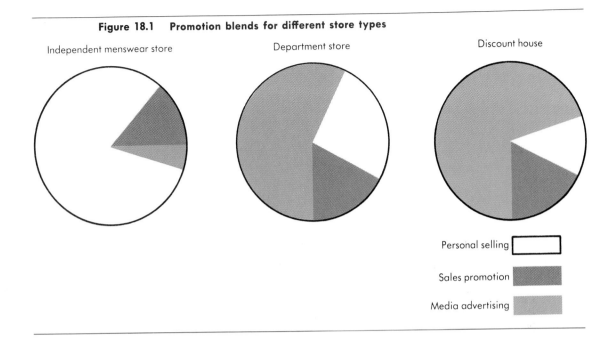

Figure 18.1   Promotion blends for different store types

Independent menswear store   Department store   Discount house

Personal selling

Sales promotion

Media advertising

provide information

sell additional merchandise to customers

tell people about upcoming sales and other events

Developing the Store Image

Consumers form mental images of retail companies, whether or not they have patronized them. Mere exposure to the store's location and premises provides input. In addition to other aspects of operation, advertising and sales promotion help strengthen these images.

Many years ago, Pierre Martineau's classic article about the personality projected by a store appeared in the *Harvard Business Review*.[3] In it, he indicated some of the factors that combine to produce this personality: layout, architecture, advertising, salespeople, and others. Since that time, the consumer's ability to conceive images of stores has been demonstrated time and again and well documented in the literature.[4]

We have also observed that "Other factors being equal, consumers will seek out those stores whose image most closely, correlates with the self status image."[5] In brief, the shopper's self-image also plays a role in store patronage. There is even evidence that shopping behavior can be predicted from store image data collected from consumers by telephone.[6]

Store image is a complex phenomenon. Most of the factors that contribute to the consumer's perception may be loosely grouped under: (1) store characteristics, (2) merchandise and services attributes, (3) promotional activity, and (4) customer characteristics. A list of those factors that appear to influence the image is given below alphabetically, with no particular emphasis given to any one:

advertising	salespeople (availability, knowledge, courtesy, and so on)
clientele	
decor	services offered
displays	signing
layout	size of store
location	store atmosphere
merchandise (assortment, quality, brand names, and so on)	store hours
	store policies (credit, returns and adjustments, and so on)
parking facilities	
physical premises	special events (exhibits, sales, promotions, and so on)
price levels	

We know, too, that department store shoppers are able to form fairly distinct images of the clienteles of competitive department stores.[7] Indeed, store patronage is closely related to store image. In one study, shoppers ranked the following patronage factors highest in importance: the price/value relationship, store specialization, merchandise quality, salesclerk service, and store location.[8] Another study revealed the more significant image aspects for a department store: dependable products, fairness in adjustments, high value for the money, and high-quality products.[9] Research into consumer images of a women's specialty clothing chain pointed up the importance of effective salespeople and a heavy "fashionability" dimension.[10] In addition to the sales personnel, shoppers' satisfaction or dissatisfaction with a particular firm can be affected by the store environment, merchandising practices, customers, promotions, and other aspects.[11] With regard to pharmacies, store location, price, the pharmacist, and merchandise quality appear to be the consumer's four most important criteria for selection.[12]

As a last point, it has been suggested that patronage of any one retail outlet is not only a function of consumers' images of that store, but also of their images of other stores.[13]

Sales Promotion

So vital to retail success are advertising, display, and personal selling that each component of the promotion mix calls for extended treatment in subsequent chapters of this book. The balance of this chapter is devoted to sales promotion. We will also discuss public relations and publicity. These two aspects are usually considered with the advertising function in most textbooks. Because most retail firms are small independent enterprises, with few or no funds available for media advertising, publicity and PR can be valuable assets to a store's promotion. Indeed, in recent years, the growth of retail sales promotion has outpaced that of media advertising.

Need for a Year-Round Program

For optimum effectiveness, all promotional activities need to be coordinated into a continuous, year-round program. Goal setting, planning strategy, outlining tactics, and organizing and scheduling all elements require the attention of specialists—at least in the larger retail organization. In a department store chain, a director or vice president of promotion may be responsible for coordinating all elements of the promotion mix. This person is frequently assisted by specialized subordinates: an advertising manager, a display coordinator (or director of visual merchandising), and a manager of sales promotion. To round out the department, the staff may include 5 to 15 more people.

Independent store merchants typically handle the entire promotion area alone. Sometimes they seek outside assistance from part-time window trimmers, independent sales promotion consultants, or small advertising agencies.

Large departmentized operations often tie promotion dollars to individual departments. They assign more funds to departments that record a higher sales volume per square foot of selling area and lesser amounts to those that yield a lower volume.

In these situations, advance promotion planning is essential. Usually this planning is well integrated with store merchandise and merchandising policy. Many small and medium-sized independents and some of the larger retailers follow many of the suggestions in the promotional calendar issued annually by the National Retail Merchants Association. Others prepare six-month and one-year calendars of their own. Retailers engage in many other promotional activities. For example, some retailers have gone so far as to distribute their own magazines to reach customers. Younker Brothers (a chain of 29 department stores), Sakowitz, Inc. of Houston, and Dallas, Neiman-Marcus have gone this route.[14]

Frequently, the tenants of a shopping center present promotional events jointly. All stores participate in both costs and benefits. These events can bring crowds of shoppers to the center.

Techniques of Sales Promotion

Retailers can draw from a large pool of accepted methods of sales promotion. One major area, display, is of such importance as to warrant separate, in-depth treatment in Chapter 20. Store services, especially consumer credit, also have promotional facets to them. Services are discussed in Chapter 17.

Advertising specialties are inexpensive articles given away free to promote a business. The retailer's address and phone are usually imprinted somewhere on the item—in this case, on the backs and spines of the matchbooks (not shown).

Sales promotion techniques run the gamut from advertising specialties and audiovisuals to trade-ins and trading stamps. Brief descriptions of the more popular types are presented in this section. By no means are all possibilities exhausted.

Advertising Specialties

Advertising specialties are inexpensive articles given free to shoppers to promote the firm or announce a special event. The store's logotype (name), address, and telephone number are usually imprinted on the item. The ad specialty may also carry a brief message. Examples of the articles merchants distribute include balloons, bumper stickers, calendars, flags, key chains, pencils, rain bonnets, and rulers.

Occasionally, retailers receive somewhat more expensive advertising specialties from their suppliers. Ashtrays, calendar books, desk sets, LED watch-pens, paperweights, T-shirts, and other popular items are frequently given out. Manufacturers and wholesalers distribute this merchandise to place or keep their company name before the retailer; to announce a new product, line, or promotion; or simply as gestures of goodwill.

Audiovisual Methods

Audiovisuals have repeatedly demonstrated their value as sales promotion tools. Many retailers use slides, films, tapes, and projectors to promote their merchandise and services. The equipment may be used to show and tell shoppers how to take care of specific articles, explain the manufacture of complex products, present the major selling points behind an item, teach viewers how to prepare a meal or set a table, or entertain the in-store audience. To a large extent, audiovisuals have supplanted the more costly personal demonstration. Films, for example, have been rated about 80 percent as effective as actual demonstrations, yet they cost only about one fifth as much.[15]

Catalogs

A major source of additional sales, **catalogs** are more properly a direct-mail or advertising vehicle. As such, they are discussed in more depth in Chapter 19 along with package enclosures, brochures, and other mailing pieces. Catalogs and other direct-mail materials extend stores' trading areas. Distant prospects are often more easily reached by catalog than by local newspaper advertising.[16]

Consumer Information and Instruction

All retailers, even the smallest independent, can provide customers with information. They may distribute printed materials furnished by suppliers; helpful literature to accompany technical products; directions enclosed with merchandise sold unassembled; instructions for sewing, knitting, or crocheting; and so on. Larger firms frequently offer informative talks on a wide range of topics. Popular subjects include home cooking, table arrangements, gardening, fashions in clothing, pre-retirement planning, investments, and proper diet. Some retailers offer courses in sewing, bridge, hair care, decorating, and other subjects.

Contests and Games

A perennially popular category of promotional activity includes both **contests** and **games.** Chains and independents alike favor them for creating excitement and generating heavy store traffic. Themes are inexhaustible; some are more familiar than others because they are used so often. There are the endless variations of bingo, the completion of a phrase, the solving of a puzzle, guessing the number of jelly beans in a huge jar, explaining in 25 words or less why you prefer to shop at Store X, composing a jingle, and the like. Contests and games have legal ramifications to consider. Local and state laws prohibit the retailer from requiring shoppers to make purchases in order to enter. Rules must be clearly stated, prizes to be given out described, the closing date announced in advance and adhered to strictly, and the odds of winning a prize delineated.

Perhaps the most popular contest form is the **sweepstakes,** largely because it requires a minimum of shopper effort. In its simplest form, consumers are invited to come into the store, complete an entry form, and deposit the slip in a fishbowl, box, barrel, or other container. Drawings are made at a later date, and the winners notified. A general tendency is to award one or several major prizes, more secondary prizes of sufficient merit, and a sizable number of additional prizes to convince consumers that they have a fair chance at winning something.

Prizes may take the form of cash or checks, gifts, travel, store merchandise, services, and the like. Retailers sometimes distribute quantities of trading stamps that can be exchanged for merchandise at a stamp redemption center. By promising window display space and in-store advertising to participating merchants, independent firms are often successful in persuading other local retailers to join in a promotion. Movie houses, for example, can often be counted on to provide a quantity of free passes as prize awards. Restaurants may offer free lunches or dinners for two; hotels can provide rooms for two days to a week or more; neighborhood bakeries may be happy to donate cakes; and so on.

An Example Consider the specifics of a "Hawaiian Holidays Sweetstakes" promoted by a manufacturer-retailer of confectionery products. The company's marketing manager designed the contest to improve sales one January in this regional chain. In the retail candy industry, January is normally the slowest month of the year. Some excellent prizes were obtained free of charge by offering to publicize the contributing companies in newspaper advertisements and store displays. Several trips for two to Hawaii by ocean liner were the top awards. These included an all-expense-paid two-week stay in Hawaii at a fine hotel and some spending money. Other prizes included 50 dinners for two at a Hawaiian-style restaurant in New York, 100 records of Hawaiian music, and several hundred gift certificates exchangeable at the stores for boxes of chocolate.

To enhance promotional impact, merchandise had been developed at the company's plant. Among the more novel candy creations were tempting pineapple cream delights, toasted coconut buttercrunch, and macadamia-nut candies. There were also one- and two-pound packages of "Hawaiian Holiday" assorted chocolates. Illustrations and descriptions of the new items appeared on the contest entry blanks with the rules and list of prizes. Throughout the chain, show windows and store interiors were gaily decorated with banners, grass mats, flowers, leis, and colorful travel posters depicting scenes of the islands. Models of the cruise ship were displayed in the firm's two busiest stores.

During that particular January, the chain enjoyed a fourfold increase over normal sales.

Coupons In recent years, **coupons,** especially the cents-off variety, have enjoyed a tremendous surge in popularity among consumers. (See Figure 18.2.)

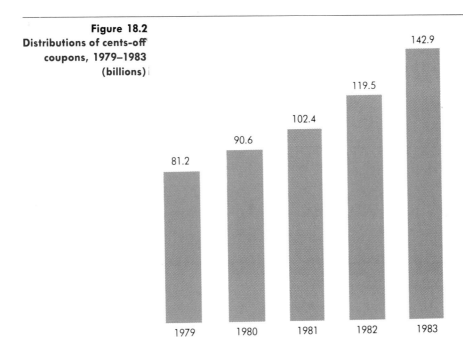

Figure 18.2
Distributions of cents-off coupons, 1979–1983 (billions)

Source: Clearing House Services Group, division of A.C. Nielson Company, *The NCH Reporter* (Number 1, 1984), p. 3. Reprinted with permission.

Their potency as a sales promotion tool seems to be enhanced during periods of inflation and when the economy passes through difficult times. Most coupons are distributed by manufacturers. Retailers use them to promote traffic and/or sales by placing them in their advertisements, shopping papers, or by distributing them in some other fashion. Manufacturer coupons are often printed on packages or enclosed within them. Procter & Gamble, Nestle, General Foods, Colgate-Palmolive, and other major producers of consumer goods each distribute millions of coupons every year.[17] Some coupons offer free merchandise or discounts that are stated in percentages. Most, however, are of the cents-off type. These bear a specific amount that the retailer is expected to deduct from the price of an item on presentation by the consumer. Years back, coupons usually carried a 5-cents-off figure. In today's economy, they range from as little as 5 or 10 cents to as much as 70 or 80 cents. Of course, many millions of coupons are not redeemed. Some of the factors that influence their redemption are indicated in Figure 18.3. It should be noted that retailers who wish to distribute coupons should seek prior legal advice. There are places in the nation where coupons may be prohibited by law or licensed, taxed, or restricted.

Cents-off coupons have a stronger impact on retail sales than either

Figure 18.3
Factors influencing
coupon redemption

1. Method of distribution.

2. Product class size.

3. Audience reached by coupon.

4. Consumer's need for product.

5. Size of brand's consumer franchise.

6. Degree of brand loyalty.

7. Brand's retail availability.

8. Established or new brand.

9. Design and appeal of coupon ad.

10. Face value of coupon.

11. Discount offered by coupon.

12. Area of country.

13. Competitive activity.

Source: Clearing House Services Group, division of A.C. Nielson Company, *The NCH Reporter* (Number 1, 1984), p. 7. Reprinted with permission.

premiums or bonus packs.[18] Moreover, coupon promotions tend to improve consumer judgments about the quality of a brand.[19]

Coupon Fraud Fraud is a major problem in couponing. Cheating by retailers as well as consumers is common. Estimates of the total cost to our economy of coupon misredemption run in the hundreds of millions of dollars.[20] Some 20 percent of all coupons submitted for redemption may be improper. In a fraudulent approach known as gang cutting, store owners purchase multiple copies of the local newspaper, clip out the coupons, and send them to the manufacturers for redemption. Producers have tried to combat this type of fraud by requiring retailers to buy enough merchandise in the first place to justify the quantity of coupons turned in. Similar approaches are sometimes used by retail cashiers, who substitute clipped-out coupons for cash in the store's register.

Demonstrations   Retailers welcome demonstrators sent in by suppliers. Demonstrators show and distribute merchandise to store shoppers. This method of promotion can add significantly to sales, especially in the case of technical or complex products. When a **demonstration** is in progress, people usually gather to watch, ask questions, and make purchases. Among the items which lend themselves easily to this technique are kitchen utensils of novel design or purpose, workshop tools, electric organs, rug-cleaning machines, home computers and video games like Atari and Intellivision, vacuum cleaners and other home appliances, and sporting goods or equipment. At times it may pay the retail firm to

From The Wall Street Journal, with permission of Cartoon Features Syndicate.

"When it gets in the middle of the tub, this little valve opens and presto, you have an oil spill."

have an employee put on a show several times each day to boost the sales of a specific article.

Demonstrators may also be used outside the store, in the vestibule, or even in the show window itself to attract the attention of shoppers. This is often seen in shopping malls, where, for example, a demonstrator plays an electric organ right in a store's entranceway, especially during the busier hours. Fudge- and candy-making machines, popcorn and pretzel-twisting equipment, doughnut makers, and the like, all have great drawing power.

Exhibits and Shows   Within the retailing industry, some confusion exists over these two terms. They are often used interchangeably. Technically speaking, however, **exhibits** are articles—or collections of articles—placed on display. For example, visitors to the Smithsonian in Washington are often delighted to observe an astonishing display, behind glass panels, of some of the world's most notable diamonds. **Shows** have a less static quality about them. They project excitement, movement, and an air of entertainment. The popular antique, handicraft, or other "shows" often promoted at shopping malls might more properly be called exhibits (or exhibitions). They are shows, of course, if artisans and craftspeople are on the premises actively crafting new works.

Retailers offer shows and exhibits to generate excitement, produce more shopper traffic, foster good public relations, and create a more

Retailers offer shows like this Christmas concert to foster good public relations, create a more pleasant shopping environment—and to help put shoppers into the Christmas gift-buying spirit.

Eleanore Snow

pleasant shopping environment. Among the better-known types are fashion shows, antique exhibitions, exhibits of oil paintings or metalcraft, displays of children's sketches and drawings, karate shows, and puppet shows.

Premiums and Giveaways

Premiums are articles distributed free or at a nominal cost with the purchase of one or more merchandise items. Suppliers give premiums to dealers to encourage them to carry their products in the first place or to persuade the merchants to promote the goods in their displays and/or media advertising. (See Figure 18.4 for a more extended list of reasons why manufacturers use premiums.) In turn, retailers may offer premiums to consumers to build good public relations, increase traffic, induce shoppers to buy, and keep customers coming back to the store.

To introduce a new flavor or to stimulate sales, an ice cream parlor may give away a pint of ice cream with the purchase of a quart package of your favorite flavor. A supermarket may display a set of dishes, offering one setting to each person who accumulates $300 worth of the store's register tapes. Or the store may offer the same articles at an attractive, below-wholesale price to shoppers who present $150 worth of tapes and would rather not wait any longer to collect their premium. A fast-food restaurant may distribute novelty drinking glasses at cost to customers who buy a cheeseburger and fries. Occasionally, a supermarket will tie into a mutual promotion with local

Retailers offer premiums in the form of free merchandise (in this case, a slab of barbecued ribs) to stimulate sales and increase store traffic.

Courtesy Jim Pasqualoni

merchants in a novel type of premium approach: The back of the register tape is preprinted with discount coupons. These may be redeemed for merchandise within a specified time at stores in the neighborhood.

Personal and home articles are popular premium items. Among others, these include kitchen utensils, purses, cosmetic bags, wallets, toys, tools, records and tapes, dishes, pots and pans, and T-shirts.

A common form of premium is the **giveaway:** an item that is presented to customers free of charge. Like the advertising specialty, it may be distributed solely as a goodwill gesture. More often than not, however, the aim of the promotion is either to introduce a new item or to generate additional store traffic. Premiums normally do not carry advertising messages. Indeed, premiums may be distinguised from ad specialties by this characteristic and by two others: (1) they are given out only to buyers, not to all shoppers in the store and (2) they are typically more expensive articles. Premiums can cost the retailer as little as 50 cents or a dollar, or as much as several hundreds of dollars. For example, a dealer may offer a set of silver flatware or encyclopedias at cost to customers who make a major purchase such as a complete living-room suite or bedroom set. In this case, the retailer uses the premium as a **self-liquidator.** Since the item's cost is paid by the customer, the merchant neither loses nor gains by selling the premium.

Premium users distinguish between the **single-offer** and the **continuity-offer** premium. The first term is self-explanatory; the second applies to a promotion designed to encourage shoppers to keep returning to

Figure 18.4
Some purposes for premiums

The use of premiums can often serve to:

1. **Give an opportunity for consumer sampling.** When getting the consumer to try your product for the first time is the major consideration, any of several types of premium promotion can serve.

2. **Introduce a new product effectively.** This is a specific area where initial sampling can be effected at far lower cost through premiums than by direct sampling or discount coupons.

3. **Encourage displays at point of sale.** Dealers respond to special promotions and will go along if the deal offers them something concrete in the way of sales gains.

4. **Meet a competitive merchandising program.** Sometimes the need is basically that of making a lot of noise in a concentrated fashion, to offset the other fellow's noises. If this is a prime problem, a premium can often fill the bill.

5. **Stimulate the sales force.** The need to push a consumer promotion to the trade will get the salespeople on their toes in many cases where boredom or inertia may have set in.

6. **Level seasonal variations in sales.** A well-planned premium campaign in an off season can boost volume.

7. **Boost slow products.** Premiums can be used to encourage full-line movement, giving the stepchildren of your product group a shot in the arm by skillful association with better-selling items.

8. **Increase the purchase unit.** New sales dollars and more intensive sampling can result when you tie the premium offer to a multiple purchase of your product.

9. **Build continuity of purchase.** Several types of premium deals are designed to keep em coming back for more, tending to establish the all-too-scarce brand loyalty we would all like to think we owned.

10. **Obtain a prospect list.** Whether by mail or in direct selling, premiums have proved highly effective at getting customers to provide names of friends who may be better-than-average prospects. And premium respondents themselves may constitute a useful list for some purposes.

11. **Get copy attention.** If your objective is to reach readers who don't normally respond to your kind of copy, a premium can catch their eye for you.

12. **Increase ad readership.** Figures compiled by Daniel Starch show your ad may win up to two and a half times as much thorough readership as a comparable ad without the premium.

13. **Promote new use of product.** A premium related to the new use for your product can open up a fresh market for expanded sales.

14. **Test your media.** The direct-response factor in a mail-in premium offer is the key to simple testing of media pull, provided copy and premium are designed to appeal to your principal desired audience.

15. **Reach adults through their children.** Often an appeal to the kids will get a message to parents in the most direct manner possible.

16. **Increase distribution.** A premium's stimulation of consumer demand can add new retail outlets.

17. **Build traffic for retailers.**

Figure 18.4
(concluded)

18. **Offset price competition.** A premium will often take the consumer's mind off price as a prime factor, reducing the advantage of a price-slashing competitor.

19. **Substitute for cash trade-in.** The trade-in premium will give you a much more favorable dollar picture, while actually increasing the consumer's appreciation.

20. Twenty is a neat number on which to end any list, and this leaves room for you to add the important sales objective which is most suited to *your* needs.

Source: George Meredith, ed., *Premiums in Marketing* (Rutherford, N.J.: National Premiums Sales Executives Inc., 1971), pp. 22–23.

the store to buy repeatedly. The earlier example involving the accumulation of register tapes is one type of continuity offer.

Manufacturers frequently distribute premiums inside their packaged products. In such cases, the package itself generally carries some announcement about the premium within. On-pack and combination-pack approaches are other possibilities.

Push Money and Other Incentives

PMs, or **spiffs,** are small sums paid to salespeople to encourage additional selling effort, usually on specific articles of merchandise.[21] The initials stand for Push Money. Suppliers may provide money to retail management to give to salespeople who push their products. Or retailers themselves may set aside their own funds to use for a similar purpose. Thus, token payments may be made to employees for selling slow-moving merchandise, clearing out seasonal items after the season has ended, and so on. Additional sales volume may also be the objective. The owners of a women's shoestore, for example, may offer a spiff of $2 to their sales staff on every purse sold with the purchase of a pair of shoes.

Retail firms often substitute store merchandise, gifts, home appliances, or even travel awards for spiff money. They may set in place a points-award system, rewarding sales personnel who demonstrate above-average selling effort with certificates for specified amounts of points. Employees save the certificates until they have accumulated enough points to exchange them for a prize of their choice. Prizes are usually displayed in a catalog supplied by the premium or incentive house. Trading stamps may also be used for this purpose. Such an incentive program can also be tied into various aspects of personnel administration. Certificates can be awarded to employees with superior attendance records, who have shown initiative, or who have contributed worthwhile suggestions, and so on.

Rain Checks

Although these are more properly an element in the retailer's service mix, **rain checks** need to be mentioned briefly as a promotional technique. They do, after all, help to promote sales. Rain checks are forms given to shoppers when a store has run out of specific merchandise, especially goods that have been advertised or placed on sale. They authorize the shopper to purchase the product at the promotional price when additional quantities arrive at the store. Many of the better establishments will alert the shopper by mail or telephone when the stock has been replenished.

Sampling　　The basic rationale behind this old-time favorite is to get consumers to try the merchandise. Manufacturers of cigarettes, soaps, and household products have resorted to **sampling** programs for many decades. Free samples were delivered from door to door and through the mail. In recent years, the popularity of this technique has been waning. More and more, manufacturers have been turning to couponing as a less costly alternative. Yet suppliers of many products still provide retailers with samples, swatches of material, designs, and the like, so interested consumers may make appropriate buying decisions. Examples include the pieces of formica for selecting kitchen counters and table tops, printed slips with color samples for choosing household paints, imported or new cheeses to be demonstrated in bite-sized slices at food stores, and bottles of spray cologne for shoppers to pick up and sample at the department store's perfume counter.

Store merchants use sampling methods to persuade consumers to try and buy. Groceries, fruit and vegetable stands, bakeries, delicatessens, and other stores commonly employ this technique. As an illustration, a cookie store in a regional shopping center distributes thousands of miniature cookies to passersby. Each cookie is tucked into a little cellophane bag with the store name and the name of the cookie.

Special Promotional Events　　This broad-ranging category includes sales and other price events; grand openings, anniversaries, and other store-related promotions; publicity stunts; community-oriented programs; and many other types of activities. The price events may be presented by themselves when discounts, rebates, trade-ins, or leader-price promotions are employed to attract shoppers. It is more likely, however, that they are tied into a holiday theme or some other occasion. Popular types are store manager's and buyers' sales, pre- and post-holiday promotions, early-bird and moonlight madness events, anniversary sales, and the like.

Elaborate exhibitions, shows, and even parades often form part of the large company's calendar of special events. One such notable event is the traditional Macy's parade in New York City. Each Thanksgiving, thousands of onlookers throng Manhattan's 34th Street to thrill to the excitement generated by the colorful, stories-high balloons, decorated floats, and marching bands. Simultaneously, millions of TV viewers enjoy this hours-long extravaganza in their living rooms.

Many malls sponsor special promotional events, such as picture-taking sessions with Santa Claus, shown here at the Palm Beach Mall.

Courtesy Palm Beach Mall, West Palm Beach, FL

Retailers of any size may sponsor a Little League or other local team, proclaim an occasional open-house promotion, or invite shoppers to meet and greet local dignitaries, show-business people, and sports celebrities. Both Santa Claus and the Easter Bunny are ever-welcome personalities. Neighboring merchants or a shopping center's tenants' association may cooperate in sponsoring block parties, fairs, carnivals, country or pop music concerts, firework shows, dance contests, parades of antique cars, and the like.

Tie-in Promotions   A cost-effective technique for retailers is the **tie-in promotion.**[22] This type of arrangement involves two or more firms sharing both the costs and the benefits of promotional effort. Even the smallest independent can profit by this tactic. Apparel retailers, for example, know that consumer demand becomes frenetic during the three or four weeks leading up to Easter Sunday. To encourage more in-store traffic as well as more sales, a shop that sells clothes for teenagers may strike a deal with a local fast-food operation. The restaurant provides coupons good for a free hamburger or frank and a soft drink. The apparel store distributes the coupons to customers who spend $25 or more on clothes. Both retailers will, of course, advertise the tie-in promotion in their stores and perhaps in the local newspaper.

Tie-ins between theaters and many types of retailers are distinct possibilities. A bank may enter a mutual promotion with a department store or other large retailer in the area. People who open new bank accounts receive certificates valued at $10 or $15 which they can redeem for merchandise at the store.

Trading Stamps   A somewhat unique sales promotion technique is the distribution of **trading stamps.** Long a favorite ploy among supermarkets, they may also be distributed by service stations, dry-cleaning establishments, drugstores, general merchandise outlets, and other retail types. Merchants give stamps to their customers to gain a competitive advantage and to encourage shoppers to continue to buy at the same store.

Gummed on the back, trading stamps carry denominations printed on the face. Usually these range in value from 10 cents to $1. They are distributed with each purchase in amounts that correspond to approximately 10 percent of the purchase value. A shopper who buys $50 worth of groceries, for example, will receive stamps with a total face value of $5. Stamp-saving consumers are provided with blank booklets to fill at home by pasting in the stamps according to their values. A sufficient number of filled booklets can be exchanged for merchandise at a stamp redemption center.

Evidently, then, trading stamps are a special type of premium. Viewed from another angle, they constitute a form of discount, with the savings available to the consumer as partial credit toward the purchase of goods, rather than cash.

In the United States, trading stamps have had a long history of waxing and waning public interest. The earliest known instance of their distribution occurred back in 1891 at Schusters' Department Store in Milwaukee. In 1896, the Sperry and Hutchinson Company set up shop as the first independently organized trading stamp firm in the nation. After the turn of the century, the stamp concept enjoyed increasing popularity with both consumers and retailers. Several other stamp companies entered the scene. The industry suffered major setbacks, however, during both World Wars and the harsh years of the Great Depression.[23] Pacing the rapid expansion of the young supermarket chains, trading stamps showed a strong spurt of activity all during the 1950s and well into the 1960s. In more recent years, retailer interest has been declining in favor of other forms of sales promotion such as couponing and premiums. Total stamp sales fell from their peak of $950 million in 1968 to only $400 million by 1976. Trading stamps appear to be in the decline stage of their life cycle.[24]

Trade-in Promotions   More properly a promotional pricing device than a sales promotion technique, **trade-in promotions** merit only brief mention in this section. Shoppers who intend to buy a new car, TV set, pair of snow tires, or appliance to replace a used product are encouraged to trade in the item at the store. The merchant then gives the buyer an allowance

This retailer encourages in-store traffic by offering free trading stamps, merchandise markdowns, and the sale of lottery tickets.

Eleanore Snow

or rebate for the old merchandise in the form of a cash discount deductible from the article's retail selling price.

Public Relations

A business enterprise cannot operate in a vacuum. The moment it has been physically situated, people in the area begin to acquire knowledge of it and develop opinions, feelings, and eventually attitudes about it. Regardless of type, all companies need to concern themselves with **public relations.** This holds true whether or not the firm devises a well-planned and coordinated PR program.

Public relations specialists take a broad view of management concern. For the most part, they regard it as open, honest, two-way communication between a company and the public. They pluralize the word and speak in terms of various publics. Employees and stockholders represent two of the firm's internal publics; shoppers, local government, fraternal and charitable organizations, and the media are among the company's external publics. A PR program aims at maintaining a positive company image among the many groups.

Defining Public Relations

Because of their closeness to the customer, retail companies occupy the limelight more often than other types of businesses. The retail firm needs to project the kind of image that will lead to its acceptance as a welcome participant in, and contributor to, the surrounding community. For a clearer grasp of what public relations entails, consider the following brief statements:

. . . the planned effort to influence opinion through good character and responsible performance, based upon mutually satisfactory two-way communications.[25]

. . . a broad area of company behavior, expressive of the firm's attitudes toward others. In the main, it consists of meaningful, two-way communication between the company and its many publics.[26]

Communication to correct erroneous impressions, maintain goodwill of the firm's many publics, and explain the firm's goals and purposes.[27]

The retailer's public relations program must begin with an attractive, well-kept facility. Merchandise offered for sale should match customer needs and be fairly priced. Displays ought to be tasteful and interesting. Shoppers should be attended to promptly by courteous salespeople. The organization should maintain cordial and fair relationships with employees and suppliers. Management ought to encourage the staff to participate actively in community affairs and organizations of their choice. Staff should listen to customers, ask their opinions, and answer their complaints promptly. Management needs to keep up with public opinion about the company. At all times it should have a clear picture of its image—and be ready to take measures to adjust that image where it deviates from the one that management prefers to project. As indicated in Figure 18.5, this holds true regardless of the firm's size.

Publicity

A vital component of the retailer's public relations program is **publicity.** Because it is free, favorable publicity can prove a marvelous boon to the new enterprise struggling to earn recognition in the community. It is just as essential for the established merchant as well; it keeps the company's name and image alive and in the limelight. Because it reaches consumers as news, rather than as advertising, publicity is generally more believable.[28]

This giant birthday cake depicting the world's only Corn Palace was baked in celebration of the Mitchell, South Dakota, centennial by Randall Stores. Such public relations gestures project a favorable image of the retailer to the surrounding community.

Courtesy Randall Stores, Inc., Mitchell, SD

Publicity has been defined as: "Any *unpaid* form of non-personal presentation of ideas, goods, or services."[29] Another definition is: "Communication in news story form, regarding an organization and/ or its products, that is transmitted through a mass medium at no charge."[30]

Community residents and visitors alike want to know, and appreciate finding out about, what is going on with local business operations. The news media continually search for events that may interest their

**Figure 18.5
Public relations can
benefit the small
business, too**

In today's ever tightening economy, the small businessperson must struggle for recognition. A sound public relations program, often thought of as something only the giant corporations can afford, can give the added strength needed for the small business to become known and recognized by those people who use and need its product or service.

Public relations could very well be defined as "the projection of a desired image." Large corporations employ entire staffs devoted to this purpose, and many retain outside counsel to tell them how to build their images. But the same principles used by large organizations to project their images to millions of people around the world can be used by the corner grocery-store owner to communicate an image to neighbors down the street.

Source: L. Kim Garvey, "Public Relations for Small Business," *Small Marketers Aids No. 163* (Washington, D.C.: Small Business Administration, December 1977), p. 2.

Source: Copyright 1981 Time Inc. All rights reserved. Reprinted by permission from TIME.

Figure 18.6
Translation services as a
public relations gesture

A Gift of Tongues

Anyone who has ever tried to explain that he wants a thingamajig that goes on the end of a doohickey understands the problem of trying to get a whatchamacallit in a foreign language. So did the merchants of northern Chicago's Lincoln Village Shopping Center. To fill the needs of customers who increasingly speak only such languages as Japanese, Spanish, Hebrew, French, and Greek, Lincoln Village has opened Language Line, a linguistic service that can help locate gizmos for speakers of foreign tongues.

Each store in the shopping center has a telephone hot line and a poster showing ten Asian and European flags. Customers signal their languages by pointing to a flag, and the merchants dial a translation service. University students at the other end listen to the customer requests and translate them into English for sales clerks.

The new service cost an initial $25,000 plus monthly maintenance charges that the merchants are totting up, but they believe it is money well spent. Says Pharmacist Franklin Lee: ''The response has been overwhelming.'' Even tongue-tied doctors, policemen, and school officials have expressed interest in the service, and Lincoln Village officials are considering adding more languages.

audiences. (See Figure 18.6.) Among the many kinds of stories that can form part of the retail company's PR program are:

stories that tug at the heartstrings or induce nostalgia
descriptions of unusual events
grand opening ceremonies
appearances at the store by local dignitaries, entertainers, or other celebrities
stories of people: store employees, store owners, or customers
store anniversaries/birthday parties
the introduction of new merchandise lines or new services
special promotions and sales events
cooperative drives by retailer and community involving civic associations, charities, religious organizations, and the like
open house
A few other possibilities are listed in Figure 18.7.

The Publicity Release Publicity can inform and excite consumers only if the retail company succeeds in getting the proper information to the news media. The details given in a **publicity release** should be complete. To ensure that all necessary facts are included, retailers can avail themselves of the five Ws of the professional journalist. These are the invaluable yet tiny questions that stimulate thinking about all aspects of an occurrence: *Who? What? Where? When? Why?* A sixth question is usually appended, even though it does not begin with a w: *How?*

Figure 18.7
Some community
relations techniques

In the final analysis, what is the core of effective community relations? Basically it is merely being a good neighbor. An individual becomes a good neighbor by doing good deeds in various ways, at various times. So does a business.

By capitalizing on assets and trying to strengthen weak spots in either case, each achieves the goal of good neighborliness. Assets and community situations, of course, differ. For that reason, there is no one formula for producing the proper community relations. . . . In conclusion, then, here are a dozen reminders of community relations activities available to small businesses:

1. Charitable contributions and participation in community fund-raising drives; for example, Community Chest, Red Cross.

2. Blood donor programs.

3. Membership and active participation in community organizations; for example—in addition to the civic, service, political, and religious groups already mentioned—veterans' and parent-teacher associations.

4. Sponsorship of activities in the fields of fire protection, water purification, noise abatement, smoke-fume elimination, accident prevention.

5. Speech making by owner and employees before community groups.

6. Plant tours and open-house events.

7. Community-oriented institutional advertising.

8. Sponsorship of cultural and sport activities of the community; for example, promotion of little theater groups, library-enlargement campaigns, park and civic statute improvements, Little League baseball, industrial bowling team sponsorship.

9. Membership and active participation in professional groups—especially local and regional chapters of such groups.

10. Student on-the-job training and summer employment for local students.

11. Participation in special days and/or weeks; community-sponsored events and celebrations; for example, junior government days, National Employ the Physically Handicapped Week, picnics for underprivileged children, Christmas toy distributions.

12. Publicity for achievements by local citizens—especially your own employees; for example, years-of-service pins, awards for the accumulation of sick leave, Young-Person-of-the-Year presentations.

Source: Robert W. Miller, "Profitable Community Relations for Small Business," *Small Business Management Series No. 27* (Washington, D.C.: Small Business Administration, 1961), pp. 33–34.

Figure 18.8 shows a sample news release from one large retail organization.

In preparing a release—for example, for a grand opening—the retailer reviews the five Ws to generate all details and to make certain that no pertinent fact is accidentally omitted. *Who* will be involved in the event? *What* activities will take place? *When* and *where* will these occur?

The mechanics of writing the release are simple. The publicity item, or story, should be typed on company stationery that measures 8½

Figure 18.8
First page of a publicity release

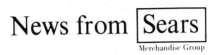

Ernest L. Arms
National News Director
Sears Merchandise Group
Sears, Roebuck and Co.
Sears Tower
Chicago, Illinois 60684
Phone: (312) 875-8371

FOR IMMEDIATE RELEASE
Nov. 8, 1983

CHICAGO, Nov. 8 . . . Sears, Roebuck and Co. today announced plans to invest $1.7 billion in a five-year remodeling and expansion program for the Sears Merchandise Group.

Edward R. Telling, chairman and chief executive officer of the company, said the "Store of the Future" program calls for remodeling of more than 600 stores and construction of 62 new stores, reflecting a shift in emphasis from new stores to modernization of existing facilities.

The program was approved today by the company's board of directors, who recently toured Sears first "pure" Store of the Future in King of Prussia, Pa.

"Sears strategy recognizes a dramatic decline in the number of desirable new shopping mall locations and the competitive importance of upgrading existing facilities to generate sales and profit growth," Telling said.

"This is the largest program of its type in Sears history," he said, "and we are confident it will produce great benefits for our employees, shareholders and the 36 million American families who shop at Sears."

-more-

F51144

Source: Sears, Roebuck & Co.

by 11 inches. Type on only one side of the page, leaving ample margins all around. Avoid errors of spelling, erasures, or white-outs that may affect the quality of copies made from the original. If the release runs over one page in length, type the word **MORE** in capital letters in the bottom margin, three lines below the last line of copy. Signify

Figure 18.9
Suggestions for writing
the news release

1. Before you begin writing copy, visualize your customers. What are these people like? What do they like? Think about their needs, preferences, and dislikes. Hold this picture firmly in mind as you begin to write.

2. Always compose a publicity release as if you are speaking directly to one person.

3. Present facts clearly and simply. Avoid any inclination to exaggerate or sell.

4. Stifle the natural compulsion to write fancy prose. Stick to a basic vocabulary, the kinds of words you would use in everyday conversation.

5. Write in words of one and two syllables. Replace polysyllabic words and obtuse expressions which only a few people will understand.

6. Sentences and paragraphs should be short and to the point.

7. Avoid the passive tense. Use active verbs and nouns that pinpoint exactly what you mean.

8. Make certain that all proper names used in your story are correctly spelled.

9. Excise all words and phrases that do not make a direct contribution to the story. These are excess baggage!

10. Don't write a news headline for your story; that is the editor's job.

11. After finishing the release, put it aside for an hour or so. Then reread it with an eye to cutting it down—to telling the story even better in less space. The shorter the release, the better its chances of being published or broadcast.

the story's end by typing the sign # or the number *30* four or five lines after the final line of copy. Duplicate the release and mail the copies in #10 envelopes that carry the firm's corner card and the words *News Release* typed toward the bottom, below the corner card. Mail the releases to all area newspapers (daily and weekly) and to all local radio and TV stations.

Figure 18.9 contains some helpful hints for the retailer.

Summary

Promotion is goal-oriented communication designed to tell consumers about the company, its products, and its services. It both projects and contributes to the company's image. Retailers depend on it to stimulate sales, build repeat business, and develop a loyal clientele over time.

Advertising, personal selling, and sales promotion are three distinct communication approaches. Sales promotion is the generic term that includes the many types of promotional activity that cannot clearly be designated as either advertising or personal selling. Retail firms use an extensive range of promotional objectives. Goals vary from generating store traffic and introducing new merchandise to fostering goodwill between the company and the community.

Consumers form images of retail companies. Many aspects contribute to these images: the location, store characteristics, merchandise and services offered, price/value relationship, the salespeople, store policies, advertising and sales promotion, and even the shoppers. It also appears that consumers prefer to shop at stores that have images that correlate with their self-images.

Retailers need to plan a solid, year-round program for sales promotion. They can draw on a wide variety of promotional tools and techniques. Among others, these include advertising specialties, audiovisual methods, catalogs, consumer information, contests, coupons, demonstrations, exhibits, premiums, push money, sampling, special promotional events, trading stamps, and trade-in promotions.

Public relations may be thought of as ongoing, two-way communication between a company and its publics, both internal and external. Its major purpose is to project a positive company image. A good PR program is founded on an attractive store, good-quality merchandise, and fair prices. Salespeople need to be courteous and attentive to shoppers. Management should maintain cordial and fair relationships with all groups.

Publicity is a cost-free method of communicating information about a firm to many people. It keeps the company's name before the public.

Key Terms

promotion	giveaway
advertising	self-liquidator
personal selling	single-offer premium
sales promotion	continuity-offer premium
store image	spiffs
advertising specialties	PMs (push money)
audiovisuals	rain checks
catalogs	sampling
contests and games	tie-in promotion
sweepstakes	trading stamps
coupons	trade-in promotions
demonstration	public relations

exhibits   publicity
shows   publicity release
premiums

Review
Questions

1. Identify and briefly describe the components of the promotion mix.

2. Propose five specific promotional objectives useful for a newly launched toy and novelty store in a neighborhood shopping center.

3. What is a store image? Name at least eight aspects of a retail operation that affect the firm's image.

4. List a minimum of seven sales promotion techniques that retailers often use.

5. What is a sweepstakes? How does it work?

6. Comment on the problem of coupon fraud by store merchants as well as by consumers.

7. Trace the growth of trading stamps as a promotional tool since their inception in the late 19th century.

8. What is *push money?*

9. Suggest three sales events that a K mart store might successfully promote.

10. Why do you suppose that sampling as a promotional technique has largely been replaced by coupon distribution?

11. Define and contrast the terms *public relations* and *publicity.*

12. Identify some types of publicity stories the news media may be interested in.

13. Give at least six useful suggestions for writing news releases.

Discussion
Questions

1. Check your neighborhood for any store that has an attractive show window. Draw a diagram of the window to approximate scale. Indicate those features in it that you found most attractive. Then make a list of the entire contents of the window.

2. How would the promotion mix for a dress shop differ from that of a neighborhood delicatessen? From that of a large, freestanding discount store?

3. For one week, check your daily newspaper for cents-off coupons. Clip them out. At the end of the week, list the values of all coupons, total them up, and determine how much the average coupon saves the shopper. Also, try to ascertain the percentage of offers that appeal to you, considering the total as 100 percent.

4. What benefits might the owner of a children's shoestore reap from sponsoring a youngsters' art contest? What problems do you envision for the retailer?

5. Suggest five merchandise ideas that might be suitably distributed as premiums by a regional supermarket chain.

6. Work out the details of an upcoming fashion show to be sponsored by a retailer of women's sportswear.

7. The management of a national chain of variety stores is contemplating a choice between the use of a trading stamp program and a promotional campaign involving the distribution of cents-off coupons. Which approach would you prefer? Why?

8. Some merchants frown on the use of the trade-in approach, considering it unethical. There are also consumers who suspect that retailers may artificially inflate the prices of merchandise to cover the goods traded in. What is your feeling about this promotional technique?

9. You are the advertising and publicity director for a small but growing chain of costume jewelry boutiques. Prepare a brief publicity release for the grand opening of a fifth store unit in the same metropolitan area.

Notes

[1] Joel R. Evans and Barry Berman, *Marketing* (New York: Macmillan, 1982), p. 412.

[2] Carl McDaniel, Jr., *Marketing: An Integrated Approach* (New York: Harper & Row, 1979), pp. 351–52.

[3] Pierre Martineau, "The Personality of the Retail Store," *Harvard Business Review* 36 (January–February 1958), pp. 47–55.

[4] Leonard L. Berry, "The Components of Department Store Image: A Theoretical and Empirical Analysis," *Journal of Retailing* 45 (Spring 1969), pp. 3–20; Eleanor G. May, "Practical Applications of Recent Retail Image Research," *Journal of Retailing* 50 (Winter 1974–75), pp. 15–20*ff.*

[5] W. Bruce Weale, "Measuring the Customer's Image of a Department Store," *Journal of Retailing* 37 (Summer 1962), pp. 40–48. See also: D. N. Bellenger et al., "Congruence of Store Image and Self-Image as It Relates to Store Loyalty," *Journal of Retailing* 52 (Spring 1976), pp. 17–32.

[6] Edgar A. Pessemier, "Store Image and Positioning," *Journal of Retailing* 56 (Spring 1980), pp. 94–106.

[7] Irving Burstiner, "A Three-way Mirror: Comparative Images of the Clienteles of Macy's, Bloomingdale's; and Korvettes'," *Journal of Retailing* 50 (Spring 1974), p. 33.

[8] Marvin A. Jolson and Walter F. Spath, "Understanding and Fulfilling Shoppers' Requirements: An Anomaly in Retailing?" *Journal of Retailing* 49 (Summer 1973), p. 41.

[9] Robert A. Hansen and Terry Deutscher, "An Empirical Investigation of Attribute Importance in Retail Store Selection," *Journal of Retailing* 53 (Winter 1977–78), pp. 59–72*ff.*

[10] Ronald B. Marks, "Operationalizing the Concept of Store Image," *Journal of Retailing* 52 (Fall 1976), pp. 37–46.

[11] Robert A. Westbrook, "Sources of Consumer Satisfaction with Retail Outlets," *Journal of Retailing* 57 (Fall 1981), pp. 68–85.

[12] Ponpun Nickel and Albert I. Wertheimer, "Factors Affecting Consumers' Images and Choices of Drugstores," *Journal of Retailing* 55 (Summer 1979), pp. 71–78.

[13] V. Parker Lessig, "Consumer Store Images and Store Loyalties," *Journal of Marketing* 37 (October 1973), p. 74.

[14] "Stores Try Publishing Their Own Magazines," *Business Week,* 27 July 1981, p. 34.

[15] "AV Stops Them in the Aisles," *Sales and Marketing Management* 119 (12 December 1977), pp. 51–53.

[16] See: William R. Darden, John J. Lennon, and Donna K. Darden, "Communicating with Interurban Shoppers," *Journal of Retailing* 54 (Spring 1978), pp. 51–64.

[17] Marketing Research Group USA. A. C. Nielsen Company, *The Nielsen Researcher* no. 4, (1979).

[18] Alfred Gross, "Cents-off: A Critical Promotion Tactic," *MSU Business Topics* 19 (Spring 1971), pp. 13–20.

[19] Patricia Margaret Hopkins, "Cents-off Coupon as a Promotional Tool to Change Judgments and Preferences" Ph.D. dissertation, Claremont Graduate School, 1977.

[20] Niles Howard, "Coping with Coupon Fraud," *Dun's Review* 151 (May 1978), pp. 74*ff.*

[21] See: Dale Varble and L. E. Bergerson, "The Use and Facets of PMs—A Survery of Retailers," *Journal of Retailing* 48 (Winter 1972–73), pp. 40–47.

[22] Al Kaufman, "Tie-in Promotions: How to Make Them Successful," *Advertising Age* (19 November 1979), pp. 54*ff.*

[23] U.S. Federal Trade Commission, *Economic Report on the Use and Economic Significance of Trading Stamps* (Washington, D.C.: FTC, January 1966); Harold W. Fox, *The Economics of Trading Stamps* (Washington, D.C.: Public Affairs Press, 1968).

[24] Louis E. Boone, James C. Johnson, and George P. Ferry, "Trading Stamps: Their Role in Today's Marketplace," *Journal of the Academy of Marketing Science* 6 (Winter 1978), pp. 70–76.

[25] Scott M. Cutlip and Allen H. Center, *Effective Public Relations,* 5th ed. (Englewood Cliffs, N.J.: Prentice-Hall, 1979), p. 16.

[26] Irving Burstiner, *The Small Business Handbook: A Comprehensive Guide to Starting and Running Your Own Business* (Englewood Cliffs, N.J.: Prentice-Hall, 1979), p. 202.

[27]William F. Schoell and Thomas T. Ivy, *Marketing: Contemporary Concepts and Practices* (Boston: Allyn & Bacon, 1982), p. 495.

[28]Philip Kotler, *Marketing Management: Analysis, Planning, and Control,* 4th ed. (Englewood Cliffs, N.J.: Prentice-Hall, 1980), p. 470.

[29]E. Jerome McCarthy and William D. Perreault, Jr., *Essentials of Marketing,* 3d ed. (Homewood, Ill.: Richard D. Irwin, 1985), p. 327.

[30]William M. Pride and O. C. Ferrell, *Marketing: Basic Concepts and Decisions,* 2d ed. (Boston: Houghton Mifflin, 1980), p. 458.

RETAIL ADVERTISING

Your Study Objectives

After you have studied this chapter, you will understand:

1. The role of advertising in the retailer's promotion mix.
2. The federal government's stance against exaggeration or fraud in advertising.
3. The value of cooperative advertising effort to retailer and supplier.
4. The methods and procedures retail companies use to budget and allocate advertising funds.
5. The major characteristics of the advertising media.

Advertising for Retailers   Manufacturers advertise to enlist the support of wholesalers and retailers in distributing their goods and services. They may also advertise directly to consumers to encourage them to visit stores in search of these offerings.

In the retail sector, advertising fulfills a somewhat different role. Retailers advertise to attract the attention of consumers and persuade them to come to their stores. Once a shopper has stepped inside, merchandise displays and salespeople are relied on to take over and close the sale.

Advertising Defined   **Advertising** is one of the three components of the promotion mix. To understand its meaning more clearly, consider this pair of concise definitions borrowed from two authoritative sources:

Advertising is a method of delivering a message from a sponsor, through an impersonal medium, to many people.[1]

Advertising consists of *nonpersonal forms of communication conducted through paid media under clear sponsorship.* [2]

The two statements are quite similar. Those characteristics that differentiate advertising from personal selling and sales promotion are readily apparent:

Communication is involved. A *source* sends messages to many *receivers.*

The messages are *sponsored:* a specific organization or person arranges for the advertising and pays for the service.

Channels of communication *(media)* are used to carry the messages to people.

The process is impersonal, or nonpersonal, in the sense that no salesperson delivers the messages.

Advertising Management   Like all other phases of business administration, the advertising function must be properly planned, organized, directed, and controlled. Sequential decisions must be made. As shown in Figure 19.1, they start with an appraisal of the advertising opportunity in light of company objectives. The last step is an assessment of advertising results. Figure 19.2 is a detailed view of the information and decision processes.

Objectives of Retail Advertising   Retail advertising may be classified as *promotional* or *institutional,* according to its purpose. Most advertisements are of the **promotional,** or **direct action,** type because they promote quick consumer response. Objectives may be to increase store traffic, move merchandise off the shelves, announce special sales, and so on. Promotional advertising

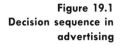

**Figure 19.1
Decision sequence in
advertising**

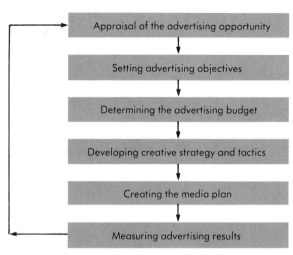

Appraisal of the advertising opportunity

Setting advertising objectives

Determining the advertising budget

Developing creative strategy and tactics

Creating the media plan

Measuring advertising results

Source: Charles H. Patti, "Evaluating the Role of Advertising," *Journal of Advertising* 6 (Fall 1977), p. 31. Reprinted with permission from *Journal of Advertising.*

is often referred to as product advertising because it displays specific merchandise. Price is frequently the major factor in drawing customers to the store. The familiar supermarket advertisements that appear in your newspaper each week, usually on Thursday mornings or Wednesday evenings, are good examples.

Retail advertising often features specific merchandise items priced to draw customers to the store, as for the grand opening sale of this franchise.

Courtesy Naked Furniture

Figure 19.2
Sequence of information gathering and decisions in marketing communication

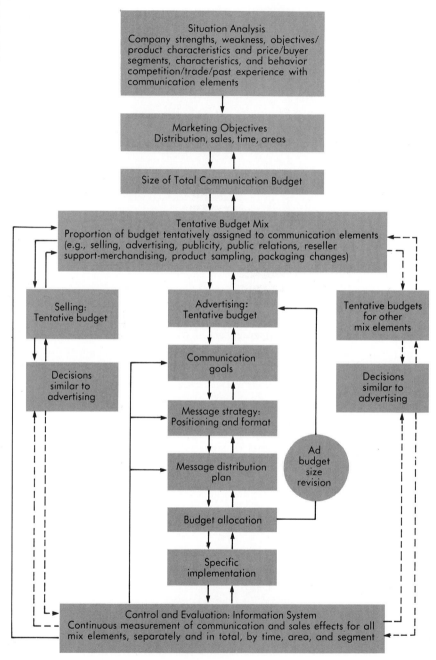

Source: Michael L. Ray, "A Decision Sequence Analysis of Developments in Marketing Communication," *Journal of Marketing* 37 (January 1973), p. 31.

Institutional advertisements appear far less often. They keep the retail company's name before the public to promote community goodwill and store loyalty. For these reasons, they are also known as **image-building** or **attitude advertising.** Including the firm's signature, or **logotype (logo),** in a promotional advertisement is an institutional element.

Among the many objectives that retailers may set for advertising are:

to announce new merchandise items
to attract new customers
to clear out overstocked or end-of-season goods
to counter the advertising of competitors
to create excitement about upcoming promotions
to encourage applications for store charge accounts
to enhance the company's reputation
to generate more in-store traffic
to help clarify the firm's image
to increase sales volume
to inform the public of special events
to introduce a brand-new store
to retain old customers
to keep the store's name in the public eye
to move goods off the shelves
to strengthen store-community ties

Before objectives can be set, retailers must define their business, their customers and what they are like, and their own attitudes toward retailing. A short, helpful guide for the small-store owner can be seen in Figure 19.3.

Truth in Advertising

A series of federal statutes spanning six decades set the stage for today's emphasis on honesty and fairness in advertising.

In 1914, Congress passed the Federal Trade Commission Act. This law prohibited unfair methods of competition and established the Federal Trade Commission (FTC). The Wheeler-Lea Act of 1938 amended the earlier statute to include false and deceptive practices, a category that embraces false or misleading advertising as well. The role of the FTC was further strengthened over the next several decades with the enactment of various labeling laws, the Flammable Fabrics Act, the Fair Packaging and Labeling Act, and other consumer protection laws. Stepping up its activities against deceptive advertising during the 1970s, the FTC took pains to ensure that advertised claims could be substantiated by valid evidence.

Although they appear infrequently, instances of fraudulent or deceptive advertising by retail companies may be significant enough to war-

**Figure 19.3
A profile checklist for
the small retailer**

The first step in evaluating the various ways of telling your story to your public is that of deciding *who you are* and *who your public is*. This profile checklist may be helpful:

1. **What Quality of Merchandise Do I Sell?** Are my price lines high? In the middle? Too low? Are my customers' incomes increasing rapidly so that they are prospects for higher price lines?

2. **How Do I Compare with Competition?** Am I priced competitively? Or do I stress quality and service? Are my merchandise lines as broad and varied as my competitors'?

3. **What Selling Techniques Do I Use?** Are my employees trained to sell related items? To sell higher-profit lines? Or are they just friendly clerks?

4. **What Customer Services Do I Feature?** Do I extend credit? Do I deliver? Do I offer a money-back guarantee or item substitution? Do I repair merchandise? Do I stay open nights? Do I offer adequate parking space?

5. **Am I Accessible to the Public?** Am I located on a busy street with lots of foot traffic? Or do I have to promote harder so as to *pull* people to an out-of-the-way location? Am I long in business and well known? Are there many people who still don't know me?

6. **Who Makes Up My Market?** Do I sell to men? Women? Teenagers? Tots? Do they have pronounced tastes? Are my customers' incomes high, low, or average? Are more young families with more children moving into my neighborhood? Do they all live near the store? Within a one-mile radius? Do they come from all over the city?

7. **Why Do People Buy from Me?** Do I know why my *best* customers continue to buy from me? Have I asked them why? Do they like me for reasons that could be featured in my advertising?

8. **Why Don't People Buy from Me?** Have I ever asked a customer who *stopped* shopping why he quit my store? Do I take an objective look at my windows, my displays, counters, lighting? Is the store clean? Are the employees courteous and well informed?

After you've studied these questions, fix the things you don't like about your store. Capitalize on what you *do* like. Decide who your customers should be. Then decide what kind of face you're going to present to them in your advertising.

Source: Charles T. Lipscomb, Jr., "Checklist for Successful Retail Advertising," *Small Marketers Aids No. 96* (Washington, D.C.: Small Business Administration, 1974), pp. 1–2.

rant concern.[3] Some retailers, for example, resort to **bait-and-switch advertising.** This involves promoting a well-known article—such as a famous-brand TV or room air conditioner—at a ridiculously low price. The purpose is to attract shoppers to the store. The retailer does not really intend to sell the item. When shoppers request the merchandise, they are informed that the goods have sold out. The salesperson then attempts to sell the shopper another, more expensive item of the same type. In ethical operations, disappointed consumers are issued rain checks on out-of-stock merchandise. The store will honor the advertised sale price when the stock has been replenished.

Retail advertising is part of the company's image. The retail firm intent on surviving and strengthening its position in the community will try to project an image of solid respectability. Because public

8888888

trust is built on truthfulness, retailers must avoid deceit and exaggeration in their promotional efforts.[4]

Cooperative Advertising

In **cooperative advertising,** two or more firms share the advertising costs. Two approaches are seen in the retail sector: horizontal and vertical. **Horizontal cooperative advertising** is less common. In these situations, two or more retailers advertise jointly, each contributing funds toward the project. This takes place in planned shopping centers, where each store makes a proportional contribution to the center's promotion budget. The individual merchant's share may be based on store size or annual sales volume. Associations of independent stores may also engage in horizontal co-op advertising. For example, a few confectionery chains with store units in the same metropolitan area may get together for a mutual promotion, such as for Mother's Day, in the newspapers and/or on radio.

Vertical cooperative advertising is by far the more common form. In this form, different channel members, such as a manufacturer and a retailer, share advertising costs in promoting one or more of the manufacturer's products. The primary advantage for the producer is that more advertising exposure is gained for the outlay of funds. Newspaper space or air time can be purchased at lower local, rather than national, rates. Local advertising can be obtained for as little as 50 percent of the cost of national advertising.

How Retailers Benefit

Typically, suppliers reimburse retailers for half the expenses incurred in advertising their products. In some instances, the manufacturer may pay up to 100 percent of the cost. Record-keeping is essential. To be reimbursed, the retailer must submit tear sheets of the advertisements. These are newsprint copies provided by the newspaper. If radio or TV is used, affidavits from the station denoting broadcast times are required.

Retail firms welcome this kind of support for their modest budgets.[5] At lowered expense, co-op advertising increases sales volume and stock turnover. Manufacturers often provide retailers with professionally prepared newspaper advertisements in the form of mats or proofs. These aids allow space for the store's name, address, and telephone number. Point-of-purchase signing, radio copy, display materials, trained demonstrators, and other promotional help may also be furnished.

The Advertising Budget

Advertising is a standard expense in the budget. As such, it must be monitored carefully by management to keep all costs within reason. Yet advertising expenses are also an investment designed to nourish

The retailer's advertising budget will take into account the amount, quality, and effectiveness of their manufacturers' advertising.

Courtesy The Goodyear Tire & Rubber Company

a business and help it grow. Each year, then, retailers face the same question: "How much should we allocate to our advertising budget?" Executive judgment is called on to strike a balance between cost constraints and the desire to stimulate sales. There is no simple resolution to this recurrent problem. No single budgeting approach is demonstrably best for all retail companies.

Factors to Consider   Here are some of the many factors that retailers consider in developing their advertising budgets:

the position of advertising and its goals in the store's basic promotional
    policy
the amount, quality, and effectiveness of manufacturers' advertising
the length of time the store has been in the area
the location of the store
the nature of the market
the physical nature of the trading area
the media available and their rates
the competition
the effect of business cycles on the trading area
the perishability of the store's merchandise
the size of the store and the variety of products carried.[6]

Establishing the Advertising Budget

In this section, we describe five of the more popular methods that retail firms use to determine their advertising budgets: the percentage-of-sales, arbitrary decision, what-we-can afford, meet-our-competition, and objective-and-task methods.

Percentage of Sales Simplicity probably accounts for the wide use of the **percentage-of-sales method.** Retailers like it because they, or their accountants, are attuned to calculating and analyzing ratios for just about every expense category on their operating statements. The ratios are expressed in relation to net sales: rent to sales, payroll costs to sales, advertising to sales, and so on. Under this approach, the company compares last year's sales with last year's total advertising expenditure. This yields the advertising-to-sales ratio:

$$\text{Advertising-to-sales ratio} = \frac{\text{Dollars spent on advertising}}{\text{Net sales}}$$

Assume that Store A spent $20,000 on advertising last year and ended up with $250,000 in net sales. Using the formula, this works out to an advertising-to-sales ratio of 8 percent, as follows:

$$\text{Advertising-to-sales ratio} = \frac{\$20,000}{\$250,000} = .08 = 8\%$$

Frequently, the budgeting procedure is refined by tallying both advertising costs and sales for several years. Thus, an average advertising-to-sales ratio is derived which may be of more value in planning. Sales projections for the coming year may also be added to past years' results. This adjustment takes long-term trends into consideration.

New retailers have no sales history to base their budget planning on. In such situations retailers acquire industry ratios from the trade association, Dun & Bradstreet, or some other source. The firm can then adopt this percentage until it has accumulated sales data. However, new-store owners often spend well above the industry average during their first year of operation to launch their business.

Critics of the percentage-of-sales method point out that it is illogical, because the technique suggests that advertising *depends on* sales, instead of the other way around. Yet the approach, "if properly used, can be as sophisticated as the objective-and-task method."[7] (This last technique will be described later.)

Arbitrary Decision Calling the **arbitrary decision technique** a *method* for setting advertising budgets stretches the truth somewhat. The proprietor (or company president) who uses this approach simply announces: "Next year, we will spend x dollars on our advertising." The amount decided on may well have depended on how the decision maker felt at that time or the evening before. If sales have recently been brisk, management may be encouraged to set a figure that is higher than last year's. The reverse may also take place.

What We Can Afford Most likely, the retailer who employs the **what-we-can-afford method** recognizes the need for advertising but is unsure of its rewards. Consequently, the total company budget is reviewed to make certain that planned sales will materialize and that the gross profit earned will more than reimburse the firm. Whatever surplus is expected, after allowing for planned profit, is then allocated to the advertising budget.

Clearly, serious planning is missing here. Each new year's budget can be higher or lower than that of the previous year.

Meet Our Competition A firm that uses the **meet-our-competition method** first tries to learn how much in advertising dollars its major competitor(s) spend. Then the company will allocate approximately the same level of funding to its own media advertising. However, it is often difficult for retailers to obtain this kind of information. It is sometimes available from the media, and many firms will ask their trade associations for industry data on their particular type and size of store. In so doing, they are really reverting to the percentage-of-sales approach mentioned earlier.

The method does contain flaws. For one thing, a retailer's competitors may be targeting at somewhat different consumer segments. To reach their audience, more (or fewer) promotion dollars may be required. For another, competitive firms may have far more (or less) financial resources at their command. They may also be pursuing different company objectives. Finally, the competition itself may be following the same approach.

Objective and Task Also known as the build-up or job-requirement approach, the **objective-and-task method** is a planned, management-by-objectives technique that makes considerable sense. The company first establishes a specific sales objective for the period. Management then designs an advertising program that will bring in the targeted sales figure. Decisions are made about media selection, advertisements to be used, and the advertising schedule (timing, frequency, and so on) needed to accomplish the firm's objective. All projected costs are then totaled to derive the budget.

Allocating Advertising Funds In industry, advertising dollars may be divided in various ways; for example, by media types, by product categories, by location or sales territories, by departments, or by calendar periods. Retailers plan their advertising around the calendar. Department, chain, and discount store

From *The Wall Street Journal*, with permission of Cartoon Features Syndicate.

organizations tailor their efforts to conform with six-month or seasonal merchandising plans. They break these down further into monthly and weekly advertising plans. The process also takes into account representative appropriations for individual departments.

Many independent merchants follow much the same procedure. They prepare an annual, semiannual, or quarterly schedule and divide the program into months and/or weeks of advertising activity. The common denominator most often applied is the percentage-of-sales approach. Each month's advertising expenditure is made to conform in percentage with the month's usual contribution to annual sales.

Assume, for example, that the firm's sales history reflects these average monthly percentages of total annual sales:

January	5.7%	July	5.2%
February	6.1	August	5.4
March	8.5	September	7.7
April	7.4	October	8.3
May	6.9	November	9.8
June	5.6	December	23.4

Assume that the advertising budget for the firm is $50,000. In planning the budget for January, 5.7 percent of $50,000, or $2,850, will be allocated for the month. This is how the entire year's breakdown would come out:

January	$2,850	July	$ 2,600
February	3,050	August	2,700
March	4,250	September	3,850
April	3,700	October	4,150
May	3,450	November	4,900
June	3,800	December	11,700

In practice, two modifications of the procedure are often made. One useful tactic is to set aside some percentage of the total year's budget, perhaps 5 to 10 percent, as a **contingency fund.** This adds flexibility. Retailers may, for example, want to take advantage of unexpected co-op advertising dollars, introduce new lines, or get rid of overstocked goods. If the contingency concept is used, monthly allocations are derived from a somewhat lower annual budget: in this case, $45,000 rather than $50,000.

A second change may be introduced because of an individual merchant's philosophy. Some retailers believe that little advertising is called for during stronger selling periods, such as before Christmas or Easter. At such times, they cut back on advertising and shunt excess funds into weaker periods to bolster sales. Other firms differ; they believe in spending disproportionately more during the busy seasons, knowing that large numbers of consumers are already in a buying mood.

Table 19.1 shows monthly sales percentages and publicity (advertising) cost percentages of sales for a group of men's store retailers. Similar results of operating experiences are often made available to retailers by their trade associations.

Advertising Media

An **advertising medium** is a vehicle that carries promotional messages to customers, actual or potential. Newspapers, magazines, TV, and radio are known as **mass media** because they deliver messages to large numbers of consumers. (See Table 19.2.) Other media categories include direct mail, the position media (billboards, car cards, and the like), advertising specialties, classified telephone directories, and so on.

Media Strategy

In choosing among media, the advertiser is concerned with: (1) audience characteristics, (2) reach, (3) impact, and (4) cost. Of these, only reach and impact require further explanation. **Reach** refers to the size of the audience contacted: number of households, number of people. **Impact** is the intensity of the effect that the medium has on its audience. A TV commercial, for example, ordinarily has a far stronger impact on its viewers than a radio announcement or newspaper advertisement would have on its audience.

Media strategy remains an art, despite attempts by some large corpo-

Table 19.1   **Monthly sales and publicity percentages, 1983: Menswear retailers**

| | Firms Handling Menswear Only | | | | | |
| | Distribution of Sales by Month (51 Firms) | | Publicity Cost as a Percent of Monthly Sales (42 Firms) | | Distribution of Publicity Cost by Month (42 Firms) | |
	Range of Common Experience	Median Firm	Range of Common Experience	Median Firm	Range of Common Experience	Median Firm
February	5.1– 6.7	5.9	3.1–5.5	4.2	4.8– 8.8	6.7
March	5.5– 7.2	6.1	2.5–5.1	3.7	5.3– 9.0	7.1
April	6.3– 7.8	7.0	2.1–5.0	3.2	5.0– 7.3	6.2
May	6.7– 8.0	7.2	2.6–5.4	3.6	6.1– 8.5	7.3
June	7.8– 9.5	8.7	2.7–4.7	3.4	6.0–11.4	8.4
July	6.3– 8.8	7.5	2.8–5.0	4.1	6.3–10.8	8.6
August	5.2– 6.8	6.0	2.2–5.5	3.4	3.9– 8.2	5.8
September	5.8– 7.6	6.5	2.2–5.6	3.6	5.0– 9.3	7.5
October	7.0– 9.2	7.9	1.8–5.2	3.8	5.0–10.9	8.4
November	8.5–10.7	9.3	2.8–5.1	3.9	7.4–13.6	9.3
December	16.1–20.7	18.6	1.9–3.8	2.5	9.4–19.4	12.4
January	6.0– 9.0	7.7	3.1–6.1	4.4	6.2–12.4	8.2
Total		100.0%				100.0%

Source: Menswear Retailers of America, *1983 Annual Business Survey: Men's Store Operating Experiences* (Washington, D.C.: Menswear Retailers of America, 1984), p. 38.

rations and advertising agencies to be scientific. Sophisticated computer models have been devised which build in many variables in addition to reach, impact, frequency, audience characteristics, and the like.[8]

Figure 19.4 displays total estimated advertising expenditures for 1983 in the different media.

In promoting their products, manufacturers of consumer goods often use **multimedia approaches** because: (1) they cater to regional or national markets and (2) they depend on wholesalers and retailers for help in distribution. Not so with retail companies. Most retailers rely on local newspapers to carry their messages throughout the community. Radio, direct mail, and other media are occasionally used to supplement newspaper advertising.

Print Media   Newspapers and magazines constitute the **print media**. Newspapers typically attract the greatest share of a store's advertising dollars. In

Table 19.2   The mass media: Strengths and weaknesses

		Strengths	Weaknesses
Television		Broad reach	Little demographic selectivity
		Creative opportunities for demonstration	Commercial clutter
		Immediacy of messages	Short advertising life of message
		Entertainment carry-over	Decreased viewing in summer
		A compelling medium	Some consumer skepticism toward claims made
		Negotiable costs	High cost
		Frequent messages	
	Network	Association of prestige with programming	Long-term advertiser commitments
	Local	Geographic selectivity	High reach more difficult on independent stations
		Association with programs of local origin and appeal	High cost for broad geographic coverage
		Short notice to schedule	Ad can be preempted
Radio		Low cost	No visual treatment
		High frequency	Short advertising life of message
		Immediacy of message	Background sound
		Short notice to schedule	Commercial clutter
		Relatively no seasonal change in audience	
		Highly portable medium	
		Negotiable costs	
		Short-term advertiser commitments	
		Entertainment carry-over	
	Network	Lower absolute cost for national coverage	Difficult to accumulate reach of a large audience
			No geographical flexibility
			Limited demographic selectivity
			Limited programming variety
			Clearance problems
			Variation in audience by market
	Local	Excellent demographic selectivity	High cost for broad geographic coverage
		Good geographic flexibility	
		Personality identification	
Magazines		Good reproduction, especially color	Long-term advertiser commitments
		Permanence of message	Slow audience buildup
		Demographic selectivity, reaches affluent audience	Limited demonstration capacities
		Regional	Less compelling than other major media like television
		Local market selectivity	Lack of urgency
		Special interest possibilities	Long closing dates
		Readership not seasonal	Not a frequency medium (unless used specially with multiple units in same issue)
		Relatively long advertising life (one week, one month)	
		Informational	
		Editorially compatible environment	
		Secondary readership	
		Merchandising programs	
Newspapers		Geographic selectivity and flexibility	Little demographic selectivity
		Short-term advertiser commitments	High absolute costs for national representation
		News value and immediacy	Limited color facilities
		Advertising permanence	Variable color reproduction
		Readership not seasonal	Different local and national rates
		High individual market coverage	Little secondary readership
		Local retailer-dealer identification	
		Merchandising programs	
		Co-op and local tie-in availability	
		Short closing	

Source: Reprinted by permission of the *Harvard Business Review*. An exhibit from "More for Your Money from the Media," by Stephen R. Fajen (HBR, September/October 1978). Copyright © 1978 by the President and Fellows of Harvard College; all rights reserved.

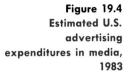

**Figure 19.4
Estimated U.S.
advertising
expenditures in media,
1983**

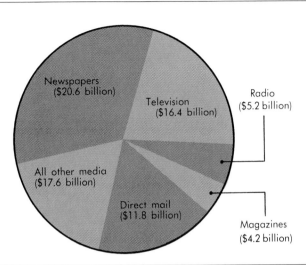

Source: Prepared for *Advertising Age* by Robert J. Coen, McCann-Erickson, Inc.

turn, most newspaper advertisements are from retailers. Magazines are primarily used by manufacturers and other national or regional companies.

Newspapers Of the approximately 1,700 daily newspapers published in the United States, three out of four are evening papers. Weeklies, often a more practical medium for the small-budget retailer, number in excess of 7,000.[9] Four out of five adults are newspaper readers, and readership rises with both education and income level.[10]

Why Newspapers Are Popular among Retailers The local newspaper is the shopper's primary and most trusted source of news and local information. Recognizing this fact, retailers look to the medium for informing the community about their stores, merchandise, and services.

The medium has a number of advantages. Newspapers provide intensive coverage of the retail firm's trading area. They are read at a leisurely pace. Consumers may reread ads several times and even clip them out for later reference. This last point is of special value when coupons are used. The cost per lead is low, and results are almost immediate. Only a short lead time is required. The retailer can design an advertisement today, and it will appear in tomorrow's edition. Copy, art, or publication date can quickly be changed. Most newspapers will help the small independent merchant prepare layout and copy and can often furnish appropriate artwork from stock **cuts** (illustrations). However, the newspaper does have its drawbacks. Excessive waste circulation can be a significant factor. Only a small percentage

Because the local newspaper is the shopper's primary and most trusted source of news and local information, retailers use this medium to inform the public about their stores, merchandise, and services. This ad appeared in the Sunday magazine section of a community newspaper.

Courtesy Omnibus Clock Shop

of readers are likely prospects for a given store. There is also **clutter:** many other advertisements in the paper compete for the reader's attention.

Costs Newspaper space is sold by the **agate line** (14 agate lines to the column inch) and by inches, columns, or fractional and full pages. Retailers pay local rates; these are substantially lower than the rates charged to national advertisers. Newspapers provide would-be advertisers with their latest rate cards. Figure 19.5 illustrates a section of one publication's rate card. The Standard Rate and Data Service compiles and issues rates for all newspapers in the United States and for other media. A sample page from a recent issue of their "Newspaper Rates and Data" can be seen in Figure 19.6.

Combination rates are available: weekdays and Sunday editions, morning plus evening editions, and so on. So are **contract rates,** based on the total linage used and/or the frequency of advertising. Rates are quoted for **run-of-paper (ROP);** that is to say, the newspaper decides where to place the advertisement. If a **preferred position** is re-

Figure 19.5
Excerpt from newspaper retail rate card

Retail Advertising Rates Full Run	Standard Advertising Unit System	
Contract Size (Total Column Inches)	Rates Per Column Inch	
	Weekdays	Saturday
Open—Gross	$206.40	$166.65
Net Rates Within One Year		
25 Column Inches or 6 Times	117.20	110.75
50 Column Inches or 13 Times	109.65	93.55
125 Column Inches or 26 Times	104.30	87.10
250 Column Inches	101.05	83.85
500 Column Inches	96.75	82.80
1,000 Column Inches	93.55	81.70
1,500 Column Inches	84.95	79.55
2,000 Column Inches	81.70	77.40
2,500 Column Inches	80.65	76.35
3,750 Column Inches	77.40	75.25
5,000 Column Inches	74.20	67.75
7,500 Column Inches	70.95	64.50
10,000 Column Inches	67.75	60.20
12,500 Column Inches	66.65	58.05
15,000 Column Inches	62.35	53.75

Full page ads will be discounted 8%.

Source: From retail rate card effective January 1, 1985, *New York Post*, p. 4.

quested—such as the top right-hand corner, or a specific page—there is an additional charge.

Milline Rates Frequently, retailers want to choose the better buy or best buy among papers. Comparing them according to their **milline rates** is a useful aid in decision making. These rates are calculated using the following formula:

$$\text{Milline rate} = \frac{\text{Agate line rate} \times 1,000,000}{\text{Circulation of newspaper}}$$

To demonstrate its use, let us consider this brief example: Newspaper A quotes the retailer a line rate of $1.80. It has a total circulation of 215,000. Newspaper B's rate comes to $3.05 per line and its circulation is 380,000. We apply the formula:

$$\text{A's milline rate} = \frac{\$1.80 \times 1,000,000}{215,000} = \$8.37$$

$$\text{B's milline rate} = \frac{\$3.05 \times 1,000,000}{380,000} = \$8.03$$

Comparing the two, we see that the milline rate for B is lower. It would seem to be the better choice. It should be pointed out, though, that milline rate comparisons neglect two important considerations:

(1) the number of readers of each paper who reside in the store's trading area and (2) the quality of those readers insofar as demographics, lifestyles, and other consumer characteristics are concerned.

**Figure 19.6
Excerpt from Standard
Rate and Data Service
page**

NEBRASKA

Fremont

Dodge County—Map Location G-3
See SRDS Consumer market map and data at beginning of the state.

TRIBUNE
A Gannett Newspaper
P.O. Box 9, 135 N. Main St., Fremont, NE 68025.
Phone 402-721-5000.

(ABC)

Media Code 1 128 2825 6.00　　　　Mid 016903-000
EVENING (except Sunday)
Member: INAME; NAB, Inc.
1. PERSONNEL
Publisher—Sara M. Bentley.
Advertising Manager—Steven Hively.
2. REPRESENTATIVES and/or BRANCH OFFICES
Gannett Newspaper Advertising Sales.
3. COMMISSION AND CASH DISCOUNT
15% to agencies; 2% 10th following month.
4. POLICY-ALL CLASSIFICATIONS
30-day notice of any rate revision.
Alcoholic beverage advertising accepted.
ADVERTISING RATES
Effective May 28, 1984.
Received July 16, 1984.
5. BLACK/WHITE RATES
SAU open, per inch 7.98
NEWSPLAN—SAU
Pages　　　　　　　% Disc. Eve. Inches
6 .... 10 7.28 774
13 .... 15 6.79 1,677
26 .... 33 5.46 3,354
See Newsplan Contract and Copy Regulations—items 1, 4, 6, 7, 8, 9, 10, 14, 22, 23, 24, 31.
7. COLOR RATES AND DATA
Available daily (except Sunday).
Use b/w rate plus the following applicable costs:
　　　　　　　　b/w 1 c b/w 2 c b/w 3 c
Extra 85.00 154.00 201.00
Closing dates: Reservations and printing material, and cancellation dates 3 days before publication date.
11. SPECIAL DAYS/PAGES/FEATURES
Best Food Day: Tuesday.
Farm Page, Monday; Building Page, TV Tab, Saturday.
12. R.O.P. DEPTH REQUIREMENTS
Ads over 19" deep charged full col. (21-3/4").
13. CONTRACT AND COPY REGULATIONS
See Contents page for location of regulations—items 1, 3, 6, 10, 11, 21, 25, 27, 34, 35.
14. CLOSING TIMES
5:00 p.m. 2 days before publication.
15. MECHANICAL MEASUREMENTS
For complete, detailed production information, see SRDS Print Media Production Data.
6/12-8/10—6 cols/ea 12 picas 8 pts betw col.
16. SPECIAL CLASSIFICATIONS/RATES
POSITION CHARGES
Next to reading 15%; full position 25%.
17. CLASSIFIED RATES
For complete data refer to classified rate section.
19. MAGAZINES
TV Journal
SATURDAY.
Effective May 28, 1984.
Received July 16, 1984.
BLACK/WHITE RATES
Flat, per inch 7.98
COLOR RATES AND DATA
Use b/w rate plus the following applicable costs:
　　　　　　　　b/w 1 c b/w 2 c b/w 3 c
Extra 85.00 154.00 201.00
CLOSING TIMES
Reservations and cancellations Tuesday prior to publication.
MECHANICAL MEASUREMENTS
Page size 10-1/2" x 8" deep. 6 cols to page.
20. CIRCULATION
Established 1868. Per copy .25.

ADVERTISING RATES
Effective July 1, 1984.
Received October 31, 1984.
5. BLACK/WHITE RATES
Open, per inch 6.86
Inches charged full depth: col. 21-1/2; pg. 129; dbl truck 279-1/2.
NEWSPLAN
Pages　　　　　　　% Disc. EorS Inches
6 .... 5 6.52 774
13 .... 7.5 6.34 1,677
26 .... 10 6.17 3,354
52 .... 12.5 6.00 6,708
65 .... 15 5.84 8,385
78 .... 16 5.77 10,062
91 .... 17 5.70 11,734
104 .... 18 5.63 13,416
See Newsplan Contract and Copy Regulations—items 1, 2, 4, 7, 8, 9, 10, 14, 22, 23, 24, 31.
6. GROUP COMBINATION RATES-B/W & COLOR
Nebraska Out-State Newspaper Unit Buy—see listing at beginning of State.
7. COLOR RATES AND DATA
Available daily (except Wed.) Only Red available Wednesday.
Use b/w rate plus the following applicable costs:
　　　　　　　　b/w 1 c b/w 2 c b/w 3 c
Extra 110.00 160.00 200.00
Standard ANPA inks used; extra charge for special order inks.
Closing dates: Copy, printing material and cancellation dates 6 days in advance.
11. SPECIAL DAYS/PAGES/FEATURES
Best Food Day: Wednesday.
Farm Pages, Tuesday; Church Pages, Home and Building, Saturday.
12. R.O.P. DEPTH REQUIREMENTS
Ads over 19 inches deep charged full col.
13. CONTRACT AND COPY REGULATIONS
See Contents page for locations of regulations—items 3, 10, 13, 14, 19, 21, 23, 26, 31, 32, 34, 35.
14. CLOSING TIMES
2 days before publication.
15. MECHANICAL MEASUREMENTS
For complete, detailed production information, see SRDS Print Media Production Data.
PRINTING PROCESS: Offset.
6/12-5/9—6 cols/ea 12 picas-5 pts/9 pts betw col.
Inches charged full depth: col. 21-1/2; pg. 129; dbl truck 279-1/2.
16. SPECIAL CLASSIFICATIONS/RATES
Business Opportunity and Mail order—general rates apply. Subject to approval; no coin-operated machine copy accepted.
17. CLASSIFIED RATES
For complete data refer to classified rate section.
19. MAGAZINES
Leisure Times
SUNDAY.
Received May 7, 1984.
BLACK/WHITE RATES
Flat, per inch 6.86
ROP DEPTH REQUIREMENTS
As many inches deep as columns wide.
CLOSING TIMES
Noon, Tuesday prior to publication date.
MECHANICAL MEASUREMENTS
PRINTING PROCESS: Offset.
Page size 10-1/4" x 13" deep. 5 cols to page 1 col. 11-1/2 picas.
20. CIRCULATION
Established 1869. Per copy .25.
Net Paid—A.B.C. 3-31-84 (Newspaper Form)
　　　　　　Total CZ TrZ Other
Eve 28,592 12,052 12,822 1,018
Sun 26,500 12,218 13,267 1,015
For county-by-county and/or metropolitan area breakdowns, see SRDS Newspaper Circulation Analysis.

Hastings

Adams County—Map Location E-4
See SRDS Consumer market map and data at beginning of the state.

TRIB...

NEWSPLAN
Pages
6 ....
13 ....
26 ....
52 ....
See Newsplan Contract and Copy
6. GROUP COMBINATION RATES
Also sold in combination with TV
7.70.
Circulation: Sworn 3-31-84: Tota
Nebraska Out-State Newspaper
beginning of State.
7. COLOR RATES AND DATA
Use b/w rate plus the following
Extra
Closing dates: Reservations 6
material and cancellation dat
11. SPECIAL DAYS/PAGES/FE
Best Food Day: Wednesday.
Church, Happenings TV Tab
Saturday.
12. R.O.P. DEPTH REQUIREMEN
Ads over 19 inches deep will be
13. CONTRACT AND COPY REG
See Contents page for location
3, 5, 6, 11, 12, 14, 18, 19, 20, 2
14. CLOSING TIMES
Noon. 2 days before publicatio
15. MECHANICAL MEASUREM
For complete, detailed produ
SRDS Print Media Production
PRINTING PROCESS: Offset.
6/12-6/8—6 cols/ea 12 picas-
Inches charged full depth: col. 2
1/2.
16. SPECIAL CLASSIFICATIONS/
Mail order—general rates apply.
POSITION CHARGES
Next to reading 25%; under and
Minimum for position 28 lines.
17. CLASSIFIED RATES
For complete data refer to class
18. COMICS
Daily Comic Page—B/W
Accepted in cartoon style at regu
Vertical 1/2 page color ads accep
20. CIRCULATION
Established 1905. Per copy .25.
Net Paid—A.B.C. 3-31-84 (News
　　　　　　　　　　　T
Eve 17
For county-by-county and/
breakdowns, see SRDS Newspa

Holdrege

Phelps County—Map Location
See SRDS Consumer market map
the state.

CITIZEN
P.O. Box 344, 418 Garfield,
Phone 308-9f

(ABC)

Media Code 1 128 4520 1.00
EVENING (except Saturday and
(Not published Jan. 1, May
Thanksgiving or Christmas.)
Member: INAME; NAB, Inc.
1. PERSONNEL
Publisher—Dwight King.
Assoc. Pub.—Harley Lofton.
Advertising Manager—Barba
2. REPRESENTATIVES and/
Branham/Newspaper Sales.
3. COMMISSION AND CASH
15% to agencies; 2% 10th fo
4. POLICY-ALL CLASSIFICATI
60-day notice given of any rate
Alcoholic beverage advertising

Source: Standard Rate and Data Service, *Newspaper Rates and Data* 66, no. 8 (12 August 1984), p. 466.

Truline Rates Some of the difficulty can be alleviated by comparing the newspapers' **truline rates.**[11] Calculations are made with essentially the same formula, except that in the denominator of the fraction, the newspaper's circulation *within the trading area,* replaces the total circulation figure:

$$\text{Truline rate} = \frac{\text{Agate line rate} \times 1,000,000}{\text{Circulation in trading area}}$$

Working with truline rates presupposes that the firm can arrive at usable trading area estimates, either through newspaper-sponsored surveys or its own research.

Magazines Store retailers seldom use magazine advertising. Nationally circulated publications are clearly out of the question, except perhaps for national chains. Some magazines, however, publish regional editions which may be useful to regional retailers. Mail-order houses, banks, hotels, and various service retailers may include magazines in their media mix.

Among the attractive features of the medium are:

the long life of the advertisement: results may flow in for months or even years

secondary readership: magazines may lie around the home, office, or waiting room for lengthy periods

the possibility of reaching many different kinds of readers and special interest groups: homemakers, business executives, sports enthusiasts, amateur photographers, do-it-yourselfers, and so on

remarkably good reproduction of photographs

the availability of color to enhance many products

Magazine Space Costs Advertising space in magazines is sold by the column inch or by fractional and full pages. For evaluating buys among these publications, there is a counterpart to newspaper milline rates, the **cost per thousand** (readers):

$$\text{Cost/M} = \frac{\text{Single page rate} \times 1,000}{\text{Circulation of magazine}}$$

This measure is also useful for making comparisons across different media, for example, when evaluating radio, TV, and magazines.

Categories Magazines may be designated as consumer, business, or farm publications. Another approach to their classification follows, along with a few examples of each type:

Type	Examples
Beauty and fashion	*Glamour, Harper's Bazaar, Mademoiselle, Vogue*
Business	*Business Week, Dun's Review, Forbes, Fortune, Nation's Business*
Farm	*Farm Journal, Successful Farming, Progressive Farmer*
Special interest	*Baby Talk, Crafts Magazine, Family Health, Horticulture, Popular Ceramics, Popular Science*
Sports	*Field & Stream, Golf Magazine, Inside Sports, Ski, Sports Illustrated*
Women's	*Cosmopolitan, Family Circle, McCall's, Redbook, Self*

Broadcast Media   Radio and television are the **broadcast media.** In the years following World War II, radio lost much of its popularity among advertisers with the advent of commercial television. However, interest in radio has been gaining ground in recent years.

Radio Radio is often used in retail media planning, although it typically occupies a subordinate role to newspapers. A nearly universal medium, radio reaches just about every household in the country. We wake up to clock radios, listen to the kitchen radio while having breakfast, remain tuned to car or portable radios on our way to work or school, and keep in touch with what's happening by listening to radio while on vacation.

In 1984, over 8,300 commercial radio stations were broadcasting. Of these, more than 4,700 were AM stations and the balance FM stations.[12] Most are local stations, although many belong to a major network such as ABC (American Broadcasting Company) or CBS (Columbia Broadcast System).

Retail advertisers can target at many different audiences: football or baseball fans, lovers of country or classical music, nationality or racial groups, young people, and so on. Syndicated services such as Arbitron Radio and Burke Rating Research provide detailed audience research in the major markets.

Advantages of Radio Radio's attractions for the retail firm include the following:

Consumer reaction is almost immediate.
It is relatively inexpensive on a cost-per-thousand basis.
It is flexible: changes are easily made and lead time is short.
It is a selective medium: the advertiser can appeal to specific target groups.
Audience loyalty is strong.

Disadvantages The major drawbacks to radio are:

Radio announcements are short-lived, and messages are quickly forgotten.
The listener cannot refer back to an advertisement as can the newspaper or magazine reader.
Radio commercials appeal to only one sense. Words and sounds must do the entire selling job.
In some areas, many stations compete for listeners. Thus, the total audience is fragmented, and only a small percentage may hear the announcement.
Many listeners live well outside the store's trading area.

Broadcast Rates Advertisers generally purchase air time, whether on radio or TV, in one-minute segments. Also available are 30-second, 10-second, and other spot lengths. Rates vary according to **time class—**

the time of day or night scheduled. **Morning drive time,** roughly defined as from 6 to 10 o'clock, is the most costly. Saturday and Sunday rates are usually much lower than weekday rates.[13]

Television Nearly all households have at least one TV set, if only a black-and-white model. The majority have color sets. As early as 1976, more than one out of every seven households had subscribed to cable TV.[14] By 1984, the figure had reached nearly one third. Americans watch a great deal of TV. Heavy viewers watch more than 100 hours of prime-time TV each month.[15]

Because of cost considerations, retail advertising on network TV is mostly limited to the nationwide chains and direct-selling companies. Yet because television appeals to two senses—sight and hearing—its impact should be superior to that of radio. It is an excellent vehicle for showing store merchandise and the store itself. In recent years, the volume of local retail TV advertising has increased sharply. Today's firms are more proficient in applying concepts such as reach and frequency. Local TV stations provide them with valuable details about the demographics and habits of their audiences.[16] Restaurants, drive-in theaters, furniture stores, car dealers, car repair shops, banks, and many other types of retailers often use local TV.

Advantages and Disadvantages Among the benefits of advertising on TV are:

extensive reach: covers most households in the broadcast area
fast results
flexible scheduling
tremendous audience impact
substantial contribution to store image
increased sales by tying commercials into point-of-purchase materials and store display[17]

These are some of the drawbacks:

extremely costly air time[18]
high production costs: professional help may be needed
short message life
mental tuning out by many viewers or they see what other channels are offering
excessive waste; most viewers are outside the store's trading area

Direct Mail The most personal medium of all is **direct mail.** It is one-to-one communication. It resembles personal selling except that the retailer's messages are delivered by the U.S. Postal Service instead of by a salesperson. Direct mail is versatile and flexible. Advertising messages can be tailored for selected market segments representing fertile sales potential. To mention just a few possibilities: apartment dwellers or home owners; students or teachers; accountants, engineers, lawyers, and other professionals; young men or middle-aged women; physical culture enthusiasts or health food faddists; people interested in woodworking, crocheting, model-building, or stamp collecting; and so on.

It is true that the results of a mailing do not show up as rapidly as those induced by the newspaper advertisement or radio or TV commercial. However, the delay is a short one, and action may be sustained for an extended period. Direct-mail messages also do not usually have to compete with surrounding, competitive advertisements as is true of print media advertising.

Drawbacks Media planners often point to the high cost per thousand, relative to other media, as direct mail's most serious disadvantage. Costs for a direct-mail package encompass: *(a)* printing the typical contents—sales letter, brochure, order form, and outside and return envelopes; *(b)* renting or buying the mailing list; *(c)* addressing, collating, folding, stuffing, sealing, metering, and delivery to the post office; and *(d)* postage. The end result is a cost of, perhaps 75 cents, $1, or more per piece. When multiplied by 10,000 or more units, this may represent an investment well beyond the reach of most small independents.

There are other drawbacks. Because many people dislike receiving junk mail, the merchant's messages may be discarded without being read. Specialists may need to be hired at considerable cost to develop a professional mailing program. The difference between a successful and an unsuccessful mailing often depends on the list used. Usually, the firm's own customer list is the most productive of all. Lists may also be derived from public records (voter registrations, car licenses, tax rolls, and the like) and from in-store contests and other promotions where shoppers are asked to register their names and addresses. Retailers can obtain worthwhile lists from any number of directories (of clubs, fraternal, and other organizations), church groups, the Yellow Pages, and so on. They can also rent or buy from mailing-list houses or brokers. Such lists can be supplied on labels or typed directly on the retailer's envelopes.

Because some 20 percent of the population can be expected to move each year, mailing lists must be kept up to date.

Catalogs These can be important assets in generating company sales. Department stores and other large organizations may issue four or more different catalogs during the year, one for each season. Catalogs are in third place behind newspaper and radio among the media used by department and specialty stores.[19] Consumers read catalogs, and they create both mail-order sales and increased store traffic.[20]

Because of the considerable costs entailed in printing and distributing catalogs, some large companies now analyze their customer lists by computer to pinpoint and segment the most likely customers for various kinds of catalogs.[21]

Position Media   The term **position media** refers to outdoor and transit advertising, posters, illuminated exterior signs, and other methods of presenting promotional messages from a fixed position. The **outdoor advertising** category includes the billboards seen on buildings and along highways as well as moving or stationary illuminated signs.

Outdoor advertising is of interest to various retailers, especially restaurants, places of entertainment, motels, and service stations. Billboards are often used to inform consumers of the location of these places or to provide directions such as "18 Miles Ahead, at State Road 54." Billboards must carry brief messages. They are passed by too quickly for car occupants to register more than a few words. One suggestion is that copy should appear to the right of the illustration or other art. This is because "perceptual speed differences seem to be a real source of distortion."[22]

Advertising displayed on posters or cards in railroad and bus terminals, airports, subways, taxicabs, and buses is known as **transit advertising.** When contracting for such space, local retailers can purchase full or partial runs. The medium's chief advantage is that captive and repeat readership is assured. Messages carried can, of course, be longer than those that appear on billboards.

Position media include stationary outdoor signs like this retailer's ad on a building in Chicago.

Eleanore Snow

Evaluating Advertising Effectiveness

Retailers are pragmatists. They feel that money spent on advertising should translate readily to additional sales rung up at the cash register. This is how they would like to measure results. Unfortunately, advertising—like other forms of promotion—is just another mode of communication with consumers. Except, perhaps, for mail-order and direct-mail advertising, only rough approximations of results can be made. Retail companies attempt to measure the effectiveness of their advertising by investigating message clarity, extent of the reach accomplished, impact of their messages on intended audiences, and so on.

Most retail budgets lack the funds to finance more sophisticated evaluation methods. Some approaches for appraising the outcome of advertising that the independent retailer may find useful can be seen in Figures 19.7 and 19.8.

Figure 19.7
Evaluating the results of store advertising

Tests for Immediate-Response Ads

In weighing the results of your **immediate** response advertisements the following devices should be helpful:

Coupons brought in. Usually these coupons represent sales of the product. When the coupons represent requests for additional information or contact with a salesperson, were enough leads obtained to pay for the ad? If the coupon is dated, you can determine the number of returns for the first, second, and third weeks.

Requests by phone or letter referring to the ad. A hidden offer can cause people to call or write. Include—for example, in the middle of an ad—a statement that on request the product or additional information will be supplied. Results should be checked over a 1-week through 6-months or 12-months period because this type ad may have considerable carry-over effect.

Testing ads. Prepare two ads (different in some way you'd like to test or set for different stations or broadcast times) and run them on the same day. Identify the ads—in the message or with a coded coupon—so you can tell them apart. Ask customers to bring in the coupon or to use a special phrase. Run two broadcast ads at different times or on different stations on the same day with different discount phrases. Ask a newspaper to give you a split run—that is, to print Ad A in part of its press run and Ad B in the rest of the run. Count the responses to each ad.

Sales made of particular item. If the ad is on a bargain or limited-time offer, you can consider that sales at the end of 1 week, 2 weeks, 3 weeks, and 4 weeks came from the ad. You may need to make a judgment as to how many sales came from in-store display and personal selling.

Check store traffic. An important function of advertising is to build store traffic which results in purchases of items that are not advertised. Pilot studies show, for example, that many customers who are brought to the store by an ad for a blouse also bought a handbag. Some bought the bag in addition to the blouse, others instead of the blouse.

You may be able to use a local college or high school distributive education class to check store traffic. Class members could interview customers as they leave the store to determine: **(1)** which advertised items they bought, **(2)** what other items they bought, and **(3)** what they shopped for but did not buy.

Source: Elizabeth M. Sorbel, "Do You Know the Results of Your Advertising?" *Small Marketers Aids No. 169* (Washington, D.C.: Small Business Administration, 1979), pp. 4–5.

Figure 19.8
**Checklist for newspaper
advertising**

*Merchandise	Does the ad offer merchandise having wide appeal, special features, price appeal, and timeliness?
Medium	Is a newspaper the best medium for the ad or would another—direct mail, radio, television, or other—be more appropriate?
Location	Is the ad situated in the best spot (in both section and page location)?
Size	Is the ad large enough to do the job expected of it? Does it omit important details, or is it overcrowded with nonessential information?
*Headline	Does the headline express the major single idea about the merchandise advertised? The headline should usually be an informative statement and not simply a label. For example, "Sturdy shoes for active boys, specially priced at $6.95," is certainly better than "Boys' Shoes, $6.95."
Illustration	Does the illustration (if one is used) express the idea the headline conveys?
*Merchandise information	Does the copy give the basic facts about the goods, or does it leave out information that would be important to the reader? ("The more you tell, the more you sell.")
Layout	Does the arrangement of the parts of the ad and the use of white space make the ad easy to read? Does it stimulate the reader to look at all the contents of the ad?
Human interest	Does the ad—through illustration, headline, and copy—appeal to customers' wants and wishes?
*"You" attitude	Is the ad written and presented from the customer's point of view (with the customer's interests clearly in mind) or from the store's?
*Believability	To the objective, nonpartisan reader, does the ad ring true, or does it perhaps sound exaggerated or somewhat phony?
Type face	Does the ad use a distinctive typeface—different from those of competitors?
*Spur to action	Does the ad stimulate prompt action through devices such as use of a coupon, statement of limited quantities, announcement of a specific time period for the promotion or impending event?
*Sponsor identification	Does the ad use a specially prepared signature cut that is always associated with the store and that identifies it at a glance? Also, does it always include the following institutional details: store location, hours open, telephone number, location of advertised goods, and whether phone and mail orders are accepted?

* The seven items starred are of chief importance to the smaller store.
Source: John W. Wingate and Seymour Helfant, "Small Store Planning for Growth," *Small Business Management Series No. 33,* 2d ed. (Washington, D.C.: Small Business Administration, 1977), p. 69.

Common Methods of Appraisal

Efforts to evaluate advertising concentrate mostly on communication rather than sales results. Two general approaches are in common use: pretests and posttests.[23] These are also known as before and after tests—before the advertisement appears and after it has been seen or heard by the consumer. One form of **pretest** involves showing alternative advertisements to small groups or to individuals in advance of publication. Viewers are then questioned or asked to judge the advertisements in some manner. Rating scales, rank-ordering, and projective measures are often employed. The **posttest** category includes both **recall tests** and **recognition tests.** In the first instance, consumers who have been exposed to advertisements are asked to relate what they can remember about them. In the second type, the respondents review a collection (portfolio) of advertisements. They are asked to indicate those they recognize. Before and after tests may also be used to evaluate broadcast advertising.

The Advertising Agency

An **advertising agency** is a firm that specializes in planning, preparing, and placing advertisements with the media for clients. As with most industries, the majority of the 5,000-plus agencies are small companies. Several hundred large organizations account for the major portion of the nation's ad billings each year.

Internal agency activities are grouped into departments such as account services, creative services, research, and media buying. As far as the client company is concerned, the real strength of an agency's contribution lies in its creative services section—the department that handles copywriting, art, and production.

For obvious reasons, most independent retailers have little need for an advertising agency. Sales are simply too low for them to be able to afford agency services. Across all of retailing, the percentage of sales usually allocated to advertising averages somewhere between 1 and 2 percent. The typical small store has an annual sales volume of under $125,000 annually. If we juxtapose the two figures, we come up with less than $2,000 available for advertising. This is hardly the kind of expenditure that calls for agency expertise. Nor would such a small budget attract much interest among agencies as a desirable account.[24]

Independents occasionally seek small agencies or direct-mail specialists for help in setting up major promotions. Even the retail organization with a sizable budget may encounter difficulty hiring a larger agency. Advertising agencies are usually reimbursed for their services by the media, not by their client companies. The standard rebate from the media is a 15 percent discount from the cost of space or air time. If not enough advertising is placed, the agency may work with a retail firm on a fee basis. Use of the fee approach has been growing.[25]

Figure 19.9   Advertising operation of a large department store

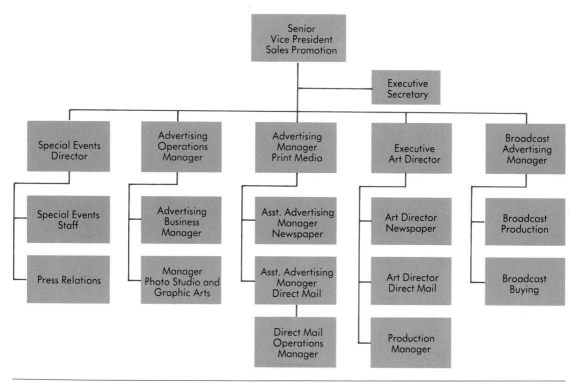

Source: Norman A. P. Govoni, *Otto Kleppner Advertising Procedure,* 7th ed., (Englewood Cliffs, N.J.: Prentice Hall, 1979), p. 521. © 1979, reprinted by permission of Prentice-Hall, Inc.

Clients also commonly reimburse their agencies for expenses incurred in connection with advertising production: the costs of preparing artwork, layouts, TV storyboards, engravings, and so on. The client is also charged for auxiliary services rendered: publicity efforts or research projects. Such expenses are calculated at agency cost plus a percentage of the cost, usually 17.65 percent, or more, to cover overhead.

Many department stores, supermarket chains, discounters, and other large-scale retail companies maintain in-house advertising departments. This is because of the heavy volume of advertising they generate and place. Figure 19.9 shows an organization chart for a retailer's advertising department. Across industry in general, the in-house agency has been adjudged better in creativity than the outside advertising agency.[26]

Summary   Advertising is one of the three components of the retailer's promotion mix. Proper management of the advertising function calls for proper planning, organization, direction, and control. Most retail advertising is promotional, emphasizing products and/or services. Institutional, or image-building, advertising is used occasionally. Retail companies choose from a long list of objectives for their advertising efforts. These range from the introduction of new merchandise and generating store traffic to strengthening community ties.

The legal climate for advertising stresses honesty and fairness. The Federal Trade Commission monitors the area and takes action against deceptive or fraudulent advertising.

In cooperative advertising, two or more companies share the costs. Retailers benefit because their suppliers pay for part of their expenses. Suppliers obtain more exposure for their products and services because they are charged local, not national, rates by the media.

In preparing their advertising budgets, retailers follow a variety of methods. The most popular approach is the percentage-of-sales procedure. Other common methods include the arbitrary decision, what-we-can-afford, meet-our-competition, and objective-and-task techniques. Many firms plan their advertising seasonally. Often, they allocate funds according to expected monthly sales (as a percentage of the total year's sales).

Retailers are concerned with four aspects of the media they use to deliver their messages: audience characteristics, reach, impact, and cost. Their principal medium is the newspaper. It provides intensive coverage of the store's trading area at relatively low cost. Magazines are rarely used by retailers, other than national and regional chains. Many firms make use of radio and television. The use of direct mail, the most personal of all media, has also been growing. A few types of retail firms rely on outdoor or transit advertising to carry their messages to the public.

Retailers attempt to measure the effectiveness of their advertising by evaluating message clarity, reach, impact, and other aspects. In this connection, pretests and posttests are valuable. They can be used to evaluate broadcast as well as print advertising. The posttest category includes recall and recognition tests.

Advertising agencies are firms that specialize in planning, preparing, and placing advertisements with the media for clients.

Key Terms

advertising	cuts
promotional advertising	clutter
direct action advertising	agate line
institutional advertising	combination rates
image-building advertising	contract rates
attitude advertising	run-of-paper (ROP)

logotype (logo)
bait-and-switch advertising
cooperative advertising
horizontal cooperative advertising
vertical cooperative advertising
percentage-of-sales method
arbitrary decision technique
what-we-can-afford method
meet-our-competition method
objective-and-task method
contingency fund
advertising medium
mass media
reach
impact
multimedia approaches
print media

preferred position
milline rates
truline rates
cost per thousand
broadcast media
time class
morning drive time
direct mail
position media
outdoor advertising
transit advertising
pretests
posttests
recall tests
recognition tests
advertising agency

Review Questions

1. Distinguish between product and institutional advertising.

2. Comment on the need for truth in advertising.

3. List at least six advertising objectives that retailers might set.

4. What benefits does cooperative advertising hold for *(a)* the manufacturer and *(b)* the retailer?

5. Distinguish between horizontal and vertical cooperative advertising.

6. Cite five factors that management needs to take into account when developing an advertising budget.

7. Identify and briefly explain four methods of setting advertising budgets.

8. What advantages and disadvantages do the following media have for the retail advertiser: *(a)* newspapers, *(b)* TV, *(c)* direct mail?

9. Distinguish between *milline* and *truline* rates. Why may the latter be of more value to the retailer?

10. Contrast these two media terms: *reach, impact.*

11. How do retail companies judge the effectiveness of their advertising?

12. Why does the independent store owner rarely use the services of an advertising agency?

13. What is the creative services function in an advertising agency?

Discussion Questions

1. Discuss the role of advertising in retail promotion.

2. Check through a copy of your local newspaper. Select two examples each of direct action and institutional advertisements and clip them out. Explain why you believe each is the type you have specified.

3. For each of the four advertisements you clipped, write one or two advertising objectives you believe the company had in mind. Defend your answers.

4. Demonstrate a method whereby the retailer can compare advertising costs among several newspapers.

5. Show how a national drugstore chain might derive monthly advertising costs from its planned annual budget figure.

6. A large discount house does 42 percent of its sales during the first half of the year and 58 percent during the last six months. Do you think management ought to allocate its advertising budget in the same manner? Why or why not?

7. For each of the following store types, suggest two media you believe would be best suited to their advertising:
   a. A freestanding souvenir and gift shop along a major highway.
   b. A neighborhood hardware store.
   c. A menswear store in a regional shopping center.
   d. An elite jewelry store in the suburbs.

8. Look around your neighborhood for examples of outdoor advertising. Make rough sketches of three, noting details of the art, copy, and layout. Suggest creative changes that would improve their impact and effectiveness.

9. What elements of a modest direct-mail program could be used by a fine seafood restaurant located just outside a busy community shopping center.

Notes   [1]Otto Kleppner and Norman A. P. Govoni, *Advertising Procedure,* 7th ed. (Englewood Cliffs, N.J.: Prentice-Hall, 1979), p. 23.

[2]Philip Kotler, *Principles of Marketing* (Englewood Cliffs, N.J.: Prentice-Hall, 1980), p. 519.

[3]James R. Krum and Stephen K. Keiser, "Regulation of Retail Newspaper Advertising," *Journal of Marketing* 40 (July 1976), p. 33. See also: J. Barry Mason and J. B. Wilkinson, "Addendum: Are Supermarket Advertisements Designed to Deceive Consumers?" *Journal of Advertising* 7 (Winter 1978), pp. 56–59.

[4]For background reading, see: Robert E. Wilkes and James B. Wilcox, "Recent FTC Actions: Implications for the Advertising Strategist," *Journal of Marketing* 38 (January 1974), pp. 55–61; David M. Gardner, "Deception in Advertising: A Conceptual Approach," *Journal of Marketing* 39 (January 1975), pp. 40–46; Jacob Jacoby and Constance Small, "The FDA Approach to Defining Misleading Advertising," *Journal of Marketing* 39 (October 1975), pp. 65–68.

[5]See: Michel Chevalier and Ronald C. Curhan, "Retail Promotions As a Function of Trade Promotion: A Descriptive Analysis," *Sloan Management Review* 18 (Fall 1976), pp. 19–32.

[6]William Haight, *Retail Advertising: Management and Technique* (Glenview, Ill.: Scott, Foresman, 1976), pp. 128–30.

[7]This technique is described later on. See: Donald S. Tull, James H. Barnes, and Daniel T. Seymour, "In Defense of Setting Budgets for Advertising As a Percent of Sales," *Journal of Advertising Research* 18 (December 1978), p. 49.

[8]For a brief introduction to this area, see: Philip Kotler, *Marketing Management: Analysis, Planning, and Control,* 4th ed. (Englewood Cliffs, N.J.: Prentice-Hall, 1980), pp. 514–16; Leo Bogart, "Media Models: A Reassessment," *Journal of Advertising* 4 (Spring 1975), pp. 28–30.

[9]*'80 Ayer Directory of Publications* (Bala Cynwyd, Pa.: Ayer Press, 1980), p. viii.

[10]Kleppner and Govoni, *Advertising,* p. 165.

[11]James E. Littlefield and C. A. Kirkpatrick, *Advertising: Mass Communication in Marketing,* 3d ed. (Boston: Houghton Mifflin, 1970), p. 398.

[12]Radio Advertising Bureau, *Radio Facts* (New York: RAB, 1984).

[13]Harvey R. Cook, "Selecting Advertising Media: A Guide for Small Business," *Small Business Management Series No. 34* (Washington, D.C.: Small Business Administration, 1969), p. 67.

[14]Arnold M. Barban and Deal M. Krugman, "Cable Television and Advertising: An Assessment," *Journal of Advertising* 7 (Fall 1978), p. 8.

[15]Kathryn E. A. Villani, "Personality/Life Style and Television Viewing Behavior," *Journal of Marketing Research* 12 (November 1975), pp. 432–39.

[16]"What's Behind New Look in Local TV?" *Marketing & Media Decisions* 14 (November 1979), pp. 110–20.

[17]John P. Dickson, "Retail Media Coordination Strategy," *Journal of Retailing* 50 (Summer 1974), pp. 61–69.

[18]Because of the high cost of TV time, experiments have been conducted with time-compressed commercials. In these announcements, the speed of speech is electronically increased without producing the Donald Duck effect. See: James MacLachlan and Priscilla LaBarbera, "Time-compressed TV Commercials," *Journal of Advertising Research* 18 (August 1978), pp. 11–15.

[19]"NRMA Media Survey Details Costs, Uses," *Stores* 59 (September 1977), p. 29.

[20]Danny H. Bellinger and Jack R. Pingry, "Direct-mail Advertising for Retail Stores," *Journal of Advertising Research* 17 (June 1977), pp. 35–39.

[21]Linda A. Gluck, "New Look at Catalogs," *Stores* 59 (September 1977), pp. 23–35*ff.*

[22]Jonathan Gutman, "Tachistoscopic Tests of Outdoor Ads," *Journal of Advertising Research* 12 (August 1972), p. 27.

[23]For an introduction to these and other tests of advertising effectiveness, see Chapter 19 in: Harper W. Boyd, Jr., Ralph Westfall, and Stanley F. Stasch, *Marketing Research: Text and Cases,* 4th ed. Homewood, Ill.: Richard D. Irwin, 1977).

[24]Agencies may be interested in small enterprises that demonstrate growth potential. See: Jack Dart, "The Advertising Agency Selection Process for Small Business: Tips from the Agencies," *Journal of Small Business Management* 18 (April 1980), pp. 1–10.

[25]Stephen Dietz and Rodney Erickson, "How Agencies Should Get Paid: Trend is to 'Managed' Systems," *Advertising Age* 48 (17 January 1977), pp. 41–42.

[26]Edward C. Bursk and Baljit Singh Sethi, "The In-house Advertising Agency," *Journal of Advertising* 5 (Winter 1976), p. 27.

RETAIL DISPLAY

Your Study Objectives

After you have studied this chapter, you will understand:

1. The significance and purposes of retail display.
2. The principles of design embodied in effective displays.
3. The basic patterns employed in displaying merchandise.
4. The nature of color and its effects on human psychology.
5. The appropriate selection and use of color schemes.
6. The uses and treatment of show windows.
7. Interior displays and the allocation of space.

The Power of Display

Palm Beach Mall is typical of hundreds of planned shopping centers around the country. Located in the fast-growing city of West Palm Beach, this large climate-controlled complex has a most pleasing ambience. It has gardens laden with subtropical vegetation, waterfalls, and pools. There is even a small footbridge for shoppers to cross over. There are main and secondary entrances and wide internal walkways flanked by rows of attractive storefronts. Contributing to the mall's drawing power are parking spaces for hundreds of cars. Bus transportation brings shoppers in from all over.

Branches of some major department store and mass merchandising organizations are located here. At one end stand Jordan Marsh and J. C. Penney. Lord & Taylor is near the center, and Sears, Roebuck marks the other end. The tenant mix is excellent; the majority of stores offer shopping and specialty goods. Intermingled with units of regional and national chains are many independent retailers. There are jewelry stores, beauty salons, apparel shops, fast-food places, banks, variety stores, restaurants, and theaters.

Now, visualize throngs of shoppers in this picturesque environment. As they stroll along the walkways, their senses are assailed from all directions. Consumers receive impressions from colorful illuminated signs and merchandise in the show windows. They look into the stores' well-furbished interiors and stroll past kiosks interestingly set at intervals along the center of the mall. Sounds and music pour out from some of the shops. Occasionally, pleasant odors waft their way through the air, like those from the popcorn stand, the fudge-making machine, or the frankfurter counter. Shoppers pass the video arcade and hear the beeping and buzzing of Pac-Man and other machines. Or they stop in front of the organ store to listen to a rousing medley of Rodgers and Hammerstein melodies played by the demonstrator.

What dazzling impact on the consumer's senses and emotions! And what an amazing testimonial to the power of display in the modern retailing environment.

Retail Display

To understand the purposes and value of display on a more modest scale, we need only to visit a department store. The store projects a quieter, more elegant atmosphere than the mall. It conveys a sense of proper planning and layout and attention to consumer needs. Muted store fixtures accent the merchandise. Departments are easily identifiable, and store signing serves as guides for the shopper and advertisement.

Retail display's overriding objectives are much the same as the other elements of the promotion mix. Display attracts attention and informs consumers about the store, its merchandise, and its services. It aims at stimulating the desire to buy. Displays also set scenes,

A bird's-eye view of Palm Beach Mall, West Palm Beach, Florida.

Courtesy Palm Beach Mall, West Palm Beach, FL

project a firm's personality, create specific atmospheres, and trigger moods. Indeed, displays can and do induce sales transactions.[1]

Among the larger retail companies, the popular term today for display is **visual merchandising.** Retailers count on visual merchandising to help make personal selling easier and to reinforce impressions made on consumers by their media advertising. Many merchants regard displays as silent salespeople for the store and as worthy substitutes for newspaper and radio advertising.[2] Display costs are much lower than advertising costs.

Display Management

Most independent retailers put up their own in-store displays. Often, they train employees to assist them in display work. Some owners trim the show windows themselves. Many hire outside decorators occasionally. These people may be professional window trimmers or retailing students attending a local school or college.

Characteristically, chain store organizations develop their own display staffs. These trained professionals plan, organize, and direct displays for all store branches. They design window displays in a mock window setup at the home office. They send photographs or diagrams

Visual merchandising helps make personal selling easier in this "Wall of Eyes" in Sears' Store of the Future.

Courtesy Sears, Roebuck & Co., Chicago

of the model windows to the branches with all needed materials. In many instances, traveling window dressing crews are dispatched to units where the personnel cannot trim their own windows.

In the department store, visual merchandising is the responsibility of an executive who reports to the vice president for advertising and sales promotion.[3] An entire department may be supervised by the director of visual merchandising. Some duties are also delegated to display managers at branch stores. Large retailers also maintain sign shops where all needed cards, posters, banners, and the like are prepared.

Concerns of Display Management

Display personnel follow certain guidelines. Displays must be kept clean and fresh. Occasional changes must be made. Proper care has to be taken of stands, fixtures, and display materials. The right merchandise must be selected. When a display is taken apart, all components must be returned to their proper locations in the storeroom. Merchandise must be marked properly before returning it to the selling stock.

Thus, there are two basic dimensions to retail display management: (1) the planning and design phase and (2) the execution phase. Planning and design are by far the more difficult. Management will need to consider many aspects, including:

costs
frequency of changes
display objectives
criteria for merchandise selection
choice of appropriate display
    patterns
color schemes
selection of proper fixtures,
    materials, and accessories

themes
use of lighting, motion, and other
    special effects
tie-in possibilities (to advertising
    and other sales promotion)
positioning displays effectively
messages and art for signing

Item Selection Decisions must be made about what merchandise should be shown. Retailers favor brand-new or popular articles and items that have been advertised in the newspaper or on TV. Many merchants select goods that carry above-average markups and will contribute more gross margin dollars. They prefer to display impulse items near cash registers or on tables or racks in the front of the store.

Accumulation of Display Materials Over time, many retailers build up an inventory of display goods and accessories. Many materials can be used to cover the window platform. These run the gamut from satins, burlap, and felt to mirrors, grass cloth, and papers of different designs and colors. Care is exercised to keep these materials clean and safely stored to avoid deterioration. Retailers also accumulate a myriad of other accessories. Examples include baskets and bunny rabbits; cornucopia, turkeys, goblins, and scarecrows; straw hats (for Father's Day) and carnations (for Mother's Day), posters, and window banners.

Stores often show point-of-purchase displays furnished by suppliers. Among others, these include racks, countertop display cartons, and floor stands. Revlon, L'Oreal, Timex, and L'Eggs are among the many companies that offer such displays.

Basic Design Principles Effective displays show the same characteristics as other creative products that please our senses. A photograph, magazine advertisement, stage setting, sculpture, painting, or other work of art all reflect the same elements of design. Each contains a plan, scheme, pattern, or motif—an arrangement of parts that fit together properly. Almost interchangeable with the word **design** is the term **composition.** A composition is a work of creation ordered to satisfy and appeal to the people it is intended for.

Retail displays are both designs and compositions. All parts are arranged to accomplish their objectives: to interest, attract, please,

Displaying furniture in a sectionalized room vignette emphasizes composition— a motif or an arrangement of parts that fit together properly

Courtesy Sears, Roebuck & Co., Chicago

and motivate shoppers to buy. Fixtures, stands, sign tickets, display cards, color, and motion can all contribute to a display's proper design.

Effective displays follow the principles of unity, balance, proportion, dominance, and contrast. (See Figure 20.1 on page 602.)

Unity   A display reflects **unity** if its various elements are placed to impart the complete concept to viewers. In other words, it appears unified; it is easily seen to be a whole and complete unit. Its elements—merchandise, stands, signs, and accessories—are perceived to belong together, rightfully and properly.

Balance   An attractive composition also shows **balance,** a state of equilibrium among all components. The effect is a harmonious arrangement. Balance may be formal or informal. Like the balance scale, formal balance in a design is accomplished by assigning the same weight to both sides. One way we can judge formal balance is to mentally divide the display straight down the center. If the two halves appear symmetrical, formal balance is present. If, on the other hand, one side bears a heavier concentration of merchandise, shapes, colors, or materials than the other, the display is informally balanced.

Consider setting up a window display of four men's sport jackets. If we position two on each side (at different heights, of course) so

An effective display reflects the principle of unity.

Courtesy Gingiss Formalwear, Tampa, FL

that the right half of the window duplicates the left, we show formal balance. If, on the other hand, we place three jackets on one side and only one on the other, we have informal balance. Informally balanced, asymmetric displays are used occasionally to generate more viewer interest.

Proportion The design principle that has to do with the relationships among a display's elements is **proportion.** Each component must be in proper proportion to the other parts and to the entire unit. When determining such relationships, we consider attributes like shape, size, quantity, and color. No part ought to stand out more than the others. Exceptions may, of course, be made. As an illustration, the decorator may feature one element over the rest by displaying it in a position of dominance.

Dominance The **dominance** concept connotes power and command. The retailer may, for example, decide to feature a sample designer dress. This can be accomplished in a variety of ways. The dress may be placed over the others on display in a dominant position. Ribbon streamers can cascade down from the ceiling to the garment. A spotlight may be aimed at it or a feature card displayed with it. Even the selection

Figure 20.1   Basic principles of design

1. Unity

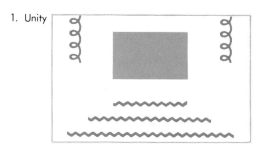

2. Balance (formal)

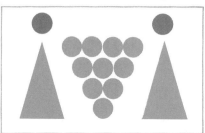

Balance (informal)

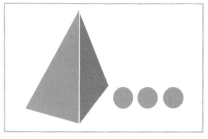

3. Proportion

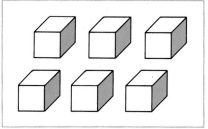

4. Dominance

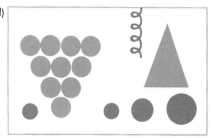

5. Contrast

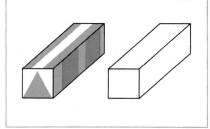

of quieter colors for the other merchandise shown will accomplish the desired effect.

Contrast   The difference between one element and the rest of a display can also be stressed through the principle of **contrast.** A dark object may be set against merchandise of a lighter hue or against a light background. A large item can be placed behind, in front of, or next to smaller articles. An elongated shape will produce contrast when inserted among a quantity of round shapes. Contrast may also be accomplished with color, lighting, location, and other approaches. The technique adds interest, and often excitement, to a display.

Figure 20.2   Display patterns

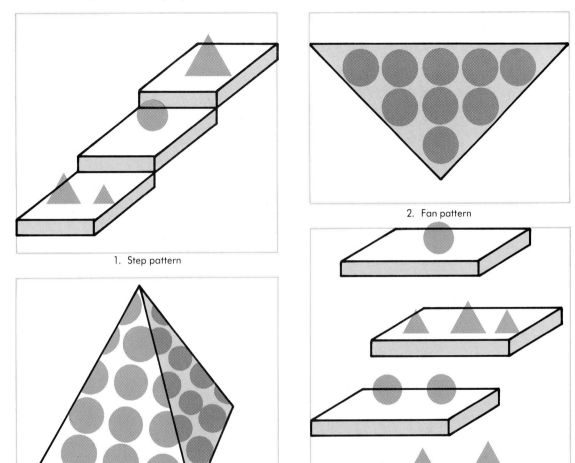

1. Step pattern

2. Fan pattern

3. Pyramid pattern

4. Zigzag pattern

Patterns for Displaying Merchandise

Different arrangements are available for displaying goods. Most designs fall into one of four basic **display patterns:** the step, fan, pyramid, or zigzag. (See Figure 20.2.)

Step Pattern

A popular and versatile arrangement for many kinds of products is the **step pattern.** With the help of pedestals or other supports, several trays are positioned one above the other. This produces a multitiered effect. The trays may be of glass, wood, plastic, or some other material. Each tray is set a bit back from the one below; the effect resembles a series of steps. Merchandise is then displayed attractively on each step. Circular, oval, or square trays may also be used.

Fan Pattern   The interesting **fan pattern** is often used to draw the shopper's attention to a main, or featured, item. When set up vertically, a small and concentrated merchandise grouping appears at the base of the fan. From the base, the design rises up and widens (fans out) drastically as the height increases. An array of hand-knitted sweaters in the window of a knit shop may reflect this pattern. So may a display of watercolors in an art store or an array of boxed chocolates in a confectionery shop. The fan arrangement can also be used horizontally or at an elevated plane.

Pyramid Pattern   A three-dimensional geometric design, the **pyramid pattern** has a pleasantly solid appearance. It is useful for exhibiting a quantity of goods in a relatively small area. To viewers, each of the pyramid's four sides presents an attractive triangular face. Widest at the base, it narrows in height to the apex.

Fixture set up in pyramid fashion sells confections and nutmeats for a popular franchise.

Courtesy Confectionery Square Corp., Morganville, NJ

Zigzag Pattern   Less frequently employed than the pyramid, but nonetheless compelling, is the **zigzag pattern.** This arrangement borrows elements from both step and pyramid designs. The base is broad and full, and the display grows narrower toward the top. However, each level in the pattern overlaps, or is indented from, the level immediately below. In short, the merchandise displayed appears to zig and zag along the way. The resulting asymmetric exhibit clearly possesses informal balance.

Color and Display   Color is an essential component of most displays. It is used to show merchandise to its best advantage. Color imparts life and drama to displays. It calls attention to, and highlights, goods. Color can accentuate the vividness of fabrics, reveal the beauty of fine woods and marbles, and dramatize the richness of gems.

The Nature of Color   The phenomenon we call *color* is a property of light. This is easily demonstrated with the aid of a prism, a three-sided glass or crystal. When light passes through the prism, it is dispersed into a spectrum of colors. The spectrum follows a set arrangement according to the length of the light waves that are emitted. The colors range from infrared (the longest wavelength) to ultraviolet (the shortest wavelength), neither of which can be detected by the human eye. Those colors we can see run from red through violet, with orange, yellow, green, and blue in between.

Red, yellow, and blue are known as the **primary colors.** By combining any two of these, **secondary colors** are produced. If we mix red and yellow, we obtain orange. Combining yellow and blue yields green; a mixture of blue and red produces purple. White is a mixture of all colors; black, the absence of color. Looked at from another viewpoint, white is the lightest and brightest of all colors, and black the darkest and least bright. White and black can be combined in differing proportions to obtain various shades of gray.

Every color, or hue, can appear in many gradations. We are familiar with such blues as sky, copen, teal, and royal. Among the greens, we recognize apple, avocado, kelly, mint, moss, nile, and others.

Colors and Human Psychology   The sensory impressions we receive from colors in our environment seem to affect our feelings and attitudes. We learn to associate certain qualities and different meanings with various colors.

Consider this abbreviated list:

Color	What It Signifies
Red	Power, warmth, patriotism, strength, vitality, intensity, vibrancy
Orange	Warmth, affection, relish, drama, Halloween, enthusiasm
Yellow	Springtime, summer, laughter, gaiety, brightness, cheerfulness
Green	Peacefulness, nature, the ocean, the countryside, grass, relaxation
Blue	Placidity, calm, the sky, water, masculinity, childhood

We think of pink and violet as feminine colors; these are traditionally popular in Mother's Day displays. Brown and gray are held to be more masculine and often appear in store windows before Father's Day. Green, rust and brown are colors that can be found in autumn leaves. We associate them with the months of October and November. Yellow, green, and pink are linked with Easter and springtime.

A combination of red and pink is favored for the Valentine's Day display. A touch of gold and/or white may be added. St. Patrick's Day calls for a shamrock green. For several weeks before the Christmas season, the entire store may be festively trimmed in reds, greens, and dabs of white. Santas, sleighs and reindeer, holly, giant plastic candy canes, bells, and other decorations create more holiday excitement. The colors of our flag are appropriate for showing merchandise on all patriotic occasions: Washington's Birthday, Memorial Day, Independence Day, and so on.

To avoid detracting from the goods on display, store fixtures often reflect soft, neutral shades. Grays and beiges are popular. Color is infused into displays in various ways. Among others, these include materials used as backdrops or bases (satins, netting, papers, velvets, grass mats, leaves), signing (cards, posters, backgrounds, banners, sign tickets), and special lighting.

Color Schemes Combining the right colors can be a challenge. Too many colors in a display may prove confusing, even annoying, to shoppers. Some combinations are unpleasant because the colors clash so badly. Happily, far more combinations please the eye than displease it. Selecting the right **color scheme** for a display becomes a simpler task if the decorator relies on any one of the three tried-and-proven approaches to color harmony. **Complementary colors,** for instance, make for attractive displays. These are any two colors that lie opposite each other on the color wheel—a distribution of hues around a circle in order of the spectrum. Examples are red with green, blue with orange, and purple with yellow. The contrasting effect is compelling. The **monochrome,** or **monochromatic display,** blends two or more shades of one color. Using light pink, red, and dusky rose enhances a presentation. So does combining two or more values of yellow, green, or purple. Finally, there are the **analogous color combinations.** Each of the colors employed shares some quality in common with the other (s). Analogous colors lie near each other on the color wheel. Blue, blue green, and green are analogous colors. So are red, red orange, and yellow.

Black and white can be used with most colors. Yet except for a deliberate black-and-white display, the two are used sparingly in visual merchandising, to add emphasis. As a final point, it should be understood that the items selected for display often affect the choice of color scheme.

Show Windows and Their Treatment

Today, many store premises have open fronts rather than show windows. We see many such stores in shopping malls. Other retail outlets seem to prefer large glass panels. Most supermarkets and many mass merchandisers are built this way. Occasionally, these retailers try to set up a rudimentary window display by placing tables or racks of merchandise close to the window glass. There are also storefronts that are completely enclosed—except for entrances and exits—by stone, masonry, brick, or other building materials. Like TV commercials, newspaper advertisements, and radio announcements, attractively dressed window displays can and do generate more store traffic and lead to increased sales.

For many kinds of stores, show windows are a valuable asset. Locations in central and secondary business districts, where both pedestrian and vehicular traffic are heavy, benefit greatly by the effective use of window display. So do many outlets in neighborhood shopping streets and in all types of planned shopping centers.

A store's window represents the consumer's first point of contact with the retailer. Through its displays, changed at regular intervals to expose passersby to new merchandise and settings, the public quickly forms impressions about the firm and its personality (store image).

Of interest at this point is a study of store windows conducted some years ago in New York City. The researchers investigated the drawing power of show windows along several major Manhattan thoroughfares. They found that the majority of people walking along those streets in both directions never glanced at the stores' windows. Nevertheless, lookers ranged from a low of 26 percent to a high of 33 percent if the displays were particularly attractive. Depending on the store, between 5 and 10 percent actually approached the window to look at the display.[4] Unfortunately, no tallies were made of the number of viewers who actually entered the store.

These percentages raise some interesting possibilities. Let us assume, for example, that a good display attracts the attention of 30 percent

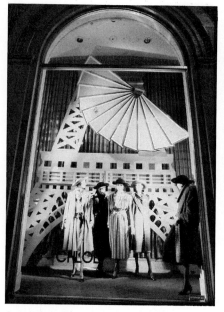

Courtesy Bethco Fragrances, Inc., New York City

The public quickly forms impressions about a retailer's image and personality as projected by its window treatments.

of the passersby and that 5 percent of these people come up to examine the display. We translate these percentages into real numbers on the basis of, say, 300 passersby an hour. Each hour, then, some 90 people will look at the window and 15 will be drawn to it. Depending on their reactions, perhaps five or six of them may go inside the store.

Thus, the challenge to the enterprising retailer becomes one of increasing the ranks of lookers, window studiers, and entering shoppers. Often, adding movement in the window through the use of turntables, ceiling turners, mechanical displays, and the like will sharply increase the percentage of lookers. So will special lighting or sound effects. Displays that evoke curiosity or that show articles of current interest will induce more shoppers to approach the window. Exhibiting goods in popular demand or that represent the latest fashions at fair prices will invite more of them to step inside. (See Figure 20.3 for some pointers on window displays.)

Types of Window Displays

While most small independent stores have a single window, many have two or more. In these instances, the larger of the two or the one to the right of the entrance is often dubbed the main window. Merchants expect the main window to capture the major share of public attention. Other, or secondary, windows are typically reserved for displaying limited assortments or several small features. Although

"*They sell junk food under the counter.*"

most window displays are designed to sell merchandise, they are sometimes used to promote the firm itself. This is similar to media advertising which, though product-oriented for the most part; can also be institutional in nature.[5]

Department stores and other large retail establishments may have up to six or eight windows or more. Such *banks* of windows readily lend themselves to distinct treatment. All, for example, may be trimmed as *independent displays,* with different merchandise shown in each. Or several adjoining windows may be linked together by displaying related goods in them, such as fall fashion apparel or home furnishings. These are known as *serial displays.* Occasionally, the retailer will display no merchandise, devoting the windows to holiday scenes and animated displays as gestures of goodwill. This is frequently seen during the Christmas season.

Window Themes   A show window is like a stage setting. Properly filled with interesting backgrounds, the right props, characters (the merchandise), and an attractive overall design, it can create excitement and arouse the emotions. A valuable technique for tying together, or unifying, the entire stage production is the selection of a **theme** for the display. Themes are topics, or subjects, around which artistic creations are woven. Musical compositions and oil paintings have themes. Themes make store displays more compelling and more effective.

Figure 20.3
Pointers on window
displays

1. Shoppers will regard your storefront and show window as the face of your retail business. Therefore, the window treatments should always convey the impression of quality, style, and distinctiveness which you would like to project.

2. Displays should be kept clean and neat in appearance at all times. A crowded display contributes nothing but clutter; instead, use air (or breathing) space between merchandise groupings.

3. Whether you engage the services of a professional window trimmer or you do the displays yourself, your windows should be changed frequently. At least 10 to 15 changes each year are recommended. (Hint: You might be able to hire someone with window display training from the local high school's distributive education program.)

4. Window displays are generally more effective when built around a single, unifying theme (Going-Back-to-School, Mother's Day, Christmas, Springtime, Vacation Fun, Travel, and so on).

5. Merchandise, materials, display stands, mannequins (if required) and signs or posters should be carefully selected and prepared ahead of time so that the window may be completely trimmed without incident within a few hours' time.

6. In selecting appropriate merchandise to put into the window, pay careful attention to the seasonality factor, to product sales appeal, and to individual gross markups.

7. Color is an essential ingredient of display. The color combinations used in the window should be attractive and harmonious.

8. Window bases (platforms) are usually covered with appropriate materials which contribute to the overall effect of the display—satins, netting, burlap, paper, artificial grass mats, and so forth. The retailer ought to build up a stock of such materials over time.

9. All point-of-purchase materials, such as sign tickets, posters, banners, and the like, should look professional and be kept perfectly clean.

10. Special effects, such as motion, lighting, and sound, can be used profitably in connection with your display to draw attention to the window. As a simple example, motion can be imparted to a section of your display through use of a small electric (or battery-operated) turntable or ceiling turner.

Source: From the book, *The Small Business Handbook* by Irving Burstiner © 1979 by Prentice-Hall, Inc. Reprinted by permission of the publisher.

Many themes, like those in Table 20.1, are quite popular. There are holiday themes such as Easter, Washington's Birthday, and Halloween. Other kinds of themes are also familiar to consumers. Back to School, Spring Clearance, White Sale, and Winter Festival are examples.

Many more unusual themes are available to retailers. During the month of January, for instance, they might select National Hobby Month or the Cotton Bowl Classic as window themes. Or in September they can choose National Singles Week and set aside an April window for National Bubble Gum Week.

For theme selection, a helpful almanac and guide for retailers is *Chase's Calendar of Annual Events.*[6]

	Month	Holidays	Other Themes

Table 20.1
Holiday and other
popular themes
	January	New Year's Day
		Martin Luther King's
		  Birthday
			January–March:
			  Buyers' Sale
			  Cruising
			  Dollar Days

	February	Lincoln's Birthday
		Valentine's Day
		Washington's Birthday
			Fun in the Sun
			  Manager's Sale
			  Midnight Madness Sale
			  Travelin' South

	March	St. Patrick's Day	Winter Jamboree

	April	Passover
		Easter
			April–June:
			  Buyers' Sale
			  Dollar Days

	May	Mother's Day
		Armed Forces Day
		Victoria Day (Canada)
		Memorial Day
			Flower Festival
			  Goin' Fishin'
			  Manager's Sale
			  Midnight Madness Sale
			  Open House

	June	Flag Day Father's Day	Spring Festival Summer Preview

	July	Dominion Day (Canada)
		Independence Day
			July–September:
			  At the Beach
			  Backyard Barbecue
			  Country Vacation

	August	—	Dog Days of Summer
			    Sale
			  Dollar Days

	September	Labor Day
		  Rosh Hashanah
			Fall Preview
			  Manager's Sale
			  Midsummer Madness Sale
			  Open House
			  Pre–Labor Day Sale
			  Summer Clearance Sale
			  Summer Cruises
			  Travelin' North

	October	Yom Kippur
		Columbus Day
		Thanksgiving Day
		  (Canada)
		United Nation's Day
		Halloween
			October–December:
			  Autumn Fun
			  Buyers' Sale
			  Dollar Days
			  Fall Clearance Sale
			  Football Season

	November	Election Day
		Veterans' Day
		Thanksgiving Day
			Happy New Year
			  Harvest Time
			  Holiday Preview
			  Manager's Sale

	December	Hanukkah Christmas	Midnight Madness Sale Open House

An example of a Neiman-Marcus in-store visual presentation.

Courtesy Neiman-Marcus, Dallas, TX

Interior Store Display

Clearly, the objectives of most window displays are to gain the attention of people outside the store and spark sufficient interest to motivate them to step inside. Interior, or in-store, displays must also accomplish these two goals. Their most important contribution, however, is to assist in the selling process by preconditioning the shopper. Sometimes they sell directly, as in the self-service operation.

When designing store layout, management will allocate space for selling, display, stockroom, and other necessary activities. Once the layout has been decided, there still remains the problem of how to maximize the value of both selling and display areas. For proper display, two other dimensions are of concern: (1) where to place in-store displays and (2) what merchandise to show. Only the first is considered here; choosing items for interior display involves the same criteria as those for window display.

In small stores, goods are displayed in showcases, on the tops of counters, and in the aisles. There may also be wall and ledge displays. Most retailers know that there are two or three **key spots** in the store, where traffic is heaviest. These may include the register well, both sides of the counters that flank the register, and locations near the store entrance. Some shops have one or more **shadow boxes** along one wall. These are small display areas set inside or affixed to a wall. Frequently illuminated from within, they make attractive settings for featured items. Larger retailers, especially those who sell apparel, set up additional display areas throughout their stores. They employ many types of display fixtures. These include freestanding racks, pegboard frames, round metal or plastic stands, A-frames, T-bars, and the like. Easels, jumble baskets, island displays, forms of all types, and mannequins are also commonly used. Most displays are **open displays;** shoppers can touch, pick up, and examine the merchandise. Some are **closed displays,** kept under lock and key to prevent theft or damage.

The Allocation of Display Space

A common approach to space allocation involves placing convenience goods in key spots and relegating other merchandise to locations in the store with less traffic.[7]

Retailers know that by putting items on display, they will sell more of that merchandise. Supermarkets, for example, have found that the total amount of shelf space (in linear feet) and the volume of freezer space (in cubic feet) bear a direct relationship to sales performance. So do the number of facings of the article on the shelves and the placing of merchandise at eye level. Merchants also know that a display's pulling power can vary considerably from one product to the next.[8] Not only does sales effectiveness vary among product groups, but price reductions can positively affect sales volume.[9] This is especially true of items in the maturity stage of their life cycles.

Many retailers talk about *space elasticity,* defined as the ratio of relative change in unit sales to relative change in shelf space. Of all kinds of merchandise, impulse goods are probably the most responsive to space changes.[10]

Managements are frequently worried that displays of particular items or brands will cut sharply into the regular sales of other, competitive brands or items. Yet a study of supermarket displays over a four-month period revealed "no adverse effects on sales of substitute products in the same category."[11] In fact, most of the stores' sales increases appeared to be from additional sales made.

Modern retailers show keen interest in making their displays more productive. More and more, the attention of visual merchandisers is focused on the bottom line.[12] We have also seen a definite and growing trend toward higher displays to increase space productivity. Another interesting merchandising concept growing in popularity is that of **classification dominance.** This involves "identifying a particular merchandise category—such as toasters, tennis rackets, or men's dress shirts—and displaying the items in a manner that suggests to the consumer that the firm has the largest possible assortment of merchandise in that category."[13]

Signing

Signs help to complete the story for interested shoppers. Some interior signing is designed to give directions or to identify departments or sections. Other signs are used to announce present or forthcoming

Top, open displays
encourage shoppers to
examine merchandise;
bottom, *pegboard racks
enable retailers to display
quantities of goods while
leaving aisles free.*

Courtesy K mart Corporation. K MART and ACCENTS are service marks of
K mart Corporation, Troy, MI

Courtesy White Stores, Inc., Wichita Falls, TX

events. Most, however, are intended to help sell merchandise. (See
Figure 20.4.) The value of signing has been documented by research.
In a supermarket chain, for example, the use of a plain, hand-lettered
sign increased the sales of instant coffee.[14] The sign showed the brand,
weight, and price and bore the words *No Limit.* That simple sign

Figure 20.4
Thoughts about signs and fixtures

Signs Tell the Story

Signs do the talking for a display. They give significant details about the article, such as size, styles, colors. Thus, as silent salespeople, signs answer customers' questions about price, features, and tell where the goods are located in the store.

The following suggestions may be helpful in thinking about the signs you use on your interior displays.

1. Make your signs informative. The wording should be compact and, when possible, sparkling.
2. They should look professional. Compact printing machines are available if you prefer to do your own signs.
3. See that they are not soiled or marred. Nothing spoils merchandise quicker in the customer's eyes than a soiled sign.
4. Keep signs timely by changing them often.
5. Try to make your signs sell customer benefits rather than things. Signs for clothes, for example, should sell neat appearance, style, and attractiveness rather than utility. For furniture, they should sell home life and happiness rather than just lamps and tables.

Fixtures That Display

Fixtures should show your merchandise in the most advantageous manner. Although the type of fixtures you use depends on the kinds of goods you sell, you may find this rule of thumb helpful: The most practical and economical fixture is one that permits you to display goods in the *proper arrangement* for each category or line with the *least distracting elements* and at the maximum exposure.

For example, cellophane bags of apples can be arranged properly in stacks on a float or table. Nothing else is needed other than a price sign. On the other hand, a proper arrangement of shirts has to be one which considers sizes. If you sell twice as many size 16 as 14, for example, your fixture should take that fact into account.

An example of a distracting element might be a moving display near a book counter. The motion keeps pulling the customer's eye away from the books he's trying to examine.

The following questions may be helpful in selecting and using fixtures to achieve an effective presentation of merchandise:

What sort of merchandise do you plan to display on the fixture?

How much area will you allot on each fixture level—deck, counter top, shelf or rack—for each category of merchandise to be displayed?

In order to stimulate buyer attention and at the same time make selling easy, what is the best kind of fixture? For example: Do you need bargain tables, platforms, counters, card-holders, displayers, forms, or mannequins? Or do you need fixtures which will allow for each restocking of sizes—fixtures such as showcases, gondolas, racks, wall cases, or island cases?

If you use shelves for display purposes, what size do you need to hold the merchandise, its assortment, package, or container?

What changes might occur because of seasonal or promotional shifts? Can you rearrange the unit or section of the fixture to meet such changes?

How can you get the best possible sales volume per square foot of display space? How much merchandise exposure can the fixture give per dollar fixture expenditure? Bear in mind that a well-designed, efficient fixture, which gives maximum exposure of goods is cheaper in the long run than a lower-priced fixture which does not allow for effective display. The efficient fixture helps to bring the biggest sales turnover.

Source: Gabriel M. Valenti, "Interior Display: A Way to Increase Sales," *Small Marketers Aids No. 111* (Washington, D.C.: Small Business Administration, reprinted May 1974), pp. 2–3.

brought in more revenue than a reduction of 20 cents in the price of the coffee. Even higher sales were obtained when both the sign and the price reduction were used together.

In another experiment, the effectiveness of in-store signing in a department store was studied under three different conditions. Presentations of six products were made at both regular and sale prices. Best results were obtained with signs that pointed out product benefits. It was also observed that at the sale price "both a price-only and a benefit sign will increase sales over a no-sign condition, with benefit signing being the most effective."[15]

Summary

Today's successful planned shopping centers testify to the impact and effectiveness of display in creating attractive shopping environments. Display, or visual merchandising, is an essential element of the promotion mix. For the individual retail company, its basic purposes are to attract the attention of consumers, inform them about the firm, its merchandise, and its services, and stimulate their desire to buy. Displays can set scenes, create specific atmospheres, and trigger moods.

Although many rely on outside window trimmers for their show windows, most retailers put up their own displays. Many chains and most large companies have their own display staffs. Display management requires attention to: (1) planning and design and (2) execution. In the planning and design area, retailers must make decisions about costs, frequency of changes, objectives, merchandise selection, color schemes, selection of materials, use of lighting and/or motion, and other aspects. They prefer to display new or popular items and advertised merchandise. Articles that carry higher markups are also favored. Over time, retailers purchase, save, and maintain a stock of materials for use in display work.

Effective displays use design and composition to please viewers. In creating them, display people bear in mind the basic principles of design: unity, balance (formal or informal), proportion, dominance, and contrast. The more frequently used arrangements for showing merchandise are the step, fan, pyramid, and zigzag patterns.

Colors make displays more attractive. They are used to highlight merchandise and contribute vitality and drama to a display. The primary colors are red, yellow, and blue. Secondary colors like orange and green are obtained by mixing two primary colors. White is a mixture of all colors; black, the absence of color. Colors affect our emotions. We associate different meanings with different hues. Retailers select appropriate color combinations, or color schemes, for their displays. Color harmony may be attained by using complementary or analogous color combinations or a monochromatic scheme.

The main purposes of a show window are to attract the attention of passersby and induce some to enter. While a typical store has only one, many have two or more. Multiple windows can be trimmed as independent or serial displays. The use of a theme, or topic, around which the display will be built helps to unify a display and adds to its appeal.

Interior displays assist in the selling process by arousing shopper interest. In self-service operations, they may complete the entire selling job. Merchandise may be displayed in showcases or shadow boxes, on counter tops or in the aisles, alongside the register, or in other key spots. Wherever they are located, displays sell goods. Their pulling power depends on factors such as the amount of space used, the items displayed, and the prices. Today's retailers want productive displays. There are trends toward higher displays to increase space productivity and toward classification dominance. In-store signing is often used to give directions, for identification purposes, and to announce forthcoming events. Signs also do the talking for displays and help increase sales.

Key Terms

visual merchandising	primary colors
design	secondary colors
composition	color scheme
unity	complementary colors
balance	monochromatic display
proportion	analogous color combinations
dominance	theme
contrast	key spots
display patterns	shadow boxes
step pattern	open displays
fan pattern	closed displays
pyramid pattern	classification dominance
zigzag pattern	

Review Questions

1. Comment on the purposes and effects of retail displays.
2. Cite some examples of the types of display materials that might be found in a typical dress shop.
3. List at least five criteria that retailers use in selecting merchandise to place on display.
4. Distinguish between formal and informal balance.
5. In display design, explain the terms: *(a)* proportion and *(b)* contrast.
6. Name and describe four common display patterns used by store merchants.
7. What is a prism? What happens to light when it passes through a prism?
8. Give two examples of analogous color combinations.
9. Suggest some steps that retailers can take to induce a greater number of passersby to look at and approach the show window.
10. Identify at least five window display themes that can be appropriately used during the spring/summer season.
11. What is a serial window display?
12. Explain the significance of *classification dominance*.

Discussion Questions

1. Which approach would be preferable for a five-store chain of children's shoestores—developing its own display crew or hiring outside window trimmers? Why?
2. Visit a specialty store in your area. Review with the store owner the kinds of fixtures, materials, and accessories used to create window and interior displays. Make a list of these, describing them in some detail.
3. Check the show windows of stores in a regional or community shopping center for two clear examples each of the step and zigzag patterns of displays. Draw

simple diagrams of these displays, noting both the kinds and amounts of items in each.

4. On your next visit to the supermarket, note how few packages, cans, or labels bear designs that are printed predominantly in black or in white. Why do you think this is so? What meanings do black and white have for us?

5. Suggest at least five useful window display themes for the month of November.

Notes

[1]The highlights of a number of display studies are summarized in: James F. Engel, Roger D. Blackwell, and David T. Kollat, *Consumer Behavior,* 3d ed. (Hinsdale, Ill.: Dryden Press, 1978), pp. 263–67.

[2]For a useful introduction to retail display methods, see: Emily M. Mauger, *Modern Display Techniques* (New York: Fairchild Publications, 1964).

[3]Insights into how department stores structure visual merchandising may be gleaned from: Richard Carty, *Visual Merchandising: Principles and Practices* (New York: MPC Educational Publishers, 1978), pp. 87–96.

[4]Melvin Unger, "Window Display Study" (Internal study, Baruch School of Business, City College of New York, March 1964).

[5]For an informative discussion of display treatments, see: Charles M. Edwards, Jr. and Carl F. Lebowitz, *Retail Advertising and Sales Promotion,* 4th ed. (Englewood Cliffs, N.J.: Prentice-Hall, 1981), pp. 427–44.

[6]By William D. Chase and Helen M. Chase, compilers. Available from the Apple Tree Press, Inc., Box 1012, Flint, MI 48501.

[7]See: John S. Wright and Jac L. Goldstucker, "Stimulating Impulse Buying for Increased Sales," *Small Marketers Aids No. 109* (Washington, D.C.: Small Business Administration, 1965).

[8]Charles W. Hubbard, "The 'Shelving' of Increased Sales," *Journal of Retailing* 45 (Winter 1969–70), pp. 75–84.

[9]Michel Chevalier, "Increase in Sales Due to In-store Display," *Journal of Marketing Research* 12 (November 1975), pp. 426–31.

[10]Ronald C. Curhan, "Shelf Space Allocation and Profit Maximization in Mass Retailing," *Journal of Marketing* 37 (July 1973), pp. 54–60.

[11]Michel Chevalier, "Substitution Patterns as a Result of Display in the Product Category," *Journal of Retailing* 51 (Winter 1975–76), pp. 65–72*ff.*

[12]Edward S. Dubbs, "Upping Productivity: A Major Goal," *Stores* 62 (May 1980), p. 62.

[13]Albert D. Bates, *Retailing and Its Environment* (New York: Van Nostrand Reinhold, 1979), p. 131.

[14]Arch G. Woodside and Gerald L. Waddle, "Sales Effects of Instore Advertising," *Journal of Advertising Research* 15 (June 1975), pp. 29–33.

[15]Gary F. McKinnon, J. Patrick Kelly, and E. Doyle Robison, "Sales Effects of Point-of-Purchase In-store Signing," *Journal of Retailing* 57 (Summer 1981), pp. 49–63.

CHAPTER 21

PERSONAL SELLING IN THE STORE

Your Study Objectives

After you have studied this chapter, you will understand:

1. The persuasive power of personal selling in a company's promotion mix.
2. The three distinct categories of selling jobs in our economy.
3. The value to the retailer of employing competent salespeople.
4. The four sequential phases in the retail selling process.
5. The contribution that effective suggestion selling can make to the firm's overall sales volume.
6. The roles of training and supervision in improving the effectiveness of salespeople.

The Importance of Personal Selling

Personal selling is often the most significant element of a company's promotion mix. Many manufacturers maintain their own field sales forces. Among them are producers of machinery and metal products, drugs and medicines, food, apparel, furniture, home appliances, paper products, sporting goods, and hundreds of other product lines. Some manufacturers, especially the smaller ones, rely on agents or outside sales organizations to take care of the selling job. They prefer to devote their energies to running the production end of the business.

Similarly, most merchant wholesalers have their own sales staffs. Examples include distributors of petroleum products, used cars, groceries, lumber, hardware, medical supplies, clothing, and other goods. With manufacturers and wholesalers alike, the annual advertising budget typically averages between 1 and 2 percent of sales. Contrast this with the selling budget, which often runs as high as 10 to 15 percent of each year's revenue.

The size of the field sales operation ranges widely. There are tiny one- and two-person sales staffs. There are statewide, regional, national, and international sales forces with thousands in the field. To manage a sizable selling component, management must set into place a supportive organization. Administrative and supervisory positions must be created and filled.

The sales complements of retail firms roughly parallel those of other kinds of companies. Since the majority of retailers in the United States are small-scale enterprises, their selling staffs are usually comprised of only a few employees. One or more of these may work part time. Large retail companies may employ hundreds or thousands of salespeople. These employees are organized along somewhat different lines than their counterparts in manufacturing and wholesaling.

Personal Selling: Two-way Communication

Personal selling has long been recognized as the single most powerful form of promotion. Because it involves face-to-face, two-way communication, it outperforms other elements of the promotion blend. Neither advertising nor sales promotion provide for this high-level interaction between seller and potential buyer. Selling has been defined as "the process of determining the needs and wants of a prospective buyer and of presenting a product, service, or idea in such a way that the buyer is motivated to make a favorable buying decision."[1]

Interaction is the key factor in personal selling's capacity for persuasion. Salespeople can ask questions, pinpoint problems, and determine customer needs. They can tailor their sales presentations in the light of prospects' needs, likes and dislikes, preferences, wishes, and so on. Through experience, they develop a sensitivity to physical cues and a capability for sensing changes in buyers' moods. They learn how to modify and improve their selling ability. During an interview, a salesperson can provide far more detail than can be conveyed in a

In-person product demonstrations are an effective way to involve the customer in the selling process.

Courtesy The Gillette Company

full-page advertisement. Advertising has other limitations. These include cost considerations, clutter, and competition from surrounding advertisements and news items. An in-person demonstration is superior to the demonstration seen on a TV screen because the latter involves only two of the viewer's senses: sight and sound. During a two-way discussion, the salesperson might appeal to the potential buyer's sense of touch. And depending on the merchandise being offered, even the prospect's sense of taste or smell can be brought into play.

Types of Selling Jobs

The many different kinds of selling jobs in our economy can be grouped into three categories: order takers, order getters, and supporting salespeople.[2] Most numerous are the **order takers.** These are relatively untrained workers who need little selling ability to perform their everyday tasks. Simply put, they take orders and fill them. In this category are those who serve us hamburgers and soft drinks in fast-food restaurants. So are the youngsters who routinely drop the daily newspaper at our front doors and the route-people who regularly deliver milk, pretzels, potato chips, and other items to our homes. **Order getters** must know how to sell. They are, of necessity, more creative. They need to locate prospective buyers of the goods and/or services they sell. They initiate contacts with prospects, conduct sales interviews, and obtain orders. Order getters sell machinery and machine parts, life insurance and pension plans, home swimming pools, roof repairs, office equipment and supplies, and many other goods and services.

Competent salespeople are often the principal key to building a loyal, regular clientele.

Courtesy W. R. Grace & Co.

Finally, the **supporting salespeople** help in securing orders. Technical sales representatives for a computer manufacturer or a chemical plant provide the know-how and advice needed to assist regular salespeople in making sales. Manufacturers of a new soft drink or an over-the-counter headache remedy employ missionary salespeople to convey information to dealers and to druggists.

Retail Selling

These days, most retail selling involves the routine processing of customer requests. It has been characterized as responsive selling because the salesclerk responds to customer requests and originates few sales.[3] In specialty shops and department stores, however, selling is not quite as routine. This is also true of retailers who sell complex equipment, such as the new computer stores.

Some retail salespeople are excellent, no matter what type of store they work in. These top performers add to the dignity of the sales profession.[4] Among others, they include "the furniture salesperson who has studied home decorating, the vacuum cleaner salesperson who knows carpeting, the book salesperson who reads widely," and the like.

An evident de-emphasis on personal selling in retailing has been apparent for many years. This can be traced back to the realization by merchants that the sales payroll often constitutes the largest single operating expense in the budget. Today, self-selection and self-service have largely replaced personal selling in most department stores and

---

Figure 21.1
Personal selling for the
independent retailer

Good personal selling in retail stores is getting harder and harder to find today. This is particularly true in the large multiunit retail establishments that have increasingly stressed self-service at the expense of good personal selling.

The de-emphasis of personal selling by large scale retailers leaves a gap in customer service that the small retailer is in a good position to fill. By emphasizing good personal selling, the small retailer can gain a competitive edge not easily matched by the bigger stores. It is much easier for your larger competitors to dominate in such areas as merchandise assortments, pricing, and advertising, than to provide a well-developed personal selling effort.

Good personal selling, however, does not automatically occur simply because the retail store is small. Nor does high quality personal selling result merely by paying salespeople more money. Rather, good personal selling results from a carefully developed program which accounts for the major elements necessary in all successful personal selling programs. . . . Personal selling in retailing is essentially a matching of the customer's needs with the retailer's merchandise and services. . . . There are three basic skills needed by salespeople to make this match effectively:

1. Salespeople must be skilled at learning the needs of the customer.
2. They must have a thorough knowledge of the merchandise and service offered by the retailer.
3. They must have the ability to convince customers that the merchandise and service offered by their store can satisfy the customer's needs better than that of their competitors.

*   *   *   *   *

Developing a program for improving these three basic selling skills in your salespeople is the essence of building a better personal selling effort for your store. The framework for the program consists of three basic elements: (1) selecting people who are suitable for particular sales positions, (2) providing training, and (3) devising an appropriate compensation plan.

Source: Bert Rosenbloom, ''Improving Personal Selling,'' *Small Marketers Aids No. 159* (Washington, D.C.: Small Business Administration, reprinted April 1980), pp. 2–4.

---

chains across the country. Still, personal selling can be a significant factor in retail success. It can be a valuable asset for the independent especially, in distinguishing a firm from its competitors. Competent salespeople are often the key to building a regular, loyal clientele. (See Figure 21.1.) Customers receive their initial, most enduring impressions about a retail company from its sales staff.

Significance of the Retail
Salesperson

Retailers and shoppers alike know how valuable a capable sales contingent can be. Salespeople can increase business or turn shoppers away. They can build the firm's customer bank, increase the size of the average sale, and sell additional merchandise to many customers. They can make the shopper's stay more pleasant. They can initiate friendly long-term relationships that lead to quicker acceptance of the company by the community and enhance the public's image of the store as a pleasant place to visit.

By the same token, an uncaring, rude, or improperly trained salesperson can turn customers away. Some years ago, a survey of former customers revealed that 68 out of every 100 stopped shopping at the store because of employee indifference or lack of interest.[5] Another 14 were lost because of complaints that were not properly taken care of.

The quality or caliber of sales personnel is a strong determinant of the store's image. Patronage factors are those which cause consumers to favor one store over another. At a shopping center in Maryland, customers were asked to rank 14 such factors. Salesclerk service placed fourth and rated more important to patronage than location, the store's atmosphere and layout, or the assortment of merchandise carried.[6]

Since the early 1970s, researchers have been probing consumer satisfaction with retail outlets. In-home interviews with women department store shoppers in Tucson, Arizona, revealed that satisfaction with the selling staff was the single most important contributing factor in this area.[7] Of importance were the salespeople's civility, warmth, and helpfulness, as well as the number available for service. Other components of shopper gratification included satisfaction with special sales, the products and/or services purchased, the store environment, and value-price relationships.

More and more, modern retailers are considering the addition of new services to their usual merchandise offerings. Some larger stores have already installed welcome service departments. Among these are dental and/or optometrical services, income tax preparation, drivers' education, travel agencies, insurance agencies, and the like.[8]

Selecting the Right Retail Salespeople

Many retailing executives claim that good salespeople are hard to find. Although salespeople are not born with the necessary skills and attributes, training can, happily, do wonders with most people who are willing to learn. Of course, trainers need to have basic material to work with. Direct-selling companies like Stanley Home Products, Tupperware, Avon, and Amway must mount massive recruiting efforts each year to obtain large numbers of salespeople. Their turnover rate approximates 100 percent annually.[9]

Store retailing is as demanding of the recruitment effort as is direct-to-home retailing. Unfortunately, top management often pays more attention to buying, merchandise management, and other aspects than to staffing and training salespeople. Several guidelines for the selection of sales personnel may be gleaned directly from the interactive nature of the retail selling process. Applicants should be neatly groomed, able to communicate with relative ease, and project a pleasant, friendly personality. Other desirable characteristics are emotional stability, enthusiasm, honesty, an interest in retail work, and a willingness to

Table 21.1 Characteristics sought in applicants for sales positions				
Rank	**Characteristic**	**Number of Stores Reporting**	**Percent of Total**	
1	Honest	45	77.6	
2	Dependable	35	60.3	
3	Enthusiastic	31	53.4	
4	Neat	30	51.7	
5	Self-motivating	28	48.3	
6	Hardworking	24	41.4	
7	Friendly	23	39.7	
8.5	Alert	21	36.2	
8.5	Cooperative	21	36.2	
10	Intelligent	20	34.5	

Source: Irving Burstiner, "Current Personnel Practices in Department Stores," *Journal of Retailing* 51 (Winter 1975–76), p. 10.

put forth effort. With the proper training, recruits who possess such traits can become productive salespeople. They will, of course, need to learn all they can about the merchandise, prices, company, and selling. Effective salespeople also need sharply developed leadership skills and an understanding of the communication process.[10]

Department store personnel managers in California and New York were asked to indicate the traits they looked for in sales applicants.[11] They were also asked to order these characteristics in ranks. As can be seen in Table 21.1, their top three choices were honesty, dependability, and enthusiasm.

The interaction between prospective buyers and salespeople has been described as a *dyadic* relationship. Research has revealed that perceived similarities between the two participants in the *dyad* may have a positive effect on the outcome.[12] It may well be that retailers should hire salespeople who belong to the same age and/or income bracket as the store's regular clientele, or who resemble them in physical appearance, or who dress in the same sort of clothing.[13] This may be especially true in selling fashion merchandise.

In the next section, we view the selling process in general and then examine the specifics of the *retail* selling process.

The Selling Process in General

Many sales managers and writers in the field of professional selling concur on the desirability of using a by-the-numbers approach in teaching the art of selling. They recommend breaking the process down into a series of steps so that novice salespeople can easily grasp the many details. After learning the process, they can work out acceptable patterns of behavior that lead to a higher level of sales.

Authorities differ over the number of steps involved.[14] Many practitioners, however, agree on the six briefly described below:

1. **Prospecting** In this initial phase, salespeople search for likely buyers of the company's products or services. They cull through directories, place advertisements to obtain leads, canvas homes or businesses, ask other people for recommendations, and avail themselves of many other sources.

2. **The Preapproach** This step "involves (1) finding out all you can about your prospect prior to the interview and (2) getting the specific interview, either through prior appointment or without an appointment."[15] Once a list of prospective buyers has been drawn up, there is still need to qualify those people or organizations. Salespeople attempt to find out whether the prospects need, want, or can use the merchandise or services being offered. They need to determine if the prospects can afford to buy and to find out who will make the decision to buy. At the same time, they try to learn as much as they can about each potential customer. This enables them to tailor the sales interview to each one's needs.

3. **The Approach** Loosely defined as the first minute or so preceding the sales presentation, the approach is the salesperson's initial face-to-face contact with the prospect. A good working relationship, or **rapport,** must be set up quickly with the potential buyer.

4. **The Presentation** This is the main portion of the sales interview, where the entire proposition is submitted. During the presentation, the salesperson outlines the features of the product or service and suggests reasons why the prospect ought to buy. Experienced salespeople demonstrate product use and try to involve the prospect in the demonstration. They answer questions readily and effectively handle any objections that are raised.

5. **The Close** The sale is closed when the salesperson, having written up the order, secures the customer's signature on the order form. A variety of closing techniques are available; descriptions of many are found in books on selling.

6. **The Follow-up** This final step aims at building repeat business and a healthy, long-term association with the customer. When thanking the customer, the salesperson reassures the customer that the decision to buy was indeed wise. Then follows a promise to check with the customer after delivery has been made to make certain that all is satisfactory.

The _Retail_ Selling Process

Selling efforts in the retail setting do not quite parallel the professional selling process we have described. As is indicated in Table 21.2, there are striking differences between the two. For one thing, store salespeople are relieved of the prospecting chore. That is taken care of by

	Department Stores	Industrial Packaging Manufacturers	Distributors of Gift Items	Insurance Companies
Table 21.2 **Tasks in the selling** **process: selected** **industries**				
Prospecting	1%	3%	17%	31%
Contacting	6	31	23	20
Stimulating	9	11	19	6
Closing	18	18	14	12
Retaining	35	29	27	24
Other*	31	8	—	7
	100%	100%	100%	100%

* In the case of department store salespeople, "other" activities include such sales-related duties as occasional packing and wrapping, merchandise replenishment, inventory control, store housekeeping, interbranch transfers of merchandise, and arrangement of displays. Industrial salespeople perform missionary work while insurance salespeople are active in estate planning, proposal preparations, and the handling of claims.

Source: Adapted from Marvin A. Jolson, "Standardizing the Personal Selling Process," *Marquette Business Review* 18 (Spring 1974), p. 18.

the firm's media advertising, window displays, and other forms of promotion.

Because the retail selling process is somewhat simpler than industrial selling, some retail managements believe that just about anyone who is willing to work and appears presentable can do the job. Unfortunately, a few believe that sales training efforts may be a waste of the firm's funds. The National Retail Merchants Association differs with this thinking and offers sales training programs and other aids to their member stores. NCR Corporation, for decades a powerful ally of the retailer, maintains: "Good selling is more than the ability to talk—a 'gift of gab.' It is more than a friendly smile. It is an orderly series of steps which lead from greeting the customer to bidding him or her goodbye."[16]

One college textbook lists these six steps in the retail selling process:

1. Approaching customers.
2. Determining customer needs and wants.
3. Presenting merchandise.
4. Avoiding and handling objections.
5. Closing the sale.
6. Selling by suggestion.[17]

In actual practice, it is often difficult to distinguish these steps clearly. For example, steps 3 and 4 may occur almost simultaneously. Even steps 1 and 2 are not quite distinct. Effective salespeople begin to size up shoppers from the moment they come in.

Although our own approach may be somewhat similar, it is perhaps more holistic. We visualize the **retail selling process** as involving four sequential phases:

1. Shopper contact.
2. The sales dialogue.
3. Completing the sale.
4. Suggestion selling.

Shopper Contact Professional sales trainers in industry typically label this step "The Approach." Retail managers refer to it as "Greeting the Customer" or "The Salutation." Whatever the title, it is only part of the first phase of the retail selling process. The **shopper contact** stage is complex. It begins when an alert salesperson spots a shopper entering the department or store. A heightened awareness and sense of anticipation follows. The salesperson notes the shopper's gait, posture, manner of dress, and other cues. A preliminary judgment must be made. Is the shopper merely browsing or signaling a readiness to accept prompt and courteous attention? Does he or she need or want more time to look around? Might the shopper resent too early an approach? (See Figure 21.2.) As experience is gained, errors of judgment are made more infrequently.

Good selling practice suggests that the salesperson should generally initiate the opening conversation.

The Opening Conversation If initial contact with the shopper is to be at all meaningful, the salesperson needs a precise understanding of the situation. The shopper should be regarded as the store's guest. As a representative of the firm, the salesperson should fulfill the role of host skillfully and with tact.[18] A friendly, good-humored approach quickly places the shopper at ease. The salesperson should project a quiet, assured professionalism that will help establish rapport.[19] Gaining the consumer's confidence is the immediate goal of the opening conversation.

Unfortunately, the first few words uttered by many retail salespeople are insipid and trite. They reflect a singular lack of imagination. Some years ago, some 100 apparel stores were visited to learn what opening phrases salespeople commonly used to break the ice with shoppers. Most used was the trite question: May I help you? And, of course: Can I help you?[20] At the very least, prefacing the question with a "Good morning, Mrs. Rafferty," or a "Good afternoon, Mr. Cummings. So nice to see you again!" would offer a welcome, although modest, improvement. To shoppers, nothing is more appealing than being recognized, greeted with a warm smile, and addressed by name. Motivated salespeople try their best to learn their customers' names quickly and they repeat them again and again during the sales dialogue.

Figure 21.2
Learning by studying
the customer

Study Your Customer

There are certain helpful things you may learn by studying your customer. She may be:

the customer who knows exactly what she wants. You should find it for her as quickly as possible.

the customer who has a general idea of what she wants. You should help her decide what she wants by bringing out merchandise which seems most likely to please.

the customer who will want something later and is just looking around. By showing your merchandise well and pointing out its good features you may be able to make the sale now. Or you can at least lay the foundation for a later sale.

the customer who has nothing definite in mind but is just "shopping." You may show her new and attractive merchandise and arouse her interest. You may make a sale at the time or prepare for a future sale.

She may change from one type to another during the sale.

In addition you may sometimes form an opinion about your customer's wants by observing her age, appearance, her interest in your merchandise, her expression, and other signs that may help you serve her more intelligently. Do not be too sure that an opinion based on these observations is right, however, and watch for changes.

Guard against the habit of classifying customers in certain ways as lookers, shoppers, and purchasers. Many sales have been lost by salespeople who classed an undecided customer as a looker and failed to give helpful information or show enough merchandise.

Treat every customer as a possible purchaser and do your best to make a sale without being over-insistent.

Source: NCR Corporation.

Experienced salespeople soon develop a pool of useful phrases with which to begin conversations. They learn to avoid approaches that may bring about a negative response or contradict what the customer is thinking. If, for example, a consumer has been studying a display of power drills, the salesperson might pick up one and hand it to the shopper, exclaiming: "This is our most popular drill. You'll find it's just the thing for your home workshop." Or: "Try the grip on this one. It weighs less than half as much as some of the other models. Yet it performs just as well." Or: "This model was featured in our newspaper ad; it's on sale this week."

For other articles of merchandise, many starters can be originated. To mention just a few of the possibilities:

"That color would look well on you."

"Cleaning the material is so easy."

"This style is very much in vogue right now."

"See what fine workmanship has gone into this."

"We sell so many of these."

From *The Wall Street Journal*, with permission of Cartoon Features Syndicate.

"Nothing thanks, just browsing."

Obviously, properly trained sales employees know their merchandise and keep abreast of changing styles.

The Sales Dialogue

Once effective shopper contact has been made, an atmosphere of mutual respect should result. Now the main portion of the selling process swings into play. During the **sales dialogue,** the salesperson determines the shopper's needs and begins to present suitable merchandise. Effective salespeople review the selling points of the item and try to show how its features will benefit the shopper.

By placing a few well-chosen questions designed to elicit the information, the salesperson tries to target rapidly on what the shopper may be looking for. Careful listening is essential. Having interpreted the shopper's need, the salesperson may lead the shopper to the area where the merchandise is displayed or perhaps bring over several samples to show the shopper.

Suppose, for instance, that a woman expresses interest in purchasing a pair of gloves. More commonly heard reactions to this kind of situation include: "What size do you wear?" "Are they for evening wear?" and "What color are you interested in?" More preferable might be the statement: "We have an excellent assortment of gloves. Let me show them to you." As the shopper slips on a pair that appears to fit perfectly, the salesperson might say, "Those suit you quite well." On the other hand, if the gloves are evidently tight and the woman

Effective salespeople review the selling points of the item and show how its features will benefit the shopper.

Courtesy 3M

can use a larger size or seems to prefer another pattern, the salesperson is ready and quick to accommodate. If several price lines are available, it is generally better to begin by showing the shopper those in the middle range. The salesperson can then judge the woman's reaction and decide, if necessary, to **trade up** to a higher-priced pair or **trade down** to less expensive gloves.

Stressing the Selling Points Better salespeople know intuitively to bring out the positive aspects of goods as selling points. These should be tied to the satisfaction of needs. A woman may buy gloves to protect her hands while operating a machine at a factory or while at home doing housework. She may use gloves to keep her hands warm during the cold winter months, to look dressy when she goes out in the evening, or simply to be in fashion.

Physical well-being and comfort are two powerful motives behind our buying behavior. We also purchase goods and services to satisfy basic needs like hunger, thirst, and the desire for rest. We buy to indulge ourselves, be "in" with others, secure the approval of family or friends, acquire status, occupy leisure hours, or express our individuality. As is pointed out in Figure 21.3, we look for proper value in repayment for the money we spend and the degree of quality we feel the merchandise ought to have. In the apparel we buy, we demand suitable material, quality work, and up-to-date styling. We want clothes that will wash and wear well and look presentable.

Salespeople need a fair grasp of basic psychology. They also need

Figure 21.3
Consumers look for
quality and taste

In the past several years, some marked developments have taken place in consumer living patterns, consumer incomes, and consumer spending habits. The result has been that millions of families today are looking for sound quality in the merchandise they buy. They are also stressing good taste and are avoiding shoddy, cheap, and tasteless items.

One reason for the increased emphasis which customers put on quality and taste is: Many can *afford better things* because their discretionary incomes (money which is left after buying essentials) have increased. They have the cash or credit to buy *better* cars, *better* clothing, *better* housing, *better* furnishings, *better* food, and *better* recreation.

Another reason is education. People are better educated and informed than they were formerly. One result of this increased knowledge is an appreciation of good taste—what is beautiful, appropriate, in good proportion, and excellent. Excellence and good taste are more important than price when such people shop.

A third factor in the increased emphasis on quality and taste is the *desire for self-expression*. The customer seeks to identify his or her own personality and to make himself or herself stand out from the masses. Purchasing quality products offers a way to be an individual in the crowd and to create a self-image which will give satisfaction and pride.

In short, many customers are looking for quality merchandise that is in good taste.

Source: Robert H. Myers, "Quality and Taste as Sales Appeals," *Small Marketers Aids No. 113* (Washington, D.C.: Small Business Administration, reprinted April 1974), p. 1.

to know what people seek in the products they buy. They need to show shoppers how the merchandise will respond to and satisfy wants and motives. Often, a salesperson will demonstrate how the item works, fits, is strong or resilient, will not rip or tear, improves appearance, and the like. Effective salespeople try to involve several of the shopper's other senses besides sight. They encourage shoppers to touch, feel, or smell the product (depending on what the merchandise may be). A useful technique is to help the prospective customer visualize comments or claims made about the item. After all, we are far more impressed by what we can witness ourselves than by what we are told.[21] Figure 21.4 shows a typical situation.

Shopper Objections In any selling situation, it is only natural to expect that the prospect will raise one or more **objections** along the way. Voicing objections is often a way for prospects to let salespeople know they are smart shoppers who cannot be taken advantage of easily. Some consumers regard sales dialogues as adversary contests. They expect salespeople to try harder to convince them. Most objections, however, originate in attitudes or feelings toward the merchandise, price, or brand. There is a world of difference between the types of objections heard in the retailing environment and those encountered by sales representatives who sell to industry. Purchasing agents for manufacturing plants, wholesalers, government agencies, and department or chain stores are typically well-trained, knowledgeable people.

Figure 21.4
Visualization: aid to
personal selling

A salesperson in the radio-TV department of a large store is trying to convey, orally, the enjoyment and ease of operation the shopper can expect with a particular color TV set that works by remote control. Far more impact would result if the salesperson would:

a. set up an easy chair in the proper spot so the shopper can view the set in operation,
b. suggest that the shopper sit down comfortably, and
c. hand over the control device with simple instructions for its use.

The prospective buyer will then realize how simple it is to turn the TV on and off from a distance, tune into the right channel, and adjust the volume.

These skilled professionals maximize their buying efforts. They realize that their suppliers operate in a highly competitive environment. Thus, they are far more likely than consumers to express objections when suppliers present their wares. Alternative sources of supply are almost always readily available.

In the industrial selling situation, objections to the price of a product or service are perhaps the most common type. This is understandable; a difference of even 20 cents per unit can result in tremendous savings to the firm when multiplied by the 50,000 or 100,000 units that must be purchased. In retailing, however, price objections are less commonly voiced, although they do occur. We hear such statements as "I didn't plan on spending quite that much," "Do you have one that's less expensive?" or "This isn't worth the price you're asking." As an example of how this last comment might be handled, consider: "I'm sure you would find any comparable product with these features costs as much or more."

More commonly, however, shoppers object to product attributes such as the quality of the material or work, its durability, the color or design, how the item fits, and the like. With appliances, questions of guarantees and warranties may be raised. Salespeople soon learn to anticipate the more frequent objections and develop techniques for responding to them. Most helpful in this regard is a thorough knowledge of the merchandise—and of competitive offerings. In addition, there are many books on professional selling that can be consulted. Most include substantial sections, if not entire chapters, devoted to suggested methods for handling objections. Interested readers are exposed to the finer nuances of such commonly used techniques as the "Yes, but . . . Method," the "Question Approach," and the "Boomerang Technique."

Completing the Sale Although technically still part of the sales interview, this important step—**completing the sale**—culminates all prior activity. The salesperson asks for the order and gets it, consummating the sale. *Precisely* *when* the sales interview should move into this phase will differ from one selling situation to the next. Capable salespeople seem to know when prospects are ripe, or ready to buy. This may be because they have used **trial closes** to test the shopper's readiness for sale completion. Trial closes often take the form of short, one-sentence questions. Here are a few examples:

"Which of the two do you prefer?"

"Would Thursday be a good day for us to deliver the merchandise?"

"Don't you feel, Ms. Harris, that this article represents an excellent buy?"

"Wouldn't you agree that your daughter will enjoy wearing this bracelet?"

Once it becomes evident that the shopper is ready to become a customer, an attempt is made to complete, or close, the sale. In retailing, the most popular of all closing techniques is the **assumptive close.** The salesperson simply begins to fill out the sales slip, on the assumption that the shopper has decided to buy. At this point, effective salespeople attempt suggestion selling, a sales-building technique described in the next section.

Resourceful salespeople are familiar with other, alternative closing methods. They employ them in situations where the assumptive close may not do the job.[22] Two of the more popular techniques are the **SRO** or **standing room only, close** and the **balance sheet close.** The latter is also known as the **T-account close.** The SRO close can be used if the salesperson knows of an upcoming event and feels that, by passing along this information to the consumer, that person might buy. As an illustration of the technique, the salesperson might say: "If you buy this garment now, you'll be saving $8. It goes off sale tomorrow." Or "These are such great sellers. I can't promise we'll have any left later on in the week. And we don't expect another shipment in."

The balance sheet technique may be used if shoppers cannot seem to make up their minds about a major purchase. Buying a boat, car, home freezer, or word processor are examples where this might apply. To help the consumer think things through, the salesperson draws a line down the center of a sheet of paper. The benefits of owning the article are listed on one side of the sheet; the disadvantages of buying the item on the other side. The idea is to demonstrate to the indecisive shopper how the advantages far outweigh the drawbacks.

Suggestion Selling After the closing, the professional salesperson will suggest other merchandise. These suggestions are frequently successful, and many shoppers leave the store carrying two—or more—items instead of one. Properly presented, **suggestion selling** can boost sales. Additional mer-

Suggestion selling—an important part of the retail selling process—can boost sales at this luxury product boutique in a Paris department store.

Courtesy The Gillette Company

chandise can be sold to from 10 percent to as many as 25 percent or more of all customers.

Related or accessory items are usually the easiest to suggest. To the customer who purchases a gallon of wall paint, suggesting a paint roller, pan, or can of turpentine may serve as a helpful and welcome reminder. Figure 21.5 presents some natural suggestions for other merchandise.

Among the kinds of suggestions that might "make the customer's shopping excursion more complete" are related items, a larger quantity, higher-priced or better-quality merchandise, newly arrived stock, specially advertised items, new and different uses for merchandise, and items for special occasions.[23]

Once a sales transaction has been completed, the shopper expects prompt and efficient postsale attention. The merchandise should be neatly wrapped or bagged and the sale properly recorded. If policy so dictates, the salesperson will bring the item over to the register or checkout point. Customers should be assured of the wisdom of their buying decisions and thanked with sincerity. In some of the better stores, the salesperson will accompany the customer to the door.

Improving Sales Effectiveness

Retail sales management plans, organizes, directs, and controls the selling staff. It aims at improving sales effectiveness. To accomplish this, all facets must be well managed: recruitment and selection proce-

Figure 21.5 **A suggestion selling checklist**		
When you have sold:		**Consider suggesting:**

When you have sold:	Consider suggesting:
bath towels	a bath sheet, face towels, washcloths
a bicycle	a bell, a bicycle pump, a rearview mirror, reflectors, a taillight
a camera	film, filters, flashbulbs
a cup of coffee	a muffin (bran, corn, English), a doughnut
an evening gown	a pair of gloves, a purse, evening shoes
a hammer	nails, a screwdriver, pliers
a hoe	a rake, garden gloves, a shovel, a spade
a houseplant	plant food, potting soil, a planter, a sprinkling can
liquor	club soda, ginger ale, cocktail mixes, liqueurs
paint	masking tape, brushes, a pan, a roller, sandpaper, spackle, turpentine
pajamas	a bathrobe, slippers
paper plates	napkins, paper cups, plastic utensils
a shirt	a necktie, socks
shoes	hosiery, a purse, slippers
slacks	a belt, a blouse or shirt, a jacket, a pair of socks
a sport jacket	a shirt, neckties, a sweater
a tape recorder	tapes
a toaster	a toaster cover
a toothbrush	dental floss, toothpaste or powder, mouthwash
a typewriter	ribbons, carbon paper, correction fluid, typing paper, a service contract
writing stationery	a pen, pencils, an eraser, envelopes

dures, training, supervision, and periodic employee evaluation. Perhaps the most stress should be placed on the starting point—the personnel selection process. It is at this juncture that management can ensure a steady supply of potentially fine salespeople.

There is some indication that older, more experienced, and better educated salespeople are often more productive.[24] In retailing, productivity is typically measured by relating selling costs to sales volume.[25] Assume, for instance, that a furniture warehouse maintains ten salespeople on its payroll. These employees receive a total of $250,000 annually in commissions, and sales for the year total $2 million. Thus, the average salesperson accounts for $200,000 in sales at a cost of $25,000 or 8 percent of total volume. Store management may then compare the current year's ratio of 8 percent to the prior year's results to see whether productivity has gone up or down. Or they may check how much in sales was produced last year by the average salesperson. Such performance results may also be checked against trade association figures to determine whether results compare favorably or unfavorably with other furniture outlets of the same type and size.

Training the Sales Staff   The importance of sales training cannot be overestimated. In one of the rare instances where training program outcomes have been documented, the productivity of department store salespeople reportedly increased by more than 40 percent after only four hours of training.[26] In the experiment, productivity was defined as total sales volume divided by the total number of hours worked by the salespeople.

Unfortunately, the main thrust of most training for sales personnel centers on store merchandise and systems/procedures. If offered at all, instruction in selling methods occupies no more than one or two hours of training time.

As alternatives to lectures, demonstrations, films, and other customary teaching techniques, behavioral approaches such as those discussed in Chapter 12 often yield impressive outcomes.[27]

Motivating, Evaluating, and Controlling Sales Employees   Essential to the proper motivation of the selling staff are effective leadership, pleasant working conditions, a satisfactory compensation plan, fair treatment by management, and the promise of a promotional ladder. Management must establish desirable levels of performance and procedures for evaluating sales personnel. Some retail organizations have introduced **management by objectives (MBO) programs.** This approach to business administration involves "a clear-cut strategic plan and its translation into departmental and personal goals which are reviewed when results are obtained."[28] The process involves four steps:

1. Superiors and subordinates decide jointly on specific objectives.
2. Cooperatively, they develop a plan of action.
3. Progress is reviewed periodically.
4. Superiors appraise performance and evaluate results against the established objectives.[29]

Summary   For many types of retailers, personal selling may prove to be the most valuable element in the promotion mix. Competent salespeople are assets to the retail firm. Frequently, company success will depend on selecting the right sales trainees. Good salespeople are made, not born. Training can work wonders with most people who are willing to learn how to sell.

In industry, the selling process is often described in six steps: prospecting, preapproach, approach, presentation, close, and follow-up. The four sequential phases in the *retail* selling process are shopper contact, the sales dialogue, completing the sale, and suggestion selling.

During the sales dialogue, the salesperson determines the shopper's needs and begins to present suitable merchandise. Effective salespeople review the selling points. Along the way, shopper objections are to be expected. These objections may be raised about the merchandise, price, brand, or other aspects. Most experienced sales employees learn how to meet and counter these objections.

Trial closes may be used to test the shopper's readiness to buy. During the sales completion step, the salesperson asks for the order and gets it, consummating the sale. After the closing, the professional salesperson will suggest additional merchandise. The suggestions are frequently successful. Other goods can be sold to perhaps 10 to 25 percent or more of all customers.

Training and supervision are important for improving sales effectiveness over time. To motivate their employees, retailers need to provide effective leadership, pleasant working conditions, a satisfactory compensation plan, fair treatment, and the promise of a promotional ladder. Management also needs to establish desirable levels of performance and procedures for evaluating sales personnel.

Key Terms

order takers	shopper contact
order getters	sales dialogue
supporting salespeople	trading up or down
prospecting	shopper objections
preapproach	completing the sale
approach	trial closes
rapport	assumptive close
presentation	SRO close
close (closing)	balance sheet (T-account) close
follow-up	suggestion selling
retail selling process	management by objectives (MBO) programs

Review Questions

1. Why are life insurance salespeople and sales representatives who sell drill presses to manufacturing companies referred to as *order getters*?

2. Explain the term *responsive selling*. Give some examples of salespeople you have met who sell responsively.

3. List at least four factors that influence shopper satisfaction toward retail stores.

4. Outline the six basic steps in the industrial selling process.

5. Distinguish between the *preapproach* and the *approach* in the industrial selling process.

6. Name and briefly describe the four phases of the *retail* selling process.

7. Cite several different types of objections a salesperson may expect to hear from shoppers.

8. When a salesperson uses *visualization* with a shopper, what does this mean?

9. Differentiate among the *assumptive, balance sheet,* and *SRO* closing techniques.

10. Explain the term *suggestion selling* and illustrate by example how it may be used to increase store sales.

11. Show how management can determine the productivity of its sales personnel.

12. Specify the procedure for instituting management by objectives in an organization.

Discussion Questions

1. Think of an instance when a salesperson turned you off. Try to recall what happened and why you were dissatisfied. How should the salesperson have handled the situation?

2. Speculate on the likely role of personal selling in department stores fifteen years from now. Explain the reasoning behind your thinking.

3. Many direct-selling organizations have an excessively high turnover rate among sales representatives. What recommendations can you make that may help to reduce the turnover rate?

4. Propose a list of qualities you would look for in applicants for a sales opening in your own neighborhood sporting goods store.

5. Assume that you are a salesperson employed by a major appliances retailer. A shopper who is interested in a particular model of a famous-name dishwasher has just told you that the price, $550, is too high. How would you try to overcome this objection?

6. Department stores and other large-scale retail companies often sell goods over the telephone. Suggest four or five creative ideas for a small store owner to successfully use the telephone to generate additional business.

Notes

[1] John W. Ernest and Richard D. Ashmun, *Selling: Principles & Practices,* 5th ed. (New York: McGraw-Hill, 1980), p. 5.

[2] E. Jerome McCarthy and William D. Perreault, Jr., *Basic Marketing: A Managerial Approach,* 8th ed. (Homewood, Ill.: Richard D. Irwin, 1984), pp. 504–9.

[3] Ben M. Enis, *Personal Selling: Foundations, Process, and Management* (Santa Monica, Calif.: Goodyear Publishing, 1979), p. 10.

[4] B. Robert Anderson, *Professional Selling,* 2d ed. (Englewood Cliffs, N.J.: Prentice-Hall, 1981), p. 9.

[5] P. L. Pfeiffer, "Where Do Your Customers Go?" *Stores* 55 (February 1973), p. 30.

[6] Marvin A. Jolson and Walter F. Spath, "Understanding and Fulfilling Shoppers' Requirements: An Anomaly in Retailing?" *Journal of Retailing* 49 (Summer 1973), pp. 38–50.

[7] Robert A. Westbrook, "Sources of Consumer Satisfaction with Retail Outlets," *Journal of Retailing* 57 (Fall 1981), pp. 68–85.

[8] Ronald D. Michman, "Changing Patterns in Retailing," *Business Horizons* 22 (October 1979), pp. 33–38.

[9]Michael Granfield and Alfred Nichols, "Economic & Marketing Aspects of the Direct Selling Industry," *Journal of Retailing* 51 (Spring 1975), pp. 33–50*ff.*

[10]Frederick E. Webster, Jr., "Interpersonal Communication and Salesperson Effectiveness," *Journal of Marketing* 32 (July 1967), pp. 7–13.

[11]Irving Burstiner, "Current Personnel Practices in Department Stores," *Journal of Retailing* 50 (Winter 1975), pp. 3–14*ff.*

[12]Franklin B. Evans, "Selling as a Dyadic Relationship—A New Approach," *American Behavioral Scientist* 6 (May 1963), pp. 76–79; Edward A. Riordan, Richard L. Oliver, and James H. Donnelly, Jr., "The Unsold Prospect: Dyadic and Attitudinal Determinants," *Journal of Marketing Research* 14 (November 1977), pp. 530–37.

[13]Gilbert A. Churchill, Robert H. Collins, and William A. Strang, "Should Retail Salespersons Be Similar to Their Customers?" *Journal of Retailing* 51 (Fall 1975), pp. 29–42*ff.*

[14]For additional background, an excellent elaboration of the process may be found in Chapters 6–18 of: Frederic A. Russell, Frank H. Beach, and Richard H. Buskirk, *Textbook of Salesmanship*, 10th ed. (New York: McGraw-Hill, 1978).

[15]Allan L. Reid, *Modern Applied Selling*, 3d ed. (Santa Monica, Calif.: Goodyear Publishing, 1981), p. 138.

[16]"Better Retail Selling" (Dayton, Ohio: NCR Corporation), pp. 3–4.

[17]David L. Kurtz, H. Robert Dodge, and Jay E. Klompmaker, *Professional Selling*, 4th ed. (Plano, Tex.: Business Publications, 1985), pp. 370–76.

[18]Russell et al., *Salesmanship*, p. 381.

[19]Reid, *Modern Applied Selling*, pp. 348–49.

[20]William H. Bolen, "Customer Contact: Those First Important Words," *Department Store Management* (April 1970), pp. 25–26.

[21]Richard H. Buskirk, *Retail Selling: A Vital Approach*, (San Francisco: Canfield Press, 1975), pp. 97–98.

[22]Ten or more closing techniques are described in: Charles A. Kirkpatrick and Frederick A. Russ, *Effective Selling*, 7th ed. (Cincinnati: South-Western Publishing, 1981), pp. 273–79.

[23]Ernest and Ashmun, *Selling*, p. 317.

[24]Robert J. Paul and Robert W. Bell, "Evaluating the Retail Salesman," *Journal of Retailing* 44 (Summer 1968), pp. 17–26; Charles N. Weaver, "An Empirical Study to Aid in the Selection of Retail Salesclerks," *Journal of Retailing* 45 (Fall 1969), pp. 22–26*ff.*

[25]David J. Rachman and Robert J. Robichaud, "How Large Stores Measure Employee Sales Productivity," *Journal of Retailing* 37 (Spring 1961), pp. 1–5.

[26]Ann Karlsson, "Does Retail Training Pay?" *Training in Business and Industry* 6 (February 1969), pp. 25–28.

[27]Frank W. Bonheim, "Dual Purpose Training," *Training and Development Journal* 32 (May 1978), pp. 40–42; Don Jerry Helms, "Some Correlates of Worker Perception and Performance in Selected Retail Sales Personnel" Ph.D. dissertation, University of Arkansas, 1977; Malcolm W. Warren, "Using Behavioral Technology to Improve Sales Performance," *Training and Development Journal* 32 (July 1978), pp. 54–56.

[28]Robert C. Appleby with Irving Burstiner, *An Essential Guide to Management* (Englewood Cliffs, N.J.: Prentice-Hall, 1981), p. 21.

[29]For a discussion of the problems involved in instituting an MBO program and a description of the process, see: Richard Hise and Peter L. Gillett, "Making MBO Work in the Sales Force," *Atlanta Economic Review* 27 (July–August 1977), pp. 32–37.

Case 6.1
Plant City

Since 1981, Amy and Owen Whittier have opened nine plant shops in regional centers in two midwestern states. All units are interestingly decorated, well-stocked kiosks that stand in the mall's main passageway. Despite their small size, annual sales at these installations have been averaging well over $200,000 annually. The entrepreneurial couple is planning to open still another place, their 10th. This time, however, they are departing from their customary approach by renting a large store rather than a kiosk. The new outlet, Plant City, will have nearly 2,100 square feet of selling space.

In the past, the Whittiers' opening promotions consisted of little more than: *(a)* displaying "Coming Soon" signs on the fence that surrounded the kiosk during the construction phase, *(b)* mailing out publicity releases to the local media, and *(c)* placing a quarter-page advertisement in the shopping newspaper that the center distributed to area residents. Amy and Owen are anxious to do much more for Plant City's grand opening. They would like to devise a program that would be both exciting and effective in its impact.

Questions

1. Of the various types of sales promotion tools you are now familiar with, which four do you believe would prove most exciting and effective for Plant City's grand opening? Explain your reasoning.

2. Outline a creative promotional program for the store's First Anniversary Celebration.

Case 6.2
The Craft Depot

Today, most residents of one small Pennsylvania town are familiar with the Craft Depot. It is a hobby shop on Main Street with an unusual "Early Yankee" flavor to both storefront and interior decor. It is run by the Harrisons, a pleasant couple in their late 30s.

Before his plant closed down, Walter Harrison had worked as a welder in a large factory in Pittsburgh. In his spare time, Walter had always been an enthusiastic hobbyist. He especially enjoyed wood-

Exhibit A Subscriber profiles	Magazine A	Magazine B
Median income	$36,780	$29,545
Own home	90.3%	68.5%
Own vacation home	16.6%	3.2%
College graduate	51.2%	37.9%
Some college	83.6%	64.4%
Business owner or executive	55.5%	36.1%
Professional	18.8%	9.6%
Leisuretime pursuits:		
Antiques (collecting)	11.2%	9.7%
Boating	17.5%	10.5%
Fishing	23.9%	27.3%
Gardening	19.2%	12.5%
Golf	30.2%	20.6%
Tennis	18.6%	22.2%

working, metalcraft, and jewelry making. His wife, Phyllis, was equally talented with her hands. Expert in sewing, needlecraft, and designing patterns, she made most of her own clothes as well as those of their two small children. Shortly after Walter lost his job, the two opened The Craft Depot. They sell all types of materials, tools, kits, and accessories for a wide variety of crafts.

During their first nine months in business, neither Phyllis nor Walter drew a salary. They used up most of their savings to redesign, furnish, and stock the store and to manage their personal expenses. First-year sales totaled slightly over $70,000. After deducting their cost of goods, rent, utilities, and other operating expenses, their income statement showed a loss of about $500. By the end of the following year, however, they were in the black—and both were earning modest salaries. They built up a loyal clientele by offering quality merchandise at fair prices, prompt and friendly attention, and demonstrated expertise. A major contributor to their success was their willingness to take time out to answer questions and explain the more complicated aspects of craftwork to their customers.

Because of their location, however, the Harrisons felt that growth was limited. Both had read a number of books on mail-order selling. They were intrigued by its possibilities. It seemed to offer a way to expand their business without detracting from store sales. With a large basement in the building, they felt they had enough room to set up a fair-sized mail-order operation.

They budgeted $8,000 for their initial venture. They planned to offer two of their most popular kits in one magazine advertisement that would run one-sixth of a page. Their schedule called for inserting the ad for two successive months, starting with the November issue. Phyllis wrote away for cost and readership information to about 10 consumer publications she felt would be suitable for their purpose. After comparing all details, the Harrisons narrowed the field down to two. (Subscriber profiles for both are shown in Exhibit A.) The cost of space would run approximately the same in either magazine. However, the national circulation of magazine B is nearly 60,000 more than magazine A's circulation of 227,000.

Questions

1. If you were advising the Harrisons, which of the two magazines would you choose? Why? Explain your reasoning.

2. Do you agree with their plans to offer two kits, rather than one, in their ad? Why or why not?

Case 6.3
Cathy's Jewelry
Boutique

Last year, Timothy and Catherine Neill revisited a regional shopping center in southern Texas not too far from San Antonio. A small, empty store caught their eye. Apparently, the previous tenant had recently closed down. The two felt that this would be an excellent spot for the fashionable jewelry shop they had been planning to open. Undaunted by the stiff competition they would face from three much larger stores in the mall, they signed a long-term lease. Two of the competitive outlets were units of well-known chains. The third was an independent retailer.

After a strong opening in mid-November, Cathy's Jewelry Boutique had an excellent Christmas season. The Neills attributed much of their holiday volume to their attractive window display. In their single large show window, they had introduced a New England winter scene, replete with miniature pine trees, a snow-covered window base, reindeer and sleigh, and a mechanical Santa. Gift-wrapped watches, necklaces, and other jewelry items were tastefully arranged throughout. The display drew praise not only from shoppers but from other mall retailers as well.

Right after the New Year, Tim and Marie changed the display to a "Pre-Valentine's Day" theme. Dressing the window in red, pink, and gold, they adorned the jewelry on display with little Cupids, hearts, and bows and arrows. A giant heart-shaped background sign, pierced with a large golden arrow, added to the total effect. Even the hand-printed price tickets were heart-shaped. The fan-shaped center display featured a compelling array of gold bracelets of many different designs. The bracelets were set into large trays covered with white satin.

Again, many favorable comments were forthcoming. Before February 14th arrived, the Neills were confident they had discovered a significant differential advantage that was bound to distinguish their store from those of their competitors. They decided they would trim their window twice each month. This way, the throngs of mall "regulars" would be continually exposed to new settings and different merchandise. At home, one Sunday afternoon, they set about devising a promotional calendar for the three-month period beginning March 1st. First, they divided the period into segments, each approximately two weeks in length. Then, they searched for interesting window themes for those segments. After dinner that evening, they began to talk about appropriate color combinations, materials, and props to use in connection with each theme they had selected.

Questions
1. Refer to the current calendar. Prepare a schedule of biweekly window changes for the months of September, October, and November.

2. Suggest an interesting theme to use for each window display.

3. Select an appropriate color scheme for each change.

Case 6.4
Microtech Home
Computers, Inc.

Established in 1978, Microtech Home Computers, Inc., is a thriving family owned business with 12 midwestern stores and annual sales of more than $6 million. Stephen Straussberg, Microtech's president, was becoming increasingly dissatisfied with what he perceived to be weak selling skills on the part of the stores' salespeople. He believed that his sales staff were knowledgeable enough about the various brands of home computers, printers, software, and supplies they carried in stock. The professional training program they had gone through when first hired assured their competency in the merchandise and service areas. He was convinced, though, that with improved selling capability, company sales would increase by as much as 25 percent.

Last week, Stephen decided to hire Albert Fisch, a college classmate and close friend of his eldest son. Albert holds a bachelor's degree from one of the top business schools with a specialization in human resources. Albert's initial assignment is to devise an effective sales training program for the company. Never having had sales experience, Albert found it quite difficult to plan a sensible and worthwhile approach to the problem. Finally, he came up with the following procedure:

1. Call a meeting at the central office with the top-producing salespeople in the company.
2. Explore their views as to: *(a)* the sales training needs of both present and new salespeople, *(b)* tentative goals for the training program,

(c) the more important topics to be covered, and *(d)* estimates of the time needed to adequately cover each topic.

3. After the meeting:
   a. Set specific program objectives—in behavioral terms.
   b. Devise a program outline and time schedule.
   c. Specify the instructional methods and prepare the materials to be used.
   d. Decide who will give the instruction.
   e. Propose a valid method of evaluating program outcomes.
   f. Do a cost analysis of the entire project.
   g. Sell the project to Mr. Straussberg.

Questions
1. Evaluate Albert's approach. Does it appear thorough? Do you agree with all of his steps? Can you think of anything you would like to add to it?

2. In your judgment, what instructional methods would be best suited to a sales training program?

The Bettmann Archive, Inc.

RETAILING FOR THE NEXT 20 YEARS

Courtesy American Air Lines

22   **Looking Forward in Time**

Courtesy Sears, Roebuck & Co., Chicago

LOOKING FORWARD IN TIME

Your Study Objectives

After you have studied this chapter, you will
understand:

1. The more evident trends in demographics and the
   implications they hold for tomorrow's retailers.
2. Some of the technological and socioeconomic
   developments we can expect between now and
   the early years of the 21st century.
3. Predictions about vital components of the retailing
   mix for the next several decades.
4. How a number of different retail types are likely
   to fare in the next several decades.

Epilogue

By now you have already learned much about modern-day retailing. You were introduced to a wide variety of retail organizations and to some characteristics of the environments they must operate in: socio-economic, technological, and legal. You learned about the four basic managerial functions, strategic and tactical planning, sales forecasting, and retail research. You have gained insights into both the psychological and sociocultural aspects of human motivation and shopping behavior, and various segmentation approaches used by retailers. You were shown some of the financial aspects of business management. Operational details were clarified for you: location choice and facility construction, the management of human resources, merchandise budgeting and control, pricing, retail buying, store services, and management of the promotion mix.

Prologue to the 21st Century

In this concluding chapter, we speculate about conditions that retail companies are likely to face between now and the early years of the 21st century.[1] To accomplish this, we have tried to evaluate current trends and then extrapolate them into the future. Of course, we recognize that considerable, even radical, changes may take place—for change is an inevitable attribute of life. It is also a prime quality of modern retailing. Certainly, tomorrow's successful retailers will be those who anticipate and adapt to environmental change.[2]

Demographic Predictions

An appropriate point of departure for speculation across the next few decades might well be a review and interpretation of consumer demographics. Although we certainly will have to confront other, unpredictable moderating factors, we can begin by extending trends already apparent by the early 1980s. In Chapter 3, we pointed out a number of specific and ongoing changes in our nation's demographics. Now, in the pages that follow, we conjecture about the near future with regard to these trends. They are discussed in the same order as in Chapter 3. For further understanding, you may wish to refer back to some of the charts and tables that accompanied the earlier discussion.

Perhaps many of the comments will prove valid—all the way through to the year 2010.

Our Population Will Continue to Grow

Early in the 21st century, world population will most likely surpass the seven-billion mark. Our own growth rate appears rather modest when compared to those of many other nations, especially the less-developed countries. Based on current trends in our birth and death rates, an assumption of 1 percent growth in the country each year

Continued population growth will lead to increased demand for home-improvement services like explanatory literature and in-store representatives along with the do-it-yourself merchandise.

Courtesy Sears, Roebuck & Co., Chicago

between now and the year 2000 would appear reasonable, even conservative. With some 226 million people recorded by the 1980 census, we can expect to be 245 or 250 million strong by 1990. By the end of the century we can look forward to 275 million consumers. Chances are that this number may be even higher, since another baby boom along the way is a distinct possibility.[3] These projections, of course, preclude the outbreak of a major war or other catastrophe.

Such potential promises well for all types of retailers. Goods and services must be provided for an additional 25 or 30 million people. Sales at general merchandise outlets and stores that supply the basics (food, clothing, household furnishings and supplies, and the like) should trend steadily upward. So should the sales of service retailers, especially those who offer health, shelter, and transportation services. The volume of discretionary buying will rise along with growing consumer affluence. Purchases of cars, furniture, major appliances, private homes, boats, and other luxury goods will tend to keep pace with the growing sales of necessities.

Marriage Will Remain Popular, but the Divorce Rate Will Continue to Rise

Over the next 25 years, the marriage rate should not deviate much from the 10 marriages per 1,000 population figure around which it has hovered since the early 1900s. Long-term divorce trends, however, reveal a different story. Were divorces among Americans to continue in the same fast track we have witnessed since the 1960s, the rate may reach 7 or 8 per 1,000 well before the year 2000.

What are the implications for the retailing sector? Among other things, there will be need to provide millions of apartments or homes for the newly divorced. These residences must then be equipped with household furnishings, appliances, and other goods and stocked with food and supplies. Dining out, whether in fast-food or sit-down restaurants will grow increasingly popular. Demand is also certain to increase for products and services that have special appeal for divorced people.

Millions of New Households Will Be Formed

Between 1960 and 1970, the number of households in the country expanded by about 20 percent. Since 1970, the household formation rate has accelerated further, with the nonfamily type increasing much more rapidly than the traditional family household. If we project a growth of only 1 percent a year for family households and double that percentage for the nonfamily variety, this is how our future might look:

	By 1990 (000)	By 2000 (000)
Family	65,959	72,859
Nonfamily	26,363	32,136
Total	92,322	104,995

Moreover, the average household size has been shrinking and will most likely continue to shrink. From some 2.73 people per household in 1981, we may see it drop to 2.3 by the year 2000. As a result of these changes, most of the implications for retailers already discussed will apply. We might also expect that, over time, smaller residences will become popular. Moreover, because of steadily rising construction costs, more and more individuals and families will be tempted to share their apartments and homes with others. Demand should also increase for smaller-sized packages of foods, detergents, and other household necessities.

Urban Population Will Continue to Grow

Thousands more Americans will move to our metropolitan areas. This movement will give rise to even heavier concentrations of population than we see today. In response to this continuing influx, revitalization efforts will accelerate. There will be programs aimed at rebuilding and renovating older structures, improving and expanding public services, and curbing crime. Local governments will offer outside business organizations special inducements to set up new facilities in town. The renewed growth of our larger cities will present new opportunities for retailers.

Geographical Shifts Will Continue

Both the North Central and Middle Atlantic regions will continue to lose population. Consumers will gravitate toward other areas, with large numbers settling in the South and West. At least in the near term, the Mountain States will reflect the most rapid percentage of population growth of all regions. Leading the pack among all states in attracting new residents will be Nevada, Arizona, Florida, Wyoming, and Utah. These substantial geographical shifts will create pressures for retail organizations to relocate. Where areas show continued population decline, we can expect the volume of retail trade to diminish.

Consumers Will Be Better Educated than Ever Before

By the year 2000, nearly three fourths of our adult population will be high school graduates. Perhaps 25 percent or more will have completed four years of college. Shoppers will be more sophisticated and seek value for their money even more than they do today. To succeed, retailers will have to carry the kinds of merchandise their customers want and at the right selling prices. They will also need to take pains to ensure better communication with their publics.

Life Expectancy Will Continue to Rise, and Age Groups Will Show Significant Changes

The median age of our population, pegged at 30 by the 1980 census, may reach 36 or higher by the end of the century. There will be millions more Americans between the ages of 35 and 64 than we find today. The ranks of senior citizens will also swell. The entire economy will feel the repercussions of an aging society.

Rising Incomes Growing affluence can be expected, since population growth will be highest in those age brackets where household income is ordinarily well above the median. More disposable income will translate to steadily rising sales of luxury goods. At the same time, there will be proportionately fewer young adults in the nation's labor force. This fact alone spells trouble for our national Social Security system. With fewer young workers paying into the system, and millions more consumers drawing out funds, the system's long-term viability is in doubt. With people living longer, the normal retirement age will gradually be extended past 65. More senior citizens will continue to work, ensuring higher levels of spending. As technological improvements are made and new types of jobs open up, the need for retraining large numbers of workers will grow.

American Consumers Will Become Even More Affluent

Almost doubling during the 1970s, the median annual household income for the nation had exceeded $16,500 by 1979. If we project no more than a 50 percent rise over the 1980s, median income will exceed $25,000 by 1990. By the end of the century, it may well have gone beyond the $37,000 mark. In 1979, more than one fourth of all households had annual incomes in excess of $25,000. Up from 4 percent in 1970, this represented a sevenfold increase.

Of course, these figures are expressed in current, not constant dollars. According to one estimate, family incomes are expected to rise to more than $23,000 *in 1974 dollars* by the mid-1990s.[4] By 1990, our work force may consist of some 116 million people. Our annual GNP (gross national product) is likely to surpass $3 trillion before the century's end. Thus, we can look forward to above-average growth in discretionary buying.[5]

More Married Women Will Be Employed than Ever Before

Over the decades, there has been a dramatic increase in the numbers of married women who hold jobs outside the home. Nearly one half of all married women were in the work force by 1980. The figure will most likely reach or exceed 60 percent by the 1990s.

In general, wives who are employed have had more education than those who are not. To working wives, convenience becomes extremely important. They tend to seek individualism and personal identity. When shopping, they are interested in being more efficient.[6]

To meet the needs of these consumers, forward-looking retailers will try to establish outlets that are conveniently located and open for business during suitable hours. These stores should be well run and staffed by courteous and efficient salespeople. They must offer prompt and courteous attention, useful services, and quick checkout.

The Environments of Retailing: General Predictions

Of one thing we can be sure: the retail sector will continue to be affected by its several environments. Retail companies will need to devise strategies to deal with ecological concerns, technological change, economic factors, and the sociological milieu.

Ecology

Undoubtedly, American consumers will express even more concern over ecology in the years ahead than they display today. An air tinged with pessimism may spread through the land. Uppermost in the minds of city planners will be the urgent need to develop more effective methods of combating air, noise, and water pollution. Water shortages will plague many communities. In many states, experimental programs aimed at purifying lakes, streams, and rivers—and at converting saltwater to drinking water—will be well underway. In the 1990s, controlling the excessive air traffic will pose a serious problem. To relieve today's crowded terminals, secondary airports will need to be constructed at some distance from our major metropolitan centers and much of the traffic rerouted to these smaller airports. On the ground, too, vehicular traffic will have become enormously congested. We may expect that

Technological innovations in selling: This racetrack wagering terminal features a high-speed mark-sense reader, optional cash validation, CRT display, and extended keyboard. It prints wagering tickets in less than half a second.

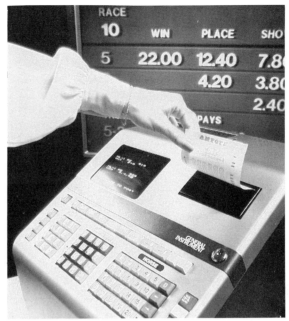

Courtesy General Instrument

local governments will search actively for ways of breaking frequent traffic jams.

Confronting the dual energy-related problems of rising costs and depletion of reserves, the federal government will encourage experimentation with new energy sources. Despite public protestations, strong emphasis will be placed on nuclear facilities for generating electricity.

Among the nation's producers, recyclable and biodegradable packaging will become the norm. Resource conservation will be of paramount concern to federal, state, and local governments, as well as to business and other organizations. As we enter the 21st century, we can expect that many shortages, now bothersome, will become critical. Increasingly, attention will be devoted to locating or devising useful substitutes for wool, cotton, wood, tin, chrome, aluminum, silver, and other substances. Eventually, the rationing of materials essential to national defense may have to be instituted.

Technological Factors Long before the century's end, advances still to come in computer technology will have been introduced into many household appliances. Computer-run air conditioners, microwave ovens, washing machines and dryers, TVs and other equipment will operate more efficiently, using far less electricity. Cable TV will be enjoyed daily in 60 to 70 percent of all households. By the late 1990s, there may be microcompu-

Technological innovation—like this wand scanner widely in use today—will continue to upgrade the effectiveness of the retailer's operation.

Courtesy NCR

ters in one out of every three households. Teleshopping by consumers will be commonplace. In the world of industry, corporate management will be preoccupied with robotizing production facilities. Advances in transportation will bring faster airplanes and trains, new and improved metropolitan mass transit systems hovercraft on our inland waterways, and the like.

In the retail sector, point-of-sale terminals, computer-assisted retail buying and merchandise management, and a considerable degree of automation will be seen almost universally in the larger firms. Automated telephone and mail-order selling methods will be responsible for a substantial percentage of retail sales.

Socioeconomic Factors   Despite possible improvements over the next 10 to 15 years, we can predict that pollution, congestion, and crime will continue to plague many of our cities. On the whole, adults at the start of the 21st century will probably exercise more strenuously and more often than do today's consumers. They are also likely to subscribe to improved nutrition, follow more natural lifestyles, and generally enjoy better health. They will tend to avoid food additives, artificial flavors, excess sugar, and high-cholesterol products. They will consume less meat and more fish, poultry, vegetables, and fruits.

Families will be smaller. A sizable majority of married women will be employed outside the home. The average work week will be somewhat shorter, 34 or 35 hours long. Despite a gradual increase in the

Tomorrow's consumer will eat more vegetables, fruits, and fish—and less meat, food additives, sugar, and high-cholesterol products.

Reprinted with permission of Safeway Stores, Inc., © 1985/Henry Moore, Jr., photo

Adults in the 21st century will show more interest in physical fitness and exercise and will generally enjoy better health.

Courtesy Sears, Roebuck & Co., Chicago

age eligibility requirements for Social Security payments, early retirement will have become popular. As the median age continues to rise, we will witness larger numbers of people making mid-life transitions in their careers and many more older people and senior citizens in attendance at colleges and universities.

For the balance of the 1980s and well into the 1990s, our economy will expand at a slower pace than it has in past decades. Most likely, our GNP will register growth of less than 5 percent each year. The continuing high cost of capital will retard business expansion. Although considerably slowed, inflation's impact on discretionary spending will still be felt.[7] Consumerism will be alive and well and constitute a more potent force affecting both industry and government at all levels. Retail companies will pay closer attention to consumer action groups.

The federal government will continue to exert a ponderous influence on the business world. In spite of numerous attempts to reduce required reporting, the paperwork burden will remain onerous. We can expect that the powers of the Federal Trade Commission will be strengthened further, and antitrust problems examined and acted on with more dispatch. Violations of equal opportunity legislation will lead to prompt action. The institution of a federal freeze on prices and wages remains a possibility in the event of a lengthy period of runaway inflation.

Specific Predictions for Retail Management

In the foreseeable future, we can assume that the majority of successful large retail organizations will continue to exercise their usual vigilance, remaining ever alert to potential opportunities. As always, they will demonstrate an adaptability to environmental change. Experienced top-management teams will become even more sophisticated, relying on computer-assisted techniques to ensure better planning of both long-term strategy and short-range tactical moves. We can ascribe part of the increase in managerial professionalism to intensifying competitive pressures. Another contributing factor may be the realization that executives will have to deal with occasional recessionary drops in consumer spending. Confronted with ever-mounting expenses, managements will demand ever-higher levels of performance. More stringent internal controls will be set into place. We can expect more thorough employee training, a strengthening of oversight measures, and improved strategic goal setting and planning.

Because of their inherent advantages, more vertical marketing systems will be established, become successful, and expand in size. Retailer portfolios will also grow, and new conglomerates will be created. As more of the technical problems of international retailing are worked out, American franchising organizations will seek further and more rapid expansion abroad.[8]

Retail Locations

By the 1990s, our metropolitan areas will be more congested than ever before. The quality of public services like transportation, police and fire protection, trash removal, and bridge and highway maintenance will have deteriorated even further. Yet despite these drawbacks,

By the 1990s, construction of shopping centers like Eastgate Mall in Cincinnati is expected to slow drastically except in a few fast-growing areas.

Courtesy Jacobs, Visconsi & Jacobs Co., Cleveland, OH

rents will continue to rise, with those in even the secondary business districts becoming prohibitive for many independent merchants. Competition will have intensified. Many retailers will seek new locations in smaller cities and towns and in less-populated sections of the country. Some movement into metropolitan CBDs can be expected, however, as downtown districts are revitalized.

Already oversaturated in many places by the mid-1980s, shopping center construction will grind to a near-halt, except in a few fast-growing areas. Many older malls will undergo renovation, and changes in the tenant mix are to be anticipated. As local demographics change, some neighborhood strip centers and community shopping centers will close.

Store Construction Some of today's trends in store construction will continue well into the next century. We can expect to see the units of many chain organizations multiply, despite escalating costs of capital, labor, materials, construction, and equipment. To minimize their investments, retailers will show increasing preference for second-use facilities—those premises formerly used by other retail firms. Renovating and refurbishing these facilities costs a great deal less than new construction. As we have already observed with companies like K mart, Sears, Edison Brothers, and others, new chain store units are likely to be smaller. Reduced interior space translates directly to curtailed energy expenditures. To maximize sales per square foot, retail firms will cut down on nonselling areas, leaving more room for merchandising and selling activities. Movable interior walls and partitions, greater use of boutique and freeform layouts, and flexibility in fixturing will characterize the new stores.

Retail Personnel

Effective management of human resources will remain a high priority with large retail organizations. We will see more sophisticated approaches and techniques used in this area, along with a strengthening of recruitment and selection systems. A bachelor's degree will have become the minimum educational requirement for openings in middle management. Preference may be extended to applicants who possess a master's degree. More women will be found in middle management positions. Some will have successfully penetrated the domain of top management. Minority group members, too, will have made substantial inroads into the ranks of middle and upper management. Nevertheless, shortages of top executives may be commonplace, and manager recruitment efforts will be hectic. To reduce internal theft, retailers will institute improved methods for screening prospective employees. The polygraph will be frequently used, and internal security systems will be tightened. There will be closer supervision of employees. To increase productivity, management will evaluate and upgrade training programs. Greater use will be made of self-instruction methods, programmed aids, tape and videocassette recorders, and microcomputers. Supervisory training will be enriched with modeling techniques and advanced programs in motivational methods.

Buying and Merchandising

Over the next few years, many resourceful independents will adapt personal computers to their business needs or will purchase more powerful equipment. Computer applications to bookkeeping and payroll will generally come first. Eventually, the retailers will integrate inventory management and other functions. Among the larger companies, efficient merchandise management and control systems will be in place. These are of value in monitoring stock movement and ensuring a more rapid rate of inventory turnover. The procedures will also aid the buying function. Consumer preferences and dislikes can be tracked and store needs for merchandise determined. Item and classification movement can be monitored to assist in managerial decision making. Purchase orders will be prepared by computer.

Many companies will strive to simplify their assortments. At the same time, they may add new services that can be profitably sold. A majority of firms will have adopted the retail method of inventory valuation.

Good use will be made of vendor rating and analysis systems. In their search for new sources of supply, retailers will turn to computer applications. Buyers will participate in seminars and workshops aimed at increasing their negotiating skills.

Customer Services

Over the next 20 years, we will notice little change in the retail sector in the more traditional service offerings. Some further expansion of store hours can be expected, especially where merchants face strong competition or declining sales or are eager to differentiate their firms. Already, free delivery is almost a thing of the past. We will see further increases in the delivery fees now charged by department and chain stores. Similarly, the charges for gift wrapping merchandise will at least double before the turn of the century. Returned goods policies will reflect tighter managerial oversight and control. The use of purchase credit by consumers will reach new highs. Many retailers will continue to offer open credit, installment, and layaway plans. Large companies with sizable numbers of charge account customers will more actively promote revolving credit and/or option terms plans. Some will relinquish their present credit arrangements in favor of bank card systems like VISA and MasterCard. These are less troublesome and less costly alternatives.

Other firms will discontinue long-established consumer services because they fail to return sufficient profit for the required investment in labor, equipment, and selling space. Coffee shops, hairstyling services, and watch repairs are among the potential candidates for discontinuance. On the other hand, some easily handled, low-cost services will become more available. A possible example would be the distribution of manufacturer-supplied printed materials and samples designed to help shoppers make purchase decisions.

Overall, however, we can expect that by the year 2000 services will account for a much larger percentage of total retail sales than they do now. Favored will be those services on which the firm can earn healthy gross margins. Among the more likely ones are all types of financial, health, insurance, and advisory services, beauty clinics, and classes on diverse subjects of current public interest.

Promotion

On the eve of the 21st century, a substantial majority of retail companies will still be relying on the percentage-of-sales method for determining their promotion budgets. They will, however, evaluate the effectiveness of their promotional efforts more carefully. To maximize their advertising investment, more thorough intermedia comparisons and analyses of results will be made. While newspapers will still attract the largest share of the retailer's advertising budget, direct mail, TV (regular and cable), and radio will be used much more often than they are today. In the display area, more emphasis will be placed

Sears Store of the Future places its cosmetic boutique in the center of the apparel floor. Super-sized backlit graphics provide both an introduction and an invitation to the well-stocked cosmetics lines.

Courtesy Sears, Roebuck & Co., Chicago

on lifestyle merchandising and boutique arrangements. Retailers will prefer their displays to be built up high and to be well packed.

To help offset climbing labor costs, retailers will convert more interior space to self-selection and self-service. They will also employ more part-time salespeople. To help upgrade their employees' selling skills, many retailers will contact outside professional training groups.

Tomorrow's retailers are likely to pay close attention to consumer complaints. They will evidence more concern over the ecology and refuse to sell merchandise that might contribute to environmental pollution. They may be expected to participate more actively in the community.

Speculating about the Future

We conclude this final chapter by speculating about what is likely to occur between today and the end of this century in some specific retail types. We make these predictions in the light of projected population estimates, the rapid growth rate of new households, probable technological advances, known socioeconomic trends, and other indicators.

The predictions are set forth in Table 22.1, arranged so you can review them readily. We hope some interested persons may save them until the year 2000, to be checked against actual events.

Table 22.1 **Predictions regarding** **some retail types**	Boutiques	The continued popularity of small, attractive boutiques is certain. To woo specific consumer segments, many merchants will attempt to position their stores more precisely. By offering more personal attention, they will strengthen their rapport with their clienteles. To create more shopper interest, larger stores will devote more space to boutique arrangments. This will be a welcome relief from the traditional gridiron layout.
	Catalog stores	The costs of small appliances, jewelry, and other merchandise customarily offered by the catalog store will continue to rise. This factor, along with sporadic bouts of inflationary pressure, will ensure continued strong consumer interest. Business should be brisk for many years to come.
	Chains	Established chains are certain to pursue expansion—the majority by adding units, others through acquisitions and mergers. Their managements will firm up systems and strengthen internal controls. Simultaneously, we can look forward to a shaking out of the weaker organizations. More selective targeting of consumer groups is indicated. Experimentation with new store prototypes will take place. Additional chain operations will be founded; these will include service as well as specialty retailers. Look for rapid growth in many of these new companies.
	Department stores	These large-scale organizations will continue to experience strong competition from mass merchandisers and specialty chains. In wrestling with the problems of normally high markups, managements will strive to exercise more stringent controls over all business aspects. This will be especially true in areas such as personnel, merchandise management, and shrinkage. Portfolio strategies will reflect interest in diversifying into alternate forms of retailing. Direct marketing activity should be brisk, and more use will be made of TV. Service offerings will account for a healthy share of the sales volume.
	Discount stores	Discount stores will face intensifying competition from the fast-growing complex of off-price specialty chains. They will gradually evolve into promotional department stores. Struggling to maintain adequate gross margin levels and obtain reasonable end-of-year profits, they will upgrade their merchandise assortments. New lines will be added. Popularly priced goods will be replaced with higher quality merchandise. Once again, the wheel of retailing will apply.
	Franchises	Unfavorable publicity associated with franchising companies will occasionally hit the nation's press. However, the retail franchise will remain an attractive investment vehicle. Competition will intensify. In each major retail field, weaker franchising organizations will lose market share to the top two or three companies. Franchise arrangements will be

Table 22.1
(continued)

	seen more frequently in nontraditional merchandise areas, the retailing of services, and nonstore approaches.
Independents	Over the next 25 years, independent retailing will most likely reflect much the same picture as it does today. Several hundred thousand new ventures will still be launched annually, and roughly similar numbers of store closings will take place. Overall, however, we can look forward to a slow and gradual attrition among independents as chains and franchise organizations continue to expand.* Accelerating growth in nonstore methods of retailing will also contribute to the decline of the small-scale operator.†
Leased departments	Between now and the year 2000, we can expect large departmentized stores to concentrate on paring their operating costs. Managements will try to maximize space productivity and enhance higher-volume/higher-gross margin departments. These retailers will then seek to lease the less profitable sections to capable outside individuals and firms. Thus, the total number of leased departments should increase considerably. Many lessees will grow into strong chain organizations.
Mass merchandisers	The ranks of mass merchandising retailers will continue to swell, if only because of population growth and the rapid rate of household formation. Moreover, these organizations will experiment with adding new lines even as they drop less productive merchandise from their stores. To keep labor and overhead costs down, many will install warehousing equipment and supermarket methods.
Nonstore retailers	Although vending machine operators will remain a comparatively small segment of American retailing, we can look forward to some expansion in the entertainment field. The numbers of companies and individuals involved in house-to-house selling will shrink, even as the well-established party plan organizations increase their sales volume and consolidate their hold on the market. Modest growth may be expected among mail-order houses. Greater growth potential lies in those direct marketing firms that make use of the air media: TV and radio. Although the catalog store will continue to flourish over the next decade or so, it is bound to give way before the exploding field of interactive communications.
Service retailers	We visualize a bright future in the service sector. Health care, communications, and educational services will make impressive gains over the next quarter of a century. Already, government deregulation has brought competition in both air transportation and banking services to a feverish pitch. We can expect occasional price wars among the airlines and rate wars among the nation's banks. New types of service retailers will appear on the scene. Hotels, motels,

Table 22.1 *(concluded)*		and other lodging places will vie with one another to attract a larger share of the market. Movie theaters will fare poorly, diminishing in number and gradually giving way to newer forms and places of entertainment.
	Specialty stores	By the year 2000, there will be many more single-line and limited-line specialty retailers. An important consideration in the expansion of successful specialty chains will be proper positioning. Middle market locations will prove popular for many of the new units. Their managements will emphasize personal service.‡
	Supermarkets	As in other fields of retailing, we will see some weaker grocery operations fail. Overstored conditions presently exist in many cities. Yet there are still fast-growing areas where additional store units are needed, for example: parts of the South, the West, and the mountain states. Supermarkets will still suffer from short markups on the bulk of their merchandise and intense competition for the consumer's food dollar. To counter these problems, they will continue to seek innovative approaches and technology. More box stores, combination stores, and newer types will appear. Supermarkets will increase their scrambling by adding entire new lines, services, and departments. We have already witnessed sizable increases in the cubic footage of their frozen food cabinets and the introduction of take-out prepared foods, salad bars, bakeries, prescription pharmacies, garden centers, banking facilities, and other innovations.
	Warehouse stores	Demand for furniture, home furnishings, and appliances of all types will strongly increase by the end of the century. A large proportion of new households will be established by young people with limited financial backing who are just starting out on their careers. This should lead to increasing numbers of furniture showroom-warehouses with higher individual sales volume. The same holds true for home furnishings and appliance stores.

* John F. Cady, "Structural Trends in Retailing: The Decline of Small Business," *Journal of Contemporary Business* 5 (Spring 1976), pp. 67–90.

† Elizabeth C. Hirschman and Larry J. Rosenberg, "Emerging Retail Systems: A Public Policy Perspective," *The Growth of Non-store Retailing: Implications for Retailers, Manufacturers, and Public Policy Makers* (New York: Institute of Retail Management, New York University, 2 January 1979), p. 51.

‡ Malcolm P. McNair and Eleanor G. May, "The Next Revolution of the Retailing Wheel," *Harvard Business Review* 56 (September–October 1978), p. 86.

Health care services will make impressive gains in the next 25 years.

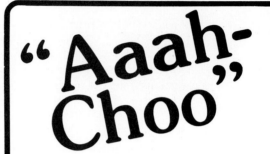

"Aaah-" Choo

Sneezes and sniffles
  fever and flu
Why does it always seem
  to happen to you

Just when your doctor isn't there
  Is when you need our Urgent Care

No appointment is needed
  there's no need to fear
We're open till eleven
  every night of the year.

Suburban Heights
Medical Center

URGENT CARE CENTER

333 Dixie Highway, Chicago Heights, IL — **756-0119**

Courtesy Suburban Heights Medical Center

Summary

In addition to keeping abreast of trends, retailers over the next two decades must remain adaptable to change. We may expect many of today's trends in our national demographics to continue: population growth, an increasing divorce rate, millions of new households, urban expansion, geographical shifts, better-educated consumers, changes in age groupings, rising life expectancy, more affluence, and a greater proportion of working wives.

Change and progress will also be noted with regard to ecology and our technology. Among the many socioeconomic aspects bound to affect the retailing sector are more natural lifestyles, better diets, smaller families, early retirement, and more midlife transitions. We can also expect slower economic growth, continued consumerism, and improved retailer response to that movement.

New directions may be expected, too, in management's retailing mix. More retailers will gravitate new stores to smaller cities and towns and to revitalized CBDs. Shopping center construction will slow down, weaker centers will be weeded out, and many older malls will be renovated. Store construction will accent flexibility and more use of freeform and boutique layouts. Personnel will concentrate on improved selection methods, better training and supervision, and more women and minority group members in middle management. Many independent retailers will adapt the personal computer to their business needs. We can also anticipate that retailers will drop marginal services, raise fees for those they retain, and make more use of credit. Financial, health, insurance, and similar profit-producing services will account for a larger proportion of total retail sales than they do today. Retailers will evaluate their promotional efforts more carefully. Although newspapers will remain the major retailing medium, more use will be made of direct mail, TV, and radio.

Review Questions

1. Specify at least five of the predictions outlined in the chapter for consumer demographics. Briefly discuss their implications for the retailer.

2. Name four states that appear to be attracting large numbers of residents.

3. Briefly describe retailing's technological environment on the eve of the 21st century.

4. List a few of the *(a)* sociological factors and *(b)* economic conditions that we may encounter in the near future.

5. With regard to new store locations, where are tomorrow's retailers most likely to look?

6. How may new store construction during the 1990s differ from that of the past?

7. Identify three specific predictions for the retailer in each of these areas: *(a)* human resources management, *(b)* buying and merchandising, and *(c)* customer services.

8. Suggest at least three commonly offered services that are likely to be discontinued in the next decade or so.

9. Give examples of four services that may offer considerable profit potential for the retail company.

10. Comment briefly on retail management's probable attitude toward advertising and sales promotion in the future.

11. Briefly indicate the likely prospects of each of the following types of retailers:
    a. Catalog stores.
    b. Discount stores.
    c. Leased departments.
    d. Service retailers.

Discussion Questions

1. By the year 2000, there may be as many as 100 million households in the country. What do you think the rapid growth in household formation portends for the retailer? Be specific.

2. In the future, we can expect retailers to pay even closer attention to consumers than they do today. Give an opinion about the possible reason(s) for this.

3. What advice do you have for department store management in light of each of the following statements?
    a. Consumers will be better educated than ever before.
    b. American consumers will become even more affluent.

4. List three or four ecological problems. Speculate about the steps a major retail chain like Sears, Roebuck or K mart might take to help improve the situation.

5. Suggest a list of personal and educational qualifications that would be useful in screening candidates for retail management positions.

6. Propose an outline for the content of a training program aimed at:
    a. Producing effective salespeople for a chain store.
    b. Developing store managers.

7. As the president of a small chain of supermarkets, you are aware of the consumer trend toward more natural lifestyles and improved diets. What steps might you take toward applying this knowledge?

8. A department store branch faces severe local competition in its apparel lines from a popular mass merchandiser and two off-price outlets. Make some recommendations about how store management might meet this challenge.

Notes

[1] For fascinating glimpses into what life in general and the retailing sphere in particular may be like in the future, see: William Lazer, "The 1980s and Beyond: A Perspective," *MSU Business Topics* 25 (Spring 1977), pp. 21–35; "Mary Wells Lawrence Looks at Consumers in the Year 2000," *Advertising Age* 48, (1 August 1977), pp. 39*ff*; "The Shape of Things to Come," *Stores* 60 (June 1978), pp. 49–51; George J. Stolnitz, "Our Main Population Patterns: Radical Shifts, Cloudy Prospects," *Business Horizons* 25 (July–August 1982), pp. 91–98; "What Life Will Be Like Twenty Years in the Future," *U.S. News & World Report,* 14 (January 1974), pp. 73–75.

[2] Ronald D. Michman, "Changing Patterns in Retailing," *Business Horizons* 22 (October 1979), p. 38.

[3] Lazer, "1980s and Beyond," p. 32.

[4] "What Life Will Be Like," pp. 73–75.

[5] Lazer, "1980s and Beyond," p. 28.

[6] Suzanne H. McCall, "Meet the 'Workwife'," *Journal of Marketing* 41 (July 1977), pp. 55–64. See also: Fred D. Reynolds, Melvin R. Crask, and William D. Wells, "The Modern Feminine Life Style," *Journal*

of Marketing 41 (July 1977), pp. 37–45; Leonard L. Berry, "The Time-Buying Consumer," *Journal of Retailing* 55 (Winter 1979), pp. 58–69.

[7]Rajan Chandran, Don Desalvia, and Allan Young, "The Impact of Current Economic Forces on Small Business," *Journal of Small Business Management* 15 (January 1977), pp. 30–36.

[8]Bruce J. Walker and Michael J. Etzel, "The Internationalization of U.S. Franchise Systems: Progress and Procedures," *Journal of Marketing* 37 (April 1973), p. 46.

APPENDIX: RETAILING AS A CAREER

Getting your college education will represent a long, arduous, but vital preparation for your eventual career. *Before* you graduate, however, you will need to make one or two important decisions. At the very least, you should decide on the field of endeavor you would like to enter. At some future point, of course, you may shelve your early plans in favor of a completely different career objective. Yet it is never too early to plan that first step. You also need to determine the kind of position best suited for your talents, personality, and skills. It is often difficult for college students to think through these two problems. Many wrongly postpone their decision making until after they graduate.

Bear in mind that you do not graduate alone. Many others will be graduating along with you. Moreover, even larger numbers will be leaving other colleges and universities throughout your state during the same month. All this means that many young people, newly equipped with degrees, will be looking for job openings at approximately the same time of year.

This is exactly the kind of situation where the early bird axiom applies. It would certainly make sense to conduct your job search early, well before your graduation date. It would also make sense to plan an effective job-hunting program in advance. We hope you will find this appendix of assistance.

Even now, though graduation may be far off, you ought to devote some time to objective self-appraisal. Give some thought to what you believe to be your more significant strengths and weaknesses. List them on a sheet of paper. Also put down your answers to such questions as:

- What areas will my academic education prepare me for?
- What special talents do I have? Abilities? Aptitudes? Skills?
- Where do my interests lie?
- What are my short-term goals? My primary objective? Secondary objectives?
- Where do I see myself five years after graduating from college? Ten years afterward?

When you have finished, put your responses away for a week or two. Then reconsider them. Improve on them so that they are even more precise. The clearer the self-portrait you manage to paint, the more able you will be to make an appropriate decision when the time approaches for you to launch your career.

Is Retailing for You?

Before deciding on the kind of career you wish to pursue, you owe it to yourself to examine both the advantages and the disadvantages of a retailing career.

What Has Retailing to Offer?

One fact is certain: opportunities abound in retailing. The industry consists of more than 1.6 million organizations. Collectively, these companies depend on more than 13 million employees to produce over $1 trillion in sales each year. While the majority are independent retailers, there are many thousands of chain store organizations. Many chains count their store units in the hundreds. Some, like Radio Shack, have thousands of stores. Practically every unit is headed by a store manager and staffed with other personnel. Management people of all types and levels work at their central offices. Sears, the country's largest retailer, has more than 450,000 employees. K mart employs a quarter of a million people. J. C. Penney employees number 175,000.

At any one time, the outlook for gainful employment in retailing is certainly bright. Retail organizations are located everywhere and numerous job openings are always available. There is also an astonishing variety of retailing environments from which to choose. There are many department stores; Dayton-Hudson, Macy's, Dillard's, Marshall Field, Foley's, and the May Company are some examples. There are giant mass merchandisers like Zayre and K mart. There are discount, specialty, drug, food, and home improvement chains, voluntary and cooperative chains, and franchise operations. There are direct selling organizations, mail-order houses, and other nonstore retailers. There is also the huge and still-expanding realm of service retailing with its own, nearly unlimited, diverse environments.

Opportunities for advancement are excellent. For capable performers who learn quickly and work hard, promotion into higher management ranks can be rapid. One explanation for this is that, in retailing, a *manager* of some kind is needed for every seven or eight people employed by a company. By way of comparison, the ratio of managers to the rank and file in manufacturing runs about 1 in 14.

In the retailing industry, women and minority group members can look forward confidently to upward mobility within the organization. The larger companies carefully follow affirmative action principles. They take pains to avoid any suspicion of discrimination among employees because of sex, age, race, marital status, or similar factors.

Many people thoroughly enjoy retail work. It gives them the opportunity to meet other people—employees as well as customers—of many different types. Working conditions, too, can be favorable. Many facilities are modern, aesthetically pleasing, air-conditioned during the summer months, and properly heated in cold weather. Another benefit they enjoy is the employee discount on store merchandise. (Of course, the discount percentage offered will vary from one firm to the next.)

There is one last, significant benefit of a retailing career to be mentioned. After having gained sufficient experience, you might consider starting a retail enterprise of your own. Ease of entry is a singular characteristic of the industry.

There Are a Few Drawbacks   What are the disadvantages involved in a retailing position? Two well-known drawbacks are the hours and the pay. Either may discourage some people from entering the field. Store retailers must arrange their store hours to suit consumer needs. Weekends are busy shopping times. So are evenings during the week. Often, stores are open for six or seven days a week and for a 10- or 12-hour day. Many shopping centers are open during the week from 9:30 or 10 A.M. until 9:30 at night, on Saturdays from 9:30 A.M. to 6 P.M., and even on Sundays (often, from noon to 5 P.M.). Rotating shifts are usually necessary to cover the store. Department managers and other middle managers may be required to work Saturdays, evenings, and some Sundays. Central office personnel may be off on weekends, but in many sectors of retailing it is traditional for executives to be present at peak selling periods to look after the store.

It is true that the salaries of salespeople and other entry-level retail workers are lower than those offered in other industries. In your case, though, you will not be starting at the bottom. Young people with college backgrounds are usually assigned to an executive training program. These programs lead to higher levels of management and possibly to top management in time. It should be mentioned, too, that retail companies prefer applicants with some experience—all the more reason for you to consider part-time employment with a retailer while attending college or during the summer. Experience will help you land a position more easily.

In any industry, starting salaries are affected by a variety of factors: the size of the company, the kinds of products and/or services it offers, where the firm is located, and so on. For example, the salary offered a management trainee by a West Coast retailer may be higher than that paid for an identical position in the South or Midwest. Generally, retail employees in metropolitan areas will command higher salaries than those in more rural areas.

Salaries for college graduates vary widely. Those offered by chain store organizations may range between $900 and $1,400 a month.

Many of the better department stores start trainees with bachelor's degrees at annual salaries from $15,000 to $18,000. An applicant with a master's degree may be offered $20,000 to $24,000.

Remember, though, that if you produce, promotion to higher positions will come fast. In the larger chains, store managers can earn from $35,000 all the way up to $70,000 and more.

There is a third drawback to the chain store organization for you to consider. Promotion often means that you are assigned to another, usually larger, unit. Your new store may be located in another city or another state. Thus, there is the ever-present possibility that you may have to relocate.

Characteristics Needed for Success in Retailing

A college degree does not ensure career success. It is true that modern companies do prefer to hire candidates with a higher education for executive development. Retailers also look for specific personality traits, aptitudes, and skills that they believe will contribute to a successful career. The characteristics they seek depend on the type of opening—and these, of course, vary from one kind of company to the next.

They especially seek people who present a good appearance, are able to learn quickly, show initiative, seem willing to work hard, can communicate easily with others, and display good interpersonal relations. They want applicants who are:

adaptable	resourceful
creative	self-confident
enthusiastic	self-disciplined
mature	self-starting
pleasant	stable
poised	willing to accept responsibility
reliable	

The self-rating chart shown in Figure A.1 lists the personal attributes that Abraham and Straus department stores feel are vital to retailing success.

Retailers also look for leadership qualities and skills. They seek people who can exercise good judgment, lead others, make decisions, plan and organize, and set priorities.

Consider the J. C. Penney Company, one of the nation's largest retailers of general merchandise. Its organization comprises more than 170,000 employees who staff over 1,600 stores and the corporation's headquarters. As Figure A.2 indicates, Penney seeks executive trainees who are "achievement-, people-, and opportunity-oriented."

Ways to Get Started

Basically, there are four avenues to a career in retailing:

1. You can go to work for a retail firm.
2. You can start your own retail business.

Figure A.1
Personal attributes vital to success in retailing

RATE YOURSELF AS A RETAIL EXECUTIVE

Consider each attribute individually. First, think about your past experiences—in-school, on-the-job and extracurricular. Have you used the particular attribute for any of these activities? (With "stress tolerance," for instance, perhaps you've had to meet multiple deadlines at the same time.) When you used the attribute, do you feel that you did it well? (If you've experienced "stress" periods, did you

remain cool and organized?) In other words, does your experience, no matter how minimal, indicate that you definitely have the attribute in question? If so, place a checkmark in the "ability" column.

In your experience, did you enjoy utilizing one of the attributes listed? If you did, consider the retailing environment descriptions for the attribute. Would you want to be responsible for using the attribute in this way on a continuing basis? Does it sound exciting to you? If yes, place a checkmark in the "desire" column.

When you've finished this process for all nine attributes, take a hard look at the descriptions again. Are there any individual attributes you do not possess or would not want to find as a requirement in your career? Does the overall description of the retailing environment excite you? Do you have the ability and desire to utilize a majority of the attributes described on a continuing basis?

If so, you might be the kind of person we need—and we might have the kind of opportunity and experience you seek.

ATTRIBUTES REQUIRED	ability	desire	IN THE RETAILING ENVIRONMENT
ANALYTICAL SKILLS: ability to solve problems; strong numerical ability for analysis of facts and data for planning, managing and controlling.			Retail executives are problem solvers. Knowledge and understanding of past performance and present circumstances form the basis for action and planning.
CREATIVITY: ability to generate and recognize imaginative ideas and solutions; ability to recognize the need for and to be responsive to change.			Retail executives are idea people. Successful buying results from sensitive, aware decisions, while merchandising requires imaginative, innovative techniques.
DECISIVENESS: ability to make quick decisions and render judgments, take action and commit oneself to completion.			Retail executives are action people. Whether it's new fashion trends or customer desires, decisions must be made quickly and confidently in this ever-changing environment.
FLEXIBILITY: ability to adjust to the ever-changing needs of the situation; ability to adapt to different people, places and things; willingness to do whatever is necessary to get the task done.			Retail executives are flexible. Surprises in retailing never cease. Plans must be altered quickly to accommodate changes in trends, styles and attitudes, while numerous ongoing activities cannot be ignored.
INITIATIVE: ability to originate action rather than wait to be told what to do and ability to act based on conviction.			Retail executives are doers. Sales volumes, trends and buying opportunities mean continual action. Opportunities for action must be seized.
LEADERSHIP: ability to inspire others to trust and respect your judgment; ability to delegate and to guide and persuade others.			Retail executives are managers. Running a business means depending on others to get the work done. One person cannot do it all.
ORGANIZATION: ability to establish priorities and courses of action for self and/or others; skill in planning and following up to achieve results.			Retail executives are jugglers. A variety of issues, functions and projects are constantly in motion. To reach your goals, priorities must be set, work must be delegated to others.
RISK-TAKING: willingness to take calculated risks based on thorough analysis and sound judgment and to accept responsibility for the results.			Retail executives are courageous. Success in retailing often comes from taking calculated risks and having the confidence to try something new before someone else does.
STRESS TOLERANCE: ability to perform consistently under pressure, to thrive on constant change and challenge.			Retail executives are resilient. As the above descriptions should suggest, retailing is fast-paced and demanding.

Courtesy Abraham & Straus

3. You can buy an existing retail business.
4. You can contract with a franchisor to open your own franchised unit.

The pros and cons of the last three alternatives have been discussed elsewhere in this book. Since college graduates who enter retailing usually choose the first approach, the rest of this appendix deals with securing a position with a retail company.

Figure A.2
Successful managers at
J. C. Penney

Who We're Looking For

As a college graduate, you don't need prior work experience to become a JCPenney associate. But we are looking for particular kinds of people. People who can apply their interests and talents and develop the management skills needed to run our complex organization.

Our most successful managers tend to be. . .

Achievement Oriented
They're skilled in finding the best ways to get a job done. They have the initiative to get it started, as well as the urgency and stamina to see it through without regard for the amount of work required. They have a commitment to their work and aren't satisfied with average results.

People Oriented
They're able to get the job done through the best use of people. They are tactful and outgoing. They communicate clearly and are sincerely interested in the development of those they supervise. They're good team players and have a healthy sense of competition.

Opportunity Oriented
They're open to new ideas no matter where they come from. They aren't averse to changing their plans of action if better ones present themselves. They're not tied down to one location but are ready to move elsewhere in the company for greater challenges and more opportunities.

If you have these qualities, you are a potential JCPenney associate. And, we hope you'll get to know us better.

Courtesy J. C. Penney

Targeting at a Retail Career

Retailing represents a gigantic slice of the American economy. Each year, the field accounts for well over one third of our gross national product. In this tremendous arena there are all kinds of career opportunities. Many large retail companies employ a variety of professionals: accountants, legal experts, architects, engineers, real estate people, nurses, and so on. Your background and personal objectives may lead you toward any number of different positions. A few examples are listed below.

If your interests lie in:

Merchandising and sales: buyer, department manager, group manager, merchandise manager, sales manager, store manager

Operations: customer service manager, maintenance manager, receiving department manager, security manager, warehouse manager

Finance: accountant, bookkeeper, controller, credit manager, EDP manager

Promotion: advertising manager, display manager, promotion manager, public relations manager

Personnel administration: personnel manager, training manager

Your Prospects with Independents and Smaller Retail Chains

Some graduates shy away from the large retail organizations, convinced that they stand a better chance of getting ahead more quickly in a smaller firm. They feel that in large companies the competition for higher positions is too keen and the environment too impersonal. Some remain with the firm that they worked for while attending college.

There is something to be said for opportunities in a small firm or local chain. For one thing, with fewer college-trained executives in the company, opportunities for advancement may be greater. Provided, of course, the person can deliver. For another, there is no doubt that you will gain valuable experience working for a smaller company. You are likely to be assigned to a variety of tasks and given responsibility more rapidly. This training can prepare you well for an eventual shift to a larger organization.

However, your compensation package will probably be smaller than those offered by the bigger retailers. Your long-term potential, too, may be quite limited. Most small and medium-sized companies are sole proprietorships, partnerships, or closely held corporations. Positions in upper management may be barred to you. Normally, you should regard a position in a family-owned business as a dead-end job. Sometimes, though, an opportunity to buy out the owner(s) presents itself.

Your Prospects with Larger Retail Organizations

Major department stores, specialty chains, and other large retailers aggressively recruit college graduates on campus for management training or executive training programs. These are well-coordinated programs that may extend for a number of months, a year, or even longer. Newly hired trainees follow preordained career paths. After an initial orientation, they are exposed to the many facets of the business through job rotation. They gain experience in sales, buying, and merchandising, serve as assistant department managers, and so on. It is common to assign new recruits to sponsors, who assist in their development. Classroom instruction is interspersed with lots of on-the-job training.

Large organizations keep close track of the progress of their trainees and evaluate them regularly. The promotional ladders are clearly established. Provided executive trainees meet management expectations, they can look forward to moving up the ladder to more responsibility. Naturally, the higher up one goes, the fewer the job openings—and the keener the competition.

Career Paths

Being young is no barrier to a retailing career. Your successful performance as an executive trainee can lead to a rapid ascent into management ranks. The retailing world is filled with young people. Many store managers and senior merchandise managers are in their early 30s. Many vice presidents—and even CEOs (chief executive officers)—are in their 40s.

Figure A.3 contains a diagram of the career path of an executive trainee at Abraham & Straus, a top-quality department store chain. The chart shows two basic lines of development: central and store merchandising. The newly hired trainee may be assigned to either

Figure A.3   **Career path chart: Abraham and Straus**

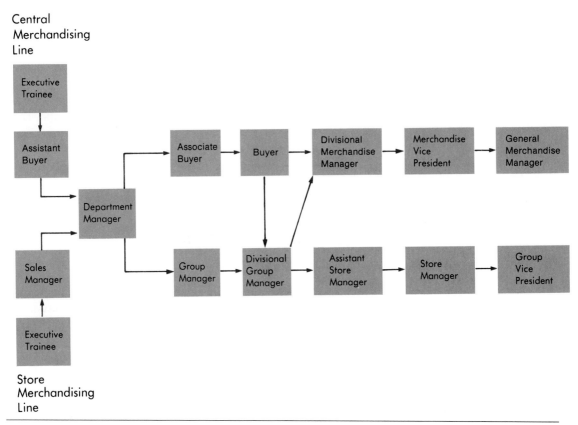

Central
Merchandising
Line

Store
Merchandising
Line

Courtesy Abraham & Straus

the assistant buyer program or the sales manager program. In the first program, for example, the trainee undergoes a 10-week orientation to the buying office and is then made an assistant buyer. In three months, the new assistant buyer is held responsible for an entire merchandise classification. The next promotion is to department manager. From there, he or she may go on to become an associate buyer or group manager. As the chart indicates, still higher positions in management remain as objectives. Like most large retailers, Abraham & Straus pursues a policy of promotion from within the company.

To illustrate still another approach, consider the executive training programs offered by B. Altman's, a fine Fifth Avenue department store. Their programs provide assignments in both merchandising and operations. New merchandising trainees are exposed to the receiving function, advertising, fashion coordination, retail accounting, inven-

**Figure A.4
Growth projections:
Edison Brothers Shoe
Stores, Inc.**

Edison Brothers Shoe Stores, Inc.
PROJECTION & GROWTH CHART
1979-1990

Chandlers, Bakers, Leeds, Burts, The Wild Pair, Joan Bari, & Leased Departments

Year Ending December 31	1979	1980	1981	1982	1983	1984	1985	1986	1987	1988	1989	1990	
Number of Stores	1,037	1,078	1,121	1,166	1,213	1,262	1,312	1,364	1,419	1,476	1,535	1,596	Total New Stores 559/53.9%
Approximate Number of Store Employees	10,370	10,681	11,001	11,331	11,671	12,021	12,382	12,753	13,136	13,530	13,936	14,354	Inc. # of Employees 3984/38.4%
Total Number of Regions	51	53	55	57	59	62	65	68	71	74	77	80	Inc. # of Regions 29/56.9%

ADDITIONAL PROMOTIONS NEEDED TO FILL THE OPPORTUNITIES AVAILABLE BY 1990

Year	1979	1980	1981	1982	1983	1984	1985	1986	1987	1988	1989	1990	Totals
Home Office Executives	28	24	25	26	27	28	29	30	32	33	34	36	352
Regional Managers	7	3	4	5	4	5	4	5	5	6	5	6	59
Store Managers	162	132	138	144	150	156	162	167	175	182	189	197	1954
Assistant Managers	369	314	327	340	355	369	382	397	415	431	448	465	4612
Total Promotions	566	473	494	515	536	558	577	599	627	652	676	704	6977
Promotions Per Day	1.6	1.3	1.4	1.4	1.5	1.5	1.6	1.6	1.7	1.8	1.9	1.9	1.6

Growth projections: Edison Brothers Shoe Stores, Inc. Courtesy, Edison Brothers Shoe Stores, Inc.

tory, and branch store operations. Altman's expects their trainees to reach senior assistant buyer status at the end of their first year. Those assigned to the operations program learn about personnel, accounting, materials handling, finance, and other areas. Performance appraisals are scheduled regularly, and the trainee's potential for advancement is considered at each evaluation.

Chains　Chains are highly centralized operations. They must be able to draw continually from a pool of management talent to staff the new units they open. They also need to replace those who retire or resign. As an illustration, consider the chart of growth projections for Edison Brothers Shoe Stores shown in Figure A.4. In addition to leased departments and other chain store organizations, this leading retailer owns and operates the popular Baker's, Burt's, Chandler's, The Wild Pair, and Leed's stores. Note carefully the firm's projections for additional promotions needed through to 1990. The buying function in the chain store organization is highly centralized, the same as in department stores. The promotional path for the new college graduate is directed toward store management, merchandising, and buying. The trainee may spend six months or more in training, then be assigned as a store manager, with opportunity to advance to merchandiser, buyer, auditor, regional manager, and so on.

The huge J. C. Penney organization has positioned itself as a national retailer of quality fashion merchandise. Annual sales have already surpassed the $13 billion mark. Executive trainees may start in a number of areas: store management, merchandise buying, inventory management, or systems. Training methods used include informal day-to-day coaching, on-the-job experience, classroom instruction, and regular performance appraisals. The successful trainee may rise through merchandise management ranks to personnel manager (or operations manager), and to store manager, district manager, and so on.

Figure A.5 traces the career ladder in merchandise buying at J. C. Penney. Buyer trainees begin as assistant buyers, then move to associate buyer, buyer, merchandise manager, and divisional merchandise manager.

What Sources Can You Turn to?

Use all the possible sources of job information at your command. Visit your college placement office. Arrange for as many on-campus interviews as you can. Ask your professors for advice and leads. They may know of companies that are currently looking for college graduates. Frequently, too, they are acquainted with company executives. Study the want ads in your local newspaper for job openings which interest you. Talk about your career plans with relatives, friends, and acquaintances. They may be able to recommend firms to visit and people to see. Perhaps they may even arrange an interview for you. Register with a private employment agency. Make telephone calls and personal visits to several local retailers to discuss possible employment opportunities. Some firms make brochures available to jobseekers.

A Program to Market Yourself

You should develop a sound marketing program—to market yourself! You need to plan, organize, and set into motion a systematic approach.
    Here are a few suggestions to help you get interviews:

1. Decide on the type of retailer you would like to work for.
2. Decide on the kind of position you would like to obtain.
3. At your college library, check reference works for the names, addresses, and telephone numbers of 10 to 12 companies that fit your criteria.
4. If the firms are local, telephone each of them. Ask for the name and exact title of the person in charge of executive training.

**Figure A.5
Buying career path:
J. C. Penney**

Courtesy J. C. Penney

5. Prepare an effective resume and cover letter. (These are described in a later section of this appendix.)
6. Three months *before* you graduate, send out resumes to the companies on your list. You can use clean, clear copies of your resume, but each cover letter should be individually typed.

Cover Letters and Resumes

Two essential tools for your job search are your resume and its cover letter. If you have prepared both well, mailing them out to selected companies will certainly lead to personal interviews. You should make sure to put your best foot forward.

Needless to say, all correspondence you send out should bear a professional look. Always buy typing paper and envelopes of good quality. Avoid using erasable bond paper. Your letters must look clean, crisp, and freshly typed. Never write them on an old, faulty typewriter or use a ribbon that is worn and faded. Learn to leave ample space around every letter you send. Often, the recipient will want to jot down notes in the margins. In a professional presentation there is no room for typographical errors, mistakes in spelling, or confusion in placing punctuation marks. Good writing is simple and lucid. It should convey, clearly and in organized fashion, precisely what you intend to convey. Be concise, selective, and economical. Place on the sheet only the information that is necessary—no more, no less. Use basic vocabulary; words of one and two syllables are preferable to three- and four-syllable words.

Cover Letters   Be sure to send a cover letter with each resume you distribute. Bear in mind, too, that cover letters are sales communications. Their purpose is to sell the reader on you—to stimulate enough interest for that person to grant you an employment interview. Thus, basic selling principles apply to the letter just as they do to a TV commercial. You need to quickly gain your prospect's attention, arouse interest, stimulate a desire to learn more, and obtain action (in the form of an appointment for a personal interview).

Your letter should be brief and to the point. State that you are applying for a specific position with the company. Outline your major selling points. Mention the enclosed resume, and request an interview. There is little need to be more expansive; after all, your resume contains more specifics. So, as you can see, your cover letter should contain no more than three or four short paragraphs. The first should act as a hook to gain the reader's attention. You might mention, very briefly, your main qualifications for the position. Then, perhaps, indicate your belief that you can indeed make a fine contribution to the company. In the second paragraph, expand on your promise by providing a few of the more significant details about your education and work experience. Be sure to emphasize your strengths. A brief reference to your resume should then follow. The final paragraph should be, preferably, a single sentence. In it, request an interview at the reader's earliest convenience. Then, sign *Sincerely yours,* and add your name.

Your Resume   Preparing an effective resume is not an easy task. You should start working on it a few months before graduation. You owe it to yourself to leaf through several books on resume preparation—you will become acquainted with a variety of formats and come across some worthwhile ideas. This research should help you develop a well-organized resume that presents your selling points clearly in a minimum of space. Visit your college placement office, too. They will furnish you with useful materials and the names and addresses of employers who are looking for college graduates. You should also attend any seminar that may be offered on resume preparation or on being interviewed. Bear in mind, too, that once you have designed your resume, you might ask one or two of your professors for their comments. They will be happy to make suggestions for improvement.

A recommended format for the new graduate is shown in Figure A.6. After you have been in the work force for several years, we recommend a different format completely—one that places more emphasis on your work experience and accomplishments, rather than on your academic preparation.

Figure A.6

Name   Telephones:
Address   Home: (xxx) xxx-xxxx
City, State, ZIP   Office: (xxx) xxx-xxxx

RESUME

Objective: An appointment as executive trainee with a major retailing organization, leading to a career in merchandising or store operations.

EDUCATION   Bachelor of Business Administration, June 1985.
                     Baruch College, 17 Lexington Avenue, New York, NY
                     10010
                        Major: Retailing and Sales
                        Dean's List, 1984, 1985.
                        Advanced courses in: Buying and Merchandising,
                        Selling, Retail Management, Consumer Behavior.

                     Associate of Arts, June 1983.
                     Queensboro Community College, Bayside, NY 11364
                        Major: English.

EMPLOYMENT   Assistant Store Manager
                     Kevin's Sportswear, 158 Broadway, New York, NY
                     10002
April 1984   Duties: Selling; supervise four salesclerks, handle
to   customer returns and adjustments; put up displays;
Present   open and close store.

July 1982   Salesclerk
to April 1984   Burger Town, 166 Main Street, Flushing, NY 11354
(part time)   Duties: Serving customers; training new salesclerks.

PERSONAL DETAILS   Vice president, Baruch Retailing Society
                     Member: American Marketing Association
                     Interests: baseball, hockey, skiing
                     Willing to relocate.

REFERENCES   Available upon request.

At this juncture, let us briefly review the major parts of the resume:

Heading At the top left-hand corner, give your name, address, city, state, and ZIP code. On the right-hand side, show your home telephone number (and area code). If you are employed and do not mind being called while working, list your office number as well. Then, skip a few lines and center the word *RESUME.*

Objective Center the statement regarding your job objective. This should be indented at least 10 spaces from the right-hand margin. If possible, couch your objective in a single, clear sentence.

Education At this stage of your life, your academic background will most likely be your principal asset. Specify the name of the degree you will have earned. Indicate the month and year the degree will be awarded. Underline this information. On the next line, show the name and location of the college or university that will grant the degree. Give your major (and minor, if applicable). List, too, the titles of three or four advanced courses that are clearly applicable to the position you are seeking. Also, add any special awards or honors you received for your academic work. If you have earned more than one degree, begin the education section with your highest degree. Work backward, listing lesser degrees below. If you have had any other professional training, show the details here.

Employment List your employment record in reverse chronological order, beginning with your present (or last) position. Use separate copy blocks for each job you have held. Indicate the dates of employment and your job title (underlined). Identify each firm you worked for, giving its name and address. Briefly describe your major duties and responsibilities. If you have had other paid employment, including military experience, indicate this information as well.

Personal Details In this section, list the organizations you belong to and the offices, if any, you hold (or have held). Indicate your membership on college teams and outstanding campus activities you may have participated in. Briefly list your major interests, hobbies, and special skills.

References You need not list these here, but be sure to obtain permission in advance from those people you plan to name as references later on.

Interviews: What to Expect

Hiring decisions are not made without one or more employment interviews. Employers (or their representatives) want to see and talk with job applicants. Only through an interview can they appraise a person's poise, posture, manner, and ability to communicate. They want to be convinced that the applicant is indeed qualified above other applicants for the position. They need to probe aspects that cannot readily be interpreted from a typed resume. They need to understand the abilities, skills, and work attitudes the applicant will bring to the company.

Before the Interview   Never go to an interview unprepared. Find out in advance all you can about the company. If the retailer has local outlets, visit one or two stores. Check into the kinds and quality of the merchandise and services they offer. Get to know something about the storefront, signing, interior layout, displays, and salespeople. If a company is a public corporation, try to secure a copy of its latest annual report. Read it carefully; it will contain a great deal of worthwhile information. You might also check the *Business Periodicals Index* at your college library for recent articles about the company.

You will find that such preparation will be helpful during your interview.

At the Interview   Go to the interview neatly—and conservatively—dressed, not overdressed. Arrive at least 10 or 15 minutes before your appointment time. As you enter the interviewer's office, be sure to maintain your poise. Approach the desk briskly, with an air of confidence and a pleasant smile (but not a grin!) on your face. As you reach the desk, say: "Good morning (or Good afternoon), Mr. (Ms.) Smith. Thank you for granting me this interview."

The interviewer gains a crucial first impression from your dress, poise, posture, and approach.

During the interview, be sure to sit upright—erect but not rigid—in your chair. Do not slouch or lounge. Be alert and attentive to what the interviewer has to say; be a good listener. When you are asked questions, do not feel pressured for time. Think a bit, then answer to the best of your ability—candidly and honestly. Avoid boasting or exaggeration. Try not to respond to questions with a simple yes or no. Use full sentences.

Most interviews last from 15 to 30 minutes or longer. Some are structured; others are not. At the end of your talk, be sure to thank the interviewer for the time and consideration extended to you. If the company's evaluation is a positive one, another interview may be scheduled for you. Often, the second interview is held by an executive in the department to which you may be assigned.

The following is a list of major U.S. retailers you might consider
as you think about embarking upon a career in retailing.

Abraham & Straus
420 Fulton Street
Brooklyn, NY 11201
(718) 875-7200

Albertson's, Inc.
250 Park Center Boulevard
Boise, ID 83726
(208) 344-7441

Alexander's
500 Seventh Avenue
New York, NY 10018
(212) 560-2121

Allied Stores Corp.
1114 Avenue of the Americas
New York, NY 10036
(212) 764-2000

B. Altman & Company
Fifth Avenue at 34th Street
New York, NY 10016
(212) 679-7800

Ames Department Stores
2418 Main Street
Rocky Hill, CT 06067
(203) 563-8234

Associated Dry Goods Corporation
417 Fifth Avenue
New York, NY 10016
(212) 679-8700

L. S. Ayres & Company
1 West Washington Street
Indianapolis, IN 46206
(317) 262-4411

Bamberger's
131 Market Street
Newark, NJ 07102
(201) 565-1234

BATUS—Retail Division
1270 Avenue of the Americas
New York, NY 10020
(212) 399-0700

Bergdorf Goodman & Company
754 Fifth Avenue
New York, NY 10019
(212) 753-7300

Bloomingdale's
Lexington Avenue at 59th Street
New York, NY 10022
(212) 705-2000

Bonwit Teller
1120 Avenue of the Americas
New York, NY 10036
(212) 764-2300

Bradlees
1 Bradlees Circle
Braintree, MA 02184
(617) 770-8000

The Broadway
3880 North Mission Road
Los Angeles, CA 90031
(213) 227-2000

Broadway Southwest
4000 Fiesta Mall
Mesa, AZ 85202
(602) 835-4500

Burdine's
22 E. Flagler Street
Miami, FL 33131
(305) 835-5151

Caldor Inc.
20 Glover Avenue
Norwalk, CT 06852
(203) 846-1641

Carson, Pirie, Scott
1 South State Street
Chicago, IL 60603
(312) 744-2000

Carter Hawley Hale Stores, Inc.
550 South Flower Street
Los Angeles, CA 90071
(213) 620-0150

Chess King
44 Hammond Street
Worcester, MA 01610
(617) 798-8553

Contempo Casuals
5433 W. Jefferson Boulevard
Los Angeles, CA 90016
(213) 936-3131

Cornet Stores
411 South Arroyo Parkway
Pasadena, CA 91109
(213) 681-6725

D&L Venture Corporation
227 Main Street
New Britain, CT 06050
(203) 223-3655

Davison's
180 Peachtree Street, N.W.
Atlanta, GA 30303
(404) 221-7221

Dayton-Hudson Corporation
777 Nicollet Mall
Minneapolis, MN 55402
(612) 370-0948

The Denver Dry Goods Company
16th & California Streets
Denver, CO 80201
(303) 534-2111

Dillard Department Stores, Inc.
900 West Capitol Avenue
Little Rock, AR 72203
(510) 376-5200

Dillard's
9315 North Broadway
San Antonio, TX 78217
(512) 821-7611

Duckwall-Alco Stores, Inc.
401 Cottage Street
Abilene, KS 67410
(913) 263-3350

Jack Eckherd Drug Company
P.O. Box 4689
Clearwater, FL 33518
(813) 397-7461

Edison Brothers Shoe Stores, Inc.
P.O. Box 14020
St. Louis, MO 63178
(314) 444-6000

Famous-Barr
601 Olive Street
St. Louis, MO 63101
(314) 444-3111

Federated Department Stores
7 West Seventh Street
Cincinnati, OH 45202
(513) 579-7000

Filene's
426 Washington Street
Boston, MA 02101
(617) 357-2100

Foley's
P.O. Box 1971
Houston, TX 77001
(713) 651-7038

G. Fox & Company
960 Main Street
Hartford, CT 06115
(203) 522-1920

Foxmoor Casuals
P.O. Box 855
Brockton, MA 02403
(617) 588-7820

The Gap
900 Cherry Avenue
San Bruno, CA 94066
(415) 952-4400

Gimbel's East
Broadway & 33rd Street
New York, NY 10001
(212) 564-3300

Goldblatts
333 South State Street
Chicago, IL 60604
(312) 786-2000

Gold Circle Stores, Inc.
6121 Huntley Road
Worthington, OH 43085
(614) 438-4141

Gold Triangle Corporation
4600 West 18th Court
Hialeah, FL 33012
(305) 558-2410

Gottschalk's
Kern & Fulton Streets
Fresno, CA 93718
(209) 485-1111

Grand Union
100 Broadway
Elmwood Park, NJ 07407
(201) 794-2000

The Great Atlantic & Pacific Tea Company
2 Paragon Drive
Montvale, NJ 07645
(210) 573-9700

Paul Harris Stores, Inc.
6003 Guion Road
Indianapolis, IN 46268
(317) 293-3900

Hecht's
Seventh & F Streets, N.W.
Washington, DC 20004
(202) 628-5100

Higbee's
100 Public Square
Cleveland, OH 44113
(216) 579-2580

D. H. Holmes Company, Ltd.
819 Canal Street
New Orleans, LA 70160
(504) 561-6611

Joseph Horne Company
501 Penn Avenue
Pittsburgh, PA 15222
(412) 553-8000

Idaho Department Store Company
523 Main Street
Caldwell, ID 83605
(208) 459-4606

Jefferson Ward
15800 N.W. 13th Avenue
Miami, FL 33169
(305) 620-2400

Jordan Marsh
450 Washington Street
Boston, MA 02205
(617) 357-3000

Jordan Marsh
1501 Biscayne Boulevard
Miami, FL 33132
(305) 377-1911

Kaufmann's
400 Fifth Avenue
Pittsburgh, PA 15219
(412) 232-2000

K mart Corporation
3100 West Big Beaver Road
Troy, MI 48084
(313) 643-1000

Kroger
1014 Vine Street
Cincinnati, OH 45201
(513) 762-4000

Lazarus
South Town & High Streets
Columbus, OH 43216
(614) 463-2121

Lerner Stores Corporation
460 West 33rd Street
New York, NY 10001
(212) 736-1222

Liberty House of Hawaii
P.O. Box 2690
Ala Moana Center
Honolulu, HI 96845
(808) 941-2345

Limited, Inc.
1 Limited Parkway
Columbus, OH 43216
(614) 475-4000

Lord & Taylor
424 Fifth Avenue
New York, NY 10018
(212) 391-3344

Lucky Stores
6300 Clarke Avenue
Dublin, CA 94566
(415) 833-6000

Maas Brothers
P.O. Box 311
Tampa, FL 33601
(813) 223-7525

R. H. Macy & Company, Inc.
34th Street and Herald Square
New York, NY 10001
(212) 695-4400

Macy's Atlanta
180 Peachtree Street, N.W.
Atlanta, GA 30303
(404) 221-7221

Macy's California
Stockton at O'Farrell
San Francisco, CA 94120
(415) 397-3333

Marriott Corporation
1 Marriott Drive
Washington, DC 20058
(301) 897-9000

Marshall Field & Company
111 North State Street
Chicago, IL 60690
(312) 781-1000

The May Company
158 Euclid Avenue
Cleveland, OH 44114
(216) 664-6000

Melville Corporation
3000 Westchester Avenue
Harrison, NY 10528
(914) 253-8000

Mervyn's
25001 Industrial Boulevard
Hayward, CA 94545
(415) 785-8800

Montgomery Ward
1 Montgomery Ward Plaza
Chicago, IL 60671
(312) 467-2000

National Tea
9701 West Higgins Road
Rosemont, IL 60028
(312) 693-5100

Neiman-Marcus
Main and Ervay Streets
Dallas, TX 75201
(214) 741-6911

Nordstrom
50 South Main Street
Salt Lake City, UT 84144
(801) 322-4200

Ohrbach's
5 West 34th Street
New York, NY 10001
(212) 695-4000

Osco Drugs, Inc.
1818 Swift Drive
Oak Brook, IL 60521
(312) 887-5000

Parisian
1101 26th Street, North
Birmingham, AL 35234
(205) 251-1300

J. C. Penney Company, Inc.
1301 Avenue of the Americas
New York, NY 10019
(212) 957-4321

H. C. Prange Company
727 Plaza Eight
Sheboygan, WI 53081
(414) 457-3611

Rich's, Inc.
Broad and Alabama Streets
Atlanta, GA 30302
(404) 586-4636

Richway Stores
P.O. Box 50359
Atlanta, GA 30302
(404) 586-2800

Robinson's
600 West Seventh Street
Los Angeles, CA 90017
(213) 488-5522

Ross Stores, Inc.
8333 Central Avenue
Newark, CA 94560
(415) 790-4400

Safeway Stores, Inc.
201 Fourth Street
Oakland, CA 94660
(415) 891-3000

Saks Fifth Avenue
611 Fifth Avenue
New York, NY 10022
(212) 753-4000

Saks Fifth Avenue
9600 Wilshire Boulevard
Beverly Hills, CA 90212
(213) 275-4211

Sanger-Harris
303 North Akard Street
Dallas, TX 75201
(214) 749-3990

Sears, Roebuck & Company
Sears Tower
Chicago, IL 60684
(312) 875-2500

Skaggs Companies, Inc.
P.O. Box 30658
Salt Lake City, UT 84130
(801) 487-4531

Stop & Shop
393 D Street
Boston, MA 02210
(617) 463-7000

SupeRx Drug Stores
175 Tri County Parkway
Cincinnati, OH 45246
(513) 782-3000

Tandy Corporation
One Tandy Center
Fort Worth, TX 76102
(817) 390-3700

Thalhimer Brothers
P.O. Box 26724
Richmond, VA 23261
(804) 643-4211

Thrifty Drug
615 Alpha Drive
Pittsburgh, PA 15238
(412) 781-5373

Von's Grocery Company
P.O. Box 3338, Terminal Annex
Los Angeles, CA 90051
(213) 579-1400

Walgreen Company
200 Wilmot Road
Deerfield, IL 60015
(312) 948-5000

Wal-Mart Stores
P.O. Box 116
Bentonville, AR 72712
(501) 273-4000

John Wanamaker
1300 Market Street
Philadelphia, PA 19101
(215) 422-2000

Weiboldt Stores, Inc.
1 North State Street
Chicago, IL 60602
(312) 782-1500

Weinstock's
Sixth & K Streets
Sacramento, CA 95801
(916) 449-8888

Wickes Companies, Inc.
1010 Second Avenue
San Diego, CA 92101
(714) 238-0304

F. W. Woolworth Company
233 Broadway
New York, NY 10279
(212) 553-2000

Younkers
71 Walnut Street
Des Moines, IA 50397
(515) 244-1112

Zayre Corporation
770 Cochituate Road
Framingham, MA 01701
(617) 620-5000

GLOSSARY

ABC analysis inventory control technique that categorizes goods into three groups according to their rate of movement.

acid-test ratio see **quick (acid-test) ratio.**

accountability employees are answerable to their supervisors.

accounts receivable monies due from charge customers.

advertising nonpersonal communication conducted by the retailer through paid media; a form of nonpersonal selling that aims at large numbers of potential buyers.

advertising agency firm that specializes in planning, preparing, and placing ads for clients with the media.

advertising medium a vehicle that carries promotional messages to actual or potential customers.

advertising specialties inexpensive articles given free to shoppers to promote the firm or announce a special event.

agate line measure by which newspaper advertising space is sold; 14 agate lines equal one column inch.

agents and brokers intermediaries who fulfill a channel function by acting as representatives of manufacturers, wholesalers, or retailers and receive fees or commissions for their services; see also **brokers.**

allowances offered by manufacturers to reduce buyers' costs by providing advertising help, free merchandise, displays, product demonstrations, and so on.

alterations tailoring wearing apparel to fit; customer service performed by retailer's employee.

alternative evaluation purchase decision stage in which consumers use their own criteria to weigh various possibilities.

analogous colors lie near each other on the color wheel: blue, blue-green, green; or red, red-orange, yellow; etc.

anchor store(s) principal tenant(s) of a shopping center.

anticipation dating credit arrangement in which an additional discount is given to encourage buyers to pay their bills before the cash discount period ends.

AOG and ROG dating invoicing terms under which the customer can obtain a cash discount by paying within a specified time after **R**eceipt (**A**rrival) of **G**oods.

approach the first minute or two of saleperson's initial face-to-face contact with the prospect.

arbitrary decision technique budgeting decision based on proprietor's intuition or experience rather than on facts and figures.

assemblers wholesalers who assemble products they usually purchase from a number of sources, then box or can them and ready the goods for shipment to retailers or warehouses.

assessment center used in management development programs to identify employees' work-related strengths and weaknesses in order to devise training plans for their long-term development.

assets the physical resources the company owns: cash, securities, accounts receivable, inventories, equipment, and so on.

associated (cooperative) buying office resident buying office set up to serve a group or association of retail firms, which manages it.

assortment the number of different choices offered in a particular retail line.

assumptive close salesperson begins to fill out sales slip or order blank on the assumption the shopper has decided to buy.

atmospherics retailer's effort to design store environment to produce specific emotional effects in the buyer.

attitude advertising see **institutional advertising.**

attitudes the way we think, feel, and act toward some aspect of the environment; attitudes are learned, not inborn, responses.

auction company broker authorized by sellers to dispose of goods at any price attainable above pre-established minimums.

audiovisuals slides, films, tapes, and projectors used by retailers to promote their merchandise and services; have replaced more costly personal demonstrations in many cases.

authority implies power, wielding influence over others, enforcing decisions, and controlling workers' activities.

autocratic leaders rule subordinates through fear; are tough, domineering, and demanding.

automatic replenishment system fill-in inventory reordering method that uses the $Q = (T_1 + T_2)R - I$ formula to determine how much stock to reorder.

average markup useful computation in determining average of all markups placed on individual merchandise lines, classifications, price lines, additional purchases, etc.

bait-and-switch advertising unethical promoting of a well-known article at a very low price to attract shoppers to the store (bait) and then attempting to switch shoppers to a higher-priced item of the same type; also called **bait pricing** or **bait-and-switch.**

balance in design, a state of equilibrium among all components of a display; may be formal or informal.

balance sheet an accounting statement that describes the financial condition of a business at a given time.

balance sheet (T-account) close salesperson lists advantages and disadvantages of buying to show indecisive shopper that advantages of buying outweigh disadvantages.

bar coding Universal Product Code (UPC) markings on product wrappers or containers that allow computer scanners to record prices and other information at checkout registers.

basic human needs five ascending sets of needs described by Maslow in 1943: physiological, safety, love and belongingness, esteem, and self-actualizing.

basic stock method carries basic inventory throughout a period, then adds enough merchandise to cover each month's expected sales.

basic stock plan lists the entire inventory to be carried by the retailer to meet sales projections; broken down by categories into classifications and subclassifications.

behavior modification training technique used in management training.

benefit segmentation marketing approach that targets consumers according to the benefits they seek in a product.

blind check method of checking deliveries in which the checker must count cartons and list label information without use of packing slip, invoice, or purchase order.

bottom-up (build-up) planning forecasting method in which top management delegates responsibility for preparing projections to individual executives or operating personnel in the firm.

bottom-up theory opposite of **trickle-down theory:** proposes that innovative fashions (like jeans and tank tops) originate with lower-class consumers, are made popular by upper-class consumers, then are adopted by the large numbers of the middle class.

boutiques small specialty shops that feature a narrow range of exclusive, fashionable merchandise in an attractive atmosphere; a **boutique layout** approach is also adopted by many department stores as a variation from conventional departmental layouts.

box stores low-priced food stores that carry much narrower assortments than supermarkets, operate on self-service, and offer no services.

breadth the width of a merchandise assortment; the number of different styles, colors, sizes, and other variants a retailer carries.

break-even point the point at which all necessary expenses are covered, showing neither profit nor loss.

broadcast media radio and TV.

brokers intermediaries who buy or sell goods on behalf of their principals (the people or companies they represent); see also **agents and brokers.**

building standards lease legal contract in which the landlord puts up a strip of stores with identical fronts, heating, restrooms, etc., and the tenants must complete the installations.

business format franchising most common kind of franchising; an ongoing relationship that includes the entire business format: marketing and strategy plan, operating manuals and standards, quality control, and continuing two-way communication between franchisor and franchisee.

canvassing door-to-door selling.

capital term usually substituted for **net worth** or **owner's equity** when a firm has been incorporated.

capital budgeting budgetary approach to management decision making about purchasing equipment, installations, or other substantial property.

cash-and-carry wholesaler limited-service wholesaler who maintains ample stock in warehouses for area merchants who come in to buy, pick up, pay for, and take out needed goods.

cash discount a small, stated percentage of the amount due, given to customers who pay bills early.

cash flow budget detailed forecast of projected receipts and expenses for each month over a specified time; used to predict periods during the year when the business may need additional financing.

catalog direct-mail or advertising promotional vehicle; may be used to extend the retailer's trading area.

catalog showroom retail outlet that sells name-brand goods at prices below those of other stores; offers high-markup goods like cameras, jewelry, and small appliances through full color catalogs and sample displays.

central business district (CBD) downtown shopping area in the core of the city; usually the oldest shopping section in town.

central processing unit (CPU) executes computer program instructions, compares and controls data flow, performs calculations, etc.

centralized buying buying offices located at corporate headquarters to maintain control over costs and production.

chain store organization owns and operates two or more outlets that carry essentially the same merchandise, closely resemble each other physically, use identical operating systems and procedures, and have a centralized management and buying function.

choice purchase decision stage that occurs after the consumer has evaluated, judged, and compared product and brand attributes.

classical conditioning rooted in Pavlov's experiments in which animals learned to associate a stimulus (ringing of a bell) with the appearance of food, causing a predictable response (salivation); also called **stimulus-response theory.**

classification dominance displaying merchandise items in a way that suggests the retailer has the largest possible assortment of items in a category.

close (closing) occurs when salesperson, having written up the order, secures customer's signature on the order form.

closed-back window retail store display window closed at the back to avoid shoppers' distraction by a view of the store interior.

closed displays merchandise displays kept under lock and key to prevent theft or damage.

clutter the many ads in a newspaper that compete for the reader's attention.

coaching (sponsor method) new employee is assigned to experienced worker, who assists the trainee by answering questions, demonstrating procedures, and so on.

color scheme planned color design in a display; may use complementary, monochrome, or analogous colors.

combination method expense allocation approach that combines the net profit and contribution plans.

combination plan catch-all label for salary/commission, salary/bonus, quota/bonus, and other compensation plans.

combination rates newspaper advertising costs based on ads appearing in more than one edition of the paper.

combination stores retail outlets that combine drugs and pharmaceuticals or general merchandise with a supermarket operation; generally double or triple the conventional supermarket size.

commission house see **commission merchant (house).**

commission merchant (house) differs from other agents in that they take in and store goods until they have been sold; they earn commission on goods sold for farmers, growers, and other small producers.

commission plan employee compensation plan, usually reserved for salespeople, who receive some percentage of sales rather than a salary.

committee buying buying approach characteristic of the supermarket industry; typically includes the merchandise manager, promotion manager, sales manager, and other specialists who (as a group) approve or disapprove merchandise proposals submitted by suppliers.

communication interaction; all the processes in which there is interchange of facts, ideas, feelings, and actions by which people influence one another.

community shopping center smaller version of regional shopping center; about 10 acres that serves 30,000 to 50,000 shoppers; anchored by a large variety or junior department store.

comparative pricing promotional pricing technique that attempts to lead consumers to believe the retailer's prices are lower than those of competitors, or that selling prices have been marked down.

comparison shopping done by retailers to keep abreast of competitors' offerings; includes checking window displays and ads and visiting competing stores.

complementary colors lie opposite each other on the color wheel: red-green, blue-orange, purple-yellow.

completing the sale third stage of the retail selling process, in which the salesperson asks for and gets the order.

composition created work whose elements have been arranged to satisfy and appeal to its intended audience; see also **design.**

concentrated marketing marketing approach that aims at only one part (segment) of the consumer market.

conglomerchant a retail conglomerate (large organization) that owns a variety of retail businesses.

consignment buying retailer acts as agent for the supplier, taking title to and paying only for merchandise sold.

consumer behavior the study of consumer psychology: what, when, why, where, and how consumers buy.

consumer cooperative (usually) a food store established by consumers who pay regular market prices but receive dividends, which in effect reduce their food costs.

consumer goods the merchandise retailers sell to consumers (rather than to organizations).

consumer panel small group of representative consumers who evaluate a store's merchandise, policies, services, and advertising for the retailer.

consumer services performed to satisfy the needs and wants of consumers, rather than those of organizations.

consumerism social movement that seeks to augment the rights and powers of buyers in relation to sellers.

contests and games promotional activity favored by chains and independents to create excitement and generate heavy store traffic.

contingency fund budgeting method that sets aside some percentage of the total year's budget for extra or emergency advertising during the year.

continuity-offer premium ongoing promotion designed to encourage repeat buying by shoppers.

contract rates newspaper advertising costs based on total linage used or the frequency with which ads are placed.

contrast design technique used to stress the difference between one element and the rest of a display and to add interest and excitement.

contribution method expense allocation approach in which only direct expenses (those within the department manager's control) are charged to the department.

controlling managerial function of evaluating methods, behaviors, and outcomes and taking action to correct deviation from plans.

convenience goods generally low-priced products that are available in many stores; includes impulse, staple, and emergency goods.

convenience store mini-grocery with strong convenience appeal for a local community; carries limited assortment of groceries and impulse goods and has extended store hours, often around the clock.

conversion franchising conversion of an independent business to a franchise.

cooperative advertising two or more firms share advertising costs.

cooperative buying office see **associated (cooperative) buying office.**

correlation techniques forecasting methods that attempt to relate company sales to other independent variables in the environment, like customer income and plant productivity.

cost of goods sold (COG sold) dollar amount determined by calculating the total cost of all merchandise available for sale during an accounting period and deducting from it the value of any inventory left at the end of the period.

cost per thousand measure used to evaluate advertising buys among magazines; a counterpart to the newspaper milline rate.

country-club billing invoicing method similar to **descriptive billing** except that original sales slips for all transactions are enclosed with the customer's statement.

coupons sales promotion tool especially effective during periods of inflation and difficult economic times; improve consumer judgments about brand quality.

cue stimulus that arouses an organism to respond.

culture values, ideas, attitudes, and other meaningful symbols that are created by people to shape human behavior and are transmitted from one generation to the next.

cumulative markup the sum total of all markups placed on individual articles during a particular period.

cumulative quantity discount granted to buyers for purchasing goods in quantity over a period of time.

current assets assets that may be relied on or actively used in operating the business during the coming year.

current liabilities debts the organization must pay within the year following the balance sheet date.

current ratio liquidity measure derived from balance-sheet information using the formula: Current ratio = Current assets ÷ Current liabilities.

customer discount offered to special groups (neighboring merchants, charities, students, senior citizens, etc.).

cuts stock illustrations used as artwork in newspaper advertising.

dating refers to the way credit arrangement with accounts are handled; includes ordinary (regular) dating, future dating, extra dating, etc.

decision making includes defining the problem, obtaining information, developing and evaluating alternative solutions, and choosing the best solution.

decline stage the fourth and last stage of the product life cycle (PLC).

Delphi method modification of jury of executive opinion forecasting in which executives' individually prepared estimates are reconsidered and a decision is made after the final round of refining.

democratic leaders encourage communication, seek member participation in decision making, and show a high degree of respect for individual workers.

demographic segmentation marketing approach that targets groups of prospects by factors like sex, age, marital status, income, occupation, family size, education, and so on.

demonstration promotion technique in which demonstrator shows and distributes merchandise to store shoppers; can add significantly to sales, especially in case of technical or complex products.

department stores large retail institutions that offer a variety of merchandise lines and are organized by departments.

departmentizing organizing merchandise into groupings or departments.

depreciate to drop in value over time.

depth the number of pieces stocked of the different styles, colors, sizes, and other variants in each line a retailer carries.

descriptive billing invoicing method in which every transaction made during billing period is entered on customer's statement; debit and credits are totaled and balance due on account is shown.

design plan, scheme, pattern, or motif; an arrangement of parts that fit together properly; see also **composition.**

desk jobbers (drop shippers) limited-service wholesalers who maintain no inventory; they secure orders from retail accounts and place them with manufacturers or other suppliers.

developmental training given to employees to promote on-the-job growth.

differentiated marketing marketing approach that seeks out two or more large groups of potential buyers.

diffusion process process by which the adoption and use of an innovation spreads through our economy over time.

direct-action advertising see **promotional advertising.**

direct check method of checking deliveries in which cartons are counted and labels checked against the packing slip, invoice, or purchase order.

direct investment a domestic firm infuses both capital and management know-how into the construction and subsequent operation of an overseas facility.

direct mail one-to-one sales communication from retailer to consumer via the mail.

direct selling most costly and most personalized nonstore retailing engaged in by firms and individuals who work with customers on a one-to-one basis.

directing managerial function of instructing, guiding, training, presenting ideas to, and supervising employees.

discount a reduction from the selling, or list, price of merchandise.

display patterns patterns used to display merchandise, such as the step, fan, pyramid, and zigzag.

dissonance consumer's tension or anxiety that sometimes results from a purchase.

dollar control tracks merchandise inventory in terms of cost or retail prices rather than by units.

dominance design concept denoting power and command in which a certain part of a display is emphasized.

drawing account (draw) usually a flat sum advanced to a salesperson against unearned commissions; earned commissions are credited and advances debited to salesperson's account, and overages are paid to employee at end of period.

drives urgent needs that induce compelling states of inner tension and drive us in the direction of their potential satisfaction.

drop-shipper see **desk jobbers.**

dual-factor theory Herzberg's theory that the work environment holds two sets of factors that affect workers' outlooks: motivators and hygiene factors.

durable goods last for long periods; bought less often than nondurables; generally offered at high unit prices.

Early Adopters next consumer group to follow the Innovators in buying and trying a new product or service.

early-bird discount extended to customers who place orders early.

Early Majority with the Late Majority, the largest group of consumers; they follow the Innovators and Early Adopters in buying and trying a new product or service.

80–20 principle suggests that 80 percent of annual sales volume is brought in by 20 percent of the merchandise items carried; see also **ABC analysis.**

electronic checkout provides better customer service, generates sales revenue increases, and reduces labor costs through faster processing of checkout lines in retail stores.

emergency goods purchased only when a need suddenly becomes pressing.

emotional motives in retailing, consumer behavior prompted by emotions or feelings rather than by logic or reasoning.

employee compensation includes basic pay plan and supplemental benefits.

employee discount given to retail personnel on merchandise they buy from the store.

employment application selection technique used by the firm to gather information about job applicants.

employment interview selection technique in which retailer seeks more information from applicant than is found in the employment application.

esteem needs need to be recognized and respected by others; need for status and prestige.

even pricing setting selling prices that end in even numbers.

exhibits promotional technique in which articles or collections of articles are placed on display.

experimental method data collection method that involves setting up one or more experiments to test some aspect or variable of a retail operation.

expectancy theory holds that worker motivation is a function of *(a)* individual expectancies of reward for effort and *(b)* the employee's perceived value of specific rewards.

expense budget plan that details projected operating expenses for a specific period.

expense center classification of expenses in which each type of business activity is appraised as a separate business; used by department stores and other large departmentized operations.

extrinsic motivation influence that comes from forces outside of an individual.

fads fashions or other goods with relatively short life spans that may not go through all phases of the normal product life cycle.

fair trade laws once allowed manufacturers to dictate the prices at which their products could be sold; now prohibited in interstate commerce.

fair-practice laws state laws that generally prohibit franchisors from terminating or failing to renew a franchise without good cause.

family life cycle concept that generalizes about the phases the typical American family passes through.

fan pattern vertical or horizontal merchandise display that draws shoppers' attention to a main or featured item.

fashions styles or designs that large numbers of consumers come to accept and continue to use for some time.

FIFO first-in, first-out method of determining cost of goods sold.

fixed assets resources the firm will use over the years to come: buildings, vehicles, machinery, equipment, and so on.

fixed pricing the prices of goods are set, and all shoppers pay the same price.

fixed rental lease legal contract that requires retailer to pay a stipulated sum monthly or yearly.

follow-up salesperson thanks buyer, reassures buyer that buying decision was wise, and promises to check after delivery to make sure that all is satisfactory.

follow-up training given to employees to reinforce initial job training.

forecasting predicting or anticipating what is to come; in retailing, forecasts of future sales volume are based on estimates of consumer demand.

franchisee an individual or firm that contracts with the parent company (the franchisor) to operate a unit.

franchisor company that offers distribution to individually owned businesses (franchisees) that operate as though part of the company chain, complete with trademarks, uniform symbols, design, equipment, and standardized services or products.

freeform layout store design in which aisles and department boundaries curve in graceful arcs and irregular shapes that please the eye; popular among retailers of specialty and shopping goods.

freestanding store a single building, usually surrounded by ample parking space; used by discount stores, restaurants, and other retailers.

full-disclosure laws state laws that mandate disclosure of the background of franchisor principals, financial statements, franchise fees, royalties, termination provision, and any requirement to purchase supplies from the franchisor.

full-service wholesaler merchant wholesaler who provides all expected services for channel members.

functional expenses classification of expenses according to the particular business functions in which they are incurred, like occupancy, buying, merchandising, and so on.

furniture warehouses large, promotional mass-merchandising operations that combine warehouse facilities with an extensive showroom operation.

general merchandise house full-service distributor who offers an extensive variety of merchandise lines.

general merchandise retailers carry an extensive variety of merchandise lines: family apparel, accessories, home furnishings, appliances, hardware and household items, health and beauty aids, and other types of goods; include department stores, variety stores, and discount houses.

general store a small retail outlet that dates back to the 18th century; stocked groceries, household items, farm equipment and supplies, animal feed, tools and hardware, medicines, and other goods.

generics unbranded, plainly packaged, no-frills items sold at lower prices in supermarkets.

geographic segmentation marketing approach that targets groups of prospects in one or more specific areas of the country.

gift certificates customer service item usually printed in several denominations for shoppers unsure about gift buying.

giveaway premium presented to customers free of charge as a promotion.

gondolas high vertical displays that maximize shopper exposure to merchandise and encourage impulse buying.

grid(iron) layout store design with straight aisles and 90-degree turns that compel shoppers to move much like vehicular traffic moves along city streets; exposes shoppers to the most amount of merchandise.

gross margin the difference between the cost of an item and its actual selling price; also, dollar amount determined by subtracting the cost of goods sold from net sales during an accounting period.

gross margin return on investment (GMROI) a planning and control formula that shows the firm's return on *inventory* investment: Gross margin dollars ÷ Average inventory.

gross sales the total of all monies collected for merchandise sold during an accounting period.

group or cooperative buying independents and small chains band together to increase their purchasing power.

growth stage the second stage of the product life cycle (PLC).

hardware the computer itself and its cabinet, electronic circuits, electromechanical devices, and other components.

horizontal cooperative advertising two or more retailers advertise jointly, each contributing funds toward the project.

human resource planning management process that assures the right number and kinds of people at the right places at the right time to complete the tasks necessary for the organization to achieve its overall objectives.

hypermarket successful in Europe; huge general merchandise retail outlet that combines the equivalent of a large discount house, supermarket, drugstore, furniture and appliances, and automotive repairs under one roof; requires 40 or more checkout stations.

image-building advertising see **institutional advertising.**

impact refers to the intensity of the effect an advertising medium has on its audience.

impulse goods items purchased on impulse when they are seen by a shopper without prior intent to buy.

independent buying office resident buying office that services client retailers.

Index of Retail Saturation describes sales volume per square foot of selling space in a given area for specific products.

industrial goods products purchased by industrial, commercial, agricultural, nonprofit, governmental, and other organizations (as opposed to *consumer goods,* which are purchased by individuals).

industrial services performed for and consumed by business and other organizations.

initial markup calculated amount placed on incoming merchandise using the formula: Initial markup percentage = Expenses + Profits + Reductions ÷ Net Sales + Reductions × 100 percent.

initial training given to new employees to quickly familiarize them with their jobs and company policies.

Innovators first consumers to buy and try a new product or service.

inseparability an attribute of services; inability to separate the service from the person who performs it or from the employees with whom we must speak.

installment credit plan customer makes down payment on article purchased and pays balance owed in series of installments.

institutional advertising keeps retail firm's name before the public, to promote community goodwill and store loyalty; also called **image-building** or **attitude advertising.**

intangibility an attribute of services, something that cannot be touched or felt.

interactive communications computer-assisted two-way communication.

intrinsic motivation influence that comes from within an individual.

introductory discount offered to induce buyers to try new items.

inventory turnover (stockturn) the number of times a retailer's average inventory is bought and sold over a period of time.

job analysis written analysis that examines kind of work being done, work conditions, knowledge and skills required, organizational relationships, and so on.

job description written definition of the job that lists duties, responsibilities, authority limits, working relationships and conditions, and other details.

job rotation used in management development programs; employees are periodically shifted to different positions in the company.

job specifications written summary of the job to be done that specifies skills, abilities, education, and other attributes the job holder must possess.

joint venture involves a domestic firm entering a partnership with a foreign company to jointly establish facilities overseas.

jury of executive opinion forecasting method in which company executives meet to formulate projections; in retailing, this might include the firm's top manager, buyers, merchandise managers, controller, and sales managers.

key spots places in store where customer traffic is heaviest; excellent locations for displays.

keystone markup selling price set by doubling the cost of merchandise.

knock-out factors information brought out in an employment interview that causes interviewer to reject the applicant—poor communication ability, excessive job-hopping, unexplained gaps in employment history, or poor emotional control.

Laggards with Nonadopters, the last consumer group to buy and try a new product or service.

laissez-faire leaders provide little direction, encouragement, guidance, assistance, or training to workers; are rare in retail sector.

Late Majority with the Early Majority, the largest group of consumers; they follow the Innovators and Early Adopters in buying and trying a new product or service.

layaway plan customer service in which shopper makes down payment on article, pays balance due in installments, and retailer retains ownership until customer has paid in full.

leader pricing reduced pricing on a popular item; used to draw customers into the store.

leadership in business, the *process* of influencing work groups in goal setting and achievement, or management's *ability* to induce subordinates to work toward group goals.

lease legal contract that spells out the details of a rental agreement between landlord and tenant.

leased departments sections in discount houses, department stores, and other large outlets that are rented to and managed by outside individuals or firms.

legal form of business includes sole proprietorship, partnership, and corporation.

liabilities obligations or debts the company must repay: bank loans, promissory notes, balances due suppliers, taxes, and so on.

license plate analysis determining a retailer's trading area by analyzing residence addresses of vehicles parked near the business.

lifestyle segmentation psychographic marketing approach that groups consumers by their activities, interests, and opinions.

LIFO last-in, first-out method of determining cost of goods sold.

limited-line retailers specialty retailers who typically have smaller stores and carry fewer number of offerings in one line than do single-line retailers.

limited-service wholesaler a merchant wholesaler who provides only some of the services that channel members need; includes desk jobbers, dropshippers, truck jobbers, mail-order distributors, rack jobbers, and cash-and-carry wholesalers.

line positions have organizational responsibility and authority to make decisions; a vertical (hierarchical) arrangement that delegates power to give instructions and orders.

liquidity ratios quotients or rates that measure how capable the business is of paying off all its obligations.

loan credit individual consumer borrows money and promises to repay the lender at some future date or according to set schedule.

long-term liabilities obligations that the firm must repay in the more distant future than current liabilities.

logotype (logo) firm's signature.

loss leader goods that a retailer sells at a loss (below its cost) to draw customers into the store.

love and belongingness needs need to give and receive affection; to belong to and be accepted by others.

luxury goods items looked upon as frills or extras by large numbers of people, and that must be purchased out of the consumer's discretionary income.

mail-order distributor sends out catalogs and direct-mail literature to prospective buyers and ships goods directly to the stores.

maintained markup net sales minus the gross cost of goods sold during a period.

management by objectives (MBO) used by some retailers to establish desired levels of sales performance and procedures for evaluating sales personnel.

management development programs training programs designed to enable employees to reach their fullest potential, give the firm flexibility, and ensure a continuing supply of managers.

management information system (MIS) usually includes internal accounting, marketing intelligence, marketing research, and marketing management–science systems.

managerial functions include planning, organizing, directing, and controlling.

manufacturers' representatives independent businesspeople or small firms who act as agents, under contract, for manufacturers.

manufacturers' sales branches operate like manufacturers' sales offices except that orders are filled from stock on hand.

manufacturers' sales offices wholesale places where company products are displayed for buyers and orders are shipped later from company warehouses; no inventory is maintained on the premises.

markdown a reduction in the selling price of merchandise.

market positioning denotes the location a product occupies in the public's mind in relation to similar, competitive products.

market segmentation market targeting approach that includes differentiated and concentrated marketing.

marketing channel all the institutions that cooperate in bringing the goods to consumers: manufacturer, agent, wholesalers, and retailers.

marketing concept holds that a firm's activities should center around its customers' needs.

marking affixing prices and other details to items before they are forwarded to the selling or reserve stock areas.

markon see **markup.**

markup amount added to the selling price by distributors and manufacturers to cover overhead expenses and produce profit; the difference between the cost of an article and what it is sold for; also called **markon.**

mass media deliver messages to large number of consumers; include radio, TV, newspapers, magazines, direct mail, position media, etc.

mass merchandisers outlets presenting a discount image, handling at least three merchandise lines, and having at least 10,000 square feet of floor space.

maturity stage the third stage of the product life cycle (PLC).

meet-our-competition method budgeting method in which a firm tries to determine how much the competition is spending on advertising and matches that amount.

memorandum buying similar to **consignment buying,** except that the retailer owns the goods.

merchandise budget planning and control device that shows forecasted sales, planned inventory levels, expected retail reductions, and purchases that will be needed.

merchandise classification grouping of similar articles or goods near each other in a store; basic groups are further grouped into categories.

merchant wholesalers intermediaries between producers and the retailing and/or industrial sectors.

military commissary large, retail grocery outlets operated by military installations for service personnel at prices generally below regular consumer supermarket prices.

milline rates useful in determining the best buy among two or more newspapers.

minimum-maximum reorder point approach inventory reordering method that establishes minimum and maximum inventory levels for every item in the retailer's assortment.

mixed-use complexes a number of grouped buildings that include offices, stores, hotels, and recreational, entertainment, and cultural facilities.

model stock a written record that serves as a planning guide for a retail buyer for a specified period.

modeling training technique that largely involves learning through imitation.

monochromatic display blends two or more tints or shades (values) of one color.

morale describes psychological state of individuals and groups of people who work together; the group's esprit de corps.

morning drive time roughly from 6 A.M. to 10 A.M.; most expensive time for radio advertising.

motives needs, impulses, urges, or drives toward goals.

multimedia approaches variety of advertising media used by manufacturers who cater to regional or national markets and depend on wholesalers and retailers for distribution.

multi-use projects renovating and remodeling an old building or several adjacent buildings into stores and offices.

natural expenses classification of expenses by their commonly accepted categories, like salaries, rent, electricity, advertising, and so on.

necessities essential products like food, basic clothing, shelter, and household furniture.

needs internal forces, conditions, or tensions that impel us toward some action.

neighborhood shopping center 10 to 20 stores on four or five acres that serves 5,000 to 35,000 or more shoppers; often anchored by a large drugstore or supermarket.

neighborhood shopping streets rows of retail stores and service businesses nestled between blocks of apartment houses or private residences.

net profit method expense allocation approach in which each selling department is charged with the expenses it incurs plus a proportionate share of indirect costs like rent, maintenance, and other overhead expenses.

net sales amount that remains when the retail value of all goods returned by customers and allowances granted by the retailer have been deducted from the gross sales amount; shown as Gross sales − Returns and allowances = Net sales.

net worth (owners' equity) the amount that remains if all the firm's liabilities were to be paid out of total assets.

new-product development process the stages a new concept passes through before it becomes a product in the marketplace: idea generation, product screening, concept testing, business analysis, product development, test marketing, and commercialization.

Nonadopters with the Laggards, the last consumer group to buy and try a new product or service.

noncumulative quantity discount a one-shot discount allowed on a single large order.

nondirected interview informal, open employment interview that does not follow a set pattern.

nondurables popular, fast-moving items that consumers purchase repeatedly throughout the year.

noninsurance management decision *not to insure* against minor or trivial risks.

nonstore retailing three major categories include direct selling companies, vending machine operators, and mail-order houses.

objective-and-task method MBO budgeting technique that designs advertising program to meet specific sales objectives.

observation method research technique in which trained individuals (or mechanical or electronic devices) observe consumers' behavior and draw inferences from the actions observed.

odd pricing setting retail selling prices that end in odd numbers.

off-price retailers offer popular, name-brand merchandise at prices considerably below those found in department stores and specialty shops.

open-account (regular) credit no down payment required; payment in full usually due 30 days after purchase.

open-back window display window without a back so that shoppers can see inside; the retail facility itself becomes part of the display.

open displays items arranged so that shoppers can touch, pick up, and examine the merchandise.

open front storefront design in which no door or window barrier exists between shoppers and the store; often found on shops in enclosed malls.

open-to-buy (OTB) amount of dollars available to complete inventory needs; calculated as:

OTB = Projected purchases − Stock on order − Stock already received.

operant conditioning theory that the individual plays a more participative (operant) role in learning than the stimulus-response pattern would indicate.

operating expenses costs a retailer incurs in the day-to-day running of the business: salaries, rent, utilities, insurance, advertising, supplies, and so on.

operating profit dollar amount determined by subtracting operating expenses from the gross margin.

operating statement accounting document that tells how profitable (or unprofitable) the business operation has been for a stated period; also called an *income statement* or *profit and loss statement (P&L)*.

opportunity analysis evaluation of market demand, including environments internal and external to the firm.

option-terms credit combines open-account and revolving credit; customer can pay in full in 30 days or make partial payments over time.

order getters salespeople who locate prospective buyers, conduct sales interviews, and obtain orders.

order takers relatively untrained salespeople who take orders and fill them.

ordinary dating credit arrangement in which no cash discount is offered.

organization the *framework* comprising the positions and people structured into a company; or the administrative *process* of structuring a firm.

organization development process that applies behavioral science techniques to induce change in order to improve organizational effectiveness.

organizational chart depicts on paper the formal structure of a company—the jobs and relationships among those who fill the jobs.

organizing managerial function of selecting and setting into place all elements essential to implementing organizational plans.

outcome purchase decision stage in which consumer experiences satisfaction or dissonance with the purchase that was made.

outdoor advertising billboards and moving or stationary illuminated signs.

output device usually some kind of a printer for computer output.

outshoppers in contrast to *inshoppers,* people who prefer to go out of their local areas to do their buying.

owner buying independent retailers make all purchasing decisions for their business.

owners' equity see **net worth (owner's equity).**

party-plan selling nonstore retailing in which merchandise is shown in the home (or office) to a group of neighbors and friends (or co-workers), orders for merchandise are taken from the guests, and the host receives one or two token gifts.

patronage motives any aspect of the retail company that contributes toward its image and appeals to its patrons (steady customers).

patterned interview structured employment interview in which interviewer follows a set of questions that have been planned and ordered in advance.

pay range minimum and maximum compensation rates established for a job.

percentage lease legal contract in which the renter pays the landlord a stated percentage of gross sales instead of a regular, fixed amount.

percentage lease with minimum guarantee legal contract in which the landlord establishes a minimum rental figure as a protection against tenant's possible low sales in a percentage lease agreement.

percentage-of-sales method budgeting method in which last year's net sales are compared to total advertising expenditures to determine the amount allocated for the current year.

percentage variation method inventory planning technique used when average inventory is expected to move out rapidly; retailer works entirely from average stock figures for the season, expected monthly sales, and average monthly sales.

perception process by which we select, organize, and interpret stimuli into a meaningful and coherent picture of the world.

performance evaluation program periodic and objective appraisals of each worker's performance.

perishability an attribute of services, in that unlike tangible goods, services cannot be warehoused or stored.

perpetual inventory keeping continuous track of stock by manual, mechanical, or electronic methods.

personal selling involves one or more salespeople making a presentation to an individual or small group.

personality the sum total of an individual's traits that makes that person unique.

petroleum bulk plants wholesalers who sell mainly to gasoline stations and fuel oil dealers.

physical inventory involves checking and counting every item of merchandise in the selling area, on display, in storage, and en route to customers.

physiological needs lowest, or most basic, order of needs required for physical survival.

planned shopping center merchandising unit comprising a deliberately chosen mix of retail businesses.

plans (planning) proposed schemes for future actions; the managerial function of forward thinking: forecasting situations and conditions, formulating objectives, devising strategies, tactics, and procedures, and making decisions to bring about the desired future situation.

PMs (push money) or spiffs small sums paid to salespeople to encourage additional selling effort, usually on specific articles of merchandise.

portfolio building acquiring other types of stores and/or diversifying into different industries.

position media outdoor and transit advertising, exterior signs, and other fixed, in-place advertising media.

posttests recall and recognition tests in which consumers are tested on how well they remember or recognize an ad.

preapproach industrial selling technique that involves (1) learning as much as possible about a potential customer prior to the sales interview and (2) getting the interview.

preferred position additional charge quoted when retailer requests specific positioning of an ad.

premium (insurance) fee paid by the insured party to the insurer for accepting certain risks or perils.

premiums (promotional) articles distributed free or at cost with purchase of one or more merchandise items.

preretailing the buyer types the selling price directly on the purchase order, which is then used by the marking section to mark the articles when the shipment is received.

presentation main part of sales interview, during which salesperson outlines features of product or service and suggests reasons why prospect should buy.

prestige pricing pricing merchandise to sell above the market to appeal to status-conscious and quality-seeking shoppers.

pretests ads shown before publication to small groups or individual consumers, who are asked to rate or judge the ads.

price elasticity economic principle that more units of a product are purchased when prices are reduced, and sales tend to fall as prices are raised.

price lining pricing system in which similar goods are separated into several grades or groupings according to quality, fabric, cost, etc., and are priced accordingly.

price points in price lining, the specific prices set by the retailer in the belief that these are the prices customers prefer to pay for different grades of a product.

price-quality relationship shows that higher prices usually signify higher quality; the relationship is stronger for durables than for nondurables.

primary colors red, yellow, and blue.

primary data describes original information that researchers must gather themselves.

primary groups groups we deal with face-to-face; as the most powerful of our reference groups, they have a profound effect on our behavior.

primary motives can be satisfied by a variety of products.

print media newspapers and magazines.

private buying office resident buying office owned and directed by a single large retailer.

problem recognition first stage of purchase decision; occurs when we realize the existence of a need or want.

product introduction stage the first stage of the product life cycle (PLC).

product life cycle (PLC) the probable sales history of a typical new product: introduction, growth, maturity, and decline.

product or tradename franchising franchising primarily of a product, service, or trademark rather than an entire business format; engaged in by soft-drink bottlers, car dealers, and gasoline stations.

profitability ratios quotients or rates that describe the extent to which profits are earned by a business.

promotion any form of communication used by a firm to inform, persuade, or remind people about its products, services, image, ideas, community involvement, or impact on society; includes media advertising, personal selling, and sales promotion.

promotional advertising product advertising designed to promote quick consumer response; also called **direct-action advertising.**

proportion design principle that each display component must balance the others and the entire unit.

prospecting searching by salespeople for likely buyers of a company's products or services.

psychographics quantitative research that groups consumers on psychological (rather than demographic) dimensions.

psychological pricing using price in a psychological manner, thus appealing to shoppers' preferences and emotions; includes odd-even pricing, prestige pricing, leader pricing, comparative pricing, and price lining.

public relations area of management concern aimed at maintaining a positive company image among the many groups that make up its publics.

publicity unpaid component of a retailer's public relations program that reaches consumers as news rather than as advertising.

publicity release information for consumers given to the news media in the hopes that the media will report the information as news.

purchase credit customer buys merchandise without paying in full at time of purchase; interest charges may or may not apply.

purchasing agent buyer for industry, commerce, government, and non-profit organizations; counterpart of the retail buyer.

pure risk risk situation in which there is only the possibility of loss and no gain.

pyramid pattern three-dimensional geometric merchandise display used to exhibit a quantity of goods in a relatively small area.

quantity discount offered to customers who buy in large quantities.

quick (acid-test) ratio a variation of the current ratio that determines liquidity by using the formula: Acid-test ratio = Cash + Securities + Accounts receivable ÷ Current liabilities.

rack jobber see **rack merchandiser.**

rack merchandiser (rack jobber) limited-service wholesaler who sets up, stocks, and services floor stands or display racks at no charge to the retailer and then collects from the retailer the wholesale cost of whatever goods have been sold.

rain checks forms given to shoppers when a store runs out of advertised or sale merchandise; allows shopper to buy later at the promotional price.

rapport a good working relationship with customers or co-workers.

rational motives prompted by logic or reasoning rather than by emotions or feelings.

reach advertising term that refers to the size of the audience contacted: number of households, number of people, etc.

recall tests consumers are shown ads and then asked to relate what they can remember about them.

receiving department checks incoming shipments against the packing slip or invoice and checks for damage to cartons of merchandise.

receiving log record maintained by the receiving department of the date, time, and other pertinent information about incoming shipments.

recognition tests consumers review a portfolio of ads and are asked to indicate the ones they recognize as having seen before.

reference groups groups we belong to (family, friends, work, etc.) that condition our ways of thinking and behaving.

regional shopping center largest of planned centers, often 30 to 100 acres that serves 100,000 to 200,000 shoppers; includes many small retail stores and service businesses anchored by one or more department stores.

Reilly's Law of Retail Gravitation holds that the drawing power of towns and cities stems from the interaction of population and distance.

remarking required where the original price ticket has been torn off the article or can no longer be read by shoppers because of excessive handling.

resident buying maintaining buying specialists in major market centers; see also **resident buying office.**

resident buying office firm that buys merchandise for the retailers it represents; located in major market centers.

responsibility obligation of employees to perform assigned duties to the best of their ability and be accountable to supervisors.

retail clusters three to six retail businesses located at the corner of a block of apartment houses or private residences.

retail method of inventory valuation accounting procedure based on the retail selling prices of merchandise.

retail reductions reductions in stock due to employee discount buying, markdowns, customer discounts, and stock shortages.

retail research marketing research that involves the purposeful and orderly collection of facts that are carefully analyzed and interpreted to assist retail management in problem solving and decision making.

retail selling process involves four sequential phases: shopper contact, sales dialogue, completing the sale, and suggestion selling.

retailer cooperative association or federation of independent retailers selling similar merchandise who set up a wholesale operation to buy in quantity at lower prices, share a common warehouse and advertising expenses, and may issue their own private-label products.

retailing form of *distribution* that involves selling goods or services to final consumers to fill their needs and wants; all the *activities* that must take place before the retailer can sell the goods (services), and including an *exchange process* between consumer and retailer.

revolving credit shoppers buy up to a set credit limit; as payment is made, they may make additional purchases up to the credit limit.

right of recission consumer's right to cancel an order within three working days after signing a contract.

ROG dating see **AOG and ROG dating.**

role ambiguity occurs when employee is inadequately trained or lacks knowledge or information about some job aspect.

role clarity occurs when employees receive preparation and training for assigned responsibilities and know the kinds of behavior expected of them.

role conflict occurs when superiors make conflicting demands on the employee.

run-of-paper (ROP) newspaper advertising rates quoted when the paper decides where to place the retailer's ad.

safety needs need to feel secure from physical and emotional threat.

safety stock reserve stock added to reorder quantities to reduce the likelihood of stockouts.

salary plan compensation plan in which employees are paid a set amount of money, usually on a weekly basis.

sale-and-leaseback arrangement plan by which retailer builds premises to its own specifications, then sells building to realty firm who leases it back to the retailer.

sales dialogue second stage of retail selling process; salesperson determines shopper's need and begins to present suitable merchandise.

sales force composite method forecasting method in which the firm uses sales representatives' combined experience and knowledge to predict future sales volume.

sales forecast an estimate or prediction of future sales volume.

sales per square foot measure of productivity that divides annual sales volume by the total square footage assigned to the department or section.

sales promotion a wide variety of promotional techniques used to complement and supplement advertising and personal selling.

sampling promotional technique used to persuade customers to try and buy merchandise.

scalar principle assigns duties, responsibilities, and authority to positions in the company in a vertical structure or hierarchy.

scrambled merchandising a policy of adding other, more profitable lines to a store's variety.

search second stage of purchase decision; may be internal (mental) or external.

seasonal discount extended to customers who place orders in advance of the season.

secondary business district shopping area located along main roads leading out of downtown.

secondary colors combine two primary colors: red + yellow = *orange;* yellow + blue = *green;* blue + red = *purple.*

secondary data facts that have been researched, organized, and issued by other organizations and individuals.

second-use facilities retail premises originally built for and occupied by other tenants.

selective motives impel consumers toward their final purchase choice.

self-actualization needs need to fulfill our potential, to be what we were destined to be and want to be.

self-concept our self-image; our mental picture of what we are like—which may or may not be as others see us.

self-insurance management decision to absorb possible losses by setting up a separate internal fund to cover such eventualities

self-liquidator premium offered at retailer's cost to customers who make major purchases; retailer neither gains or loses, since customer pays for the item.

selling agent contracts with manufacturers to represent them with wholesalers and retailers; responsible for selling the manufacturer's entire output.

semantic differential research instrument; shoppers rate a store or a product on scales consisting of pairs of opposite (polar) words or phrases; the responses are tallied to form a composite shopper opinion or attitude.

semiblind check method of checking deliveries in which the names but not the quantities of all goods in the shipment are listed on a printed form, and the checker fills in the quantities.

services activities, benefits, or satisfactions offered for sale or provided in connection with the sale of goods.

shadow boxes small retail display areas for featured items set inside or affixed to a wall.

shell-and-allowance lease legal contract in which the landlord offers only the building shell and a token contribution to the tenants, who finish off the premises at their own expense.

shipping department prepares orders for outgoing shipments.

shopper contact first stage of retail selling process; salesperson makes preliminary judgment and greets shopper.

shopper objections usually originate in attitude or feelings toward the merchandise, price, or brand.

shopping goods often represent a major household purchase; shoppers compare values for the same article in several stores before buying.

show window retail display area whose main purpose is to attract passersby; can be significant sales generator.

shows promotional technique that is less static than exhibits; project excitement, movement, demonstration, or entertainment.

shrinkage (shrink) stock shortages determined by discrepancies between book and actual inventory values.

single-line retailers specialty retailers who offer a broad selection in one category of merchandise plus an assortment of related items.

single-line store 19th-century precursor of today's single-line and specialty stores; carried only one type of merchandise, like men's clothing, hardware, or drugs.

single-line wholesaler stocks a complete assortment of goods in one major line of trade, such as groceries, hardware, or drugs.

single-offer premium a promotional premium that is offered only one time.

social class relatively permanent divisions in a society by which people sharing similar values, lifestyles, interests, and behavior can be categorized.

software programs and instructions that tell the computer hardware how to operate.

source marking done by suppliers at their plants or warehouses before shipment, usually at the retailer's request.

space productivity ratios show the typical dollar sales per square foot of selling space for different merchandise classifications.

span of control (span of authority) principle holds that the number of people who report to a manager must be limited.

specialization of work principle calls for breaking down total work load into groupings of activities.

specialty goods possess one or more unique characteristics that so strongly attract consumers that they are unwilling to consider a substitute.

specialty wholesaler specializes in a narrow product range (like seafood, meat, or spices) in a single merchandise line.

specification buying occurs when a company requests changes in products according to its own specifications.

speculative risk risk situation in which there is a possibility of gain as well as loss.

spiffs small sums paid to salespeople to encourage additional selling effort, usually on specific articles of merchandise; also called **PMs (push money).**

sponsor method see **coaching.**

SRO (standing room only) close selling technique used when salesperson knows of upcoming event (end of sale, possibility of stockout), and passes information on to shopper so that person might buy.

staff positions organizational advisors, technical personnel, and specialists who exercise authority only over their own staffs.

staffing management function of locating, screening, and selecting personnel for job vacancies in the organization.

staple goods items bought regularly by the consumer to be used during the year.

status a person's rank or position in the entire social system.

step pattern multi-tiered merchandise display.

stimulus-response theory another name for **classical conditioning.**

stock-to-sales ratios describe relationship between inventory on hand at the start of any given month and sales volume for the month.

stockkeeping unit (SKU) number assigned to every stock variant a retailer carries; used to keep track of every article and for reordering.

stockouts running out of some items and being unable to fulfill customer requests.

stockturn (inventory turnover) the number of times a retailer's average inventory is bought and sold over a period; Net sales ÷ Average inventory.

store equipment items used to carry on necessary support (nonselling) activities and to facilitate store traffic.

store fixtures showcases, small display cases, gondolas, racks, pegboard displayers, and other articles or accessories in stores that are affixed or attached to other things or structures.

store image a complex phenomenon involving shoppers' conception of a store's personality, based on factors like store characteristics, merchandise and service attributes, promotional activity, and customer characteristics.

strategic plans outline the rationale for the firm's operation and overall objectives.

subcultures groups of people based on demographic (race, nationality, age, religion) or geographical or cultural differences.

suggestion selling sales technique in which, after closing the sale, salesperson suggests additional related or accessory items for the shopper to buy.

supermarkets large, high-volume, multi-line, departmentized stores that carry wide assortments of groceries, dairy products, meats, household supplies, and other nonfood and convenience items.

superstore larger than a combination store; includes complete super-market, drugs and pharmacy, and many other merchandise lines, snack shops, and service operations.

supplemental benefits part of employee compensation plans; once called fringe benefits, now common in retailing; include paid vacations, paid holidays, sick leave, and employee discounts.

supporting salespeople help order getters secure orders; include technical experts and missionary salespeople.

survey method of gathering primary data about customer preferences, demographics, reaction to advertising, and so on; may be conducted by personal interviews, by mail questionnaires, or by telephone.

sweepstakes most popular contest form; requires minimum shopper effort; involves a drawing to award prizes to shoppers who enter contest.

syndicate buying office resident buying office similar to **associated buying office** but with more authority and control over the member stores with respect to merchandising and procedures.

tactical plans for attaining short-range goals.

tare weight of packing cartons in which bulk goods are shipped; the tare is deducted from the total weight to determine the weight of the merchandise.

theme topics or subjects around which retail displays are designed.

Theories X and Y McGregor's theory that management holds either negative (Theory X) or positive (Theory Y) attitudes toward workers in general.

three Cs of credit credit department criteria used to evaluate the *character, capacity* to repay, and *capital* of credit applicant.

tickler method similar to the **ABC analysis** inventory technique.

tie-in promotion sharing of costs and benefits of promotional effort by two or more retail firms.

time class time of day or night that broadcast media advertising is scheduled.

time series extrapolation forecasting method in which historical sales information forms the basis for projections.

top-down planning strategic process in which management determines the organization's *overall revenue goals* and breaks them down into smaller organizational segments or units; also, a *forecasting method* in which management appraises the general state of the economy and then evaluates the retail sector to project sales.

trade discount price reductions made available to channel members for performing those activities expected of them.

trade-in allowance promotional pricing device in which a retailer "allows" shoppers to turn in an old item for allowance or rebate on price of new article.

trading area field or geographical territory from which a retail business draws most of its customers.

trading stamps promotional technique used by retailers to gain competitive advantage and encourage shoppers to continue to buy at the same store.

trading up or down selling technique in which a salesperson offers higher or lower priced article to shopper, depending on shopper's reaction to item initially offered.

traffic counts determining how many people pass a retail location at different times of day and on different days of the week.

transit advertising posters or cards displayed in rail and bus terminals, airports, subways, taxis, and buses.

trend analysis forecasting method in which the retailer reviews results of several preceding years as guidelines to predict future sales volume.

trial closes selling technique used to test the shopper's readiness for sale completion.

trickle-across theory holds that persons in any social class can begin a new fashion. These persons are popular among their peers, who copy and adopt the fashions.

trickle-down theory sees the fashion life cycle as embracing four stages: distinctive introduction to a few members of the upper class; emulation by a few; popularization and mass production; decline.

truck jobber limited-service wholesaler (also called a **wagon jobber**) who makes deliveries on a regular basis over a set route to grocers, supermarkets, delicatessens, and other food stores.

truline rates variation of **milline rates** that focuses on the trading area rather than on the paper's total circulation.

truth in lending Consumer Credit Protection Act of 1969 that requires retailers to make full disclosure of installment sale details.

turnkey lease legal contract in which the landlord provides all necessary construction, often to tenant's specifications, and leases the comparatively finished structure to the tenant.

undifferentiated marketing marketing approach that sees the entire consumer market as holding sales potential.

unit control inventory method that keeps track of merchandise movement by physical units.

unit pricing indicates the cost per pound, quart, or other unit of measurement in addition to the selling price of a product.

unity design principle in which display elements (merchandise, stands, signs, accessories) are arranged so that viewers can grasp the complete concept.

unity of command principle holds that no employee should work under the supervision of more than one person.

Universal Product Code (UPC) see **bar coding.**

usage-rate segmentation marketing approach that groups consumers by their rate of usage of a product or service.

value segmentation marketing approach that targets prospects according to the values buyers hold with regard to the products or services they desire; closely related to **benefit segmentation.**

variable pricing flexible pricing used by antique dealers, flea marketers, used-car dealers, and other vendors of unique or high-priced goods.

variety the number of different lines of merchandise that the retail company offers shoppers.

variety stores offer 18 to 20 different lines: variety of household items, apparel, kitchen utensils, stationery, notions, candy, etc.; display goods prominently on a self-selection, self-service basis.

vending machine operators nonstore retailing in which merchandise is sold from coin-actuated machines by operators who fill and service the machines regularly.

vendor analysis process by which retailers' buyers decide which suppliers are best to work with.

vertical cooperative advertising different channel members (like a manufacturer and a retailer) share advertising costs to promote one or more of the manufacturer's products.

visual merchandising popular term for *retail display.*

wagon jobber see **truck jobber.**

want-slip program salespeople are asked to record every customer request for an item not carried; if demand is heavy enough, the item may be added to the retailer's regular line of merchandise.

wants needs that are learned, not inborn.

weeks' supply method stock planning technique that provides sufficient inventory to cover several weeks of operation, at the average weekly sales rate expected.

what-we-can-afford-method budgeting method in which forecasted surplus funds, after profit taking, may be allocated to advertising.

Wheel of Retailing theory of the evolutionary aspects of retailing, in which a low-cost/low-margin innovation is introduced, becomes forced by competitive imitations to expand operations and raise prices until consumers no longer differentiate among the offerings, and another innovation repeats the cycle.

wholesaler-sponsored voluntary chain wholesaling company or large distributor induces retail firms in its field to become members by offering lower wholesale prices, assistance in inventory control and bookkeeping, promotional aid, etc.

zigzag pattern asymmetric merchandise display combining step and pyramid designs.

AUTHOR INDEX

SUBJECT INDEX

This book has been set VideoComp in 10 Times Roman leaded 2 points. Part and chapter numbers are 18 point Technica Light; part and chapter titles are 28 point Times Roman. The size of the type page is 36 by 50 picas.